The Social Burdens of Environmental Pollution:

A Comparative Metropolitan Data Source

BRIAN J.L. BERRY, ed.

Contributing Authors:

Susan Caris
Daniel Gaskill
Charles P. Kaplan
John Piccinini
Neil Planert
James H. Rendall III
Alexandra de Ste. Phalle

Research Assistants:

Vincent Egonmwan
Mary B. Hoyt
Karol Kennedy
Margaret McFarland
Christopher Saricks
Erich Schultz
Christine Smyrski
Bruce P. Winston

Graphics:

Douglas B. Cargo
Susan Friedman

Ballinger Publishing Company • **Cambridge, Massachusetts**
A Subsidiary of J.B. Lippincott Company

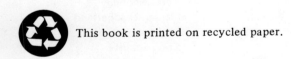

Copyright © 1977 by Ballinger Publishing Company. All rights reserved. No part of this publication may be reproduced, stored in a retrieval system, or transmitted in any form or by any means, electronic mechanical photocopy, recording or otherwise, without the prior written consent of the publisher.

International Standard Book Number: 0-88410-427-3

Library of Congress Catalog Card Number: 76-40419

Printed in the United States of America

Library of Congress Cataloging in Publication Data
Main entry under title:

The social burdens of environmental pollution.

Bibliography:
Includes index.
1. Pollution—United States. 2. Metropolitan areas—United States. I. Berry, Brian Joe Lobley, 1934-   II. Caris, Susan.
TD180.S6   363   76-40419
ISBN 0-88410-427-3

The Social Burdens of Environmental Pollution:

A Comparative Metropolitan Data Source

Contents

Acknowledgements

Many persons and organizations provided advice and information, and otherwise furthered the progress of this study. To each is due thanks, viz:

Robert Samis of the Illinois Environmental Protection Agency for the air pollution data; the City of Chicago's Department of Environmental Control for the air pollution data for the city; and the Cook County Environmental Control Department for the air pollution data for Cook County.

Roger J. Vaughan for the noise data and statistical analysis of Chicago; John Standard of the Chicago Department of Environmental Control for the Chicago noise ordinance and the background noise study for Chicago; and Major Hearn, State of Illinois EPA, Noise Section, for the complaint data for the Chicago metropolitan area.

Richard Seeley and E.J. Petkus, Engineering Sciences Division, City of Chicago's Department of Environmental Control for the 1966 and 1972 solid waste data; Emmet Garrity, Bureau of Sanitation, Chicago Department of Streets and Sanitation for the street dirt data; Celesta Jurkovich, Jim Cornovich, Douglas Ziesmer and William Lough of the Department of Streets and Sanitation, City of Chicago for information on subsidiary sources of solid waste; Sanitation and Public Works Departments for the cities of Rochester, San Diego, Baltimore, Jacksonville, Denver, and Cincinnati; and Fred Lafser of the East-West Gateway Coordinating Council of St. Louis for the solid waste management report.

Robert J. Bowden, David Rockwell, and especially Stuart Ross of the US EPA Region V office were most helpful in the water quality analysis not only for the Chicago case study but for comparative analysis; the various regional EPA offices for the cities studied; and the Northeastern Illinois Planning Commission for the land use data for the Chicago case study.

Bill Robinson, Department of Health Education, Chicago Board of Health for the rat bite data; Mr. Stanton, Department of Statistics, Chicago Board of Health for the Chicago poisoning data; and Maria-Louise Bayer Pesticides Branch, U.S. EPA Region V, for the 1972 pesticide study report.

✳ *Chapter 1*

The Problem Stated

That poor residents of inner-city neighborhoods bear the greatest burdens of environmental pollution has been suggested in a series of studies commissioned by the Environmental Protection Agency. Examples include Improving the Inner City Environment (January, 1971) and Our Urban Environment (September, 1971). More recently, William Kruvant has compared maps of air pollutants with maps showing the spatial distribution of different social groups in Washington, D.C. and concluded that "families with high incomes contribute more than their share to air pollution. Families with low incomes, on the other hand, are far more likely to be on the receiving end of air pollution." (Incidence of Pollution Where People Live in Washington, Washington Center for Metropolitan Studies, 1974). How general is this relationship? Does it apply equally to air, water, noise, solid wastes and other pollutants? Are the same groups afflicted to the same degree by the same pollutants in all metropolitan regions in the United States? These are the principal questions addressed in the present work, in which a detailed case-study investigation of the Chicago

region is followed by comparative analyses of the situation in a care-
fully-selected national sample of twelve other metropolitan areas.

If the answer to the first group of questions is affirmative,
two others logically follow: What will be the ramifications of uniform
enforcement of federal pollution controls for inner-city residents?
What will be the implications of achieving federal environmental
quality standards for the inner city resident, and for the inner city?
EPA's 1972 Summer Fellows said that the evidence available to them
at that time enabled them to deduce a series of tentative hypotheses
about these ramifications and implications (Studies in Environment,
Vol. III: Pollution and the Municipality, February, 1974). Effective
uniform enforcement leading to achievement of national standards
would, they argued:

. . . decrease mortality rates in central city
      locations
. . . increase the population under age 10 and
      over age 50 in the central city
. . . increase the birth rate in the central city
. . . increase central city transportation prob-
      lems for the poor and aged
. . . increase central city housing problems,
      especially increasing housing abandonment
. . . decrease the labor force participation
      through increased unemployment, especially
      for the black population
. . . increase regional and local out-migration
      over the long term
. . . decrease central city population densities
. . . increase regional central city and suburban
      industries
. . . shift the economic base of the central
      city, causing severe unemployment problems
      in certain sectors.

The Fellows' work was tentative and highly speculative. Clearly,
much more work on such questions is required -- but only after the
first group of questions has been resolved satisfactorily, for as we
show, the relationships between the social geography of metropolitan
regions and patterns of environmental pollution are neither as clear

cut nor as straightforward as the simple assertions argue them to be. It follows that the burdens and benefits of pollution control programs and of achieving high quality urban environments are likely to be far more complex and far more variable across the nation's metropolitan network than has been thought to date.

That however, must be the subject of future research. Before we can get to that point a variety of prior evidence must be as assembled, and that is the purpose of this report. Chapter 2 provides backdrop information by dealing descriptively and cartographically with the social geography of Chicago and of the twelve metropolitan regions selected for comparative study: Baltimore, Washington, D.C., Providence, St. Louis, Rochester, Cincinnati, Jacksonville, Birmingham, Oklahoma City, Denver, Seattle, and San Diego. Chapters 3 and 4 are devoted to a discussion of water quality-- Chapter 3 to the Chicago case, and Chapter 4 to the comparative analysis. Chapter 5 combines the case-study and comparative materials on air quality and Chapters 6 and 7 do likewise for noise and solid wastes. Chapter 8 then addresses the question of the social burdens of pollution: Which residential groups are afflicted by poor quality central city environments and to what extent?

The point of departure for the investigation was a prior study undertaken by the same research group for the Environmental Protection Agency, published as Brian J.L. Berry, et.al., <u>Land Use</u>, <u>Urban Form and Environmental Quality</u> (Department of Geography Research Paper No. 155, the University of Chicago, 1974). In that study, a careful survey was undertaken of the nature of environmental pollution, environmental monitoring systems, and of studies of the health and welfare effects of specific pollutants. In addition, the nation's metropolitan areas were classified into relatively homogeneous types on the basis of their pollution characteristics. The twelve metropolitan regions analyzed in this study were selected to represent each of these types.

Thus, our comparative generalizations extend over the entire range of national experiences.

To serve as a bridge between the prior study and our comparative analysis, the first six months of the present investigation (which extended over twenty-four months) were devoted to a detailed case-study of relationships in the Chicago region. There were several reasons for this strategy. Firstly, there were few methodological guidelines available for the kind of comparative analysis we wished to undertake. We simply had to come to terms with the research issues in a case which was close at hand, where data and resource personnel were readily available. Moreover, we had to systematize and to simplify. For example, many water quality parameters are monitored and measured. Which of these might be redundant in that they indicate the same things about the nature, causes and impacts of pollution? Which key parameters should be analyzed in each of the twelve regions to be compared? Which might safely be eliminated? Similarly, many variables might be used to describe the residential patterns of different social groups within metropolitan regions. Which of these are redundant, in that they reflect the same elements of residential choice and social differentiation? The purpose of the case study was to range broadly, to produce a methodology for the comparative inquiry, and to train new research staff. Presentation of the case study materials early in each section that follows is designed to show how we selected, systematized and simplified -- to indicate why we chose to use certain variables and not to use others.

The basic source of the social data was the 1970 Census of Population and Housing, supplemented by a variety of local data sources in the Chicago case. Air quality data came from SAROAD, the National Aerometric Data Bank, again enriched by local data sources and reports wherever possible. Water quality information came from EPA's STORET system, from reports by the U.S. Geological Survey and from relevant

state and local agencies. Information concerning noise and solid
wastes was all derived from local agency sources. Because so few of
the sample regions had actually undertaken surveys of these two pollutants, Chapters 6 and 7 differ from the preceding ones in that complete 12-region comparisons are not possible. Since SAROAD and STORET
are still in their developmental stages, we found it unwise to attempt
to base our analysis upon the limited information they included for
the years 1969-70. Instead, we elected to use environmental quality
data for the years 1971-3 as a means of ensuring both broader network
coverage and greater consistency of monitoring procedures. In the
noise and solid wastes cases, we were grateful for any data we could
get, just as we were in dealing with metropolitan land use patterns.

With each variable included in the case study and in the comparative analysis, the first step in the research process was the same:
to prepare a map that showed the spatial pattern of the social or
environmental indicator in question. Many such maps are included in
what follows. Indeed, Chapters 3-7 come close to being a comparative
metropolitan atlas of environmental quality, with a text that discusses
the nature of the pollutants, their spatial patterns and causes, while
Chapter 2 has a similar quality with respect to urban social geography.
The atlas-like quality is intentional. We found there to be a dearth
of good comparative evidence on environmental pollution, systematically
prepared and presented, a situation conducive to hasty overgeneraliza-
tion about the nation's environmental health. All of the maps in
Chapters 3-7 share one thing in common: symbolism related to national
environmental quality standards, where such standards have been specified. Thus, one can tell by looking at the maps exactly which areas
have substandard environments, as measured by federal criteria, how
substandard the conditions are, and how the spatial patterns of substan-
dardness vary from one metropolitan region to another.

The cross tabulations laid out in Chapter 8 are based upon comparisons of selected social and environmental maps to determine the numbers of people, for example, of different income levels living in areas, for example, exceeding federal primary standards for particulates, exceeding secondary standards but not primary ones, or in areas meeting both primary and secondary standards. We were instructed by our program officer in the Environmental Studies Division, Washington Environmental Research Center of the Environmental Protection Agency that these comparisons should be restricted to the central cities, because they were specifically concerned with the question of the impact of uniform enforcement of national environmental quality standards on the inner-city poor. However, our discussion in earlier chapters and in our conclusions does extend to central city-suburban differences. These permit us to look at both the direct and the indirect effects of pollution abatement programs on the inner-city poor.

✳ *Chapter 2*

Metropolitan Social Patterns

The social geography of metropolitan America can best be understood as a series of polarities -- between rich and poor, young and
old, black and white, Catholic and Protestant. These find their expression in the residential fabric through the choices of individuals
seeking a home and neighborhood reflective of their personal desires
and aspirations, played out against a backdrop of the activities of
profit-seeking home builders, subsidized and regulated by governments
at several levels. Mobility enables individuals to sort themselves
out into relatively homogeneous neighborhoods and communities. Home
builders respond by constructing subdivisions in response to demand
pressures, or they try to shape and influence the directions of individual choice by innovations in housing style, community plan and mar-
keting strategy. New construction forces a continuous reevaluation
of the bases of homogeneity and, combined with mobility, leads simulta-
neously both to neighborhood change and to resistance to change by
community groups. As Homer Hoyt remarked almost 40 years ago in The
Structure and Growth of Residential Neighborhoods in American Cities

8

(Washington, D.C.: Federal Housing Administration, 1939):

> The erection of new dwellings on the periphery
> sets in motion forces tending to draw population
> from older houses and to cause all groups to
> move up a step, leaving the oldest and cheapest
> houses to be occupied by the poorest families
> or to be vacated. The constant competition of
> new areas in itself a cause of neighborhood
> shifts. Every building boom, with its crop of
> structures equipped with the latest modern de-
> vices, pushes all existing structures a notch
> down in the scale of desirability. The high
> grade areas tend to preempt the most desirable
> residential land, intermediate rental groups
> tend to occupy the sectors in each city that
> are adjacent to the high rent area. Occupants
> of houses in the low rent categories tend to
> move out in bands from the center of the city
> by filtering up. There is a constant outward
> movement of neighborhoods because as neighbor-
> hoods become older they tend to be less desir-
> able. A neighborhood composed of new houses in
> the latest modern style, occupied by young fam-
> ilies with children, is at its apex. Physical
> deterioration of structures and the aging of
> families constantly lessen the vital powers of
> the neighborhood. The steady process of deteri-
> oration is hastened by obsolescence; a new and
> more modern type of structure relegates all
> existing structures to lower ranks of desirability.

The continuing validity of Hoyt's insights is illustrated no more clearly than in the social geography of the case-study region, Metropolitan Chicago, as may be seen in the sequence of maps that follows. These maps were selected from a much larger group that had been prepared as part of the case study as being particularly indicative of factors and forces bearing upon the question of social differentiation of urban regions.

These factors and forces include, first of all, stage of growth. The period in which a community grew largely determines its housing types, densities, and community design -- and hence, according to Hoyt, its degree of obsolescence and its status in the ranking system of communities. Thus, Figures 2.1 to 2.4 reveal that the areas which developed earliest in Chicago have the highest population densities today, but also are zones of population decline. And the older areas rely to a greater extent on public transportation and upon jobs in the central business district (Figures 2.5 and 2.6).

A second factor involves the relationship between the stage in life cycle of a community's residents, the age structure of the community, and population mobility. The most mobile population groups are the youngest, especially families in the early stages of child-rearing who occupy the outlying ring of new suburbs (Figures 2.7 and 2.8) and minority-group members concentrated in the least desirable housing in the old city centers (compare with Figure 2.9). Between these is sandwiched a ring of older residential neighborhoods and suburbs occupied by less-mobile older families whose children have left home.

Together, stage of growth, housing type, densities and stage in life cycle give an overall ring-like structure to the metropolis. Superimposed on this is a pattern of housing preferences determined by income levels and social rank. A major determinant is occupation. The residences of blue-collar employees are concentrated in the old central cities or in rural areas beyond the belt of continuous suburbanization (Figure 2.10). Managers and executives create and concentrate in more exclusive and "desirable" clusters of suburbs, and in sub-communities within the central city richly endowed with amenities (for example, Chicago's Gold Coast and northern lakeshore -- compare Figures 2.10 and 2.11). The oldest residential developments are, in general, the multi-problem poverty communities (Figures 2.11-2.20). The question that we ultimately want to address is whether these communities, in particular, are also afflicted with the greatest burdens of environmental pollution. But before we reach that point, we want to present all the relevant evidence in maps, beginning with the social data on Chicago and on the twelve comparative case studies. The reader should proceed map by map, reading the legends and looking at the spatial distributions portrayed; the sequence of maps and legends is intended to be accumulative.

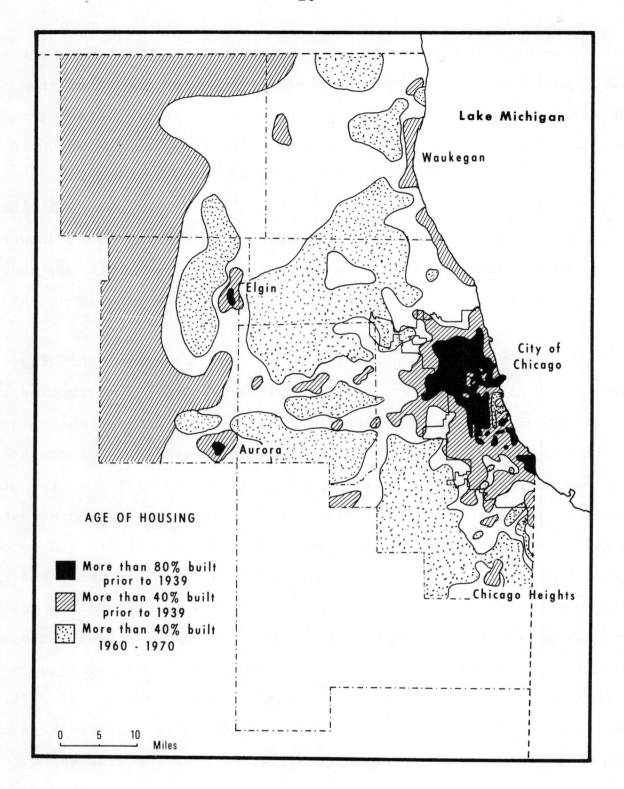

Figure 2.1. Metropolitan Chicago grew by ring-like accretion. Much of the inner city was built before 1939 -- a large part even earlier -- and it is encircled by successive "layers" of suburbs that are broken only by the older housing stock of outlying industrial satellites such as Elgin and Aurora, and the earlier developments along the Lake Michigan shoreline.

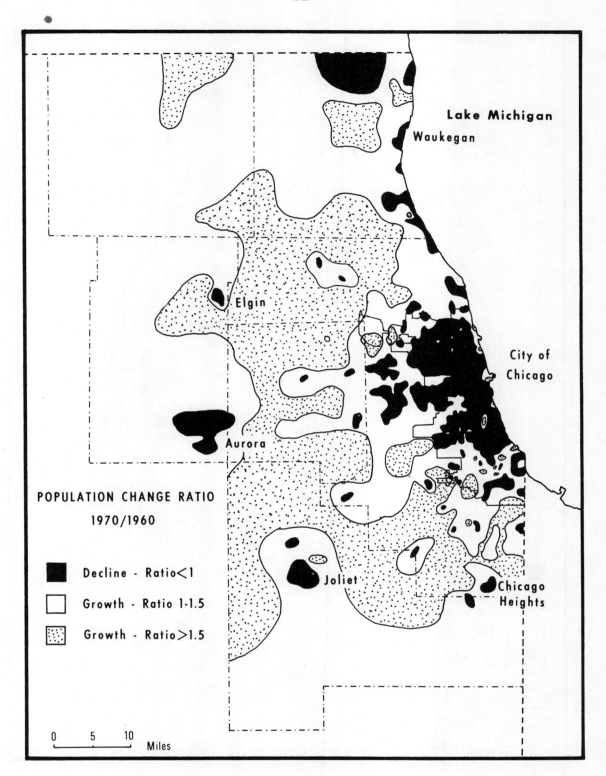

POPULATION CHANGE RATIO
1970/1960

■ Decline - Ratio<1

☐ Growth - Ratio 1-1.5

▨ Growth - Ratio>1.5

0   5   10
Miles

Figure 2.2.   The newest suburban ring increased in population much more rapidly during the 1960-70 decade than the previous layer of suburban growth, while the oldest areas of the inner city, the industrial satellites and the shoreline communities all declined as families moved to the newer residential areas, leaving behind decay and urban blight.

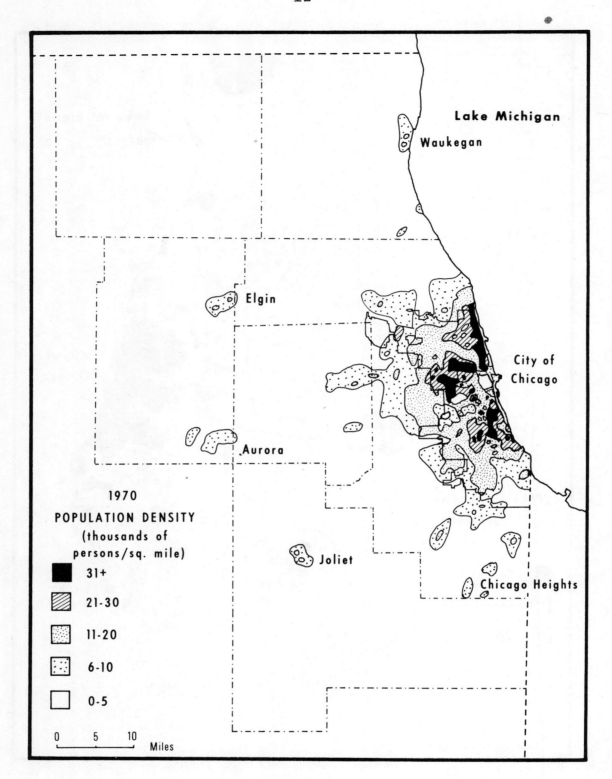

Figure 2.3. The areas of population decline during the 1960's, were the higher-density zones of the inner city and the satellite crescent. Growth was concentrated in the much lower-density communities of the suburban ring, reflecting dramatic shifts in housing preferences facilitated by the automobile.

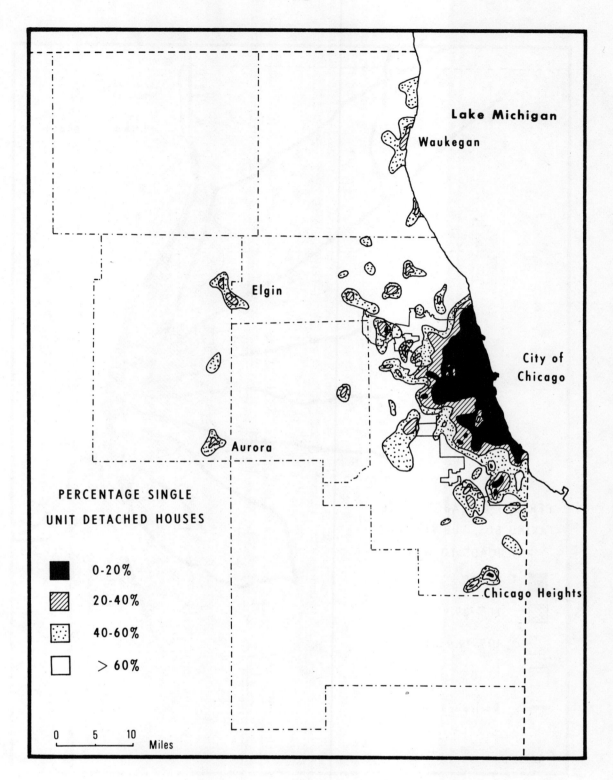

Figure 2.4. The higher population densities of the inner city and the industrial satellites were based upon older multiple-unit residential developments, as opposed to the single-family detached building styles dominating suburbia. The overwhelming preference for a single-family home on its own lot in an outlying area is clear.

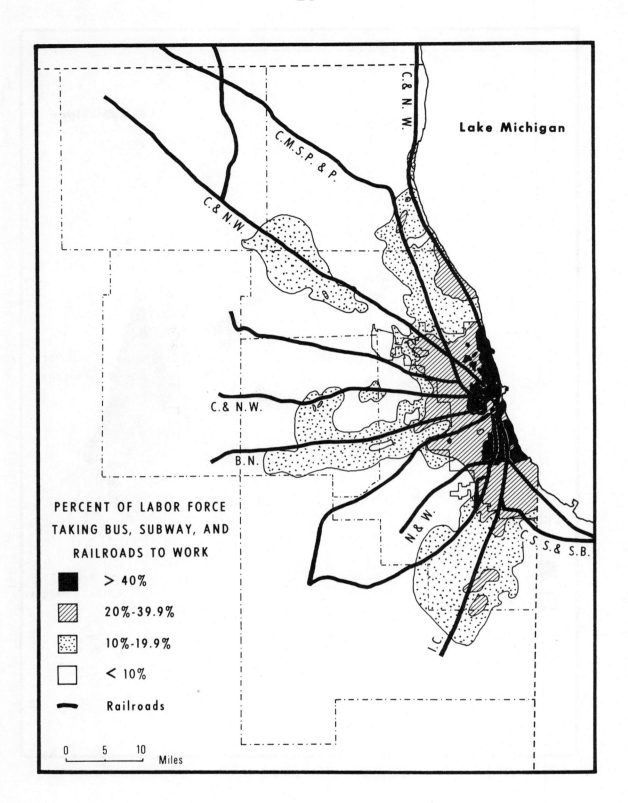

Figure 2.5. Such residential choices are supported by the automobile. Public transportation is only a significant element in the journey to work within the higher-density inner city and along the principal commuter railroads, as befits the building style and dominant transportation modes at the time these areas grew initially.

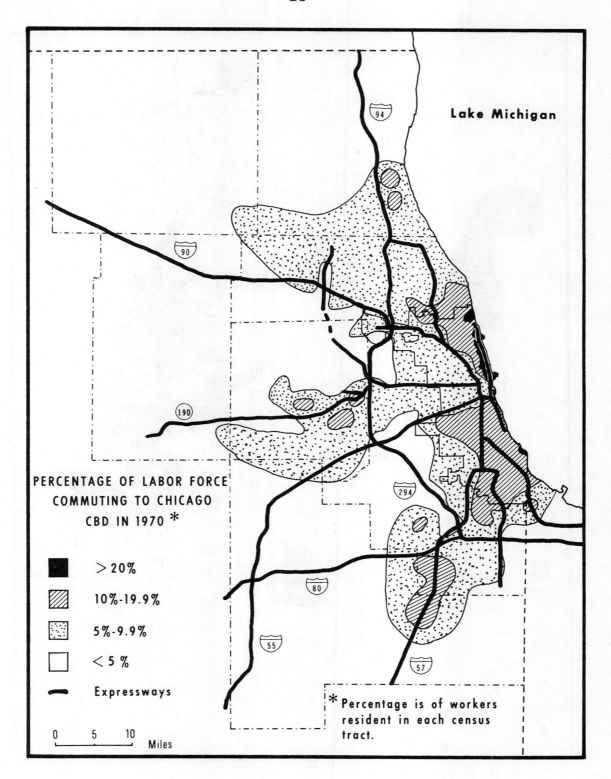

PERCENTAGE OF LABOR FORCE COMMUTING TO CHICAGO CBD IN 1970 *

■ > 20%

▨ 10%-19.9%

▦ 5%-9.9%

□ < 5%

— Expressways

0   5   10
Miles

* Percentage is of workers resident in each census tract.

Lake Michigan

Figure 2.6. Because modern suburbia is based upon the automobile, and because workplaces have decentralized too with the advent of the super highway and efficient truck transportation, the suburbs have detached themselves from traditional central-city workplaces. Indeed, only the older city and inner suburbs remain substantially core-oriented, with heavy amounts of commuting to and from the central business district. Beyond spreads a multi-centered, dispersed urban region.

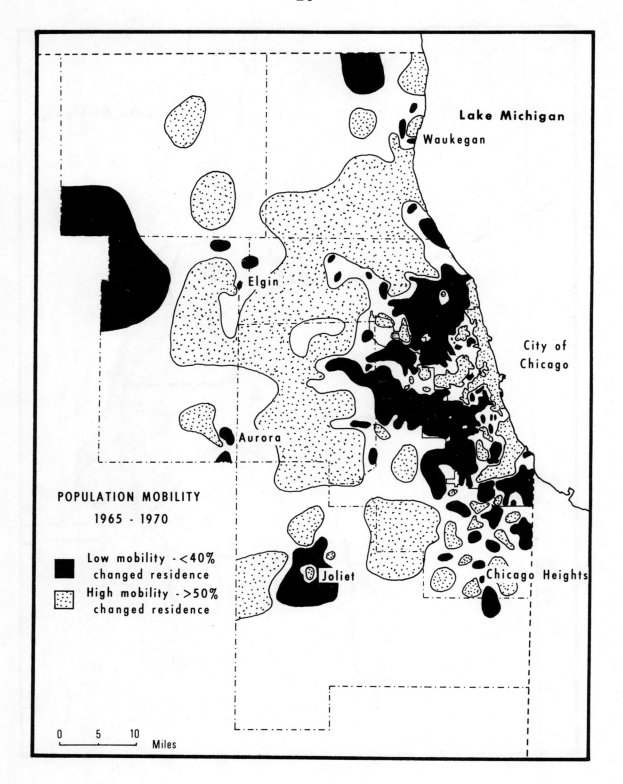

POPULATION MOBILITY

1965 - 1970

■ Low mobility - <40% changed residence

High mobility - >50% changed residence

0   5   10
Miles

Lake Michigan

Waukegan

Elgin

Aurora

City of Chicago

Joliet

Chicago Heights

<u>Figure 2.7</u>. Population mobility does not mirror the suburb-central city dichotomy exactly, however. To be sure, the new suburbs have high mobility levels. But they are flanked by a lower-mobility zone in the rural areas beyond, and they encircle a low-mobility belt of older inner suburbs. Much of the central city has very high population mobility.

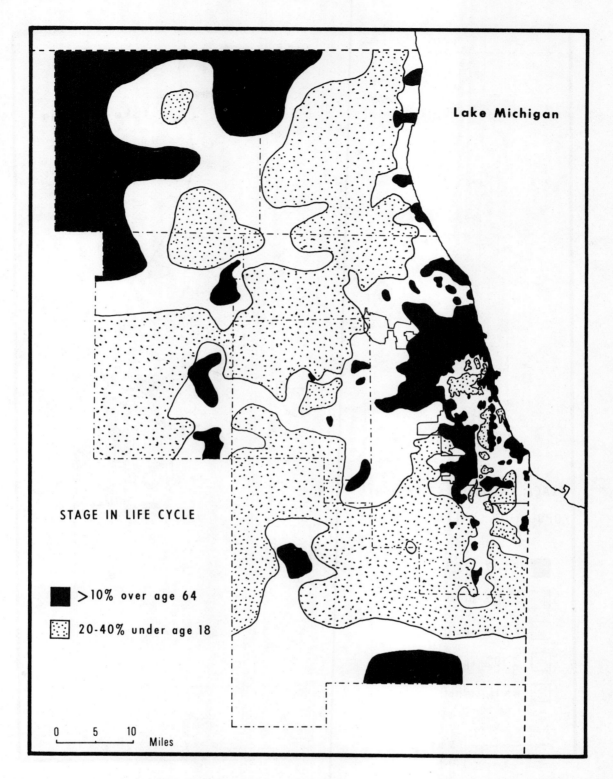

Figure 2.8. These mobility differences reflect the stage in life cycle of their residents: the high mobiles are the younger child-rearing families, and the low-mobiles create communities with a much higher proportion of the elderly. The differences seen in the preceding figure thus are between new child-rearing suburbanites, older rural families, older suburbanites whose children have gone and new concentrations of child-rearing minority families in the central city, as may be seen in the figure that follows.

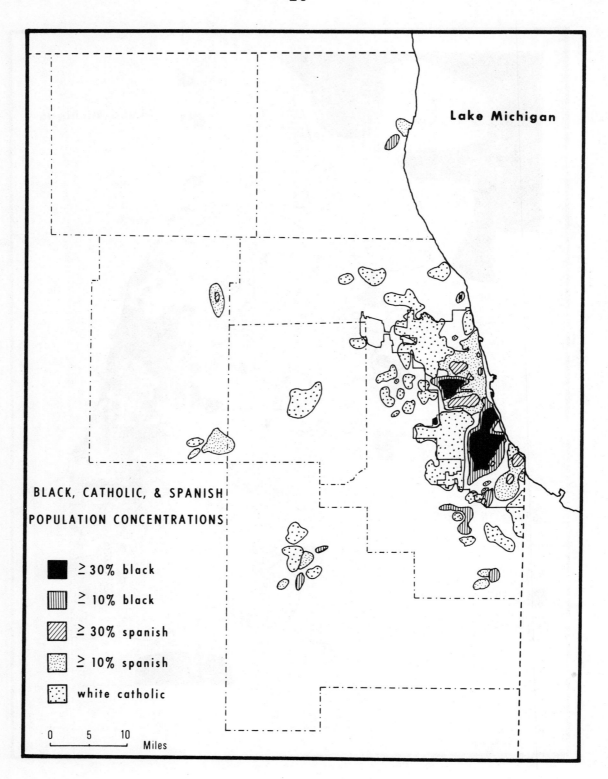

Lake Michigan

BLACK, CATHOLIC, & SPANISH
POPULATION CONCENTRATIONS

■ ≥ 30% black

▥ ≥ 10% black

▨ ≥ 30% spanish

▤ ≥ 10% spanish

⬚ white catholic

0   5   10
Miles

Figure 2.9. Within the central city, the contrast between the high-
and low mobiles reflects the polarity between the city's black and
Spanish minorities, on the one hand, and the aging communities surrounding them, occupied **by** largely ethnic populations, heavily Catholic.
This polarity is repeated in each of the industrial satellites.

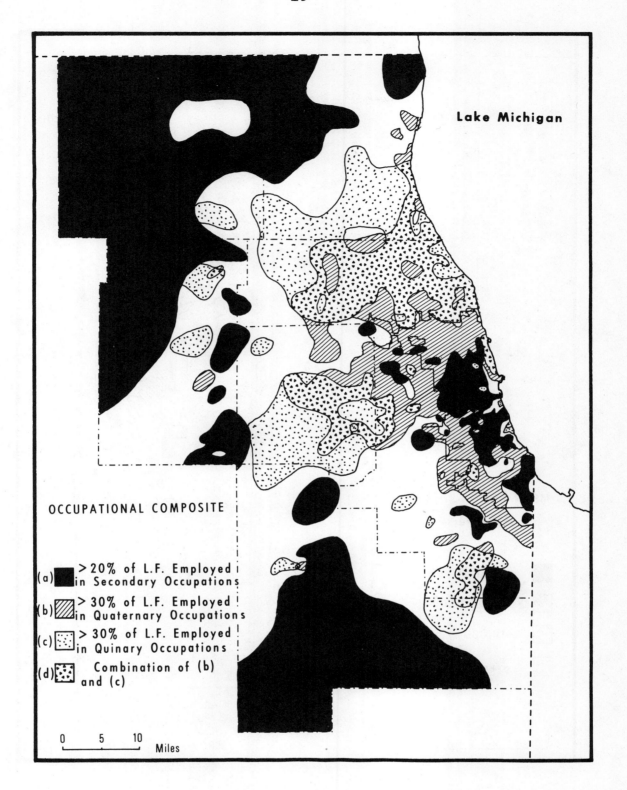

Lake Michigan

OCCUPATIONAL COMPOSITE

(a) ▮ >20% of L.F. Employed in Secondary Occupations

(b) ▨ >30% of L.F. Employed in Quaternary Occupations

(c) ▨ >30% of L.F. Employed in Quinary Occupations

(d) ▨ Combination of (b) and (c)

0   5   10
Miles

Figure 2.10. The suburbanites are dominantly employed in quaternary (white collar, information processing) and quinary (professional and executive) activities (as are the high-rise residents along the city's northern lakeshore), whereas both the rural fringe, the rest of the central city, the older inner suburbs, and the satellite crescent are the homes of blue collar employees engaged in secondary (manufacturing and similar) activities.

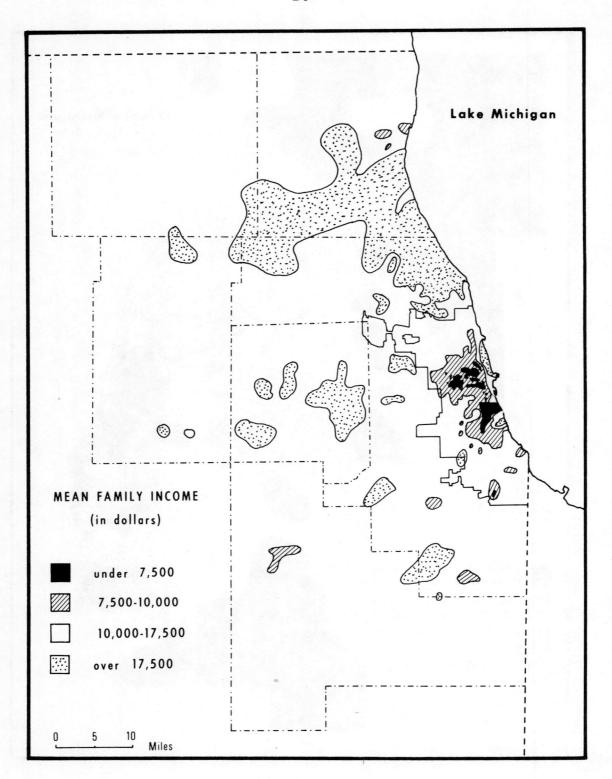

Lake Michigan

MEAN FAMILY INCOME

(in dollars)

■ under 7,500

▨ 7,500-10,000

□ 10,000-17,500

▧ over 17,500

0   5   10
|————|————| Miles

Figure 2.11. These occupational differences translate into income differences: the low-income population is concentrated in the central city, whereas the high-income professionals reside in the outer suburban ring and in the lakeshore highrises.

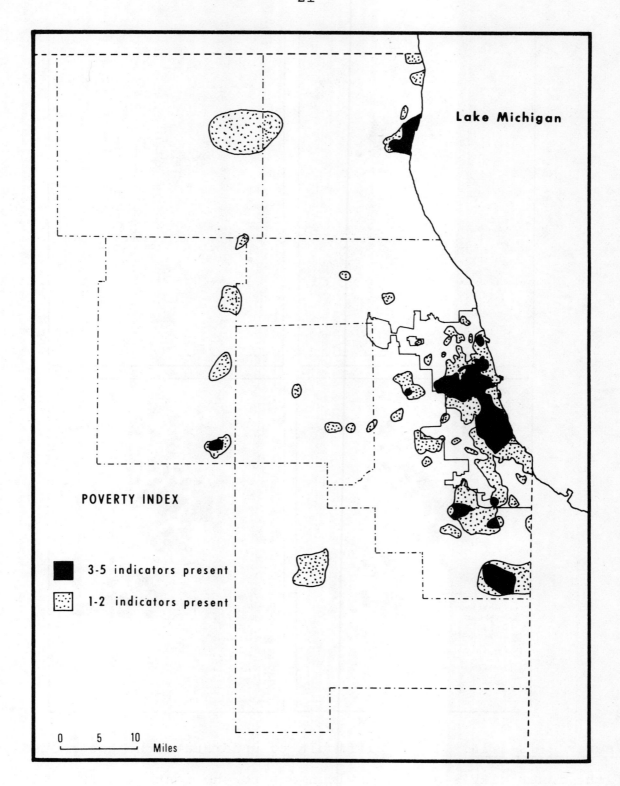

Figure 2.12. But money income alone is a poor index of poverty.
Taking five indicators (unemployed males 16-21 not in school, households with more than 1.01 persons per room, lacking telephones or
automobiles and percentage of income from public payments) a poverty
index was constructed that traces out the neighborhoods occupied by
minorities both within and outside the central city, and by the
elderly poor.

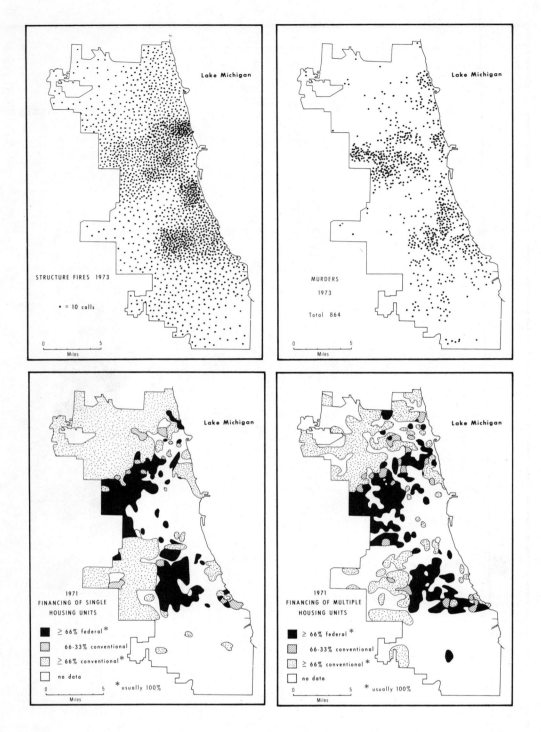

Figures 2.13-2.16.   It is difficult to understate the hazardousness
of the inner city's social environment to the central city's minority
populations, concentrated as they are in old multiple housing units
at higher densities.   The poverty areas in which they live are afflicted by frequent fires, rampant crime and personal violence, and
the fact that conventional mortgage money has been withdrawn from
them is indicative of their worth in the eyes of the city's financial
institutions.

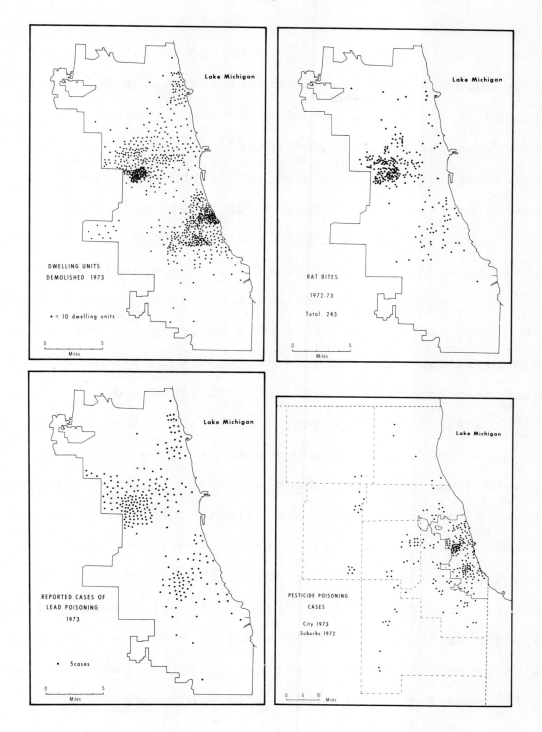

Figures 2.17-2.20. The housing stock in these inner city areas is being abandoned and demolished -- and none too soon, for these are neighborhoods in which rat bites are common, in which children eat old paint and get lead poisoning and in which careless storage or use of pesticides and rodenticides sends children to hospitals in far greater numbers than with suburban children visiting careless grand-parents.

What is to be learned from the foregoing as a prologue to examining variables relating to pollution? Several themes that are well established in the literature of urban ecology are intertwined. One is the obvious necessity of understanding the dynamics and directions of urban change -- including what is new and what is not so new in the housing stock -- as a backdrop for understanding mobility directions of the residents and the filtering of housing. Equally, density patterns, the staging of past growth and the extent to which the urban pattern is core-oriented in a traditional sense as opposed to multi-centered and diffused in a more modern sense must be appreciated as a basis for understanding the framework within which socially differentiated neighborhoods and communities develop -- because played out against the backdrop of this fabric are residential decisions that individuals make about where to live in terms of such basic factors as income and socio-economic status, family structure and stage in life cycle, and race, ethnic origins and similar variables. These factors serve to sort and sift like-minded similarly-statused individuals into relatively homogeneous neighborhoods and communities, to differentiate central city and suburban life styles, and to polarize the central city itself. But when that is said, much else is repetition -- occupation tells the same story as income, age differences indicate stage in life cycle, etc.

Accordingly, we selected six key variables indicative of the above factors and forces for use in the comparative analysis of the sample of twelve metropolitan regions noted in Chapter 1. These are: age of housing, population density, use of public transportation, stage in life cycle, minority populations, and mean family incomes. Each variable was mapped in each region. The six sets of twelve maps that resulted are presented as Figures 2.21-2.26, following immediately. They show the city-to-city variations in social patterns that are to be compared with a variety of indicators of water, air, noise and solid wastes pollution later in the book.

Marked contrasts in the social geographies of the regions emerge on simple inspection. The age of housing variable for example, clearly differentiates the older from the newer urban regions, those metropolitan areas containing substantial rural peripheries from those that do not, and those growing by ring-like accretion from those that do not. Some regions, such as Washington, D.C., have well-defined growth rings, for example, but many others do not.

Both the density and the transportation variables also serve to differentiate older and newer metropolitan regions, while both the stage in life cycle and the race and ethnicity variables call into question any highly simplistic generalizations about central city-suburb differences. Likewise the variations in the spatial patterns of incomes show there to be no simple statements about spatial patterns equally applicable to all metropolitan areas and all parts of the country. It follows that only if pollution patterns vary both equally and in the same manner, is there any reason to expect consistent relationships between the social geographies of metropolitan regions and the incidences and impacts of environmental pollution.

AGE OF HOUSING

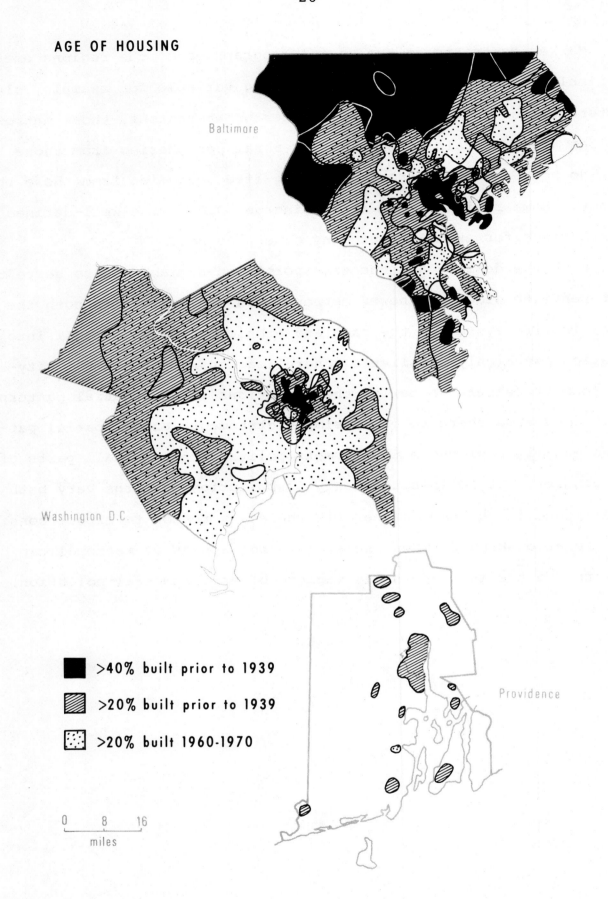

Baltimore

Washington D.C.

Providence

■ >40% built prior to 1939

▨ >20% built prior to 1939

░ >20% built 1960-1970

0   8   16
miles

Figure 2.21a. Age of Housing: Baltimore, Washington, and Providence.

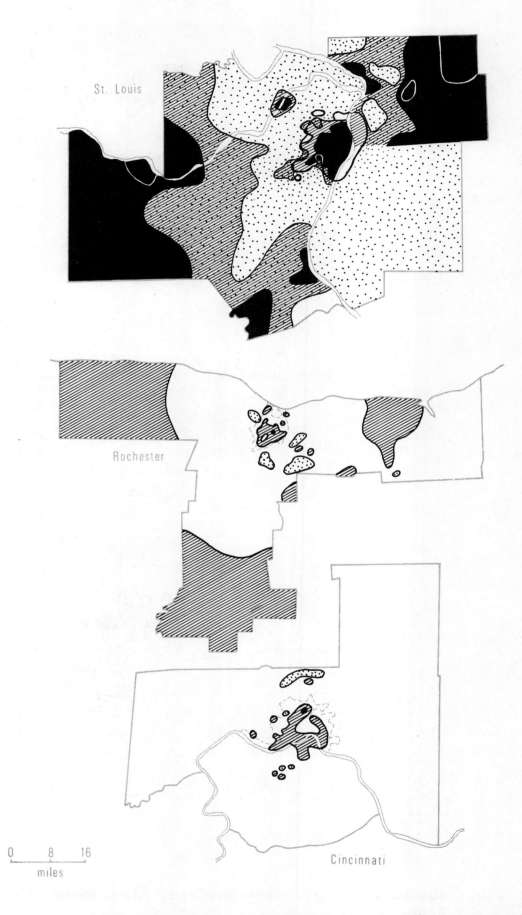

Figure 2.21b. Age of Housing: St. Louis, Rochester, and Cincinnati.

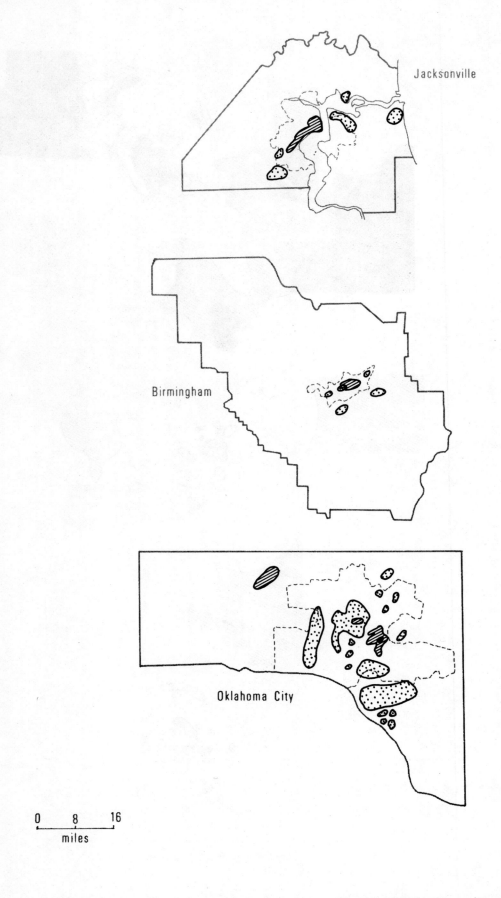

Figure 2.21c. Age of Housing: Jacksonville, Birmingham, and Oklahoma City.

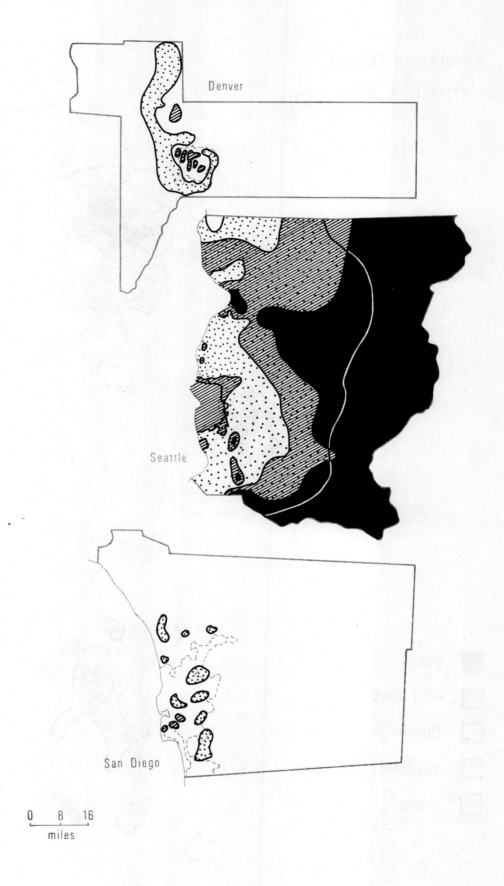

Figure 2.21d. Age of Housing: Denver, Seattle, and San Diego.

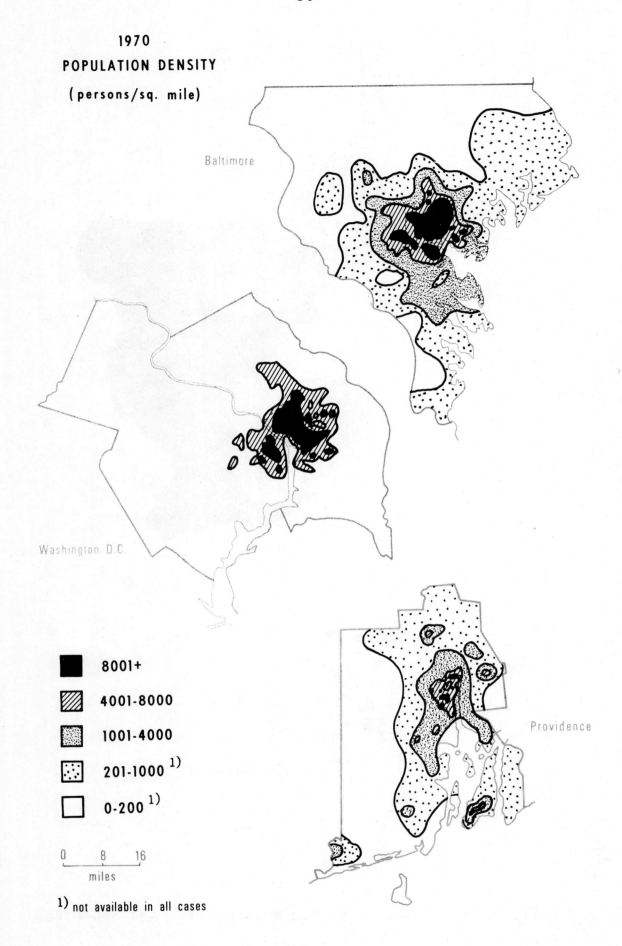

1970
POPULATION DENSITY
(persons/sq. mile)

Baltimore

Washington D.C.

Providence

■ 8001+

▨ 4001-8000

▦ 1001-4000

⬚ 201-1000 [1]

□ 0-200 [1]

0   8   16
miles

[1] not available in all cases

Figure 2.22a.   Population Density: Baltimore, Washington and Providence.

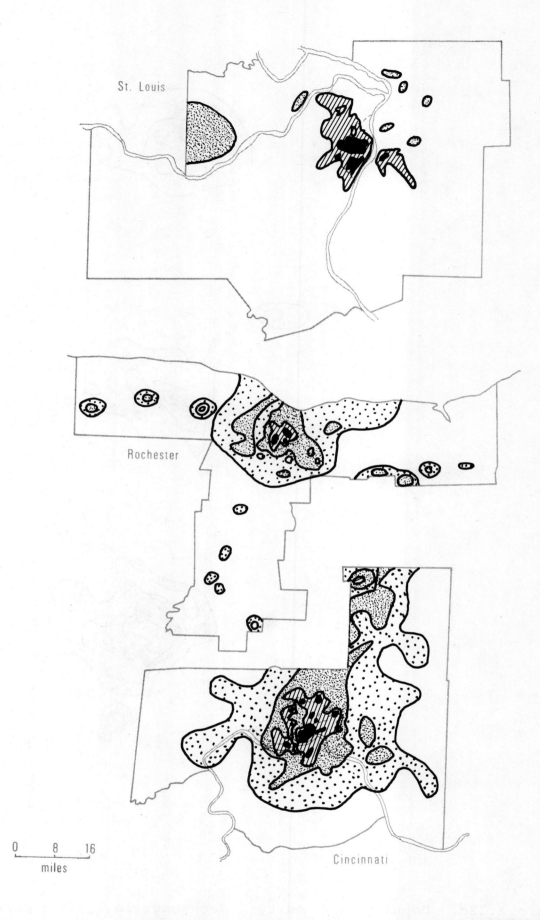

Figure 2.22b. Population Density: St. Louis, Rochester and Cincinnati.

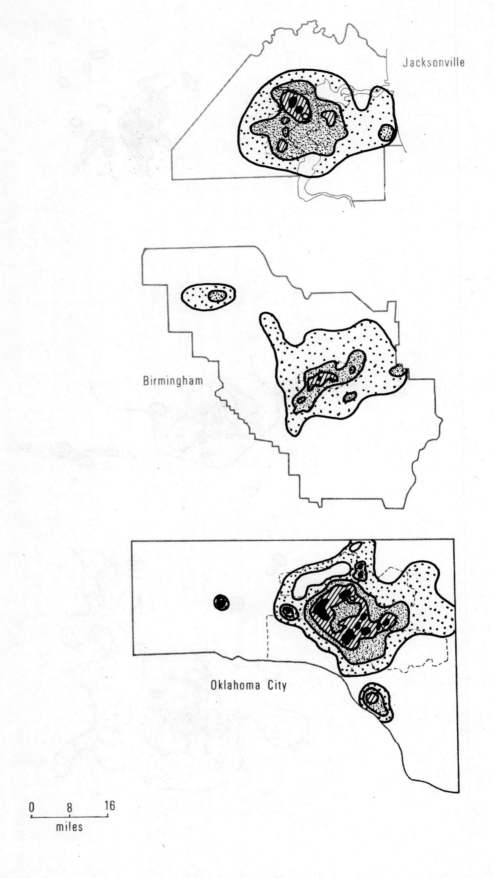

Figure 2.22c.   Population Density: Jacksonville, Birmingham and Oklahoma City.

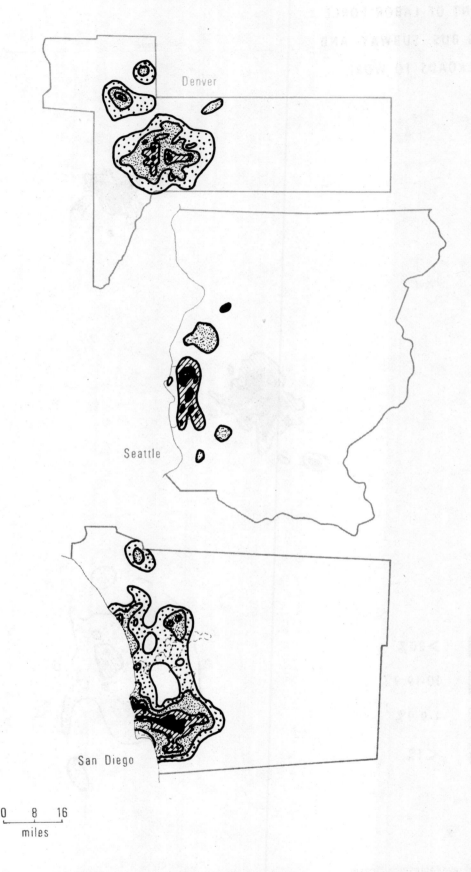

Figure 2.22d. Population Density: Denver, Seattle and San Diego.

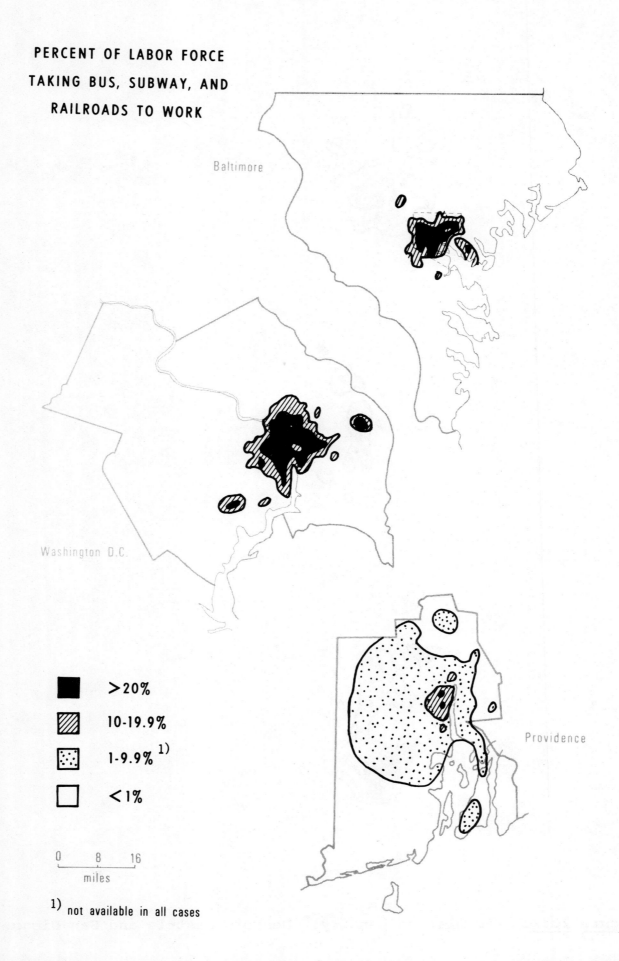

PERCENT OF LABOR FORCE
TAKING BUS, SUBWAY, AND
RAILROADS TO WORK

Baltimore

Washington D.C.

Providence

■ >20%

▨ 10-19.9%

▨ 1-9.9% 1)

☐ <1%

0 8 16
miles

1) not available in all cases

Figure 2.23a.   Percent of Labor Force Taking Bus, Subway, and Railroads
to Work: Baltimore, Washington and Providence.

Figure 2.23b. Percent of Labor Force Taking Bus, Subway, and Railroads to Work: St. Louis, Rochester and Cincinnati.

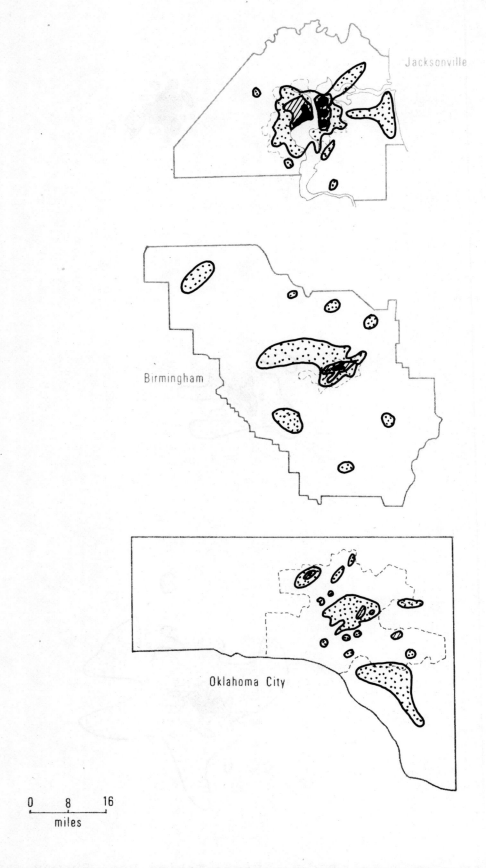

0   8   16
miles

Figure 2.23c.   Percent of Labor Force Taking Bus, Subway, and Railroads to Work: Jacksonville, Birmingham, and Oklahoma
City.

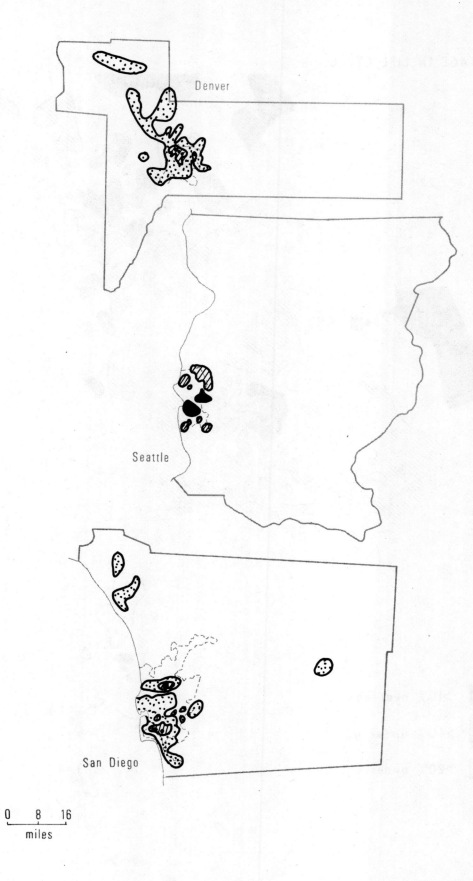

Figure 2.23d.   Percent of Labor Force Taking Bus, Subway, and Railroads
to Work: Denver, Seattle and San Diego.

STAGE IN LIFE CYCLE

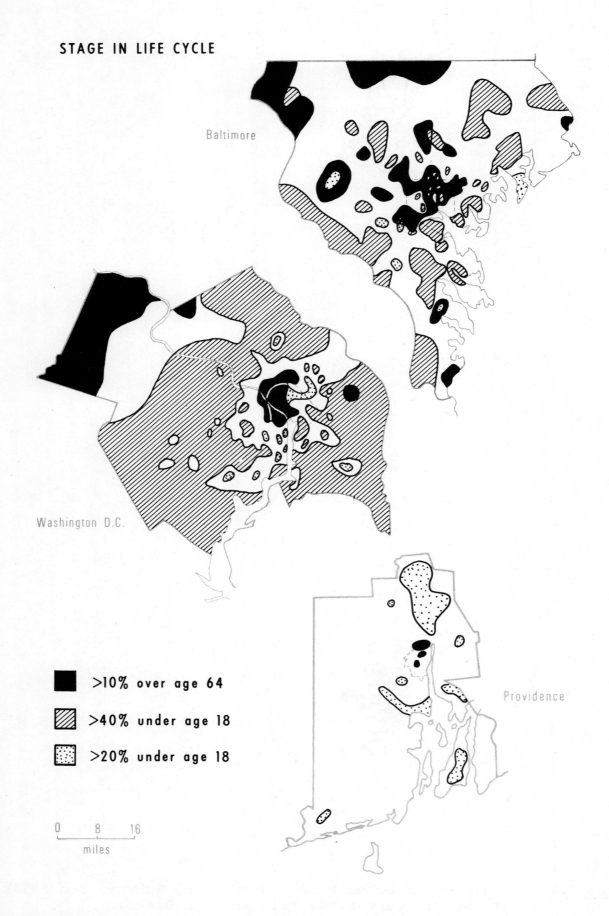

Figure 2.24a. Stage in Life Cycle: Baltimore, Washington and Providence.

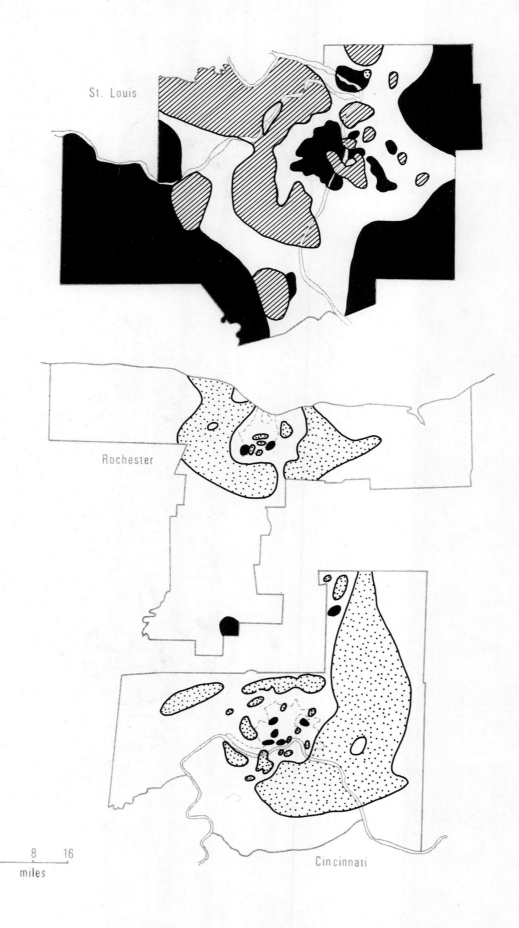

Figure 2.24b. Stage in Life Cycle: St. Louis, Rochester and Cincinnati.

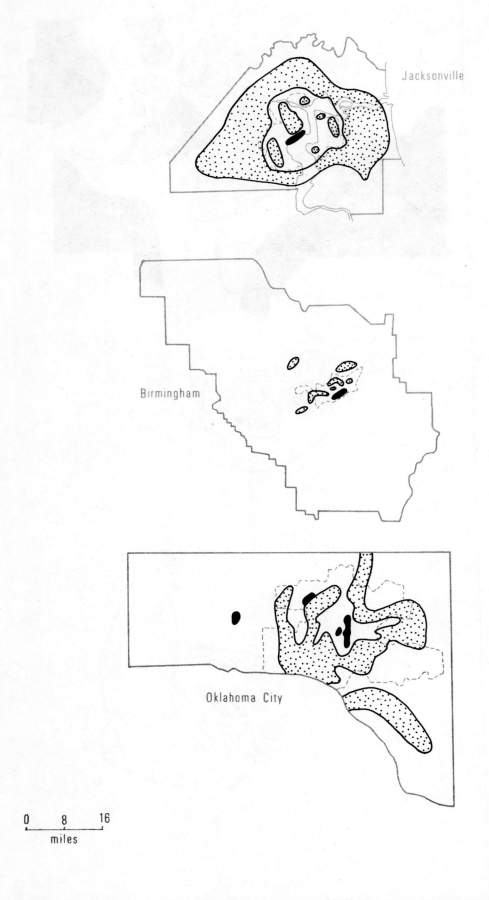

Figure 2.24c. <u>Stage in Life Cycle:</u> Jacksonville, Birmingham, and Oklahoma City.

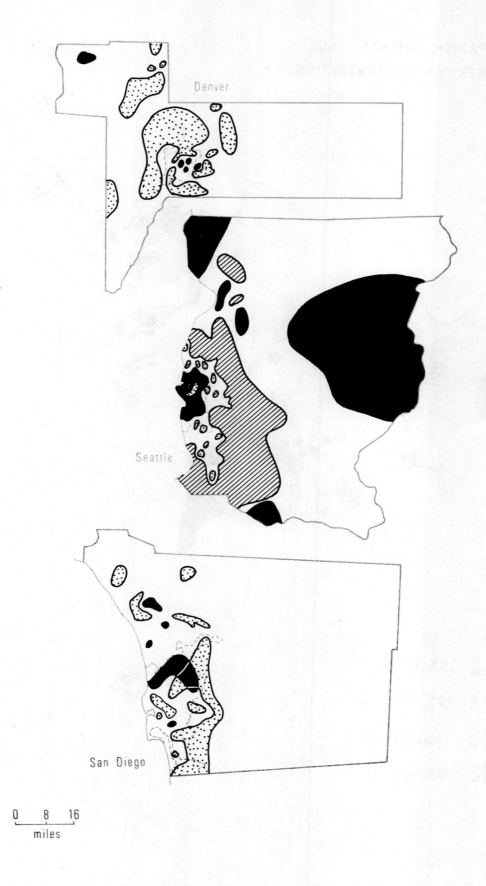

Denver

Seattle

San Diego

0   8   16
miles

Figure 2.24d. **Stage in Life Cycle:** Denver, Seattle and San Diego.

BLACK, SPANISH, ORIENTAL, AND
NATIVE AMERICAN CONCENTRATIONS

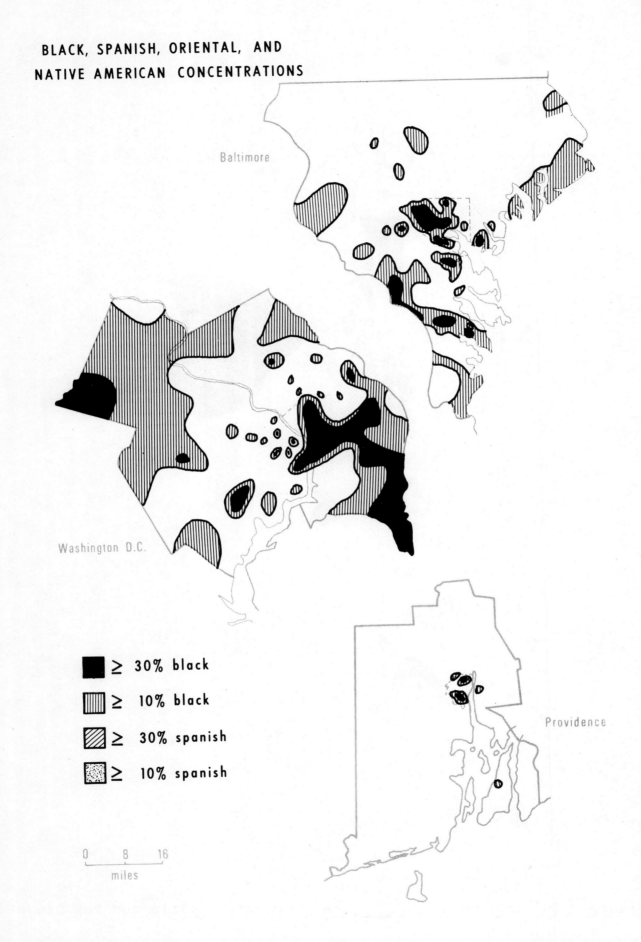

Figure 2.25a.   Black, Spanish, Oriental, and Native American Concentrations: Baltimore, Washington and Providence.

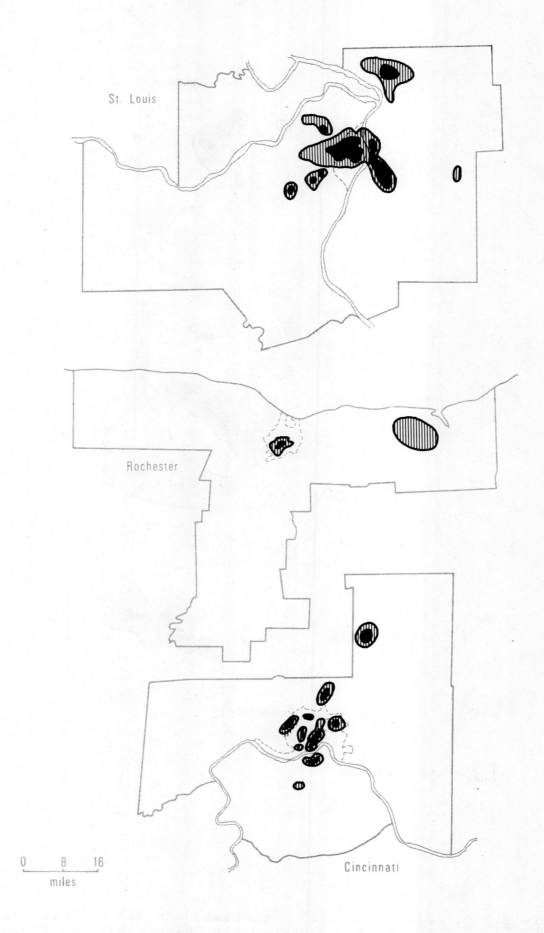

Figure 2.25b. Black, Spanish, Oriental, and Native American Concentrations: St. Louis, Rochester and Cincinnati.

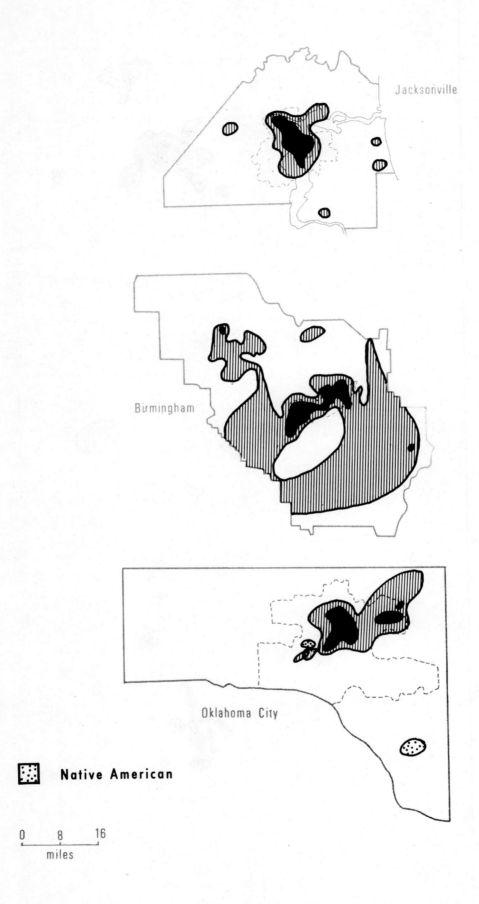

Figure 2.25c. Black, Spanish, Oriental, and Native American Concentrations: Jacksonville, Birmingham and Oklahoma City.

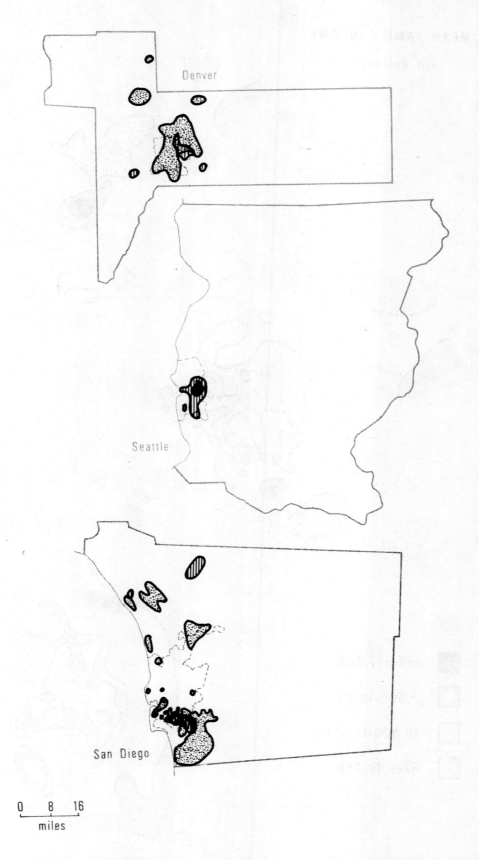

Figure 2.25d.   Black, Spanish, Oriental, and Native American Concentrations: Denver, Seattle, and San Diego.

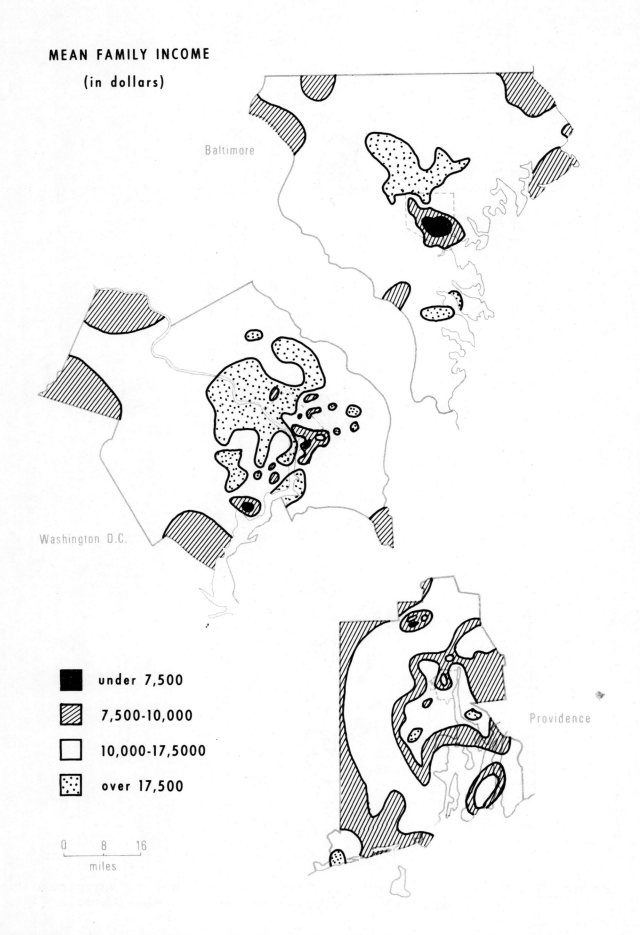

MEAN FAMILY INCOME

(in dollars)

Baltimore

Washington D.C.

Providence

■ under 7,500

▨ 7,500-10,000

□ 10,000-17,5000

▨ over 17,500

0   8   16

miles

Figure 2.26a.   Mean Family Income: Baltimore, Washington and Providence.

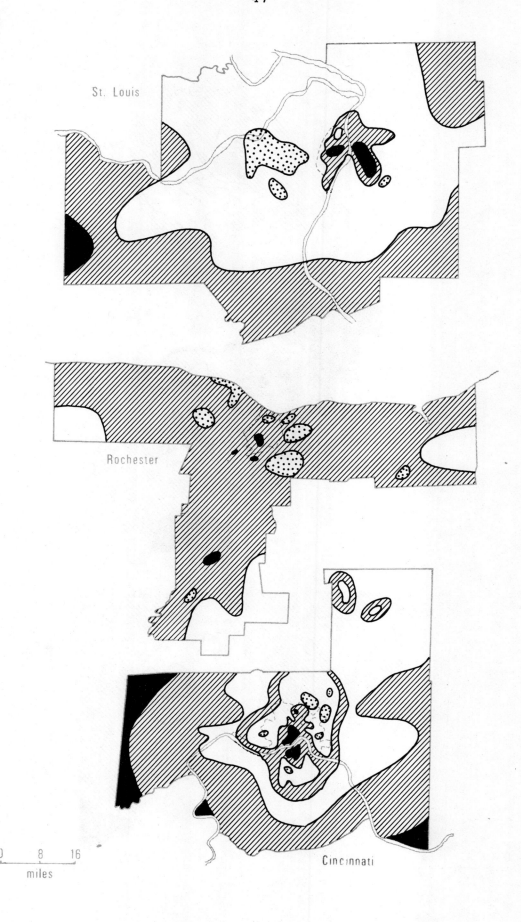

Figure 2.26b. Mean Family Income: St. Louis, Rochester and Cincinnati.

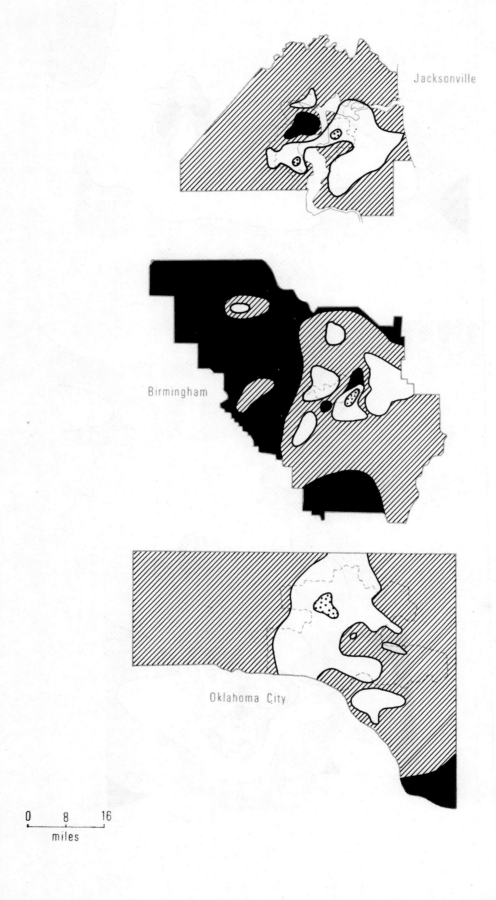

Figure 2.26c. Mean Family Income: Jacksonville, Birmingham and
Oklahoma City.

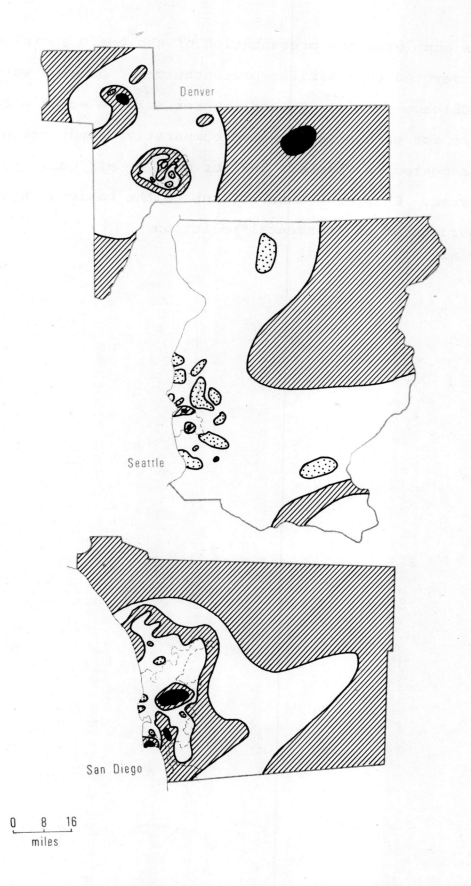

Denver

Seattle

San Diego

0   8   16
miles

Figure 2.26d. Mean Family Income: Denver, Seattle and San Diego.

This completes the presentation of the basic social maps. Chapter 3 is devoted to a similar presentation of data on water quality for the Chicago case study, and Chapter 4 to selected water quality parameters for each of the twelve comparative study regions. The process is repeated in Chapters 5-7 for data on air quality, noise and solid wastes. Chapter 8 then returns to the basic question of the social burdens of environmental pollution.

 *Chapter 3*

Water Quality: The Metropolitan Chicago
Case

We began our case-study investigations by analyzing the quality
of both drinking water and of the surface waters in the Metropolitan
Chicago region. In both cases, the ultimate water source is precipitation; the question addressed is of the nature, magnitude, spatial
pattern and causes of pollution of this water.

The amount of precipitation that falls in the Chicago watershed
averages approximately 35 inches a year. It was 28.4 inches in 1971,
a year of relatively intense storms and the study year for our Chicago water quality analysis. What happens to the water after it
reaches the ground depends upon many factors such as rate of rainfall,
topography, soil condition, density of vegetation, temperature and
the extent of urbanization. The direct runoff in Chicago is relatively great, not only because the density of impermeable pavements
and roofs permits less rain to infiltrate the ground, but also because storm sewer systems carry more water directly to the treatment
plants and the managed hydrologic network. Some of the rain that
enters the ground filters into subsurface aquifers. Before proceeding

to a discussion of areawide water supply and quality, it therefore is appropriate to gain an appreciation, in gross terms, as to the role of rainfall as an urban resource and as a potential hazard. For every inch of rain falling evenly over the acreage in the Chicago watershed, the following volumes of water are involved:

	CHICAGO WATERSHED (1600 sq. mi.)	MSD* GENERAL SERVICE AREA (890 sq. mi.)
Acres	1,024,000	550,400
Cubic Feet	3,717,120,000	1,997,952,000
Gallons	1,567,188,616,000	14,945,561,600

* Metropolitan Sanitary District

	MSD COMBINED SEWER SERVICE AREA (375 sq. mi.)	CITY OF CHICAGO (224 sq. mi.)
Acres	240,000	141,888
Cubic Feet	871,200,000	515,053,440
Gallons	6,516,960,000	3,852,826,752

Evaporation and transpiration return much of this moisture to the atmosphere. However, the fact remains that an enormous amount of rainwater is deposited which supplements Lake Michigan as a potential water supply, replenishes aquifers, presents a direct problem in terms of runoff and flooding, and if polluted, can be a major health and welfare hazard. We first discuss the question of drinking water quality, and then turn to the quality of the surface waters.

The Quality of Drinking Water

Supplies from Lake Michigan

Drinking water for the City of Chicago and for 72 of the inner-most suburbs is drawn from Lake Michigan and is provided by the City's Department of Water and Sewers. The Department of Water and Sewers operates two intake cribs 2 miles out into the Lake which bring water to the two filtration plants where water is treated before it is delivered to City residents. In terms of water quality treatment practices, the treatment process is conventional, but it is highly effective in bringing uniformly good quality water to all residents in the region who are supplied with it, which means that the inner-city poor are well-served in this regard.

In the treatment process, raw water brought to the filtration plants passes through traveling screens which remove fish, weeds and trash. Chemicals are then added to the water; chlorine is added to kill bacteria; anhydrous ammonia to stabilize the chlorine residual and to decrease the chlorinous tastes; aluminum sulphate or oxidized ferrous sulphate to produce coagulation; lime or caustic soda to adjust the pH level; activated carbon to remove objectionable tastes and odors; and fluoride to reduce cavities in children's teeth. Once the chemicals are added, water passes to mixing basins where the coagulants react chemically to form floc which, with further mixing, grow larger in size entraining sediment and microorganisms. The water then flows into settling basins where 85 to 90% of the floc are removed. Then it receives final chemical treatment - chloride, ammonia and fluoride are added, and the water passes on to the pumping stations where it is pumped to customers.

The bacteriological and mineral quality of this water at the outlet composite is well below all the 1974 federal and state standards. It also meets the very strict standards recommended by the FWCPA in 1968. This water does not change in quality as it passes through the distribution system, even though some of the pipes are more than a hundred years old, because the treatment process includes stabilization. Stabilized water reaches the consumer with no change in chemical composition and without causing any changes to the piping system. There are both physical and chemical means of stabilizing water. The Department of Water and Sewers uses both means. Old cast iron feeder mains are cleaned and lined with cement to provide a physical barrier against corrosion. Chemically, an egg-shell film of $CaCO$ along all the pipes will prevent corrosion. The Dept. of Water and Sewers adjusts the pH of the water by adding lime or caustic soda so that the water is just saturated with calcium carbonate. In this way, the water will neither be corrosive nor encrusting. A further preventitive to corrosion of bare metals is maintenance of the mineral quality of the water at an alkalinity of above 100 mg/l and at calcium levels as $CaCO$ above 50 mg/l. Chicago's water meets both the alkalinity levels and the calcium levels. Thus there is little danger of corrosion of the copper and lead service pipes which are in use, and so all Chicago residents are assured of high quality water, as are the residents of the inner suburbs which purchase water from Chicago.

Groundwater Supplies

In suburbs using groundwater to meet their drinking needs, water is not chemically stabilized, but because the groundwater in Northeastern Illinois tends to be hard and free of dissolved oxygen, the water is naturally protected against corrosion. However, those suburbs which soften groundwater that contains chloride and sulfate ions may have corrosion problems, because softening reduces the natural protection that hardness provides.

Groundwater currently serves the needs of two million people and many industries in the suburban area of Chicago. Both its quality and quantity are becoming matters of increasing concern because the most rapidly growing western suburbs rely solely on groundwater supplies for domestic and industrial consumption. Because the quality and quantity of groundwater varies with the nature of the geological structures in which it is stored and with the quality and quantity of its sources of replenishment, some discussion of these background factors is warranted. The discussion reveals that it is the more affluent suburbanite who drinks the worst quality water in the Chicago region.

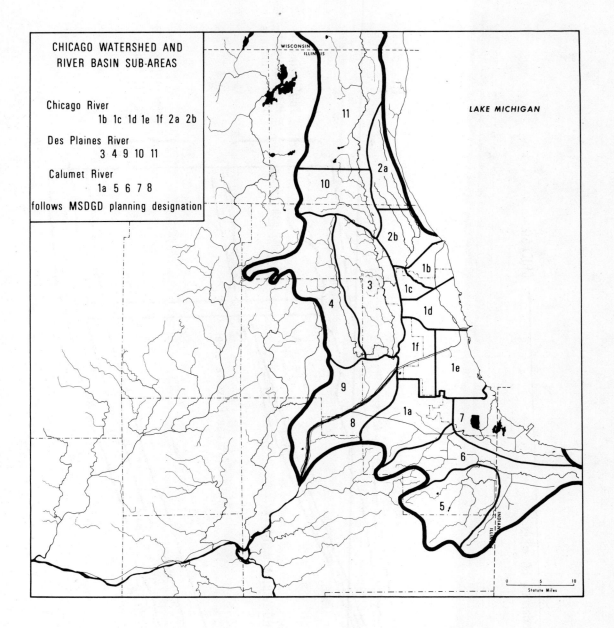

Figure 3.1 (above). The Chicago watershed encompasses 1,600 square miles and includes four counties in Illinois and one each in Wisconsin and Indiana.

Figure 3.2 (next page). There are two main sources of potable water supply for consumers in the area: The surface water from Lake Michigan and groundwater from the extensive aquifers which underlie the region. Groundwater is obtained from both the deep Cambrian-Ordovician and the shallow Silurian-Glacial drift aquifers.

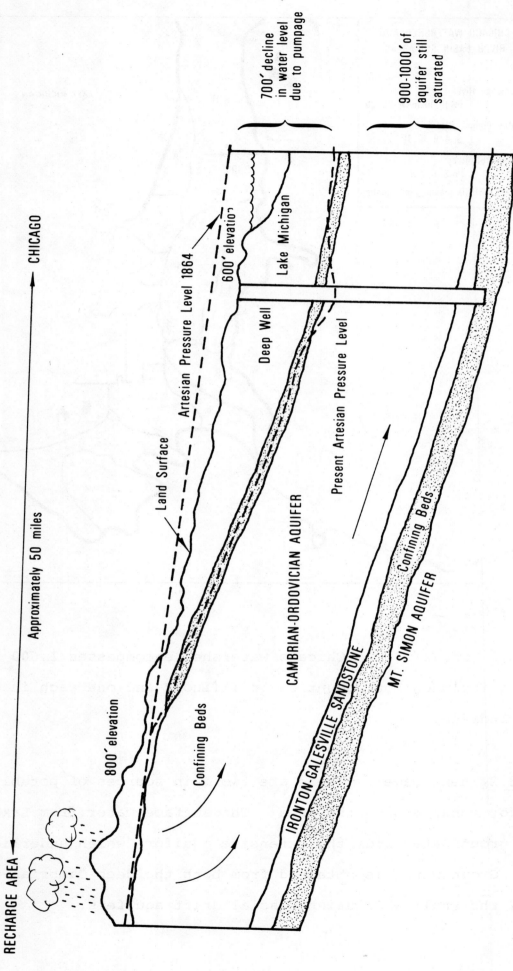

Source: Northeast Illinois
Planning Commission

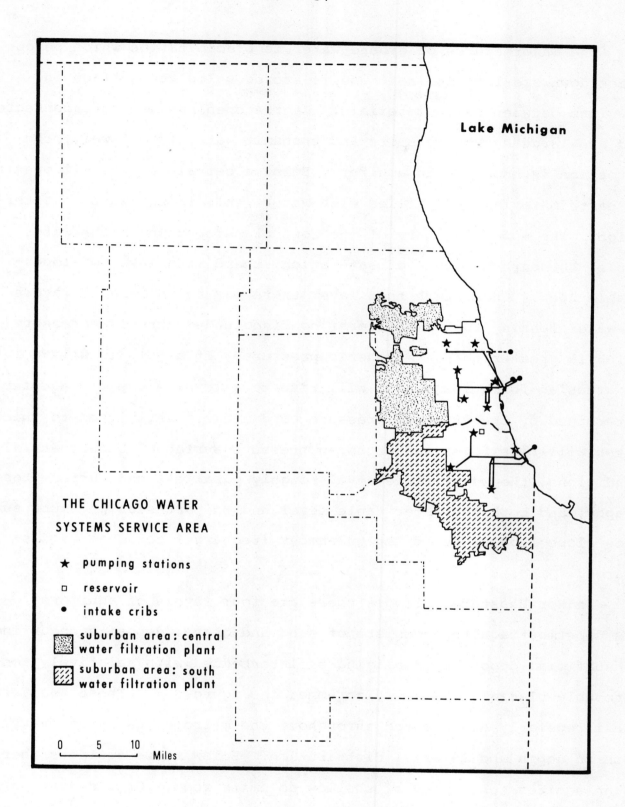

THE CHICAGO WATER
SYSTEMS SERVICE AREA

★ pumping stations

□ reservoir

● intake cribs

suburban area: central
water filtration plant

suburban area: south
water filtration plant

0   5   10
Miles

Figure 3.3. The two major water treatment plants which pump the Lake Michigan surface water are the Central Water Filtration Plant and the South Water Filtration Plant. These plants serve the City of Chicago and many adjacent municipalities. The balance of the region relies upon groundwater.

The major source of ground water is precipitation which percolates downward into the soil and is stored below the surface in openings between earth materials. If the openings are interconnected and are large enough to store and transmit water into a well, the formation is known as an aquifer. Below a certain depth, all openings in earth materials are filled with water; this is the zone of saturation. The upper boundary of the zone of saturation is the water table. Beneath the zone of saturation, there is a layer of impermeable rock. Underneath that layer there may be additional layers of water bearing rocks (aquifers) confined under artesian pressure which is greater than atmospheric pressure. If a well is driven into an artesian formation, water will rise to a level above the aquifer determined by the artesian pressure conditions. This level to which water will rise forms the artesian pressure surface. Under natural conditions, the water table level roughly parallels the surface topography, and both the water table level and the artesian pressure surface slope from areas of replenishment (recharge) to areas of discharge.

In Northeastern Illinois there are four levels of aquifers. The uppermost aquifer consists of sand and gravel deposits occurring as surficial deposits underlying or interbedded with relatively nonpermeable glacial tills as diagrammed in Figure 3.4. These aquifers are irregularly distributed throughout the metropolitan area, varying both in depth and in areal distribution. Below these aquifers there is an aquifer consisting of shallow dolomite rock. Groundwater is stored and flows through the interconnected joints, crevices and fissures of this bedrock. This aquifer underlies most of the metropolitan area and lies up to 400 feet below the surface becoming thicker as it extends toward the Indiana border. The sand and gravel aquifers and the shallow dolomite aquifers are hydraulically interrelated and considered as one unit. In some places, water flows freely from

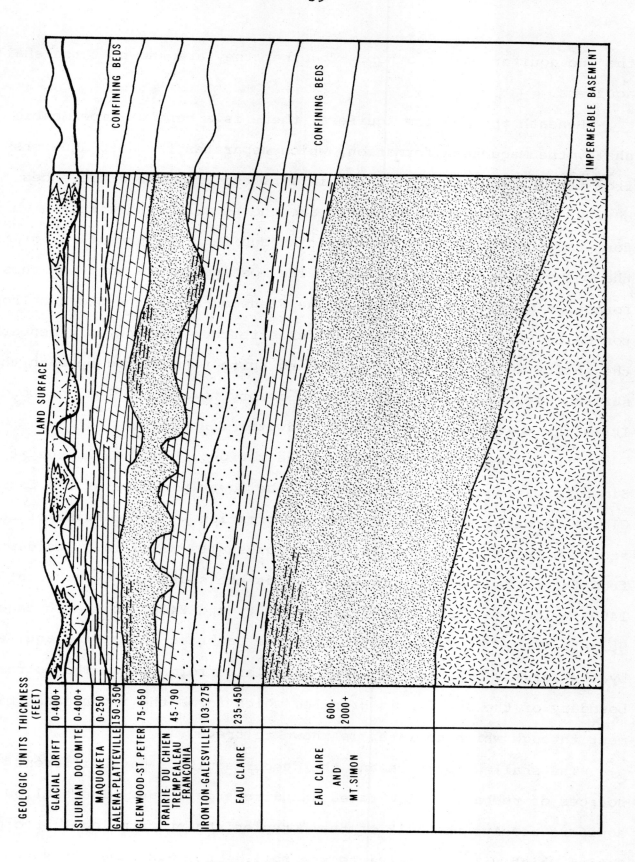

Figure 3.4. Subsurface Geology in Northeastern Illinois.

Source: Northeast Illinois Planning Commission

the one aquifer to the other. Together they are known as the shallow aquifers.

Beneath the shallow aquifers, there is a band of impermeable shale, the Maquoketa formation, which separates the deep aquifers from the shallow aquifers and maintains the pressure differences between them. Below this, there are the permeable rock strata which form the artesian Cambrian-Ordovician aquifer. Figure 3.4 diagrams the composition of this aquifer. The most permeable units of this formation are the sandstones of the Glenwood-St. Peter and the Ironton-Galesville layers. This aquifer stretches continuously beneath the entire metropolitan area becoming further submerged beneath the surface as it advances from McHenry county toward the Indiana border. It is the most heavily tapped groundwater resource.

The deepest known aquifer in the metropolitan area is the Mt. Simon formation. It is composed of the lower portions of the Eau Claire formations and the Mt. Simon formation. They consist of sandstone but with siltstones and micaceous shales mixed in. Its depth from the surface also increases towards the southeast lying about 1400' below the surface in McHenry county and 2400' in the Chicago Heights area. It is separated from the Cambrian-Ordovician aquifer by the largely impermeable upper Eau Claire formation. The bottom boundary of the aquifer is granite, which forms the impermeable basement through which no water is known to travel.

The shallow aquifers and the deeper aquifers have different sources of recharge, flow rates and discharge areas. The shallow aquifers receive the bulk of their replenishment from local precipitation which filters down into the soil. They also receive some replenishment by infiltration from some local streams and flood plains. Under natural conditions, the ground water flows through the aquifers following the downward slope of the landscape at a rate of a few feet per day. It flows out of the aquifers forming the

base flow to lower lying streams and by evapotranspiration. But the
many wells that have been built in the past hundred years have altered
the flow of the ground water. Pumpage for domestic and industrial
consumption adds another source of discharge. The water table has
been lowered in some areas, and the deep wells that have been built
have opened up holes in the Maquoketa formation allowing 4% of its
practical sustained yield to leak downward into the underlying aquifer. But despite these changes, there has been no overall decline
in the water levels of this aquifer. In 1967 pumpage from the shallow aquifers was 114 mgd or only 22% of the total of 507 mgd which
could be withdrawn from the shallow aquifers without mining water
from storage. The shallow aquifers are not used to their full capacity because of their irregular occurence, unpredictable yields and
relatively poor quality water. Local precipitation and outflow from
streams more than replaces the water that is lost through pumpage,
although there may be seasonal declines in water levels.

The Cambrian-Ordovician aquifers and the Mt. Simon aquifer are
not recharged locally. Their source of recharge is approximately
50 miles west of the Chicago Loop in western McHenry, Boone and Dekalb
counties where the uppermost layer of the Cambrian-Ordovician aquifer
outcrops at the surface. The Maquoketa formation is thin and relatively permeable as precipitation filters through it also. But the
amount of recharge it receives is only about one-tenth that of the
shallow aquifers. The Chicago area only receives about one-fifth of
that flow because of the very slow rate of flow in the aquifer, and
because of the slight hydraulic gradient. But the Cambrian-Ordovician aquifer contains vast amounts of water in storage. The Illinois
State Geological Survey estimates that it contains 209,400,000 million
gallons of "free water," i.e. that water which could drain from
rocks by gravity. Under natural conditions, the Cambrian-Ordovician
aquifer was in dynamic equilibrium because the water which was re-

charged to it was discharged upward to the Maquoketa formation by
artesian pressure, and by leakage to the Illinois River. The water
flowed in a southeasternly direction. The artesian pressure surface
in 1864 was estimated to be about 100 feet above the surface in
Chicago, for that was the elevation to which water flowed when the
first deep well was drilled.

Since that time, there has been a very drastic change in the
rate and direction of flow in the Cambrian-Ordovician aquifer. Deep
wells drilled into the aquifer create cones of depression about them
which lower the water level and the artesian pressure levels in their
vicinity as diagrammed in Figure 3.2. It has been calculated that
it takes 180 years for a cone of depression to become stabilized.
Until that time, all water taken into the well is drawn from storage
rather than from recharge flowing into the aquifer. Thus the artesian pressure levels in the Chicago area have been falling since
1864, although it was not until 1958 that pumpage exceeded the practical sustained yield of the aquifer of 44.6 mgd. In 1966, the
general flow of water was from all directions toward deep cones of
depression surrounding the pumping centers at Summit, Elmhurst,
Joliet, Elgin, Aurora , and Des Plaines. The lowering of the water
levels at these areas of heavy pumpage has steepened the hydraulic
gradients so that 20 times as much water is flowing toward these
areas than formerly, most of which is derived from storage. The
artesian pressure surface is 900 feet lower than in 1864 in some
areas. Water levels in wells are now declining so rapidly in these
areas (as much as 20' per year in Des Plaines and Joliet) that the
top layer of the aquifer, the Glenwood St. Peter is being dewatered.

This extensive mining of the Cambrian-Ordovician aquifer has
consequences for the flow and quality of ground water for current
residents as well as reducing the potential water resource for future
generations. The reduced artesian pressure increases pumping costs

and causes water to leak downward from the shallow aquifers and to leak upward from the Mt. Simon aquifer. This leakage lessens the quality of water drawn up through wells in the Cambrian-Ordovician aquifer. This mining of the aquifer can only take place for 30 years before serious dewatering will occur.

Quality of the Ground Water Aquifers

Of more immediate concern than quantity, is the quality of ground waters currently being tapped for domestic and industrial supplies, however. Each of the aquifers differs in quality because of their different storage sites and different sources of recharge. Within each aquifer there are also differences in mineral quality at different geographical locations and at different elevations.

The shallow aquifers display the most variability of mineral and bacteriological content. They tend to have a high iron content averaging 2.0 mg/l and ranging from 0 to 29 mg/l. The shallow aquifers in the western portion of the metropolitan area have low sulphate contents. Hardness ranges from less than 100 mg/l to more than 1000 mg/l; see Figure 3.5. Whether or not the hardest water (greater than 1000 mg/l) is due to natural causes is disputed. The average hardness of water in the aquifers has been increasing. In 1958 the median hardness was 275 mg/l, with half of 60 samples falling between 225 and 325 mg/l. In 1966, the Northeastern Illinois Planning Commission reported that typical values of hardness were 440 mg/l. The areas of exceptionally hard water have increased significantly in areal extent, especially along the length of the Chicago Sanitary and Ship Canal. Exceptionally hard water in Du Page County was found to have been caused by seepage from an industrial waste lagoon through 100 feet of overlying drift. Thus there is some presumptive evidence of pollution but it has not been substantiated for all of the areas with exceptionally hard water.

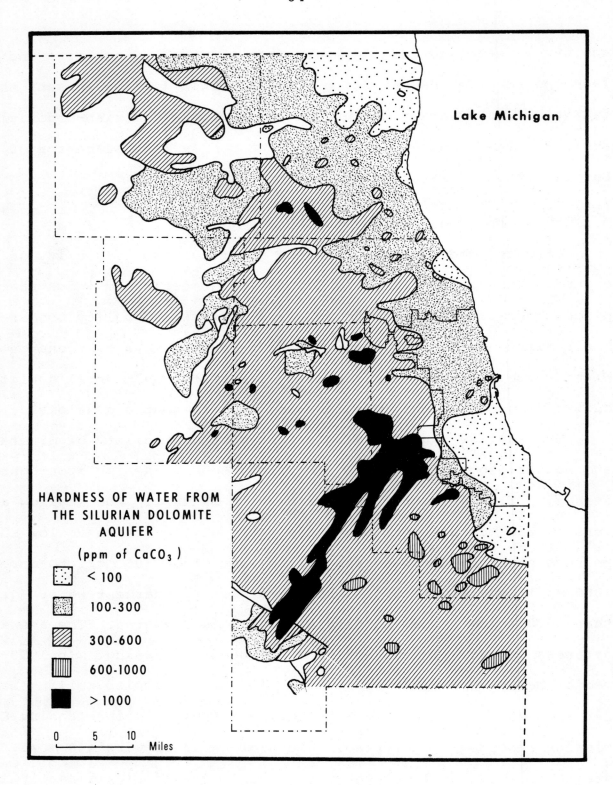

Figure 3.5. Hardness of water in the shallow aquifers gradually increases from east to west. The harder water generally coincides with the uplands produced by the Valparaiso moraine.

The shallow aquifers are susceptible to pollution from many sources. The most prevalent source of pollution is improperly placed or maintained septic systems. Figure 3.6 shows the distribution of septic systems in 1960 based on U.S. Census data. There is a ring of heavy concentration around the central city and additional areas of heavy concentration in the McHenry Chain of Lakes area to the north, the Fox River Valley and the Joliet vicinity. Since then, the 1970 census shows that the number of septic systems has remained roughly the same in the outlying counties. But there have been significant reductions of 30 percent and 15 percent in Cook and Lake Counties. Thus there has been some progress in these counties toward reducing the threat of this source of contamination.

Industrial and domestic waste oxidation lagoons pose another contamination threat to ground water. In 1963, the State Sanitary Water Board and the County Health Departments had records on 46 lagoons. There may have been others, for permits are only required of those which have surface stream outlets. According to NIPC, their number has been increasing, for they are an inexpensive and simple method of waste treatment and federal financing is available for their construction. Seepage from land fill sites have also been noted as sources of ground water pollution, but a Northeastern Illinois Planning Commission report states in 1974 that very few cases of contamination have been reported.

Other sources of shallow ground water pollution relate to stream flow and well construction. Pollutants in streams can infiltrate ground water during floods and through normal ground water recharge. Improper well construction can lead to bacteriological pollution of ground water.

But despite these many sources of potential pollutants, not all shallow ground water is in serious danger of pollution, for some of the geological environments in the metropolitan area offer protection

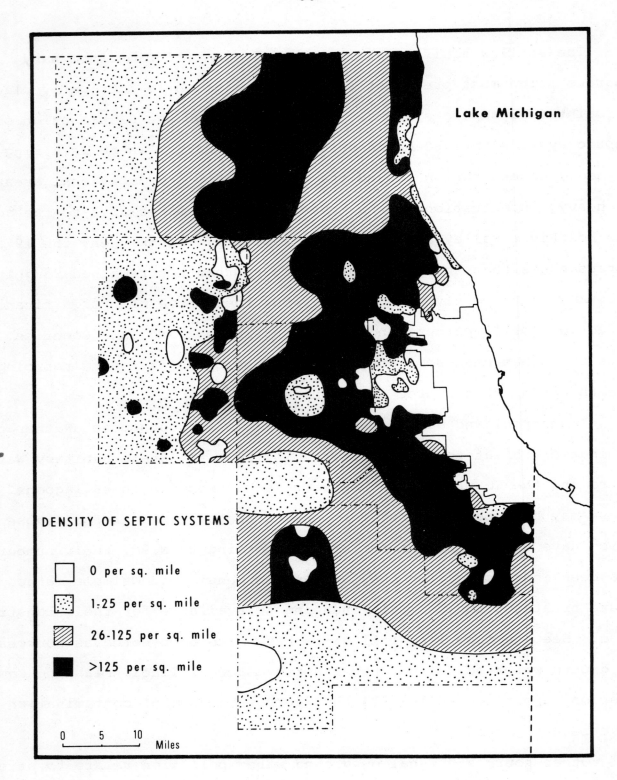

Figure 3.6. Septic tank systems in the Chicago region in 1970.

against it. Overlying soil and sand filter and purify the water as
it percolates downward. However, there are many areas within the
metropolitan area where bedrock is exposed at the surface, where there
is less than 50 feet of cover over creviced dolomite, where sand and
gravel aquifers are near the surface, and where other relatively permeable surface materials are found which offer no protection against
ground water pollution. Figure 3.7 shows the distribution of these
areas. Both bacteriological and chemical pollutants can travel particularly rapidly in creviced dolomite aquifers, for they offer little
resistance to the flow of water. Ground water has very little capacity to purify itself.

A comparison of this map with the map of the distribution of
septic systems and with maps showing the quality of the surface rivers
and streams which appear later in this chapter will point up the most
likely areas to suffer from ground water pollution. So far, there
has been no systematic survey of ground water pollution in Northeastern
Illinois, but it is known that one-third of the septic systems and
40 percent of the waste oxidation lagoons are situated in unfavorable
geological environments. Another two-thirds of the septic systems
are located in soils which the U.S. Conservation Service does not
consider appropriate for them. Many of the surface rivers are located
in areas of bedrock and dolomite exposure. And most of rural McHenry
County, which suffers the additional threat of agricultural feedlot
pollution, is located in unfavorable geological environments, and its
ground water flows towards the rest of the metropolitan area. Thus
the conditions exist for extensive ground water pollution in the
metropolitan area. But so far, there has been no systematic survey
of ground water pollution in Northeastern Illinois.

What evidence can be assembled here? The State Department of
Public Health and the Illinois State Water Survey monitor the bacteriological and chemical constitutents of public ground water supplies,

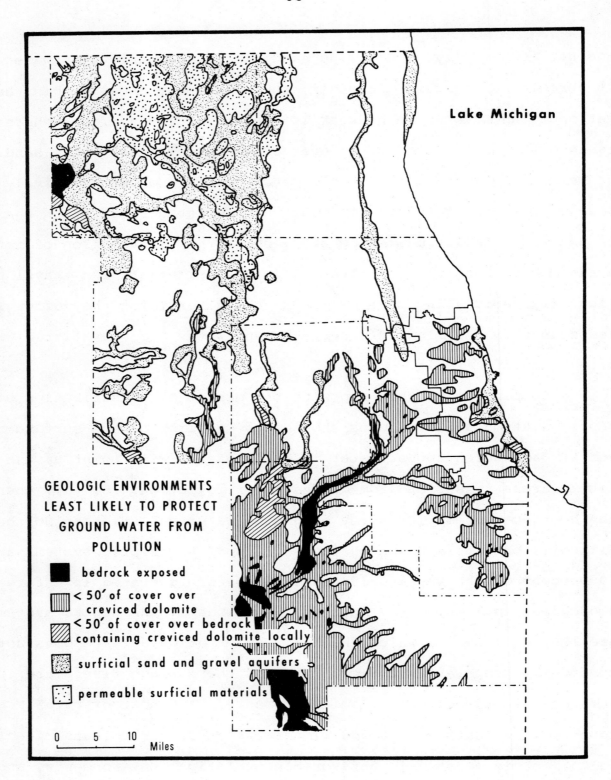

Lake Michigan

GEOLOGIC ENVIRONMENTS
LEAST LIKELY TO PROTECT
GROUND WATER FROM
POLLUTION

■ bedrock exposed

< 50' of cover over
creviced dolomite

< 50' of cover over bedrock
containing creviced dolomite locally

surficial sand and gravel aquifers

permeable surficial materials

0   5   10
Miles

Figure 3.7. Naturally hazardous environmental conditions.

but the 126,340 private wells in the SMSA are only analysed upon request. Thus, there is no thorough network of sampling points for analyzing the quality of shallow groundwater supplies. There are difficulties with using only the public supplies as an indicator of the quality of the shallow aquifers because most public wells penetrate the Cambrian-Ordovician aquifer as well as the shallow aquifers. There is some unsystematic evidence of pollution in private wells. In one county's survey of 3,000 wells, 27 percent of the household supplies were bacteriologically contaminated. In another survey of private wells, 44 percent were above the standards set for coliforms. These high percentages of contaminated wells may result not only from contaminated water but also from improper well construction. In flooding periods, there also is serious danger to private wells. In the summer of 1972, 75 to 80 percent of the private wells in Du Page County were determined unsafe for use and more than 150 wells in Cook County were found to be seriously contaminated. There have also been many instances of high nitrates and MBAS concentrations (methylene blue active substances -- indication of detergents) in private wells.

Public wells, even those penetrating the shallow aquifers alone have not had serious problems with bacteriological nitrate contamination for in general they are better constructed and are built deeper than private wells. Bacteriological pollution of the deeper shallow aquifers is not prevalent, for bacteria do not travel in solutions and thus they are easily barred passage by overlying sand. The mineral quality of the municipal water supplies using the shallow aquifers will be discussed later.

The overall mineral quality of the two deep aquifers must be discussed separately because they are very different from one another, however. The mineral quality of the major water bearing units (the Glenwood-St. Peter and the Ironton-Galesville) of the Cambrian-Ordovician aquifer is relatively uniform in the western two-thirds of the metropolitan area. As the accompanying maps (Figures 3.8-3.10) illustrate, hardness, sulphates and chlorides are relatively low until the eastern border of Du Page County is reached. Then mineralization increases rapidly toward the Indiana border as the formations become further submerged beneath the surface. The temperature also increases from 56° in the west to 62° in the east with increasing elevation. Water from the sandstones of these formations has uniformly low iron content (.2 - .4 mg/l) and a fluoride concentration of 1.0 mg/l. Because of its low mineral content, the water from the western two-thirds of this aquifer is of very acceptable quality for municipal purposes. However water is rarely drawn from these two layers alone. Small quantities of sulphurous waters from the Galena-Platteville dolomite layer may enter wells as well as waters with high iron content from the shallow aquifers and water migrating upward from the Mt. Simon aquifer.

It is the Mt. Simon aquifer that contains the greatest amount of available water, but it is of the lowest quality. There are some clear sandstone beds but its more highly mineralized water makes it a poor aquifer. Below a depth of 1,300' below sea level, the chloride content is too high for public supplies. Nevertheless, many municipal wells do penetrate the aquifer and its highly mineralized waters get mixed in with better quality water from the Cambrian-Ordovician aquifer.

Unlike the shallow aquifers, the deep aquifers are in no danger of being polluted by local ground water seepage, for the impermeable Maquoketa and Eau Claire formations effectively prevent infiltration. There is the possibility of contamination at the recharge areas in western McHnery, Boone and DeKalb Counties, but there, relatively sparse population and the very slow movement of water in the aquifer make the threat of pollution very slight. The sandstones of the aquifer effectively filter away contaminants that do percolate downward in the recharge areas. There have been no recorded instances of bacterial contamination of the two aquifers. Abandoned wells, and wells

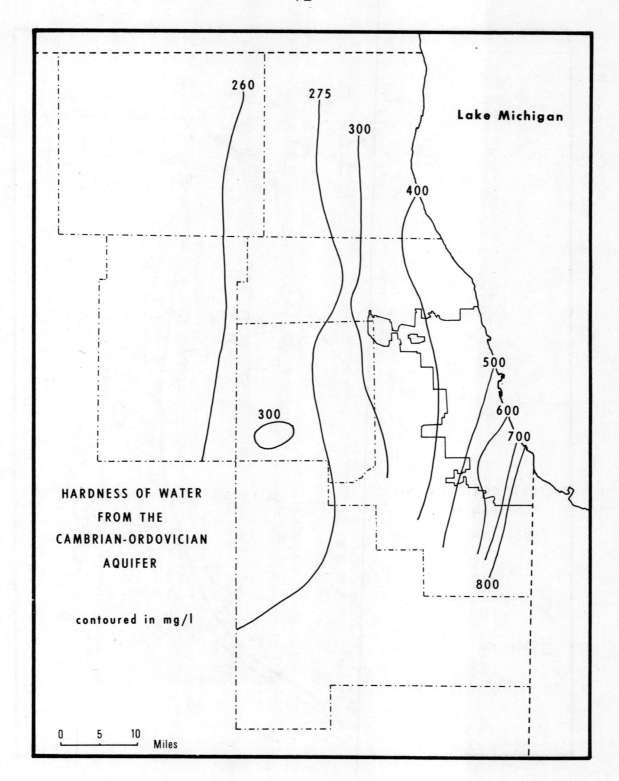

Figure 3.8. A sharp gradient is evident in the hardness of groundwater.

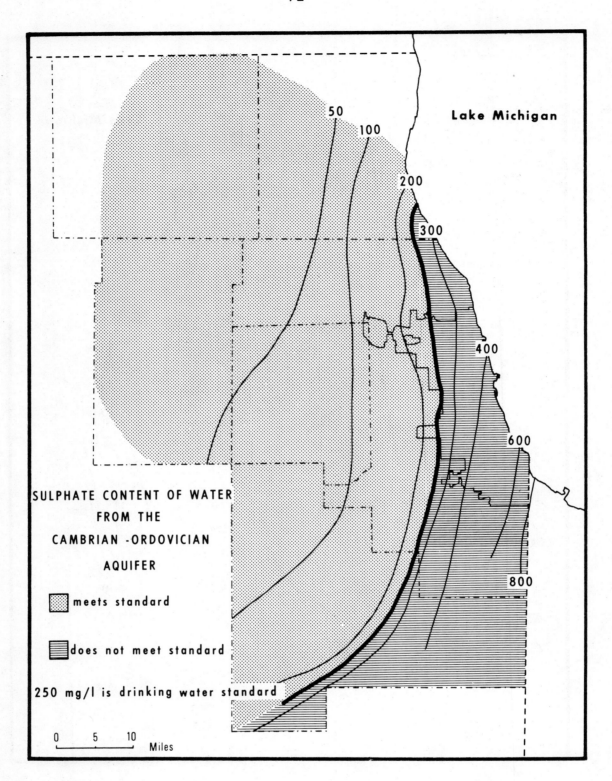

Lake Michigan

50
100
200
300
400
600
800

SULPHATE CONTENT OF WATER
FROM THE
CAMBRIAN -ORDOVICIAN
AQUIFER

meets standard

does not meet standard

250 mg/l is drinking water standard

0   5   10
Miles

Figure 3.9. Substantial parts of the groundwater supply fail to meet drinking water standards.

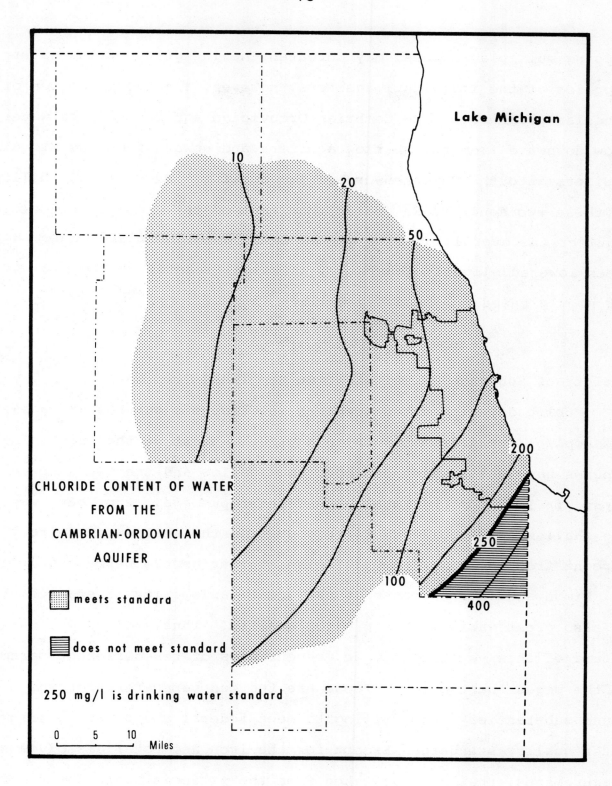

CHLORIDE CONTENT OF WATER

FROM THE

CAMBRIAN-ORDOVICIAN

AQUIFER

meets standard

does not meet standard

250 mg/l is drinking water standard

0   5   10
Miles

Figure 3.10.   Some parts of the aquifer also deliver excess levels of chlorides.

tapping multiple sources, may threaten the integrity of the water supplies of the individual aquifers, however, and the reduction of artesian pressure in the Cambrian-Ordovician aquifer induces water to flow downward from the shallow aquifers and upward from the Mt. Simon aquifers into the Cambrian-Ordovician aquifer. Because the quality of these two aquifers is poorer than that of the Cambrian-Ordovician aquifer the overall quality of the Cambrian-Ordovician aquifer has been lowered slightly generally, and significantly in the vicinity of poorly cased or abandoned wells.

Quality of Suburban Municipal Water Supplies

Public drinking water supplies in Chicago's suburbs are a mixture of supplies drawn from all three aquifers. Most of the incorporated suburbs have wells which tap both the shallow and the two deep aquifers. In 1967, of the total ground water pumpage, 12 percent was from the shallow sand aquifers, 34 percent from the shallow dolomite, 31 percent from the Cambrian-Ordovician aquifer and 23 percent from the Mt. Simon aquifer. Because of the great variability in sources, there is also great variability in water quality. Thus, to capture the nature of this variability, we present maps of ten different parameters in the pages that follow. These are the ten parameters for which we found substantial areas failing to meet federal and/or state drinking water quality standards. Except for the iron and total dissolved solids measurements, the data was taken from the Illinois State Water Survey records for 1969-73. Information relating to individual municipal wells was averaged to get a single indicator for each municipality with greater than 1,000 customer services, for each of the parameters measured by the Illinois State Water Survey. The measurements are of the _raw_ _ground_ _water_ _quality_ taken from the wells _before_ any treatment is given. Measurements for the iron and total dissolved solid content

of raw ground water and finished drinking water supplies were obtained
from the 1973 State of Illinois Public Water Supplies Data Book, published by the Illinois Environmental Protection Agency. Following
the procedures used throughout this study, the data are mapped with
regard to compliance with drinking water and public use standards.
The discussion proceeds map by map, beginning with the text and illustration for ammonia, Figure 3.11, on pages 76 and 77 immediately following.

Figure 3.11. Ammonia. Concentrations of ammonia that are above the Illinois recommended standards for drinking water of .5 mg/l display a fairly wide distribution throughout Chicago's suburbs. There are major concentrations of ammonia in the ground water wells in Du Page County, northern Will County and isolated distributions elsewhere. Since concentrations greater than .1 mg/l are usually indicative of organic pollution and most of the affected areas are located in geo- logical environments least likely to protect against ground water pollution, there is some evidence of ground water contamination in these areas. (This is certainly born out by the findings of our sur- face water analysis, see Figure 3.44 which appears later). The wide- spread distribution of high ammonia concentrations in Du Page County is probably accounted for by the heavy reliance on shallow wells.

Ammonia is not removed by the types of treatment carried out by the suburban municipalities. Hence the raw ground water levels may be regarded as the effective concentrations in drinking water. Ammonia is not toxic to humans at these levels but it is corrosive to pipes and increases the amount of chlorine needed for disinfection.

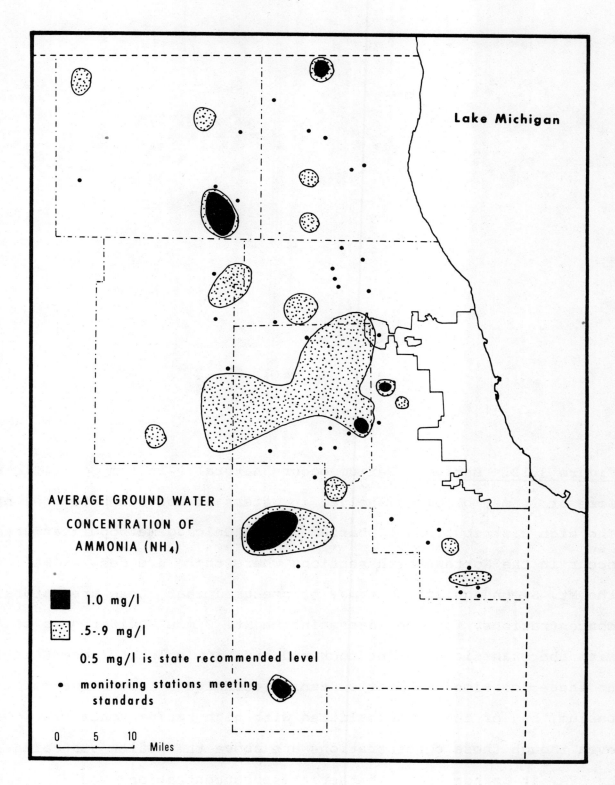

Lake Michigan

AVERAGE GROUND WATER
CONCENTRATION OF
AMMONIA (NH₄)

1.0 mg/l

.5-.9 mg/l

0.5 mg/l is state recommended level

• monitoring stations meeting
standards

0   5   10
Miles

Figure 3.12. Barium. Barium occurs naturally in some granitic rock. Some of it may become dissolved in waters of low sulphate content. The high distributions of barium in the Chicago metropolitan area occur in the Northwestern sections where there are deep wells tapping the Mt. Simon aquifer. It may be presumed that these are natural concentrations, for the waters in the Mt. Simon aquifer have contact with the granitic basement rock and have low sulphate concentrations at these locations. Water softening techniques remove most of the barium, but of the municipalities with high barium concentrations even though these concentrations are above the health standards set by EPA, it is not known whether these concentrations would have harm-ful health effects. Very high barium concentrations have serious toxic effects to heart, blood vessels and nerves.

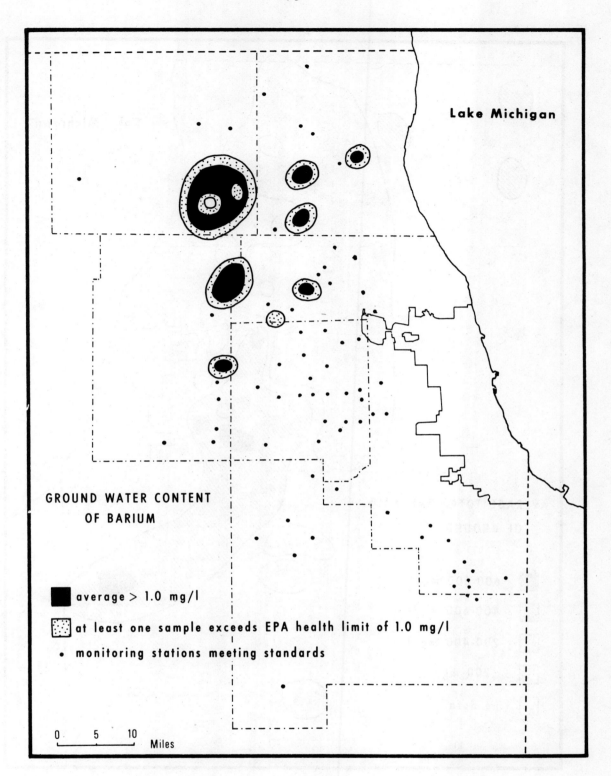

Lake Michigan

GROUND WATER CONTENT
OF BARIUM

■ average > 1.0 mg/l

▨ at least one sample exceeds EPA health limit of 1.0 mg/l

• monitoring stations meeting standards

0   5   10
Miles

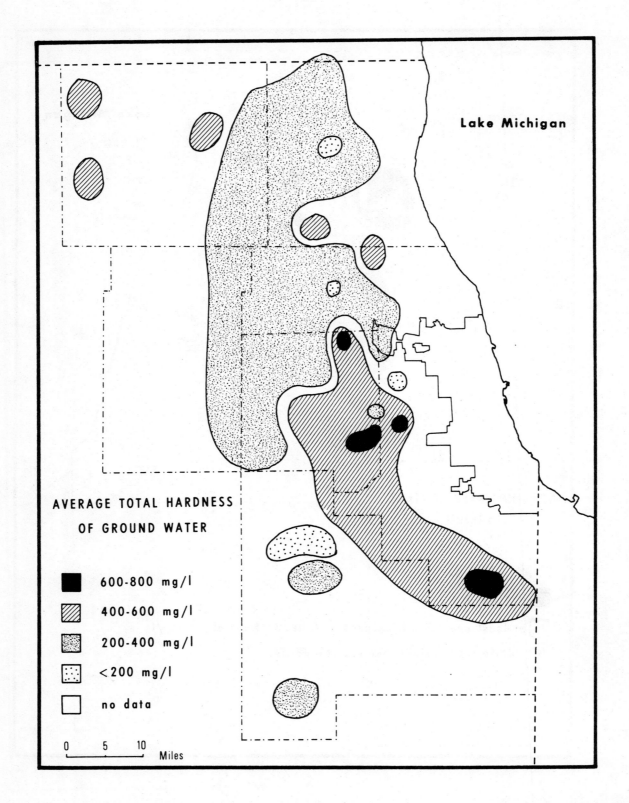

Lake Michigan

AVERAGE TOTAL HARDNESS
OF GROUND WATER

■ 600-800 mg/l

▨ 400-600 mg/l

▒ 200-400 mg/l

⋮ <200 mg/l

□ no data

0   5   10
Miles

<u>Figure 3.13. Hardness of Groundwater</u>. The variation in hardness of
groundwaters used for municipal supplies is roughly a composite of
the hardness of the Cambrian-Ordovician aquifer and the shallow aquifers: hard water in Du Page County reflects reliance on the shallow
aquifers, and in south Cook County both the naturally hard water of
the Cambrian-Ordovician aquifer and the hard water in the shallow dolomite aquifers.

81

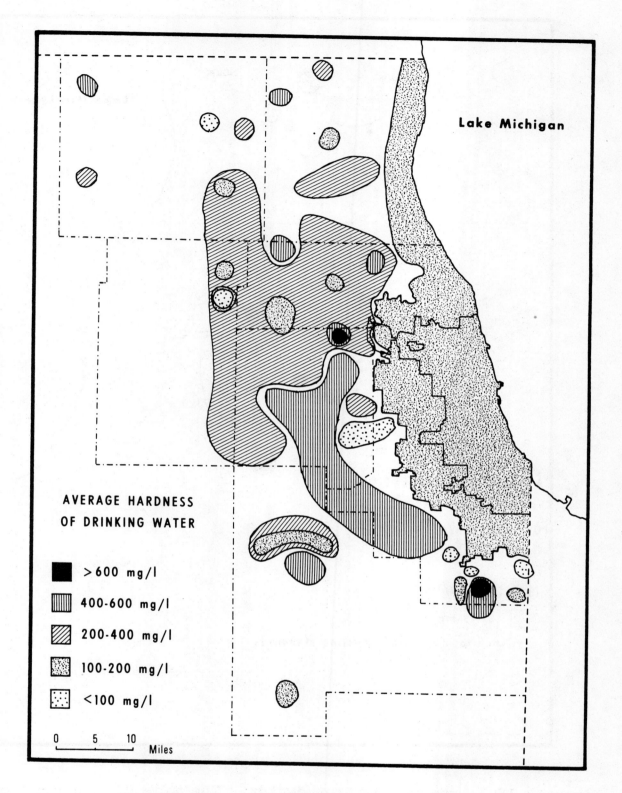

AVERAGE HARDNESS
OF DRINKING WATER

Lake Michigan

> 600 mg/l

400-600 mg/l

200-400 mg/l

100-200 mg/l

< 100 mg/l

0   5   10
        Miles

Figure 3.14.   Average Hardness of Drinking Water. This pattern is
much less systematic than that of the raw groundwater, but this is
simply explained.   Some suburban municipalities have decided to soften
their water and others have not.   The drinking water in the suburbs
served by Chicago and along the lake front reflects the hardness of
Lake Michigan.

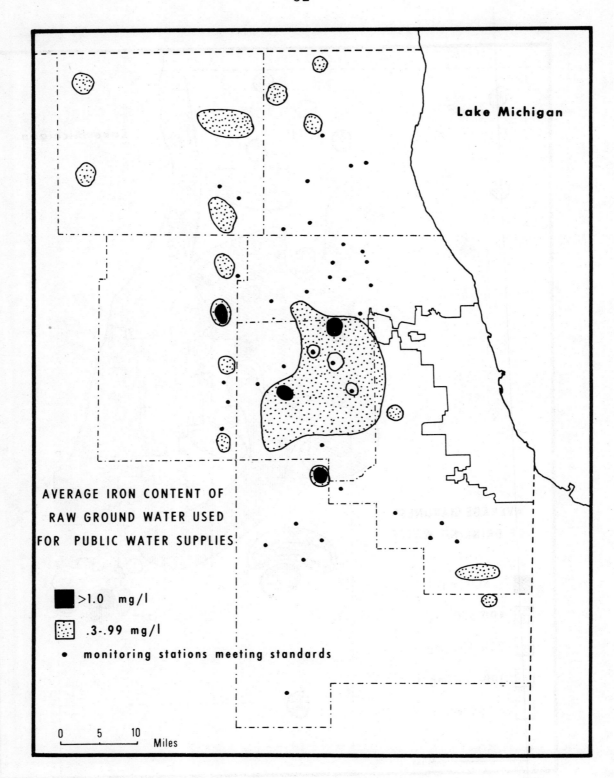

Figure 3.15.   Iron in Raw Groundwater.   The wide distribution of high iron content in the municipal groundwater supplies is indicative of reliance on the water from the shallow aquifers.

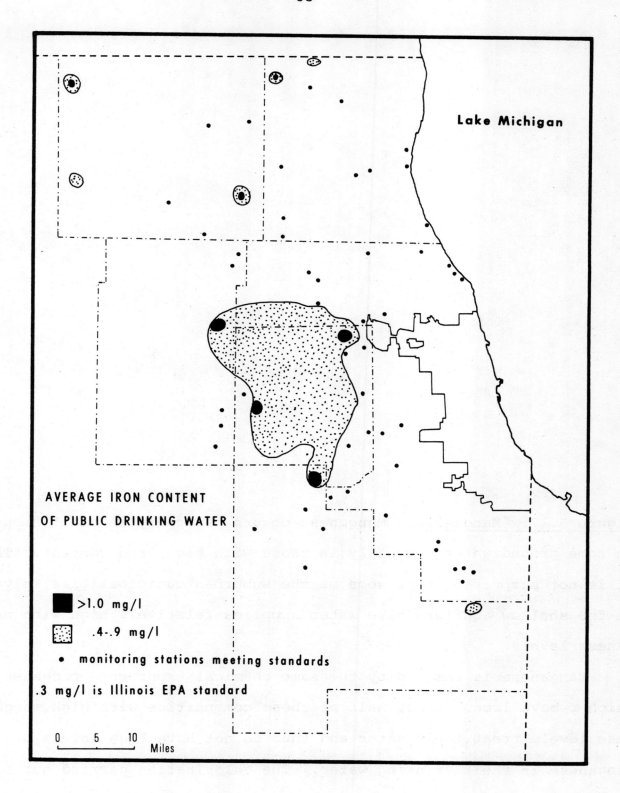

AVERAGE IRON CONTENT
OF PUBLIC DRINKING WATER

■ >1.0 mg/l

▨ .4-.9 mg/l

• monitoring stations meeting standards

.3 mg/l is Illinois EPA standard

0   5   10
Miles

Lake Michigan

Figure 3.16. Iron in Public Drinking Water. The difference between this map and Figure 3.14 is that some municipalities remove iron from the water.

Figure 3.17. Manganese. Manganese occurs naturally in small amounts in some ground waters, usually in those with high iron content. Thus it is not surprising that some of the suburban municipalities relying on the shallow aquifers have water supplies relatively high with manganese levels.

Manganese is removed by the same chemical treatment processes which remove iron. About half of those communities with high manganese levels treat their water and thus do not have high levels of manganese in their drinking water. The chlorination carried out by the remaining communities has no effect on the high manganese levels.

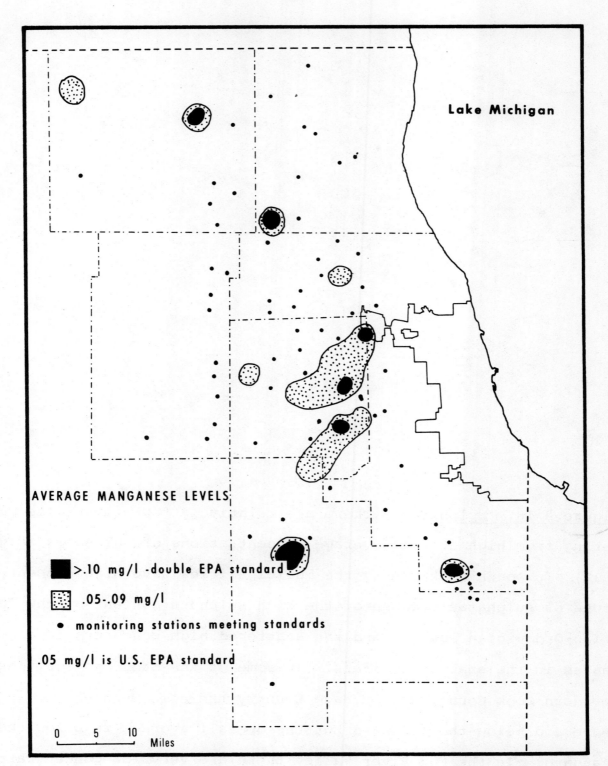

Lake Michigan

AVERAGE MANGANESE LEVELS

■ >.10 mg/l -double EPA standard

▦ .05-.09 mg/l

● monitoring stations meeting standards

.05 mg/l is U.S. EPA standard

0   5   10
Miles

Figure 3.18. Sulphates. There are relatively few communities suffering from high overall average concentrations of sulphates (Figure 3.18). In south Cook County the municipalities have high concentrations of sulphates because of the high sulphate content of the Cambrian-Ordovician aquifer and the scattered high concentrations of sulphates in the shallow aquifers. In some of the other communities in northern Cook County and Du Page Country there is much variation above and below the standard but the overall average is below the standard. In the Fox River Valley there are very low concentrations of sulphates because of the low sulphate content of the Cambrian-Ordovician aquifer in the western half of the metropolitan area. Sulphates are not removed by the water treatment processes carried out by the suburban municipalities so that these may be presumed to be the final drinking water concentrations.

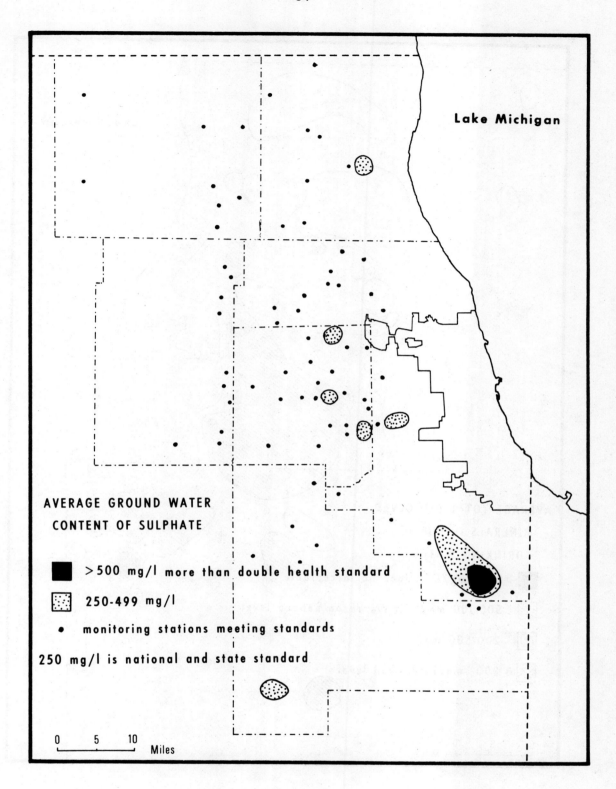

Lake Michigan

AVERAGE GROUND WATER
CONTENT OF SULPHATE

■ >500 mg/l more than double health standard

▨ 250-499 mg/l

• monitoring stations meeting standards

250 mg/l is national and state standard

0   5   10
Miles

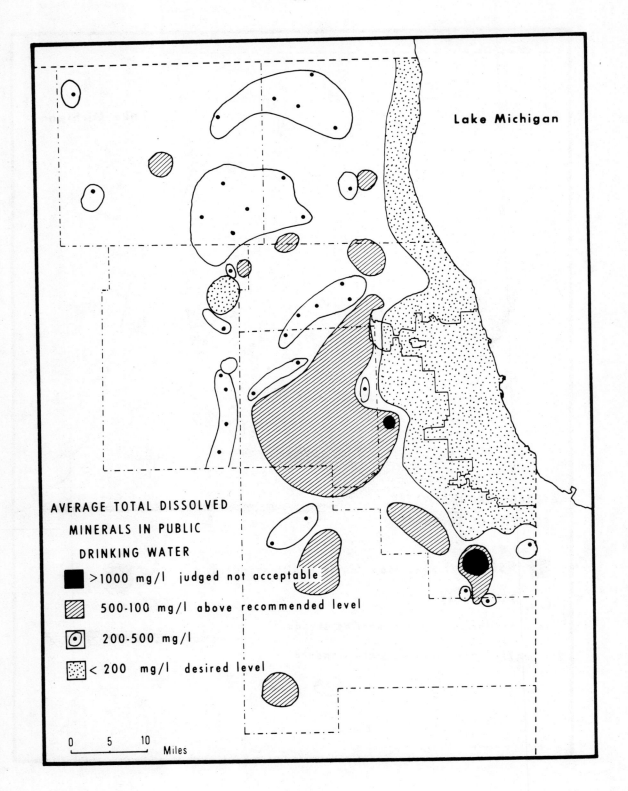

Figure 3.19. Total Dissolved Solids. Major areas of Du Page County and southern Cook County have high concentrations of total dissolved solids, explained in part by heavy reliance on the more mineralized shallow aquifers, but may reflect contamination from surface streams, which show similar TDS patterns (see Figure 3.33).

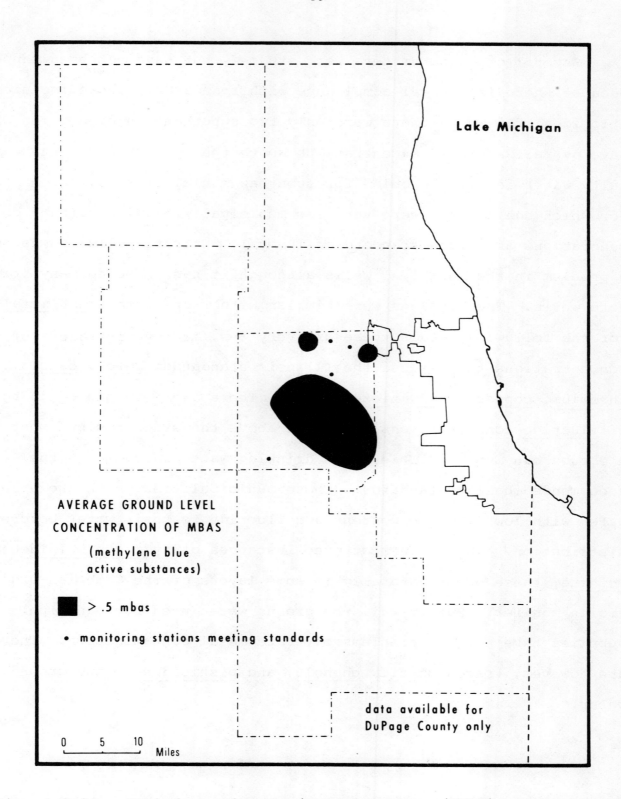

Figure 3.20. Methylene Blue Active Substances (MBAS). Data are only available for Du Page County. The widespread high concentrations of MBAS in Du Page County are an indication that there has been ground-water contamination by septic systems or surface streams. Pollution from the latter source is strongly implicated in the study done on surface water contaminants (see Figure 3.40).

Several other parameters were studied, but have not been mapped because there is general compliance with standards. These include chlorides, for which there were only two suburban municipalities which have overall average concentrations above the standards, so that salty water is not a problem for suburban municipalities, and nitrates, for which again there were very few municipalities with nitrate concentrations above the standard of 10 mg/l. Nitrate pollution is not a problem in the municipal wells although it has infected many private wells. The findings were similar with respect to trace metals. For the following metals there are very few, if any, instances of concentrations that exceed the Illinois standards: boron, cadmium, chromium, copper, lead, nickel, zinc. There are a couple of instances of fluoride concentrations which are above the standards but most of the suburban municipalities have drinking water which meets the recommended health standards. Those municipalities which use ground water with low fluoride content add fluoride to their water before distribution. There are scattered instances of hydrogen sulfide and methane; these occur naturally in some layers of the Cambrian-Ordovician aquifer. But overall the ground water used for municipal supplies have not had problems of trace metal contamination. There are however, traces of oil, phenols, and pesticides in the ground water.

The Quality of the Surface Waters

Earlier in this chapter, the volume of rainwater deposited an-
nually within the Chicago watershed was noted and certain ground
water relationships were explored. To complete our analysis of the
water resource cycle, a discussion of surface waters is necessary.
Here a distinction can be made between a most visible symbol and supply -- 22,400 square-mile Lake Michigan -- and the adjacent lakes
and rivers of the region. The principal drainage basins of the region
were illustrated in Figure 3.1; these basins encompass approximately
1,800 miles of shallow streams, some 700 shallow natural lakes, and
numerous swamps, marshes, and artificial lakes.

As the following discussion of surface waters will reveal, the
primary thrust of governmental policy in regards to protecting and
managing metropolitan Chicago's surface water supply continues to be
the protection of Lake Michigan. Beyond that reasonably clear-cut
goal, it is a complex task to differentiate current standards of
designated quality for other surface waters. Thus, in the tables, maps
and text which follow, we present results of the first uniform interpretation of water quality in the Chicago region. The profile of
water quality presented was prepared using standards defined by the
1973 Water Pollution Regulations of Illinois as applied to water
quality information monitored in 1971. These regulations are in har-
mony with the Federal Water Pollution Control Act which has the goal
of providing, by 1983, water in which people can swim and fish, and
by 1985, the elimination of all discharge of pollutants. Following
the surface water quality profile, we conclude the chapter by addres-
sing another important aspect of water quality -- the role of water
pollution abatement given a combined sanitary and storm sewer system
as the primary municipal response to captured storm water.

The Applicable Standards

The Federal Water Pollution Control Act outlines the basic strategy for the attainment of the goals for 1983 and 1985, with initial
emphasis placed on point source pollution control. Every point source
is subject to an effluent standard and a water quality standard, which
may or may not coincide. As explained in the related Water Quality
Strategy Paper (p.24):

> The effluent, or technology, standard states what
> is economically achievable in pollutant reduction
> for that class and type of discharger, nationally.
> The water quality standard can be used to deter-
> mine what additional pollutant reduction is envi-
> ronmentally necessary to achieve, if the particu-
> lar stretch of water on which a discharger is lo-
> cated is to be used for its designated purpose
> (drinking water supply, swimming) . . . In prac-
> tice, the technology standard is used as the base
> level for limitations . . .

The 1983 goal pertains to the water quality standard and the 1985 goal
to the technology standard. It is recognized that these goals are
somewhat idealistic (p.11):

> Indeed, . . . the present interpretation of the
> legislative caveat "where attainable" recognizes
> that naturally occurring conditions, or uncontrol-
> lable non-point source pollution, could result in
> a failure to meet the 1983 goal everywhere.

Likewise, the "universal achievement of no discharge" by 1985 may not
"be either feasible or environmentally desirable."

The Act places primary legislative and enforcement responsibilities upon the states. The 1972 amendments to the Act required that
EPA publish revised recommendations for water quality criteria by 1973.
Using the 1968 Report of the National Technical Advisory Committee to
the Secretary of the Interior (also known as the "Green Book") and a
National Academy of Sciences Report (the "Blue Book") as primary
sources, these "Proposed Criteria for Water Quality" were to serve as
a guide to the states in legislating their own standards. Where the
states filed to legislate Federally-approved standards, the "Proposed
Criteria for Water Quality" were to be used to set applicable state

standards. Thus "by June 1974, Federal/State water quality standards should exist for all navigable waters of the United States and its territories." (p.28, Water Quality Strategy Paper, Second Edition)

The Water Pollution Regulations of Illinois are the Federally-approved Illinois state standards legislated in compliance with these Water Pollution Act Amendments. Adopted by the Illinois Pollution Control Board as of July, 1973, the Regulations specify both effluent and water quality standards. The latter vary for Lake Michigan and areas with three specified water use designations: General Waters, Public and Food Processing Water Supply, and Secondary Contact and Indigenous Aquatic Life waters. The standards for Lake Michigan, which are the most stringent, are designed to maintain the high quality of the water for aquatic life and recreation involving primary contact, where the chance of accidental ingestion is high.

The Public and Food Processing Water Supply water use designation corresponds to the next most stringent set of state standards. The respective standards are designed to provide a margin of safety for water withdrawn for treatment and distribution as a potable supply or for food processing. The Regulations specify that all waters of Illinois are designated for this water use category except those de-signated as Secondary Contact and Indigenous Aquatic Life, and except for the following: (a) The Chicago River, and (b) The Little Calumet River.

Overlapping and subsuming the Public and Food Processing Water supply/water use designation is the General Use water use designation. Somewhat less stringent than the former designation, General Use waters include all the waters of Illinois except those designated as Secondary Contact and Indigenous Aquatic Life. The Regulations state that the standards pertaining to this water use designation

> will protect the States' water for aquatic life,
> agricultural use, primary and secondary contact
> use, and most industrial uses, and ensure the
> aesthetic quality of the States's aquatic envi-
> ronment. (p.7)

The last category, Secondary Contact and Indigenous Aquatic Life, sets standards appropriate for secondary contact uses and capable of supporting certain types of aquatic life. As regards "Indigenous Aquatic Life," the water use designation is somewhat confusing, since the standards are designed to protect only those aquatic life forms which are not adversely affected by:

> the physical configuration of the body of water, characteristics and origin of the water and the presence of contaminants in amounts that do not exceed the applicable standards.
> (Pollution Control Board, Newsletter #80, p.64)

In general, the standards for this water use category are the least stringent, state standards being identical in most cases with the effluent standards. The following waters, all within the study area, are designated as Secondary Contact and Indigenous Aquatic Life:

a) The Chicago Sanitary and Ship Canal;
b) The Calumet-Sag Channel;
c) The Little Calumet River from its junction with the Grand Calumet River to the Calumet-Sag Channel;
d) The Grand Calumet River;
e) The Calumet River;
f) Lake Calumet
g) The South Branch of the Chicago River;
h) The North Branch of the Chicago River from its confluence with the North Shore Channel to its confluence with the South Branch;
i) The Des Plaines River from its confluence with the Chicago Sanitary and Ship Canal to the Interstate 55 bridge;
j) The North Shore Channel, except that dissolved oxygen shall not be less than 5 mg/l during 16 hours of any 24 hour period, nor less than 4 mg/l at any time;
k) All waters in which, by reason of low flow or other conditions, a diversified aquatic biota cannot be satisfactorily maintained even in the absence of contaminants.

Figure 3.21 shows the water use designations for the Chicago study area. It can be found on p. 104, following.

A comparison of Illinois state and Federal water quality standards may be confusing since the state and Federal water use designations differ. The state designations are less specific than the Federal, and relate to them in the following manner:

State of Illinois Water Use Designation	Corresponding Federal Water Use Designation*
Public and Food Processing Water Supply	Public Water Supply Intake
General	Freshwater Aquatic Life Agricultural: Irrigation and Livestock Primary Contace Recreational Aesthetic
Secondary Contact and Indigenous Aquatic Life	Designated Recreational General (or Undesignated Recreation)

*From EPA, "Proposed Criteria for Water Quality", 1973, and FNPCA, USD1, "Report of the Committee on Water Quality Criteria, USCPO, 1972.

Legislated Illinois standards compare quite favorably with EPA's recommendations for water quality criteria (Table 3.1). The table shows the variability between state standards and federal recommendations and points also to the wide gaps in current knowledge of the effects of many of the monitored pollutants.

In addition to effluent discharge and water quality standards, the Metropolitan Sanitary District of Greater Chicago must conform to additional standards for sewage and industrial waste discharged into the District's sewerage system. As described in the Sewage and Waste Control Ordinance as Amended, the MSD's legislated purpose is:

> The protection of the public health and safety by abating and preventing pollution through the regulation and control of the quantity and quality of sewage and industrial wastes admitted to or discharged into the sewage systems, water reclamation plants and waters, under the jurisdiction of the Sanitary District.

TABLE 3.1. WATER QUALITY STANDARDS: A SUMMARY

PARAMETERS	ILLINOIS: GENERAL	ILLINOIS: LAKE MICHIGAN	FEDERAL: FRESHWATER AQUATIC LIFE	FEDERAL: AGRICULTURAL
DISSOLVED OXYGEN	Not less than 6.0 mg/1 during at least 16 hrs. of any 24 hr. period, nor less than 5.0 mg/1 at any time.	Less than 90% saturation except due to natural causes.	1) Min. acceptable limits for all water shall be based upon seasonal temperatures as in table 5: 36 5.8 mg/1 27.5 5.8 21 6.2 16 6.5 7.7 6.8 1.5 6.8 2) under extreme conditions of not more than 24 hrs. a minimum limit of 4 mg/1 is acceptable for waters above 31 C (87.8°F).	
BOD				
COD				
TOC				
CCE				
FECAL COLIFORM	Based on a minimum of 5 samples taken over not more than a 30 day period, shall not exceed a mean of 200 per 100ml nor shall more than 10% of the sample during any 30 day period exceed 400 per 100 ml.	Based on a minimum of 5 samples taken over not more than a 30 day period, shall not exceed a mean of 20 per 100 ml.		Irrigation: 1000 per 100 ml Livestock: 1000 per 100 ml maximum monthly mean. 4000 per 100 ml at any time.

PARAMETERS	ILLINOIS: LAKE MICHIGAN	ILLINOIS: GENERAL	FEDERAL: FRESHWATER AQUATIC LIFE	FEDERAL: AGRICULTURAL
TOTAL COLIFORM				Livestock: 5000 per 100 ml maximum monthly mean. 20,000 per 100 ml at any time.
PH	7.0 to 9.0, except for natural causes.	6.5 to 9.0 except for natural causes.	6.0 to 9.0.	
TOTAL ALKALINITY			75% of natural.	
TOTAL DISSOLVED SOLIDS	180.0 mg/l	1000.0 mg/l		Irrigation: 2000-5000 mg/l for tolerant plants in permeable soils or 500-1000 mg/l for sensitive crops.
CONDUCTIVITY				
TOTAL HARDNESS				
SUSPENDED SOLIDS			80.0 mg/l	
TURBIDITY			No more than 10% deviation from seasonally established norm.	
TEMPERATURE	Standards prohibit temperature changes detrimental to aquatic life, or in excess of more than 3°F of natural seasonal temperatures, except due to natural causes. Also subject to monthly limits. Extensive criteria to be met by individual pollutors.	Standards prohibit temperature changes determintal to aquatic life, or in excess by more than 5 F natural seasonal temperature, except due to natural causes. Different segments of the hydrological process are also subject to different monthly limits.	A) Criteria for maximum weekly average based on limits of acceptability for most sensitive important species. B) Maximum temperature for short term summer and spawning exposures.	

PARAMETERS	ILLINOIS: LAKE MICHIGAN	ILLINOIS: GENERAL	FEDERAL: FRESHWATER AQUATIC LIFE	FEDERAL: AGRICULTURAL
COLOR		Freedom from unnatural color.	Not more than 10% change from seasonal norm.	
MBAS				
PHENOLS		0.1 mg/l	0.05 of 96-hour C50 value; 0.1 mg/l at any time.	
CYANIDE		0.025 mg/l	0.05 of 96-hour C50 value; 0.005 mg/l at any time.	
OIL AND GREASE			a)No visible oil on surface b)Emulsified oils: 0.05 of 96-hour C50 value. c)1000 mg/kg hexane extrac-tables	
PHOSPHORUS	0.007 mg/l	Shall not exceed 0.5 mg/l in any reservoir or lake, or in any stream at the point where it enters any reservoir or lake.		
AMMONIA	0.02 mg/l	1.5 mg/l	0.02 mg/l	
NITRATES & NITRITES				Livestock: 100.0 mg/l

PARAMETERS	ILLINOIS: LAKE MICHIGAN	ILLINOIS: GENERAL	FEDERAL: FRESHWATER AQUATIC LIFE	FEDERAL: AGRICULTURAL
				NOTE: *maximum concentration for continuous irrigation. +maximum concentration for neutral and fine-textured alkaline soils for a period of not more than 20yrs.
SULFATES	24.0 mg/1	500.0 mg/1		
CHLORIDES	12.0 mg/1	500.0 mg/1		
FLUORIDES		1.4 mg/1		Irrigation: 2.0 mg/1*;15.0 mg/1 1.0 acid and sandy Livestock: 2.0 mg/1
ARSENIC		1.0 mg/1		Irrigation: 0.10 mg/1*;2.0 mg/1 Livestock: 0.2 mg/1
CADMIUM		0.05 mg/1	0.03 mg/1 in hard water 0.004 mg/1 in soft water	Irrigation: 0.01 mg/1*;0.05 mg/1 Livestock: 0.05 mg/1
CHROMIUM		1.0 mg/1 trivalent; 0.05 mg/1 hexavalent	0.05 mg/1	Irrigation: 0.1 mg/1*;1.0 mg/1 Livestock: 1.0 mg/1
COPPER		0.02 mg/1	0.10 of the 96-hour C50 value	Irrigation: 0.2 mg/1*;5.0 mg/1 Livestock: 0.5 mg/1
IRON		1.0 mg/1 total iron		Irrigation: 5.0 mg/1*;20.0 mg/1+
LEAD		0.1 mg/1	0.03 mg/1	Irrigation: 5.0 mg/1*;10.0 mg/1+ Livestock: 0.1 mg/1
MANGANESE		1.0 mg/1		Irrigation: 0.2 mg/1*;10.0 mg/1
MERCURY		0.0005 mg/1	0.0002 mg/1 at any time; 0.00005 mg/1 maximum mean; 0.0005 mg/1 maximum concentration in any aquatic organism.	Livestock: 0.001 mg/1
NICKEL		1.0 mg/1	0.02 of the 96-hour C50 value	Irrigation: 0.2 mg/1*;2.0 mg/1
SELENIUM		1.0 mg/1		Irrigation: 0.02 mg/1 Livestock: 0.05 mg/1
SILVER		0.005 mg/1 total ag		
ZINC		1.0 mg/1	0.005 of the 96-hour C50 value	Livestock: 25.0 mg/1

PARAMETERS	ILLINOIS: PUBLIC AND FOOD PRO-CESSING WATER SUPPLY	FEDERAL: PUBLIC WATER SUPPLY INTAKE	ILLINOIS: SECONDARY CONTACT AND INDIGENOUS AQUATIC LIFE	FEDERAL: RECREATIONAL AND AESTHETIC
DISSOLVED OXYGEN			Not less than 3.0 mg/1 during at least 16 hrs of any 24 hr period nor less than 2.0 mg/1 at any time, and after Dec. 31, 1977 shall not be less than 4.0 mg/1 at any time North Shore Channel not less than 5 mg/1 during any 16 hrs of any 24 hrs nor less than 4 mg/1 at any time.	
BOD				Based upon comprehensive effluent standards which vary according to four different segments of the hydrologic network. Standards include a schedule of increasingly stringent criteria to be met by specified future dates. Standards also take into account variables such as dilution ratios and waste load of individual pollutors.
COD				
TOC				
CCE	0.2 mg/1	0.3 mg/1		
FECAL COLIFORM		2,000 per 100 ml		Primary Contact Recreational: Based on a minimum of 5 samples 200 per 100 log mean. Not more taken over not more than a 30-day period, shall not exceed a mean of than 10% of samples in 30-1000 per 100 ml nor shall more than day period to exceed 400 per 10% of the samples during any 30 100 ml. day period exceed 2000 per 100 ml. Designated and Undesignated Recreational: 2,000 per 100ml mean 4,000 per ml maximum.

PARAMETERS	ILLINOIS: PUBLIC AND FOOD PROCESSING WATER SUPPLY	FEDERAL: PUBLIC WATER SUPPLY INTAKE	FEDERAL: RECREATIONAL AND AESTHETIC	ILLINOIS: SECONDARY CONTACT AND INDIGENOUS AQUATIC LIFE
TOTAL COLIFORM		10,000 per 100 ml		
PH		5.0 to 9.0	Recreational: 6.5-8.3 accep- table. In no case 5.0 or 9.0.	6.0-9.0, except for natural causes.
TOTAL ALKALINITY				
TOTAL DISSOLVED SOLIDS	500.0 mg/l			
CONDUCTIVITY				
TOTAL HARDNESS				
SUSPENDED SOLIDS				Standards specified in same manner as state BOD standards
TURBIDITY			Recreational: Clarity at least 4 ft by Seachi Disc Method. Aesthetic: Free of substances producing unnatural turbidity	Reduced to below obvious levels- free from unnatural turbidity.
TEMPERATURE		No changes that detract from potability or interfere with treatment processes	86°F maximum except where caused by natural conditions.	Temperature shall not exceed 93°F more than 5% of the time, or 100°F at any time.

PARAMETERS	ILLINOIS: PUBLIC AND FOOD PROCESSING WATER SUPPLY	FEDERAL: PUBLIC WATER SUPPLY INTAKE	FEDERAL: RECREATIONAL AND AESTHETIC	ILLINOIS: SECONDARY CONTACT AND INDIGENOUS AQUATIC LIFE
COLOR		Maximum acceptable limits= 75 platinum cobalt units	Aesthetic: Surface waters should be free of substances producing objectionable color	
MBAS	0.5 mg/l	0.5 mg/l		
PHENOLS	0.001 mg/l	0.001 mg/l		
CYANIDE	0.01 mg/l	0.2 mg/l		
OIL AND GREASE	0.01 mg/l	Should be essentially absent.	Surface waters should be free of oil.	
PHOSPHOROUS				1) No effluent discharged within the Lake Michigan Basin shall contain more than 1.0 mg/l of phosphorous after Dec. 31, 1971. 2) No effluent from any source which discharges within the Fox River Basin and whose untreated waste load is 1500 or more pop. equivalent shall contain more than 1.0 mg/l of phosphorus after Dec. 31, 1973.
AMMONIA	0.5 mg/l	0.5 mg/l		Water quality standards--based on different standards--differ for segments of the hydrologic network, time or year and pollution load of individual polluter.
NITRATES & NITRITES	10.0 mg/l	10.0 mg/l nitrate; 1.0 mg/l nitrite		

PARAMETERS	ILLINOIS: PUBLIC AND FOOD PROCESSING WATER SUPPLY	FEDERAL: PUBLIC WATER SUPPLY INTAKE	FEDERAL: RECREATIONAL AND AESTHETIC	ILLINOIS: SECONDARY CONTACT AND INDIGENOUS AQUATIC LIFE
SULFATES	250.0 mg/l	250.0 mg/l except in areas where no other drinking water supply is available.		
CHLORIDES	250.0 mg/l	250.0 mg/l		
FLUORIDES				2.5 mg/l
ARSENIC	0.01 mg/l	0.1 mg/l		0.25 mg/l
CADMIUM	0.01 mg/l	0.01 mg/l		0.15 mg/l
CHROMIUM		0.05 mg/l		1.0 mg/l trivalent; 0.3 mg/l hexavalent
COPPER		1.0 mg/l		1.0 mg/l
IRON	0.3 mg/l Total iron	0.3 mg/l		0.5 mg/l dissolved Fe 2.0 mg/l total
LEAD	0.05 mg/l	0.05 mg/l		0.1 mg/l
MANGANESE	0.05 mg/l	0.05 mg/l		1.0 mg/l
MERCURY		0.002 mg/l		0.0005 mg/l
NICKEL				1.0 mg/l
SELENIUM	0.01 mg/l	0.01 mg/l		1.0 mg/l
SILVER		0.05 mg/l		0.1 mg/l Total
ZINC		5.0 mg/l		1.0 mg/l Total

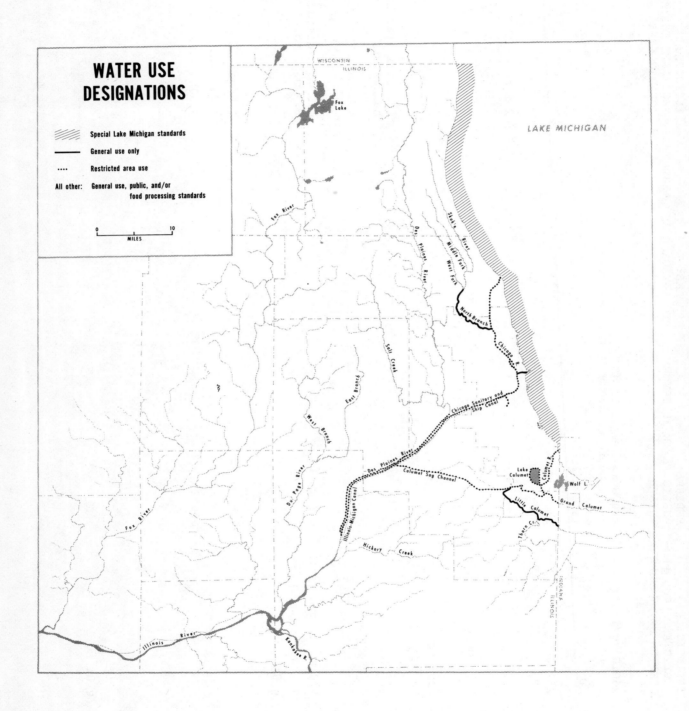

Figure 3.21

It is the intention of the Water Pollution Control Act and Amendments to delegate enforcement responsibilities, as well as legislative responsibilities, to state and local agencies. In keeping with this policy, enforcement of the standards is primarily the responsibility of the MSDGC for the waters within its boundaries, which covered the greater part of the study area. In addition to the virtues of delegating authority to appropriate state and local agencies, disadvantages also stem from this approach. For our purposes, it made obtaining a comprehensive and definitive evaluation of stream water quality difficult; the different state and local agencies employ different monitoring techniques and schedules, often monitor different parameters, and have different enforcement procedures and interpretations of their enforcement responsibilities. None of the enforcement agencies is presently concerned with enforcing point source compliance to the state water quality standards pertaining to the different water use designations (as opposed to effluent and sewer discharge standards). Because of the lack of consistency in enforcement policy, the profile of water quality presented in the following series of maps and texts has its emphasis on overall levels and patterns of water quality rather than on degree of compliance or violation with the specified water quality standards.

Methodology

Before proceeding to the analysis of surface water quality, a summary of the methodology employed is in order. Our data base was STORET -- the acronym used to identify the computer-oriented U.S. Environmental Protection Agency Water Quality Control Information System for the STOrage and RETrieval of water quality data. Various programs in this system provide data as to the date, time and type sample for water quality analyses reported in terms of requested parameter measurements. Chemical, physical and biological parameters are identifiable within the system. Station location data were retrieved utilizing a polygon with the coordinates:

1)	42°30' 88°00'		4)	41°30' 87°20'	
2)	42°00' 89°00'		5)	41°45' 87°20'	
3)	41°00' 89°00'		6)	42°30' 87°40'	

This polygon describes all STORET surface water quality stations within the drainage basins affecting the Chicago metropolitan area including surface sources of drinking water. Figure 3.22 shows the STORET station locations.

Several considerations influenced the group of parameters selected for mapping and analysis in the Chicago case study:

1. It was important to select parameters which in fact are indicators of pollution. An effort was also made to obtain parameters representative of different types of pollution. Parameters were grouped according to the general category of pollution represented.

2. An important factor was the number of stations which monitored a given parameter in the study area, and the frequency with which they monitored it. A PGM INVENT program was ordered to make these determinations.

3. Lastly, it was desirable to include parameters for which there were existing Illinois state standards, and secondly, federal (EPA) proposed criteria.

An important limitation to our data source was the unavailability of 1973 data with which to compare the 1973 Illinois Standards. We were forced to use STORET data for 1971 - the last calendar year for which complete data were available. This apparent problem was largely alleviated by our decision to emphasize over-all levels and patterns of pollution, with Illinois Standards and EPA proposed criteria as references, rather than the degree of compliance with or violation of state water quality standards.

Using the STORET station map overlaid on the regional hydrologic network and data from a PCM MEANS program, the locations of stations

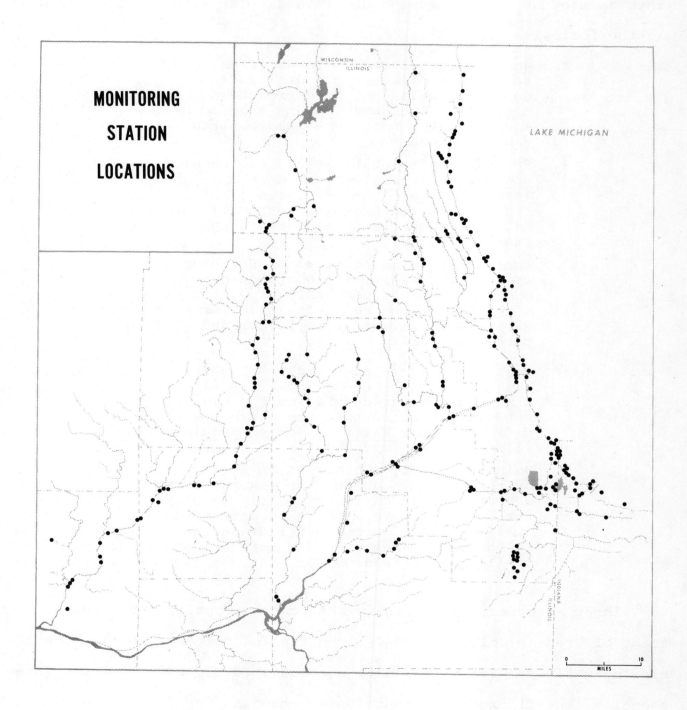

Figure 3.22

monitoring each parameter were noted and plotted for two factors:
(a) levels for each parameter, and (b) where possible, violations of
legislated state standards for water quality. Levels were determined
by taking the range of yearly mean values for each parameter divided
into as many as seven symbol-coded levels. The levels were determined
in the following manner:

1. Where Illinois state standards existed, then
    regardless of water use designation (i.e.,
    General, Public and Food Processing, Lake
    Michigan, Secondary Contact and Indigenous
    Aquatic Life) they were incorporated into the
    table of levels.

2. In addition to state standards, Federal (EPA)
    proposed criteria were used as a secondary
    reference, when they differed significantly
    from state standards, to set additional levels.
    Thus, they were utilized as a supplement to
    state standards.

3. Where there were no state or EPA proposed
    criteria, or where these standards did not
    prescribe a set numerical value, the range
    of values of the means for that parameter were
    arbitrarily divided into levels and depicted
    cartographically.

Violations of legislated state standards were determined as follows:

1. A map was prepared defining the hydrologic
    network according to water use designations
    defined by the Water Pollution Regulations of
    Illinois (see Figure 3.21)

2. Using this map, violations of state standards
    by the yearly mean and the maximum or minimum
    were indicated cartographically -- when they,
    for each parameter, could be determined. A
    small region of Northwest Indiana was included
    in the study area. We did not indicate violations
    of Illinois standards for stations in this region.

Three agencies, the Illinois EPA, the Metropolitan Sanitary District of Greater Chicago (MSDGC), and the federal EPA, were responsible for well over 90% of the data entered into STORET. Of these three
agencies, the Illinois EPA contributed the data for 80% of the stations. Minor contributions were made by various other agencies such
as the Indiana Board of Health in the Calumet area.

There was a large number of parameters available for the Chicago study area, although the number of stations monitoring certain parameters was frequently less than adequate. The low number of stations monitoring temperature over the year, combined with the difficulty in accounting for fluctuation due to natural seasonal variations, resulted in the omission of this important parameter. Pesticides and radiological pollutions were also insufficiently monitored to enable any systematic analysis. With the important exceptions of the above groups, most all of the important chemical and biological groups were available for analysis. The number of stations monitoring a given parameter was relatively high for most parameters that we studied although a sizeable fraction, especially in the case of trace metals, received poor or localized coverage.

The 267 water quality stations within the study area (Figure 3.22) provide good coverage on all major rivers and along the lake with the exceptions of the Illinois River, the Kankakee River, and the Des Plaines River below Joliet. Figure 3.22 does not show the entire polygon described earlier; no stations were listed for the portions omitted.

Many of the smaller tributary streams lacked adequate station coverage, and the existing monitoring stations throughout the polygon varied widely in the frequency with which they monitored. Many stations monitored only once or twice a year for certain parameters, a finding which limits the reliability of generalizations on water quality, particularly for small segments of a given waterway. Fortunately, there were enough stations with good monitoring frequency for most parameters. The Metropolitan Sanitary District, for instance, provides a well distributed network of 28 monitoring stations for waterways within its jurisdiction, and takes samples at a frequency of once per month. For a large number of parameters used in the Chicago study, there were enough stations to allow a comparison between data from stations which monitored relatively frequently with data from those monitoring infrequently. It was found that the data from the less frequently monitored stations generally supported and supplemented data from stations with more frequent coverage, and did not appear to distort apparent spatial differences in water quality.

The Parameter Maps and Their Interpretation

Loosely grouped according to the general category of pollution they represent, the list of parameters finally mapped was as follows:

I. Oxygen Measuring

a) Dissolved Oxygen
b) Deoxygenating Wastes: Biochemical Oxygen Demand, Chemical Oxygen Demand, Total Organic Carbon.

II. Microbiological: Total Coliform, Fecal Coliform

III. Acidity, Alkalinity: pH, Total Alkalinity

IV. Solids

a) Total Hardness, Total Dissolved Solids, Conductivity
b) Suspended Solids, Turbidity

V. Organic Chemicals

a) Cyanide
b) Methylene Blue Active Substances
c) Oil and Grease
d) Phenols

VI. Dissolved Elements, Ions, and Compounds

a) Chloride
b) Fluoride
c) Nitrogen Complexes: Ammonia, Nitrates and Nitrites
d) Phosphorus
e) Sulfate

VII. Trace Metals

a) Arsenic
b) Cadmium
c) Copper
d) Iron
e) Lead
f) Manganese
g) Mercury
h) Nickel
i) Silver
j) Zinc

In what follows we review the nature, utility and detrimental health and welfare effects of each of these parameters in turn. The best available source and our primary reference for this information is <u>Water Quality Criteria, 1972</u>, The report of the Committee on Water Quality Criteria of the National Academy of Science and Engineering. We also present the Chicago region map of each, and analyze it. The discussion begins on p. 112 with a consideration of the oxygen-measuring parameters.

I. OXYGEN MEASURING PARAMETERS

Dissolved Oxygen

Dissolved oxygen in the water is derived from surface exposure
to the atmosphere and from the photosynthetic processes of aquatic
plants. Low levels of D.O. may indicate the presence of oxygen-demanding (especially inorganic) materials in the water, which consume
oxygen in their oxidation. The effectiveness of D.O. as a parameter
depends on several variables, however. First of all, D.O. levels may
vary according to the distance of the monitoring station from the
"sag point." The sag point is defined as the point in the stream at
which the lowest level of D.O. is reached after exposure of the stream
to oxygen-demanding wastes. Because a given sag can move according
to pollutant loads, flow, season and algae blooms, monitoring stations
may not consistently measure the full extent of the pollution.

Secondly, D.O. levels may vary according to the time of day.
This occurs because the oxygen demand from the photosynthetic processes of algae and other aquatic plants are much greater during the
daylight hours. D.O. levels are not measured at the same times by
different monitoring stations, which may distort the true picture of
pollution trends in a given area. Furthermore, D.O. is rarely measured just before dawn, when D.O. levels would be expected to be
lowest.

Another variable effecting D.O. concentrations is the temperature of the water body. Saturation levels of D.O. are temperature
dependent and vary inversely. The seasonal fluctuation of D.O. levels
due to temperature differences is complicated by the marked decrease
in oxygen demand due to photosynthetic plants during the colder months
of the year.

Natural levels of D.O. are essential to preserve the integrity
of indigenous aquatic life, as well as for the decomposition of wastes.
Based upon an evaluation of the latest scientific information, E.P.A.

states: "There is evidently no concentration level or percentage of saturation to which the D.O. content of natural waters can be reduced without causing or risking some adverse effects on the reproduction of fishes inhabiting those waters."

D.O. in high concentrations is disadvantageous to industries, as it is often responsible for corrosion of pipes.

The Water Pollution Regulations of Illinois specify 3 ways of evaluating D.O. levels: 1) a level below which the mean for 16 hours of any 24 hour period cannot fall; 2) a minimum below which D.O. levels cannot fall; 3) in the case of Lake Michigan, a minimum level determined by 90 percent of total saturation. Since few stations take enough daily readings to determine an accurate 16 hour mean, the standards corresponding to this method of evaluation could not be used in our map (Figure 3.23). However, a value of 8.9 was used as a minimum value for Lake Michigan in this map. This value represents 90 percent of total saturation at 68° F. The standards used to set levels for the other water bodies in the map were: a minimum of 2.0 mg/l in areas designated as Secondary Contact and Indigenous Aquatic Life; a minimum of 5.0 mg/l for all water designated as General. The federal Proposed Criteria stipulates a minimum of 4.0 mg/l for short periods for freshwater aquatic life, and a lower limit of 5.0 mg/l is suggested for primary contact recreation by EPA (Guidelines for Developing or Revising Water Quality Standards, 1973.)

Except for Lake Michigan, dissolved oxygen was one of the better monitored parameters. The map shows frequent reporting of substandard levels. The upper east and west branches of the Du Page River, the lower portion of Salt Creek and the Des Plaines River near their confluence, the Chicago Sanitary and Ship Canal and South Branch of the Chicago River, the Cal-Sag Channel and Calumet River System, and the Thorn Creek vicinity all contained monitoring stations reporting yearly means below the Illinois General Standard and federal recommended levels for primary contact recreation and freshwater aquatic life. Numerous other stations in the hydrologic network reported yearly minimums which were in violation of the state standards. Low dissolved oxygen readings were not restricted to any specific land use. Low readings were monitored both in highly industrialized areas and in various suburban residential areas suggest both industrial and municipal effluents as likely sources.

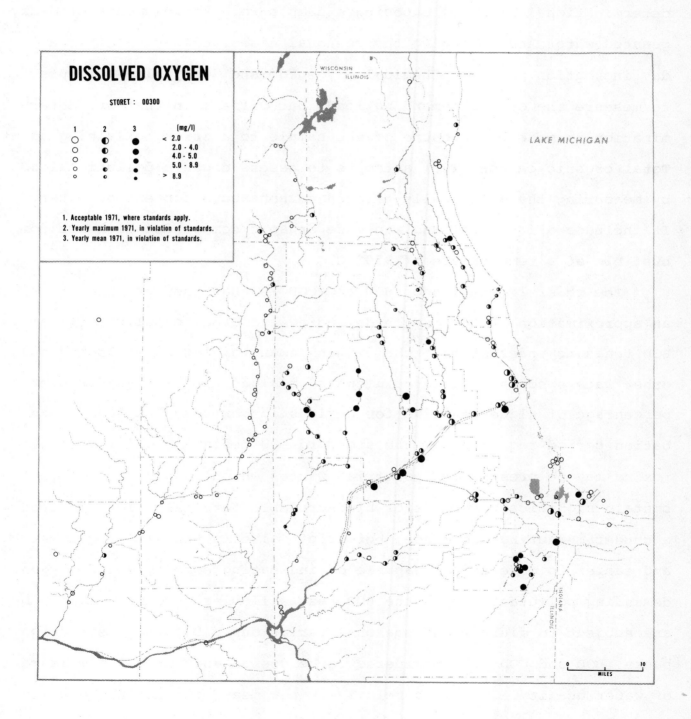

Figure 3.23

Deoxygenating Wastes: BOD, COD and TOC

Three methods are commonly used to measure the oxygen-demanding load placed on a body of water. Five day biochemical oxygen demand (BOD5) is a measure of the oxygen required to oxidize the organic material usable as a source of food by aerobic organisms. The BOD5 determination is made by exposing a sample to a known amount of deoxygenated water and measuring the residual dissolved oxygen after a 5 day incubation period. Chemical oxygen demand (COD) also attempts to measure the oxygen-demanding load, but differs in that its determination is made by exposure of the sample to a strong oxidizing agent. Total organic carbon (TOC) attempts to assess organic pollution loads by measuring the organically related carbonaceous content of water. It includes all natural and man-made organic compounds which are combustible at a temperature of 950° C.

The chief limitation of BOD and COD is that they provide only an approximation of the oxygen demanding and organic pollution loads. BOD tends to underestimate the oxygen demand of lagoon effluents and other waters containing large amounts of algae, since a significant percentage of algae can live for periods longer than the 5 day incubation period required for the standard BOD tests. Similarly, certain toxins may be present in industrial wastes which record low BOD yet contain significant amounts of biodegradable material. TOC involves a cruder measuring technique, but is of value in that it is quicker and easier to make and is capable of indicating some types of oxygen demanding pollutants which the BOD test will miss. Both BOD and COD are subject to diurnal and seasonal variations. Despite their drawbacks, BOD and COD are considered to be useful and versatile measure of water quality. TOC is a relatively new measuring technique which may provide a more comprehensive method for determining levels of organic pollution.

These deoxygenating waste parameters indicate the presence of organic pollution from sewage or industrial wastes, both of which have numerous detrimental effects on humans and aquatic life. They are a direct measure of the oxygen-demanding load placed on the water body and thus of the degree to which forms of aquatic life dependent upon high dissolved oxygen levels are adversely affected.

There are no state standards for COD or TOC and although there are state standards for BOD, they are written only for effluent discharges (no General, Public and Food Processing, etc.). Nonetheless, these standards specified are among the most comprehensive and thorough of all the parameters for which there are standards. They take into account such variables as dilution ratios and waste load of individual polluters, and they have different standards to be met by different dates and for different segments of the hydrologic network. The standards include the following limits, based on a 24 hour composite of samples averaged over any consecutive 30 day period:

1. 4.0 mg/l BOD for discharges into Lake Michigan.

2. 20.0 mg/l BOD for discharges into the Chicago River System, the Calumet River, the Illinois River, or the Des Plaines River downstream from its confluence with the Chicago Sanitary and Ship Canal.

3. 30.0 mg/l BOD for discharges into remaining waters.

Based on 5 percent of the 24 hour composite samples averaged over any consecutive 30 day period, the limits are:

4. 10.0 mg/l BOD for discharges into Lake Michigan.

5. 50.0 mg/l BOD for discharges into the Chicago River System, the Calumet River, the Illinois River, or the Des Plaines River downstream from its confluence with the Chicago Sanitary and Ship Canal.

6. 75.0 mg/l BOD for discharges into remaining waters.

This range of effluent levels was incorporated into our BOD map (Figure 3.24).

Despite these detailed standards outlined by the state for BOD levels however, there was a rather modest number of stations which monitored this parameter, with few stations along Lake Michigan, as

Figure 3.24 reveals. The worst readings were reported at a station on Pettibone Creek, at a station on the West Fork of the Chicago River, and at several stations on Thorn Creek, which generally appeared to have the worst water. Because application of the state standards depends on a number of factors, violations were not mapped.

Several times as many stations had readings for COD, which was one of the most widely monitored parameters in the study (Figure 3.25). In the absence of state or federal reference levels for COD and TOC, generalizations with regard to water quality according to these parameters must of course, be limited. It would seem however, that features of the BOD and dissolved oxygen maps are repeated on the COD map. The worst water was once again found on the West Fork of the Chicago River and around Thorn Creek. Other regions reporting poor readings were the Grand Calumet - Little Calumet River, the Cal-Sag Channel, Salt Creek and the Des Plaines River up to the Chicago Sanitary and Ship Canal, and the East Branch of the Du Page River. Following Lake Michigan, the best water was reported in the Fox River.

Even fewer stations monitored TOC than BOD, and it becomes difficult to generalize with such scanty data (Figure 3.26). The worst stations were located along Thorn Creek, the Little Calumet, the West Fork of the Chicago River, and the North Shore Channel north of its confluence with the Chicago River - findings compatible with the observed BOD and COD trends.

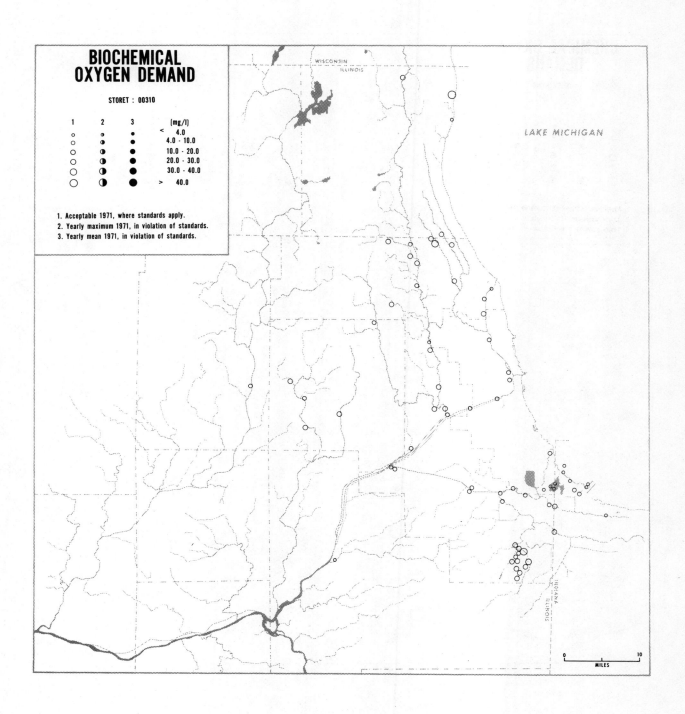

Figure 3.24

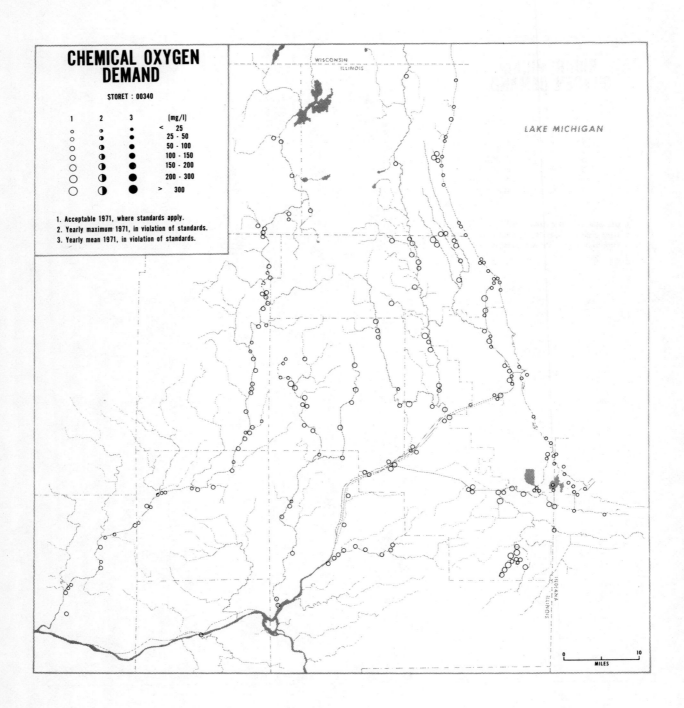

Figure 3.25

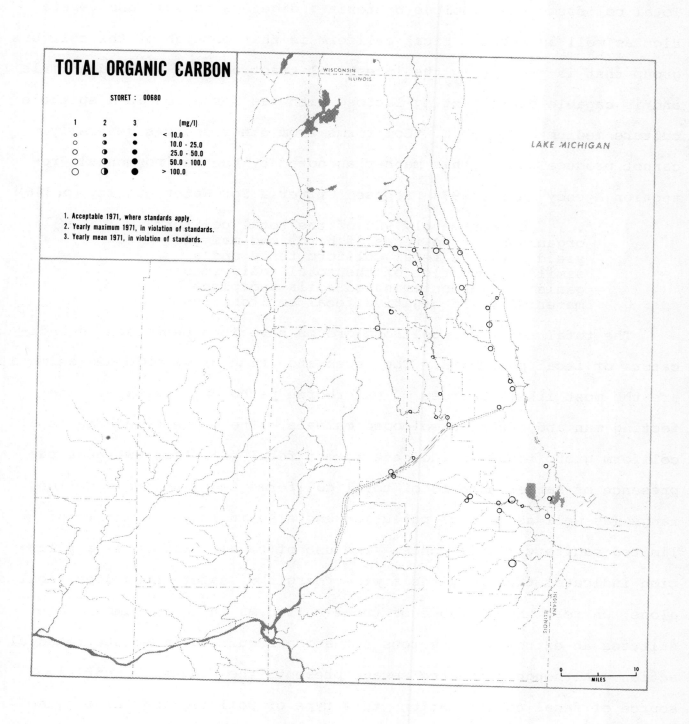

Figure 3.26

II. MICROBIOLOGICAL PARAMETERS

Total Coliform and Fecal Coliform

The total coliform group includes bacterial organisms found in sewage as well as bacteria from diverse natural sources and habitats. Total coliforms thus include bacteria indigenous to soil and vegetation as well as feces. Fecal coliform is that portion of the coliform group that is present in the intestinal tract of warm-blooded animals and is capable of fermenting lactose with gas formation in a suitable culture medium at 44.5° C. Coliforms from other sources generally cannot produce gas in this manner as noted by the Environmental Protection Agency in the 1973 Proposed Criteria for Water Quality (p.346):

> . . . approximately 95% of the total coliform organisms in the feces of birds and mammals yield positive fecal coliform tests and a similar proportion of the total coliform organisms in uncontaminated soils and plant material yield negative fecal coliform test.

The total and fecal coliform groups have long been used as indicators of fecal pollution. The feces and urine of warmblooded animals are the most likely sources of waterborne pathogens capable of infecting man and other warmblooded mammals. The presence of the fecal coliform group tends to indicate recent fecal pollution, whereas the presence of larger numbers of total coliforms tends to indicate long range (as well as recent) pollution and also includes organisms of limited sanitary significance. The use of total coliform as a pollution indicator thus provides a wider margin of safety than does fecal alone, whereas the presence of fecal coliforms in large numbers constitutes an extremely dangerous situation requiring immediate remedial action. Although untreated sewage presents the biggest potential source of fecal contamination, this type of pollution may also arise from paper, leather, meat packing, and milk processing industries.

High coliform counts present a severe hazard to humans, wildlife and livestock, facilitating the rapid spread of cholera, typhoid, dysentery, salmonella, gastroenteristis, infectious hepatitis and numerous other diseases. The health hazard exists for indirect use and water contact recreation as well as for direct use.

The State of Illinois has General, Secondary Contact and Indigenous Aquatic Life and Lake Michigan standards for permissible levels of fecal coliforms. No standards are specified for total coliforms (Figure 3.27). For the General and Secondary Contact Standards, there are two criteria to be met in each case: a maximum permissible level for the geometric mean of at least 5 samples within a 30 day period (200 per ml H_2O and 1000 per 100 ml H_2O, respectively); and a maximum permissible level for not more than 10 percent of the samples in this 30 day period. For both water use designations, the level for the value of 10 percent of the samples was twice that of the value of the sample mean. The standards for Lake Michigan were based entirely upon the value of the geometric mean for at least five samples within a 30 day period (20 per 100 ml H_2O). Our map incorporated the standards based upon the mean value over a 30 day sample period (Figure 3.28). We did not map violations, since few of the stations monitored the required minimum of 5 samples per 30 days.

Federal proposed criteria exist for both total and fecal coliforms: 5000 per 100 ml H_2O total coliform as a maximum monthly mean and 20,000 per 100 ml at any time are set as levels for livestock water supplies. 10,000·per 100 ml H_2O total coliforms is suggested for public water supplies. For fecal coliforms, 200 per 100 ml H_2O "log mean" and 400 per 100 ml for not more than 10 percent of the samples in any 30 day period are suggested for primary contact recreation. 1000 per 100 ml is suggested as a limit for agricultural irrigation and as a maximum monthly mean for livestock water supplies. 2000 per 100 ml is the suggested limit for public water supplies and the "average" for undesignated recreation. 4000 per 100 ml is the maximum suggested for undesignated recreation and livestock water supplies.

A large percentage of the stations in the hydrologic network monitored fecal coliform with about half as many monitoring total coliforms. Looking at the fecal coliform map, we see that extensive areas of hydrologic network suffer extremely polluted water. Because of the manner in which the state standards were specified, we were unable to map violations. Yet if we consider the reported values for fecal coliform levels in terms of the standards specified for the means of 30 day periods, there are virtually no extensive unpolluted regions of the hydrologic network. Extensive stretches of the water-ways are in excess of the federal reference levels as well; only the Lake Michigan shoreline meets the two primary contact recreation criteria for most of its length.

Extremely polluted fecal coliform levels were reported through-out the Chicago River System, the Des Plaines River System, the Cal-umet River System (including Thorn Creek), the East Branch of the Du Page River System, the Calumet River System (including Thorn Creek), the East Branch of the Du Page River System and Pettibone Creek. Values reported in these areas commonly exceeded 20,000 per 100 ml, ten times the standard specified for a 30 day mean in areas designated as General use by Illinois and the federal suggested criteria for public water supply intake. The water improved only slightly in the Fox River and the remainder of the Du Page River System.

The map for total coliform levels is not as informative, but shows roughly similar trends. Again, most of the areas monitored showed extremely high coliform levels. The great majority of yearly means exceeded the federal reference level for public water supply intake. Thus, the pollution pattern for total and fecal coliform, which seems to relate to the extent of urbanization, strongly sug-gests inadequate treatment facilities for municipal wastes. Since urban runoff in Cook County flows into the Chicago Sanitary District's sewage system, overflow from storm runoffs may constitute a major part of the problem. Agricultural runoffs in outlying areas may further contribute to the observed high levels.

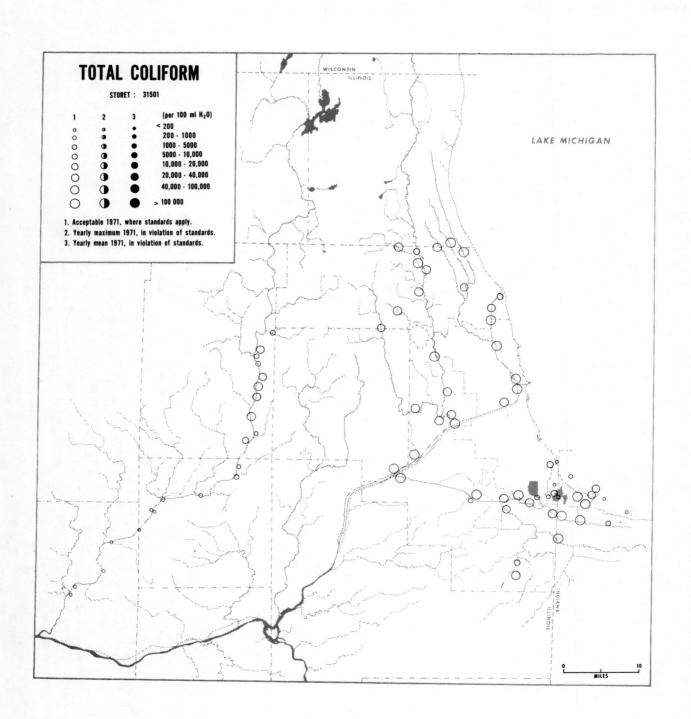

Figure 3.27

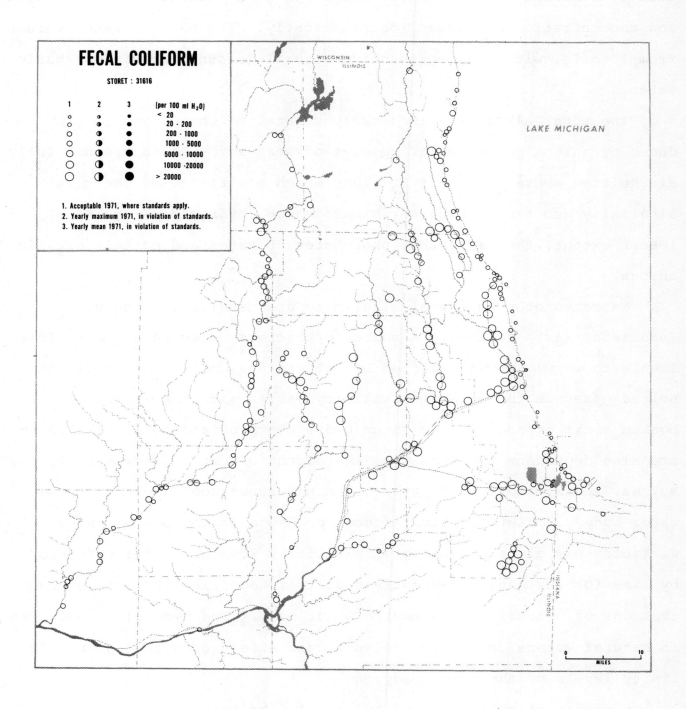

Figure 3.28

III. ACIDITY - ALKALINITY

pH and Total Alkalinity

Total alkalinity and pH are two parameters which indicate the acidity-alkalinity of the water body. pH is a measure of the hydrogen ion concentration expressed logarithmically. The pH can assume values from 1 to 14, with 7.0 representing neutral (neither acidic nor basic) water.

The total alkalinity is closely related to the pH and is produced by anions or molecular species of weak acids which are not fully dissociated above a pH of 4.5. Ions which contribute to the total alkalinity are the carbonates, bicarbonates, hydroxides, and to a lesser extent, the silicates, phosphates, borates and certain organic anions.

Extremes of pH or total alkalinity are usually indicative of industrial waste sources. A number of factors cause pH and alkalinity levels to vary: pH is modified by temperature and the ratio of dissolved gases in the water. Alkalinity varies with the amount of carbonate rocks exposed to the water body. Both pH and total alkalinity are also dependent upon the type and amount of cations (expecially Ca, Mg, Na, and K) and certain other chemical substances present in the water body. Pollution which effects a change in any one of these variables may alter pH and total alkalinity levels. Water softened by lime for instance, frequently results in addition of high concentrations of hydroxide ions to the water body. The hydroxide ion, rare in natural waters, can have a significant effect upon the pH and alkalinity levels of the water body.

Significant changes of pH and total alkalinity from natural levels can produce several adverse effects on aquatic life. Non-lethal limits are even narrower for many fish food organisms and plants such as plankton and benthic invertebrates. Many of these adverse effects are indirect; chemical reactions are generally strongly dependent upon pH levels, and altering pH levels can therefore facilitate undesirable reactions while blocking beneficial ones. For instance, adding strong alkalines to a water body can cause a substantial increase in un-ionized ammonia. Similarly, cyanide complexes can increase a thousand fold in toxicity with a drop of 1.5 pH units. Variations in pH and alkalinity directly influence the availability of nutrient substances to plants.

While moderate pH and alkalinity changes can be tolerated in drinking water, they may cause eye irritation, necessitating special requirements for recreational areas.

pH levels below 7.0 result in waters which are increasingly corrosive to water works structures, distribution lines, and household plumbing fixtures. Besides the cost of wear and tear on exposed piping, potentially harmful ions such as iron, copper, zinc, cadmium and lead are added to the water by corrosive pH levels.

State standards exist for acceptable pH levels, but not for total alkalinity levels (Figures 3.29 and 3.30). Three different criteria exist for pH levels, corresponding to the three water use categories -- Lake Michigan, General and Secondary Contact and Indigenous Aquatic Life. These criteria, which were incorporated into the pH map, specified that the pH "be within the range of 5.0 to 9.0 except for natural causes" in Lake Michigan. In the same manner, a range of 6.5-9.0 was prescribed for waters designated as General use and a range of 6.0 - 9.0 for those designated as Secondary Contact.

A range of 5.0 - 9.0 was suggested by EPA for Primary Contact Recreation and Public Water Supply Intake, a range of 6.0 - 9.0 for Freshwater Aquatic Life and Wildlife, and a range of 6.5 - 8.3 for Primary Contact Recreation areas used extensively for bathing and swimming.

The pH map immediately shows that pH was monitored by many stations and that the state standards and federal reference levels were only rarely exceeded, and then usually only by the maximum or minimum (as opposed to the yearly mean) for the station.

The total alkalinity map is somewhat more informative. Total alkalinity levels were lowest along the lake and along the waterways for a short distance downstream of their confluences with the lake. Two spots stand out with somewhat higher total alkalinity readings -- Thorn Creek and the East Branch of the Du Page River. On the whole, there was little variation in total alkalinity levels, as with the pH levels.

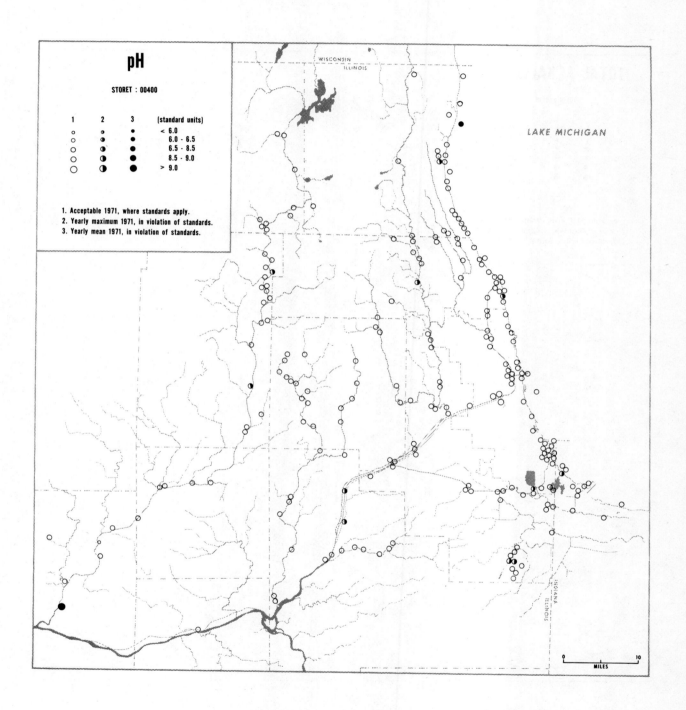

Figure 3.29

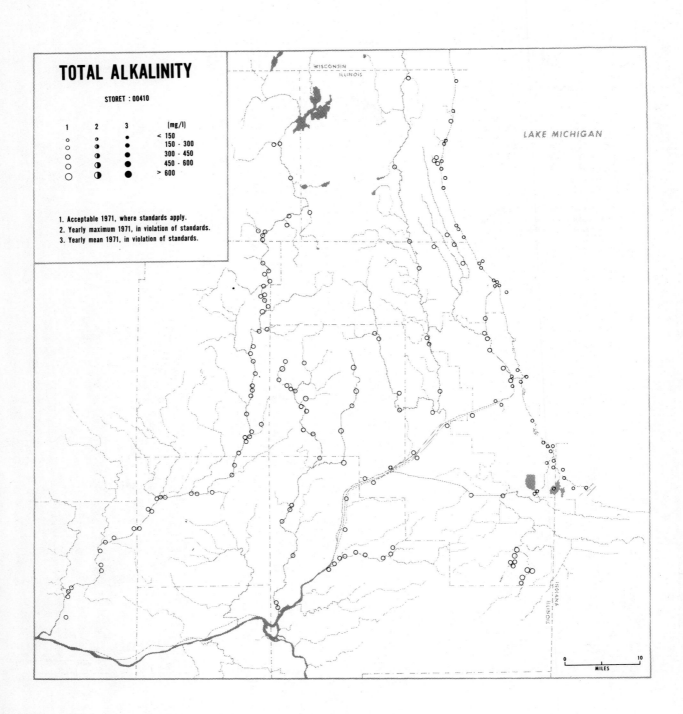

Figure 3.30

IV. SOLIDS

Total Dissolved Solids, Conductivity and Total Hardness

Substances which can pass through the pores of a 0.45 µ filter are generally considered to be dissolved. The major constituents of total dissolved solids in natural waters are the ionizable salts of anions such as carbonate, sulfate, phosphate, nitrate and chloride. Although these inorganic compounds are usually responsible for most of the total dissolved solids in water, organic matter may also contribute.

Conductivity is a measure of the ability of the water to conduct a small electrical current. The conductivity of a solution is roughly proportional to the number of charged ions present, and the conductivity is thus closely related to the amount of total dissolved solids present in solution.

Total hardness is a component of the total dissolved solids. Calcium and magnesium ion concentrations are the principal determinants of total hardness, with trace elements such as iron, copper, zinc, lead, manganese. boron and strontium contributing minimally.

Since most of the material present in both natural waters and waste waters consists of dissolved solids, unusually high TDS and conductivity readings would lead one to suspect pollution from industrial waste, municipal waste, or storm run-off. TDS is thus an important parameter for assessment of overall water quality. The conductivity parameter is somewhat less useful because its determination does not relate exactly to the total dissolved solids present in the sample. Still, its determination is easily made and gives a rough indication of the amount of total dissolved solids present after composition and other characteristics of the water body. The TDS value is normally from 0.55 to 9.75 of the conductivity value.

Although extreme hardness can also be the result of excessive pollution loads, it is somewhat less useful as a parameter because of its limited biological significance.

The composition and amount of total dissolved solids in the water are key factors in determining the quantity and quality of aquatic plant and animal life. High levels of this residual can be harmful to fish and aquatic plants, since the dissolved solids typically include toxic agents as well as nutrients.

Changes in dissolved solids concentrations can cause gastric disturbances in humans. High levels of dissolved solids, and particularly, of total hardness, are undesirable for industry, since they result in the formation of boiler scale and scale in heaters, pipes and radiators.

Although high levels of dissolved solids and total hardness are in some cases beneficial for irrigation purposes, "hard" water is often deemed undesirable because of its decreased ability to produce lather from soap.

There are no state standards for total hardness, which more often tends to be a matter of aesthetic consideration. Although there are no state standards for conductivity, the state of Illinois specified maximum levels of total dissolved solids for each of the three different categories of designated water use and Lake Michigan. A maximum level of 180 mg/l is prescribed for Lake Michigan, a maximum of 500 mg/l for waters designated as Public and Food Processing Water Supply, a maximum of 1000 mg/l for waters for Secondary Contact and Indigenous Aquatic Life. All four of these criteria were incorporated into the map of dissolved solids.

Federal proposed criteria suggest a maximum allowable range of 500 to 1000 mg/l total dissolved solids for sensitive crops and 2000 to 5000 mg/l for tolerant plants in water used for agricultural irrigation. A limit of 500 mg/l is suggested for water supply purposes in EPA's Guidelines for Developing or Revising Water Quality Standards, 1973.

Most stations monitored dissolved solids, a few less monitored total hardness, and only a few monitored conductivity (Figures 3.31-3.33). Similar patterns are seen across all three maps. The worst areas were Thorn Creek, the region near the confluence of the Calumet and Little Calumet Rivers, both branches of the Du Page River north of their confluence, and Pettibone Creek. These areas had many stations whose yearly means violated the state standards for general use for TDS. Virtually all waterways in the study areas except for Lake Michigan and the Fox River were polluted with respect to the state standard for Public and Food Processing water supply.

In summary, the maps for these three parameters indicate extreme differences between the specified state standards and the actual condition of waters. The significance of these findings is to be emphasized, since TDS and conductivity are capable of measuring most of the total amount of material in the water, and are therefore prime indicators of overall water quality. The high reported readings undoubtedly reflect natural conditions as well as a number of pollution sources, generally indicating the influence of urbanized areas on water quality. The pattern of Average Hardness and TDS levels in drinking water follow roughly similar patterns, especially regarding the high levels on the East and West Branches of the Du Page River and the Thorn Creek area (see Figure 3.19), which suggests that natural conditions may play a large role in the observed water quality patterns.

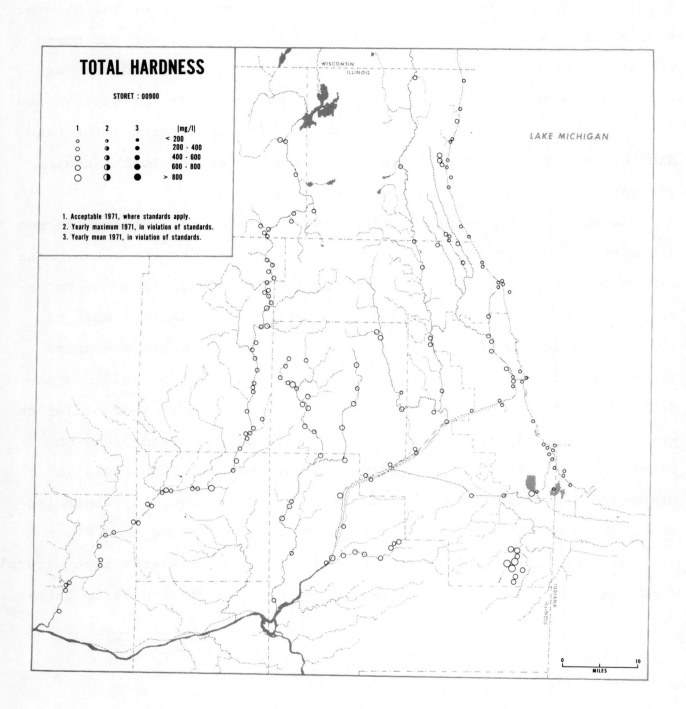

Figure 3.31

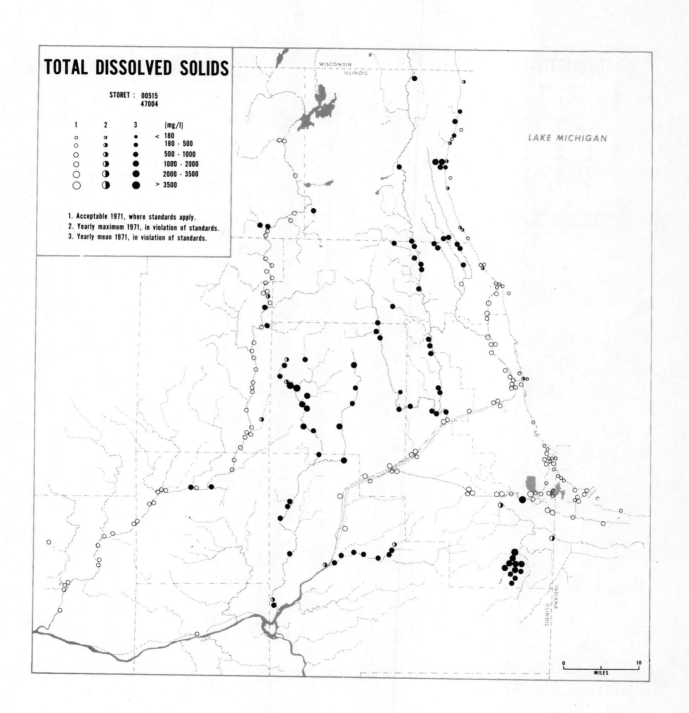

Figure 3.32

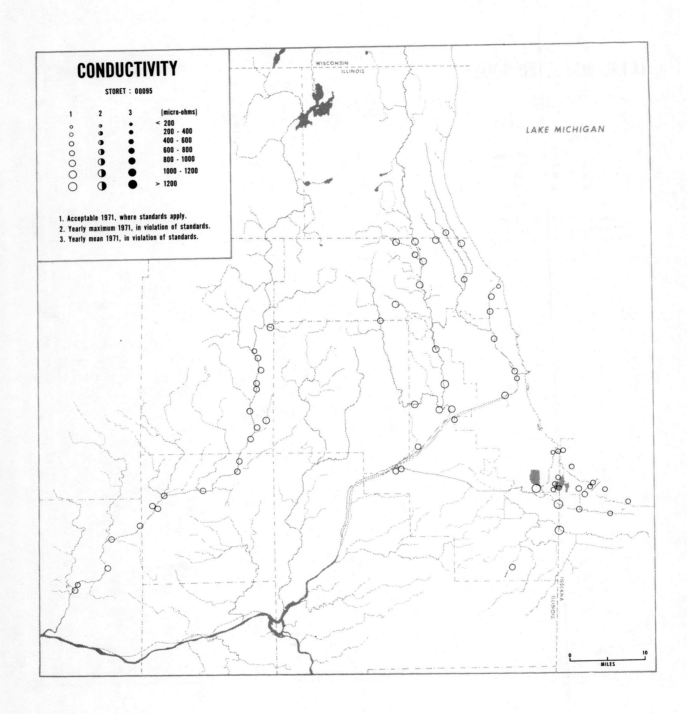

Figure 3.33

Suspended Solids and Turbidity

Suspended solids include all particles of matter larger than those defined as dissolved. They remain in suspension in water because of the upward component of turbulent currents or by colloidal suspension. Suspended solids include an inorganic fraction -- largely made up of silt, sand, and clay soil particles -- and an organic fraction, consisting both of living organic matter such as plankton and bacteria and also of finely divided dead organic matter.

Turbidity measures the extent to which the penetration of light is inhibited by the presence of suspended solids. It is a function of the type, size and concentration of the particles of suspended solids.

Much of the suspended material in the water results from the natural process of erosion and weathering. Natural levels of suspended solids and turbidity are influenced by climatic conditions such as wind intensity and rainfall as well as by topography of the drainage area and stream flow and rate. High levels of suspended solids and turbidity may very well reflect the intervention of man's activities in this natural process -- agricultural runoff, construction activities, industrial operations, storm sewers, and municipal wastes can all add considerably to the amount of suspended solids present and the degree of turbidity.

High concentrations of suspended solids reduce water transparency, thereby inhibiting photosynthesis by aquatic plants and restricting their availability as a food source for other forms of aquatic life. The suspended solids gradually settle to the bottom of the water body and may effect physical and chemical changes which may alter the types of organisms present and reduce their numbers. Finely divided particulate matter can also kill fish directly and impede egg and larvae development.

The inhibition of light penetration by suspended matter also influences temperature patterns which can have potentially adverse effects on indigenous aquatic life. Furthermore, pesticides and other toxic materials are readily absorbed into clay and other particulate matter and are thereby transported and dispersed.

Suspended solids are responsible for abrasion in pipes, pumps and turbine blades. High levels of suspended solids also contribute to clogged sewer lines, increased solids loadings at treatment plants, and shoaling of waterways.

In addition to these numerous and important adverse effects on aquatic life and industry, suspended solids and turbidity may have undesirable effects on recreational waters. Clarity is important for recreational waters for a variety of reasons among which are safety, visual appeal and recreational enjoyment. Water which is safe for use as drinking water may not be accepted by the consumer if turbidity is great.

No state standards exist for turbidity. The state standards for suspended solids are specified in the same manner as those for BOD. They are thorough, taking into account factors such as dilution ratios, waste load per individual polluter, and current water use; and they include a long range schedule for the implementation of increasingly stringent standards. They do this only for areas designated as Secondary Contact and Indigenous Aquatic Life, however; there are no standards for areas designated as General. The following standards for suspended solids are incorporated into the map (Figure 3.34); Based on 24 hour composite samples averaged over any consecutive 30 day period:

1. A maximum of 5.0 mg/l in Lake Michigan.
2. A maximum of 25.0 mg/l in waters of the Chicago River System, the Calumet River, the Illinois River, or the Des Plaines River downstream from its confluence with the Chicago Sanitary and Ship Canal.
3. A maximum of 37.0 mg/l in all remaining waters.

Based on 5 percent of the 24 hour composite over any consecutive 30 day period:

4. A maximum of 12.5 mg/l in Lake Michigan.

5. A maximum of 62.5 mg/l in the waters of the Chicago River System, the Calumet River, the Illinois River or the Des Plaines River downstream from its confluence with the Chicago Sanitary and Ship Canal.

6. A maximum of 92.5 mg/l in all remaining waters.

Federal reference levels for aquatic life suggest 50 JTU's turbidity as a limit or 10 JTU's as a "good" reference level. A proposed criterion for freshwater aquatic life is 80 mg/l suspended solids.

A large percentage of stations monitored turbidity, but far fewer measured suspended solids. Considering the turbidity map first, (Figure 3.35) the worst water was reported along Salt Creek and large portions of the Des Plaines River, along the Cal-Sag Channel, and along part of the West Branch of the Du Page River. Regions in which the water was somewhat better included the entire Fox River, Lake Michigan's north shore in the vicinity of Pettibone Creek and Thorn Creek. Many stations were in excess of the more stringent reference level in these areas, and several were in excess of the less stringent reference level as well. A general trend of increasing turbidity can be observed going north along the Lake Michigan shoreline, a trend which may well be due to natural conditions.

The highest levels of suspended solids were recorded along Salt Creek, the Des Plaines River, the North Shore Channel and North Branch of the Chicago River, and the waterways in the Calumet area.

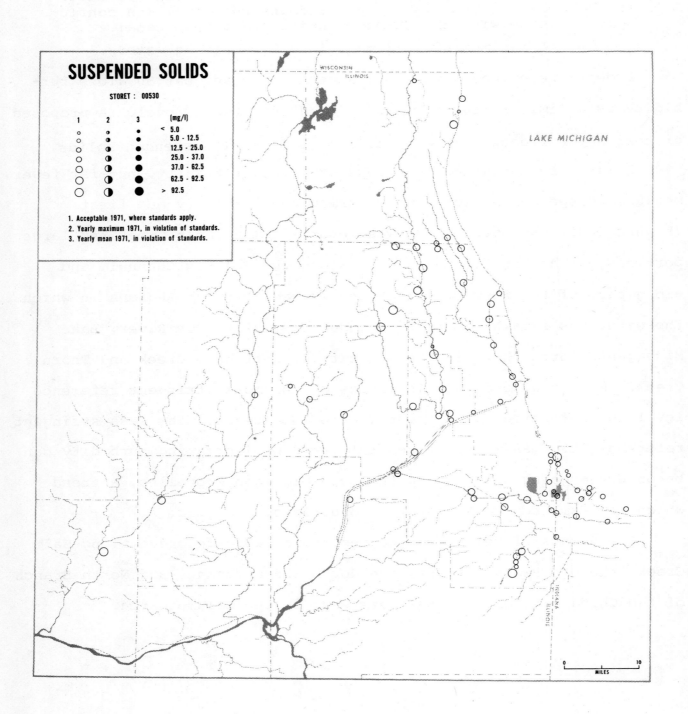

Figure 3.34

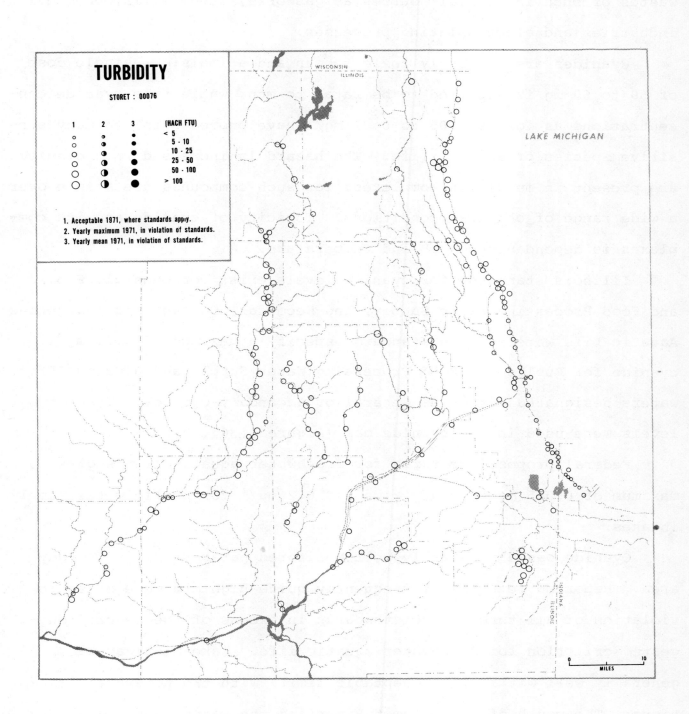

Figure 3.35

V. ORGANIC CHEMICALS

Cyanide

Cyanide (CN) is a carbon-nitrogen complex ion. Not found freely in nature, cyanide and its complexes enter water supplies through the wastes of such industrial sources as gasworks, steel mills, chemical industries and electroplating processes.

Cyanides are extremely toxic to man and animals: a single dose of 50 to 60 mg is reported to be fatal to man, while free cyanide concentrations as low as 0.05 to 0.01 mg/l have proved fatal to many sensitive species of aquatic life. The hazard is increased when cyanides are present in metal ion complexes; for such compounds are stable over a wide range of chemical conditions. Toxicity of cyanide and its complexes is dependent upon pH and temperature.

Illinois standards for cyanide levels exist for General, Public and Food Processing Water Supply, and Secondary Contact and Indigenous Aquatic Life waters. The standards specify a maximum of 0.01 mg/l cyanide for Public and Food Processing Water Supply and 0.02 mg/l for waters designated either as General or Secondary Contact. These two levels were used in the cyanide map (Figure 3.36).

Federal proposed criteria for freshwater aquatic life suggest a maximum of 0.005 mg/l at any time and 0.2 mg/l for public water supply intakes.

Cyanide was a moderately well monitored parameter in the study area. Reported levels were frequently quite high and were often in violation of all three state standards in excess of the federal suggested criterion for freshwater aquatic life. Lake Michigan was generally well within the acceptable limits with two noteworthy exceptions: The mouth of the Calumet River and the water in the vicinity of Indiana Harbor, which reported some of the worst yearly means for cyanide in the study sample. Other exceptionally high readings were reported on the Des Plaines River and on spots along the Chicago River,

North Shore Channel and the Chicago Sanitary and Ship Canal. Areas
of high readings most likely correlate with industrial effluent discharges.

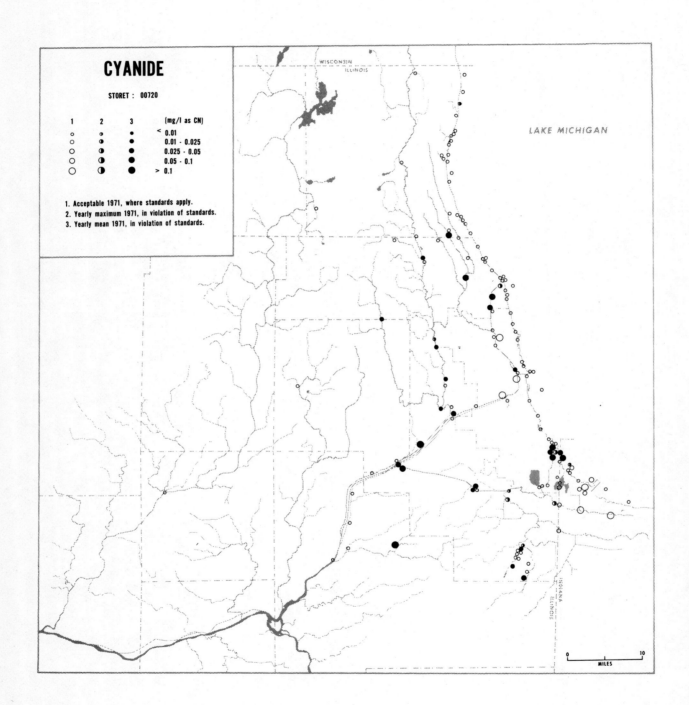

Figure 3.36

Methylene Blue Active Substances

Although MBAS does not detect cationic or nonionic surfactants, the MBAS measurement is the best available measure of anionic surfactants in the water. Most detergents, which come into the waterways from municipal and industrial waste sources, contain the anionic surfactants, which are highly resistant to chemical oxidation and biological breakdown.

In high concentrations, the toxic components of detergents are lethal to fish. In their more commonly found low concentrations, synthetic anionic surfactants and other foaming agents impart an unpleasant taste and odor to the water. Even extremely low concentrations are capable of producing unsightly masses of foam in a stream or tap water. The physiological implications of MBAS for humans are unknown.

The only state standard for MBAS is the one specified in the Public Health Service Drinking Water Standards which apply to waters designated as Public and Food Processing Water Supply. This criterion, which was used to set a level in the MBAS map (Figure 3.37), states that these waters shall contain no more than 0.5 mg/l MBAS at any time, and is the same as the proposed criterion specified for Public Water Supply Intake by EPA.

MBAS proved to be a fairly well-monitored parameter. Several regions stand out as having the worst MBAS readings: Thorn Creek, the East Branch and part of the West Branch of the Du Page River, and the whole southern region of the Fox River, which represents a break from the prevalent pattern of water quality which we have seen so far.

There were many stations for which the yearly means violated the standard. It is interesting to note that most of the violations, as well as the lowest quality waters, lie outside the MSD. Many stations in the aforementioned areas reported yearly means which were in excess of 4.0 mg/l of MBAS, a value which is 8 times the standard.

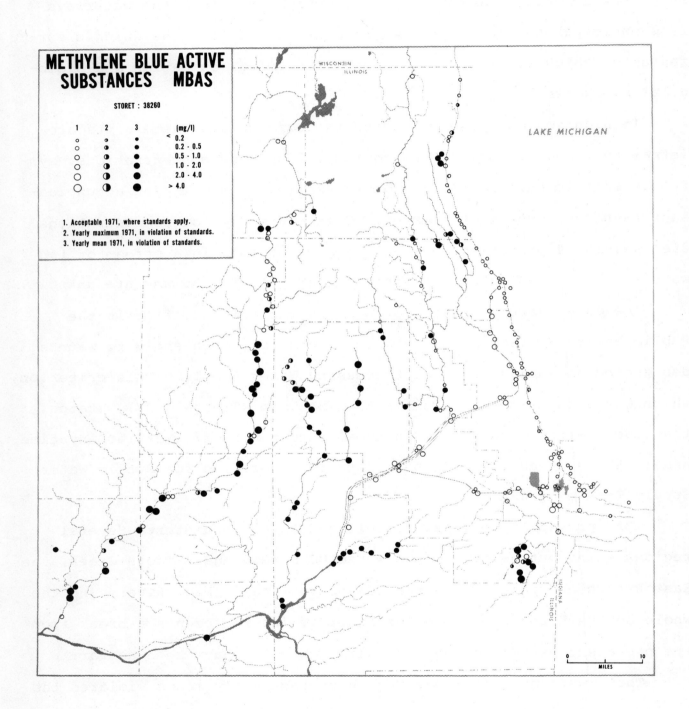

METHYLENE BLUE ACTIVE SUBSTANCES   MBAS

STORET : 38260

1	2	3	(mg/l)
			< 0.2
			0.2 - 0.5
			0.5 - 1.0
			1.0 - 2.0
			2.0 - 4.0
			> 4.0

1. Acceptable 1971, where standards apply.
2. Yearly maximum 1971, in violation of standards.
3. Yearly mean 1971, in violation of standards.

Figure 3.37

Oil and Grease

"Oil and grease" includes floating oils, emulsified oils and water soluble fractions of oils. This type of pollution enters the water from oil spills or discharges. Oil free waters are necessary to preserve the integrity of wildlife and indigenous aquatic life.

Floating oils may restrict reaeration and photosynthesis in the water body. They may suffocate aquatic organisms which are dependent upon surface oxygen. Sedimented oils may blanket the river bottom, destroying indigenous organisms and altering spawning areas. Emulsified and water soluble oils can prove extremely toxic to algae and fish. Water birds and aquatic mammals are severely affected by surface oils. Heavy mortalities of water birds have resulted from contamination of plumages by oil leading to immobility, heat loss, starvation, or direct poisoning. Taste, odor and appearance problems ensue from the presence of even small quanitites of oil and greast in public water supplies. Oils may be physiologically detrimental to man and are detrimental to conventional treatment processes.

State standard exists for Public and Food Processing Water Supply (a maximum of 0.1 mg/l oil at any time) and for Secondary Contact and Indigenous Aquatic Life waters (a maximum of 15.0 mg/l at any time). Both criteria were incorporated into Figure 3.38.

Unfortunately, only a handful of stations monitored this parameter. It is interesting to note that all but two of these stations were located in the vicinity of the Calumet and Grand Calumet Rivers and Lake Michigan in the vicinity of Indiana Harbor, areas which are heavily industrialized. Every lake station except one reported violation of the standard by the yearly mean. The lake stations typically reported reading 50 times the specified state standard.

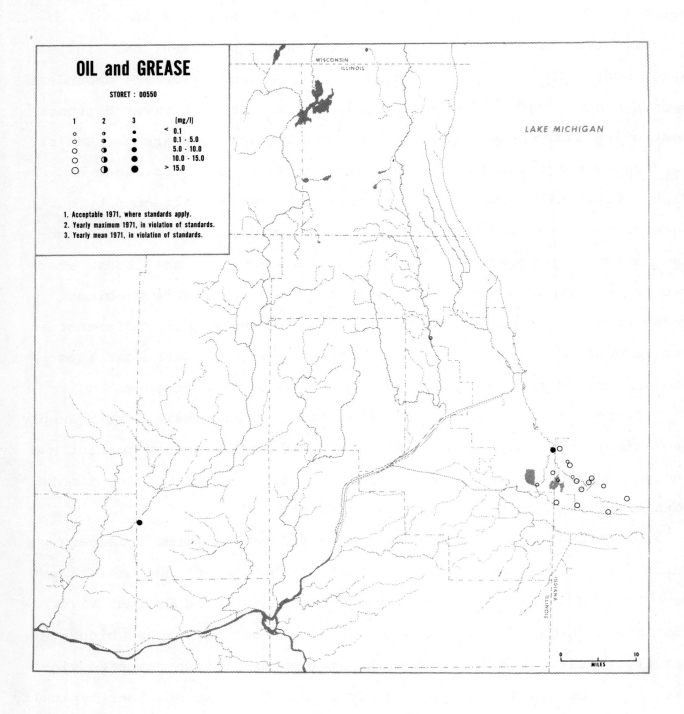

OIL and GREASE

STORET : 00550

1	2	3		(mg/l)
○	○	●	<	0.1
○	○	●		0.1 - 5.0
○	◐	●		5.0 - 10.0
○	◐	●		10.0 - 15.0
○	◑	●	>	15.0

1. Acceptable 1971, where standards apply.
2. Yearly maximum 1971, in violation of standards.
3. Yearly mean 1971, in violation of standards.

WISCONSIN
ILLINOIS

LAKE MICHIGAN

INDIANA
ILLINOIS

0   MILES   10

Figure 3.38

Phenols

Phenols, one of the hydroxyl derivatives of benzene or its homologs, are invariably the result of industrial and/or domestic pollution. Widely used as disinfectants in the synthesis of organic compounds, phenols and phenolic compounds derive from the wastes of petroleum, coke and chemical industries. They are also a by-product of wood distillation and are found in appreciable amounts in domestic and animal wastes. Phenols decompose in the presence of oxygen and microorganisms, and their persistance downstream from the point of entry is relatively short-lived. For this reason, they serve as fairly reliable indicators of local sources of pollution.

High levels of phenols are lethal to fish and other aquatic organisms. The problem is compounded by the fact that many phenolic compounds are more toxic than pure phenol. Phenols adversely affect the taste of fish at levels that do not appear to effect adverse physiological changes in the fish. At high concentrations, phenols are potentially hazardous to humans and at low concentrations they impart a disagreeable taste and odor to water. Raw water contaminated by phenols poses a problem for its use as a drinking water supply, since phenols and phenolic compounds are not easily removed by conventional treatment processes.

The Water Pollution Regulation of Illinois specify a maximum level of 0.1 mg/l phenols for all waters designated as General, a maximum of 0.001 mg/l for all waters designated for Public and Food Processing Water Supply and maximum of 0.3 mg/l for waters designated as Secondary Contact and Indigenous Aquatic Life. All three levels are shown on the map for phenols [Figure 3.39].

Federal proposed criteria suggest a maximum of 0.001 mg/l in water used for public supplies and 0.1 mg/l for freshwater aquatic life.

A fair number of stations monitored phenols. The map shows that many stations had yearly means which exceeded state and federal reference levels for public water supply. No stations exceeded the state standards for General use areas or Secondary Contact and Indigenous Aquatic Life areas or the reference level for Freshwater Aquatic Life.

The worst water was reported along Thorn Creek, the Little and Grand Calumet Rivers, Indiana Harbor, the vicinity of Pettibone Creek, the North Shore Channel and North Branch of the Chicago River and the Des Plaines River.

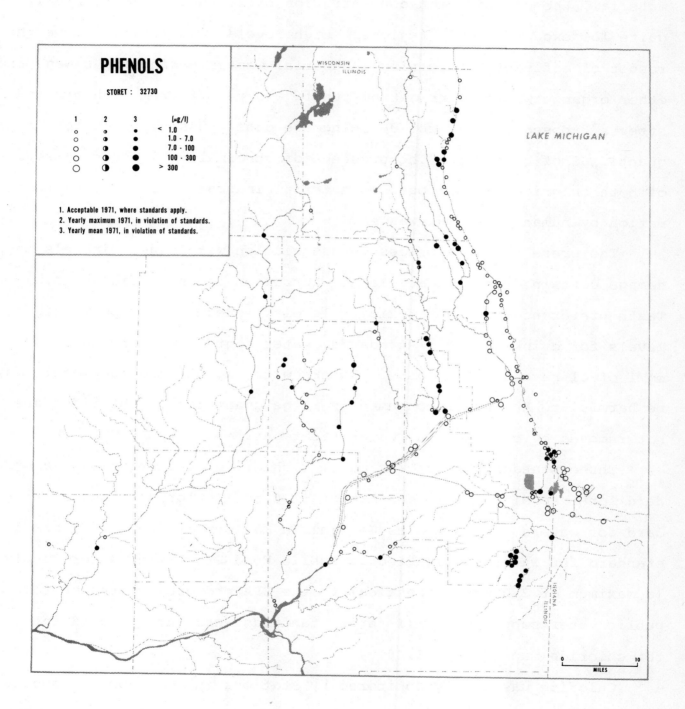

Figure 3.39

VI. DISSOLVED ELEMENTS, IONS AND COMPOUNDS

Chloride

Most commonly derived from the weathering of sedimentary rock material, the chloride ion concentration of freshwater is generally quite low except in arid regions. High levels of chloride may be the result of effluents containing industrial wastes, brine and sewage and other organic waste. Irrigation runoff and runoff from highways and streets exposed to salt for de-icing are other possibilities for large quantities of chloride. The presence of abnormally high concentrations of both chloride and nitrogenous material indicates possible contamination by human or animal wastes.

The presence of chlorides in association with other minerals may damage certain crops and accelerate corrosion in industrial uses. Taste preferences and not toxicity levels, determine the permissible levels for drinking water standards; water containing more than 250 mg/l of Cl have a salty taste. Waters with higher chloride levels may be harmful to humans if consumed in large quantities. Chlorides are not removed by conventional water treatment.

Three standards exist for maximum chloride concentrations; a standard for Lake Michigan (a maximum of 12.0 mg/l chloride); and a standard for waters designated as General (a maximum of 500 mg/l); and a standard for waters designated as Public Food Processing Water Supply (a maximum of 250 mg/l, identical to the EPA proposed criterion for public water supplies). All three standards were incorporated into the chloride map (Figure 3.40).

Chloride was widely monitored by stations in the sample, especially along the Fox River. Corresponding with pollution patterns in other maps discussed so far, stations along Thorn Creek, Pettibone Creek and the East and West Branches of the Du Page River reported the highest chloride concentrations, frequently exceeding state and federal reference levels for public water supplies. The North Branch of the

Chicago River, Salt Creek and the Des Plaines River, part of the Little Calumet River, Hickory Creek and the remainder of the Du Page River contained water of somewhat higher quality, but still reported stations with yearly maximums in excess of the state standard. Though stations in Lake Michigan reported lower levels of chloride, violations of the state standard for Lake Michigan by the yearly maximum were frequent.

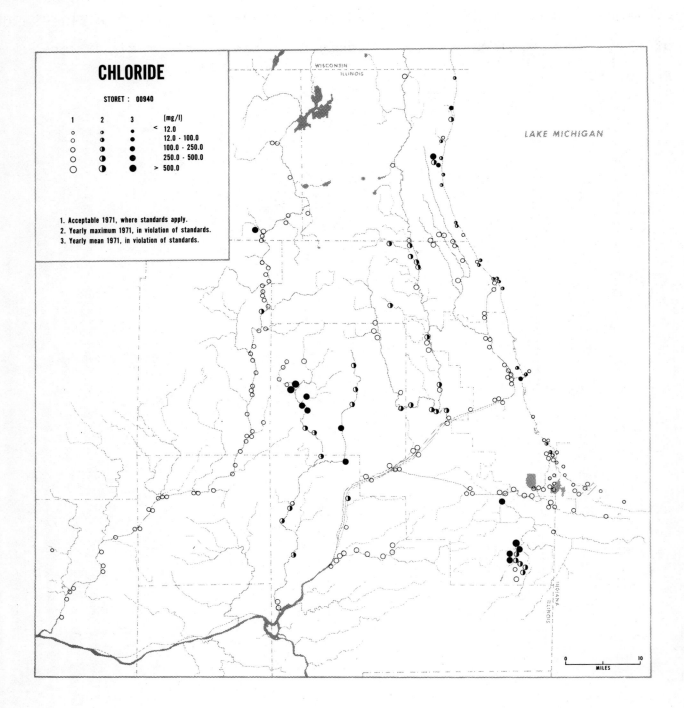

CHLORIDE

STORET : 00940

1	2	3	(mg/l)
○	◔	●	< 12.0
○	◑	●	12.0 - 100.0
○	◑	●	100.0 - 250.0
○	◑	●	250.0 - 500.0
○	◑	●	> 500.0

1. Acceptable 1971, where standards apply.
2. Yearly maximum 1971, in violation of standards.
3. Yearly mean 1971, in violation of standards.

WISCONSIN
ILLINOIS

LAKE MICHIGAN

INDIANA
ILLINOIS

0   10
MILES

Figure 3.40

Fluoride

In natural waters, fluoride is usually present only in small concentrations caused by the weathering of rocks containing fluorine.
High concentrations are often associated with volcanic or fumerolic
gases caused by recent volcanic activity and by saline water from oil
wells. In areas where there are high concentrations of fluoride in
natural water there are generally low readings in calcium. Fluoride
is found occasionally in industrial wastes, particularly in steel,
disinfectant, glass and enamels and chemical industries.

Fluoride is also added to many public water supplies to reduce
the incidence of cavities in teeth.

High concentrations of fluoride can produce chronic fluoiosis in
humans. Fluoride may also cause discoloration in teeth of children
although it does reduce tooth decay.

For all General use waters in the State of Illinois concentrations
of fluoride in excess of 1.4 mg/l are in violation. The Secondary
Contact and Indifenous Aquatic Life standards for fluoride is 2.5 mg/l.
Both state standards were incorporated as levels in the fluoride map
(Figure 3.41).

Federal proposed criteria suggest 1.0 mg/l fluoride for continuous irrigation of sandy soils and 2.0 mg/l fluoride as a maximum for
all soils or for water used as supply for livestock.

Fluoride was monitored quite extensively over the hydrologic network and few stations were in excess of state and federal reference
levels. High concentrations of fluoride were monitored at the West
Branch of the Du Page River, Pettibone Creek, Calumet Harbor and to a
lesser extent, Thorn Creek. All reference levels were exceeded by
some stations in each of the first three above-mentioned areas, but
overall, stations in the monitoring network were in compliance with
the state and federal reference levels.

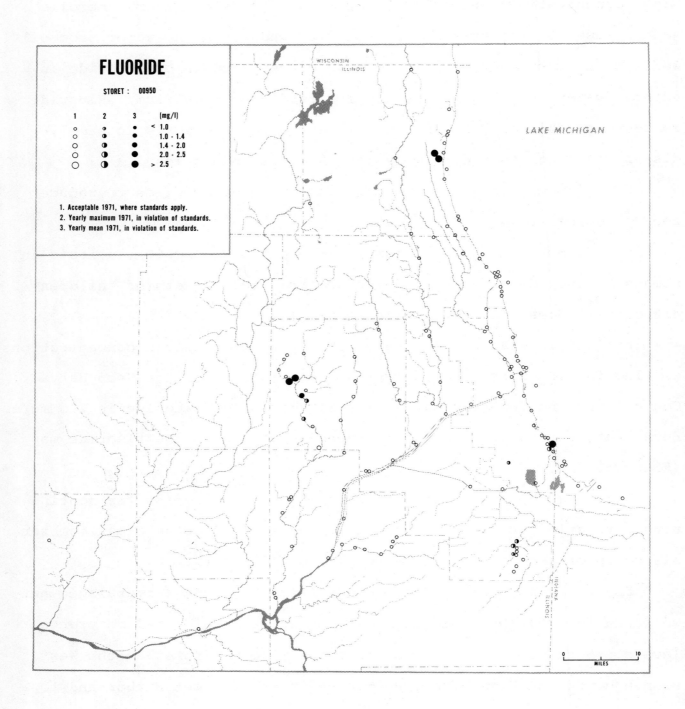

FLUORIDE

STORET :   00950

1	2	3	(mg/l)
○	◦	•	< 1.0
○	◦	•	1.0 - 1.4
○	◐	•	1.4 - 2.0
○	◐	•	2.0 - 2.5
○	◑	●	> 2.5

1. Acceptable 1971, where standards apply.
2. Yearly maximum 1971, in violation of standards.
3. Yearly mean 1971, in violation of standards.

WISCONSIN
ILLINOIS

LAKE MICHIGAN

INDIANA
ILLINOIS

0   10
MILES

Figure 3.41

Ammonia

Ammonia (NH_3) is a nitrogen complex which exists in equilibrium with the ammonium ion (NH_4+). Ammonia occupies an important position in the nitrogen cycle. Since ammonia is present in natural waters in very small concentrations, its presence in water in levels exceeding 0.1 mg/l usually indicates organic pollution. Ammonia is a product of untreated sewage, which may contain as much as one half of its total nitrogen in the form of free ammonia.

The toxicity of ammonia solutions is dependent upon the unionized fraction, which varies with the pH of the solution. The more basic the water body, the greater the hazard a given quantity of ammonia will provide. Although there is no evidence that ammonia is toxic to man or livestock, it may be extremely toxic to fish in large quantities.

In high concentrations, NH_3 has an adverse effect on the determination processes used in the treatment of water for public supply, as well as being corrosive to pipes.

The state standards specify a maximum of 0.02 mg/l ammonia as nitrogen in Lake Michigan and 1.5 mg/l in waters designated General. The General standard specified the same value recommended by EPA for Freshwater Aquatic Life. Different standards are specified for Secondary Contact and Indigenous Aquatic Life waters depending on factors such as magnitude of waste load, time of year and effective date of the standard. The General and Lake Michigan standards were incorporated into the parameter map [Figure 3.42]. An EPA proposed criterion suggests a limit of 0.5 mg/l for public water supplies.

Except for the Fox River, ammonia was a well monitored parameter. Ammonia concentrations were exceptionally high throughout the study area with all of the reference levels being exceeded by stations on all waterways in the hydrologic net. Due to complexities in the application of the state standards for Secondary Contact and Indigenous Aquatic Life, violations could not be plotted for this water use designation, yet the majority of the stations in the hydrologic net are still seen to violate the other state standards. Areas of particularly high concentrations are the East and West Branches of the Du Page River and the Thorn Creek area. Industrial and sewage effluents and the effects of storm overflow are undoubtedly factors in the observed pattern. Organic pollution is implicated, with inadequate sewage treatment and overflow due to storm runoffs being the most likely sources. Probable ramifications of the excessive ammonia levels in surface waters can be seen in the correspondingly high concentrations present in ground water (see Figure 3.11).

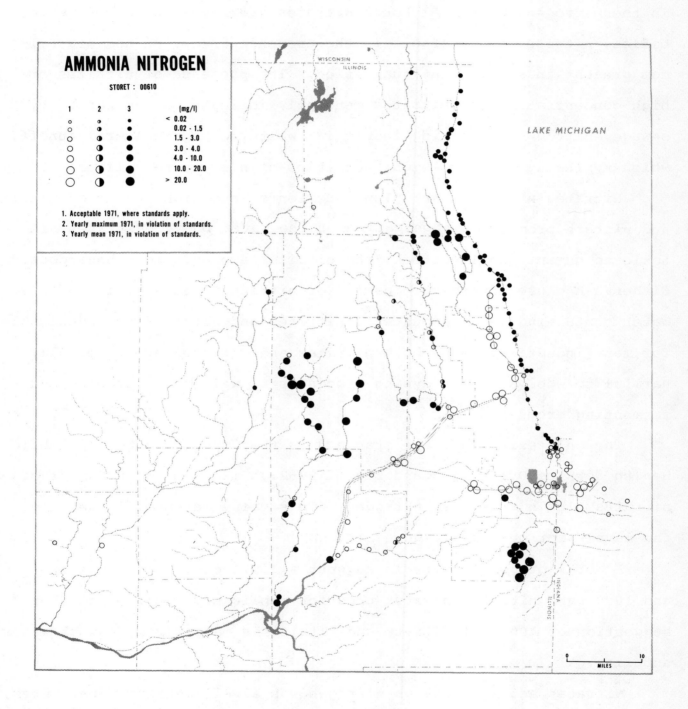

Figure 3.42

Nitrates and Nitrites

Nitrite (NO_2) and nitrate (NO_3) are nitrogen complexes which represent two consecutive steps in the nitrogen cycle. In nature, nitrite is oxidized to nitrate, which is the final oxidation product in the nitrogen cycle. Although nitrates are found in natural water bodies, nitrites are unstable in the presence of oxygen and are seldom present in significant quantities. The presence of nitrites or high concentrations of nitrates generally indicate contamination by sewage, nitrogen-containing industrial waste, or agricultural runoff, which typically contains high quantities of nitrate fertilizers.

Nitrates are important plant nutrients, and high levels of nitrite and nitrate promote eutrophication of the water body. Nitrates are toxic to humans and livestock, and nitrites are even more hazardous. Either can cause methemoglobinemia (or nitrate poisoning) in infants. Water containing large amounts of nitrites and nitrates is undesirable for many industrial uses; both nitrites and nitrates are especially harmful to wool and silk dyeing processes as well as to brewing and fermenting processes.

The only existing state standard is that specified by the Public Health Service Drinking Standards of 1962: a maximum of 10.0 mg/l of nitrates plus nitrites as nitrogen. This value was used in setting the levels for our map [Figure 3.43].

Federal proposed criteria suggest a limit of 1.0 mg/l nitrite and 10.0 mg/l nitrate in water used for public supplies. A further suggestion of 100 mg/l nitrate and nitrite is made for livestock water supplies.

Nitrates and nitrites as nitrogen was a well monitored parameter, especially along the Fox River and Lake Michigan. The worst readings were reported along the Des Plaines River. It should be noted however, that the highest readings were all taken by MSD stations, and the yearly means were relatively greater because of exceptionally high readings taken by the MSD stations on one date. This would be an error in measurement technique or STORET processing, or it could have a legitimate explanation such as the first flush effect of the run-off from a heavy storm. The Du Page River had high levels of this parameter. The Fox River also reported lower readings proceeding southward.

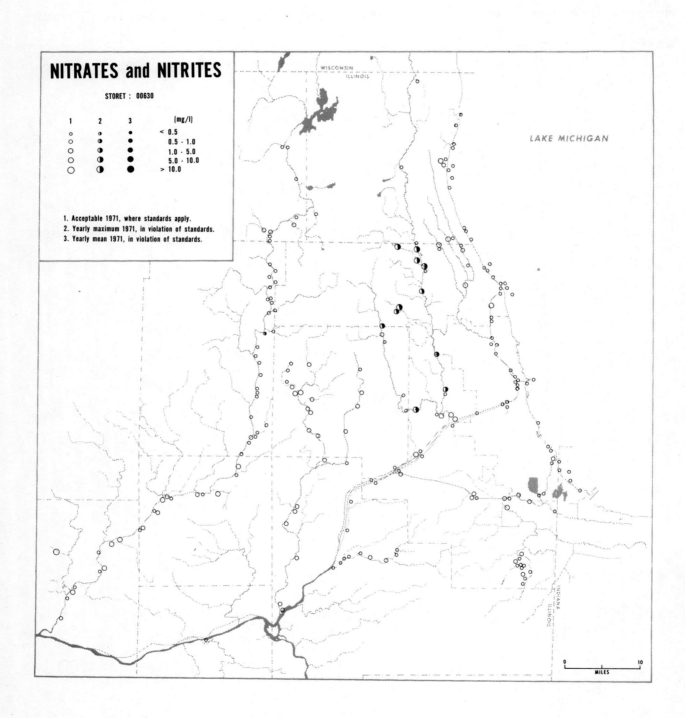

Figure 3.43

Phosphorus

Like nitrates, phosphorus is an essential plant nutrient necessary
to aquatic vegetation. Natural levels result from the leaching of
soil and rocks and from the normal decomposition processes of plants
and animals. Unnaturally high levels of phosphorus may be the result
of several likely sources of pollution: Phosphorus is always present
in untreated sewage. Both animal metabolic waste and household detergents are the sources of phosphorus in domestic waste. Industrial
effluents -- especially those containing organic wastes and phosphates
used for water treatment -- are another source of phosphorus. Agricultural runoff may also contain considerable phosphorus because of
the high phosphorus content of many fertilizers. In general, sources
that contribute nitrogen wastes are also likely sources of phosphorus.

In its elemental form, phosphorus is particularly toxic and is
subject to bioaccumulation in much the same way as mercury. Certain
marine fish have been found to concentrate phosphorus at concentrations
as low as 1 mg/l (Proposed Criteria, p.280). Phosphates can stimulate
algal blooms and contribute to the eutrophication of the water body.
In addition to creating an aesthetic nuisance, this may adversely effect the quantity and quality of aquatic life. In its 1973 Proposed
Criteria for Water Quality, EPA states: "Reducing phosphorus in lakes
and reservoirs is the single most important step that can be taken in
the control of eutrophication at this time." (p.342)

Standards exist for maximum levels, but they are specified only
for several bodies of water, most of them reservoirs or lakes. A maximum of 0.007 mg/l is specified for Lake Michigan, a maximum of 0.05
mg/l for the Fox River Basin, which is the only river or stream
governed by the state standards. These three levels were incorporated
into the phosphorus map [Figure 3.44].

A federal reference level of 0.1 mg/l is suggested as a nutrient
standard in Guidelines for Developing or Revising Water Quality Standards (EPA, 1973).

Phosphorus was well monitored, especially along the Fox River and Lake Michigan, the two bodies of water to which the standards are primarily addressed. Levels were quite high with respect to the reference levels throughout the hydrologic net, although violations could not be determined along waterways other than the Fox River and Lake Michigan. Numerous stations reported violations of the state yearly mean standard, with the Indiana Harbor region, the areas near the mouths of the entering rivers, and an extensive region north of Pettibone Creek appearing especially bad.

Over the whole area, Thorn Creek and the East and West Branches of the Du Page River stood out as having the highest levels of phosphorus with several stations reporting yearly means of more than 100 (and in several cases, over 200) times the value specified by the General Standards for lakes and reservoirs.

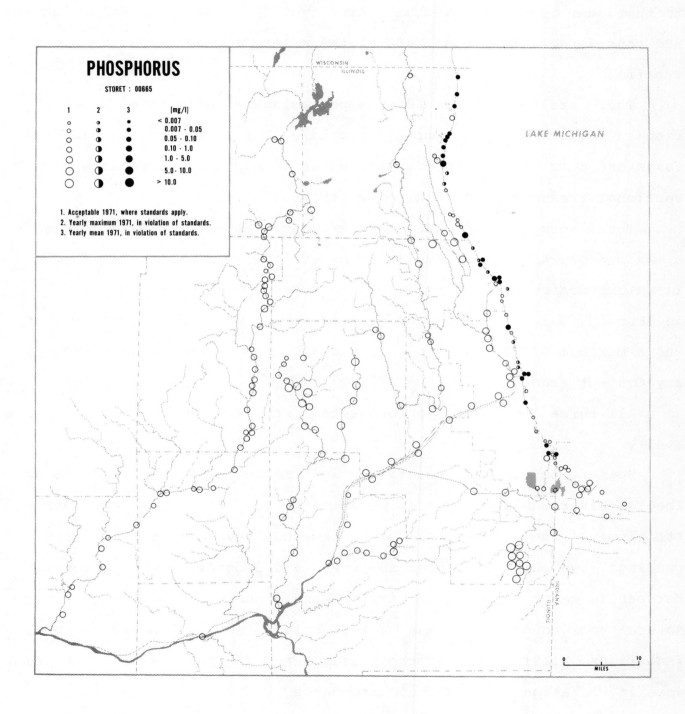

PHOSPHORUS

STORET : 00665

1	2	3	(mg/l)
○	○	●	< 0.007
○	◓	●	0.007 - 0.05
○	◑	●	0.05 - 0.10
○	◑	●	0.10 - 1.0
○	◑	●	1.0 - 5.0
○	◑	●	5.0 - 10.0
○	◑	●	> 10.0

1. Acceptable 1971, where standards apply.
2. Yearly maximum 1971, in violation of standards.
3. Yearly mean 1971, in violation of standards.

WISCONSIN
ILLINOIS

LAKE MICHIGAN

INDIANA
ILLINOIS

MILES

Figure 3.44

Sulfate

The sulfides in both igneous and sedimentary rock enter the water body through natural weathering processes and are quickly oxidized to yield sulfate (SO_4) ions. Organic material also adds sulfate to the water as a phase of the sulfur cycle. Organic pollution can add considerably to the sulfate in the water, as can excessive storm runoff.

There are no apparent adverse physiological effects of waters rich in sulfate to humans or aquatic life, but a highly objectionable taste and odor are imparted to the water at high concentrations. Conventional treatment does not remove the sulfate ion.

Three sets of state standards are specified for sulfate levels: a maximum of 24 mg/l sulfate in Lake Michigan; a maximum of 250 mg/l in waters designated as Public and Food Processing Water Supply (which is also the value suggested by EPA for Public Water Supply Intake) and a maximum of 500 mg/l in waters designated as General. No Secondary Contact standards are specified.

All three levels were incorporated into our map of sulfate (Figure 3.45).

Sulfate levels were relatively well monitored in the study area. The Fox River was particularly well monitored. Two areas stand out strikingly. The vicinity of Thorn Creek had several extremely high readings (two and three times the state and federal reference levels for public water supply), as did the West Branch of the Du Page River. Natural background levels may partly explain the high observed levels (see Figure 3.18). Many of the yearly means of stations in these areas were in violation of both state standards. After these two areas, the regions with the worst water were Pettibone Creek, the Little and Grand Calumet Rivers, the Cal-Sag Channel, the northern part of Salt Creek, the Illinois River, Hickory Creek and the remainder of the Du Page River. Although Lake Michigan generally had the best water, more than half of its stations had yearly maximums which were in violation of the state standard for Lake Michigan. The mouths of rivers and channels gave the worst readings along Lake Michigan.

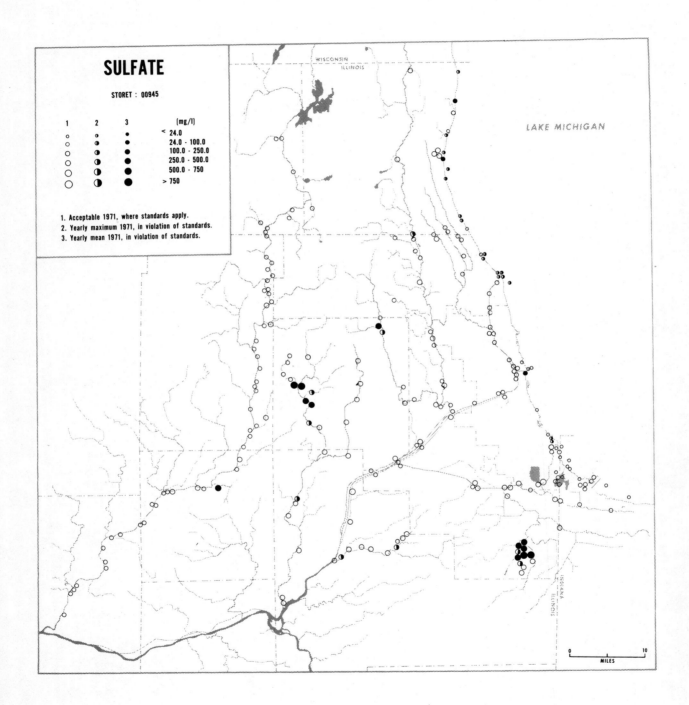

SULFATE

STORET : 00945

1	2	3	(mg/l)
○	◔	●	< 24.0
○	◓	●	24.0 - 100.0
○	◓	●	100.0 - 250.0
○	◑	●	250.0 - 500.0
○	◑	●	500.0 - 750
○	◐	●	> 750

1. Acceptable 1971, where standards apply.
2. Yearly maximum 1971, in violation of standards.
3. Yearly mean 1971, in violation of standards.

Figure 3.45

VII. TRACE METALS

Arsenic

Found at low levels in some natural water, arsenic may be introduced in higher concentrations through man's activity. Likely sources are weed killers, insecticides and industrial effluents.

Arsenic has been shown to be a dangerous cumulative toxicant. For plants, toxicity varies for different species, influenced by such factors as soil texture and absorptive capacity. For animals, it depends on the chemical form. The organic oxides are considerably more toxic than the organic forms occurring in living tissues or used as feed additives to livestock. For humans, severe poisoning can result from as little as 100 mg, and smaller dosages may be accumulated and lead to adverse chronic effects.

State Standards specify a maximum allowable concentration of 1.0 mg/l total arsenic in waters designated as General, 0.25 mg/l total arsenic in waters designated as Secondary Contact and Indigenous Aquatic Life, and 0.01 mg/l total arsenic in water used for Public and Food Processing Water Supply. These standards were incorporated into the range of values for the parameter map (Figure 3.46).

EPA suggested levels are 0.1 mg/l for public supply intakes and continuous irrigation, 0.2 mg/l for livestock water supplies, and 2.0 mg/l for irrigation of neutral and fine textured alkaline soils for less than 20 years.

Arsenic was not very well monitored in the study area, with a conspicuous absence of stations monitoring it along Lake Michigan (many stations along Lake Michigan monitor dissolved arsenic however). Reported readings were quite high with respect to reference levels just about everywhere the parameter was monitored; the great majority of stations reported yearly means in excess of the standard for Public and Food Processing Water Supply and most of these were in excess of the standard for Secondary Contact and Indigenous Aquatic Life as well.

Of the remaining stations, most reported maximum readings in violation of this standard.

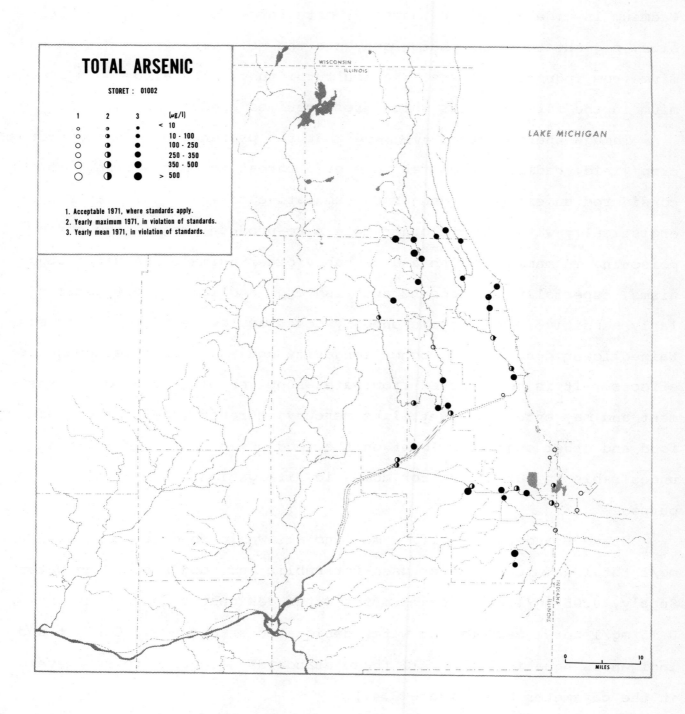

Figure 3.46

Cadmium

Under natural conditions, cadmium is present in the water at low levels as a sulfide and as an impurity in zinc lead ores. When found in higher concentrations, it is the result of man-made pollution. Cadmium is widely used in industry; metallurgy, electroplating, cersius, pigmentation and photography are the most likely sources of cadmium from industrial waste. Agricultural runoff may also contain cadmium in the form of salts which are sometimes used in pesticides.

Though there is some evidence that the presence of cadmium reduces crop yield, cadmium poses far more of a threat to animal life. It is considered an extremely dangerous cumulative toxicant which acts synergistically with certain other metals to produce progressive chronic poisoning in mammals, fish and probably other animals. Aquatic organisms, especially crustaceans and fish eggs and larvae, are particularly sensitive. Man is sickened by doses as low as 15 mg/l, and sustained lower dosages may reduce longevity and have possible mutagenic effects. It is not removed from water supplies by conventional treatment and may enter the diet, like mercury, through ingestion of seafood and other organisms lower on the food chain. Cadmium is thus undesirable in water used for domestic, irrigation and recreational purposes.

State standards specify a maximum allowable concentration of 0.01 mg/l total cadmium in water used for Public and Food Processing Water Supply, 0.05 mg/l total cadmium for water designated as General and 0.15 mg/l total cadmium for water designated as Secondary Contact and Indigenous Aquatic Life. All these standards were used to set levels in the parameter map (Figure 3.47).

Federal proposed criteria exist for freshwater aquatic life (0.004 mg/l for soft water, 0.03 mg/l for hard water), for public water supply intakes (0.01 mg/l), for continuous irrigation (0.01 mg/l) and for irrigation of neutral and fine textured alkaline soils for a period of less than 20 years (0.05 mg/l).

Rather poorly monitored, cadmium was reported to be in low concentrations at those stations which measured it. In no instance, did
a yearly mean exceed the most stringent state and federal reference
levels.

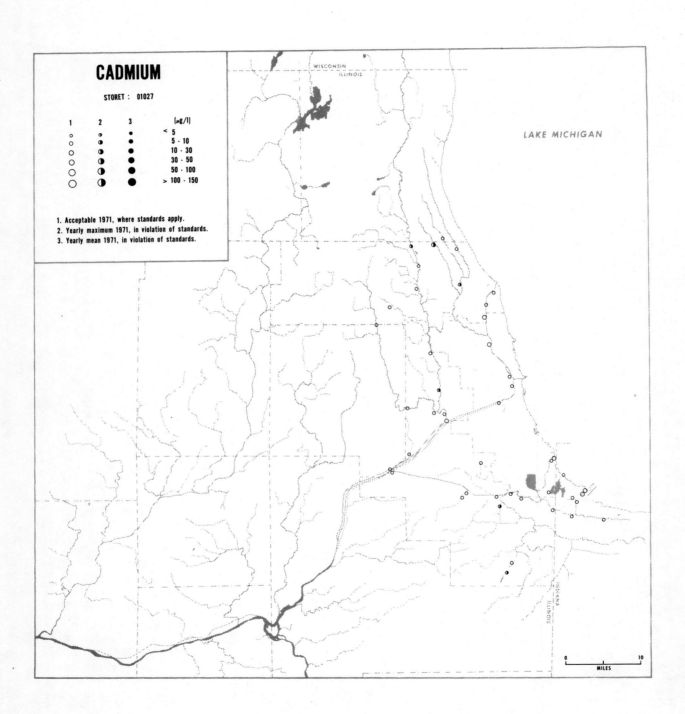

Figure 3.47

Copper

Copper is commonly found as a trace element in natural waters. When present in high concentrations, it is more likely the result of industrial effluent pollution. Corrosion of copper pipes and copper bearing equipment, mining wastes, salts used for algae control in open reservoirs and urban runoff containing salts used for snow removal constitute several common sources of pollution.

At high levels, copper is highly toxic to a large number of plants and invertebrates and moderately toxic to animals. Depending on pH and other chemical characteristics of water, as little as 0.1 mg/l can prove toxic to certain plants, although trace levels often are beneficial.

Toxicity varies to a much greater extent for different species, aquatic organisms and livestock. Trace levels are necessary in the diets of many animals. Man also requires trace levels, but as little as 1.0 mg/l impart a disagreeable metallic taste to the water. Though not considered to be a cumulative poison, large doses may produce emesis or if prolonged, result in liver damage. High levels of copper are also undesirable in water used for industrial purposes, since this leads to corrosion problems.

State standards exist for water designated as General (0.02 mg/l dissolved copper) and Secondary Contact and Indigenous Aquatic Life (1.0 mg/l total copper). Both values were used as levels in the parameter map (Figure 3.48).

Federal proposed criteria include a limit of 0.2 mg/l for continuous irrigation purposes, 0.5 mg/l for livestock water supplies, 1.0 mg/l for public water supplies intakes and 5.0 mg/l for neutral and fine textured alkaline soils for less than 20 years.

Copper was one of the more extensively monitored trace metals. The worst water was reported around Pettibone Creek and vicinity, the northern tributaries of the Chicago River, the West Branch of the Du

Page River and the Calumet-Thorn Creek region. All of these areas had stations reporting yearly means which were in violation of the General Standards (but never any of the other reference level).

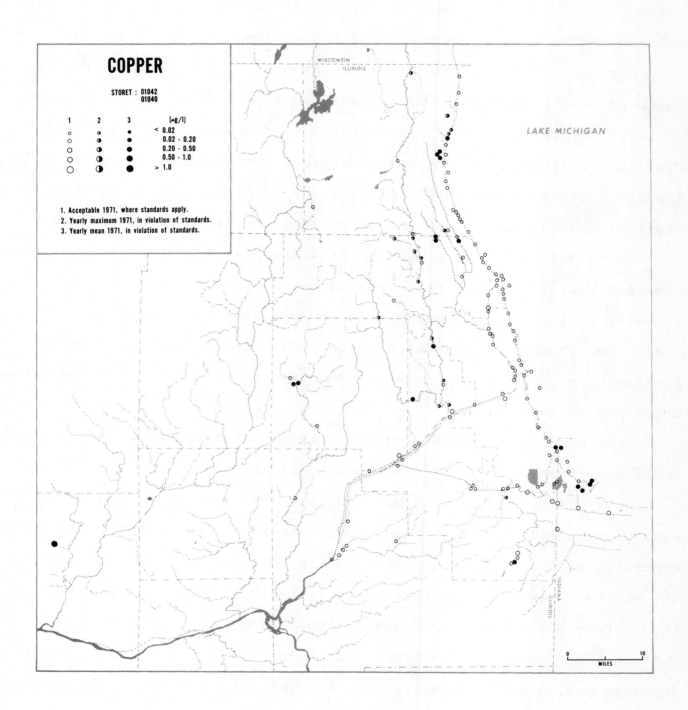

Figure 3.48

Iron

Although iron is a very common mineral and enters the hydrologic network in dissolved form from many types of rock and soil, only acidic water can usually carry more than 1 mg/l. Exposure to air of the dissolved species results in the formation of insoluble iron oxides.

Because of its low solubility in neutral to basic water, iron presents no serious hazard to most plant and animal life. Precipitation of ferric hydroxide flocs in seawater may adversely affect sediment dwelling invertebrates. At concentrations greater than 0.3 mg/l iron imparts a disagreeable taste to water and forms rust deposits which stain clothes and porcelain and accumulate in distribution systems.

State standards set a maximum of 0.3 mg/l total iron in water used for Public and Food Processing Water Supply, 1.0 mg/l total iron in water designated as General and 0.5 mg/l dissolved iron and 2.0 mg/l total iron in waters designated as Secondary Contact and Indigenous Aquatic Life. All four standards were used to set levels for the parameter map (Figure 3.49).

0.30 mg/l is a federal suggested maximum for public water supplies and 5.0 mg/l is suggested for agricultural irrigation.

Coverage for total iron was moderate over the hydrologic network with particularly good coverage along Lake Michigan. The highest concentrations of iron were reported in Pettibone Creek and vicinity, in the southern reaches of Des Plaines River and at scattered points on the Du Page River, Hickory Creek and the Calumet-Thorn Creek region. Two stations (on Pettibone Creek and at the mouth of Lake Calumet) reported yearly means in excess of the limit for total iron for Secondary Contact and Indigenous Aquatic Life waters, the least stringent reference level, and many stations exceeded reference levels for public water supply.

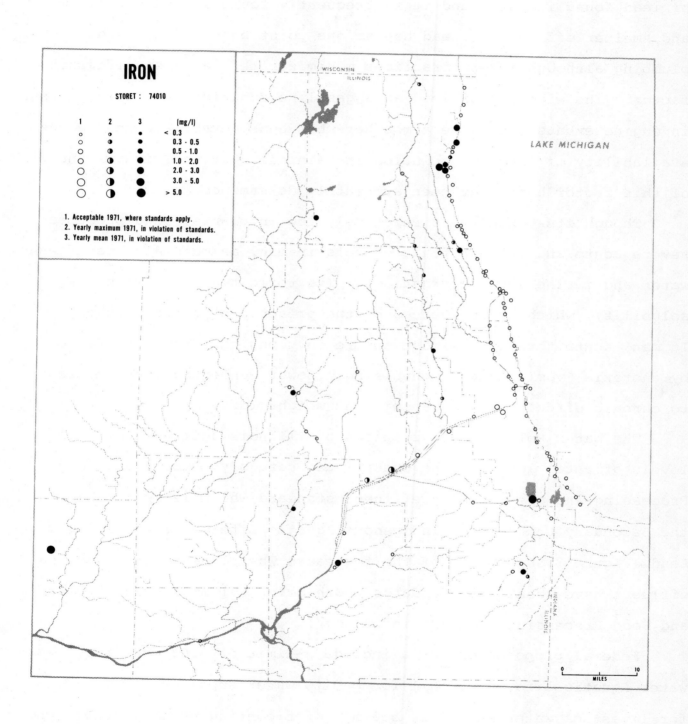

Figure 3.49

Lead

Although lead is seldomly found in natural waters, occasionally
it can be detected in areas where extensive weathering of limestone
and galen occurs. Man-made sources are responsible for the majority
of lead found in water and it is frequently found in industrial, mine
and smelter effluents. Lead had at one point been widely used in
plumbing although modern practices minimizes this as a significant
factor. The wide use of lead as a gasoline additive and its dispersal
in engine exhaust into the atmosphere has considerably increased the
availability of lead for solution in rainfall; yet the significance
of this factor has never been accurately determined.

Though its toxicity is relatively low in plants, lead produces
severe acute and chronic toxic effects in man, animals and most freshwater and marine aquatic organisms. Its toxicity varies with its
solubility, which is influenced by the presence of certain other ions.
In man, acute toxicity is most severe in young children, manifested
by anorexia, vomiting and convulsing. Lower concentrations may lead
to chronic effects such as anemia and weight loss.

The Water Pollution Regulations of Illinois define permissible
levels of total lead for the General use category, Public and Food
Processing and also give an effluent standard which is applicable to
the Secondary Contact and Indigenous Aquatic Life Water use category.
Lead (Figure 3.50) is one of the few cases where the general and the
effluent have identical standards, both being 0.1 mg/l. The Public
and Food Processing Standard is .05 mg/l.

Federal proposed criteria include a limit of 0.03 mg/l for Freshwater Aquatic Life, 0.05 mg/l for public water supplies. 0.1 mg/l
for livestock water supplies, 5.0 mg/l for contingous irrigation, and
10.0 mg/l for irrigation of neutral and fine textured alkaline soils
for a period of not more than 20 years.

Total lead was not a particularly well monitored parameter with only a handful of stations monitoring Lake Michigan, though a large number of stations monitored dissolved lead (which was not mapped). All of the stations reported yearly means in excess of the federal suggested criteria for Freshwater Aquatic Life, although only a few stations, located in the Calumet and Thorn Creek areas, exceed the state General and Secondary Contact and Indigenous Aquatic Life standards. A large number of stations monitored areas reported means in excess of the state and federal reference levels for public water supplies, which casts serious doubt on the sanitability of these waterways for this purpose and further attests to the excessively high levels of lead present in the study area.

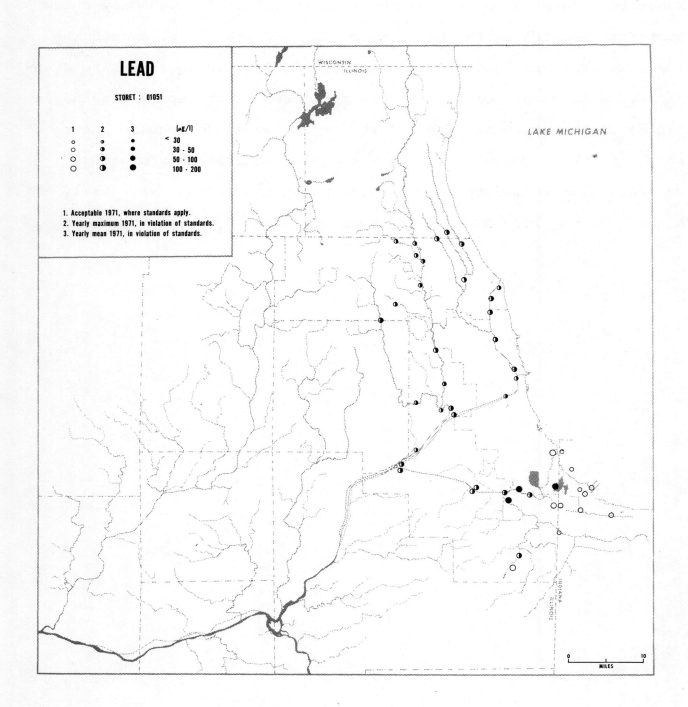

Figure 3.50

Manganese

Small amounts of manganese enter natural waters from certain ore
and mineral deposits. It is usually present only at very low levels
since the dissolved species precipitates to manganic oxide in the presence of air.

Manganese is toxic to a number of crops when present in nutrient
solutions in concentrations of a few tenths to a few milliliters per
liter. Toxicity increases with lower pH values. In high concentrations, manganese may be hazardous when present in human or livestock
water supplies. The soluble ion, which is not removed by conventional
treatment, imparts a disagreeable taste to water at concentrations as
low as 0.05 mg/l. High concentrations of manganese will form deposits
and such water is therefore undesirable for many industrial uses. It
is especially objectionable in water used for laundry work and textile
processing, causing dark stains on fabric and porcelain fixtures.
State standards exist for water designated as General and Secondary
Contact and Indigenous Aquatic Life (1.0 mg/l) and Public and Food
Processing Water Supply (0.05 mg/l). Both of these standards were
used to set levels in the parameter map (Figure 3.51).

EPA proposed criteria included a limit of 0.05 mg/l for Public
Water Supply Intake, 0.2 mg/l for continuous agricultural irrigation,
and 10.0 mg/l for irrigation of neutral and fine textured alkaline
soils.

Manganese was fairly well monitored relative to the other trace
metals. The lowest concentrations were reported along Lake Michigan,
which was the only water body consistently below the state and Federal
reference levels for water supply. Pettibone Creek and the West Branch
of the Du Page stood out as having the highest concentrations.

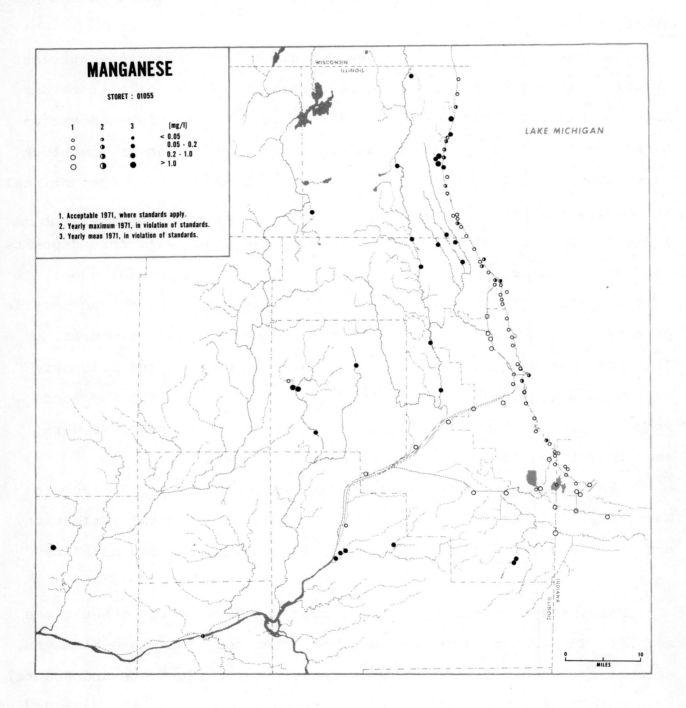

MANGANESE

STORET : 01055

1	2	3	(mg/l)
			< 0.05
			0.05 - 0.2
			0.2 - 1.0
			> 1.0

1. Acceptable 1971, where standards apply.
2. Yearly maximum 1971, in violation of standards.
3. Yearly mean 1971, in violation of standards.

LAKE MICHIGAN

WISCONSIN
ILLINOIS

INDIANA
ILLINOIS

0   1   10
MILES

Figure 3.51

Mercury

Mercury is rarely found in appreciable amounts in natural waters; natural levels have usually been found to be far less than 5 mg/l. In nature mercury is usually found in the form of cinnabar (HgS), but the main source of abnormally high concentrations of mercury is usually the highly toxic methyl mercury ($Hg(CH_3)_2$). Mercury contamination is the result of mining waste, metallurgical or other industrial waste, and runoff containing mercurial pesticides.

Mercury compounds, especially the organic forms, are virulent cumulative poisons which are readily absorbed through the respiratory and gastrointestinal tracts or through unbroken skin. The accumulation and retention of these mercurials in the nervous system, the ease with which they are transmitted across the placenta and their adverse effects on developing tissue, make them extremely dangerous to man, animals and aquatic life. They are particularly dangerous to man and other organisms high on the food chain since mercury compounds are retained and concentrated in the flesh of life forms lower on the food chain. Fish from polluted streams and lakes have thus been found to contain amounts of mercury well above the safe limits of food consumption.

A maximum allowable concentration of 0.5 mg/l is specified by the Illinois Standards for waters designated as General or Secondary Contact and Indigenous Aquatic Life. This standard was incorporated into the range of levels on the parameter map (Figure 3.52).

Federal proposed criteria include a maximum mean of 0.05 mg/l and 0.2 mg/l at any time for Freshwater Aquatic Life, 1.0 mg/l for Agricultural, Livestock and 2.0 mg/l for Public Water Supply Intake, all of which were incorporated into the parameter map.

It is surprising that mercury was not better monitored particularly along Lake Michigan; the majority of the few stations monitored (about half of which were located in the heavily industrialized Calumet area) reported yearly maximums which were in violation of the state standards, and most of these also had yearly means which were in violation. Only a handful of stations had yearly means which did not exceed the Federal reference level for aquatic life.

The worst water was reported at the mouth of the Calumet River, the canals inland from Indiana Harbor and the Calumet River System, including the Cal-Sag Channel. Several yearly means reached 0.001 to 0.002 mg/l, two to four times the permissible limit.

In light of the highly toxic nature of mercury compounds, their ability to store in the flesh of food organisms and the degree to which water samples have been found to be in consistent violation of state standards, this parameter deserves far wider monitoring than is presently employed.

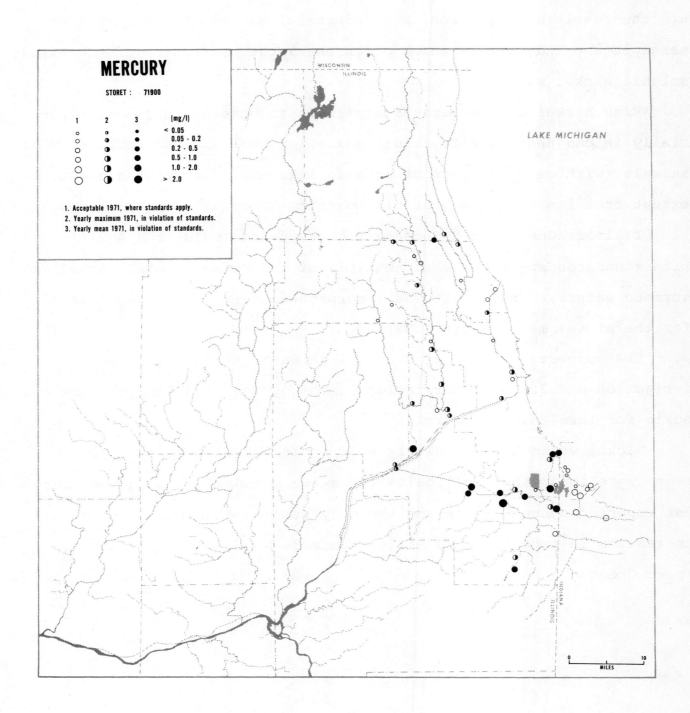

Figure 3.52

Nickel

Elemental nickel is rare in natural waters, though enough nickel may be introduced from compounds in certain ores and minerals to occasionally reach hazardous levels. Most high concentrations of nickel are the result of pollution from industrial wastes, especially from metalplating industries, which often use large quantities of the highly soluble nickel salts.

High nickel concentrations are toxic to numerous species, especially in conjunction with acidic soils. Nickel is less toxic to most animals, with certain types of aquatic life suffering to the greatest extent from its acute and chronic toxicity effects.

Illinois General and Secondary Contact and Indigenous Aquatic Life standards specify a maximum limit of 1.0 mg/l of total nickel in surface waters. This limit was incorporated into the range of levels for the nickel map (Figure 3.53).

EPA suggests a limit of 0.2 mg/l in water used for continuous irrigation and 2.0 mg/l for irrigation of neutral and fine texture soils for less than 20 years.

Nickel was not particularly well monitored and reported yearly means were invariably well below the state standards. Both the highest reported concentration and the only station ever reporting a concentration in excess of the state standards were in the vicinity of Thorn Creek.

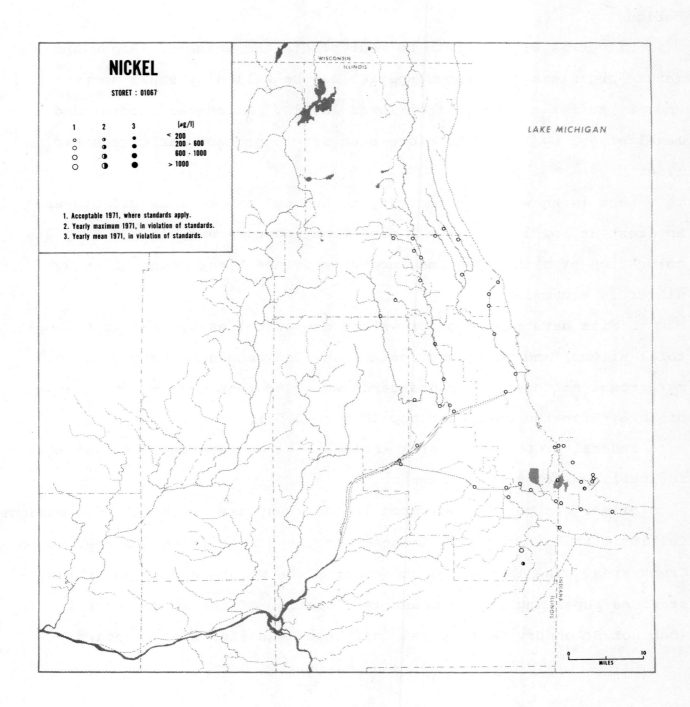

Figure 3.53

Silver

In natural waters silver is present only at very low concentrations. The presence of high concentrations is a likely indicator of industrial pollution since silver has a wide range of industrial applications.

Silver is highly toxic to most plants and animals. Algae and marine organisms of various species can be killed by small amounts and may suffer mutagenic from lower levels. A federal recommended level of 0.5 mg/l has therefore been set to protect marine aquatic life.

Less is known about toxicity to humans. No serious effects are apparent at low levels, but a condition known as argyria - a gray discoloration of skin, eyes and mucous membranes - may occur if enough silver is accumulated.

Limits have been set for waters designated as general (0.005 mg/l total silver) and Secondary Contact and Indigenous Aquatic Life (0.1 mg/l total silver). Both standards were incorporated into the range of levels for the parameter map (Figure 3.54).

Federal proposed criteria include a suggested limit of 0.05 mg/l for public water supply intakes.

Silver was poorly monitored in the study area with all the readings falling either in the Des Plaines-Salt Creek area or the Calumet-Thorn Creek area. The latter region reported the worst readings with most stations reporting yearly means in violation of the state General (but not Secondary Contact and Indigenous Aquatic Life) standard.

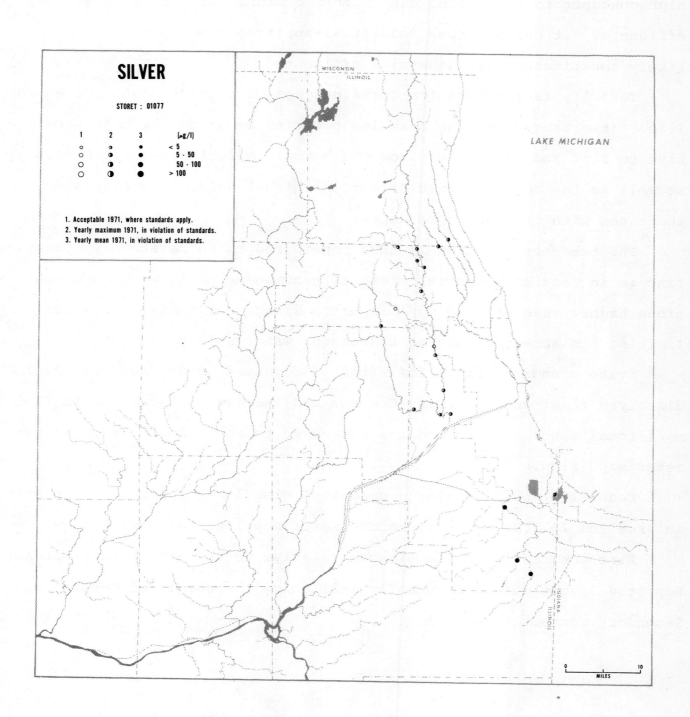

Figure 3.54

Zinc

Because its free metal oxide forms are only slightly soluble, zinc is a minor constituent of most natural waters. Somewhat higher levels may be found in excessively acidic waters, but the presence of high concentrations of zinc can be more commonly traced to industrial effluents. It has numerous industrial applications and is thus a likely constitutent of industrial effluents.

Toxicity is greatest for certain types of aquatic plant and animal life. Invertebrate marine animals appear to be among the most sensitive to zinc and may suffer from the chronic effects of lower levels as well as the acutely toxic effects of high levels. Toxicity also increases with increasing hardness.

The tendency for zinc is thus considered to be relatively nontoxic. Zinc is in fact an essential element in human metabolism. Concentrations higher than about 5 mg/l impart a disagreeable taste to water, limiting its acceptability as a drinking water supply.

State standards exist for waters designated as General (1.0 mg/l dissolved zinc) and Secondary Contact and Indigenous Aquatic Life (1.0 mg/l total zinc). The standards were used to set a level in the parameter map (Figure 3.55).

Federal proposed criteria suggest 5.0 mg/l for public water supply intakes and 25.0 mg/l for livestock water supplies.

Zinc was fairly well monitored relative to the other trace metals. Reported levels were consistently well below the specified General and Secondary Contact Standards.

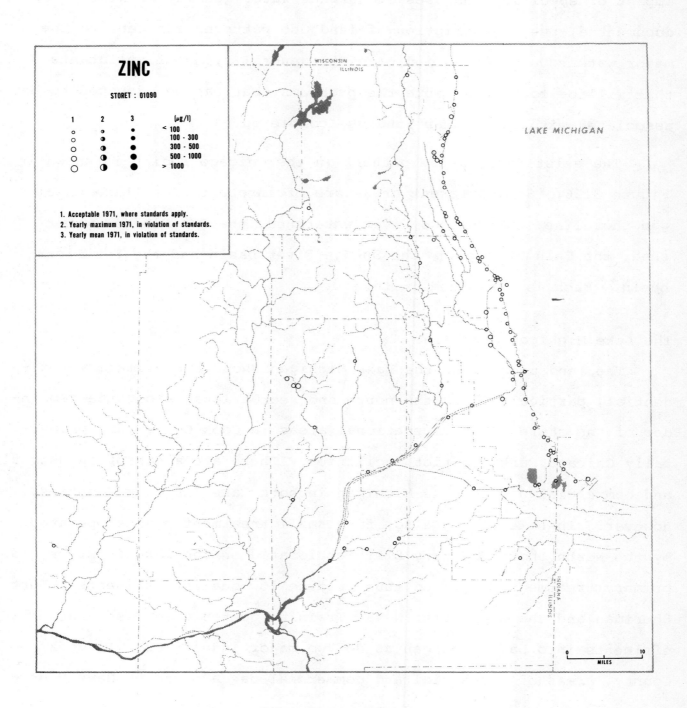

Figure 3.55

Relationships Between Surface
Water Quality and Land Use

There are a number of surface water quality problems that an analysis of existing land use patterns can help explain. The full impact of specific land uses on surface water quality remains to be documented, but a description of land use patterns adjacent to the major water courses does indicate the general types of pollutants that will be found, and thus the problems that can be expected to be associated with particular land use complexes.

The existing land use pattern in the Chicago region is shown in Figure 3.56. Six different areas are of interest: the Lake Michigan shoreline, the Chicago River watershed, the Des Plaines watershed, the Calumet region, the DuPage River basin and the Fox River basin. Each is discussed in turn.

The Lake Michigan Shoreline

The land uses along the Lake Michigan shore are primarily residential, particularly in the north and recreational along the remainder of the shore. The recreational areas in Cook County are principally Chicago Park District facilities. There are areas of industrial and commercial use on Lake Michigan in both Lake and Cook Counties, however. In Lake County also, five small treatment plants operated by the North Shore Sanitary District located on the lake front provide primary treatment only, and thus produce low quality effluents. Fort Sheridan and the Great Lake Naval Training Center also discharge effluents into Lake Michigan as do two major industries. In Cook County, areas of industrial and commercial use are in the Navy Pier area and in the U.S. Steel South Works areas.

The municipal systems currently in operation serving the residential areas of Waukegan, North Chicago and Highland Park are unable to accommodate growth or to serve the extensive area that has septic tank

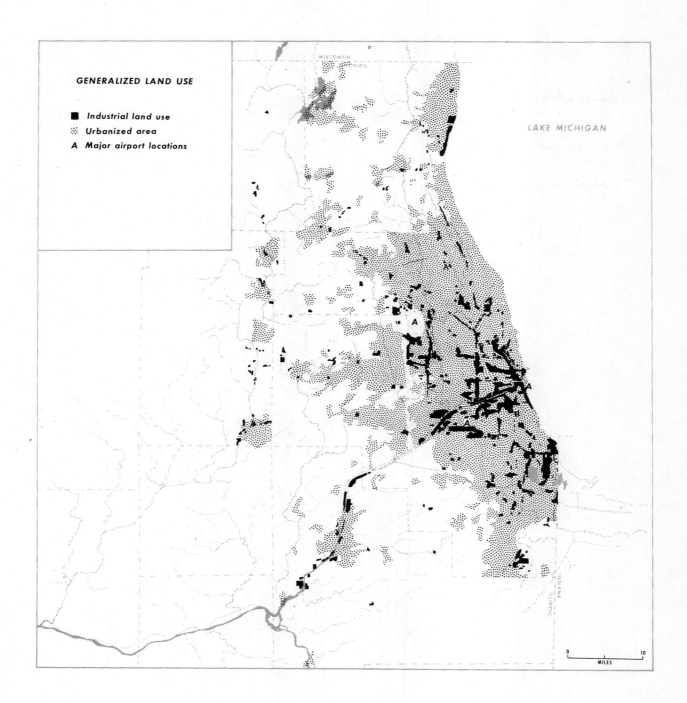

GENERALIZED LAND USE

■ Industrial land use
Urbanized area
A Major airport locations

WISCONSIN
ILLINOIS

LAKE MICHIGAN

INDIANA
ILLINOIS

0   10
MILES

Figure 3.56

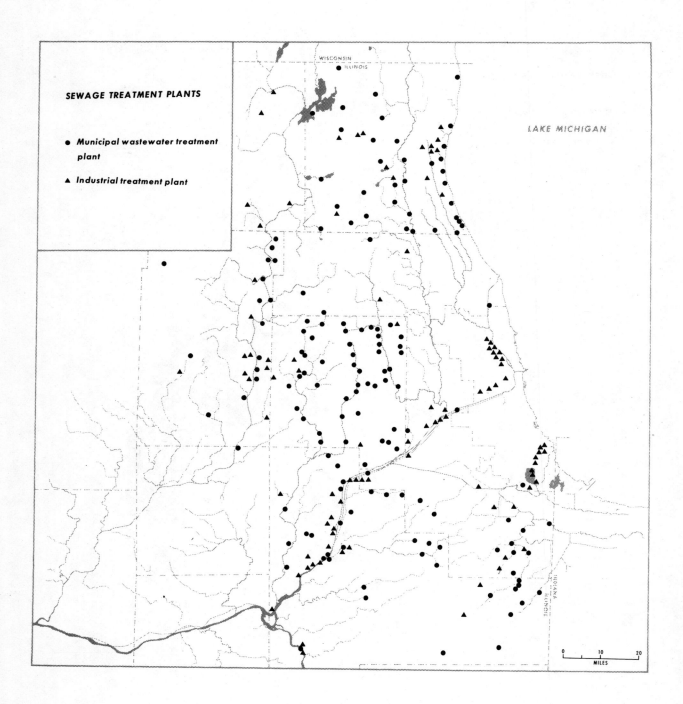

SEWAGE TREATMENT PLANTS

● Municipal wastewater treatment plant

▲ Industrial treatment plant

LAKE MICHIGAN

Figure 3.57

systems which are proving unsatisfactory. In times of wet weather, excessive infiltration in municipal systems introduces flows which exceed plant capacities and thus requires by-passing and the discharge of partially or untreated sewage into Lake Michigan.

In Cook County, as in Lake County, the principal pollution problem for Lake Michigan is the adverse effect of overflows from combined sewers during periods of heavy rains. Under normal operating conditions, no effluents are discharged into Lake Michigan in Cook County. However, during periods of heavy rainfall, treated and untreated waste flow from combined sewers and the water from the Chicago River, North Shore Channel and the Calumet River is allowed to flow into the Lake, contributing to the degradation of the Lake water.

The Chicago River System

The northern reaches of the Chicago River watershed including the East and West fork of the North Branch of the Chicago River and the Skokie River, are primarily areas of residential and recreational land use. There is interspersed industrial and commercial activity along the northern reaches. The same general land use patterns continue along the North Shore Channel and along the North Branch of the Chicago River, but with industrial and commercial concentrations increasing and becoming the predominant land uses as the waterway flows into the Loop area.

The central reaches of the Chicago River, including the Loop, are fronted by industrial and commercial land uses. The section of the Sanitary and Ship Canal from Western to McCook continues this pattern of industrial and commercial use.

The canal systems in Cook County, including the North Shore Channel, the Sanitary and Ship Canal and the Cal-Sag Channel, provide navigational facilities for boats and barges as well as serving as receiving waters for converging the flows from tributary streams and

and sewage treatment plant effluents and storm water runoff from the
Lake Michigan watershed to the Des Plaines watershed.

The influence of periods of high rainfall in 1971, the low permeability in the Loop, and the resultant overflow from the combined
sewer outfalls produced high volumes of untreated or partially treated
effluent which were discharged into the local waterways.

The Des Plaines River Valley

The land adjacent to the northern reaches of the Des Plaines in
Lake County is in a combination of agricultural/vacant and residential use. Urban development is limited, and a number of small and
inefficient wastewater treatment plants have been constructed. Because of poor soil conditions, high water tables and dense concentrations of homes on small lots around attractive lakes, the area is
prone to have water pollution problems. The drainage pattern of a
large number of lakes connected by sluggish or intermittent streams
has caused the effluents of one community to be the sequential problems of other downstream towns and cities.

Downstream, the land use abutting the river changes, with large
areas of recreational land that are part of the Cook County Forest
Preserve System. At O'Hare International Airport, there is a large
industrial complex which continues south stretching between the Des
Plaines River and Salt Creek to the west. In the Oak Park and the
Maywood reaches, the adjacent land is used for residential purposes.
There are a number of industries discharging effluents directly into
the waterways or into municipal-type sewers, with or without pre-
treatment. Several of these either involve very large quantites of
water, or solid (suspended) waste generated by sophisticated manufacturing processes.

The land use patterns along Salt Creek are a combination of
recreation and residential with industrial and commercial activities
interspersed between those dominant uses. South of the confluence

with the Des Plaines River at Lyons, there is a concentrated area of industrial and mining activities.

In the central portion of Salt Creek in Du Page County, outside of the Metropolitan Sanitary District jurisdiction, there is a high density of septic systems, and a large number of small, independent wastewater facilities whose capacities, because of the rapid growth in population, are now being exceeded. Inadequately treated effluent discharges are thereby affecting the quality of the water.

Continuing down the Des Plaines River as it flows in a southeasterly direction paralleling the Ship and Sanitary Canal from McCook to Lockport, the land uses are industrial, commercial and recreational with the remaining land in agricultural or vacant uses.

One consequence of the massive outward movement and rapid increase in employment and population in the suburban communities has been the overloading of the existing municipal treatment facilities, the capacities of many now being exceeded. The Joliet area is an example. In the Greater Joliet area there are a large number of small, independent, undersized plants which discharge low quality effluents. The larger plants in that area provide primary treatment only, with the Joliet and Lockport plants now being upgraded to provide secondary treatment. In the Fairmont area, between Lockport and Joliet, municipal type wastewater services and even septic installations are lacking. There are several sizable industries which discharge large quantities of wastewater directly into the receiving waterways. Agricultural and animal wastes also are considered to be a pollution problem in the area.

The Des Plaines River below Joliet has primarily agricultural/ vacant and recreational land uses.

The Calumet Region

Within the Calumet Region, the Cal-Sag Channel is primarily vacant with some industrial/commercial uses near its junction with the

Little Calumet River. Near its junction with the Sanitary and Ship Canal, the channel is surrounded by Cook County Forest Preserves. The Little Calumet River has residential, recreational and agricultural land uses on its shores. On the other hand, the banks of the Calumet River are highly developed, with a mix of industrial, commercial, residential and recreational land uses.

The Grand Calumet River and the Indiana Harbor Canal drainage system constitute a large source of pollutants to the lake. These streams, which have a combined length of approximately 13 miles, drain an area which contains a population approaching one half million and one of the most concentrated steel and petroleum manufacturing complexes in the nation. In excess of 90 percent of the water flowing in these stream enters via sewers as treated waste water, cooling water or as storm water overflow (Indiana Stream Pollution Control Board 1973). There are currently seven major industries discharging into the Grand Calumet and Indiana Harbor Canal and several other industries with minor discharges. These are mainly steel mills, oil refineries, a chemical company and municipal sewage treatment plants. All the major discharges currently provide some treatment of their waste water, but in some cases current treatment is inadequate.

The major population centers in the Calumet Area are the South Side of Chicago in Illinois and Whiting, Hammond and Gary in Indiana. These are centers of heavy industry, with ten major steel mills and four petroleum refineries and other major industries including Union Carbide Chemicals and E.I. Dupont. These industries are located in four major groups, along the Calumet River in Illinois, along the Indiana Harbor Canal, in Gary and in the Burns Harbor basin.

There are some outfalls along the lake shore, primarily from American Oil Co. in the Whiting area and from U.S. Steel Co. at Gary. There are also a number of combined storm sewage overflow outfalls both along the lake and on tributary streams and a high density of septic systems in areas outside of the Metropolitan Sanitary District.

Thorn Creek flows through a complex of residential areas, including South Holland, Homewood, Glenwood and Chicago Heights. There are also extensive reaches of public open space and agricultural land, as well as some industrial and commercial activities primarily at Chicago Heights. The Bloom Township Sanitary District has a treatment plant which discharges into Thorn Creek. The surrounding area also contains a high density of septic systems.

The Du Page River Basin

The two primary land uses along the Du Page River are residential and agricultural/vacant. The residential areas on the West Branch of the Du Page River include West Chicago and Naperville and on the East Branch, Glen Ellyn and Lombard and south of the confluence, the primary residential area is Plainfield. There are scattered industrial and mining activities along both branches and along the main stream.

The recent rapid growth in both Du Page and Will Counties has caused a proliferation of a large number of small independent wastewater facilities, the capacities of many new ones being exceeded. Most of the existing plants along the Du Page River need upgrading to meet the new effluent standards. A total of 34 existing treatment plants along the Du Page River need either to be replaced or expanded. Another problem is the existence of unsatisfactory septic tank systems which pose local health threats and contribute to the pollution of the waterways.

The Fox River Basin

The land uses adjacent to the northern reaches of the Fox River in McHenry County are primarily residential and agricultural. Further south in Kane County, along with extensive residential land use, there are industrial and commercial activities stretching between the industrial clusters at Elgin and Aurora. Animal waste from feedlots and concentrated poultry operations and scattered mining activities all contribute to water quality degradation.

The residential communities along the Fox River include McHenry, Algonquin, St. Charles, Geneva, Batavia and the residential satellites of Elgin and Aurora, all of which have expanded rapidly. The existing water treatment facilities need upgrading to meet effluent standards. A number of plants now receive excess flows in times of heavy rainfall. Another factor causing pollution problems along the Fox River stems from unsatisfactory septic tank systems.

The Water Quality Relationships

What then, are the major associations between surface water quality and land use? First, our analysis shows that the region's waterways are extensively "polluted," as defined by state and federal reference levels, for a number of parameters. All reaches which monitored fecal coliforms were consistently in excess of both the state reference level and the federal reference level for Primary Contact and Indigenous Aquatic Life and the federal reference level for Agricultural Irrigation and Livestock. Total coliform findings reflected this pattern of widespread pollution; all reaches consistently exceeded federal reference levels for Public and Livestock Water Supply. Ammonia levels in all reaches consistently exceeded the federal reference level for Freshwater Aquatic Life, while all reaches had scattered stations exceeding the federal reference for Public Water supply.

For total dissolved solids, all waterways except the Fox River and Lake Michigan appeared to consistently exceed the Illinois Public and Food Processing Water Supply reference level, with the East and West Branches of the Du Page River, Thorn Creek and Pettibone Creek exceeding the Illinois General standard reference level as well.

Phosphorus levels in Lake Michigan frequently exceeded the Lake Michigan standard, while all remaining waterways consistently exceeded the nutrient standard reference level.

Three parameters, dissolved oxygen, MBAS and phenols, were apparently present in high levels in the study area, but not as extensively throughout the study area as the above mentioned parameters. Dissolved oxygen levels were lower than the General standard and Freshwater Aquatic Life reference levels in most areas besides the Fox River and Lake Michigan.

Scattered areas, especially the middle and lower Fox River, the West Branches of the Du Page River and the Thorn Creek area displayed MBAS levels which were excessively high with respect to state and federal Public Water Supply reference levels. Phenol levels exceed Public Water Supply reference levels in all reaches except for the lower Du Page River and Lake Michigan outside of the Calumet and Pettibone Creek areas.

A large number of the trace elements were present in dangerously high levels in those areas which monitored them, but they were seldom monitored along the Du Page River, the Fox River, or even Lake Michigan, except in the highly industrialized areas around Pettibone Creek and in the Calumet region. Arsenic, cyanide, mercury and lead - all extremely toxic - were reported in levels which consistently exceeded reference levels for Freshwater Aquatic Life (mercury and lead), Public Water Supply (arsenic, cyanide and lead) and General use (arsenic, cyanide and lead), in the areas where they were monitored, usually focusing on the Calumet area. Most of these constituents were also frequently present in levels which exceeded Secondary Contact and Indigenous Aquatic Life Standards as well. Manganese, while not as toxic as the above, also exceeded reference levels for Public Water Supply, as did oil and grease, which was monitored only in the Calumet region.

A last group of parameters was found to exceed reference levels in more localized areas. They were chloride, copper, fluoride, iron, silver, sulfate, suspended solids, and turbidity.

Certain areas reported high levels of a variety of parameters much more frequently than the general rule. This overall "frequency of pollution" pattern is typified in the maps of dissolved oxygen and total dissolved solids (Figures 3.32 and 3.33). In these maps, the East and West Branches of the Du Page River and the Thorn Creek area stand out as the areas consistently displaying the highest levels of pollution in the Chicago study area. The Pettibone Creek area and the Calumet region display low quality water somewhat less frequently, followed by the lower Chicago River and the lower Des Plaines River and Chicago Sanitary and Ship Canal. The Lake Michigan shoreline stands out as having the best water with a noticeable decrease in water quality in the vicinity of the mouths of rivers and streams. The Fox River contains higher levels of surface water constituents than Lake Michigan, but was still found to be significantly better for most parameters than the remainder of the hydrologic network.

Surface water quality is the product of a great number of factors. Stream size, flow, assimilative capacity and other hydrologic characteristics, physical geography and geology of the area, the concentrations of groundwater constituents, climatology, especially yearly rainfall and storm patterns, runoff characteristics of the area, land use, features of industrial and municipal effluent discharges, density of septics systems, combined sewer overflows and regional and local enforcement policy are some of the many important factors which interact to form the reality of surface water quality.

Several aspects of the patterns of levels of surface water constituents are explained by rather obvious features of the area's hydrology. That levels of all constituents were lowest in Lake Michigan should come as no surprise owing to the enormous assimilative capacity of this body of water. The input of diversion water from the lake is also frequently apparent at the mouths of streams. Concentrations typically gradually decreased for a distance downstream due to this influx. On the other hand, during times of intense storms (several times a year) runoff and storm overflow necessitate the opening of locks into Lake Michigan from these streams. Thus there is a noticeable decrease in the quality of Lake Michigan in the vicinity of the entering streams.

The earlier discussion of groundwater detailed patterns of the concentrations of various groundwater constituents. Figures 3.13, 3.15, 3.17, 3.18 and 3.19 all show that the highest levels of hardness, iron, manganese, sulfate and total dissolved minerals in groundwater overlapped with the two stretches of surface water which usually showed the highest levels of those constituents: The East and West Branches of the Du Page River and Thorn Creek. Thus the observed surface water quality in those areas may partially be the result of high natural levels.

But much of the pollution is man-made, and insights into its origins can be obtained from a study of land use. From the previous section on land use, we find that the two areas abutting streams of lowest overall quality, Thorn Creek and the upper Du Page River, are occupied by extensive residential and agricultural areas, but are also areas of rapid industrial expansion as well as scattered mining activities.

The large industrial complex in the Calumet area, with its numerous steel mills and oil refineries, contains the heaviest industry in the Chicago study area, dramatically reflected by the pattern of trace metal constituents and oil and grease pollution. The influence of industrialization on water quality is also suggested by the high levels of many constituents along the lower Des Plaines River and Chicago Sanitary and Ship Canal, the Chicago River as far north as

the North Branch and the North Shore Channel and especially the northern region of Lake Michigan in the vicinity of Waukegan and Pettibone
Creek. The proximity of Great Lakes Naval Base to Pettibone Creek
suggests the possible impact of that institution upon the extremely
low water quality evidenced in that area.

Overall, the land use map shows a general association between
urban development and low quality water. Not surprisingly, the quality of surface water improves and the extent and frequency of station
monitoring decreases the further one moves from developed areas, as
is most clearly evidenced along the Fox and Des Plaines Rivers and the
Lake Michigan Shoreline. The worst areas outside the city limits,
tend to be centers of rapid urban growth and expansion. The Pettibone
Creek area, the Thorn Creek area and the Upper Du Page River area, all
quickly come to mind.

The extensive and significant organic pollution indicated by parameters measuring fecal and total coliforms and ammonia are most likely
the result of an inability to accommodate the domestic waste load of
the area's population. As was mentioned earlier, many of the developed
areas outside the central city - and particularly the new and expanding
ones - have inadequate treatment facilities. Figure 3.6 shows the
density of the area's septic systems, thought to be a major source of
pollution in the outlying areas. Once again, the problem areas are
Thorn Creek and the upper Du Page, as well as the Waukegan area and
substantial portions of Salt Creek. The Des Plaines River and the
Fox River also stand out as areas of pollution from this source.

The MSDGC has problems of its own as well, primarily due to periodic release of combined sewer effluent at various points along the
river systems due to stormwater overflow. Figure 3.58 shows the location and size of the storm overflow outfalls in the MSDGC. The problem
is compounded by the size of the area serviced by combined sewers and
the high degree of surface imperviousness in the area, particularly

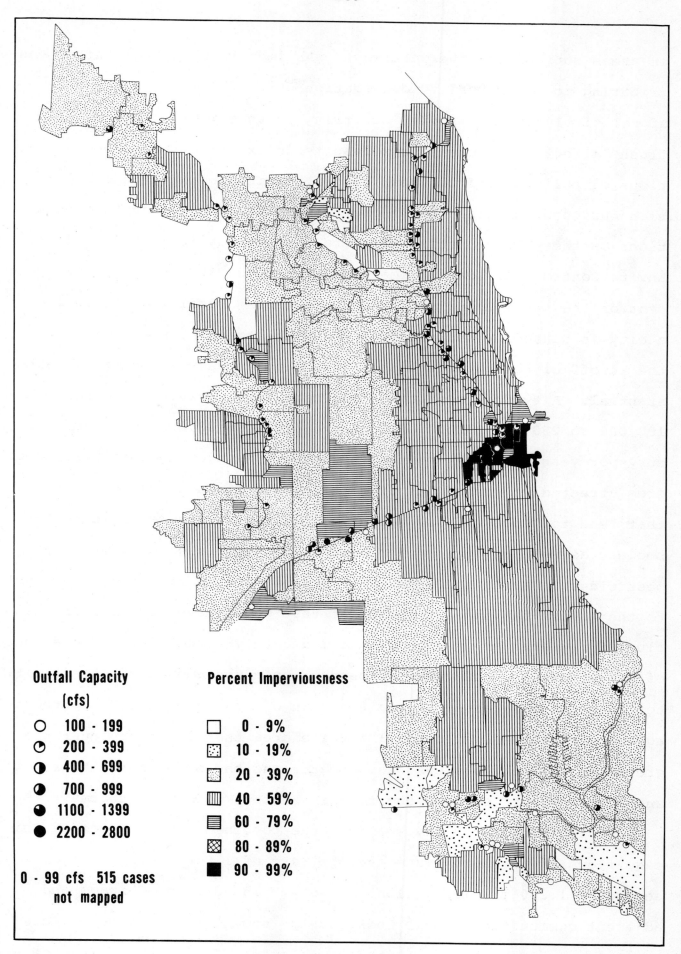

Outfall Capacity
(cfs)

○ 100 - 199
◔ 200 - 399
◑ 400 - 699
◕ 700 - 999
⬤ 1100 - 1399
● 2200 - 2800

0 - 99 cfs 515 cases
not mapped

Percent Imperviousness

☐ 0 - 9%
▒ 10 - 19%
░ 20 - 39%
▥ 40 - 59%
▤ 60 - 79%
▩ 80 - 89%
■ 90 - 99%

Figure 3.58

in areas surrounding the waterways. An important related factor contributing to water quality degradation during 1971 was the frequency of relatively intense storms occurring in that year. The "first flush" effect of severe storms results in extremely high concentrations of pollutants from urban runoff combined with the added pollution burden of combined sewer overflow and thus has major ramifications on the yearly picture of overall water quality. Nationally, Enviro Control Inc. has estimated that between 40 percent and 80 percent of the total annual BOD and COD entering receiving waters from a city is caused by sources other than treatment plants, and that the runoff of toxic pollutants, particularly heavy elements, is substantial. A typical moderate-sized city, they said, will discharge 100,000 to 250,000 pounds of lead and 6,000 to 30,000 pounds of mercury per year, to cite but two instances. Much of the material comes from street dirt washed off by rainfall and it includes substances that tend to depress dissolved oxygen levels in the receiving water bodies, as well as toxic materials, algal nutrients, coliforms and pesticides. During the first hour following a storm, the waste input to the waters far exceeds the input that would have occurred from influx of raw sanitary sewage from a moderately-sized city. The amount of street wastes received is dependent upon the amount of street litter that accumulates--itself a function of land use--and the percentage of the storm sewer outfall service area that is impervious; the greater the imperviousness, the greater and the more rapid the runoff, and thus the more serious the flushing effect of severe storms.

During periods of dry weather, the combined sewer system of Chicago flows at an approximate average rate of 1,850 cubic feet per second or 1,200 million gallons per day. The City of Chicago and adjacent communities within Cook County (some 375 square miles) are entirely served by this combined sewer system. However, even moderate rainfalls create difficulties for the existing system: first , the treatment plants are designed to handle only <u>one and a half</u> times the flow that moves through the sewers under dry weather conditions, second, the interceptors that link the sewers to the treatment plants can carry <u>twice</u> the volume of flow that the plants are prepared to treat; but third, the recorded volume of runoff from rainstorms has been <u>thirty</u> times as great as the capacity of the interceptors.

Because of the area's growth and the increase in the captured rainwater volume, the impact of intense storms thus overburdens the sewer system and treatment plants. On an average of 100 times a year, the combined sanitary and stormwater flow overloads the pipes and surges into the waterway system at over 640 discharge points (Figure 3.58). Over the past 30 years, there have been 21 occasions where storm loads have been so great that the gates of the Chicago and Calumet Rivers have had to be opened, releasing polluted storm waters into Lake Michigan whose quality is preserved most of the time at the expense of surface water quality elsewhere in the metropolitan region.

✳ *Chapter 4*

Surface Water Quality in Twelve
Metropolitan Regions

The Chicago case study reported in the previous chapter was designed to enable the research group to develop a methodology for systematic analysis of water quality in the twelve metropolitan regions
that had been selected for comparative study, to provide focus and to
raise questions.

Several lessons were learned from the investigations in Chicago.
For example, as important a question as the quality of ground and
drinking waters may be, data sources are so fragmentary and inconsis-
tent that a major nationwide effort of data system development at
least of the magnitude of STORET will have to be undertaken before
sound comparative studies can be initiated. Further, as profound a
constraint as both captured and uncaptured urban stormwater runoff
may be to the achievement of national water quality goals, so little
is known about this topic and its relationships to the organization
and efficiency of municipal housekeeping services and the collection
and disposal of solid wastes that this issue, too, should be a matter
of separate data system development before high quality comparative
studies can be undertaken.

We decided therefore, to restrict our comparative analysis to the question of surface water quality, relying upon STORET as a data source, and it is that comparative analysis that is reported in this chapter. We begin by discussing our methodology, following that with a region-by-region presentation and brief interpretation of the water quality and related maps that were prepared -- 168 in all -- and we conclude with comparative interpretations regarding variations in water quality from one region to another. As in the previous chapters, this one also has an atlas-like quality, but this is said without apology, and the same quality will appear in the three chapters that follow. Many of the maps speak for themselves, and it is critical that the basic evidence now available be presented with care by someone.

Methodology

Data Acquisition

The first step that was taken was to define a data retrieval polygon encompassing each of the twelve Standard Metropolitan Statistical Areas (SMSA's) that had been selected for comparative study. The coordinates for each polygon were determined by commuter patterns, drainage basin size and physical characteristics of the region. Polygon configurations for several cities were extended in a downstream direction to maximize the number of stations which sampled regularly and to show the extent to which urban pollution effects downstream water quality.

For each polygon for the calendar year 1971, we requested a PGM-INVENT from EPA's STORET system. The INVENT program provides a computerized listing of data available for all stations within the polygon. Data for each station included a yearly mean, maximum, minimum and time range for every parameter monitored by the station. To supplement this PGM-INVENT data, we requested a PGM-RET for selected parameters from each station in the polygon. This program furnishes raw data which one can use to correct poor readings which would impro-

perly weight the mean. Improbable or impossible readings can be recognized in the maximum or minimum levels recorded on the RI-120 (PGM-
INVENT).

Construction of Base Maps of the Hydrologic Network

AS PGM-INVENT data were received from STORET, we began to construct
maps of the hydrologic networks for the twelve sample cities. All
locatable stations were plotted by latitude/longitude coordinates on
base maps constructed from the USGS and USC & GS (U.S. Coast and Geo-
detic Survey) 1:250,000 series maps with temporary grids superimposed.
Each point was labeled with its own STORET station number. We excluded
from our base maps water quality data for wells and effluent discharge
pipes. Only surface water quality stations located on rivers, in
marine waters or on lakes and reservoirs were used. River mile index
was used to locate those stations not listed by geographical coordinates.

Quality of Data -- Station Coverage

Apparently, our data requests revealed several limitations inherent in the STORET system. These only became apparent as we constructed
our base maps. First, STORET does not include municipal data for many
cities. This may be due to financial inability to transcribe or com-
puterize the information, or it may be the result of reluctance on the
part of municipal or private concerns to submit the data to local or
state agencies. It may also be simply a function of poor urban coverage for some cities, due to limited deployment of monitoring stations
and poor location of those stations. In Washington, D.C., for example,
a substantial number of the water quality stations were located on minor tributaries whose total contribution to the volume of the main
stream was miniscule. Among the other problems were these:

1. Only three of the forty San Diego stations
were actually located on surface streams.
Most of the remainder were well stations.
This necessitated an additional data request
from the California Water Resources Control
Board which stores all water quality data
for that state.

2. Most stations within the Baltimore polygon were located on minor tributaries or on estuaries outside of the urban limits. We were informed that the Maryland State Department of Natural Resources ceased its urban water quality monitoring activities in February, 1971 in order to prepare a comprehensive basin study required by EPA for the Baltimore area. Further data was requested and received from the Maryland Department of Natural Resources which also provided supplementary data for the Washington, D.C. study area.

3. Oklahoma City stations were scattered throughout its large SMSA but not near the city. Nearly all stations were located on reservoirs far upstream or downstream from the urbanized portion of the SMSA.

4. Only thirteen stations located by geographical coordinates appeared in our initial data request for Birmingham. Subsequent retrievals from STORET provided many additional stations. Many time-consuming retrievals using several different formats were required to produce this data. In each case, station data was retrieved by a computer program which was supposed to have produced data in a different format. No Birmingham city data appeared until we obtained an effluent discharge study prepared by EPA.

5. Network coverage within or near St. Louis, Birmingham, Rochester and Jacksonville appeared limited and may indicate failure of municipal agencies to furnish water quality data to the STORET system and/or inadequate water quality surveillance.

Whatever the reason, there was one serious implication: absence of adequate central city data made it impossible to assess the social burdens of water pollution within these areas, as requested by EPA.

Quality of Data -- Parameter Coverage

The quality of data also varies both from one parameter to another, and in the frequency of sampling of any given parameter from one monitoring station to another. The most commonly monitored and most frequently sampled water quality measures were those which were simplest to perform and least costly to process. The presence of trace metals was seldom explored. The more universally-monitored parameters were often those which were dependent variables, of limited value when used as specific indicators of water pollution.

The most striking observation one can make from analysis of the water quality data is the degree of contrast in sampling frequency. An individual parameter might be monitored as often as several hundred times a year by a small number of stations but as infrequently as once a year by all others that sample it. Of the twelve cities, Denver is the extreme case in point. Dissolved oxygen in the Denver SMSA was sampled one hundred to three hundred times within the calendar year by a very small number of stations, yet less than four times a year by the majority of stations which monitored it. The time range of DO readings was often restricted to no more than one quarter of the year. This poor distribution of water quality sampling, both areally and temporally, makes comparative urban analysis difficult and intra-urban analysis awkward at best. Water quality sampling programs clearly reflect the specific needs of the individual agencies doing the monitoring.

During the mapping process, we decided that some indication of the quality of the data should be made on each parameter map to facilitate analysis of that map. Identification of those stations with poorest quality data was made by employing a "cutoff" value. All readings above the minimum number and time range were indicated by a full dot while all values below it were shown by a circle.

The cutoff value selected was four readings over at least two quarters of the year. This helped identify stations where many readings were taken within a short time span, often several days or less. This limited sampling time range makes data for that parameter less reliable, since it is not as representative of the water body as readings more evenly distributed throughout the year.

Other Problems with STORET,
and Recommendations

A variety of other problems were encountered with STORET along the way, and deserve comment:

1. The PGM-INVENT data were requested for the year 1971. Retrieval printouts often included multiple-year . The INVENT for Seattle, Providence and Birmingham on the first pass drew summarized data for the entire recording history of each station. In some cases, the period of record was longer than ten years. A second pass through the computer was frequently required to obtain the 1971 data. This also occurred when proper beginning and end dates were specified.

2. In the PGM-INVENT for several cities, duplicate retrieval of stations was common within the same polygon. For example, several series of stations belonging to individual agencies would be printed repeatedly during computer scanning and selection, as often as three or four times in a program. Other stations would be retrieved only once.

3. In several INVENT requests, stations not within the retrieval polygon appeared in the computer printout. Incorrect input information listings was probably the reason.

4. There are standard errors found in each PGM-RET raw data retrieval. The printout sometimes contains readings with improper placement of the decimal point. One is forced to determine whether the extreme level recorded for a parameter is the result of an abnormal and perhaps significant event in the water body or the result of a data transfer and storage error.

These common errors are more than likely evidence of the "bugs" in the STORET process itself--how data are coded and ultimately stored on tape--rather than mistakes on the part of programmer since both the PGM-INVENT and PGM-RET are common retrieval packages.

Nonetheless, our dealings with EPA's STORET system during the course of this study prompt us to make several recommendations for its improvement. In past years, strong reliance has been placed on physical evidence of pollution when water quality studies have been used in planning assessments. The subjective nature of that approach restricted its usefulness to those variables which are sense-detectable, and thresholds of detection vary considerably. Many chemical, aesthetic and microbiological parameters could not be measured. Trace metals and harmful organic chemicals directly related to industrial effluents were also not detectable.

The need for a quantitative approach to water quality studies has become apparent from the number of indexes developed in recent years to deal with the problem. Cartographic expression of water quality data derived from scientific measurement of contaminants also is essential. In both cases, the data must be accessible and there must be enough of it to permit proper assessment of stream quality. The designed capabilities of the STORET system are sufficient to meet these needs. However, much data from the nation's cities are not yet in the system's data bank. Water quality data from special basin studies and commissions are also lacking. If municipal participation in STORET data collection efforts was mandatory, national policy studies affecting urban water resources programs would be greatly facilitated.

A second and perhaps more important adjustment that must be made in the STORET system is the need for immediate standardization. In its developmental stages, STORET contributors received a parameter code number after they described the lab method they used. Too often, code numbers were assigned without time to check for duplication. As a result, STORET parameter code books became cluttered with thousands of numbers, many of which referred to the same lab test. It was clearly a case of data collection outpacing methodological development, all brought about by the transfer of water quality monitoring responsibilities from the federal government to the states. Priority should be given to converting data into common terms, perhaps those in which proposed federal criteria are expressed. For each officially approved EPA laboratory method, a STORET number should be assigned on a nationwide basis. All agencies monitoring that parameter would be required to use the lab technique designated by the STORET code number. Previous data can be reassigned the proper code number.

At present, potential use of STORET far exceeds actual use. The cause of this situation is the complexity of the parameter code system and the difficulties associated with data retrievals. The cost of operating the STORET system can be reduced by standardization. All STORET users should be kept informed of programming changes and methodological development. Water quality data for the entire period of record of the surveillance networks should be kept readily available as the change in emphasis from qualitative to quantitative analysis takes place.

Selection of Parameters

The dilemma confronting us was how we might compare water quality for the twelve cities, maintain some measure of scientific accuracy and yet relate our comparisons to social, economic and other environmental variables, given data derived from STORET that were subject to all of the aforementioned difficulties. We needed some immediate indication of the degree of uniformity of expression of the data base. Could any of the measures of Chicago water quality be used for an evaluation of the hydrologic networks of the other twelve cities? If so, how many? Could they be compared in the same terms or if not, were the other terms equivalent or could they be made so?

The first step was to obtain a visual expression of data quality for the sample cities. Data summaries contained in the gross sheets accompanying the INVENT program output were presented in tabular form for visual examination. The gross sheets list the number of stations, total number of observations and samples for the polygon as well as the total number of readings taken for each parameter during the year. They revealed that each water residual may be measured by more than one sampling technique and analyzed by more than one laboratory method. It may be expressed in standardized units with temperature reference levels or it may be listed in terms of the actual field readings. The data may be recorded in metric units or may be expressed in Platinum-Cobalt units for color, JTUs for turbidity or Standard Units for pH. The degree of contrast becomes obvious when one scans a parameter across many cities. Several STORET numbers may be listed for a single parameter, an expression of multiple sampling techniques used to measure different chemical states of that parameter in the water, or of the various terms in which a single reading can be recorded, each term preferred by a different user of the water quality data.

Step two involved selecting the universally-monitored water quality measures. These were characterized by a single STORET code number for each measure, or occasionally two.

The third step consisted of selecting from the above list those parameters which we felt would allow our range of indicators to correspond to the seven map groupings used in the Chicago study, based as they were upon their affiliation in nature or their common causes, as discussed in the literature. More frequently sampled parameters were selected over those for which spatial and/or temporal coverage was more limited. Total and fecal coliform bacteria, ammonia and nitrate nitrogen, and phosphorus measures were quickly added because of their importance, even though they were recorded in a multiplicity of ways. However, attempts to establish a least common denominator STORET parameter number permitted us to combine several parameter numbers on a map by converting data into the same terms using a conversion factor. Where data were recorded in the same terms but lab methods differed slightly, we obtained the best available estimates of error or difference for use in interpretation.

The fourth step involved the addition of MBAS and several toxic metals to our list, although it was apparent that a comparative analysis would be limited to the few sample cities which adequately monitored those parameters.

The final step before initiating parameter mapping was to ascertain whether there were established or proposed federal criteria from which we could derive suitable ranges of values to place on the maps.

Table 4.1 indicates the list of parameters we selected for mapping as well as the levels used and the proposed federal criteria from which they were derived. (See p.230 ff.).

Some subjectivity was necessary to keep the scope of our mapping within the time constraints set for us. In addition to the other criteria for parameter selection (availability, comparability to Chicago groupings, etc.), our selections were based on what we judged to be the most significant indicators of water quality for metropolitan regions. Our final judgments were based on an extensive survey of the literature and on the advice of EPA chemists and biologists, as well as our past experience with certain variables, viz:

Oxygen Measuring Parameters. Dissolved Oxygen was chosen as one of the best and most often monitored indicators of water pollution. Low DO levels are usually indicative of pollution in the form of oxygen-demanding wastes. Although BOD is an excellent direct measure of oxygen-demanding wastes, it was not monitored as often as its adjudged importance in the literature would warrant. However, we did map it where possible. The lack of good COD coverage was surprising and resulted in the elimination of what we felt was an important indicator of urban water pollution. Both BOD and COD are monitored more frequently now than they were in 1971, however, and future studies may choose to use these variables, or perhaps Total Organic Carbon (TOC), which requires a relatively new and sophisticated laboratory analysis, and was seldom recorded in 1971.

Microbiological Parameters. Total coliform and fecal coliform bacteria have been traditional indicators of pollution by sewage and were mapped wherever possible. Neither parameter is monitored as often in surface waters as the U.S. Public Health Service recommends for water designated for public water supply uses. Coliform organisms are tested frequently at water intakes for public consumption. Other intensive sampling is limited to problem areas such as those near sewage treatment plant outfalls, livestock pens and agricultural and recreational areas. Coliforms are measured by a plethora of methods, few of which are comparable. The membrane filter method (MFM) is becoming the EPA standard method, although data for the twelve cities were evenly divided between it and the most probable number (MPN) technique. We were advised by the Method Development and Quality Control Section of EPA (Dr. Robert Bordner, personal communication) that there has been little quality control for microbiological parameters in the past. The two groupings of lab techniques, MFM and MPN are not considered comparable to one another. The reliability of values for STORET numbers for each method is said to vary considerably.

Acidity/Alkalinity Parameters. The utility of pH as an indicator of water quality is limited in that its most significant effects become evident at the extreme ranges. However, it is a good reference parameter for all ranges when one analyzes the behavior of the other variables and it was selected as the indicator of this group. Even slight variations in pH are the basis for many chemical and biological changes in surface waters. Total alkalinity was not considered for mapping because the higher ranges of pH already give an indication of it.

Solids Parameters. Total Dissolved Solids and Turbidity were selected from the solids category for mapping. Hardness is of course, an expression of the levels of several dissolved solids, but TDS is a more comprehensive indicator of water quality. The two laboratory techniques used for drying the filtered sample, at 105°C and 180°C, cause a variation of about twenty percent in a sample analyzed both ways. The weight difference that results is due to the greater loss of the waters by hydration and the precipitation of additional trace metals at the higher temperature. Conductivity was monitored frequently but its significance lies in its indication of or possible conversion to the total dissolved solids content of the water. However, in the twelve sample cities, the conversion factor varies from .45 to 1.15 in natural waters, making conductivity of limited value. On the St. Louis TDS map, the #47004 number (TDS from Electrical Conductivity) was used to supplement other TDS parameters. In that case, the appropriate conversion factor for the area had already been applied. Suspended Solids were felt to be more significant than turbidity but the latter was monitored much more frequently. Turbidity is an aesthetic parameter but it is also an indicator of the presence of the suspended solids fraction. It is influenced by the color and iron content of the water. Several methods of measuring turbidity are in use today. The predominant methods record data in terms of Jackson Turbidity Units (JTU), Formazin Turbidity Units (FTU) or Nephelometric Units. JTUs were used in our study. Transparency measured in inches using a secchi disc is a more recent and less error-prone method. It was used only in two of the twelve cities. The third method of expressing turbidity records data in terms of milligrams per liter of S_1O_2. The three basic methods cannot be converted into common terms.

Dissolved Elements, Ions and Compounds. All members of this grouping were considered for mapping. The group contains some of the major mineral and nutrient constituents found in polluted surface waters. Nearly all parameters are sampled nationwide.

Chlorides and sulfates are each recorded by single STORET parameter numbers. Levels of both vary geographically but often indicate industrial and municipal sewage pollution. High concentrations of these residuals, especially in winter months, might be the result of urban sheet runoff after deicing. Storm sewer outlets might provide other points of surface wash discharge of these ions into the stream. We felt that mapping chlorides and sulfates would allow us to estimate their economic impacts on the urban industrial users who must withdraw the water for cooling and processing.

A single map for each city indicating the total amount of nitrogen in its several forms could not be made. No reliable test for all nitrogen was available for nationwide mapping. We therefore selected ammonia nitrogen and nitrate since both appeared to be excellent urban pollution indicators. Nitrates and nitrites were tested in 1971 but the unwieldy array of STORET code numbers for each of them forced us to confine our mapping to nitrate alone. The City of Chicago and the Illinois State standards employ the combined test for nitrate and nitrite. Our sample cities tended to present data for each ion separately. Nitrite was not recorded as often as nitrate. Had it been, we would have been required to add it to nitrate for each reading in the raw data, an arduous task. Furthermore, the recorded data for nitrite are not representative of its true concentration in the water because most of the nitrite has been converted to nitrate by the time the sample reaches the lab. When a reading for total nitrate was unavailable, dissolved nitrate was used instead. In surface water, there is no appreciable difference between the two.

All nitrogen recorded as NO_3 was converted into terms of elemental nitrogen (N). The same was true for the component forms of phosphorus which were changed into the elemental form (P). Phosphorus was monitored in one or more of its several forms throughout our sample group. The lack of a single parameter number for phosphorus would have eliminated it from the nationwide study but a comparison of phosphorus and nitrogen would evaluate the relationship of both nutrients to each other in an urban hydrologic setting. Fluoride was monitored by most of our sample cities and was also chosen for mapping.

Minor Elements and Metals. The final grouping contained the largest number of variables from which to choose. All parameters had one common characteristic: insufficient data for a comparative study. As a result, we were forced to select several metals which were considered important for urban analysis. Iron is a common metal in water quality data banks. Total iron was selected for mapping over the dissolved species although coverage was split between the two. Of the toxic metals, the only ones available in our twelve city sample were lead (dissolved), cadmium (dissolved), zinc, copper and nickel.

Temperature. Temperature was not mapped or even considered for mapping, although its importance in the water body is acknowledged by us and by major sources in the literature. It is the basis for most of the reactions and activity in the water and the levels of nearly all other water residuals are temperature-dependent. As a specific indicator of water quality, its significance is limited to detection of sources of thermal pollution. Thus temperature is not an important measure of urban water pollution. Moreover, temperature standards vary monthly, too often in light of the number of readings taken. Our experience in attempting to map this parameter in the Chicago study confirmed its limited value for comparative studies.

Mapping the STORET Data

The water quality parameters listed in Table 4.1 were mapped according to the following procedures. For each parameter in the table, one or more STORET code numbers were available. The 1971 data for each station in the PGM-INVENT listed all code numbers for that station in numerical order. The code number (or numbers) for the parameter being mapped was located on the printout sheet. For each code number, the maximum, minimum, mean and dates of coverage were examined. If the mean value or the maximum-minimum range appeared to exceed that found in natural waters, the raw data were consulted for any obvious errors such as impossible values. The mean was re-calculated if necessary.

The yearly mean value for the specific parameter number was compared to the ranges of values derived from the federal proposed criteria and violations were noted. An appropriate color was selected which corresponded to one of the ranges in the map legend.

During the mapping process, we decided that some indication of the quality of the data should be made on each parameter map to facilitate analysis of that map. Identification of those stations with poorest quality data was made by employing a cutoff value. All readings above the minimum number and time range were indicated by a full dot while all values below it were shown by a circle. We would have used a cutoff reference level of twelve readings per year, preferably one each month, but the limited nature of the data would put most of the stations below the reference level.

The cutoff value selected was four readings over at least two quarters of the year. This was used to identify stations where many readings were taken within a short time span, often several days or less. So limited a sampling time range would make data for that parameter less reliable since it would not be as representative of the water body as readings more evenly distributed throughout the year. We later observed that many stations falling below the cutoff, showed trends similar to those stations above it.

On a piece of tracing paper placed over the hydrologic network map of the city, a dot was placed at the location of the station. The color of the dot corresponded to that range of values within which the mean fell. If the mean was based on poor data, that is, if it was below the previously established cutoff level of at least four readings covering more than three months of 1971, that value was designated by an open circle of the appropriate color rather than the usual dot.

When multiple code numbers were available for the parameter being mapped, selection of the mean was based on the ranking of those numbers in Table 4.1. If the first number was not recorded, the second was used. If that was absent, the third number was used, and so on. The exception to this rule was where the number of readings for one of the secondary numbers was at least twice as great as those of the first.

If the second or third code number had several times the number of readings of the first, it was used since it increases the size of the statistical sample hence the extent of coverage throughout the year. We believe that it produced a more valid indication of water quality, albeit based on a method whose accuracy differed somewhat from that of the primary code number.

If a parameter was not represented by one of the STORET code numbers in Table 4.1, no symbol was placed on the map at the station location. When the data for a parameter were represented by multiple code numbers, several symbols were used so that one could recognized the different sampling techniques and lab methods used.

Final cartographic representations were greatly simplified over the work maps. Part of this simplification process involved drafting of graphics for black and white reproduction. Further, the reduction of the graphics for publication limited that portion of the drainage net which could be shown on the map. To create a consistent drainage net map for each city, Strahler's modification of Horton's laws of stream order and number was applied. Stream order is a measure of the position of a stream in the hierarchy of tributaries. Order 1 in such a system is a channel without tributaries; order 2 is a channel with only order 1 tributaries, but includes only the length segment between junction upstream of order 1 channel and junction downstream with another order 2 channel, etc. To show only major tributaries in the final maps, the lowest order of tributaries were systematically removed from the drainage net. The plotting stations on the drafted base map will give an indication of the completeness of monitor network coverage. Recommendations for improved sampling network distribution can be based accordingly.

Final parameter maps contain dots of varying size. Ordinarily the largest dots or circles represent the most contaminated water, while the smallest indicate the least polluted with respect to proposed criteria. There are several exceptions. The lowest dissolved oxygen values indicate highest levels of contamination and are represented by the largest size symbols. Instead of using the larger sized dots to indicate deviation of mean annual pH values from the normal range for that parameter, we chose to use smaller dot sizes for acidic waters and the larger sizes for alkaline waters. Therefore, the least polluted pH values are shown by the medium-sized dots. The dot sizes for phosphorus, cadmium and ammonia tend to run smaller than actual pollution levels warrant. The large range in proposed standards, some reference levels low, some high is responsible for this inadequate representation of water quality (see Table 4.1). The stringent Freshwater Aquatic Life reference levels for ammonia and cadmium and the nutrient reference level for phosphorus are signified by the smallest size dots. It would have been impractical for us to attempt to further subdivide these trace values to provide additional levels for mapping.

Table 4.1

LEVELS FOR PARAMETER MAPS

PARAMETER		LEVELS	CRITERIA	CATEGORY/SOURCE
1.	D.O.	$X_1 < 4.0$ mg/l	4.0 mg/l: Min. for	Freshwater (Aq. Life)
	00300	$4.0 \leq X_2 < 5.0$	short periods	Marine Water (Aq. Life)
	00299	$5.0 \leq X_3 < 6.0$	Absolute min.	
		$6.0 \leq X_4 < 7.0$	5.0 mg/l: Lower limit	Primary contact Rec.
		$7.0 \leq X_5$	6.0 mg/l: Min. except	Marine Water (Aq. Life)
			For temporary natural	
			conditions	
2.	B.O.D.	$X_1 \leq 5.0$ mg/l	30.0 mg/l	Secondary Treatment**
	00310	$5.0 < X_2 \leq 10.0$		
		$10.0 < X_3 \leq 20.0$		
		$20.0 < X_4 \leq 30.0$		
		$30.0 < X_5 \leq 40.0$		
		$40.0 < X_6$		
3.	TOT. COLI.	$X_1 \leq 1000$ per 100ml	5000: Max. monthly	Agricultural (Livestock)
	31501	$1000 < X_2 \leq 2000$	mean	
	31503 MFM	$2000 < X_3 \leq 5000$	10000	Public Water Supply
	31504	$5000 < X_4 \leq 10000$	20000: At any time	Agricultural (Livestock)
		$10000 < X_5 \leq 20000$		
	31505	$20000 < X_6 \leq 40000$		
	31506 MPN	$40000 < X_7 \leq 100000$		
		$100000 < X_8$		
4.	FECAL COLI.	$X_1 \leq 200.0$ per 100ml	200 per 100ml: "log	Primary Contact Rec.
	31616 MFM	$200 < X_2 \leq 400$	mean"	
		$400 < X_3 \leq 1000$	400 per 100ml: For not	" " "
		$1000 < X_4 \leq 2000$	more than 10% of	
		$2000 < X_5 \leq 4000$	samples in 30 day per.	
	31614	$4000 < X_6 \leq 10000$	1000 per 100ml	Agricultural (Irrigation)
	31615 MPN	$10000 < X_7 \leq 20000$	1000 per 100ml: Max.	Agricultural (Livestock)
	31617	$20000 < X_8$	monthly mean	
			2000 per 100ml	Public Water Supply
			2000 per 100ml:	Undesignated Rec.
			"average"	
			4000 per 100ml:	" "
			"maximum"	
			4000 per 100ml: At	Agricultural (Livestock)
			any time	
5.	pH	$X_1 < 6.0$	5-9 Absolute limits	Primary Contact Rec.
	00400	$6.0 \leq X_2 < 6.5$		Public Water Supply
	00403	$6.5 \leq X_3 \leq 8.5$	6-9	Freshwater (Aq. Life)
		$8.5 < X_4 \leq 9.0$	6.5 - 8.3	Primary Contact Rec.
		$9.0 < X_5$	6.5 - 8.5	Marine Water (Aq. Life)
6.	T.D.S.	$X_1 \leq 250$ mg/l	500 mg/l	Water Supply*
	00515	$250 < X_2 \leq 500$	500-1,000: For	Agricultural
			sensitive crops	(Irrigation)
	70300	$500 < X_3 \leq 1000$	2000 - 5000: For	Agricultural
			tolerant plants	(Irrigation)
	70301	$1000 < X_4 \leq 2000$		
		$2000 < X_5 \leq 5000$		
	47004	$5000 < X_6$		
7.	TURBIDITY	$X_1 < 5$	10 Jackson Turbidity	Aquatic Life*
	00070	$5 \leq X_2 < 10$	Units	
	00076	$10 \leq X_3 < 25$	"Good" reference level	
		$25 \leq X_4 < 50$	50 J.T.U.'s	Aquatic Life*
		$50 \leq X_5 < 100$		
		$100 \leq X_6$		
8.	MBAS	$X_1 \leq 0.2$ mg/l	0.5 mg/l	Public Water Supply
	38260	$0.2 < X_2 \leq 0.5$		
		$0.5 < X_3 \leq 1.0$		
		$1.0 < X_4 \leq 2.0$		
		$2.0 < X_5 \leq 4.0$		
		$4.0 < X_6$		

Table 4.1

LEVELS FOR PARAMETER MAPS (cont.)

PARAMETER		LEVELS	CRITERIA	CATEGORY/SOURCE
9. CHLORIDE		$X_1 \leq 50.0$ mg/1	250.0 mg/1	Public Water Supply
00940	50.0 <	$X_2 \leq 100.0$		
	100.0 <	$X_3 \leq 250.0$		
	250.0 <	$X_4 \leq 500.0$		
	500.0 <	X_5		
10. FLUORIDE		$X_1 \leq 0.5$ mg/1	1.0 mg/1: For continuous irrigation of acid sandy soils	Agricultural (Irrigation)
60950	0.5 <	$X_2 \leq 1.0$		
	1.0 <	$X_3 \leq 1.5$	1.5 mg/1	Marine Water (Aq. Life)
	1.5 <	$X_4 \leq 2.0$	20 mg/1: For continous irrigation of <u>all</u> soils	Agricultural (Irrigation)
	2.0 <	$X_5 \leq 2.5$		Agricultural (Livestock)
	2.5 <	X_6	15.0 mg/1: For neutral and fine textured alkaline soils for a period of not more than 20 years	Agricultural (Irrigation)
11. AMMONIA NIT.		$X_1 \leq 0.02$ mg/1	0.02 mg/1	Freshwater (Aq. Life)
(as N)	0.02 <	$X_2 \leq 0.1$	0.4 mg/1	Marine Water (Aq. Life)
00610	0.1 <	$X_3 \leq 0.2$	0.5 mg/1	Public Water Supply
71845				
(see conversions)[1]	0.2 <	$X_4 \leq 0.3$		
	0.3 <	$X_5 \leq 0.4$		
	0.4 <	$X_6 \leq 0.5$		
	0.5 <	$X_7 \leq 1.0$		
	1.0 <	X_8		
12. NITRATE		$X_1 \leq 0.5$ mg/1		
00620	0.5 <	$X_2 \leq 1.0$		
00630	1.0 <	$X_3 \leq 5.0$	10.0 mg/1: nitrate (as N)	Public Water Supply
71850	5.0 <	$X_4 \leq 10.0$	100. mg/1 $NO_2 + NO_3$ (as N)	Agricultural (Livestock)
71851	10. <	X_5		
00618				
00631				
(see conversions)[1]				
13. TOTAL		$X_1 \leq 0.05$ mg/1	0.1 mg/1 (P)	Nutrient*
PHOSPHORUS	0.05 <	$X_2 \leq 0.10$		
AND/OR	0.10 <	$X_3 \leq 0.5$		
PHOSPHATE	0.5 <	$X_4 \leq 1.0$		
(as P)	1.0 <	$X_5 \leq 5.0$		
00665	5.0 <	$X_6 \leq 10.0$		
00650[1]	10.0 <	X_7		
71886				
(see conversions)[1]				
14. SULFATE		$X_1 \leq 50.0$ mg/1	250.0 mg/1: Except in areas where no other drinking water supply is available.	Public Water Supply
00945	50.0 <	$X_2 \leq 150.0$		
	150.0 <	$X_3 \leq 250.0$		
	250.0 <	$X_4 \leq 350.0$		
	350.0 <	X_5		
15. CADMIUM		$X_1 \leq 0.004$ mg/1	0.004 mg/1: For soft water	Freshwater (Aq. Life)
01025	0.004 <	$X_2 \leq 0.01$		
	0.01 <	$X_3 \leq 0.03$	0.01 mg/1	Public Water Supply
	0.03 <	$X_4 \leq 0.05$		Marine Water (Aq. Life)
	0.05 <	$X_5 \leq 0.1$	For continuous irrigation.	Agricultural (Irrigation)
	0.1 <	X_6	0.03 mg/1: For hard water	Freshwater (Aq. Life)
			0.05 mg/1: For neutral and fine-textured alkaline soils for a period of not more than 20 years.	Agricultural (Livestock) Agricultural (Irrigation)

Table 4.1

LEVELS FOR PARAMETER MAPS (cont.)

PARAMETER	LEVELS	CRITERIA	CATEGORY/SOURCE
16. COPPER 01040 01042	$X_1 \leq 0.02$ mg/1 $0.02 < X_2 \leq 0.05$ $0.05 < X_3 \leq 0.1$ $0.1 < X_4 \leq 0.2$ $0.2 < X_5 \leq 0.5$ $0.5 < X_6 \leq 1.0$ $1.0 < X_7$	0.05 mg/1 0.2 mg/1: For continous irrigation 0.5 mg/1 1.0 mg/1 5.0 mg/1: For neutral and fine-textured alkaline soils for a period of not more than 20 years	Marine Water (Aq. Life) Agricultural (Irrigation) Agricultural (Livestock) Public Water Supply Agricultural (Irrigation)
17. IRON 01045	$X_1 \leq 0.1$ mg/1 $0.1 < X_2 \leq 0.3$ $0.3 < X_3 \leq 0.5$ $0.5 < X_4 \leq 1.0$ $1.0 < X_5 \leq 3.0$ $3.0 < X_6 \leq 5.0$ $5.0 < X_7 \leq$	0.3 mg/1 5.0 mg/1: For continuous irrigation 20.0 mg/1: For neutral and fine-textured alkaline soils for a period of not more than 20 years.	Public Water Supply Marine Water (Aq. Life) Agricultural (Irrigation) Agricultural (Irrigation)
18. LEAD 01049	$X_1 \leq 0.01$ mg/1 $0.01 < X_2 \leq 0.03$ $0.03 < X_3 \leq 0.05$ $0.05 < X_4 \leq 0.1$ $0.1 < X_5 \leq 0.2$ $0.2 < X_6$	0.03 mg/1 0.05 mg/1 0.1 mg/1 5.0 mg/1 10.0 mg/1: For neutral and fine-textured alkaline soils for a period of not more than 20 years.	Freshwater (Aq. Life) Public Water Supply Marine Water (Aq. Life) Agricultural (Livestock) Agricultural (Irrigation) Agricultural (Irrigation)
19. NICKEL 01065	$X_1 \leq 0.1$ mg/1 $0.1 < X_2 \leq 0.2$ $0.2 < X_3 \leq 0.5$ $0.5 < X_4 \leq 1.0$ $1.0 < X_5 \leq 2.0$ $2.0 < X_6$	0.1 mg/1 0.2 for continuous irrigation of all soil 2.0 mg/1: For neutral and fine textured alkaline soils for a period of not more than 20 years	Marine Water (Aq. Life) Agricultural (Irrigation) Agricultural (Irrigation)
20. ZINC 01090	$X_1 \leq 0.1$ mg/1 $0.1 < X_2 \leq 0.3$ $0.3 < X_3 \leq 0.5$ $0.5 < X_4 \leq 1.0$ $1.0 < X_5 \leq 3.0$ $3.0 < X_6 \leq 5.0$ $5.0 < X_7$	0.1 mg/1 5.0 mg/1 25.0 mg/1	Marine Water (Aq. Life) Public Water Supply Agricultural (Livestock)

1.

The following conversions were used:

1. 71845 x .777 = 00610

2. 71850 x .2259 = 00620
   71851

3. 00650 x .33 = 00665
   71886

Note: All reference levels are taken from Criteria for Water Quality, EPA, 1973 except:

* taken from Guidelines for Developing or Revising Water Quality Standards, EPA Water Planning Division, April 1973 or

** taken from the "Water Programs: Secondary Treatment Information", EPA, (40 CFR Part 133).

The Metropolitan Map Sets

We now proceed directly to a presentation of the data for the sample of twelve metropolitan regions. Analysis of the individual cases is kept to a minimum, because we are more concerned with the comparative aspects of water quality that are revealed. However, in each case we present the following:

1. A brief text describing the physical and hydrologic characteristics of the region, land use patterns, distribution and coverage by monitoring stations, the number and type of parameters monitored and the frequency and distribution of readings, a generalized summary of water quality based upon the 1971 STORET data and a comparison with other published reports on water quality in the region (where available).

2. A table that shows the parameters that have been mapped, indicating the total number of stations monitoring each parameter, the distribution in the inner city and the rest of the urban region, the percentages falling below the cutoff for adequate numbers of readings, and the numbers and percentages of stations in the central city and the remainder of the region exceeding federal reference levels (standards), by water use designation.

3. The set of parameter maps for the region.

In the text, emphasis is placed on the associations between pollution, land use and social patterns. If further research is undertaken, additional topics such as the following might be addressed:

1. Parameter associations characteristic of urbanized areas -

   (a) variables associated with municipal sewage treatment plants (nitrates, ammonia, phosphorus, chlorides, BOD, etc.)
   (b) street wash storm sewer runoff (oil, dust, solids)
   (c) oil and other pollutants added from rainwater after absorption into the atmosphere above impermeable urban street surface (possible correlation with air data)
   (d) chlorides and sulfates associated with deicing
   (e) rodenticide and insecticide residues

2. Physical and geomorphic issues -

   (a) water pollution in urban karst areas
   (b) unsewered runoff and groundwater contamination
   (c) estuary pollution
   (d) marine coastal pollution in urban areas
   (e) urban landfill site contamination of groundwater and streams

(f) groundwater inflow contamination of streams in
    cities underlain by aquifers
(g) snowmelt pollution (climate dependent)
(h) irrigation return flow contaminants (chlorides,
    TDS) in water-deficient areas

The presentation begins with three east-coast urban regions: Providence, Washington and Baltimore. Next, three mid-continent cases are examined: Rochester, Cincinnati and St. Louis. Third come two southern cases, Birmingham and Jacksonville, two plains cities, Denver and Oklahoma City and finally two west-coast cases, Seattle and San Diego. To reiterate, all of the maps refer to the year 1971.

PROVIDENCE

The physical features of Providence and vicinity are similar to those of several of our sample cities. Surface features reflect their periglacial origins. Surficial geology consists mostly of glacial out-wash sand and gravels and consolidated rock types which support a crushed stone industry. Small dams and reservoirs upstream help to regulate flow and provide drinking water for municipalities downstream. Many small lakes, abundant groundwater resources, fisheries and a series of estuaries are assets to Providence and nearby coastal cities. There is little vertical relief and coastal marshes and ponds are fre-quent. The coastal climate is modified by marine effects. In 1971, cumulative runoff was in the normal range for the first quarter of the calendar year and deficient from April to June. Runoff during the remaining half of the year was in the low-normal or deficient range.

Roughly 70 percent of the land in the polygon is unsuitable for agricultural use and has not been developed; 25 percent of the land is urbanized; and the remainder is agricultural land currently in use (Figure 4.1). The northern half of the Moshassuck River Basin is pri-marily rural in character with scattered concentrations of develop-ment, while the southern portion of the basin is urbanized with high density development occurring in Providence, Central Falls, Pawtucket and North Providence. Major industrial operations are located at the mouth of the Providence River in the central business district of Providence, where there are many effluent discharge points. The com-bined sewer overflows from the City of Providence sewerage system also are concentrated in this area in periods of heavy rainfall. There are lesser industrial concentrations located in North Providence and Smithfield. Nonpoint source pollution consists primarily of urban stormwater runoff in the areas of Providence, North Providence, Paw-tucket and Central Falls.

The 1971 water quality data from STORET provided a total of 74 water quality surveillance points in a retrieval polygon that encompassed all of Rhode Island and a small portion of the neighboring states of Massachusetts and Connecticut (Figure 4.2). Approximately two-thirds of the monitoring points were located on estuaries and bays. One large cluster of stations is ideally located at the mouth of the Providence River at the entrance to Narragansett Bay. Another major concentration of surveillance points is in Mount Hope Bay at the mouth of the Taunton River. The remaining stations are located on upstream tributaries of both major rivers. This includes a cluster of seven stations in the swampy headwater of the Taunton River. Several coastal or near-coastal stations on the Pawcatuck River are included in the polygon. These monitoring points used are well-located with respect to the Providence and Fall River urban cores, but adequate surveillance is lacking for the many tributary sub-basins. The coastal waters of Narragansett Bay around Newport are not well monitored.

The 1971 STORET data for the polygon were supplied by seven agencies, the majority by EPA Region I technical staff, who performed intensive testing over short periods during the summer months. Most stations sampled several times a year for each parameter, with the exception of DO and pH which were monitored more frequently. Few stations were sampled regularly. Instead, the readings tended to be part of a short-term series of tests performed by EPA or other agencies over a period of days in late summer. The U.S Geological Survey tested water quality at more regular although infrequent intervals. The principal parameters monitored were: DO, total and fecal coliforms, pH, turbidity, nitrates, ammonia, total phosphorus and chlorides. Trace metals, BOD and MBAS were poorly monitored. Fluorides, TDS and sulfate were not available.

Previous research on water quality in the region undertaken as part of the Rhode Island Statewide Planning Program indicates although almost all segments of the Woonasquatucket Basin are in compliance with their classification of water quality, two major problems exist within the basin. The first is combined sewer overflows from the Providence sewer system during periods of heavy rainfall. The second problem is the need for a municipal sewerage system in Smithfield, to eliminate industrial and domestic wastewater discharges to the Woonasquatucket River. With the elimination of these problems, it was concluded that pollution from surface runoff in urban areas within the basin may become the dominant problem. The same source lists water quality data obtained during a one-day sampling study along the Woonasquatucket River by the Rhode Island Department of Health in 1970. For the six sample locations, DO remained above 5.0 mg/l at all but the last downstream station where 0.0 mg/l DO was recorded. Total coliforms MPN/100 ml increased substantially from a low reading of 2,300 at river mile 5.9 to a maximum of 11,000,000 at river mile 0.25. A slight increase in BOD was observed near the mouth of the river. The low DO and high coliform counts are attributed to combined sewer overflows or surface runoff. A comparable series of tests performed in 1974 by the same agency showed similar trends except for total coliforms which were far below previous levels.

An evaluation of the Moshassuck River Basin classified it as similar in quality to the Woonasquatucket. The Moshassuck also flows through densely populated communities including Providence, North Providence, Pawtucket and Central Falls. Its waters were found to be generally in compliance with state water quality standards which have reference levels similar to the proposed federal criteria used in our own study. However, the Moshassuck is plagued by combined sewer overflows during storm periods, especially from the Cities of Providence and Central Falls. The entire City of Providence and parts of contiguous communities are served by a sewer system consisting primarily of combined sewers. Stormwater overflow is diverted to the Moshassuck,

Providence, Seekonk and Woonasquatucket Rivers, resulting in the temporary closure of upper Narragansett Bay to shellfishing. In addition, the effluent from an industrial park served by a package treatment plant is discharged into a swamp near the headwaters of the Moshassuck River. In the town of North Providence, an engineering study discovered other adverse effects of urbanization including infiltration of groundwater, through leaks, faulty connections, introduction of surface drainage and the connection of rain leaders and foundation drains.

Do the water quality maps prepared from the 1971 data confirm these conclusions? The inner City of Providence, at the mouth of the Providence River, indeed is seen in the maps to be grossly polluted for several water quality variables: phosphorus, ammonia, dissolved oxygen, total and fecal coliform bacteria. See Figures 4.4-4.12. Mt. Hope Bay and the mouth of the Taunton River in the Fall River SMSA were contaminated by high levels of ammonia, phosphorus and total coliforms. Dissolved oxygen levels exceeded reference levels for several stations at that location. Two pH stations in the vicinity had mean levels below 6.0 SU. The North River, a small stream in a marshy area near the headwaters of the Taunton River, had impaired water quality for ammonia at all sampling points. Stations on that stream showed mixed values for total and fecal coliforms, DO and pH. The Blackstone River had high ammonia levels and somewhat acidic pH values. Nitrates on that stream were slightly higher than elsewhere but still far below the 10 mg/l recommended level.

For the polygon as a whole, we can also evaluate specific parameters. See Table 4.2. Total phosphorus levels for all but two of the 44 stations used (87 percent were below the cutoff value for adequate readings) were in excess of the .1 mg/l nutrient reference value. Ammonia nitrogen readings were available for 53 stations (all below the cutoff). All four Providence inner city stations exceeded the three reference levels used. All of the 49 stations in the remainder of the polygon surpassed the .02 mg/l Freshwater Aquatic Life level. Approximately 43 percent of those stations were also above the .4 mg/l Marine Water Aquatic Life reference level. In addition, 39 percent of the 49 stations exceeded the Public Water Supply proposed standard of .5 mg/l.

Of the 52 stations that monitored pH, 10 stations (19 percent) exceeded the recommended ranges for Primary Contact Recreational and Marine Water Aquatic Life. The four inner city stations which monitored total and fecal coliforms exceeded all reference levels. In the remainder of the polygon, the Public Water Supply level for total coliforms was exceeded by 8 stations (19 percent). For fecal coliforms in the remainder of the polygon, 19 percent of the stations were above the 200/100 ml reference level and 7 percent were above the 2000/100 ml suggested level.

Dissolved oxygen readings did not meet reference levels at all inner city stations. Approximately 47 percent or 24 of the remaining 51 stations did not attain the 6.0 mg/l standard. Of those 51 stations, 14 (27 percent) fell below the 5.0 mg/l reference level and 6 fell below the least stringent 4.0 mg/l value. The low dissolved oxygen levels may have been the result of sampling during a storm or sewer overflow period. Nearly 79 percent of the total stations fell below our cutoff reference point.

Water in the Providence polygon was good for all of the remaining parameters. The chloride map simply defines the areas of fresh water and salt water. Nitrate, turbidity and BOD reference levels were met at all stations used. All five stations which sampled MBAS had readings at least twice as great as the .5 mg/l reference level. Most of those stations were located near urban concentrations.

Table 4.2

Providence

Parameter	Total N	Total P	Inner City N	Inner City P	Remainder N	Remainder P	Details By Water Use Designation Inner City WD	Inner City R	Inner City E	Inner City PR	Remainder R	Remainder E	Remainder PR
DO	56	79	4	100	51	78	FA	4	100	100	6	12	100
							MA_1	4	100	100	6	12	100
							MA_2	4	100	100	24	47	96
							PC	4	100	100	14	27	100
TOT COLI	46	89	4	100	42	88	AL_1	4	100	100	4	10	100
							AL_2	4	100	100	10	24	100
							PS	4	100	100	8	19	100
FEC COLI	47	89	4	100	43	88	AI	4	100	100	4	10	100
							AL_1	1	25	100	1	3	100
							AL_2	4	100	100	4	10	100
							PS	4	100	100	3	71	100
							UR_1	1	25	100	1	2	100
							UR_2	4	100	100	3	7	100
							PC_1	4	100	100	5	12	100
							PC_2	4	100	100	8	19	100
PH	52	77	0	-	52	77	FA	-	-	-	3	6	100
							MA	-	-	-	10	19	90
							PS	-	-	-	0	0	-
							PC_1	-	-	-	0	0	-
							PC_2	-	-	-	10	19	90
TURB	39	69	0	-	39	69	FA_1	-	-	-	0	0	-
							FA_2	-	-	-	0	0	-
CL	21	90	0	-	21	90	PS	-	-	-	7	33	86
NH3	53	100	4	100	49	100	FA	4	100	100	49	100	100
							MA	4	100	100	21	43	100
							PS	4	100	100	19	39	100
NO3	48	90	4	100	44	87	AL	0	0	-	0	0	-
							PS	0	0	-	0	0	-
P	44	87	5	100	39	87	NS	4	80	100	37	92	95

Code:

N = Number of stations
P = Percentage of stations below cutoff value
E = Percentage of stations exceeding reference level
R = Number of stations exceeding reference level
PR = Percentage of stations exceeding reference level below cutoff

Water Use Designation (WD):

AI = Agricultural, Irrigation
AL = Agricultural, Livestock
FA = Freshwater Aquatic Life
MA = Marine Water Aquatic Life
PS = Public Water Supply Intake
UR = Undesignated Recreational
PC = Primary Contact Recreational
ST = Secondary Treatment Standard
NA = Nutrient Standard

Note: Subscripts refer to different standards, where more than one standard is specified for a given water use designation.

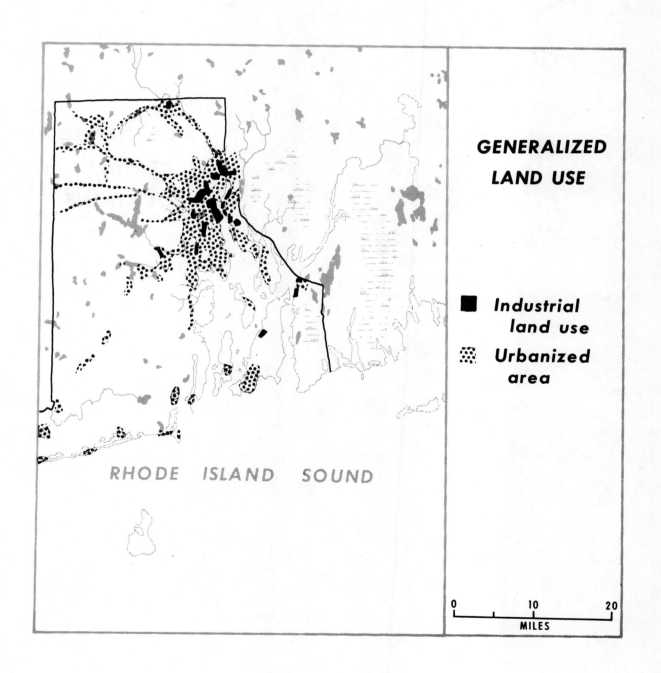

GENERALIZED
LAND USE

■ Industrial
land use

Urbanized
area

RHODE ISLAND SOUND

0   10   20
MILES

Figure 4.1

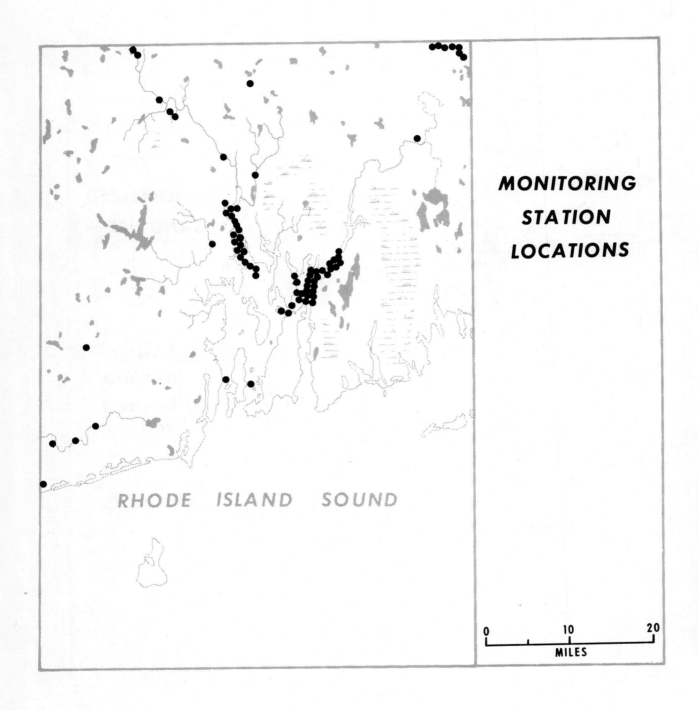

MONITORING
STATION
LOCATIONS

RHODE ISLAND SOUND

0   10   20
MILES

Figure 4.2

DISCHARGE

POINTS

● *Municipal*
discharge

RHODE ISLAND SOUND

0   10   20
MILES

Figure 4.3

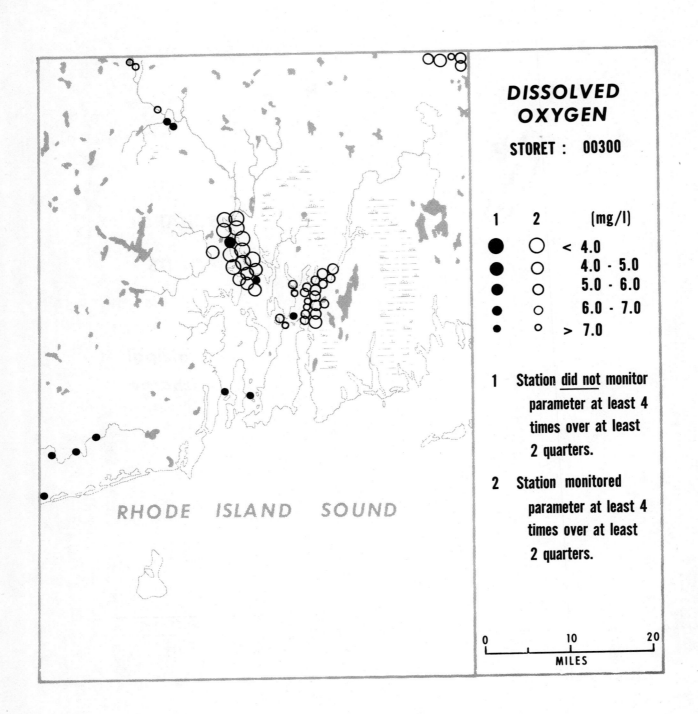

Figure 4.4

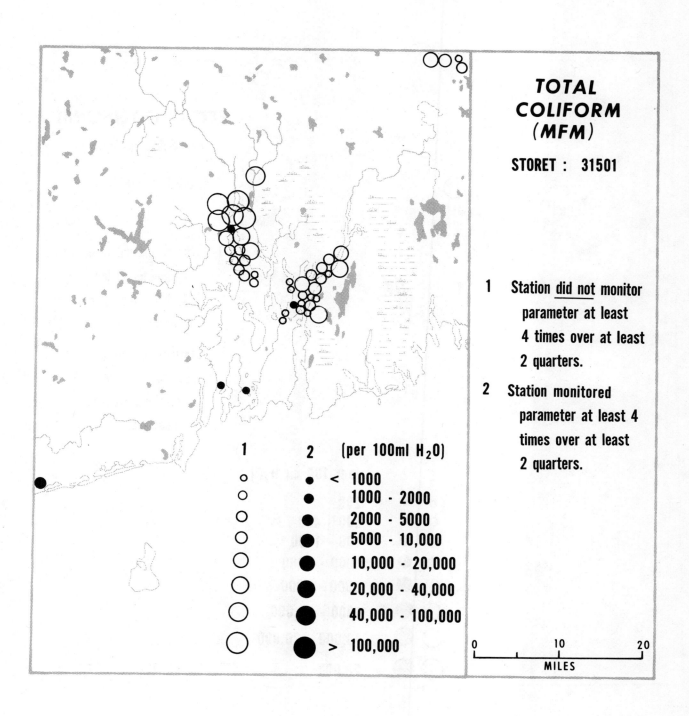

TOTAL
COLIFORM
(MFM)

STORET : 31501

1 Station did not monitor
parameter at least
4 times over at least
2 quarters.

2 Station monitored
parameter at least 4
times over at least
2 quarters.

1	2	(per 100ml H₂O)
○	●	< 1000
○	●	1000 - 2000
○	●	2000 - 5000
○	●	5000 - 10,000
○	●	10,000 - 20,000
○	●	20,000 - 40,000
○	●	40,000 - 100,000
○	●	> 100,000

0   10   20
MILES

Figure 4.5

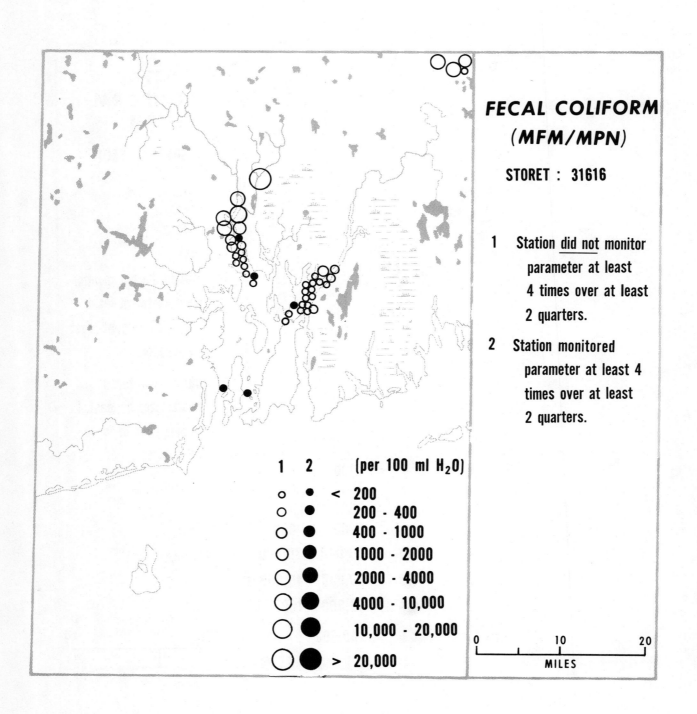

FECAL COLIFORM
(MFM/MPN)

STORET : 31616

1 Station <u>did not</u> monitor parameter at least 4 times over at least 2 quarters.

2 Station monitored parameter at least 4 times over at least 2 quarters.

1	2	(per 100 ml H₂0)
○	•	< 200
○	•	200 - 400
○	•	400 - 1000
○	●	1000 - 2000
○	●	2000 - 4000
○	●	4000 - 10,000
○	●	10,000 - 20,000
○	●	> 20,000

0   10   20
MILES

Figure 4.6

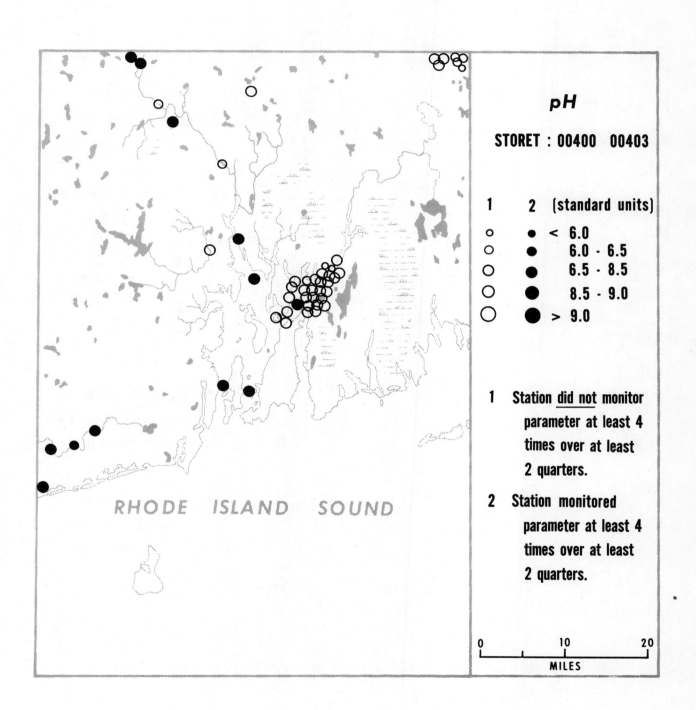

pH

STORET : 00400 00403

1	2	(standard units)
○	●	< 6.0
○	●	6.0 - 6.5
○	●	6.5 - 8.5
○	●	8.5 - 9.0
○	●	> 9.0

1 Station <u>did not</u> monitor
parameter at least 4
times over at least
2 quarters.

2 Station monitored
parameter at least 4
times over at least
2 quarters.

RHODE ISLAND SOUND

0   10   20
MILES

Figure 4.7

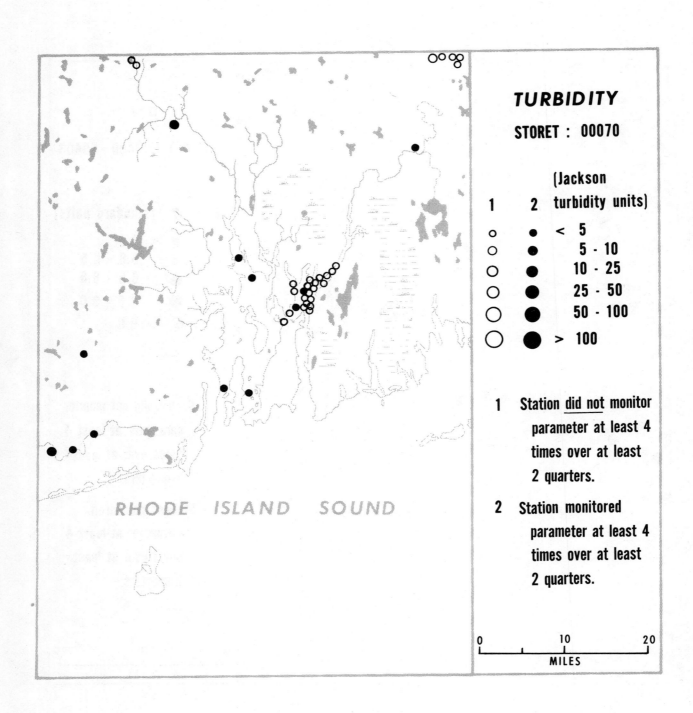

Figure 4.8

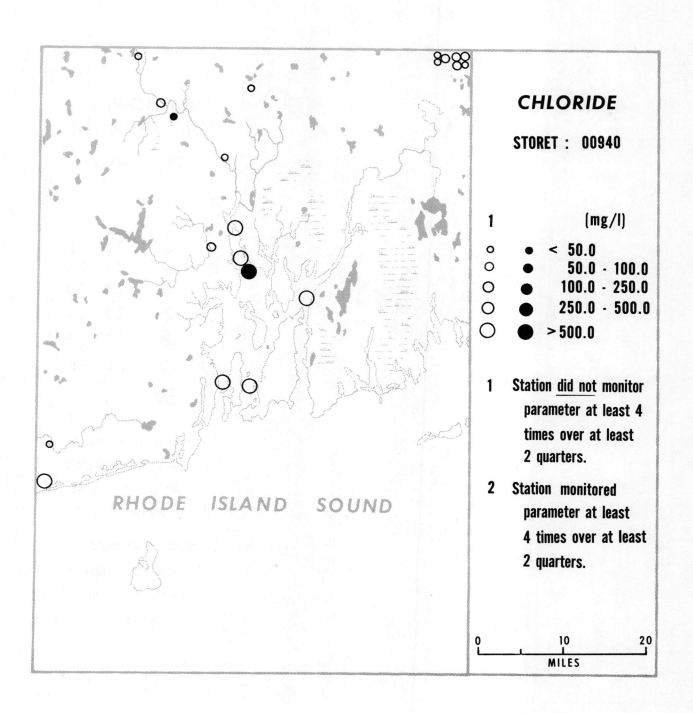

CHLORIDE

STORET : 00940

Figure 4.9

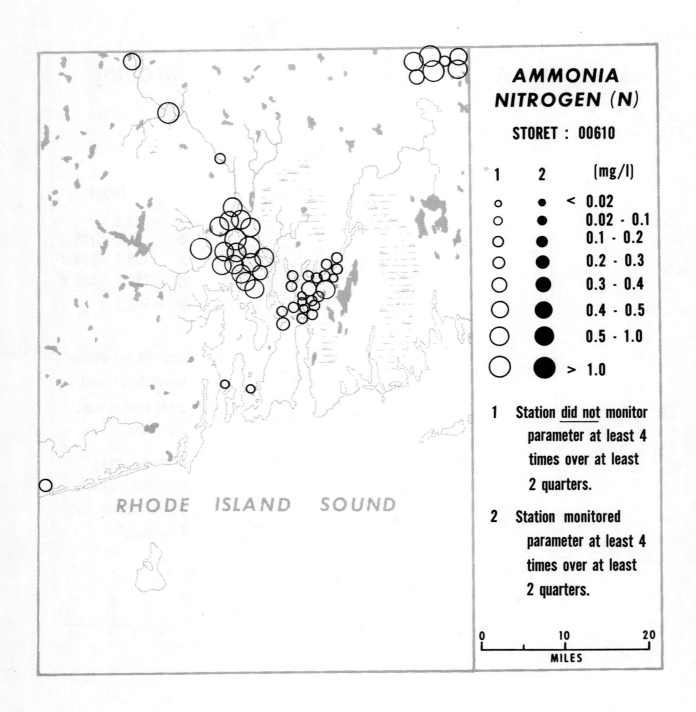

Figure 4.10

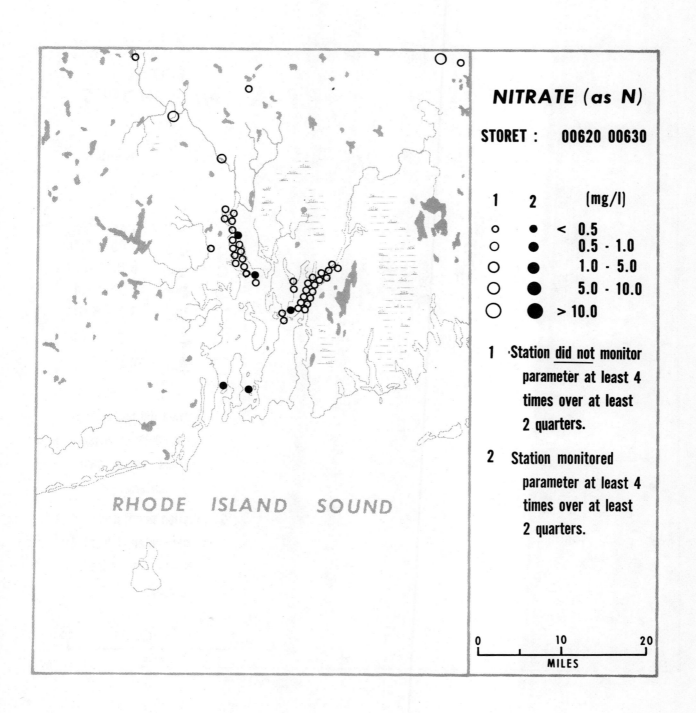

Figure 4.11

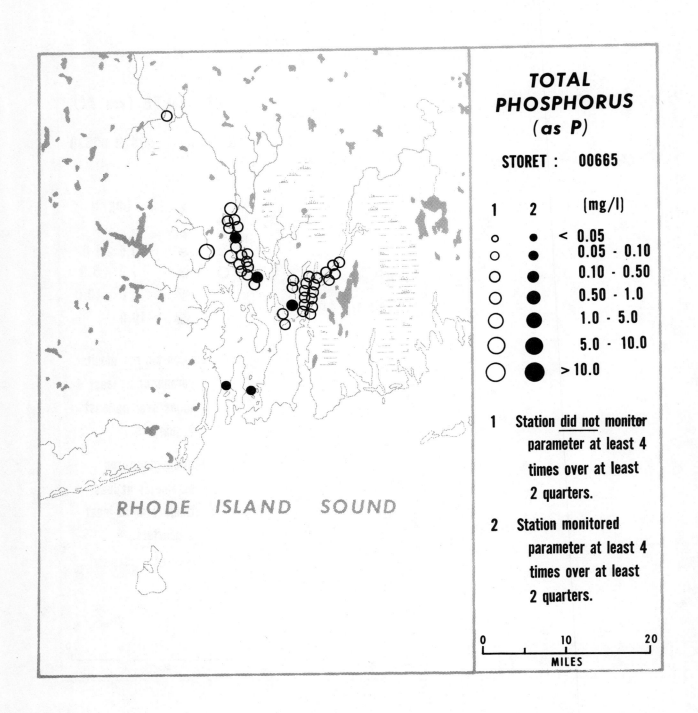

Figure 4.12

WASHINGTON, D.C.

Our STORET retrieval polygon for the Washington, D.C. area contained most of the drainage area of the Potomac River from its confluence with the Shenandoah River to its mouth at Chesapeake Bay, and extended across two physiographic provinces, the Piedmont Plateau (characterized by gently-rolling topography with occasionally steep, stream-formed slopes) and the Atlantic Coastal Plain (which is partially to strongly dissected with gently-rolling hills and broad valleys). Most soils are well-drained and suited to intensive agriculture, except where accentuated slopes limit activity to grazing. Vegetation ranged from a mixed hardwood forest throughout the region to grasses, shrubs and aquatic plants in the tidal marsh areas. The drowned river type of estuary common to the Chesapeake Bay area characterizes the mouth of the Potomac and creates a natural fishery.

The climate of the region is continental with short, moderately cold winters and long, warm summers. Average annual temperature is 55°F. Precipitation is fairly uniform throughout the year with slightly higher levels during spring and summer. The average annual precipitation in Montgomery and Prince George's counties in Maryland is 48.5 and 45 inches, respectively. Runoff and flooding in tributary basins varies from year to year. During most of the U.S.G.S. water year (Oct. 1970-Sept. 1971) streamflow was in the above normal range. Annual mean discharge ranged from 100 to 200 percent of the median. The monthly flow of the Potomac River near Washington, D.C. ranged from 402 percent of median in November (1970) to 64 percent in April (1971). The base period for the median was 1941-70. Monthly flows at the Washington station were excessive, in the upper 25 percent of recorded flows, from November to February and in June and September. Only in April was the flow deficient, in the lowest 25 percent of recorded flows. Widespread flooding occurred during the year, mostly as a result of thunderstorm activity during August and September.

Intense rainfall caused flooding and highest discharge of record on several streams in the Baltimore, Md. and Washington, D.C. urban areas.

Eighty percent of the population of the Potomac River Basin is located in the Washington Metropolitan Area. Because of the major role of the Federal Government in the Washington region's economy, there are relatively few industrial wastewater discharges in the basin.

The Seneca drainage area, with the exception of a few small urban-suburban centers, is composed primarily of agricultural farmland. There are only three major sewage treatment plants presently discharging in the Seneca watershed. However, the urbanization which has occurred and the construction which is underway have resulted in increased sediment loadings, and agricultural runoff contributes to high nutrient loadings in this area.

The five tributaries draining into the lower Potomac support a variety of land uses from scattered farmlands to major suburban and urban concentrations nearing the Washington Metropolitan area. Water quality in the Muddy Branch area is generally poor due to the combined effects urban runoff and periodic overflow of sanitary waste at the Muddy Branch pumping station. Runoff from construction sites frequently occurs in both Watts Branch and Rock Run. Sewage waste is discharged into Cabin John Creek.

Approximately 75 percent of the Rock Creek sub-basin is heavily urbanized. However, the continued preservation and controlled development of Rock Creek Park provides a quasi-buffer zone against the problems inherent to urban watersheds. Storm water runoff, heavy sediment loadings from continuing development and the possibility of sewage discharges during periods of heavy rainfall exist in this drainage area.

The Anacostia Watershed drains most of the suburban area located northeast of the District of Columbia. Major land use is categorized as 20 percent urban, 60 percent suburban development and the remaining 20 percent as woodland/agricultural. Septic system discharge occurs in the upper part of this watershed. In the tidal portion of the Anacostia, storm water runoff and periodic sewage discharge are major sources of pollution. The major industrial user of the Anacostia River is the Potomac Electric Power Company, which discharges cooling water from the operation of two electric generating stations. Extensive residential construction centered in the upper watershed has resulted in extensive stream bank erosion and runoff during periods of heavy rainfall.

Land areas surrounding the main stem of the Potomac are the most heavily urbanized of the entire region. This urban core is the focal point of the region and is the area of most intensive land use. Residential, commercial, governmental and industrial uses predominate. Surrounding the urban core is an established area which shares many of the characteristics of the core, but densities are not generally as high.

Lack of adequate facilities for controlling sewage flows in the collection system often results in overloading of collection and treatment facilities. The upper estuary receives upwards of 325 million gallons per day of wastewater from 18 sewage treatment plants. Sediment pollution from urban runoff and from construction sites is also discharged into the estuary. The inner city sewer system of the urban core tend to be the least adequate and is often overloaded.

Our STORET retrieval polygon included approximately 335 biochemical quality monitoring stations. An additional request to the Maryland Department of Natural Resources provided 67 water quality stations. The inclusion of several pesticide and radiological stations gave us over 400 stations for our monitoring network map (Figure 4.14). Over 100 of these stations were located within the Rock Creek sub-basin. The entire drainage area for Rock Creek is 76.5 square miles and the average flow at its mouth is 56.2 cubic ft. per second. Total drainage area for the Potomac near Washington is 11,560 square miles. Total average flow is 10,790 cubic feet per second at that point. Therefore, Rock Creek, although passing through a highly urbanized area in its lower reaches, is somewhat over represented in our data summary.

The main channel of the Potomac had few stations upstream from Washington, but was adequately monitored from the city to the lower reaches of the estuary. Most of the Maryland and District of Columbia tributaries to the Potomac had adequate surveillance during 1971. Coverage was almost entirely lacking for tributary streams in Northern Virginia with the exception of the Shenandoah River, for which several stations appear on our maps. The Patuxent River received limited coverage, with most stations in its drainage basin being located on tributaries. Several dozen sampling points on the Potomac and several tributaries were located at or near bridges, possibly influencing water quality readings. All stations in our sample were located on rivers.

The 1971 water quality data were drawn from eleven sources. Sampling by the agency was done frequently and on a regular basis for nearly all of its stations. In direct contrast, the University of Maryland's sample data seldom covered extensive portions of the calendar year. The number of readings taken at each of its stations varied from one to several dozen samples, all within extremely short periods of time. For the entire monitoring system within the polygon, more than 60 percent of the total 400 stations exceeded our cutoff reference level for data quality. Therefore, our parameter maps are adequately representative of existing water quality for the period of record.

The following parameters were available for mapping: DO, BOD, total and fecal coliforms (by the Most Probable Number Method), pH, total dissolved solids, turbidity, chloride, ammonia, nitrate and total phosphorus/phosphate. Fluoride, MBAS, sulfate and trace metals data were insufficient.

Examining the resulting maps (Figures 4.13-4.26), we find that the Potomac River was polluted with respect to turbidity, total and fecal coliforms and ammonia in and near the District of Columbia. The lower reaches downstream from the mouth of Mattawoman Creek had very alkaline pH averages. Farther downstream DO levels drop to below 4.0 mg/l and then rise again.

Rock Creek had high total and fecal coliform bacteria levels, particularly downstream. It also had very high turbidity levels and low DO readings at several stations. The nearby Anacostia River also suffered from poor water quality and contributed to the degraded state of the Potomac within the SMSA. Total and fecal coliform levels exceeded all reference levels at all stations within the District of Columbia. Turbidity averages were above 50 JTUs at all stations within the same segment. Ammonia and phosphorus levels also exceeded all of the reference levels for the same series of stations.

Several minor tributaries of the Potomac were also severely contaminated. Mattawoman Creek had high total coliform levels at several stations. Normal levels were attained as the stream entered the main channel of the Potomac. The pH levels for the same stream segment were in the alkaline range and caused a temporary deterioration in the pH balance of the Potomac. Another stream which empties into the Potomac, Piscataway Creek exhibited high total and fecal coliform values at stations on one of its branches.

The Patuxent River suffered from contaminated water at several locations in its drainage basin. The Calvin Branch Tributary of the Patuxent had high BOD levels, in excess of all recommended levels, at several of its stations. The same stream segment showed high total and fecal coliform averages. The Little Patuxent River was critically polluted by some of the same parameters that were in excess of reference levels for other streams. Turbidity readings at one of the upstream branches of the Little Patuxent had exceedingly high turbidity readings usually characteristic of swamps. Maximum average turbidity at one station was 654 JTUs. Total and fecal coliform levels were also high, as were ammonia levels.

For the Washington polygon as a whole, several generalizations can be made about the degree to which the area is polluted by specific water quality variables. Dissolved oxygen and BOD levels were acceptable for most water use designations. Total dissolved solids and chlorides did not exceed reference levels. The pH Primary Contact Recreation level was exceeded by 20 (15 percent) of the 277 stations outside of the central city. None of the 31 inner city stations had averages outside of the recommended range.

For total coliform bacteria 262 total stations were represented on our map (56 percent below cutoff). Approximately 87 percent or 40 of 46 inner city stations exceeded the 10,000 MPN/100 ml reference level. Outside of the city area, 56 percent or 120 of 262 stations surpassed this reference level. A similar situation existed for fecal coliforms throughout the polygon. The total number of stations used was 276, 63 percent of which were below the cutoff level for adequate numbers and distribution of samples. All inner city and most suburban stations exceeded the Primary Contact reference level of 200/100 ml. The Public Water Supply recommended level of 2,000/100 ml was surpassed by 41 (91 percent) of the inner city stations and 114 (49 percent of the stations in the remainder of the polygon.

The Freshwater Aquatic Life proposed standard of 10 JTUs was exceeded by all 27 inner city stations and 52 (91 percent of those outside the city).

All 65 stations in the polygon which monitored ammonia exceeded the stringent .02 mg/l reference level for Freshwater Aquatic Life. The Public Water Supply .5 mg/l proposed standard was exceeded by 16 (64 percent) of the inner city stations but only 9 (23 percent) of the stations outside the city boundaries. The .1 mg/l Nutrient standard for phosphorus was surpassed by 20 (61 percent) inner city stations and 79 (43 percent) outer stations out of a total of 217 stations.

Table 4.3
Washington, D.C.

Parameter	Total N	Total P	Inner City N	Inner City P	Remainder N	Remainder P	Inner City WD	Inner City R	Inner City E	Inner City PR	Remainder R	Remainder E	Remainder PR
DO	388	35	48	31	340	35	FA	1	2	100	5	2	80
							MA_1	1	2	100	5	2	80
							MA_2	2	4	100	19	6	79
							PC	1	2	100	11	3	91
BOD	167	42	27	0	140	50	ST	0	0	-	2	1	0
TOT COLI	262	56	46	41	216	59	AL_1	35	76	34	91	42	48
							AL_2	44	96	39	150	69	43
							PS	40	87	33	120	56	48
FEC COLI	276	63	45	42	231	67	AI	42	93	38	126	55	50
							AL_1	37	82	35	81	35	57
							AL_2	42	93	38	126	55	50
							PS	41	91	37	114	49	49
							UR_1	37	82	35	81	35	57
							UR_2	41	91	37	114	49	49
							PC_1	43	96	40	154	67	54
							PC_2	45	100	42	181	78	57
PH	308	25	31	7	277	27	FA	0	0	-	4	1	50
							MA	0	0	-	20	7	55
							PS	0	0	-	2	1	100
							PC_1	0	0	-	2	1	100
							PC_2	0	0	-	20	7	55
TDS	53	68	0	-	53	68	AI_1	-	-	-	0	0	-
							AI_2	-	-	-	0	0	-
							PS	-	-	-	8	15	88
TURB	84	36	27	0	57	53	FA_1	6	22	0	12	21	8
							FA_2	27	100	0	52	91	48
CL	77	45	22	5	55	62	PS	0	0	-	0	0	-
NH3	65	14	25	0	40	23	FA	25	100	0	40	100	23
							MA	21	84	0	12	30	8
							PS	16	64	0	9	23	11
NO3	126	56	25	0	101	70	AL	0	0	-	0	0	-
							PS	0	0	-	0	0	-
P	217	44	33	85	184	37	NS	20	61	85	79	43	51

Code:

N = Number of stations
P = Percentage of stations below cutoff value
E = Percentage of stations exceeding reference level
R = Number of stations exceeding reference level
PR = Percentage of stations exceeding reference level below cutoff

Water Use Designation (WD):

AI = Agricultural, Irrigation
AL = Agricultural, Livestock
FA = Freshwater, Aquatic Life
MA = Marine Water Aquatic Life
PS = Public Water Supply Intake
UR = Undesignated Recreational
PC = Primary Contact Recreational
ST = Secondary Treatment Standard
NA = Nutrient Standard

Note: Subscripts refer to different standards, where more than one standard is specified for a given water use designation.

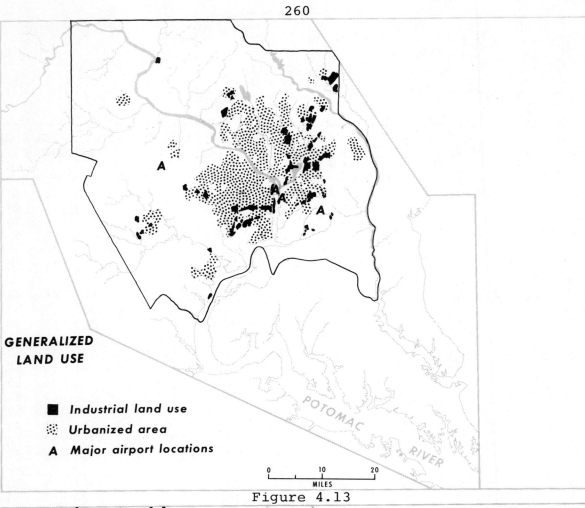

GENERALIZED
LAND USE

■ Industrial land use
░ Urbanized area
A Major airport locations

0   10   20
MILES

Figure 4.13

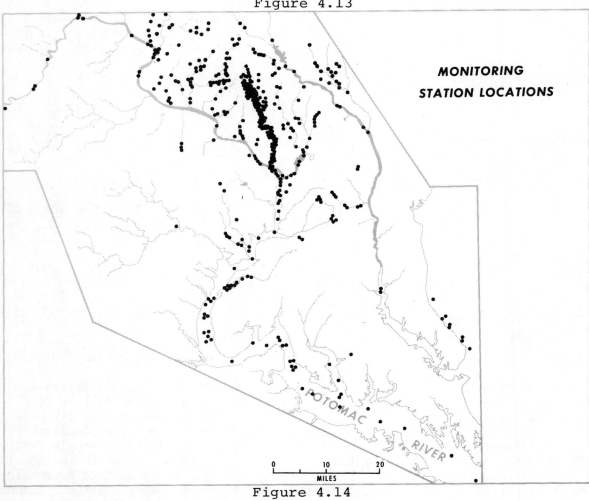

MONITORING
STATION LOCATIONS

0   10   20
MILES

Figure 4.14

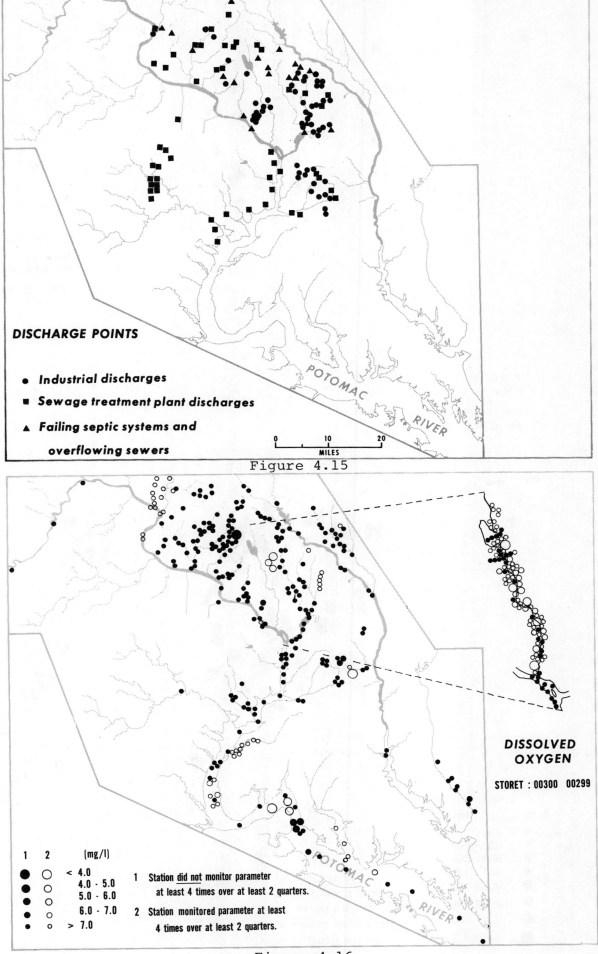

DISCHARGE POINTS

- ● **Industrial discharges**
- ■ **Sewage treatment plant discharges**
- ▲ **Failing septic systems and overflowing sewers**

POTOMAC RIVER

0   10   20
MILES

Figure 4.15

DISSOLVED OXYGEN

STORET : 00300 00299

1	2	(mg/l)
●	○	< 4.0
		4.0 - 5.0
		5.0 - 6.0
		6.0 - 7.0
		> 7.0

1   Station <u>did not</u> monitor parameter at least 4 times over at least 2 quarters.

2   Station monitored parameter at least 4 times over at least 2 quarters.

POTOMAC RIVER

Figure 4.16

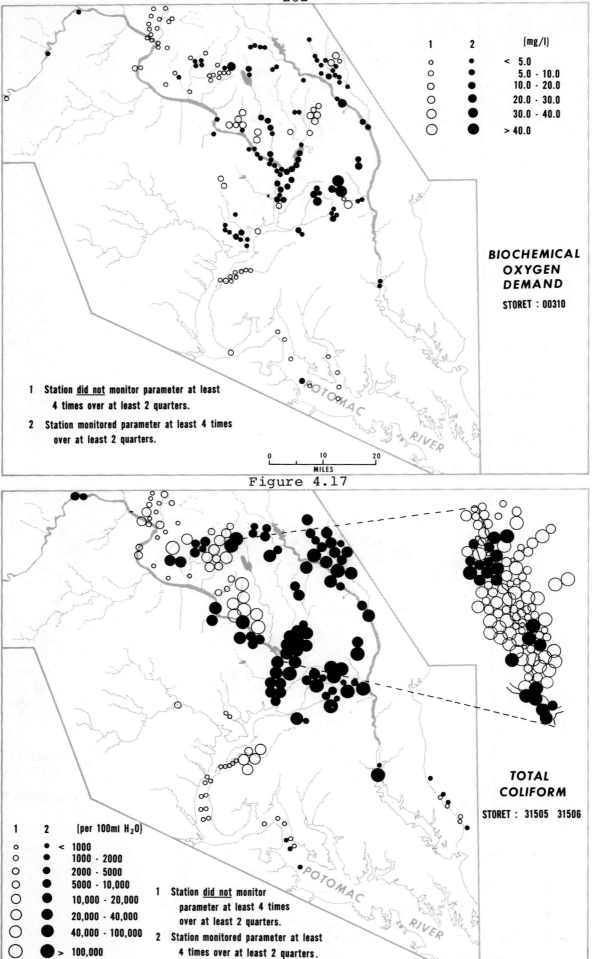

BIOCHEMICAL OXYGEN DEMAND

STORET : 00310

1	2	(mg/l)
○	•	< 5.0
○	•	5.0 - 10.0
○	•	10.0 - 20.0
○	•	20.0 - 30.0
○	•	30.0 - 40.0
○	•	> 40.0

1 Station **did not** monitor parameter at least 4 times over at least 2 quarters.

2 Station monitored parameter at least 4 times over at least 2 quarters.

0   10   20
MILES

Figure 4.17

TOTAL COLIFORM

STORET : 31505 31506

1	2	(per 100ml H₂O)
○	•	< 1000
○	•	1000 - 2000
○	•	2000 - 5000
○	•	5000 - 10,000
○	•	10,000 - 20,000
○	•	20,000 - 40,000
○	•	40,000 - 100,000
○	•	> 100,000

1 Station **did not** monitor parameter at least 4 times over at least 2 quarters.

2 Station monitored parameter at least 4 times over at least 2 quarters.

Figure 4.18

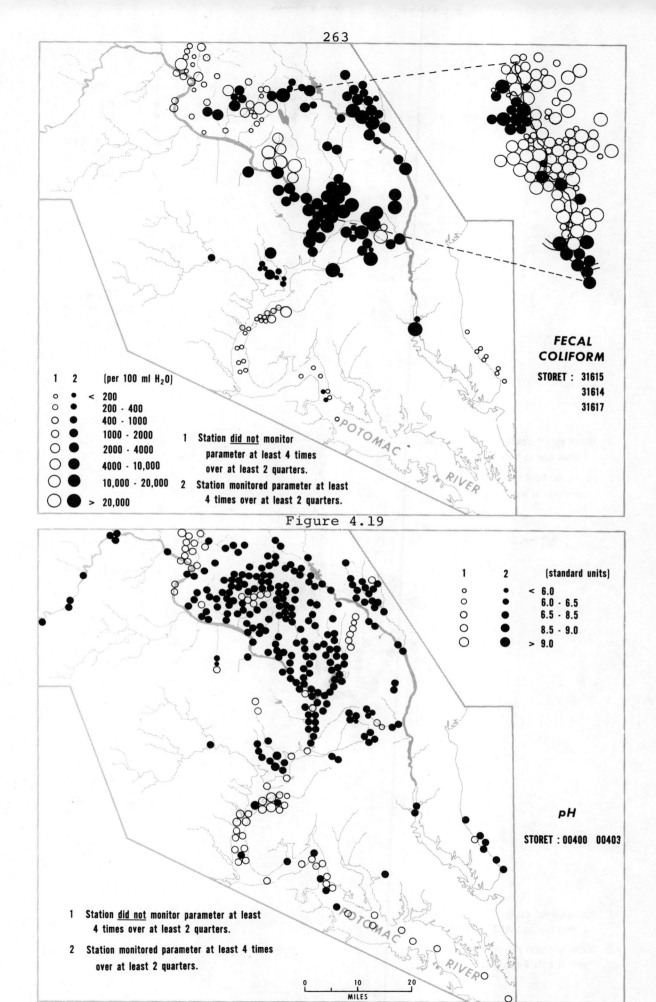

FECAL COLIFORM

STORET : 31615
31614
31617

1 2 (per 100 ml H₂O)

○ ● < 200
○ ● 200 - 400
○ ● 400 - 1000
○ ● 1000 - 2000
○ ● 2000 - 4000
○ ● 4000 - 10,000
○ ● 10,000 - 20,000
○ ● > 20,000

1 Station <u>did not</u> monitor parameter at least 4 times over at least 2 quarters.

2 Station monitored parameter at least 4 times over at least 2 quarters.

Figure 4.19

pH

STORET : 00400 00403

1 2 (standard units)

○ ● < 6.0
○ ● 6.0 - 6.5
○ ● 6.5 - 8.5
○ ● 8.5 - 9.0
○ ● > 9.0

1 Station <u>did not</u> monitor parameter at least 4 times over at least 2 quarters.

2 Station monitored parameter at least 4 times over at least 2 quarters.

0   10   20
MILES

Figure 4.20

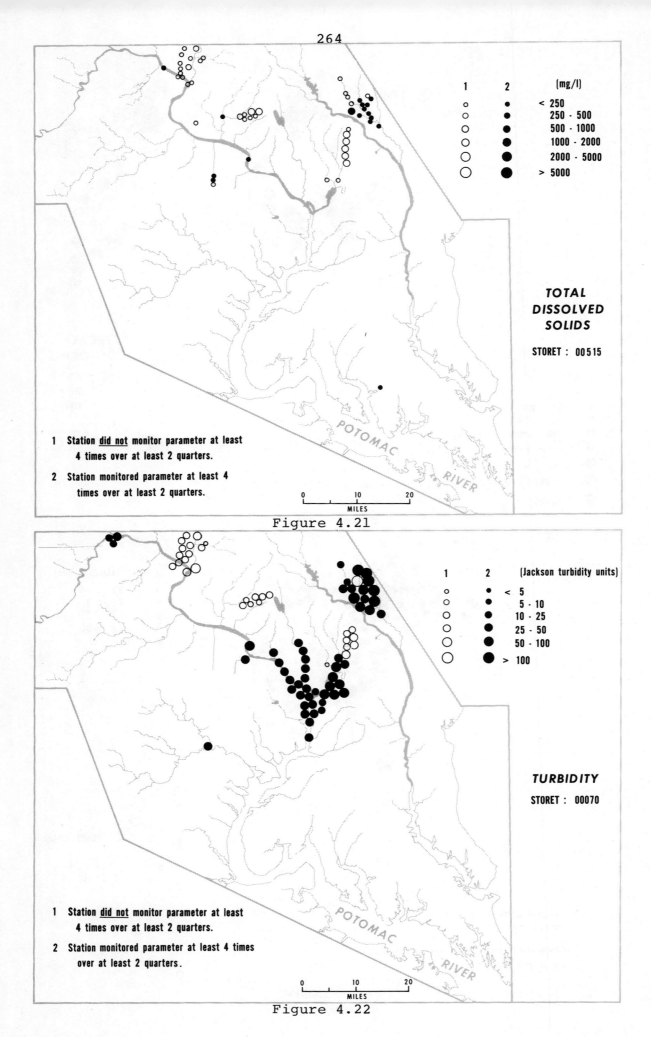

Figure 4.21

Figure 4.22

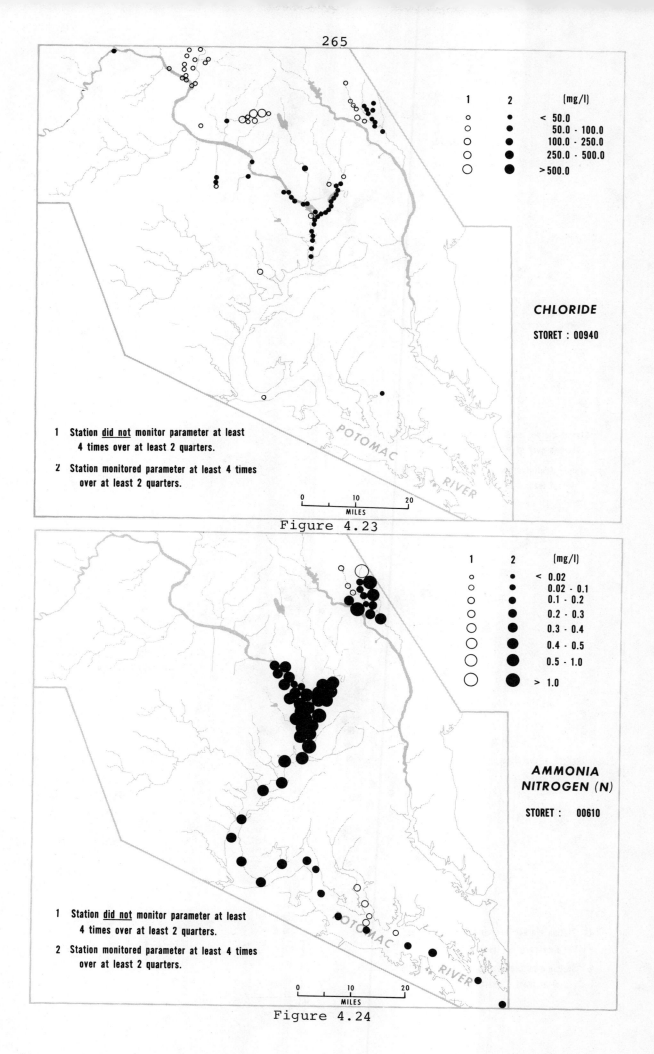

CHLORIDE

STORET : 00940

1 Station _did not_ monitor parameter at least
   4 times over at least 2 quarters.

2 Station monitored parameter at least 4 times
   over at least 2 quarters.

Figure 4.23

**AMMONIA
NITROGEN (N)**

STORET : 00610

1 Station _did not_ monitor parameter at least
   4 times over at least 2 quarters.

2 Station monitored parameter at least 4 times
   over at least 2 quarters.

Figure 4.24

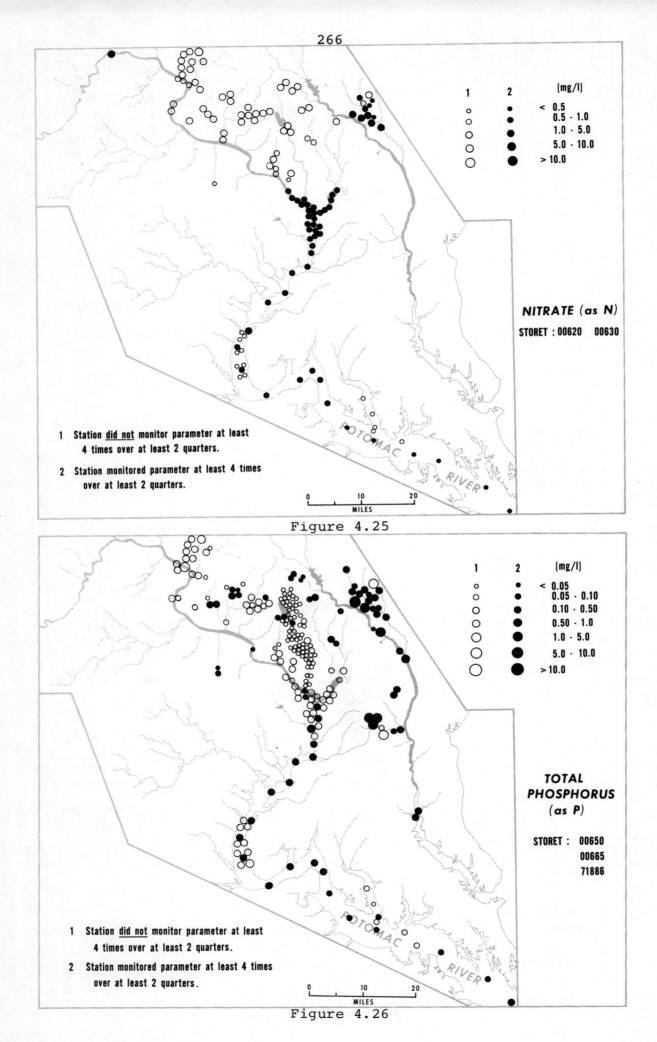

Figure 4.25

NITRATE (as N)

STORET : 00620   00630

(mg/l)
< 0.5
0.5 - 1.0
1.0 - 5.0
5.0 - 10.0
> 10.0

1 Station did not monitor parameter at least
   4 times over at least 2 quarters.

2 Station monitored parameter at least 4 times
   over at least 2 quarters.

0   10   20
MILES

Figure 4.26

TOTAL
PHOSPHORUS
(as P)

STORET :   00650
           00665
           71886

(mg/l)
< 0.05
0.05 - 0.10
0.10 - 0.50
0.50 - 1.0
1.0 - 5.0
5.0 - 10.0
> 10.0

1 Station did not monitor parameter at least
   4 times over at least 2 quarters.

2 Station monitored parameter at least 4 times
   over at least 2 quarters.

0   10   20
MILES

POTOMAC RIVER

BALTIMORE

Baltimore shares the physical setting of Washington, described in the previous section. However, the Baltimore polygon differs in that it contains much heavy industrial activity, concentrated in the urban core surrounding the estuary of the Patapsco River, and extending from this central point in finger-like radiations. The two radials with particularly heavy clusters of industry are the ones on the northeast-southwest axis. A number of important military installations are also located in Baltimore and play a significant part in the economy of the region.

Agriculture is not of particular importance to the economy of the polygon and is not a predominant use of rural lands. The exceptions to this are the Washington and Greenspring valleys, where key agricultural activities occur. Much of the rural open space is devoted to recreational activities, parks and nature preserves. Large areas of wetlands, which play an important role in the ecology of the region, are primarily wildlife sanctuaries. Much of this open space is quickly being turned over to developers as the city expands. Agricultural lands, which are often only marginally profitable in the area, easily succumb to residential and commercial development. Many wetlands have been filled in and used as industrial sites, and this practice continues.

Sewerage discharge at older, inner city locations and urban run-off end up in river estuaries and Chesapeake Bay. Industrial discharge is also a problem in these areas, while ship bilge pumping and oil spills at unloading installations add to the problem. Silt and runoff from construction sites in newly developing areas also runs into the bay and threatens to inadvertently fill up wetland sanctuaries.

Relatively few of these features appear on our maps, however. The Baltimore polygon proved difficult to study because no data were available for the City of Baltimore for 1971, due to a temporary halt in monitoring activities. Therefore most of our station data for the Baltimore retrieval polygon lacked input from that portion which was of greatest concern to our study. However, we felt that the abundance of data for Chesapeake Bay stations might indicate the presence of contaminants derived from the urbanized areas, or from Sparrow's Point where the heaviest industrial concentrations are located.

The majority of the stations for which we received data are located in marine waters of Chesapeake Bay and in the estuarine waters of coastal river mouths. Nearly one-third of the 94 total stations are located on two tributaries in the Susquehanna River Basin. The Susquehanna River contributes pollutants from mining areas and industrialized sections of Central Pennsylvania. With the exception of Chesapeake Bay and the two tributaries of the Susquehanna, station coverage for areas covered by our polygon was wholly inadequate.

Eighty-seven of the 94 total stations were contributed by the Maryland State Department of Environmental Resources. Seventy-five of those stations sampled at least 4 times per year over a two-quarter period or longer. The oxygen measuring parameters, turbidity, the nutrient parameters and total and fecal coliforms were monitored and mapped (Figures 4.27-4.36). Inorganics, chloride, fluoride and trace metals were lacking.

These are the highlights of the maps which, to reiterate, do not cover any inner-city locations: only one station exceeded the primary contact reference level for dissolved oxygen of 5.0 mg/l; of 84 total stations reporting total coliforms, only 8 exceeded the public water supply reference level of 10,000; for fecal coliforms, 9 out of 84 stations exceeded the Public Water Supply reference level, while 25 percent of the stations failed to meet standards for Primary Contact ecreation; 8 stations also exceeded the Primary Contact Recreational level for pH, while 76 percent of all stations exceeded the Freshwater Aquatic Life standard for turbidity. Thirty-five stations exceeded the nutrient standard for phosphorus.

Table 4.4

Baltimore

Parameter	Total		Inner City		Remainder		Details By Water Use Designation						
							Inner City				Remainder		
	N	P	N	P	N	P	WD	R	E	PR	R	E	PR
DO	96	19	0	-	96	19	FA	-	-	-	0	0	-
							MA_1	-	-	-	0	0	-
							MA_2	-	-	-	12	13	0
							PC	-	-	-	1	1	0
TOT COLI	84	81	0	-	84	81	AL_1	-	-	-	3	4	100
							AL_2	-	-	-	15	18	80
							PS	-	-	-	8	10	100
FEC COLI	84	85	0	-	84	85	AI	-	-	-	13	15	100
							AL_1	-	-	-	6	7	100
							AL_2	-	-	-	13	15	100
							PS	-	-	-	9	11	100
							UR_1	-	-	-	6	7	100
							UR_2	-	-	-	9	11	100
							PC_1	-	-	-	21	25	86
							PC_2	-	-	-	29	35	86
PH	72	33	0	-	72	33	FA	-	-	-	1	1	100
							MA	-	-	-	8	11	38
							PS	-	-	-	0	0	-
							PC_1	-	-	-	0	0	-
							PC_2	-	-	-	8	11	38
TURB	38	58	0	-	38	58	FA_1	-	-	-	0	0	-
							FA_2	-	-	-	29	76	48
NH3	53	13	0	-	53	13	FA	-	-	-	6	11	0
							MA	-	-	-	1	2	0
							PS	-	-	-	0	0	-
NO3	87	77	0	-	87	77	AL	-	-	-	0	0	-
							PS	-	-	-	0	0	-
P	88	23	0	-	88	23	NS	-	-	-	35	40	23

Code:

N = Number of stations
P = Percentage of stations below
    cutoff value
E = Percentage of stations exceeding
    reference level
R = Number of stations exceeding
    reference level
PR = Percentage of stations exceeding
    reference level below cutoff

Water Use Designation (WD):

AI = Agricultural, Irrigation
AL = Agricultural, Livestock
FA = Freshwater Aquatic Life
MA = Marine Water Aquatic Life
PS = Public Water Supply Intake
UR = Undesignated Recreational
PC = Primary Contact Recreational
ST = Secondary Treatment Standard
NS = Nutrient Standard

Note: Subscripts refer to different standards, where more than one standard is specified for a given water use designation.

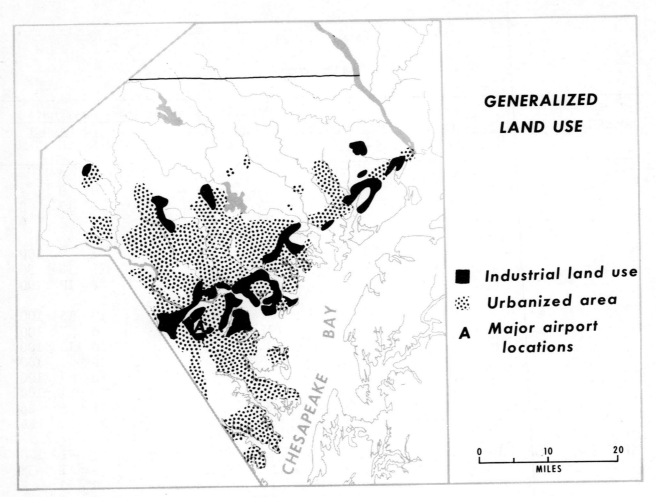

GENERALIZED
LAND USE

■ Industrial land use
⣿ Urbanized area
A Major airport
locations

0   10   20
MILES

Figure 4.27

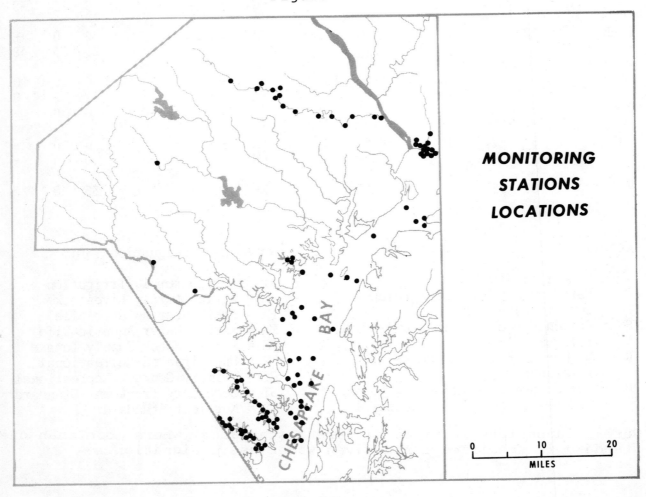

MONITORING
STATIONS
LOCATIONS

0   10   20
MILES

Figure 4.28

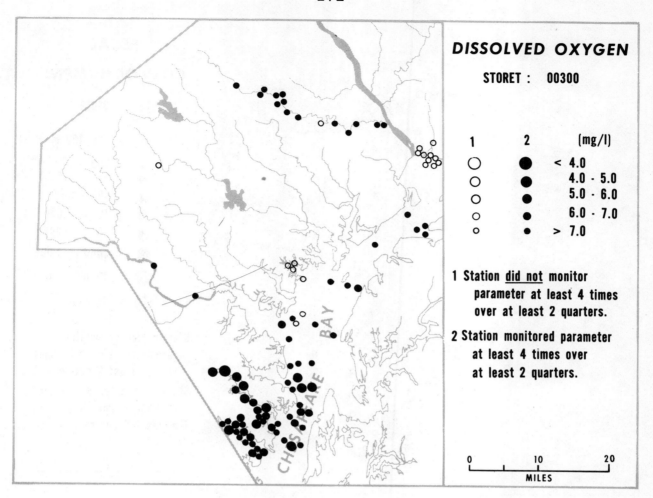

DISSOLVED OXYGEN

STORET : 00300

Figure 4.29

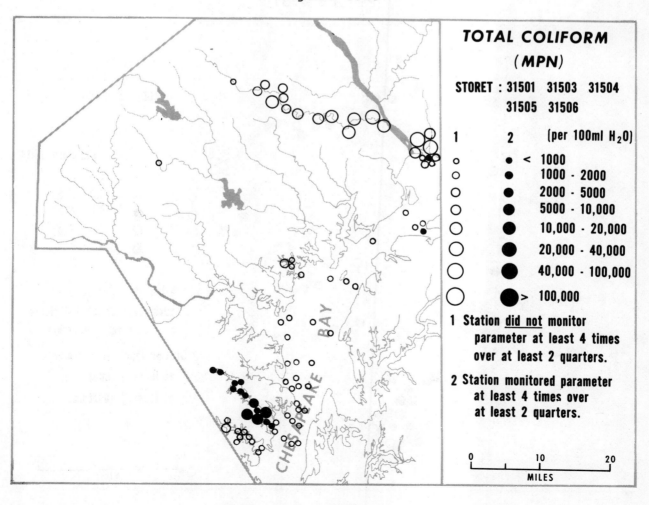

TOTAL COLIFORM

(MPN)

STORET : 31501 31503 31504
31505 31506

Figure 4.30

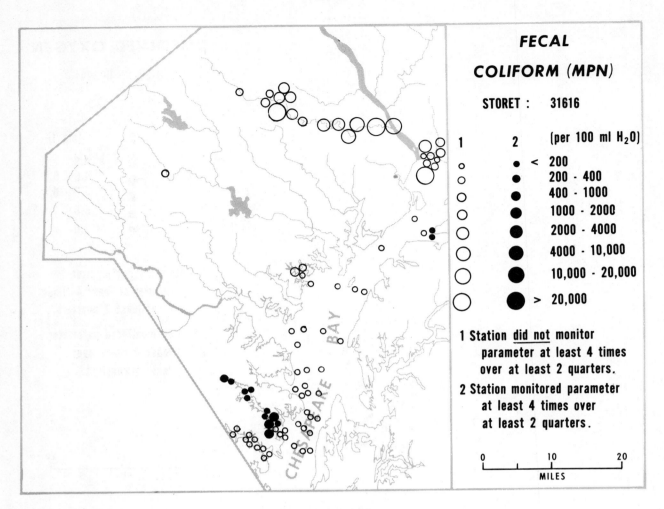

Figure 4.31

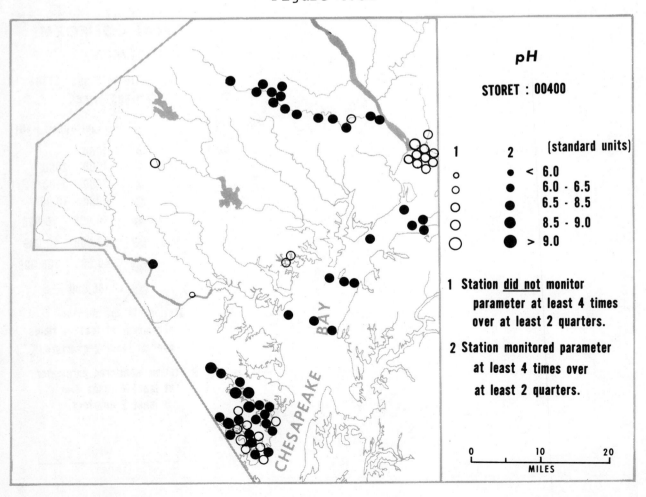

Figure 4.32

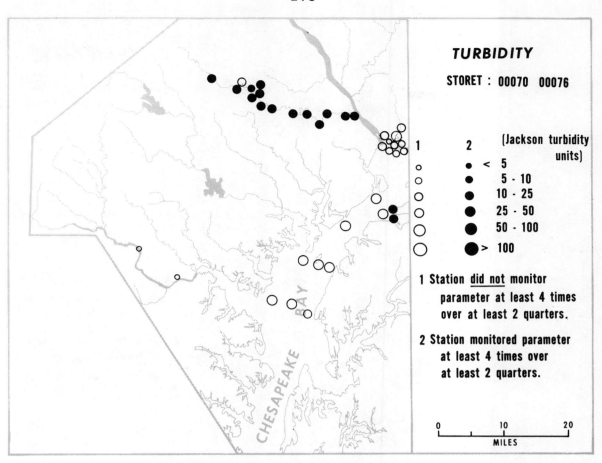

Figure 4.33

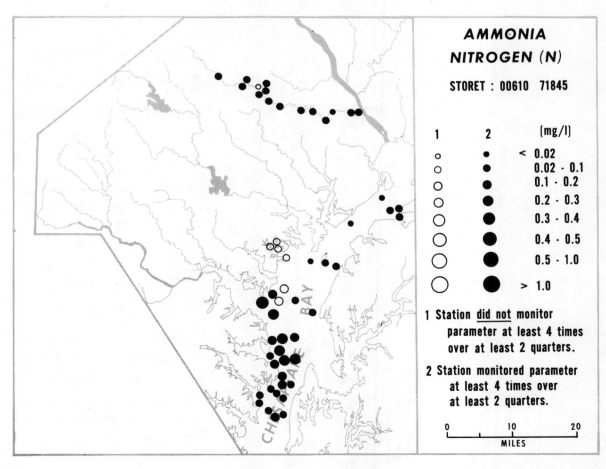

Figure 4.34

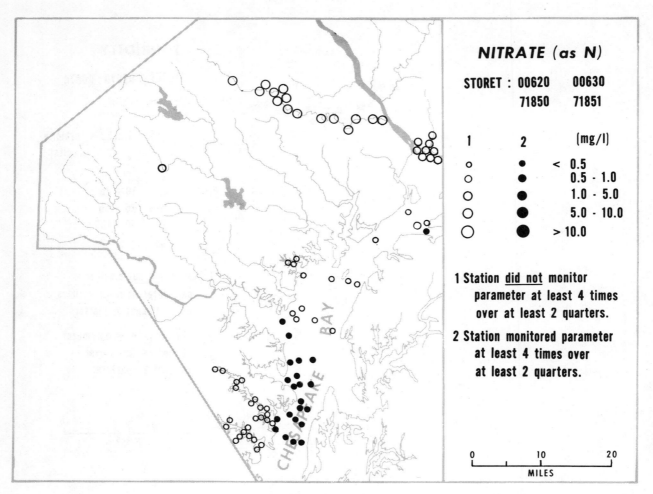

Figure 4.35

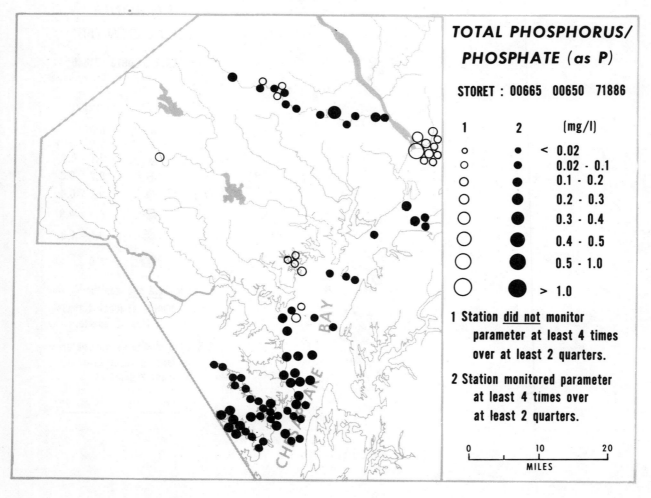

Figure 4.36

ROCHESTER

Rochester is located on the shores of Lake Ontario in the Finger Lakes region of New York. The Genesee River and Lake Ontario are the main water bodies in the drainage basin. The Genesee River originates in Pennsylvania's Allegheny Mountains and flows northward until finally terminating in Lake Ontario. The main river has 31 tributaries and there are six major lakes in the region, five of which are natural, part of the Finger Lakes chain. Flow in the Genesee is regulated by Mt. Morris Dam (40 miles south of the City of Rochester). The southern portion of the drainage basin is located in the Allegheny Plateau.

The climate of the region is temperate and is influenced by its close proximity to Lake Ontario to the north and the rugged topography to the south. The climate is also influenced by the proximity of the area to the so-called St. Lawrence storm track. Moisture originating in the Gulf of Mexico is carried to the Atlantic Ocean through the St. Lawrence Valley by means of cyclonic systems and is precipitated en-route. Average yearly precipitation in Rochester is 30 inches.

Land use patterns in the region are complex and diversified. Industrial establishments and commercial districts are located mainly in and around village population centers and in towns adjacent to Rochester; the heaviest concentration of these activities is found in Rochester itself. Industrial growth has been especially pronounced in suburban Rochester, where numerous light industrial establishments have been locating in recent years. Food products and processing is the leading type of industrial activity. Stone quarries and sand pits are prevalent to the southwest of Rochester. Salt mining and processing take place at Retsoff and Silver Springs. Oil production is a major activity around Wellsville.

Numerous state, county and municipal parks comprise public recreational lands. An important wildlife refuge and preserve is located west of Churchville; and a large state park, through which the Genesee

River flows, is located in the area. Many of the small lakes and ponds found in the polygon are recreational in character.

The Genesee River Basin is predominantly agricultural, with farming being the leading land use. The Ontario Plain, encompassing the northern portion of the basin, is given over to truck farming, with a prevalence of vegetable crops and fruit orchards. The central portion of the basin is devoted to vegetable crops and dairy farming. Vegetables are raised chiefly in the valley bottomlands, while dairy farming takes place primarily in the uplands. Dairy farming predominates in the southern part of the basin on the Allegheny Plateau, where pasturage is grown to provision cattle.

The main river and a number of its tributaries are intensively used in many places for the disposal of waste. The principal types appear to be milk and cannery process waste and municipal sewage disposal.

The Genesee River also receives sewage periodically from an overflow relief sewer, industrial waste via a village storm sewer and primary effluent from the village sewage treatment plant. Downstream at Belmont, the river takes untreated sewage from the city and wastewater from a milk plant. At Mt. Morris, the river receives heavy discharge loads of process waste from a cannery. At Avon, the river again receives waste from a food processing plant and effluent from a sewage treatment plant.

Red Creek receives discharges from a dairy and a number of private residences. There are two major discharge locations on Black Creek. At Bergen, partially treated wastes from a cannery are discharged into the creek and at Churchville the creek receives sewage from the village via multiple storm sewer outlets.

Oatka Creek takes plating and knitting mill wastes at Warsaw, together with primary effluent from the sewage treatment plant. At Le Roy, the creek receives industrial wastes and cooling water from a number of outlets and raw sewage from multiple village storm sewers and private outlets. Near Garbutt, mine drainage is conveyed to the creek; and at Scottsville, primary effluent from the village sewage treatment plant is discharged into the creek.

Lakeville discharges waste from a milk plant into nearby water-ways and Dansville village sewage treatment plant and industrial cool-ing water are discharged into a local stream. There are numerous other minor discharge points on the hydrologic network, many of which come from private residences as well as municipal and industrial sources.

Our STORET PGM-INVENT for Rochester listed 118 water quality sta-tions, well-distributed throughout the polygon. Many inner city or near-urban stations are located on the Genesee River and on Irondequoit Creek to the east. Sampling points are well located with respect to confluences and have a favorable main stream to tributary ratio. Several stations are located on Lake Ontario and three are situated on canals. Several sampling stations are on rivers which have been somewhat altered by channelization and dams.

Four monitoring agencies provided the data retrieved from STORET. The U.S. Geological Survey and the New York State Department of En-vironmental Conservation accounted for 100 of the 118 stations. All of the parameters we selected for mapping were available except fecal coliform bacteria, MBAS and all trace metals excluding iron. However, few samples were taken and the period of record at each station tended to be short.

In 1973 an investigation on the water quality of the Rochester region was undertaken by the Environmental Protection Agency. This investigation, published in 1975 by O'Brien and Gere Engineers, Inc., and entitled, Water Pollution Investigation: Genesee River and Roches-ter Area, produced a variety of interesting results that are confirmed in our maps (Figures 4.39-4.51).

They found that DO levels decreased upstream from Rochester due to the discharge of the Gates-Chili-Ogden Sewage Treatment Plant; stormwater overflows and/or dry weather flows from the combined sewer overflow network of Rochester; the heavy contribution of organic loading from parks; the Eastman Kodak Wastewater Treatment Plant; and the Barge (Erie) Canal. The report concluded that four major point source discharges have a significant effect on the DO levels present in the Genesee River. These four discharges are:

1. Oatka Creek where it enters the Genesee;

2. Gates-Chili-Ogden Sewage Treatment Plant "which contributes a significant carbonaceous and nitrogenous ultimate oxygen demand load on the River just upstream of the point of entry of the Barge Canal waters;"

3. Barge (Erie) Canal;

4. Kodak Sewage Treatment Plant discharge "which contributes a significant carbonaceous and nitrogeneous ultimate oxygen demand loading on the Genesee River just prior to its discharge to Lake Ontario;"

NH_3 and NO_3 were found to increase at the Gates-Chili-Ogden Sewage Treatment Plant, the Erie Canal, the sewage outfalls for the City of Rochester and the Eastman Kodak Treatment Plant. BOD increased in value the nearer to Rochester, from a concentration of 2.0 mg/l upstream to 3.6 mg/l near the city limits. Chlorine ranged from 64 mg/l to 139 mg/l. Chlorine loadings due to the sewage treatment plants were not significant however. Fluorides averaged .05 mg/l and the evidence was not conclusive of a particular point source.

High phosphorus levels were found near the industrial discharges (Eastman Kodak, Bausch and Lomb, Gates-Chili-Ogden Sewage Treatment Plant) and from non-point sources especially rural cropland.

Other factors influencing water quality in the Rochester area appear to be:

1. Soil erosion in the upper reaches of the Genesee resulting in extreme variations in turbidity,

2. Deteriorated water quality from the Barge Canal particularly at low flow,

3. Redredging in the Rochester Harbor,

4. Sewer overflows for the City of Rochester,

5. Industrial and municipal discharge of nutrients, heavy metals, and oxygen demanding substances,

6. Non-point sources of nutrient and oxygen demanding materials from cultivated and forest components of the drainage basin.

The report concluded that". . . It is very difficult to describe the present status of the Genesee River in qualitative terms. However, in comparing the study measured concentrations of the Genesee River prior to its intrusion into Lake Ontario, we find that the levels of most pollutants are about 2-3 times higher than the corresponding levels in the Lake measured at a point just west of the embayment area."

Table 4.5
Rochester

Parameter	Total		Inner City		Remainder		Details By Water Use Designation						
								Inner City			Remainder		
	N	P	N	P	N	P	WD	R	E	PR	R	E	PR
DO	52	58	11	45	41	61	FA	2	18	100	0	0	-
							PC	2	18	100	1	2	100
BOD	42	55	10	50	32	56	ST	0	0	-	0	0	-
TOT COLI	33	79	8	75	25	80	AL₁	5	63	100	6	24	67
							AL₂	6	75	75	13	52	77
							PS	5	63	100	9	36	78
PH	103	83	13	62	90	86	FA	0	0	-	0	0	-
							PS	0	0	-	0	0	-
							PC₁	0	0	-	0	0	-
							PC₂	0	0	-	4	5	100
TDS	68	97	4	100	64	97	AI₁	0	0	-	1	2	100
							AI₂	0	0	-	5	8	100
							PS	0	0	-	16	25	88
TURB	50	72	11	55	39	77	FA₁	1	9	100	5	13	40
							FA₂	10	91	50	24	62	75
CL	107	70	17	47	90	74	PS	0	0	-	3	3	100
F	52	96	2	100	50	96	AI₁	0	0	-	0	0	-
							AI₂	0	0	-	0	0	-
							AI₃	0	0	-	0	0	-
							AL	0	0	-	0	0	-
NH3	77	77	8	38	69	81	FA	8	100	38	60	87	80
							PS	2	25	100	4	6	100
NO3	77	78	8	38	69	83	AL	0	0	-	0	0	-
							PS	0	0	-	0	0	-
P	17	82	3	100	14	79	NS	3	100	100	8	57	100
SO4	71	76	7	29	64	81	PS	0	0	-	9	14	89
FE	63	83	6	33	57	88	AI₁	0	0	-	0	0	-
							AI₂	0	0	-	0	0	-
							PS	0	0	-	1	2	0

Code:

N = Number of stations
P = Percentage of stations below cutoff value
E = Percentage of stations exceeding reference level
R = Number of stations exceeding reference level
PR = Percentage of stations exceeding reference level below cutoff

Water Use Designation (WD):

AI = Agricultural, Irrigation
AL = Agricultural, Livestock
FA = Freshwater, Aquatic Life
MA = Marine Water Aquatic Life
PS = Public Water Supply Intake
UR = Undesignated Recreational
PC = Primary Contact Recreational
ST = Secondary Treatment Standard
NA = Nutrient Standard

Note: Subscripts refer to different standards, where more than one standard is specified for a given water use designation.

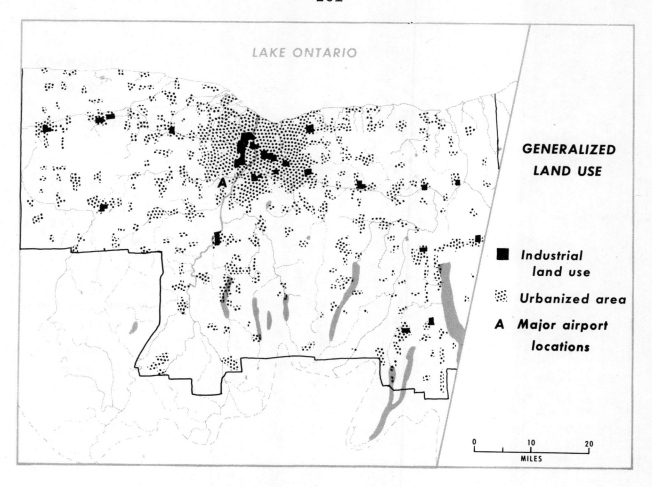

Figure 4.37

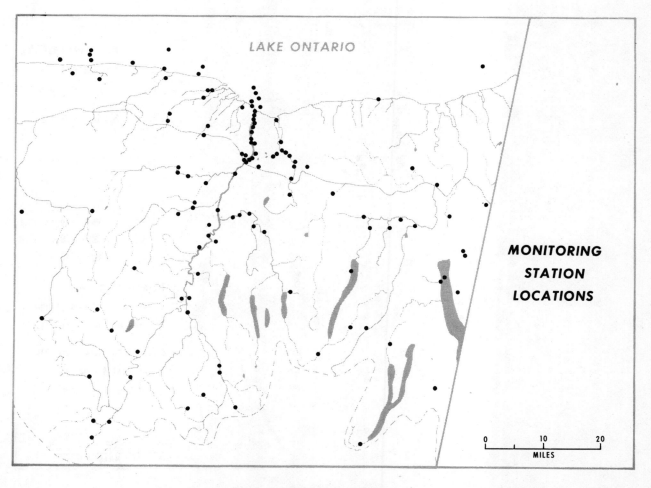

Figure 4.38

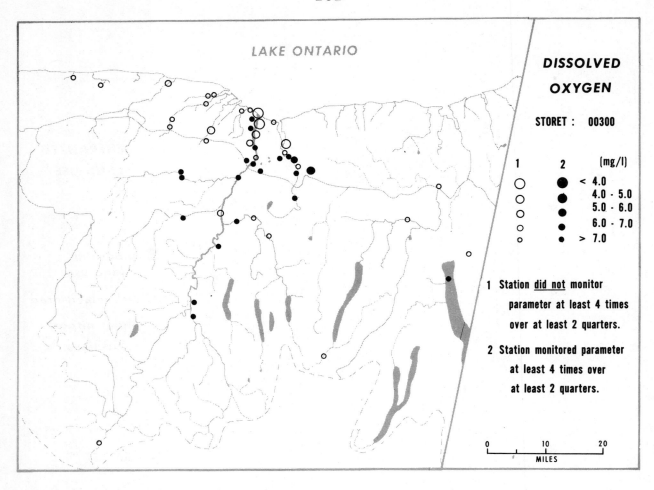

Figure 4.39

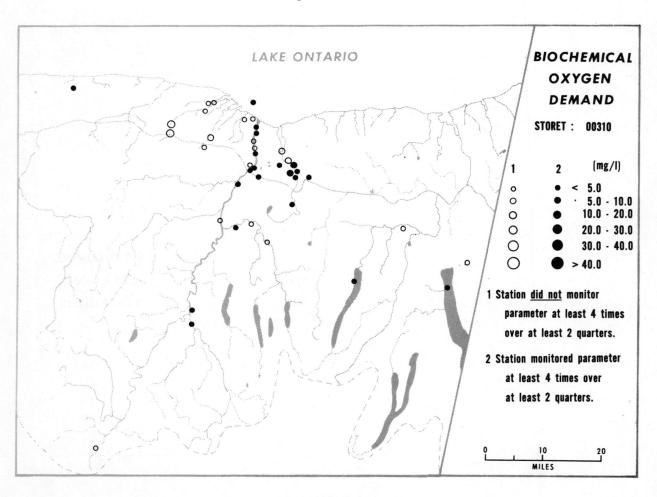

Figure 4.40

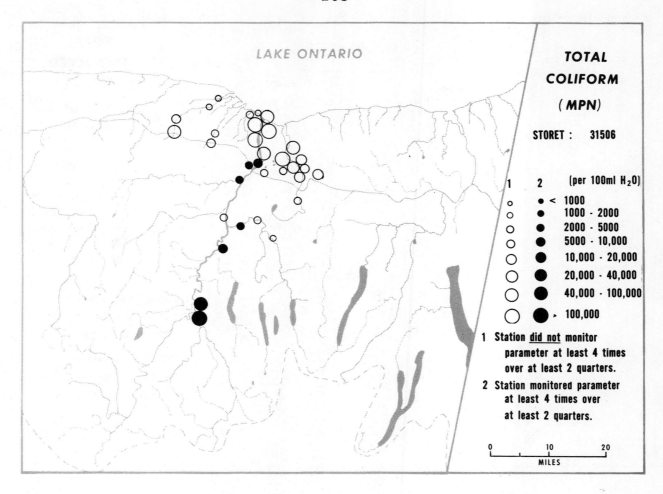

Figure 4.41

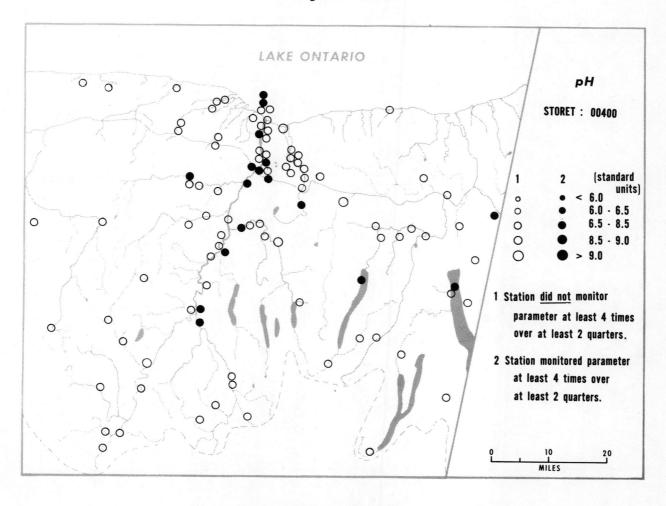

Figure 4.42

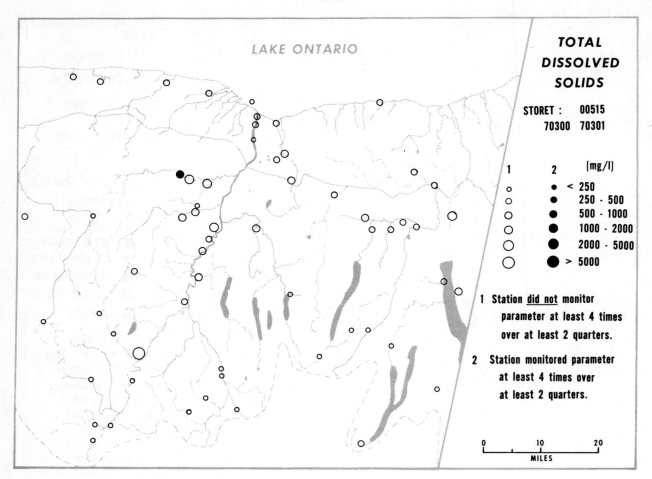

Figure 4.43

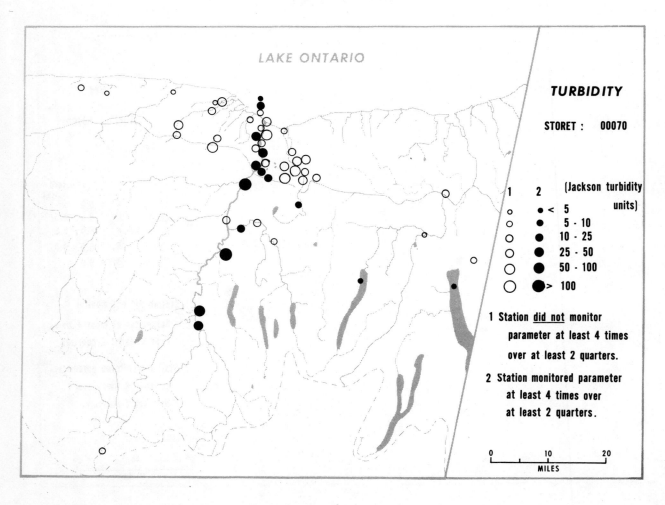

Figure 4.44

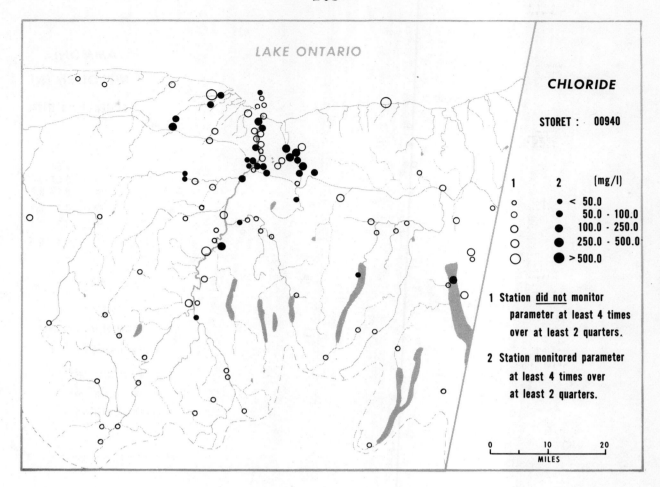

Figure 4.45

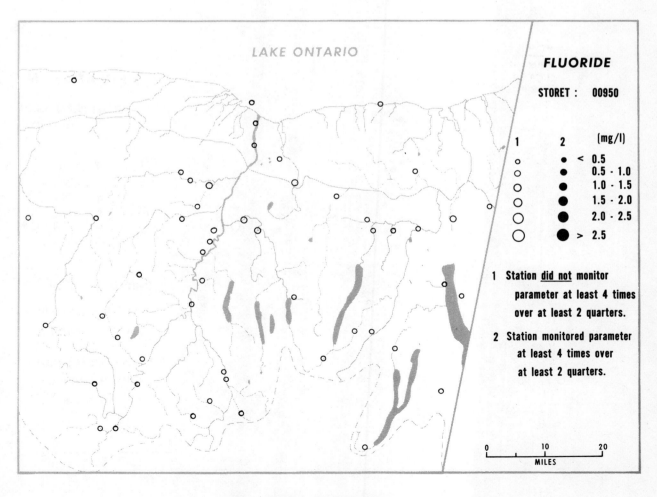

Figure 4.46

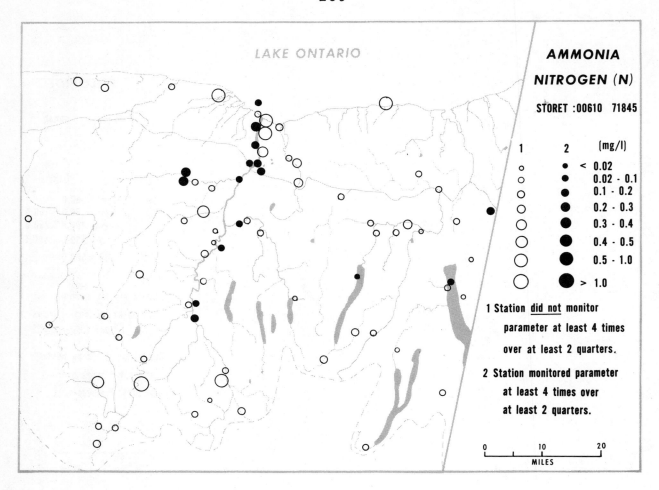

Figure 4.47

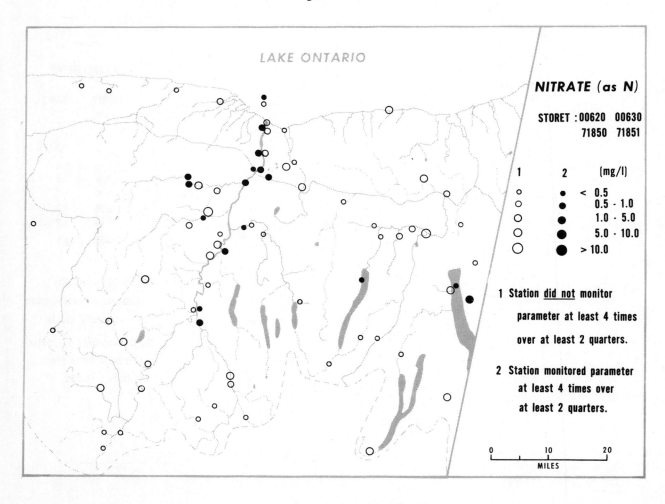

Figure 4.48

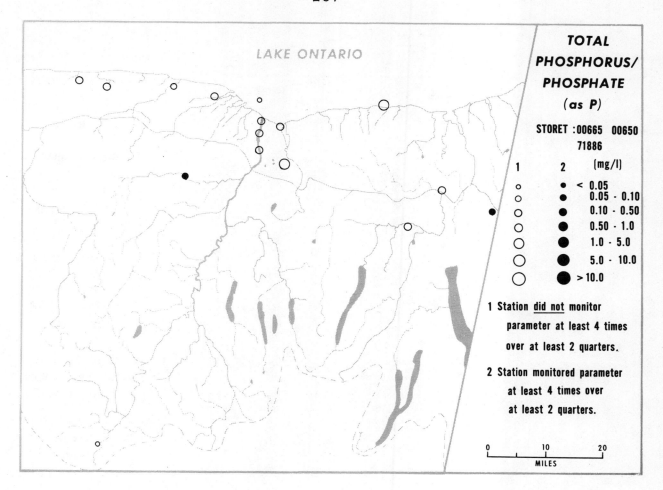

Figure 4.49

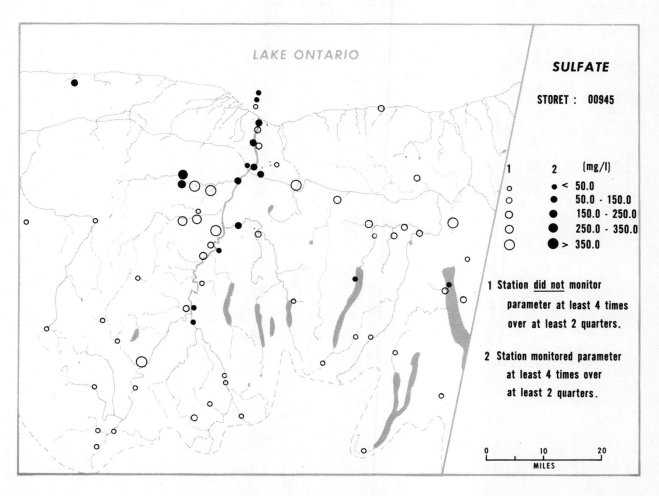

Figure 4.50

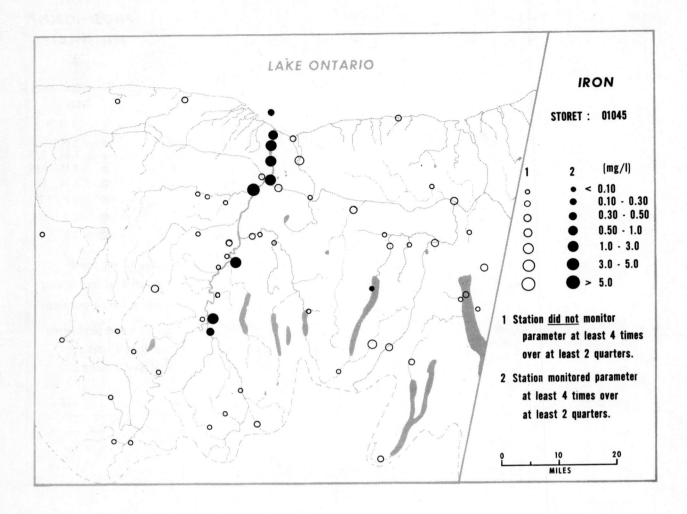

Figure 4.51

CINCINNATI

The area within the Cincinnati polygon extends across two physiographic provinces, the Interior Low Plateaus province of the Interior Plains and the Central Lowlands. Surface features range from gently rolling to more rugged terrain. North of the Ohio River, major glacial valleys run south into the Ohio and divide the area. These broad flat-floored river valleys, the Whitewater River Valley, the Great Miami River Valley, the Mill Creek Valley and the Little Miami River Valley, are where the major urban concentrations were established. The Licking River divides northern Kentucky as it flows to the Ohio.

The central portion of the Cincinnati polygon is the most heavily urbanized of the region, with industrial, residential and commercial uses tending to gravitate toward the Ohio River and the urban core of Cincinnati. The north central area between the Great Miami River and the Little Miami River is heavily urbanized throughout and contains the major industrial clusters of the polygon. The largest municipalities, including that of Cincinnati, are found in this area, which is almost totally developed. The heaviest concentration of industry is located in the core district of Cincinnati along the Ohio River and Mill Creek. The east branch of the Mill Creek drainage basin is the most heavily industrialized area outside the urban core area of Cincinnati. To the northwest of Cincinnati is a large United States atomic energy plant near the Great Miami River. On the south bank of the Ohio River, opposite the City of Cincinnati, along the Licking River, is another major industrial area, including a large steel plant.

Rugged topographic conditions in outlying areas do not permit extensive agricultural uses. Where agricultural uses do occur, the raising of livestock is the predominant form.

The areas of greatest wastewater discharge are found in the lower reaches of the Whitewater-Miami River Basin, including large amounts of both municipal discharge and stormwater runoff as well as industrial effluent. Major sewer outfalls are located on Mill Creek where it meets the Ohio, on the Little Miami just east of Cincinnati and Muddy Creek where it joins the Ohio. The sewage system is one which combines stormwater runoff and wastewater flow in the same conduit.

In 1971, there was a total of 141 water quality monitoring points within our retrieval polygon.

The Ohio state EPA accounted for 60 percent of the total number of stations for the polygon, but there were few readings per station in the STORET data. The USGS and National EPA networks accounted for most of the remainder. The total includes several stations on Kentucky tributaries to the Ohio River. The sampling points were well-distributed throughout the Ohio State portion of the drainage net. Within that section, surveillance was maintained at all confluences as well as at water intakes of small municipalities upstream from Cincinnati. Our station maps indicate that the inner portion of the central city was not heavily monitored, but the abundance of stations at the upstream and downstream margins of the core area insures representative surveillance. Nearly all testing points were on rivers or at water filtration plant intakes from streams. Few stations were located on dams, lakes or reservoirs. However, the nature of some of the many Ohio EPA stations is not clearly designated in the station location-description code information appearing on our printout. There is a possibility of data concerning partially-treated water appearing on the same maps as data from raw intake unprocessed water sampling point. The remainder of the polygon received poor coverage in the STORET data lists, especially the Whitewater River in Indiana and substantial portions of the Licking and Kentucky Rivers in Kentucky. The Great Miami River, the Little Miami River and Mill Creek sub-basins were the most extensively monitored streams. The industrialized sections along the Ohio River show only a few water quality stations.

Despite this extensive surveillance network, there was failure to adequately monitor several important parameters in the Cincinnati area in 1971, according to the STORET data, however. The oxygen demanding, microbiological and inorganic water-quality variables were seldom sampled. Suspended solids determinations were seldom performed. Dissolved oxygen, pH and conductivity were the most commonly monitored parameters. Although the percentage of stations monitoring trace metals far exceeded that for the other sample cities, the number of readings per station was low, usually one or two samples per year.

Despite these difficulties, our parameter maps do indicate an urban-oriented pollution problem with respect to several measures of water quality. Rural areas in Kentucky and Ohio had the lowest levels of contamination. Distinctly higher concentrations of pollution existed on the Great Miami River and the Ohio River just downstream from Cincinnati. The mouths of several Ohio River tributaries exhibited high levels of turbidity. The mouth of Licking Creek in Kentucky also had high levels of ammonia.

The Great Miami River appears to have had a serious microbiological and nutrient pollution problem in 1971. Dissolved oxygen readings reached their lowest point on the Great Miami River north of Middletown at New Baltimore. Total and fecal coliform levels were extremely high near the mouth of the river with the highest readings being taken in winter and spring. The Great Miami, especially the lower urbanized portion, also had high levels of the following parameters: turbidity, phosphorus and ammonia.

The main channel of the Ohio showed a marked increase in pollution concentrations immediately downstream from Cincinnati, especially turbidity and total and fecal coliform bacteria.

Most trace metals, with the exception of lead and cadmium, chloride, sulfate, fluoride, nitrate, pH and total dissolved solids had low levels in relation to their recommended criteria for most parts of the polygon. Of the measures of water quality whose values significantly exceeded the reference levels, the coliforms, ammonia and phosphorus showed the largest numbers of stations in excess.

For total coliforms, 86 percent of the inner city stations and 43 percent of the remainder exceeded both the Public Water Supply and Agricultural livestock levels. For fecal coliforms, all stations were above the most stringent Primary Contact standard of 200/100 ml. For the Public Water Supply category, fecal coliform levels surpassed the Public Water Supply reference value of 2,000/100 ml at 86 percent of the inner city and 29 percent of the remainder of the stations. All stations measuring ammonia exceeded Freshwater Aquatic Life standards, while only one inner city and three remaining stations of the total sixteen stations exceeded Public Water Supply levels. Of the 40 stations which sampled phosphorus, 11 (92 percent) of the inner city stations and 21 (75 percent) of the outer stations of the polygon exceeded the .1 mg/l reference level.

For the 97 stations which monitored turbidity, 9 inner city (33 percent) and 9 outside of it (13 percent) were above the 10 JTU recommended level for Aquatic Life. Our lead and cadmium maps, based on many stations each with few readings, showed slightly higher levels of those parameters on the Great Miami and the Ohio Rivers, and at the mouths of the Little Miami and Licking Rivers. Only a small percentage of the stations were above the reference levels.

Table 4.6

Cincinnati

Parameter	Total		Inner City		Remainder		Details By Water Use Designation						
								Inner City			Remainder		
	N	P	N	P	N	P	WD	R	E	PR	R	E	PR
DO	20	20	11	18	9	22	FA	0	0	-	0	0	-
							PC	0	0	-	1	11	0
BOD	14	14	7	14	7	14	ST	0	0	-	0	0	-
TOT COLI	14	0	7	0	7	0	AL_1	5	71	0	2	29	0
							AL_2	6	86	0	3	43	0
							PS	6	86	0	3	43	0
FEC COLI	14	0	7	0	7	0	AI	6	86	0	3	43	0
							AL_1	3	43	0	1	14	0
							AL_2	6	86	0	3	43	0
							PS	6	86	0	2	29	0
							UR_1	3	43	0	1	14	0
							UR_2	6	86	0	2	29	0
							PC_1	6	86	0	5	71	0
							PC_2	7	100	0	7	100	0
PH	124	59	32	56	92	62	FA	3	9	100	2	2	0
							PS	3	9	100	2	2	0
							PC_1	3	9	100	2	2	0
							PC_2	3	9	100	5	5	0
TDS	30	60	7	43	23	65	AI_1	0	0	-	0	0	-
							AI^2	0	0	-	0	0	-
							PS^2	0	0	-	1	4	100
TURB	97	67	27	67	70	67	FA_1	1	4	0	2	3	0
							FA_2	9	33	11	9	13	11
CL	125	60	33	52	92	63	PS	0	0	-	0	0	-
F	116	78	27	81	89	78	AI_1	0	0	-	0	0	-
							AI_2	0	0	-	2	2	50
							AI	0	0	-	5	6	80
							AL	0	0	-	2	2	50
NH3	16	0	7	0	9	0	FA	7	100	0	9	100	0
							PS	1	6	0	3	33	0
NO3	112	62	31	58	81	63	AL	0	0	-	0	0	-
							PS	0	0	-	0	0	-
P	40	53	12	25	28	64	NS	11	92	25	21	75	67
SO4	127	64	34	62	93	65	PS	0	0	-	0	0	-

Parameter	Total		Inner City		Remainder		Details By Water Use Designation Inner City				Remainder		
	N	P	N	P	N	P	WD	R	E	PR	R	E	PR
CD	93	86	27	100	66	80	AI_1	8	29	100	6	9	100
							AI_2	0	0	-	0	0	-
							AL	0	0	-	0	0	-
							FA_1	0	0	-	0	0	-
							FA_2	8	29	100	8	12	100
							PS	8	29	100	6	9	100
CU	93	86	27	93	66	77	AI_1	0	0	-	0	0	-
							AI_2	0	0	-	0	0	-
							AL	0	0	-	0	0	-
							PS	0	0	-	0	0	-
FE	101	86	27	96	74	82	AI_1	0	0	-	0	0	-
							AI_2	0	0	-	1	100	100
							PS	3	11	100	12	16	92
PB	94	81	26	96	67	76	AI	0	0	-	0	0	-
							AL	0	0	-	0	0	-
							FA	2	7	100	0	0	-
							PS	7	26	100	5	7	100
NI	91	86	27	96	64	81	AI_1	0	0	-	0	0	-
							AI_2	0	0	-	0	0	-
ZN	92	72	26	92	66	64	AL	0	0	-	0	0	-
							PS	0	0	-	0	0	-

Code:

N = Number of stations
P = Percentage of stations below cutoff value
E = Percentage of stations exceeding reference level
R = Number of stations exceeding reference level
PR = Percentage of stations exceeding reference level below cutoff

Water Use Designation (WD):

AI = Agricultural, Irrigation
AL = Agricultural, Livestock
FA = Freshwater Aquatic Life
MA = Marine Water Aquatic Life
PS = Public Water Supply Intake
UR = Undesignated Recreational
PC = Primary Contact Recreational
ST = Secondary Treatment Standard
NS = Nutrient Standard

Note: Subscripts refer to different standards, where more than one standard is specified for a given water use designation.

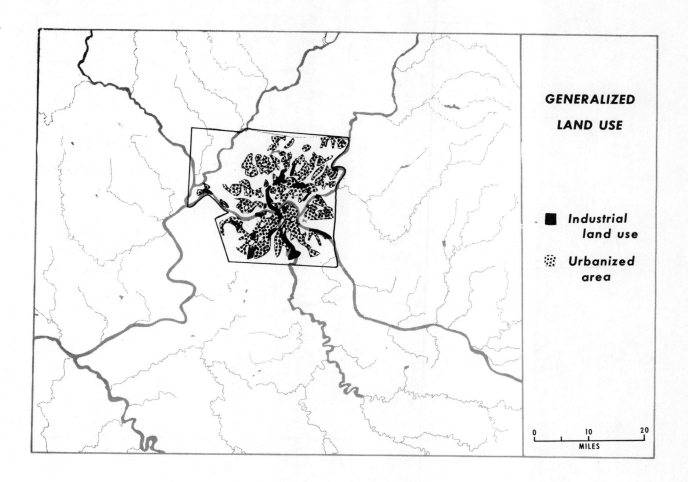

Figure 4.52

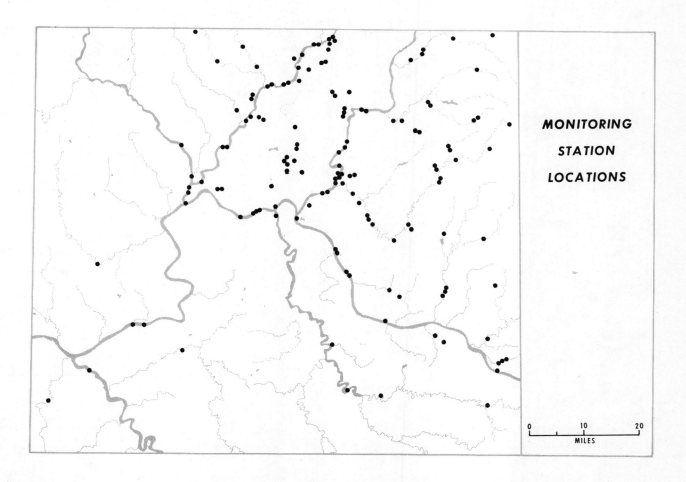

Figure 4.53

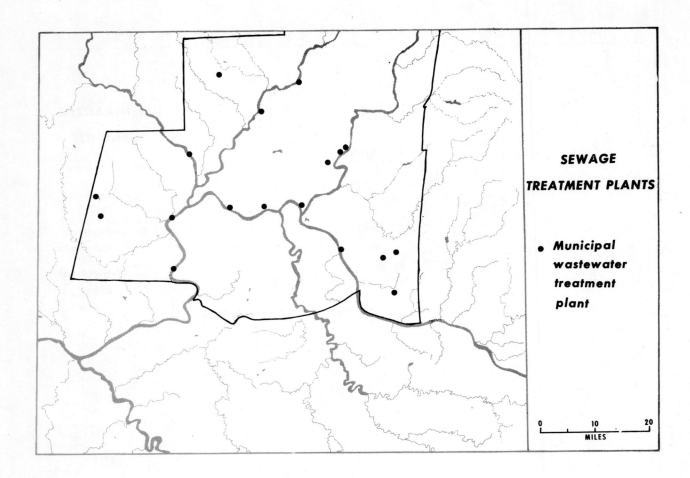

Figure 4.54

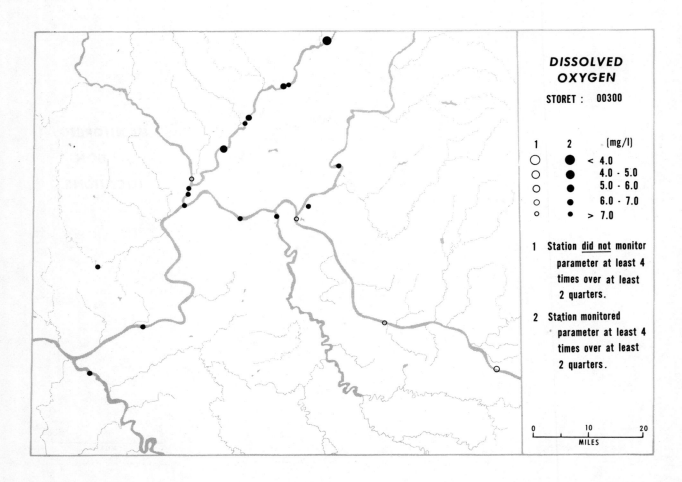

Figure 4.55

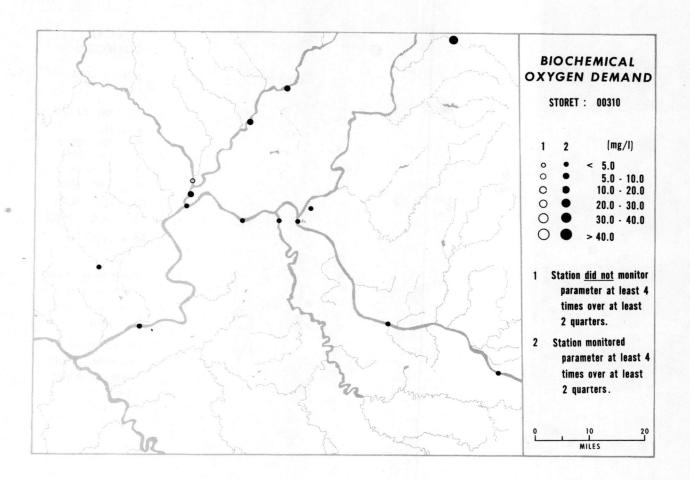

Figure 4.56

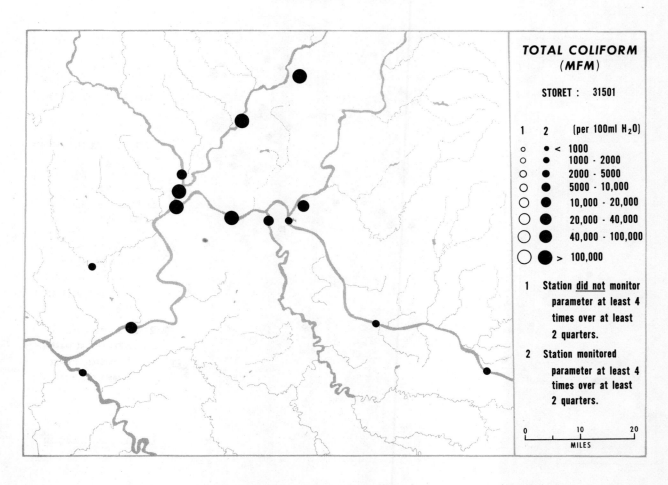

Figure 4.57

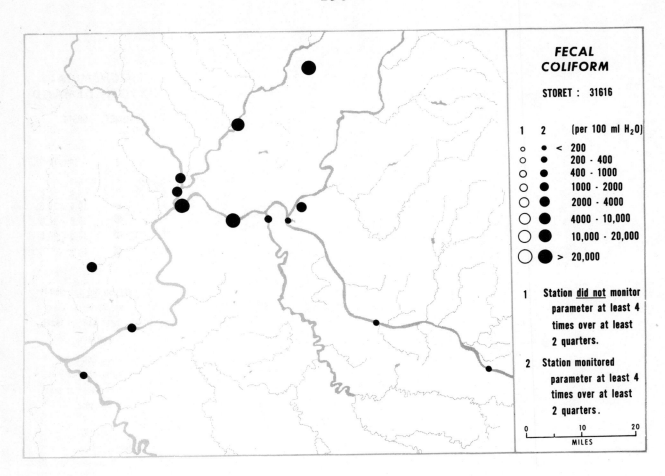

Figure 4.58

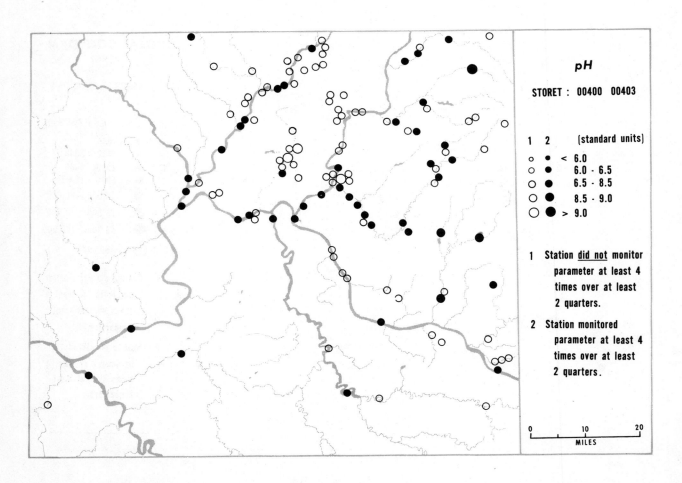

Figure 4.59

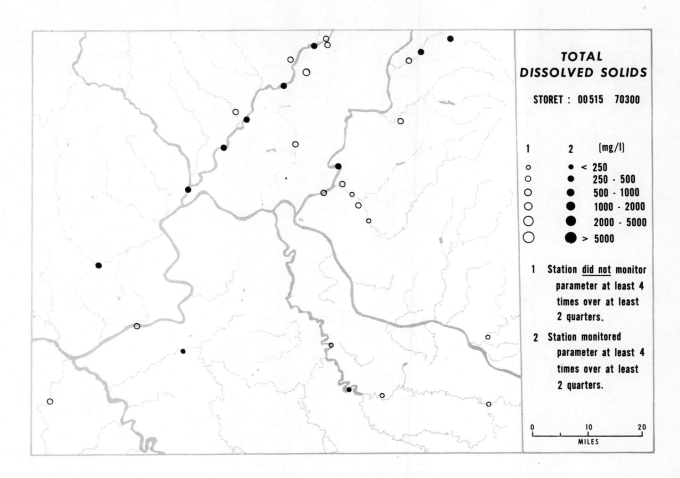

Figure 4.60

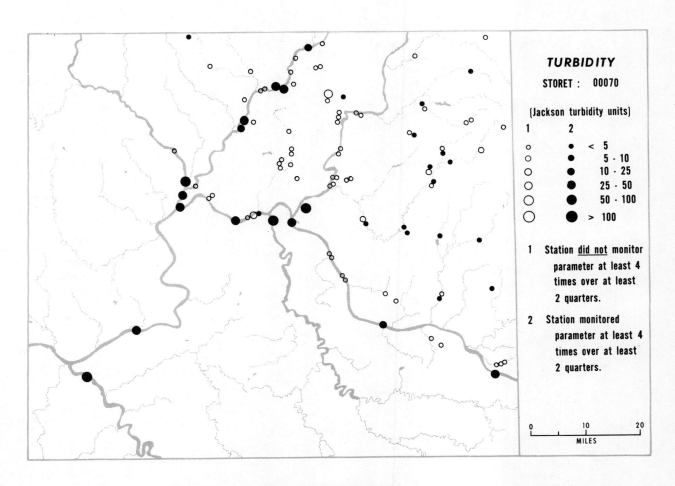

Figure 4.61

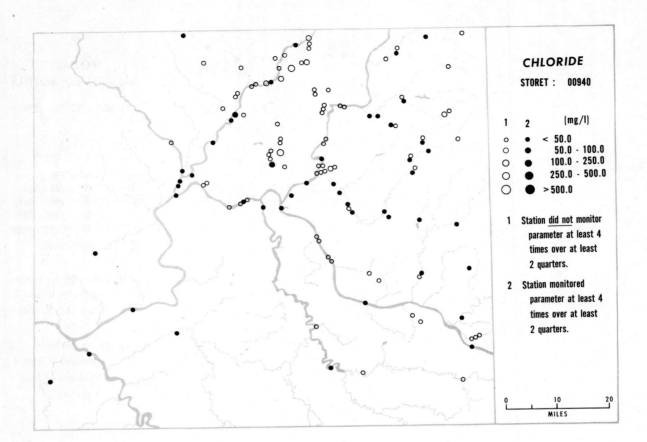

Figure 4.62

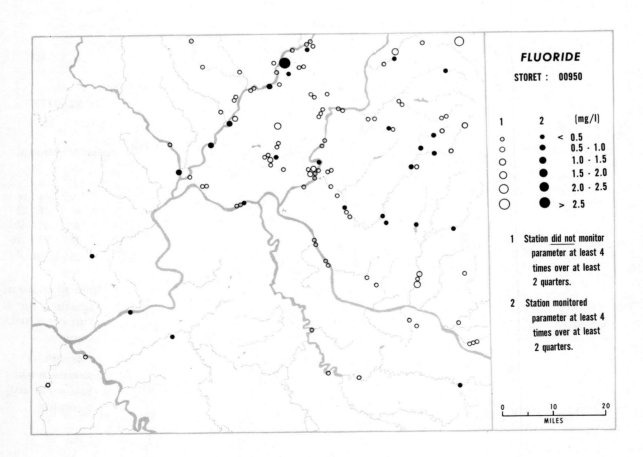

Figure 4.63

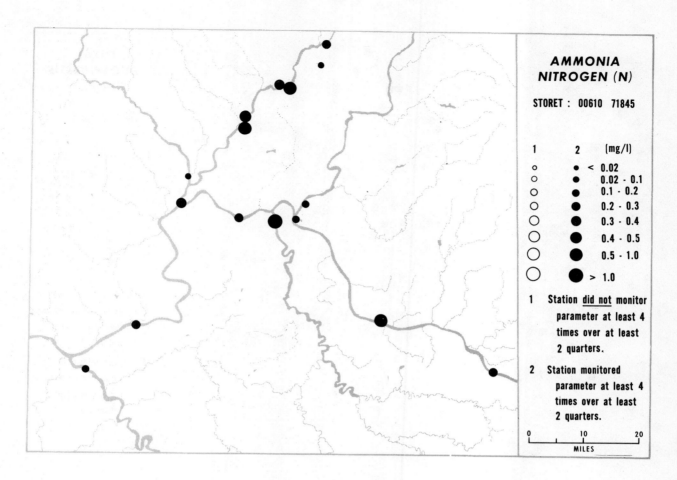

Figure 4.64

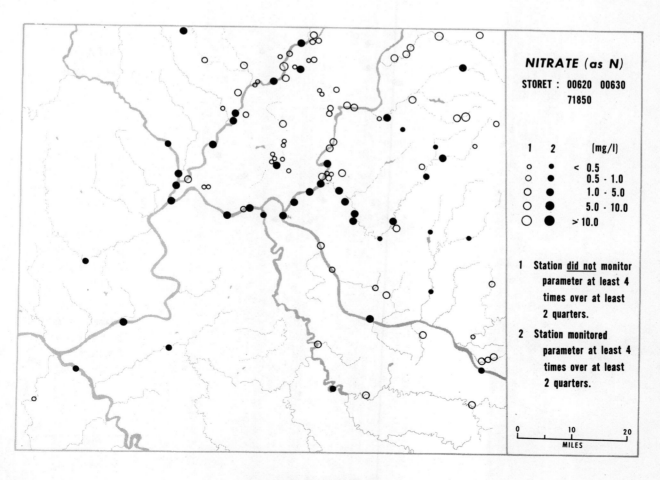

Figure 4.65

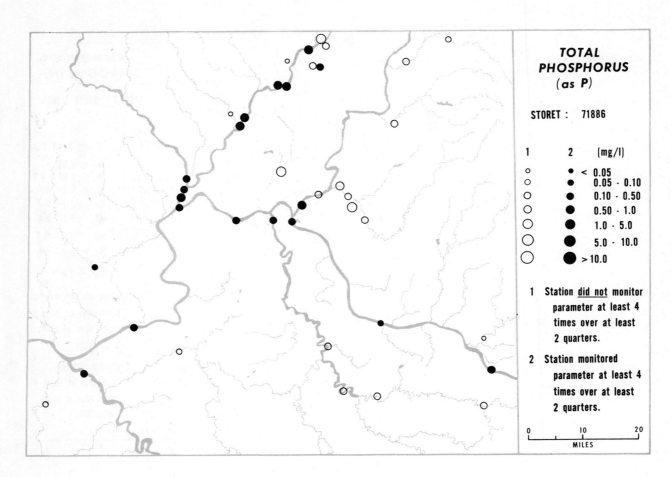

Figure 4.66

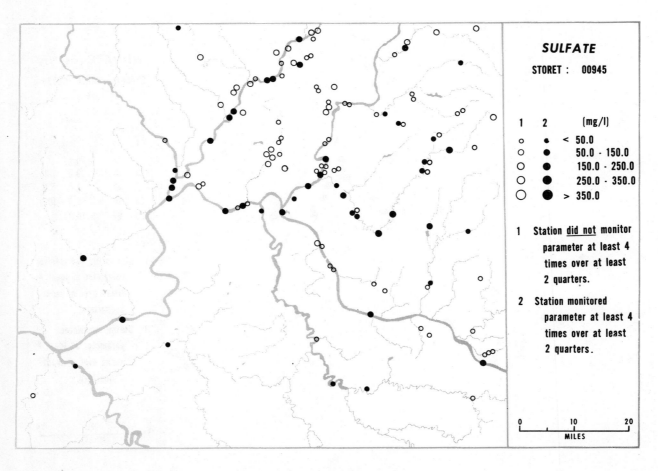

Figure 4.67

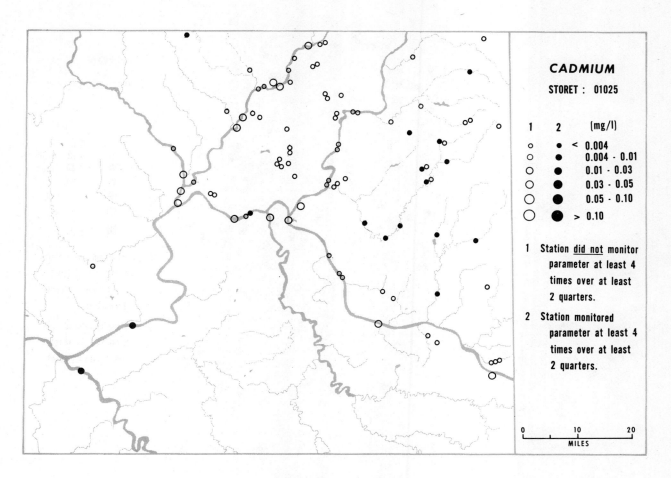

Figure 4.68

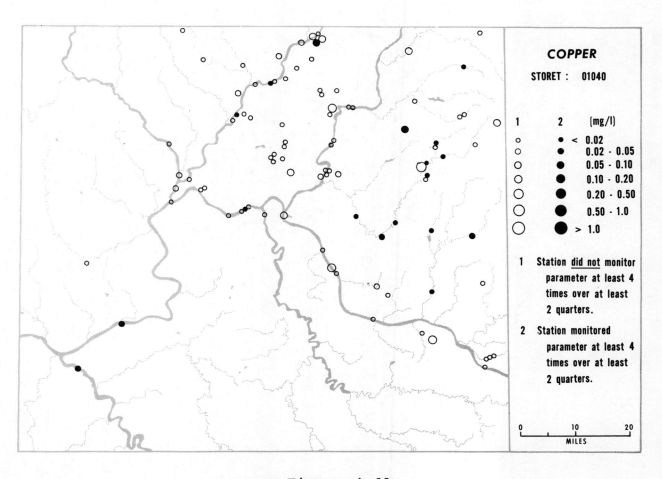

Figure 4.69

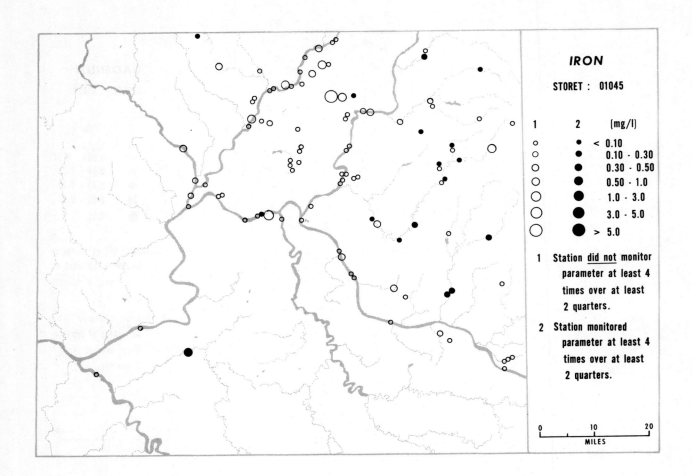

Figure 4.70

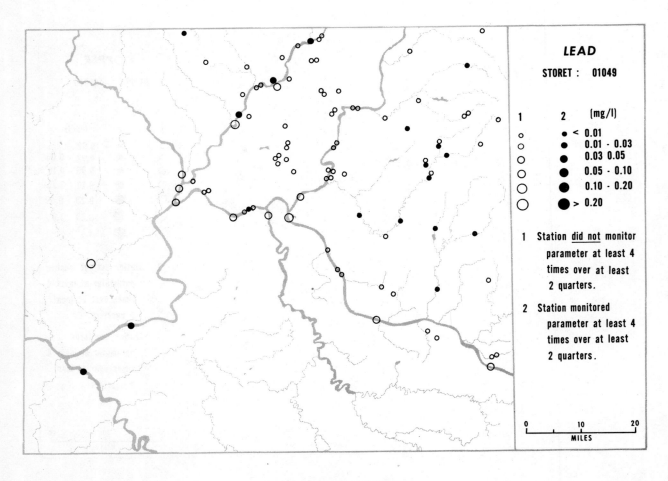

Figure 4.71

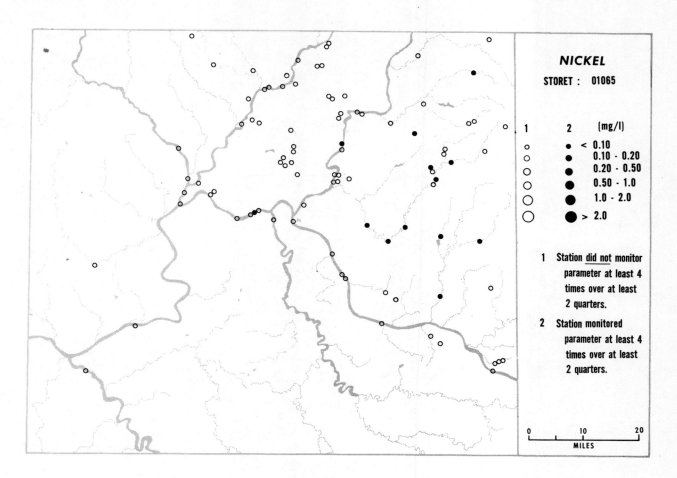

Figure 4.72

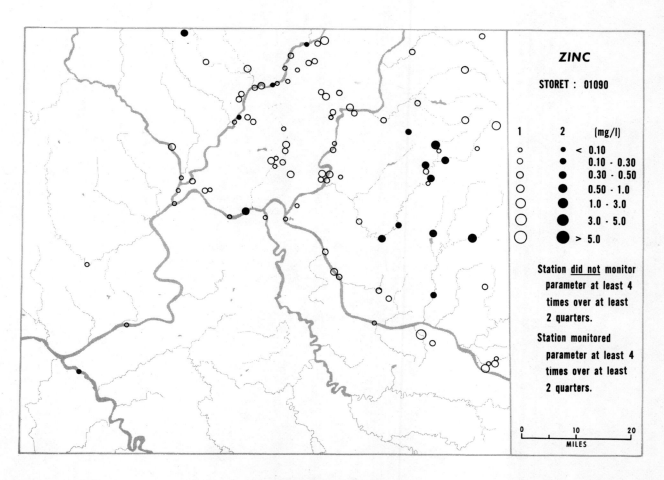

Figure 4.73

ST. LOUIS

The St. Louis area is located in eastern Missouri on the Mississippi below its confluence with the Missouri River. Dissected till plains cover the northern half of the polygon and mark the southern limit of Pleistocene glaciation. The southern half in Missouri below St. Louis is part of the Salem Plateau of the Ozarks physiographic province. Bedrock usually consists of limestone and dolomite covered by alluvium. The region is characterized by a generally hilly and sometimes forested landscape, a dendritic drainage pattern, and an interior continental climate. Temperature ranges are extreme and the majority of precipitation falls in the spring and summer months. Maximum runoff and flooding occur in the spring throughout the polygon. Natural quality of surface and groundwaters varies in hardness and total dissolved solids content depending on lithology, permeability and spring flow. Natural turbidity is low in major tributary basins but considerably higher on the Mississippi and Missouri main stems. Water supplies for the heavily urbanized St. Louis area are obtained from the two major rivers and from the Meramec. Large supplies of groundwater are available from alluvial and bedrock aquifers.

There are major contrasts in land use between the region's heavily urbanized and industrialized centers in St. Louis-East St. Louis, and the hinterlands' agricultural and mining activities. The region has many large primary manufacturing and heavy industrial operations, though most of this activity is found in the St. Louis area. Major industrial clusters occur in the urban core and in peripheral locations around the city. Mining and extractive activities are important in the city and extend off from the city in a line to the southeast. A large stock yard is located in East St. Louis near the Mississippi River. A major strip mine occurs just to the southeast of the city. Where the terrain permits, agriculture and livestock raising are common.

A recently published report of the Missouri Geological Survey and Water Resources Division describes surface water quality in the area as varying from good in the tributary streams of southern Jefferson County to very poor in the highly urbanized areas. The report indicates that the presence of streams of large flow volume alleviates water supply and waste disposal problems. However, costly and extensive treatment is required for surface waters used for domestic and manufacturing purposes. The report also indicates that urbanization has directly affected runoff and water quality in the area in several ways, viz:

1. Preliminary studies of Coldwater Creek, a 60 percent urbanized, 20 percent impervious basin reveal that average annual runoff is about twice that of a comparable rural stream.

2. Peak flows for the same basin increased one-and-a-half to two times as a result of urbanization.

3. Sewage treatment plants augment low flows of unrelated streams in an urban area.

4. Groundwater quality is also being affected by improperly located or poorly constructed septic tanks, sewage lagoons and sanitary landfills. Springs are becoming polluted.

The report concludes that the influence of urbanization on water quality of small streams is characterized by the generally deteriorated condition of the streams in St. Louis County, particularly those in the metropolitan St. Louis area.

The 1971 STORET data retrieval for the St. Louis polygon contained 55 surface water quality stations. The majority of these stations were located on minor tributaries upstream from the urbanized area or on minor streams flowing into the Mississippi, Missouri and Illinois Rivers. The principal rivers and the urban core were not well monitored. The exception to this is Marine Creek, which had several stations on the fringe of the central city. Many of the rural monitoring points are located on bridges. Several stations appearing in the data are situated on Illinois streams which enter the Mississippi far downstream from St. Louis. The USGS and the Illinois EPA were together responsible for two-thirds of the total water quality stations. Most of the monitoring agencies sampled water quality approximately three or four times per year with the exception of the USGS which tested more frequently, usually a dozen times per year. Readings by all sources are well distributed throughout the calendar year.

The fourteen effluent discharge points provided in the 1971 STORET data are surrounded by monitoring stations which maintain adequate surveillance. The flow of portions of the Missouri and Mississippi Rivers is controlled by a series of dams which may effect the levels of individual contaminants and cause backwash into nearby tributaries. Relocation of sampling stations further upstream to avoid back water flow effects is evident in the absence of stations near the mouth of streams near St. Louis.

Dissolved oxygen and pH were the most comprehensively monitored parameters. Total and fecal coliform bacteria were recorded in terms of a single STORET code number each. This is in marked contrast to Washington, D.C. and Seattle which have four or five parameter numbers each for those parameters. The map illustrating total dissolved solids is greatly augmented by using values calculated from specific conductance readings and stored in STORET. The nutrient parameters (nitrate and phosphorus) are monitored by several agencies each using a different lab technique and recording the data in terms of different STORET code numbers. Only the U.S. Geological Survey monitored trace metals.

The maps reveal that a small number of waterway segments consistently show up with the water of lowest quality. Concentrations of certain parameters were particularly high for these streams. In Illinois, Macoupin Creek was contaminated with respect to proposed federal criteria for more measures of water quality than any other stream in the polygon. It had high levels of fecal coliforms, dissolved solids and turbidity, ammonia, nitrogen, MBAS and phosphates. The Kaskaskia River and tributaries show high concentrations of sulfate, MBAS and turbidity and the Mary's River, a small tributary of the Mississippi in Illinois, had high ammonia, turbidity and TDS readings. The Big Muddy River and tributaries monitored especially high levels of sulfate, turbidity and TDS.

Forkwood Creek and the Mississippi River near Alton were particularly polluted with respect to MBAS, ammonia, nitrogen, turbidity and dissolved oxygen. In the vicinity of West Alton upstream from its confluence with the Mississippi River, the Missouri River showed exceptionally low dissolved oxygen levels and high fecal coliforms, turbidity and ammonia nitrogen levels. Maline Creek is polluted with respect to oxygen measuring parameters, fecal and total coliforms and dissolved lead. Further south Joachim Creek had especially high concentrations of nitrate, copper, cadmium and lead.

It should be emphasized that inadequate distribution of stations and the large number of parameters monitored by certain stations have much to do with the reason certain segments of the hydrologic network appear to stand out as having water of particularly low quality. In terms of overall pollution patterns, pollutants indicative of organic wastes appear to constitute the most severe problem. Based upon percentages of stations in excess of federal recommended criteria for different water use designations, total and fecal coliforms, ammonia nitrogen, phosphorus and MBAS were all found in sufficiently high concentrations throughout the polygon to present a hazard to Water Supply and Primary Contact Use and Freshwater Aquatic Life. The most extreme cases of widespread pollution were fecal coliforms, for which 81 percent of the stations exceeded a suggested primary contact standard (based on 38 stations, twelve of which were over the cutoff), and ammonia nitrogen, for which 96 percent of the stations exceeded the recommended Freshwater Aquatic Life standard (based on 47 stations, 15 of which met the cutoff). Excessively high turbidity and, to a lesser extent, low dissolved oxygen and high lead levels were also widespread.

Only two monitoring stations were located within the St. Louis City limits, yet most of the polluted water was found in the vicinity of urbanized areas or small towns. Considered together with the fact that organic pollution comprised most of the problem, sewage is implicated as a likely source. Pollution (particularly inorganic) is also heavy in areas used for industrial or extractive purposes.

Table 4.7

St. Louis

Parameter	Total		Inner City		Remainder		Details By Water Use Designation Inner City				Remainder		
	N	P	N	P	N	P	WD	R	E	PR	R	E	PR
DO	30	40	2	100	28	36	FA	0	0	–	4	14	25
							PC	0	0	–	6	21	33
TOT COLI	17	41	1	100	16	38	AL_1	0	0	–	9	56	56
							AL_2	0	0	–	14	88	43
							PS	0	0	–	10	63	50
FEC COLI	38	68	2	100	36	67	AI	1	50	100	18	50	78
							AL_1	1	50	100	12	33	75
							AL_2	1	50	100	18	50	78
							PS	1	50	100	14	39	71
							UR_1	1	50	100	12	33	75
							UR_2	1	50	100	14	39	71
							PC_1	1	50	100	28	78	71
							PC_2	1	50	100	29	81	69
PH	50	32	2	100	48	29	FA	1	50	100	1	2	100
							PS	1	50	100	0	0	–
							PC_1	1	50	100	0	0	–
							PC_2	1	50	100	4	8	25
TDS	40	43	1	100	39	41	AI_1	0	0	–	0	0	–
							AI_2	0	0	–	6	15	67
							PS	0	0	–	12	31	75
TURB	37	46	1	100	36	44	FA_1	1	100	100	20	56	25
							FA_2	1	100	100	28	78	29
MBAS	24	13	0	–	24	13	PS	–	–	–	14	58	0
CL	28	57	0	–	28	57	PS	–	–	–	0	0	–
F	18	61	0	–	18	61	AI_1	–	–	–	0	0	–
							AI_2	–	–	–	2	11	50
							AI	–	–	–	3	16	67
							AL	–	–	–	2	11	50
NH3	47	68	2	100	45	67	FA	2	100	100	43	96	67
							PS	1	50	100	10	22	60
NO3	50	56	2	100	48	54	AL	0	0	–	2	4	100
							PS	0	0	–	2	4	100

Parameter	Total N	Total P	Inner City N	Inner City P	Remainder N	Remainder P	WD	Inner City R	Inner City E	Inner City PR	Remainder R	Remainder E	Remainder PR
P	45	53	2	100	43	51	NS	2	100	100	29	67	59
SO4	26	31	0	-	26	31	PS	-	-	-	4	15	100
CD	22	41	1	100	21	38	AI$_1$	0	0	-	0	0	-
							AI$_2$	1	100	100	3	14	67
							AL	0	0	-	0	0	-
							FA$_1$	0	0	-	0	0	-
							FA$_2$	1	100	100	3	14	67
							PS	1	100	100	3	14	67
CU	18	39	1	100	17	41	AI$_1$	0	0	-	0	0	-
							AI$_2$	0	0	-	0	0	-
							AL	0	0	-	0	0	-
PB	18	39	1	100	17	35	AI$_1$	0	0	-	0	0	-
							AI$_2$	0	0	-	0	0	-
							AL	1	100	100	3	18	100
							FA	1	100	100	3	18	100
							PS	1	100	100	4	74	75
NI	16	38	0	-	16	38	AI$_1$	-	-	-	0	0	-
							AI$_2$	-	-	-	0	0	-
ZN	18	50	1	100	17	47	AL	0	0	-	1	6	100
							PS	0	0	-	1	6	100

Code:

N = Number of stations
P = Percentage of stations below cutoff value
E = Percentage of stations exceeding reference level
R = Number of stations exceeding reference level
PR = Percentage of stations exceeding reference level below cutoff

Water Use Designation (WD):

AI = Agricultural, Irrigation
AL = Agricultural, Livestock
FA = Freshwater Aquatic Life
MA = Marine Water Aquatic Life
PS = Public Water Supply Intake
UR = Undesignated Recreational
PC = Primary Contact Recreational
ST = Secondary Treatment Standard
NS = Nutrient Standard

Note: Subscripts refer to different standards, where more than one standard is specified for a given water use designation.

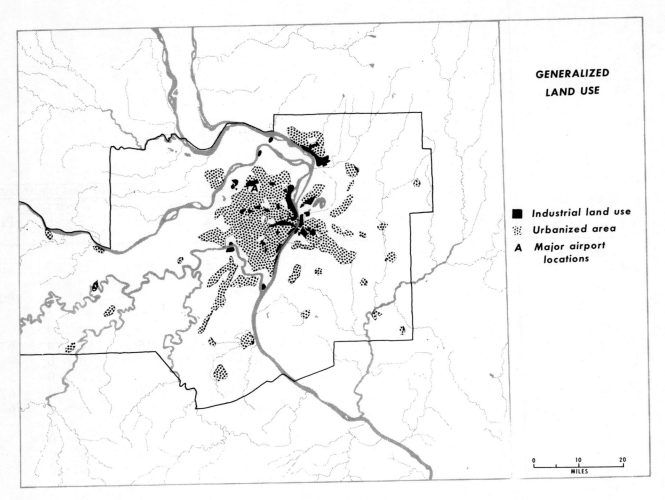

GENERALIZED
LAND USE

■ Industrial land use
⠿ Urbanized area
A Major airport
  locations

0   10   20
MILES

Figure 4.74

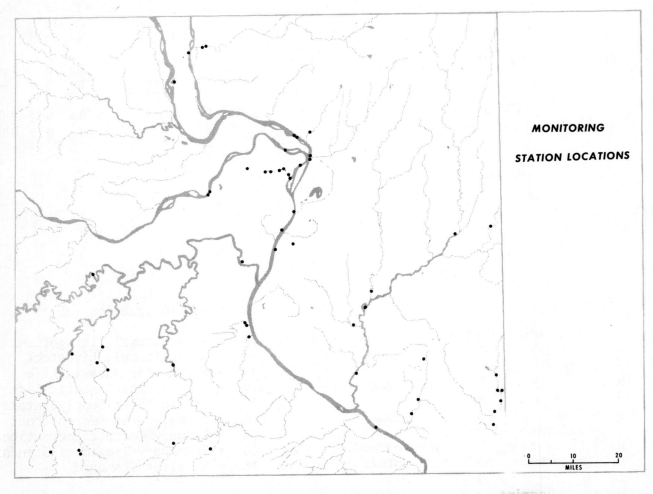

MONITORING

STATION LOCATIONS

0   10   20
MILES

Figure 4.75

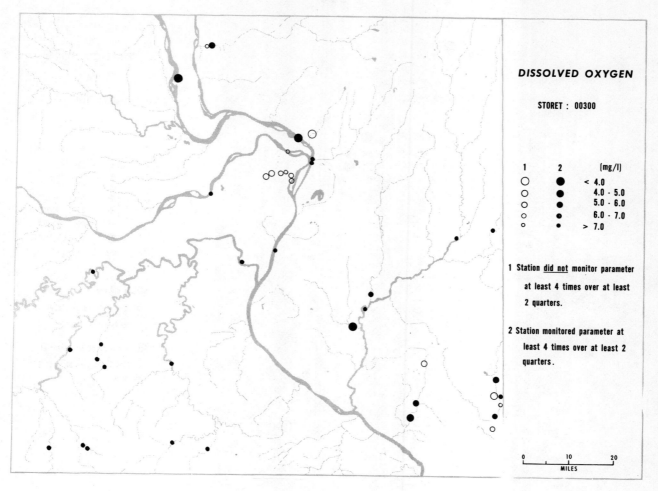

Figure 4.76

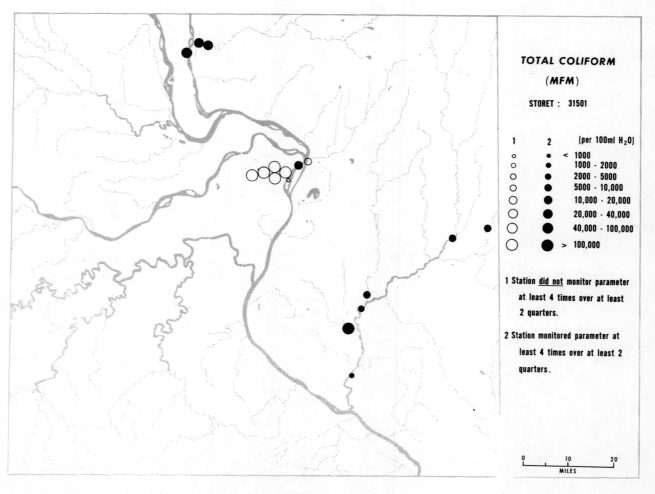

Figure 4.77

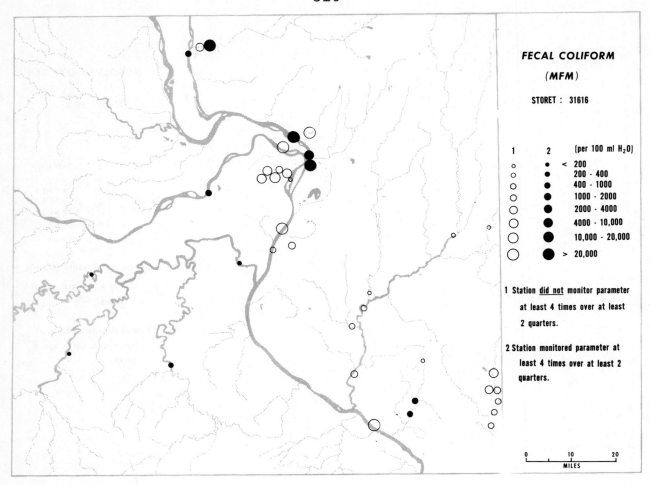

Figure 4.78

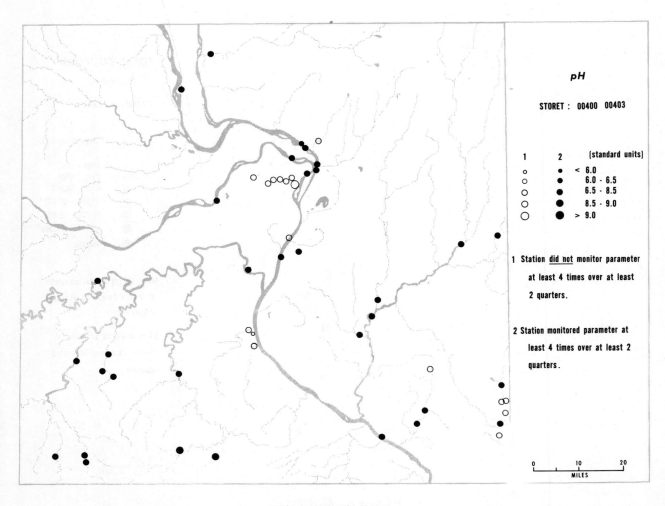

Figure 4.79

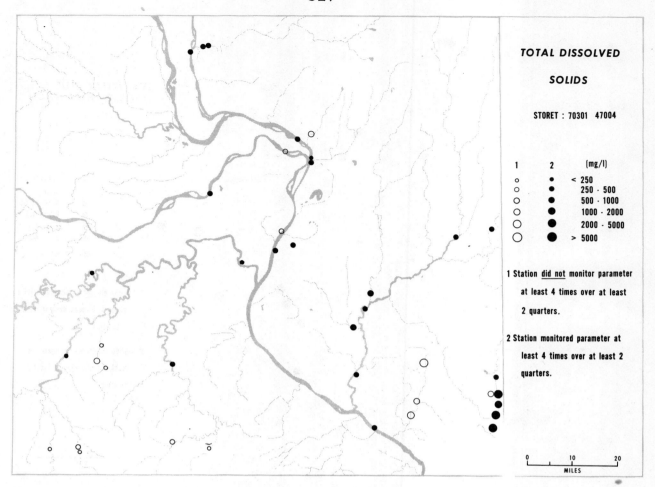

Figure 4.80

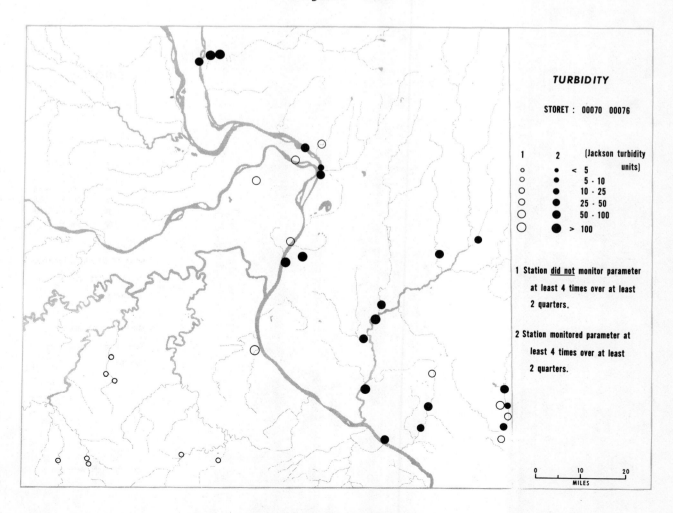

Figure 4.81

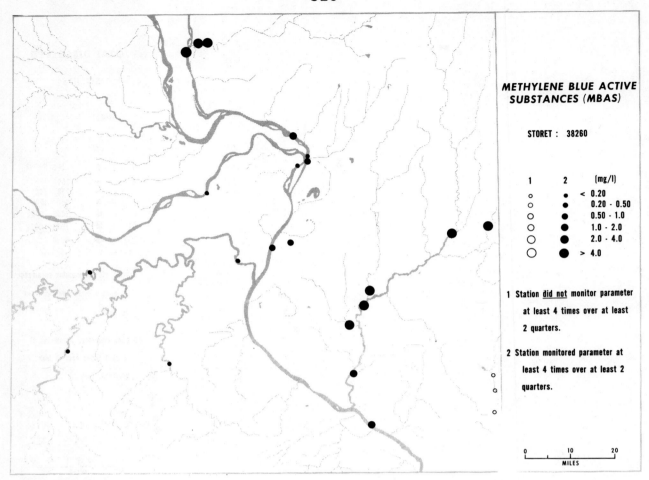

Figure 4.82

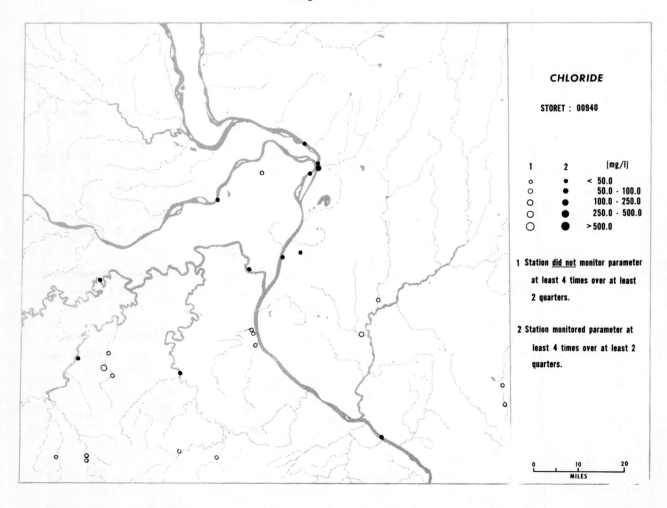

Figure 4.83

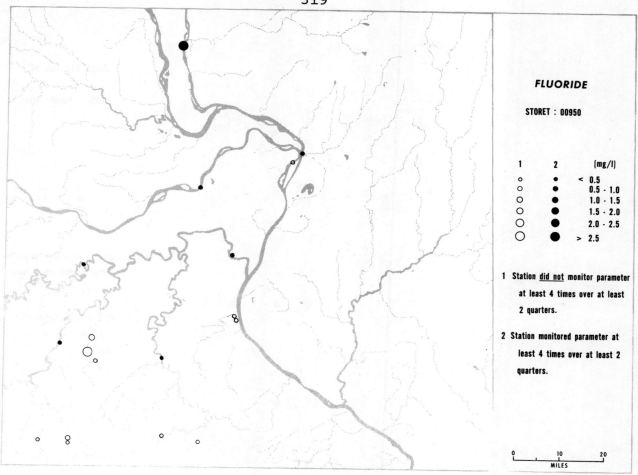

Figure 4.84

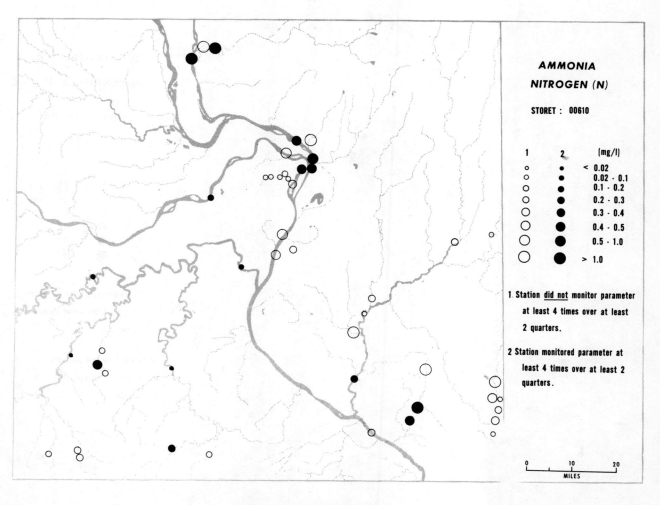

Figure 4.85

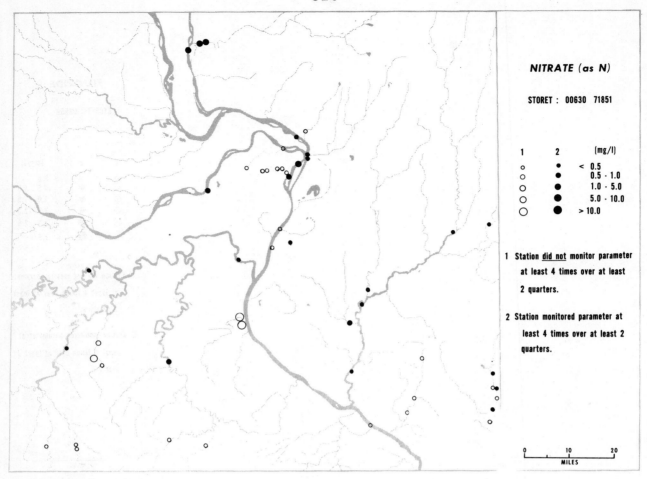

Figure 4.86

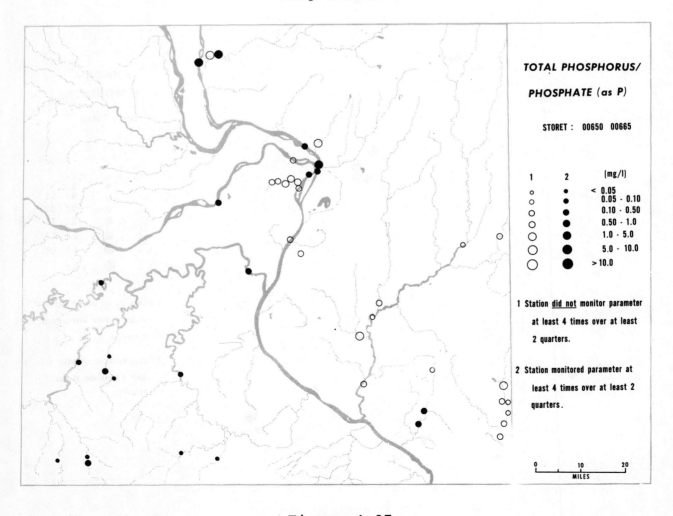

Figure 4.87

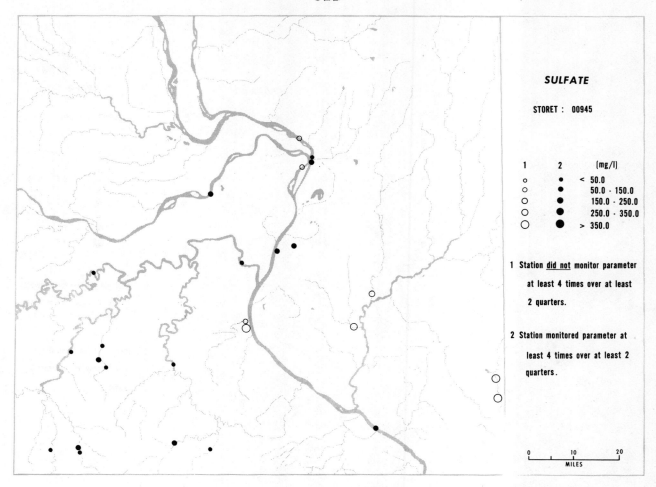

Figure 4.88

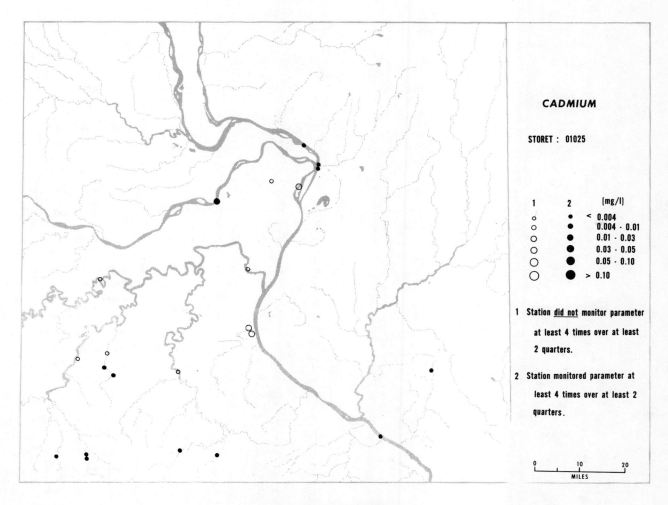

Figure 4.89

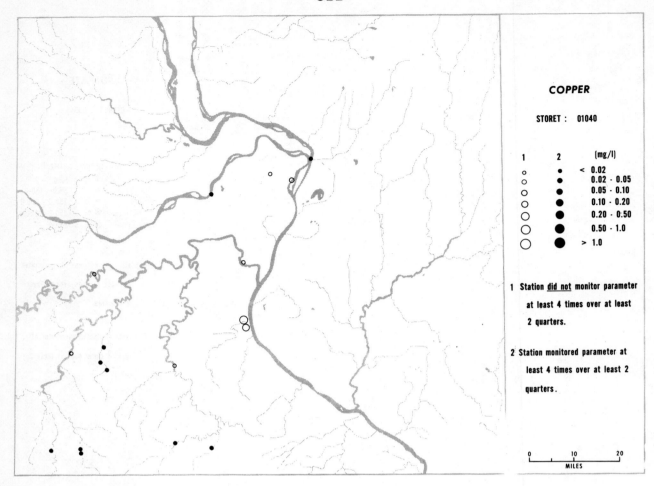

Figure 4.90

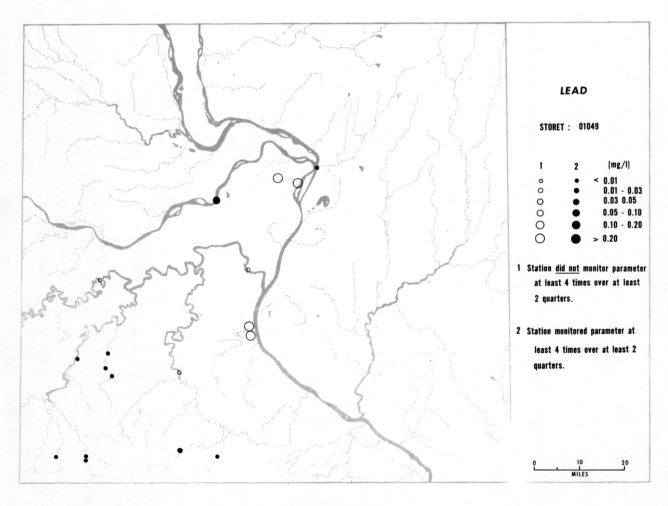

Figure 4.91

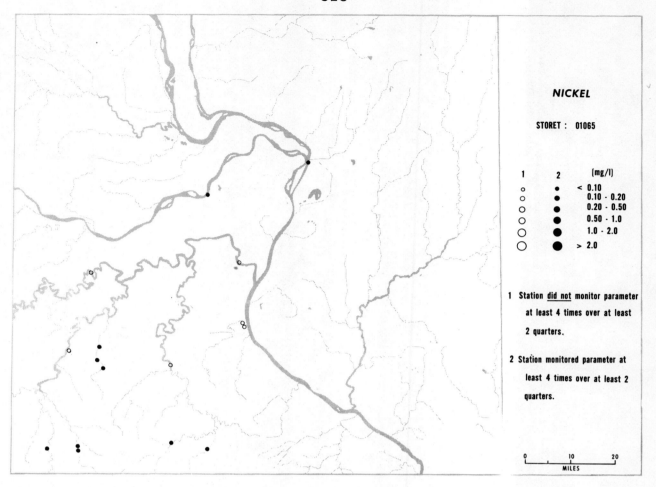

Figure 4.92

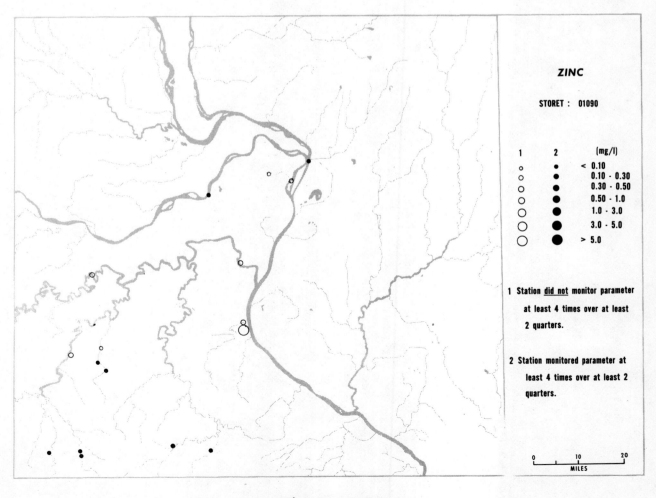

Figure 4.93

BIRMINGHAM

The dominant factor affecting the spatial pattern of urban development in the Birmingham metropolitan area has been its surface geomorphology. The SMSA lies within a diversity of physiographic units. These units include the Appalachian Plateau, the Ridge and Valley and Piedmont provinces of the Appalachian Highlands physical division and the Coastal Plain province of the Atlantic Plain. The major ridges and valleys are oriented along a northeast-southwest axis. As a result, the drainage pattern, rail and highway networks and major residential and industrial patterns tend to reflect their topographic limitations. Elevations within the polygon vary from 500 ft. to less than 2,000 ft.

The Birmingham region is susceptible to flooding. Sewerage networks are inadequate and urban concentrations are located in the flood-plains of the major rivers. Data available for the latter part of the 1971 calendar year indicated that most streams in the area had excessive flows in 1971, in the upper 25 percent of record, especially for the month of December. No outstanding floods were reported for the last few months of the year.

A total of 68 surface water quality stations was obtained from STORET after several retrieval attempts. The majority of the monitoring points are located on the Black Warrior River and its tributaries. Several stations are located on the Cahaba River. The third major northeast-southwest trending river in our polygon contains no water quality stations. Nine of the total number of stations were concentrated in the industrialized sections of the polygon. This area is southwest of Birmingham in the vicinity of Tuscaloosa and downstream from it. The remaining stations are distributed along the upstream portions of the Black Warrior River drainage basin. About ten of the 68 stations are located on dams or bridges which modify the flow characteristics of the major streams.

Very few parameters were available for mapping. Nutrient, inorganic and microbiological parameter data were completely lacking at most monitoring stations. Dissolved oxygen was sampled more times and by more stations than any other parameter used -- as often as several hundred times during the year at some stations although the median range for sampling frequency was 80-100 times per year -- but was not available for the inner city stations where trace metals were sampled: iron, copper, lead, nickel and zinc.

The seven maps that could be plotted (Figures 4.96-4.102) reveal that the industrialized portions of the Birmingham region suffer from a severe water pollution problem. We were able to evaluate the quality of the most critically polluted segment of the Black Warrior River with dissolved oxygen data. Information for the other eight parameters used in this study (six of which appear in the subsequent map section) were not available for the lower Black Warrior River upstream and downstream from Tuscaloosa. However, the large number of DO readings for each station gave what we felt was an adequate picture of the degraded water quality in the area.

All but one of the 45 stations which tested DO were located on the Black Warrior River and its tributaries. A total of 40 stations exceeded our cutoff reference level for station data quality. Of the 45 DO data stations, 18 fell below the 4.0 mg/l minimum reference level for Freshwater Aquatic Life. Thirteen stations fell below the 5.0 mg/l reference level. The cause of the DO sag point is a combination of the degenerating wastes discharged by local industry and the abundance of strip mines located around Tuscaloosa and Birmingham. Pollution sources in the upstream reaches of the Black Warrior River Basin also contribute to the degraded water quality.

The mean annual values for pH reflect the alteration of the water body by industrial effluents. These wastes appear to have had their source within the City of Birmingham. Lowered pH readings on Opossum

Creek, a tributary of Valley Creek, were obtained near mills of the United States Steel Company. Three (33 percent) of the inner city stations are in excess of the 6.5-8.5 recommended range. Two of the remaining 15 stations fail to attain the reference levels.

Trace metal data also point to industrial pollution in the inner city industrial area, based on a limited number of readings. Out of a total of 17 monitoring stations, 9 (100 percent) of the inner city and 4 (50 percent) of the remaining stations exceed the Freshwater Aquatic Life reference level of .03 mg/l. The same stations also exceed the Public Water Supply Intake level of .05 mg/l. Four of the 9 city stations and none of the remaining stations surpass even the most liberal Agricultural Livestock level of .1 mg/l. The four inner city stations are located on Opossum Creek and Valley Creek.

All stations which monitor iron (17) had mean values which exceeded the .3 mg/l Public Water Supply recommended value. Four stations on Opossum Creek and Valley Creek also exceed the 5.0 mg/l suggested level for continuous irrigation. The degree to which the reference levels were exceeded are worthy of mention. Three consecutive sampling points, two on Opossum Creek, one on Valley Creek exhibited readings of 687 mg/l, 94 mg/l and 81 mg/l in a downstream direction for a series of single grab samples.

The Public Water Supply recommended level for zinc (5.0 mg/l) was not exceeded at any of the 17 stations although higher readings were obtained on Opossum and Valley Creeks. The 1971 mean levels for copper, cadmium and nickel were within reference levels at nearly all stations in the polygon.

Table 4.8

Birmingham

Parameter	Total		Inner City		Remainder		Details By Water Use	Inner City			Designation Remainder		
	N	P	N	P	N	P	WD	R	E	PR	R	E	PR
DO	45	9	0	-	45	9	FA	-	-	-	18	40	11
							PC	-	-	-	31	69	13
PH	24	75	9	100	15	60	FA	1	7	100	0	0	-
							PS	0	0	-	0	0	-
							PC_1	0	0	-	0	0	-
							PC_2	3	33	100	2	13	100
FE	17	88	9	100	8	75	AI_1	3	33	100	0	0	-
							AI_2	3	33	100	1	13	100
							PS	9	100	100	8	100	75
CU	17	100	9	100	8	100	AI_1	0	0	-	0	0	-
							AI_2	0	0	-	0	0	-
							AL	0	0	-	0	0	-
							PS	0	0	-	0	0	-
PB	17	100	9	100	8	100	AI_1	0	0	-	0	0	-
							AI_2	0	0	-	0	0	-
							AL	4	44	100	0	0	-
							FA	9	100	100	4	50	100
							PS	9	100	100	4	50	100
NI	17	100	9	100	8	100	AI_1	0	0	-	0	0	-
							AI_2	0	0	-	0	0	-
ZN	17	100	9	100	8	100	AL	0	0	-	0	0	-
							PS	0	0	-	0	0	-

Code:

N = Number of stations
P = Percentage of stations below cutoff value
E = Percentage of stations exceeding reference level
R = Number of stations exceeding reference level
PR = Percentage of stations exceeding reference level below cutoff

Water Use Designation (WD):

AI = Agricultural, Irrigation
AL = Agricultural, Livestock
FA = Freshwater Aquatic Life
MA = Marine Water Aquatic Life
PS = Public Water Supply Intake
UR = Undesignated Recreational
PC = Primary Contact Recreational
ST = Secondary Treatment Standard
NS = Nutrient Standard

Note: Subscripts refer to different standards, where more than one standard is specified for a given water designation.

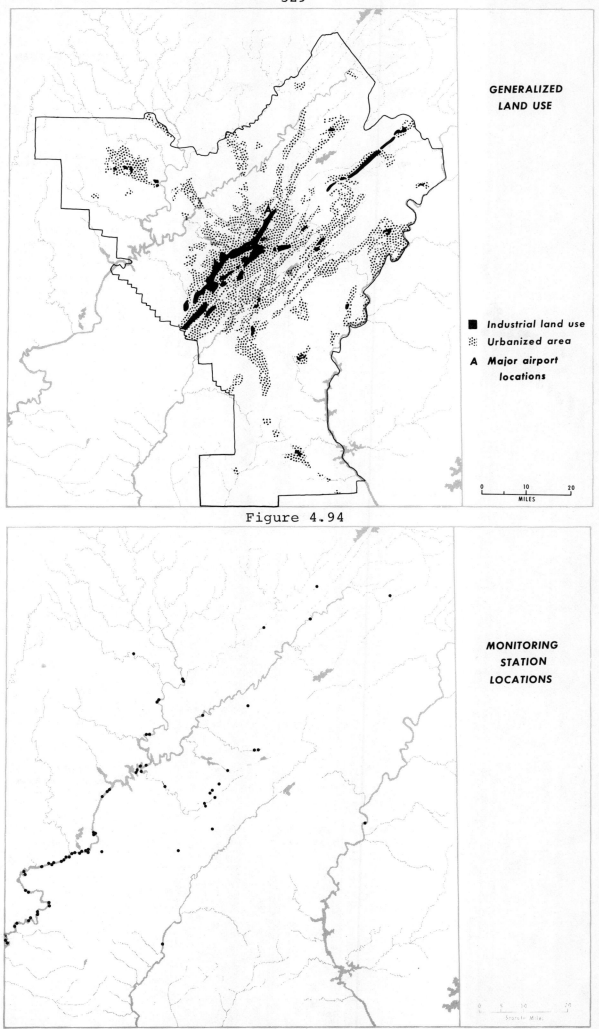

GENERALIZED
LAND USE

■ Industrial land use
∷ Urbanized area
A Major airport
locations

0   10   20
MILES

Figure 4.94

MONITORING
STATION
LOCATIONS

0   5   10   20
Statute Miles

Figure 4.95

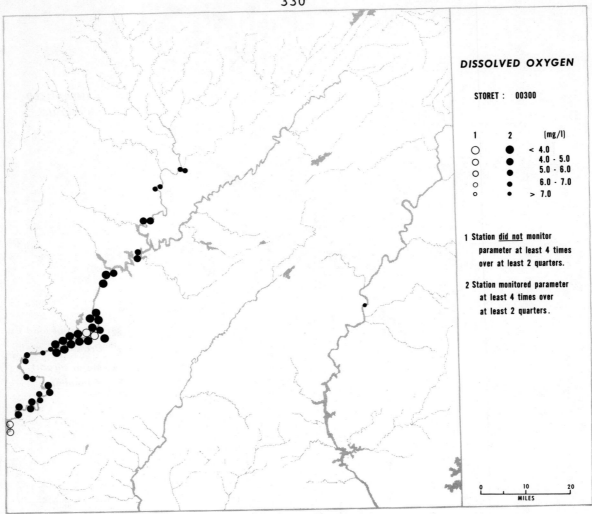

DISSOLVED OXYGEN

STORET : 00300

1	2	(mg/l)
○	●	< 4.0
○	●	4.0 - 5.0
○	●	5.0 - 6.0
○	●	6.0 - 7.0
○	●	> 7.0

1 Station <u>did not</u> monitor parameter at least 4 times over at least 2 quarters.

2 Station monitored parameter at least 4 times over at least 2 quarters.

0   10   20
MILES

Figure 4.96

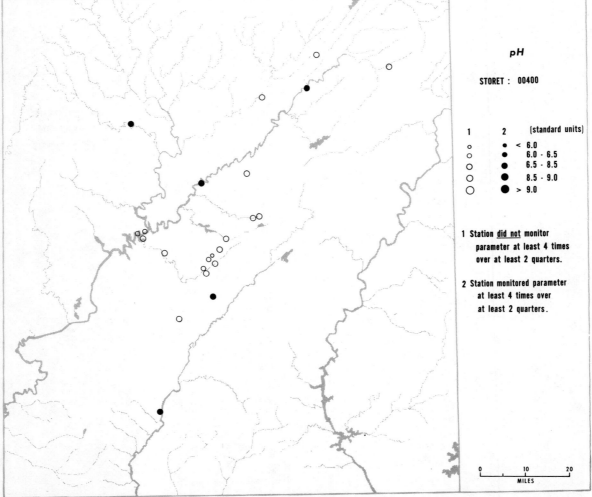

pH

STORET : 00400

1	2	(standard units)
○	●	< 6.0
○	●	6.0 - 6.5
○	●	6.5 - 8.5
○	●	8.5 - 9.0
○	●	> 9.0

1 Station <u>did not</u> monitor parameter at least 4 times over at least 2 quarters.

2 Station monitored parameter at least 4 times over at least 2 quarters.

0   10   20
MILES

Figure 4.97

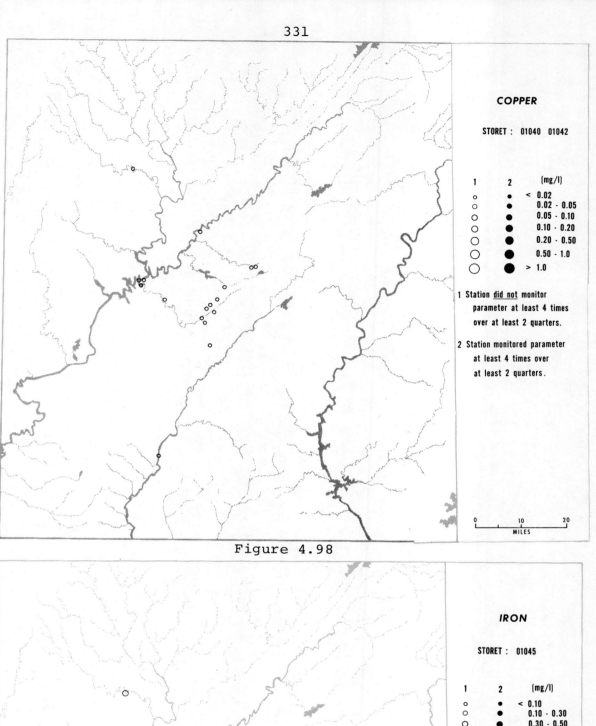

COPPER

STORET : 01040 01042

1	2	(mg/l)
○	●	< 0.02
○	●	0.02 - 0.05
○	●	0.05 - 0.10
○	●	0.10 - 0.20
○	●	0.20 - 0.50
○	●	0.50 - 1.0
○	●	> 1.0

1 Station _did not_ monitor
   parameter at least 4 times
   over at least 2 quarters.

2 Station monitored parameter
   at least 4 times over
   at least 2 quarters.

Figure 4.98

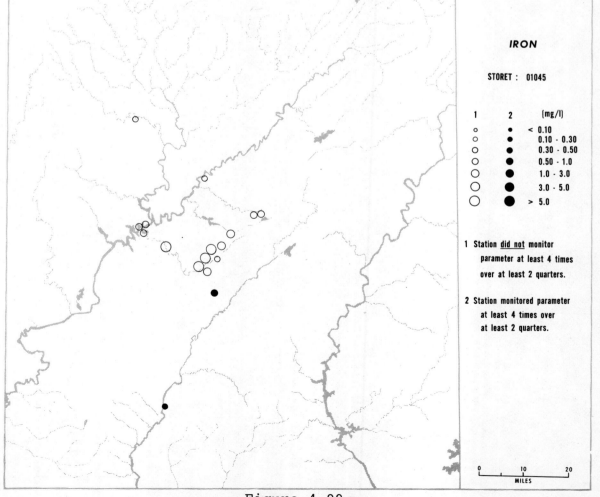

IRON

STORET : 01045

1	2	(mg/l)
○	●	< 0.10
○	●	0.10 - 0.30
○	●	0.30 - 0.50
○	●	0.50 - 1.0
○	●	1.0 - 3.0
○	●	3.0 - 5.0
○	●	> 5.0

1 Station _did not_ monitor
   parameter at least 4 times
   over at least 2 quarters.

2 Station monitored parameter
   at least 4 times over
   at least 2 quarters.

Figure 4.99

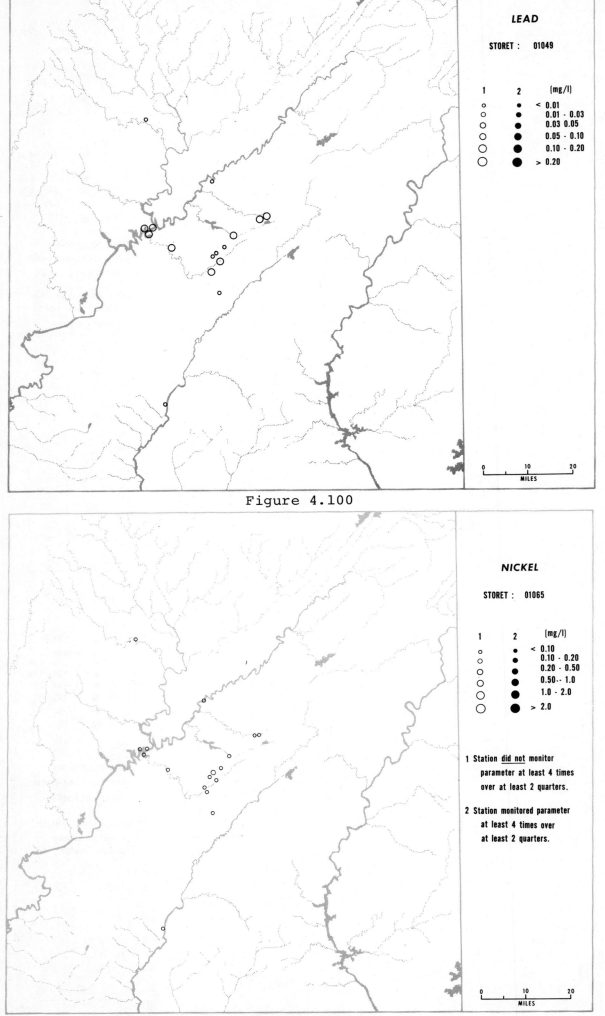

Figure 4.100

Figure 4.101

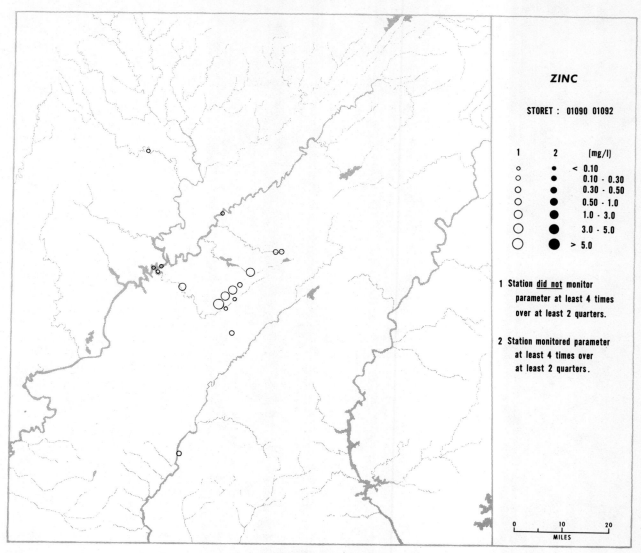

Figure 4.102

JACKSONVILLE

The Jacksonville area is part of the Atlantic coastal plain and has a humid subtropical climate. Total relief is approximately twenty feet throughout the county. During 1971, runoff was far below normal, reaching only 25 percent of normal during the USGS 1971 water year (October, 1970-September, 1971). Conditions improved slightly during the end of the calendar year but remained deficient.

The consolidated City of Jacksonville, which covers all of Duval County in northeastern Florida, is also the Jacksonville SMSA. Most of the area is drained by the St. Johns River and its small tributaries, the majority of which are fed by groundwater from shallow aquifers. The flow characteristics of the basin are unmodified by major dams or reservoirs. The effects of tidal action cause flow reversals for half of the time and occasional salt water intrusion into the estuary as far upstream as the southern city limits. Thus it is possible for the shallow aquifers to become contaminated from streams bearing conservative pollutants. Saltwater marshes and pine forests are found in the less urbanized stream basins of the polygon -- the St. Mary's, the Nassau, the Santa Fe Rivers and along the coastal margins. The surface waters of the area are brackish and used for industrial cooling. Most water for domestic use is obtained from the Florida Aquifer.

Almost all of the developed regions within our study area lie within Duval County. Within Duval County, less than 20 percent of the total land area is developed. Of the developed land, 3 percent is industrial, concentrated in three principal clusters in the central city. Liquid wastes from industrial operations are often not treated or channelled to over-burdened municipal treatment facilities. The industrial cluster in the port district of the city is primarily devoted to heavy industry. The St. Regis Paper Company, the largest individual wastewater generator in the city has a large facility in this district. Discharge from other industries and from boats and ships also contribute effluent loadings. The discharge map (Figure 4.105) shows numerous industrial discharges in the vicinity of the core district, among them the pulp and paper mill, one of the likeliest sources of effluent pollution. Within Duval County major water pollution problems also stem from 77 raw sewage outfalls, many of which also contain stromwater runoff. Most of the 400 separate point sources of waste water effluents-which have as their sources faulty septic tanks, sewage treatment plants, raw sewage outfalls and industrial outflows-are located in small streams and drainage ditches which are frequently unable to assimilate the waste.

Other pollution in the Jacksonville area may stem from agricultural activities. The principal types of agriculture in the area are dairying, beef, horses, poultry, swine and truck farming. Forty-three dairy herds and 103 hog feeding lots contribute to water quality degradation in the area.

The entire St. Johns basin, especially the eastern portion, is a valuable fish and wildlife habitat. The 50,000 acres of estuaries and marshlands provide a breeding ground for shellfish, shrimps and sportfish. In addition, both the St. Johns River and the Atlantic coast are prominent for their recreational uses.

The 1971 STORET data for the Jacksonville polygon contains 31 surface water quality stations. Nearly all of the stations are located to the south and west of the city. Half of them are distributed along the North and South Forks of Black Creek, a tributary basin on the St. Johns. The polygon also contains seven monitoring stations which are located on the Santa Fe River, which flows away from the Jacksonville SMSA. There are no stations on the main channel of the St. Johns and only one monitoring point within the Jacksonville SMSA (Duval County). The major residential and industrial concentrations, hence the major sources of pollution to the estuary are not covered.

Sewered or unsewered discharge, industrial discharge and stormwater runoff are not accounted for. Therefore the STORET data enables appraisal of water quality only on the upstream portion of the St. Johns River Basin.

Despite the limited number of surveillance stations, many of the parameters used in this study were available for mapping with the exception of trace metals and inorganics. Total coliforms were tested by the most probable number method rather than by the membrane filter method. Fecal coliform data were lacking. Few sulfate, ammonia and fluoride readings were provided.

All of the STORET data for the Jacksonville polygon were furnished by the U.S. Geological Survey and the Florida State Department of Pollution Control. Biochemical stations were nearly divided between both agencies. The location/description code numbers on the STORET printout differed between sources. The USGS uses 04 which designates location of the station on a river. The state agency uses 03 which can be the sum of 01 (ocean) and 02 (lake), possibly to distinguish stations in marshy areas. We assumed that both agencies were referring to river stations, since the printed designation for the majority of the stations described river locations.

The state agency sampled more frequently than the USGS, usually once per month at twelve of its sixteen stations. The remainder of its sampling points and those of USGS sampled very infrequently, often over a period of several days. This may be indicative of special testing periods.

The lack of data for the entire Duval County area (one station) is a serious setback to any attempt of interpretation of the area's water quality. As was mentioned earlier, the developed areas in the Jacksonville area, and particularly the vast majority of industrial and municipal effluent outfall sites, lie to the north of the monitoring stations located from STORET materials. In addition, there were

no monitoring stations on the main body of the St. John's River, the
major river draining the area.

Given the poor quality of monitoring surveillance in the areas
most likely to support pollution burdens from man's activity, high
recorded levels of certain parameters may more likely be an indication
of prevailing natural conditions in the area. The limited data suggest
high possible concentrations of phosphorus (60 percent of the station's
in excess of the Nutrient reference level) and low pH (35 percent of
the stations in excess of the more stringent reference level for Primary Contact Recreation) and dissolved oxygen readings. These findings
are not surprising given the marshy characteristics of the areas
drained by the Santa Fe River and the North and South forks of Black
Creek. The accompanying table suggests that on the basis of the scanty
data available, the area monitored does not suffer from any outstanding
water pollution problems.

Table 4.9

Jacksonville

Parameter	Total N	Total P	Inner City N	Inner City P	Remainder N	Remainder P	WD	Inner City R	Inner City E	Inner City PR	Remainder R	Remainder E	Remainder PR
DO	31	52	1	100	30	50	FA	0	0	-	1	3	0
							MA_1	0	0	-	1	3	0
							MA_2	1	100	100	59	30	33
								1	100	100	2	7	0
BOD	21	38	0	-	21	38	ST	-	-	-	1	5	100
TOT COLI	16	25	0	-	16	25	AL_1	-	-	-	0	0	-
							AL^2	-	-	-	1	6	100
							PS	-	-	-	0	0	-
PH	20	25	0	-	20	25	FA	-	-	-	5	25	0
							MA	-	-	-	7	35	0
							PS	-	-	-	0	0	-
							PC_1	-	-	-	0	0	-
							PC_2	-	-	-	7	35	0
TDS	20	40	0	-	20	40	AI_1	-	-	-	0	0	-
							AI_2	-	-	-	0	0	-
							PS	-	-	-	0	0	-
TURB	31	55	1	100	30	53	FA_1	0	0	-	0	0	-
							FA_2	0	0	-	3	10	33
CL	20	35	0	-	20	35	PS	-	-	-	0	0	-
NO3	31	58	1	100	30	57	AL	0	0	-	0	0	-
							PS	0	0	-	0	0	-
P	31	61	1	100	30	60	NS	1	100	100	18	60	50

Code:

N = Number of stations
P = Percentage of stations below cutoff value
E = Percentage of stations exceeding reference level
R = Number of stations exceeding reference level
PR = Percentage of stations exceeding reference level below cutoff

Water Use Designation (WD):

AI = Agricultural, Irrigation
AL = Agricultural, Livestock
FA = Freshwater Aquatic Life
MA = Marine Water Aquatic Life
PS = Public Water Supply Intake
UR = Undesignated Recreational
PC = Primary Contact Recreational
ST = Secondary Treatment Standard
NS = Nutrient Standard

Note: Subscripts refer to different standards, where more than one standard is specified for a given water use designation.

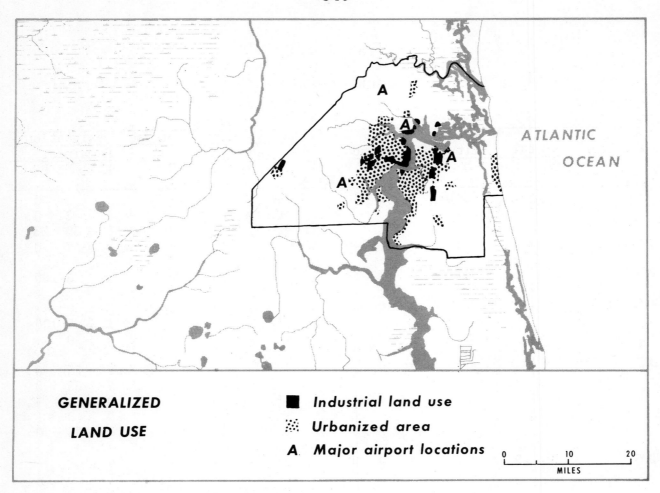

GENERALIZED

LAND USE

■ Industrial land use

⋮ Urbanized area

A Major airport locations

0   10   20

MILES

Figure 4.103

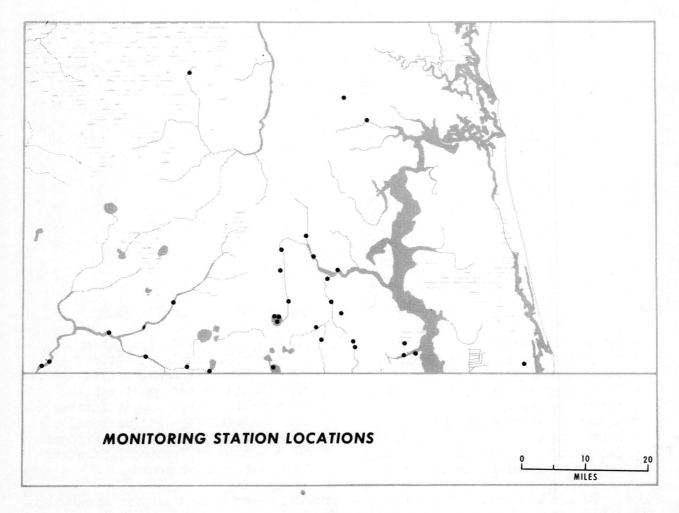

MONITORING STATION LOCATIONS

0   10   20

MILES

Figure 4.104

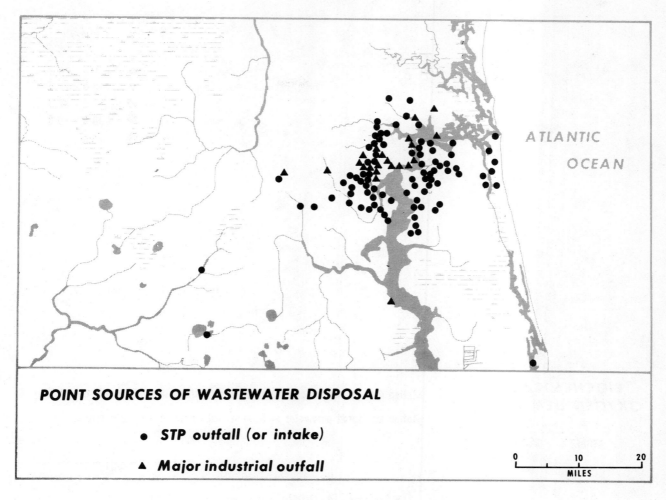

POINT SOURCES OF WASTEWATER DISPOSAL

● STP outfall (or intake)

▲ Major industrial outfall

0   10   20
MILES

Figure 4.105

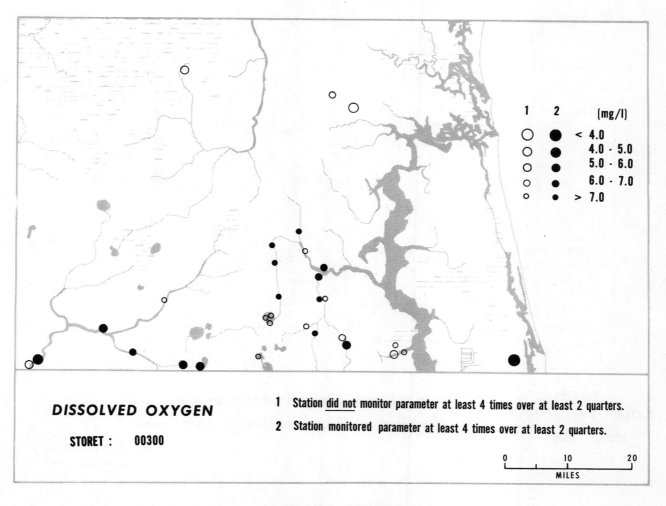

1   2   (mg/l)

○ ●   < 4.0
○ ●   4.0 - 5.0
○ ●   5.0 - 6.0
○ ●   6.0 - 7.0
○ ●   > 7.0

DISSOLVED OXYGEN

STORET :   00300

1   Station did not monitor parameter at least 4 times over at least 2 quarters.

2   Station monitored parameter at least 4 times over at least 2 quarters.

0   10   20
MILES

Figure 4.106

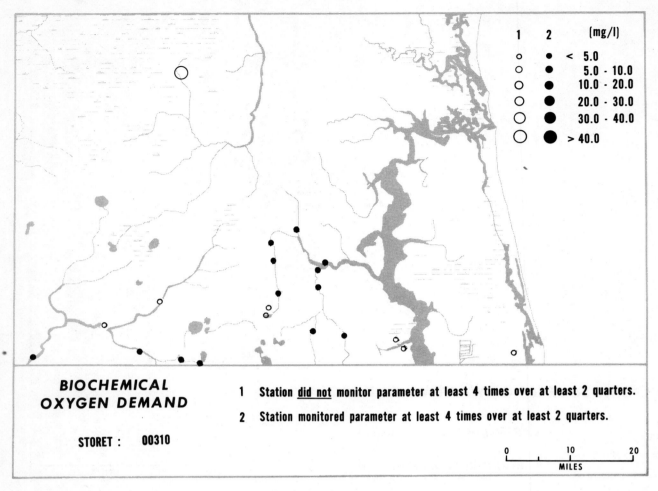

BIOCHEMICAL OXYGEN DEMAND

1 Station <u>did not</u> monitor parameter at least 4 times over at least 2 quarters.

2 Station monitored parameter at least 4 times over at least 2 quarters.

STORET : 00310

Figure 4.107

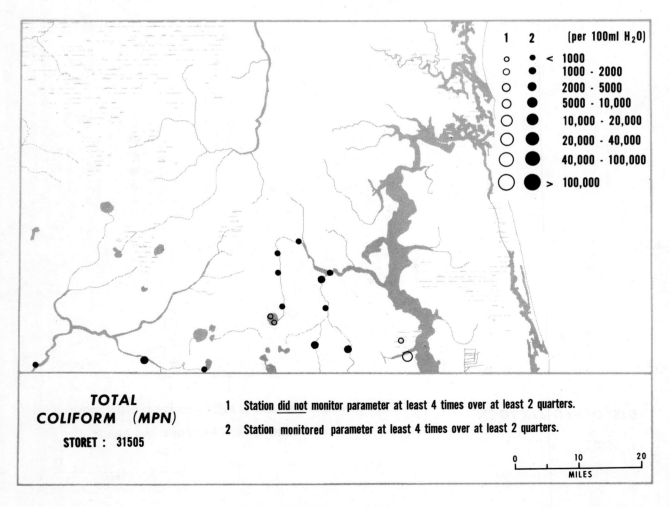

TOTAL COLIFORM (MPN)

STORET : 31505

1 Station <u>did not</u> monitor parameter at least 4 times over at least 2 quarters.

2 Station monitored parameter at least 4 times over at least 2 quarters.

Figure 4.108

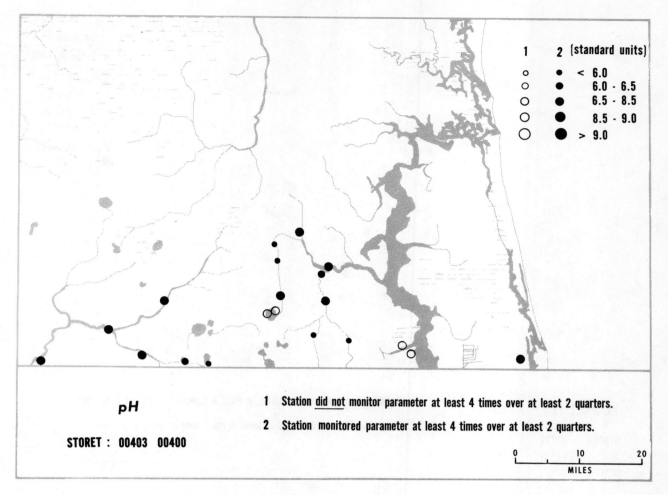

pH

STORET : 00403 00400

1 Station did not monitor parameter at least 4 times over at least 2 quarters.

2 Station monitored parameter at least 4 times over at least 2 quarters.

Figure 4.109

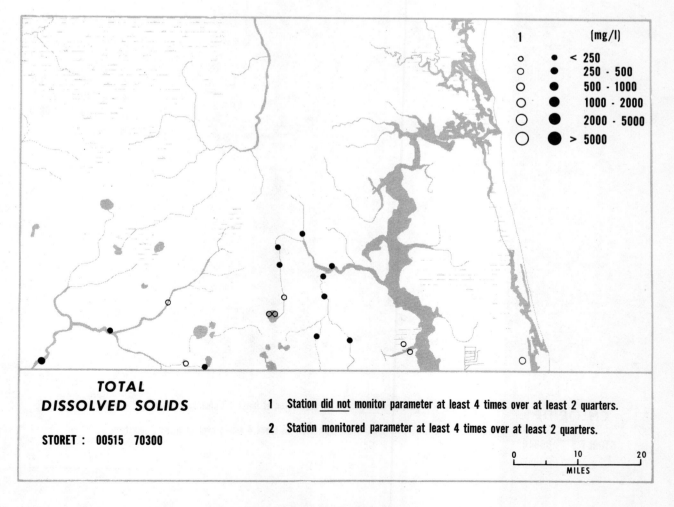

TOTAL
DISSOLVED SOLIDS

STORET : 00515 70300

1 Station did not monitor parameter at least 4 times over at least 2 quarters.

2 Station monitored parameter at least 4 times over at least 2 quarters.

Figure 4.110

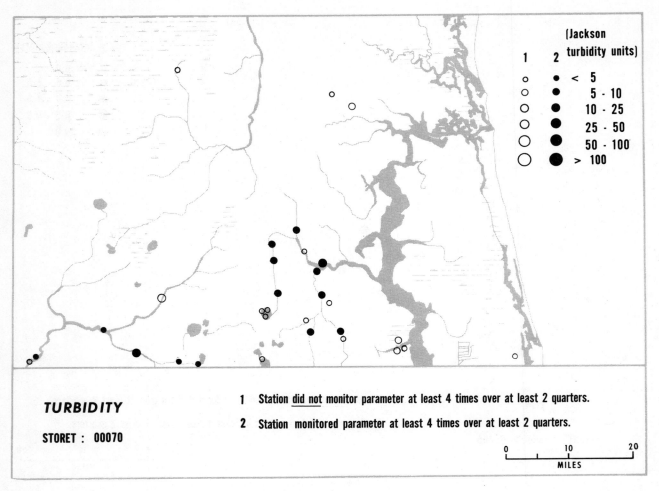

TURBIDITY

STORET : 00070

1   Station <u>did not</u> monitor parameter at least 4 times over at least 2 quarters.

2   Station monitored parameter at least 4 times over at least 2 quarters.

Figure 4.111

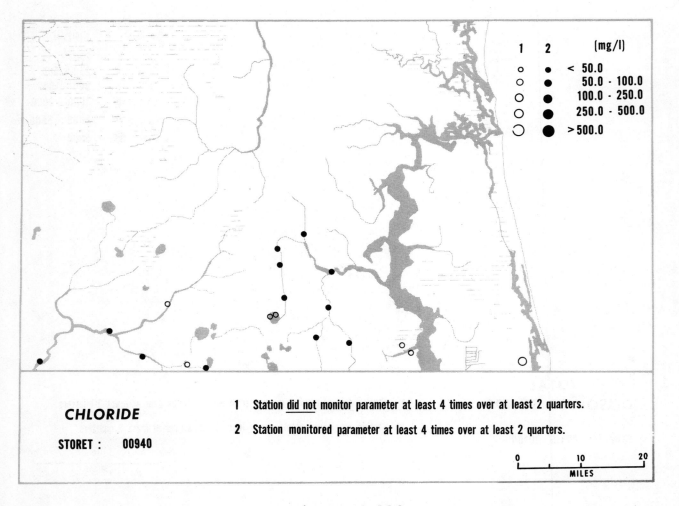

CHLORIDE

STORET :   00940

1   Station <u>did not</u> monitor parameter at least 4 times over at least 2 quarters.

2   Station monitored parameter at least 4 times over at least 2 quarters.

Figure 4.112

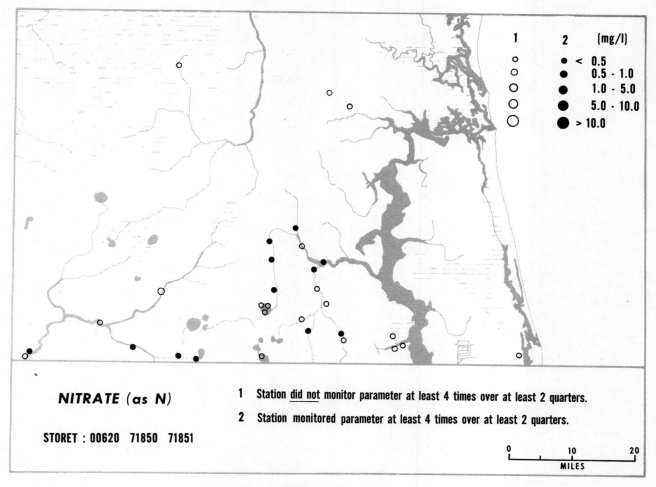

NITRATE (as N)

STORET : 00620 71850 71851

1 Station <u>did not</u> monitor parameter at least 4 times over at least 2 quarters.

2 Station monitored parameter at least 4 times over at least 2 quarters.

Figure 4.113

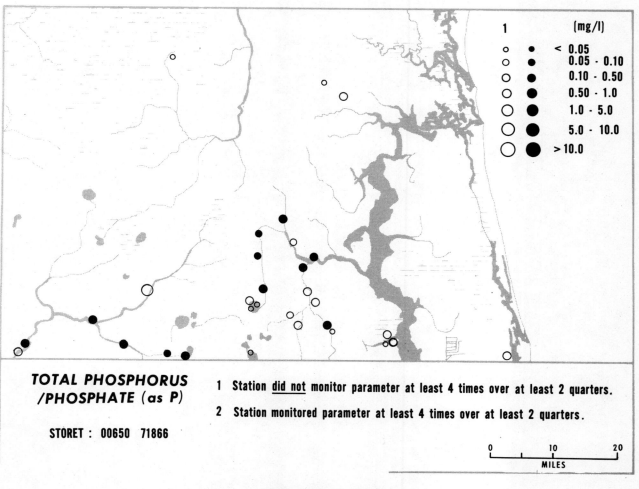

TOTAL PHOSPHORUS /PHOSPHATE (as P)

STORET : 00650 71866

1 Station <u>did not</u> monitor parameter at least 4 times over at least 2 quarters.

2 Station monitored parameter at least 4 times over at least 2 quarters.

Figure 4.114

DENVER

The Denver Metropolitan Area is located on the South Platte River. The STORET retrieval polygon for Denver contains most of the South Platte Basin to the river's confluence with the Thompson River and Cache La Poudre Creek. It includes all major tributaries which originate along the Continental Divide in the mountains west of the city.

Most of the territory covered by our retrieval polygon lies either in the Great Plains or Southern Rocky Mountains physiographic divisions. The two provinces are separated by steeply-dipping hogbacks or ridges which rise several hundred feet above the plain. Elevations within the basin range from less than 3,000 feet on the High Plains to more than 14,000 feet along the Continental Divide. Surface relief is pronounced in the mountains and flat and gently sloping in the plains where the South Platte takes on a braided appearance. Vegetation and soils range from alpine to steppe in character depending on altitude. Geology of the basin is characterized by granitic core rocks in the mountains and sedimentary (sandstone, shales and limestones) overlain by varying thicknesses of alluvium in the plains and intermontane valleys.

Climate ranges from an alpine type with more than 50 inches of precipitation in the mountains, much of it in the form of snow, to a dry semi-arid climate in the lowland plains. Precipitation tends to occur in spring and summer although in somewhat erratic patterns. Abundant surface water supplies originate in the mountains but are depleted by withdrawals for agricultural, industrial and municipal uses. Groundwater aquifers are available in parts of the basin.

The land area of the Denver polygon includes a mountainous region to the west and foothills and high plains to the east. The major drainage basin is that of the South Platte River. The area, because of its diverse land forms and climatic conditions, supports a variety of land uses.

The predominant uses in the mountainous regions are skiing resorts and similar recreation facilities, mining operations and ranching where conditions are favorable. In addition, a number of fish hatcheries are located in the mountains. In general, urbanization has not occurred to any great extent in this section of the polygon.

The most heavily urbanized regions are located on the plains at the edge of the mountainous region. In terms of population size and industrial and commerical development, the City of Denver is far ahead of other urbanized areas in the polygon. The other major urban concentrations are Boulder, Longmont, Fort Collins, Greeley and Loveland, with many smaller communities scattered throughout the polygon. The principal industrial operations of the region are sugar beets processing, meat packing, oil production, sand and gravel production and electric power generation.

The South Platte River serves as an agricultural supply source throughout the region, being used primarily for crop irrigation and livestock watering.

Important municipal discharge points are located in Denver, Greeley, Loveland and Fort Collins. Lesser discharge points are found in the mountains in resort areas and small municipalities. The use of individual septic tank units which discharge groundwater is widespread throughout the rural areas of the basin.

There are also a number of important industrial discharge points in the polygon. Discharging directly into the South Platte are two sugar beet processing plants and one electric power generating plant. Some industrial waste is channelled into municipal sewer systems before being discharged. The Cache la Poudre River receives effluents from sand and gravel operations, a steel industry, an electric power generating plant, a meat packing plant and the Great Western Sugar Company. Major discharge point concentrations occur in Greeley and Fort Collins. In the mountains, there are a number of discharge points connected with fish hatcheries and mining operations.

The most recent comprehensive study by the Colorado Department of Health dealing with the South Platte River basin, but excluding the Denver metropolitan area, listed several significant findings about water quality in the polygon:

1. The Cache La Poudre River is polluted with respect to ammonia toxicity between Fort Collins and its confluence with the South Platte River.

2. The Big Thompson River is water quality limited with respect to phosphates in its upper reach.

3. The Little Thompson River near Johnstown and segments of Coal Creek also have high ammonia nitrogen levels.

4. All other streams and river segments analyzed were found to be effluent limited.

5. Both surface and groundwaters in the area show increasing salinity levels which degrade water quality.

6. Non-point sources of pollution are considered more significant than point sources.

7. Existing water quality programs are neither coordinated nor adequate.

8. Inadequate staffing of wastewater treatment facilities by untrained personnel in small communities results in continued violation of the state's water quality standards.

Our EPA STORET materials contained chemical and biological water quality data for a total of 157 monitoring stations. Information for many sewage and water treatment plant influent and effluent points was also provided. The locations of surface chemical quality stations are shown in Figure 4.116. Effluent discharge points are shown in Figure 4.117.

All parts of the drainage basin receiving water from the mountains are covered by the extensive surveillance network. The network stations are very well distributed throughout the drainage system. The South Platte is monitored at many points along its length including confluence and reaches upstream or downstream from the Denver central city. Five stations are located within the central city. All major tributaries west of the Platte have stations well distributed along their lengths, around the confluences and on both sides of each of the smaller sewage treatment plants. The overall distribution of monitoring points is the best of all cities in the twelve-city samples and also the most representative of the drainage net. All but six of the biochemical stations are on rivers or intake pipes from rivers.

All parameters selected for mapping in our twelve sample cities were monitored by a multiplicity of water quality agencies in the Denver area. Trace metals and inorganic chemicals were the least frequently sampled parameters. Dissolved oxygen and pH were the most frequently tested. Total readings per parameter for each station varied greatly in those stations above the cutoff reference level, especially for dissolved oxygen and pH.

The parameter maps (Figure 4.118 ff) reveal that water quality in the Denver polygon varies considerably. In general, pollution levels were lowest on tributaries and in the upstream portions of the basin. They were decidedly higher downstream from the urban area. It appears that there were several severe pollution concentrations in 1971, the most noticeable being the main stem of the South Platte immediately below Denver and the confluences of the Thompson and Cache La Poudre Rivers with the South Platte near Greeley. The water quality was most polluted with respect to total and fecal coliforms and dissolved oxygen.

The stretch of the South Platte River downstream from Denver shows a very definite DO sag point about ten miles north of the city at Brighton. All stations in that section also show the highest observed fecal coliform bacteria counts. Total coliforms, ammonia nitrogen and MBAS levels were also exceedingly high. Phosphorus/phosphate levels were somewhat higher at this location.

The second major concentration of polluted water was on Cache La Poudre and Thompson Creeks near Greeley. This area had the worst total coliform readings and very high levels of fecal coliform bacteria. Many of the other tributaries in the western part of the basin had better quality water except for microbiological parameters which were mixed for total coliforms. St. Vrain Creek exhibited high turbidity and sulfate readings. Trace metals, fluorides, chlorides, nitrates, pH and turbidity had generally low readings throughout the polygon or else had too few stations to indicate any significant pollution.

Table 4.10

Denver

Parameter	Total		Inner City		Remainder		Details by Water Use Inner City				Designation Remainder		
	N	P	N	P	N	P	WD	R	E	PR	R	E	PR
DO	92	0	7	0	85	0	FA	0	0	-	3	4	0
							PC	0	0	-	6	7	0
BOD	74	72	4	25	70	74	ST	0	0	-	1	1	100
TOT COLI	93	65	1	0	92	65	AL_1	0	0	-	-	-	55
							AL_2	0	0	-	56	61	55
							PS	0	0	-	56	61	55
FEC COLI	93	47	0	-	93	47	AI	-	-	-	33	35	48
							AL_1	-	-	-	21	23	33
							AL_2	-	-	-	33	35	48
							PS	-	-	-	26	28	38
							UR_1	-	-	-	21	23	33
							UR_2	-	-	-	26	28	38
							PC_1	-	-	-	46	49	67
							PC_2	-	-	-	57	61	67
PH	127	0	3	0	124	0	FA	0	0	-	0	0	-
							PS	0	0	-	0	0	-
							PC_1	0	0	-	0	0	-
							PC_2	0	0	-	3	2	0
TDS	66	91	6	100	61	89	AI_1	0	0	-	0	0	-
							AI_2	0	0	-	20	33	85
							PS	1	17	100	30	49	80
TURB	38	71	0	-	38	71	FA_1	-	-	-	5	13	60
							FA_2	-	-	-	32	84	63
MBAS	26	54	5	20	21	62	PS	1	20	0	1	5	100
CL	42	0	4	0	38	0	PS	0	0	-	0	0	-
F	33	79	1	100	32	78	AI_1	0	0	-	0	0	-
							AI_2	0	0	-	0	0	-
							AI_3	0	0	-	9	28	78
							AL	0	0	-	0	0	-
NH3	52	79	2	50	50	80	FA	2	100	50	34	85	74
							PS	1	50	0	11	22	18
NO3	63	78	2	50	61	79	AL	0	0	-	0	0	-
							PS	0	0	-	0	0	-
P	50	92	1	100	49	92	NS	1	100	100	39	80	87

Parameter	Total		Inner City		Remainder		Details By Water Use Designation						
							Inner City				Remainder		
	N	P	N	P	N	P	WD	R	E	PR	R	E	PR
SO4	36	75	1	100	35	74	PS	0	0	-	11	31	18
CD	49	100	1	100	48	100	AI_1	0	0	-	0	0	-
							AI_2	1	100	100	24	50	100
							AL	0	0	-	0	0	-
							FA_1	0	0	-	0	0	-
							FA_2	1	100	100	31	65	100
							PS	1	100	100	24	50	100
CU	49	92	1	100	48	92	AI_1	0	0	-	0	0	-
							AI_2	0	0	-	0	0	-
							AL	0	0	-	0	0	-
							PS	0	0	-	0	0	-
FE	24	79	1	0	23	83	AI_1	0	0	-	0	0	-
							AI_2	0	0	-	-	-	-
							PS	1	100	0	2	9	100
PB	20	95	1	0	19	100	AI_1	0	0	-	0	0	-
							AI_2	0	0	-	0	0	-
							AL	0	0	-	0	0	-
							FA	0	0	-	0	0	-
							PS	0	0	-	5	26	100
ZN	54	96	3	100	51	96	AL	0	0	-	0	0	-
							PS	0	0	-	0	0	-

Code:

N = Number of stations
P = Percentage of stations below cutoff value
E = Percentage of stations exceeding reference level
R = Number of stations exceeding reference level
PR = Percentage of stations exceeding reference level below cutoff

Water Use Designation (WD):

AI = Agricultural, Irrigation
AL = Agricultural, Livestock
FA = Freshwater Aquatic Life
MA = Marine Water Aquatic Life
PS = Public Water Supply Intake
UR = Undesignated Recreational
PC = Primary Contact Recreational
ST = Secondary Treatment Standard
NS = Nutrient Standard

Note: Subscripts refer to different standards, where more than one standard is specified for a given water use designation.

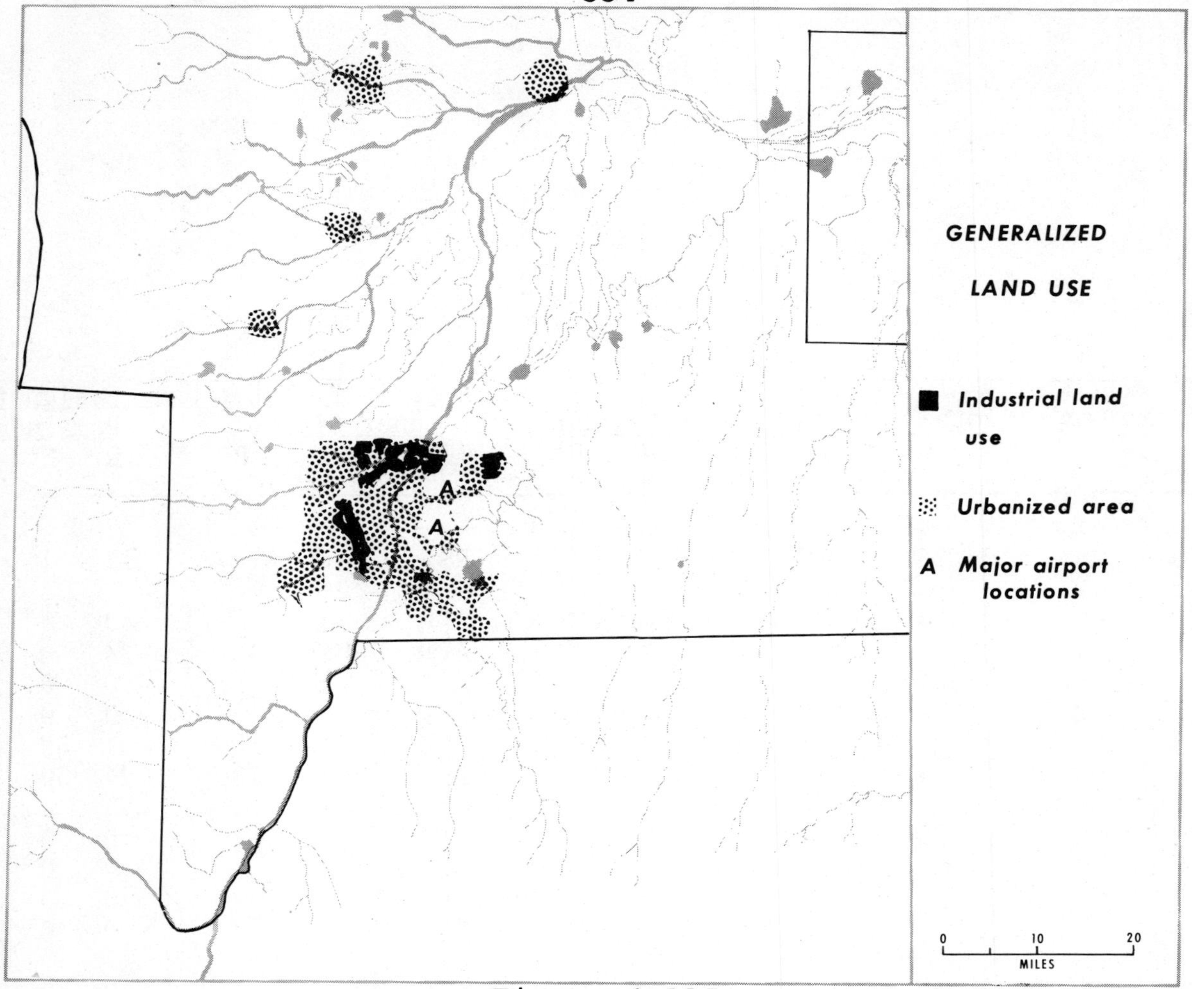

GENERALIZED
LAND USE

■ Industrial land
use

▓ Urbanized area

A Major airport
locations

0   10   20
MILES

Figure 4.115

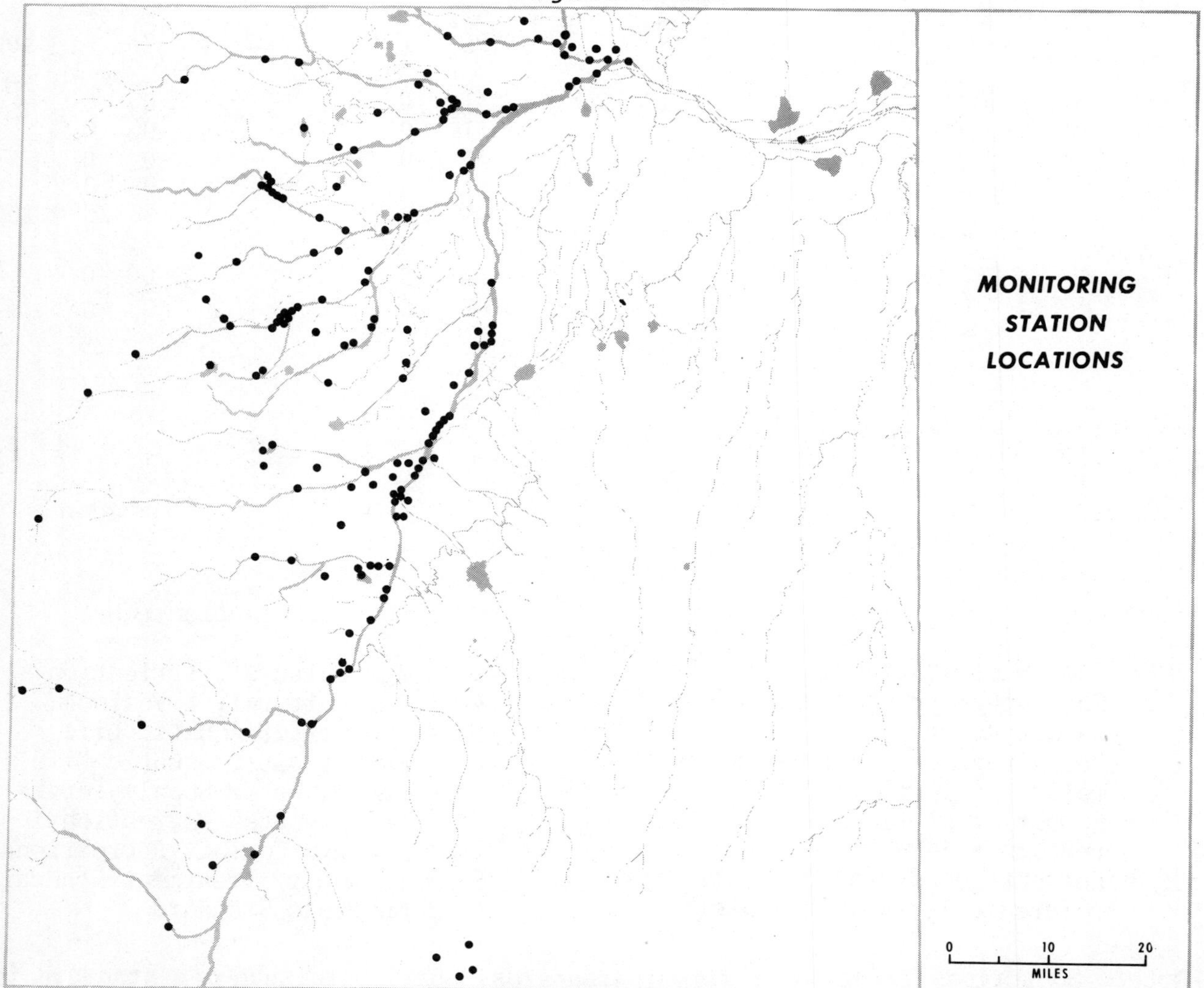

MONITORING
STATION
LOCATIONS

0   10   20
MILES

Figure 4.116

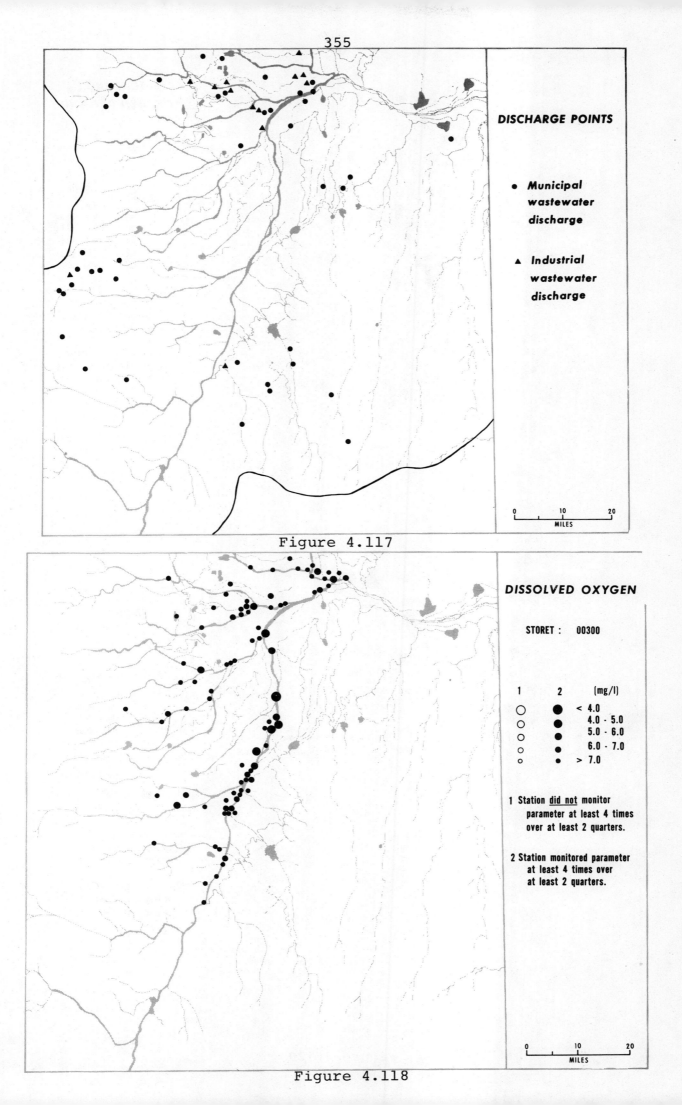

Figure 4.117

Figure 4.118

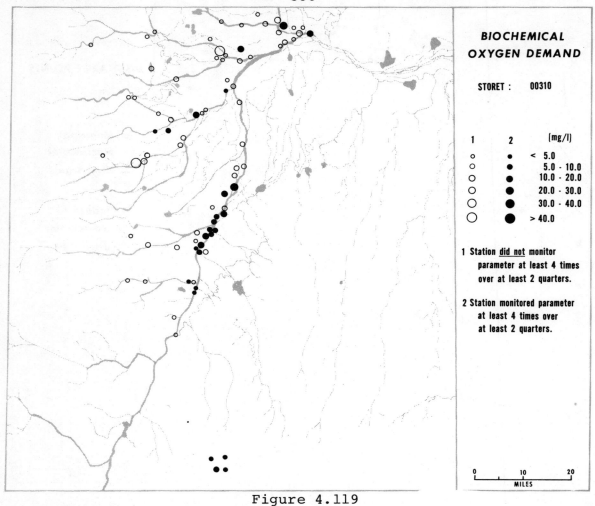

Figure 4.119

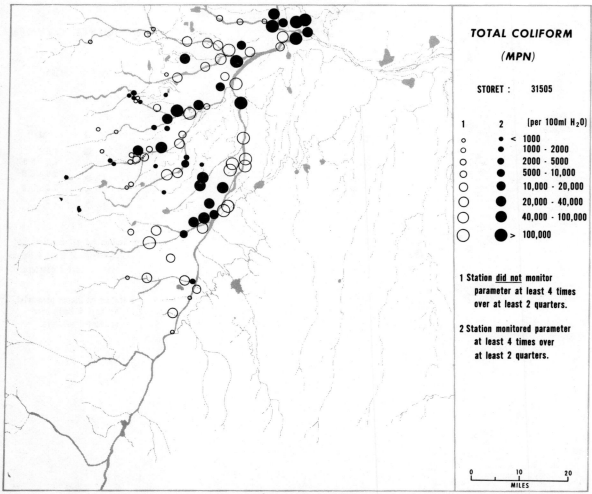

Figure 4.120

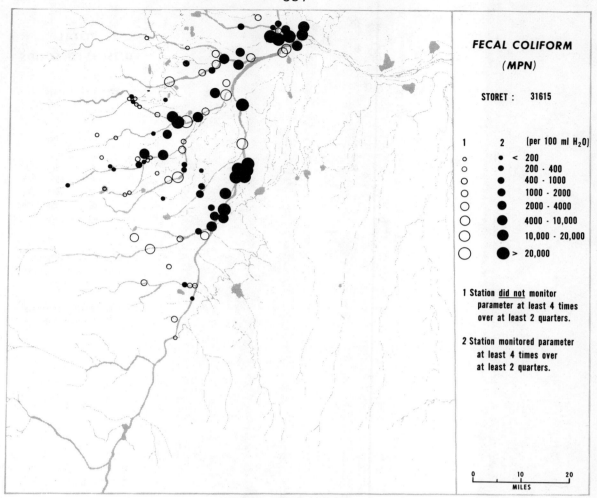

FECAL COLIFORM

(MPN)

STORET : 31615

1	2	(per 100 ml H₂O)

1   2   (per 100 ml H$_2$O)

○   •   < 200
○   •   200 - 400
○   •   400 - 1000
○   •   1000 - 2000
○   •   2000 - 4000
○   ●   4000 - 10,000
○   ●   10,000 - 20,000
○   ●   > 20,000

1 Station *did not* monitor
  parameter at least 4 times
  over at least 2 quarters.

2 Station monitored parameter
  at least 4 times over
  at least 2 quarters.

0   10   20
MILES

Figure 4.121

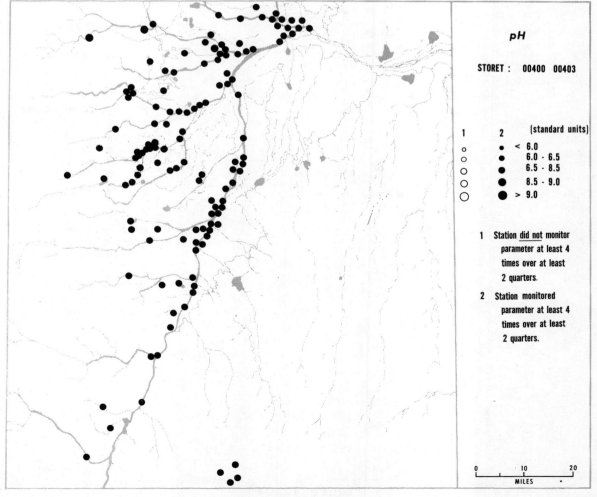

pH

STORET : 00400 00403

1   2   (standard units)

○   •   < 6.0
○   •   6.0 - 6.5
○   •   6.5 - 8.5
○   ●   8.5 - 9.0
○   ●   > 9.0

1 Station *did not* monitor
   parameter at least 4
   times over at least
   2 quarters.

2 Station monitored
   parameter at least 4
   times over at least
   2 quarters.

0   10   20
MILES

Figure 4.122

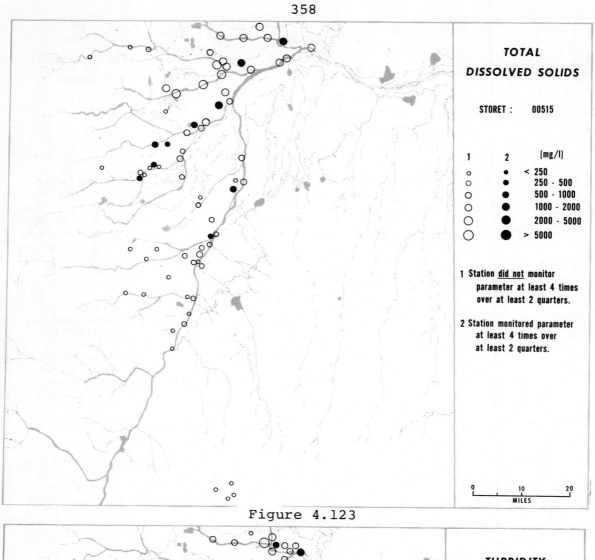

TOTAL DISSOLVED SOLIDS

STORET :   00515

1	2	(mg/l)
○	●	< 250
○	●	250 - 500
○	●	500 - 1000
○	●	1000 - 2000
○	●	2000 - 5000
○	●	> 5000

1 Station _did not_ monitor parameter at least 4 times over at least 2 quarters.

2 Station monitored parameter at least 4 times over at least 2 quarters.

0   10   20
MILES

Figure 4.123

TURBIDITY

STORET : 00070 00076

1	2	(Jackson turbidity units)
○	●	< 5
○	●	5 - 10
○	●	10 - 25
○	●	25 - 50
○	●	50 - 100
○	●	> 100

1 Station _did not_ monitor parameter at least 4 times over at least 2 quarters.

2 Station monitored parameter at least 4 times over at least 2 quarters.

0   10   20
MILES

Figure 4.124

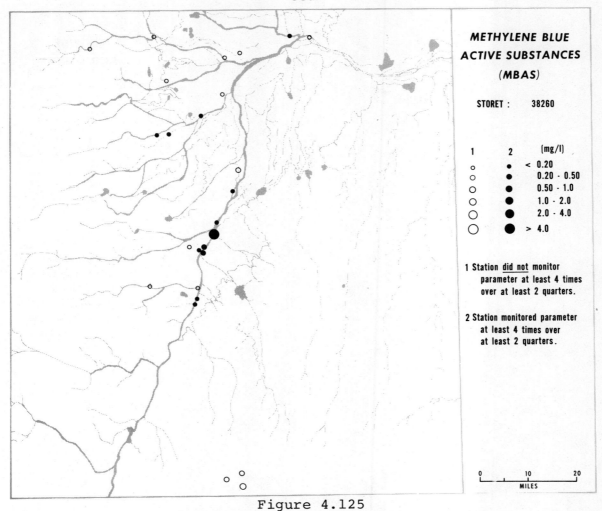

Figure 4.125

Figure 4.126

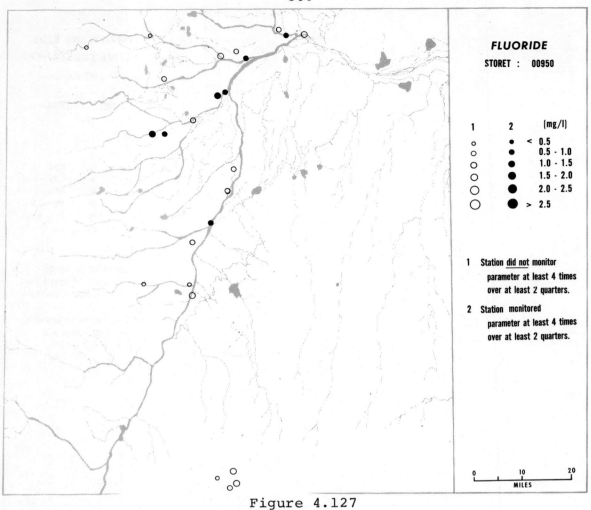

Figure 4.127

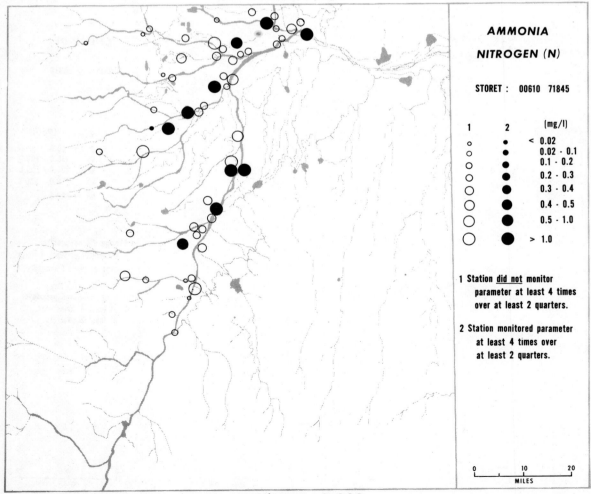

Figure 4.128

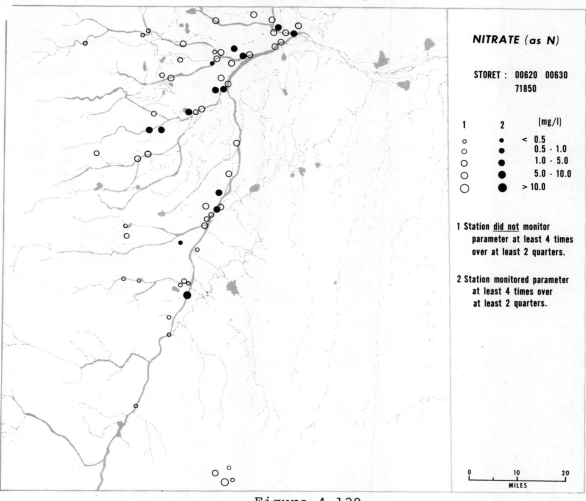

NITRATE (as N)

STORET : 00620 00630
71850

	1	2	(mg/l)
	○	•	< 0.5
	○	•	0.5 - 1.0
	○	●	1.0 - 5.0
	○	●	5.0 - 10.0
	○	●	> 10.0

1 Station <u>did not</u> monitor
  parameter at least 4 times
  over at least 2 quarters.

2 Station monitored parameter
  at least 4 times over
  at least 2 quarters.

0   10   20
MILES

Figure 4.129

TOTAL PHOSPHORUS/

PHOSPHATE (as P)

STORET : 00665 00650

	1	2	(mg/l)
	○	•	< 0.05
	○	•	0.05 - 0.10
	○	•	0.10 - 0.50
	○	●	0.50 - 1.0
	○	●	1.0 - 5.0
	○	●	5.0 - 10.0
	○	●	> 10.0

1 Station <u>did not</u> monitor
  parameter at least 4 times
  over at least 2 quarters.

2 Station monitored parameter
  at least 4 times over
  at least 2 quarters.

0   10   20
MILES

Figure 4.130

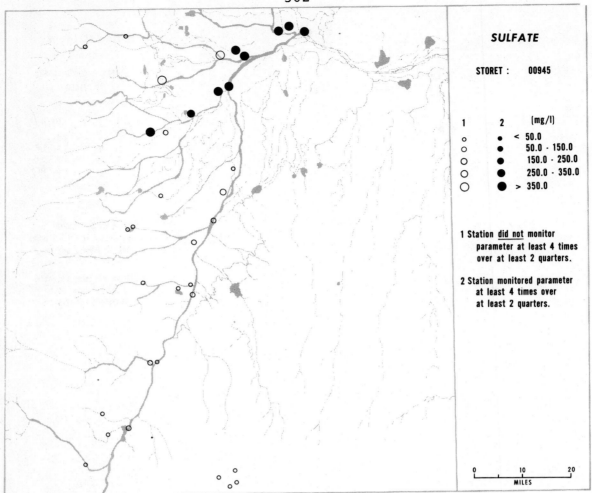

SULFATE

STORET : 00945

1	2	(mg/l)
∘	•	< 50.0
∘	•	50.0 - 150.0
○	●	150.0 - 250.0
○	●	250.0 - 350.0
○	●	> 350.0

1 Station <u>did not</u> monitor
   parameter at least 4 times
   over at least 2 quarters.

2 Station monitored parameter
   at least 4 times over
   at least 2 quarters.

0   10   20
MILES

Figure 4.131

CADMIUM

STORET : 01025

1	2	(mg/l)
∘	•	< 0.004
∘	•	0.004 - 0.01
○	●	0.01 - 0.03
○	●	0.03 - 0.05
○	●	0.05 - 0.10
○	●	> 0.10

1 Station <u>did not</u> monitor
   parameter at least 4 times
   over at least 2 quarters.

2 Station monitored parameter
   at least 4 times over
   at least 2 quarters.

0   10   20
MILES

Figure 4.132

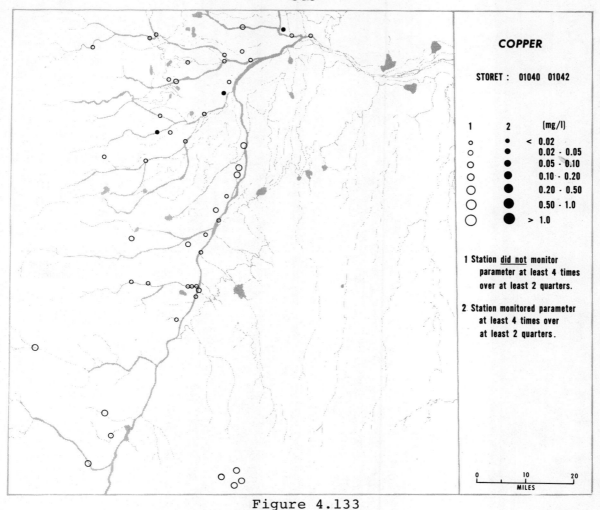

Figure 4.133

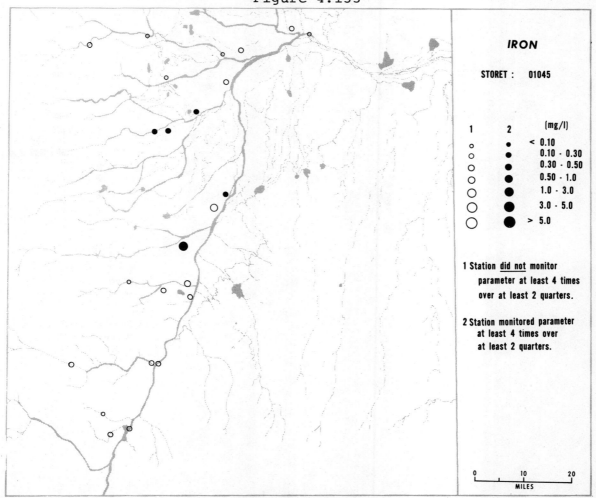

Figure 4.134

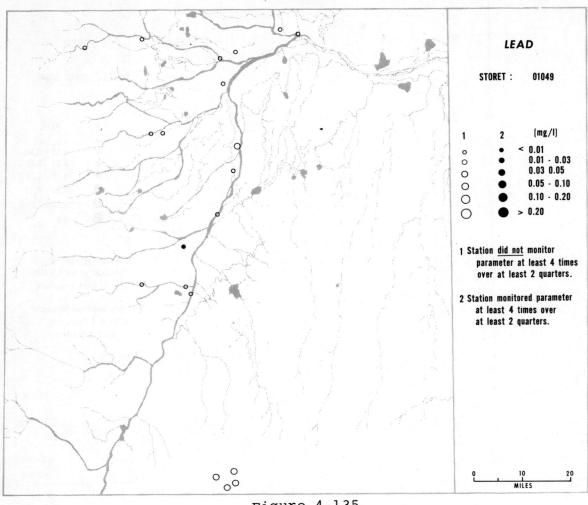

Figure 4.135

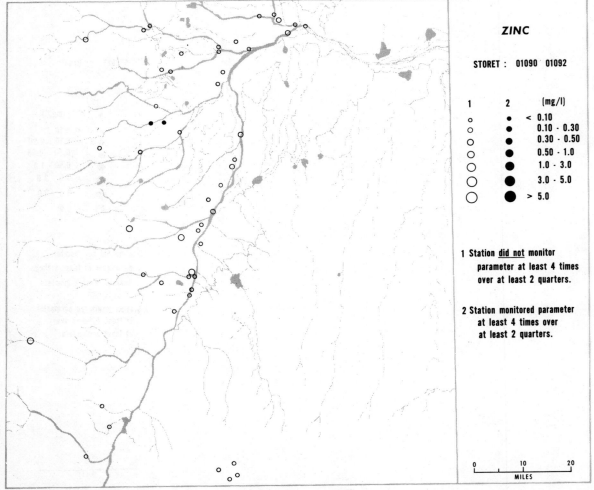

Figure 4.136

OKLAHOMA CITY

The portion of central Oklahoma within our polygon lies within the Interior Plains physiographic province. The region around Oklahoma City lies approximately 800 to 1,600 feet above sea level, with the average relief seldom exceeding 100 feet. Drainage patterns are dendritic with evenly distributed tributaries of approximately equal size. Drainage of all major streams in our polygon (North Canadian, Canadian, Cimarron, Deep Fork and Washita Rivers) is to the east. The flow of the major rivers is modified by a system of dams and reservoirs. Local climate is characterized by short, mild winters and long, hot summers with large diurnal ranges and gradual change of season. Average annual rainfall around Oklahoma City is 32 inches per year, the greatest amount of which falls in the spring months. Winds are also highest during the spring and tornados are not uncommon. Local surface geology consists of consolidated sedimentary rocks of Permian age (referred to as redbeds) and unconsolidated Quaternary alluvium terrace deposits.

During the U.S. Geological Survey 1971 water year (October 1970 to September 1971), yearly runoff was normal in east Central Oklahoma and below normal in the remainder of the state where yearly mean discharge was generally 20 percent to 50 percent of average. Reservoir storage in central and eastern Oklahoma varied within the normal range and was at least 80 percent of capacity at the end of the water year.

The Canadian River Basin contains a mixture of land uses, ranging from the commercial, industrial and residential uses of Oklahoma City, to large areas of agricultural land that is used for both truck and subsistence farming and for range land. A number of subregions in the basin contain large numbers of feed lot cattle operations. Rough estimates of gross land use percentages are as follows: 5 percent urban, 21.5 percent forest, 22.5 percent cropland, 38 percent range and 12 percent pasture.

The waters of the Canadian River and the North Canadian River, particularly above Canton Reservoir, do not meet the usually accepted water quality standards for municipal use or for irrigation. Both streams contain excessive amounts of dissolved minerals derived primarily from the soluble material in the rocks of the basin and also from farming or industrial activities.

Major concentrations of industrial effluent sources are located in Oklahoma City and immediately surrounding areas. Industrial pollution may take the form of untreated waste or heated effluent; and oil field brines are discharged into waterways in Oklahoma City and in Okmulgee County, also.

Sewage effluent and heavy metals, cyanide and nutrients discharged through storm sewers have been reported in Oklahoma City and there is substantial groundwater contamination. Mixing of land uses has resulted in scattered patches of industry among residential and commercial areas, indicating that industrial discharge is not a highly localized phenomena. Though vacant land constitutes nearly half of the total land within the urbanized area, urban runoff is a problem in periods of peak rainfall.

Monitoring stations are located on the main streams and on tributaries but are usually far apart and scattered throughout the SMSA. Many of the sampling stations are found on the Washita Rivers (Arkansas Basin) and its tributaries. Oklahoma City is not monitored, except for one radiological station within the city and one station more than ten miles downstream on the Deep Fork of the Canadian River. Chemical quality stations are found either on the far upstream or downstream margins of the city. The distances between sampling points are too great to give a representative indication of stream quality despite the large number of readings at each station. However, each station does present a good picture of water quality in its immediate vicinity. Total dissolved solids, pH, chlorides, sulfates, nitrates, phosphates and fluorides are well monitored, but the microbiological, inorganic, and oxygen measuring variables are completely lacking in the STORET data except for BOD, which was not available in sufficient numbers for mapping. Trace metals are represented only by chromium, which we did not map.

All stations in the chemical surveillance network are maintained by the U.S. Geological Survey. Data for state run stations which we observed in the literature were not available from EPA STORET. Readings at USGS stations are taken throughout the entire year in most cases and for nine months at the remainder. The average number of readings is forty per year.

Overall water quality in the immediate vicinity of testing stations was generally good, although reflecting uniformly higher levels of certain dissolved solids (C , SO , TDS). Chloride levels were higher than those for other cities, a possible illustration of conditions in semi-arid basins. These levels might also be attributed to return flow or contamination from nearby oil wells. The lowest levels of chloride, sulfate, nitrate and total dissolved solids were found on the tributaries of the Washita River; higher levels of these parameters were found on the main channel of the same stream.

For the entire polygon and the 22 stations which regularly monitored them, the following results were obtained for dissolved solids parameters. For the Public Water Supply reference level, 64 percent of the stations had mean values which were in excess for TDS, 27 percent for chlorides, and 32 percent for sulfates. For the Agricultural (Irrigation) reference level for sensitive crops (100 mg/l), 23 percent of the stations surpassed the reference level.

Six of the 13 stations monitoring total phosphate exceeded the nutrient standard of .1 mg/l. Readings for pH and fluoride were low at all stations where they were sampled. The general hardness of the water may be due to the chemical composition of rock types including high sulfate gypsum.

Table 4.11

Oklahoma City

Parameter	Total		Inner City		Remainder		Details By Water Use Designation						
							Inner City				Remainder		
	N	P	N	P	N	P	WD	R	E	PR	R	E	PR
PH	22	5	0	-	22	5	FA	-	-	-	0	0	-
							PS	-	-	-	0	0	-
							PC₁	-	-	-	0	0	-
							PC₂	-	-	-	0	0	-
TDS	22	5	0	-	22	5	AI₁	-	-	-	0	0	-
							AI₂	-	-	-	5	23	0
							PS	-	-	-	14	64	0
CL	22	5	0	-	22	5	PS	-	-	-	6	27	0
NO3	22	5	0	-	22	5	AL	-	-	-	0	0	-
							PS	-	-	-	0	0	-
P	13	46	0	-	13	46	NS	-	-	-	6	46	0
SO4	22	5	0	-	22	5	PS	-	-	-	7	32	0

Code:

N = Number of stations
P = Percentage of stations below cutoff value
E = Percentage of stations exceeding reference level
R = Number of stations exceeding reference level
PR = Percentage of stations exceeding reference level below cutoff

Water Use Designation (WD):

AI = Agricultural, Irrigation
AL = Agricultural, Livestock
FA = Freshwater Aquatic Life
MA = Marine Water Aquatic Life
PS = Public Water Supply Intake
UR = Undesignated Recreational
PC = Primary Contact Recreational
ST = Secondary Treatment Standard
NS = Nutrient Standard

Note: Subscripts refer to different standards, where more than one standard is specified for a given water use designation.

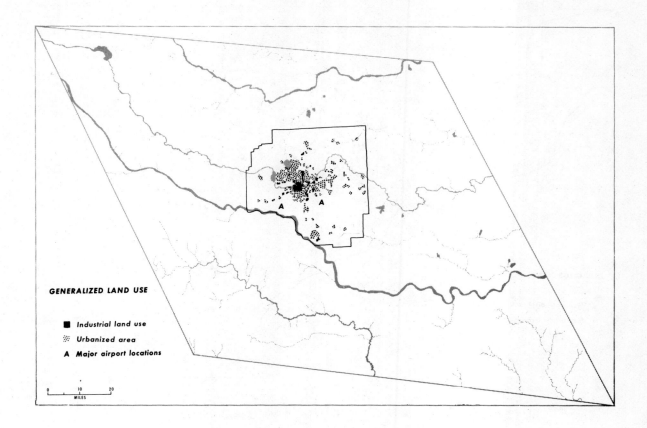

Figure 4.137

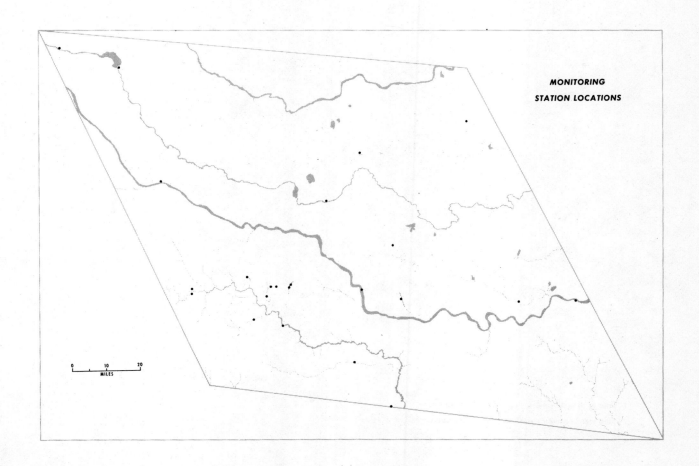

Figure 4.138

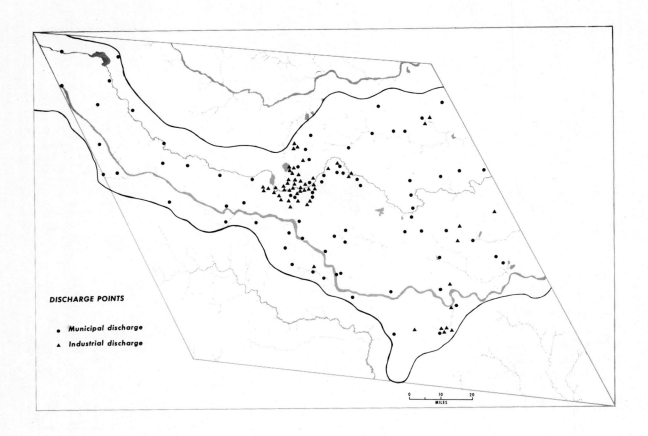

DISCHARGE POINTS

● Municipal discharge

▲ Industrial discharge

0   10   20
MILES

Figure 4.139

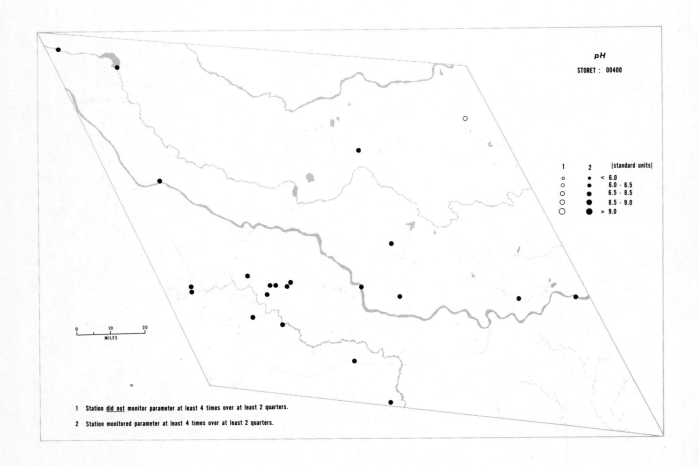

pH

STORET : 00400

1	2	(standard units)
○	●	< 6.0
○	●	6.0 - 6.5
○	●	6.5 - 8.5
○	●	8.5 - 9.0
○	●	> 9.0

0   10   20
MILES

1   Station did not monitor parameter at least 4 times over at least 2 quarters.

2   Station monitored parameter at least 4 times over at least 2 quarters.

Figure 4.140

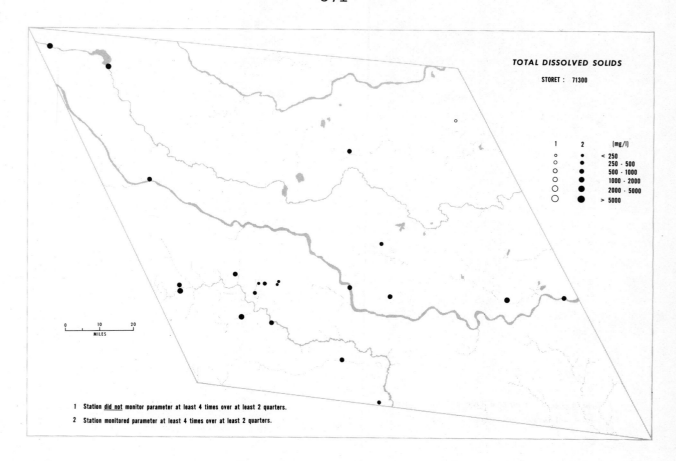

Figure 4.141

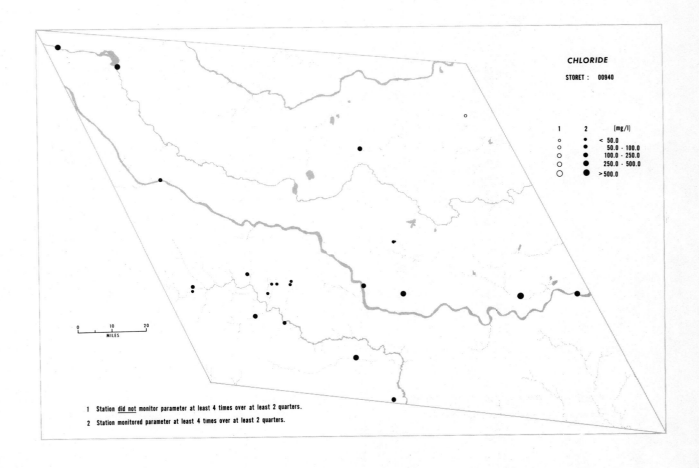

Figure 4.142

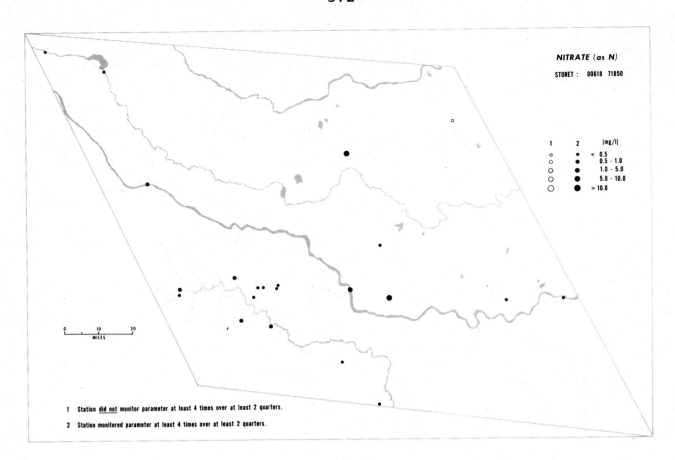

Figure 4.143

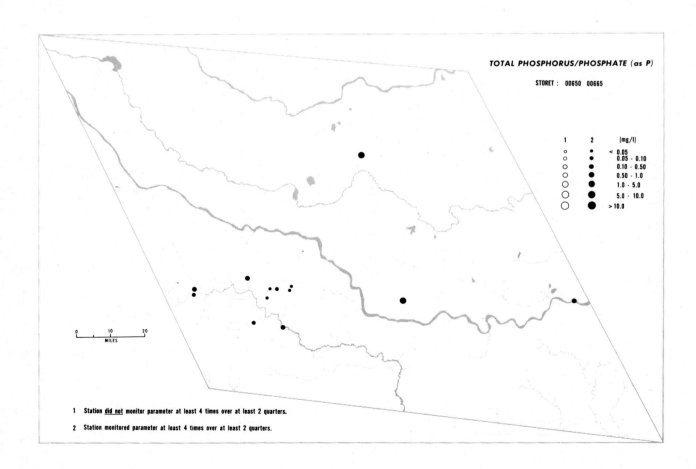

Figure 4.144

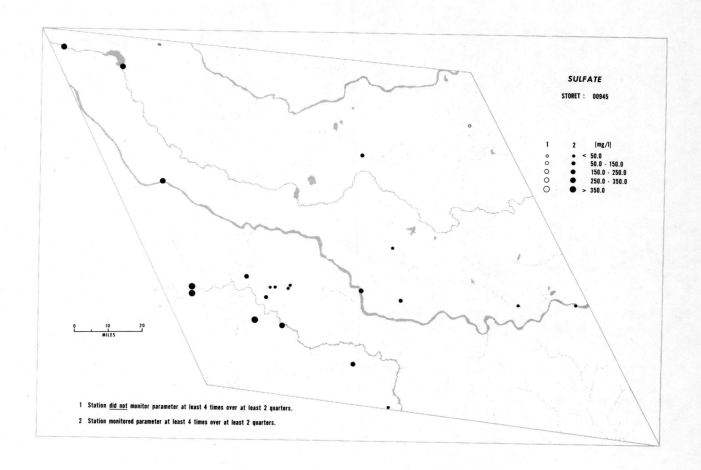

Figure 4.145

SEATTLE

The STORET retrieval polygon for the Seattle area contains Seattle and Everett, the two major urban concentrations in the two counties which comprise the Seattle-Everett SMSA. Tacoma to the south and portions of the Olympic Peninsula bordering Puget Sound are also included, since their contributions to the water body influence its quality. The major geomorphic features in the area are the Puget Sound Lowland, a series of flat-lying till plains and alluvial valleys bordering the Sound and the Cascade Range, a rugged mountainous drainage divide which provides the larger cities with water for drinking, agricultural and industrial uses. The major drainage basins in the area are the Green-Duwamish River, the Cedar-Lake Washington Basin, the Snoqualmie-Skykomish-Snohomish River systems and the White-Puyallup River Basin. Major streams are similar in natural constituents since they have a common source in the mountains.

Climate in the region varies in relation to elevation above sea level and location of the drainage divides. The lowlands have a cool-summer, mild-winter marine climate with 30 inches of rainfall. The mountainous limits of the polygon have an alpine climate with several times as much precipitation, usually in the form of snow. There is a striking decrease in precipitation and runoff in the late summer months, a situation which affects pollution concentrations in the low-lands. During 1971, streamflow in the Seattle-Everett watershed was slightly above average throughout the calendar year except for October through December when it was slightly below normal. High precipitation in January and February nearly doubled average runoff in most basins during those months. A cool period in May and June prolonged the melting period in the mountains and resulted in greater runoffs in the normally dry late summer months.

Nearly all urban and industrial concentrations in the polygon are found along the Puget Sound lowland. Heavy industry and manufacturing are located along the Duwamish estuary and the nearby eastern shore of Elliot Bay. The Seattle CBD is located on Elliot Bay immediately north of the industrial waterfront district. Additional industrial zones are: The ship canal connecting Lake Washington with Puget Sound, the southern tip of Lake Washington at Renton, the mouth of the Snohomish River at Everett and nearby portions of Puget Sound around Port Gardner (pulp mills and oil storage), and the mouth of the Puyallup River at Tacoma (pulp mills). Some major industrial discharge points, METRO sewage treatment plants and sewage and storm overflow points are shown in Figure 4.148. According to Seattle METRO, there were 338 industrial dischargers into the METRO sewerage system. Of these, 89 companies specialized in food processing.

The predominant land use along Puget Sound from Tacoma to Everett is residential. The lowland section of King County immediately east of Lake Washington is becoming increasingly urbanized and is expected to continue to do so in the future. Agricultural activity within the polygon is concentrated in the alluvial floodplains of the major rivers. The remainder of the polygon is forested and alpine in character. Its chief uses are logging and recreational with some grazing and mining.

There are approximately 460 monitoring stations in the polygon covering the Seattle-Everett SMSA. Of the total number, 180 stations are on rivers or minor tributaries, 160 are clustered around lakes and 120 are located in marine waters. Coverage of drainage basins is adequate but with many concentrations. All main streams are monitored at the confluences with tributaries. Large concentrations of stations are found along Puget Sound, the Duwamish estuary (Elliot Bay), and on minor tributaries draining into Lake Washington. There are clusters of stations around each of the major sewage treatment plant outfalls. In 1971, many of the minor lakes had multiple sampling points in accordance with a major research project in progress at the time. The headwaters of each drainage basin received limited coverage since industrial and municipal pollution sources are centered in the urbanized area at the mouth of the Duwamish River.

Four agencies were the chief contributors of Seattle area water quality information to the STORET data bank. The largest network of stations within the Seattle city limits and suburban county area is that of the Municipality of Metropolitan Seattle (METRO). That agency monitors extensively along the coast and on lakes and tributaries of importance to fish rearing and water supply. Another contributor of data to STORET was the University of Washington whose stations were concentrated on minor tributaries to the east of Lake Washington and in Puget Sound along the coast. The Washington State Department of Ecology (DOE) and the U.S. Geological Survey provided most of the river data coverage for the non-urban portions of the polygon. The USGS also sampled several lakes.

The most commonly monitored parameters in 1971 were those which were common to most of the twelve sample cities. Dissolved oxygen, total and fecal coliforms, pH, turbidity, chlorides, sulfates, nitrates, ammonia and phosphorus were frequently monitored. Trace metals and inorganics (except for mercury) were seldom sampled. Seattle was the only city in the sample set to monitor mercury extensively.

Several groups of sampling stations monitored water quality frequently and at regular intervals throughout the year. This was typical of many METRO marine stations and those river stations of the DOE and USGS located at confluence of major streams. However, for most parameters the number of readings varied considerably from station to station both in total number and yearly distribution. The extreme case in point was dissolved oxygen (00299). Seven METRO automatic monitoring stations accounted for 6,306 readings of the 11,321 total readings. Five of those same stations were responsible for 63 percent of the total pH readings. The DO map shows 259 stations and the pH map 279. Each of the automatic monitors is surrounded by other stations many of which fall below cutoff values.

Our maps prepared from the STORET data indicate that waterways in the Seattle polygon were among the cleanest in the twelve-city sample. The only parameter grossly in excess of proposed federal criteria was ammonia nitrogen for which 55 of a total of 88 stations exceeded the stringent .02 mg/l Freshwater Aquatic Life reference level. However, only one station exceeded the .4 mg/l Marine Water Aquatic Life and .5 mg/l Public Water Supply reference levels. This station was one of a cluster of stations near the mouth of the Quilicene River which had high ammonia levels.

The only significant concentration of pollution in the inner city area was located at the mouth of the Duwamish River where it empties into Elliot Bay. Several stations in this vicinity exhibit high total and fecal coliform and ammonia levels. Station coverage of the inner city was excellent. The high mean annual coliform values might have been the result of point source pollution along the waterfront, storm-water runoff, or combined sewer overflows into the Duwamish. Thornton Creek, a minor inner city stream which flows into Lake Washington, had total coliform values at two of its four stations slightly in excess of Public Water Supply reference levels. For the entire polygon, Public Water Supply levels were surpassed only in 7 out of 300 stations for total coliforms and 5 of 101 stations for fecal coliforms.

Maps for the remaining parameters show only a small percentage of stations in excess of proposed federal standards. Dissolved oxygen levels were above 7.0 mg/l at most rivers and marine sampling points. They were slightly lower on the small streams east of Lake Washington and near Port Gardner in the Saratoga Passage. Most of the DO readings still exceeded the 5.0 mg/l reference level for Primary Contact Recreational uses. The overall dissolved oxygen patterns differed for the clusters of lake stations. The variations in lake station DO levels do not reflect deteriorated water quality. They are the result of depth variation in sampling practices which lower the yearly mean for many stations when averaged in. The variations in pH levels at lake stations also reflect vertical differences in water quality.

Turbidity readings appeared to be consistently higher in the larger streams, especially downstream. The maximum levels for this parameter were obtained on Coal Creek and nearby streams. Approximately 417 of the mapped stations were above the stringent Freshwater Aquatic Life recommended level of 10 JTUs.

Nitrate levels were highest on several minor tributaries to Puget Sound, at one station on the Raging River and on Big Soos Creek below the fish hatchery. However, only 2 of 305 stations exceeded Public Water Supply criteria on 10 mg/l (N).

The chloride map illustrates the difference between freshwater and saltwater stations. None of the freshwater stations exceeded recommended levels. Sulfate and phosphorus values were low. Of the few stations available for fluorides, four had mean levels above 2.0 mg/l. These sampling points were located in Puget Sound not far from municipal sewage treatment plants. Trace metals had low readings except for lead. Extremely high levels of that parameter were found at two stations near the confluence of the Pilchuck and Snohomish Rivers at Snohomish.

These pleasing conclusions were the results of the concerted efforts to halt the degradation of water quality in the region by the Municipality of Metropolitan Seattle and by the State of Washington. Thus, METRO was itself able to report that "the major highlight of 1971 was the continued improvement of water quality levels in the marine waters of Puget Sound along Seattle's waterfront. Elliot Bay is now one of the cleanest commercial harbors in the world." The occasional high levels of total and fecal coliform bacteria in the Seattle area, particularly in Elliot Bay, are attributed to combined sewer overflows and stormwater runoff in winter. The loading factors for combined sewage overflows greatly exceed those for stormwater overflows, particularly in regard to nutrient discharge.

Table 4.12
Seattle

Parameter	Total		Inner City		Remainder		Details By Water Use Designation Inner City				Remainder		
	N	P	N	P	N	P	WD	R	E	PR	R	E	PR
DO	259	55	28	46	231	56	FA	0	0	-	7	3	100
							MA$_1$	0	0	-	7	3	100
							MA$_2$	0	0	-	21	9	100
							PC	0	0	-	11	5	100
TOT COLI	300	64	65	25	235	75	AL$_1$	1	2	0	1	1	100
							AL$_2$	10	15	50	15	6	67
							PS	4	6	50	3	1	67
FEC COLI	101	26	49	14	52	37	AI	5	10	0	1	2	0
							AL$_1$	1	2	0	0	0	-
							AL$_2$	5	10	0	1	2	0
							PS	4	8	0	1	2	0
							UR$_1$	1	2	0	0	0	-
							UR$_2$	4	8	0	1	2	0
							PC$_1$	14	29	0	4	7	0
							PC$_2$	19	39	5	6	12	0
PH	279	79	10	70	269	79	FA	0	0	-	7	3	100
							MA	1	14	100	44	16	100
							PS	0	0	-	5	2	100
							PC$_1$	0	0	-	5	2	100
							PC$_2$	1	14	100	44	16	100
TDS	64	83	4	25	60	87	AI$_1$	0	0	-	0	0	-
							AI$_2$	0	0	-	0	0	-
							PS	0	0	-	0	0	-
TURB	138	67	4	100	134	66	FA$_1$	0	0	-	5	4	100
							FA$_2$	2	50	100	55	41	69
CL	63	30	11	36	52	29	PS	11	100	36	13	25	8
NH3	88	32	3	100	85	29	FA	3	100	52	52	61	40
							MA	0	0	-	1	1	0
							PS	0	0	-	1	1	0
NO3	305	72	25	84	280	75	AL	0	0	-	0	0	-
							PS	0	0	-	2	1	0
P	134	55	3	100	131	54	NS	-	-	-	39	30	87
SO4	38	21	0	-	38	21	PS	-	-	-	0	0	-

Code:

N = Number of stations
P = Percentage of stations below cutoff value
E = Percentage of stations exceeding reference level
R = Number of stations exceeding reference level
PR = Percentage of stations exceeding reference level below cutoff

Water Use Designation (WD):

AI = Agricultural, Irrigation
AL = Agricultural, Livestock
FA = Freshwater Aquatic Life
MA = Marine Water Aquatic Life
PS = Public Water Supply Intake
UR = Undesignated Recreational
PC = Primary Contact Recreational
ST = Secondary Treatment Standard
NS = Nutrient Standard

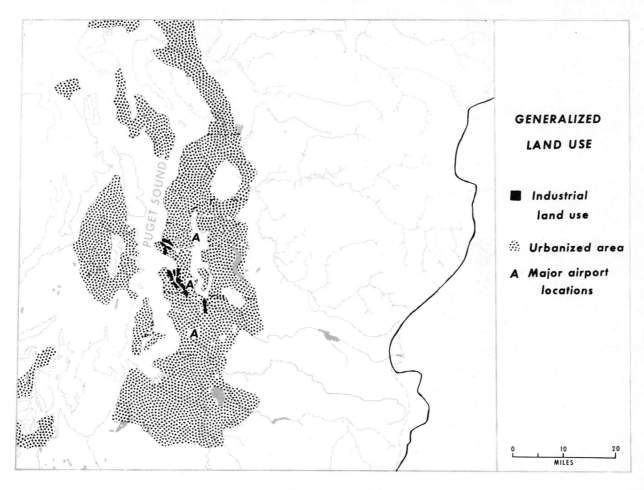

Figure 4.146

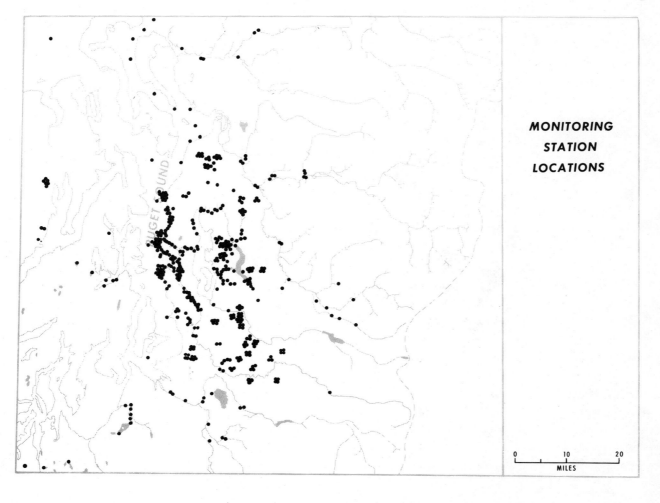

Figure 4.147

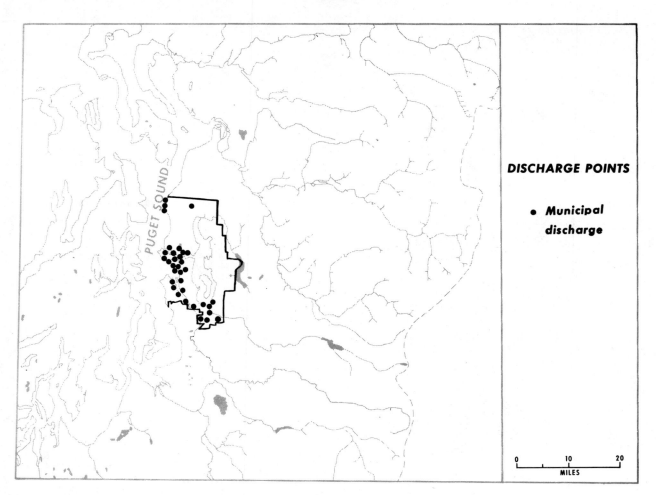

Figure 4.148

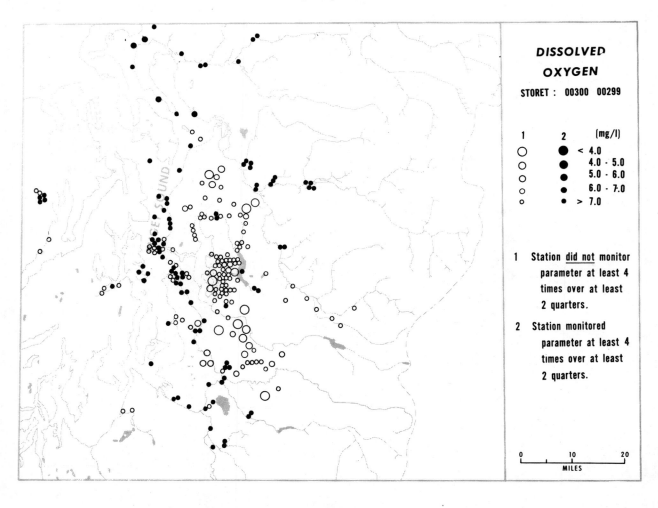

Figure 4.149

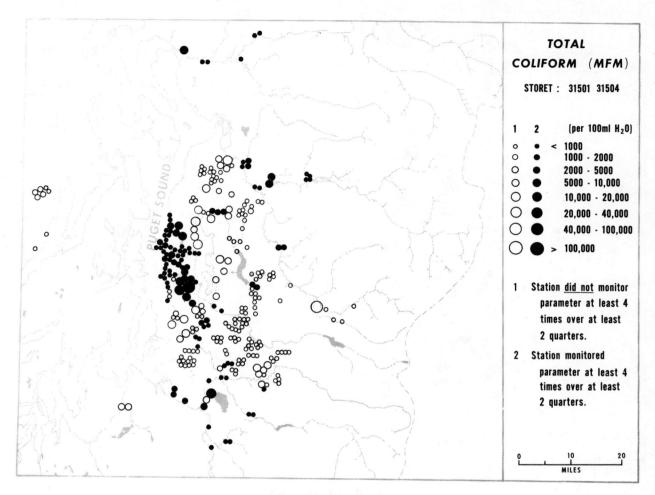

Figure 4.150

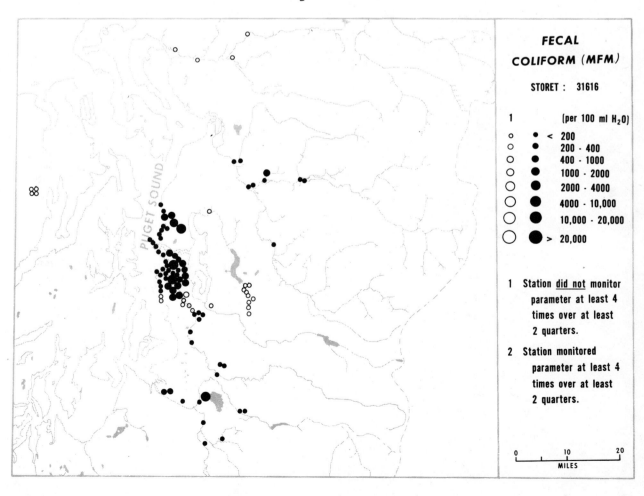

Figure 4.151

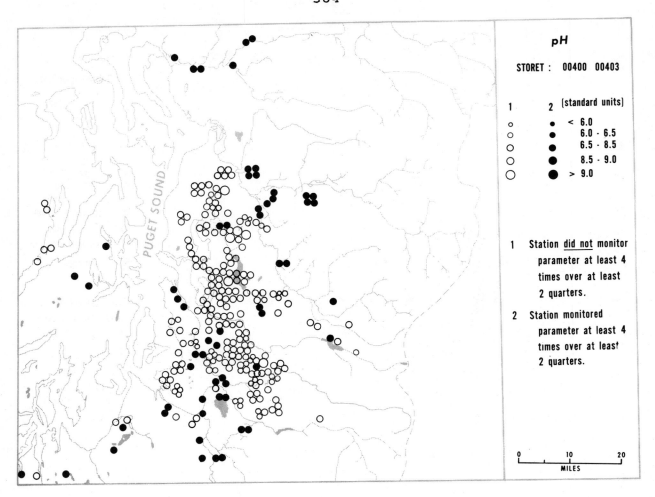

Figure 4.152

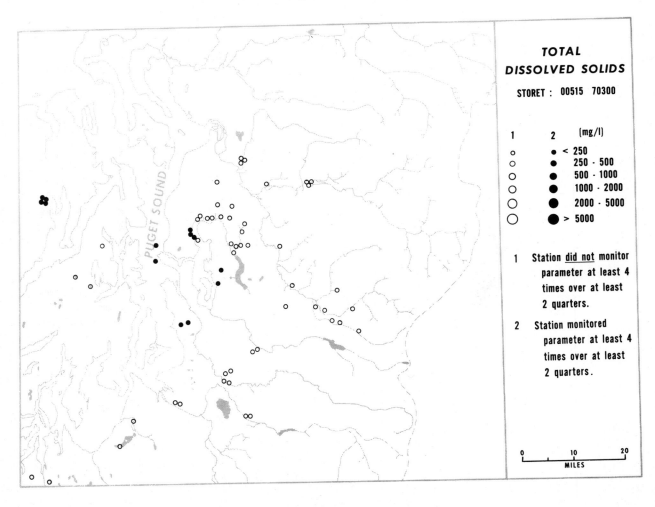

Figure 4.153

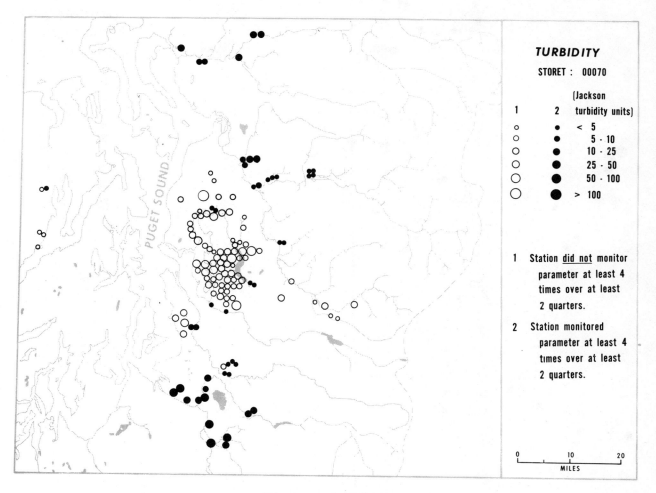

Figure 4.154

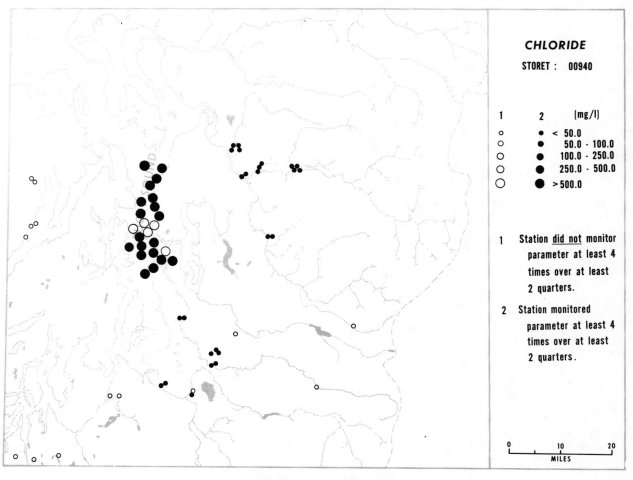

Figure 4.155

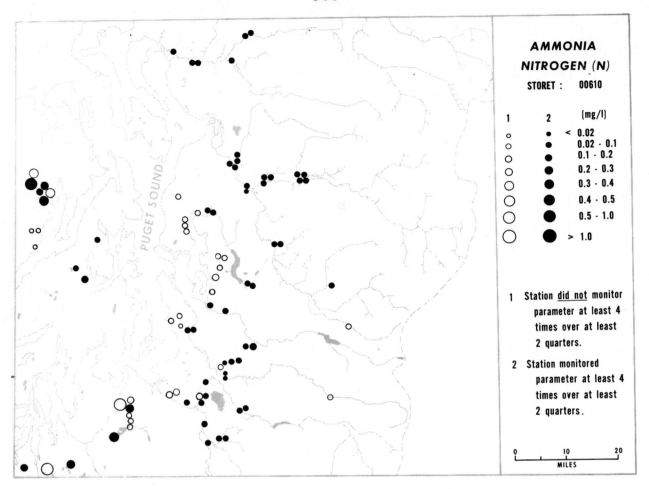

Figure 4.156

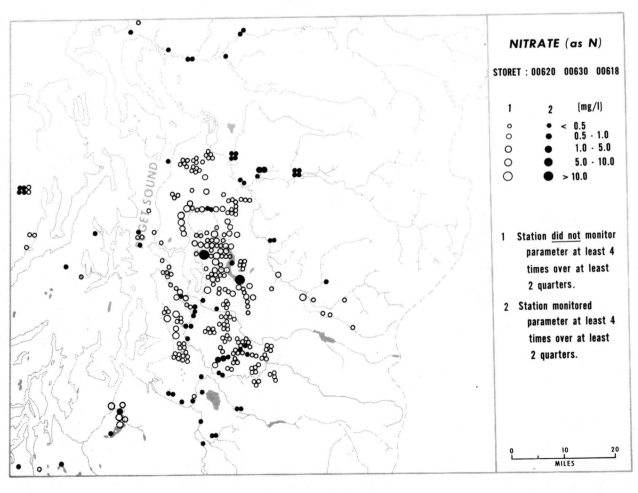

Figure 4.157

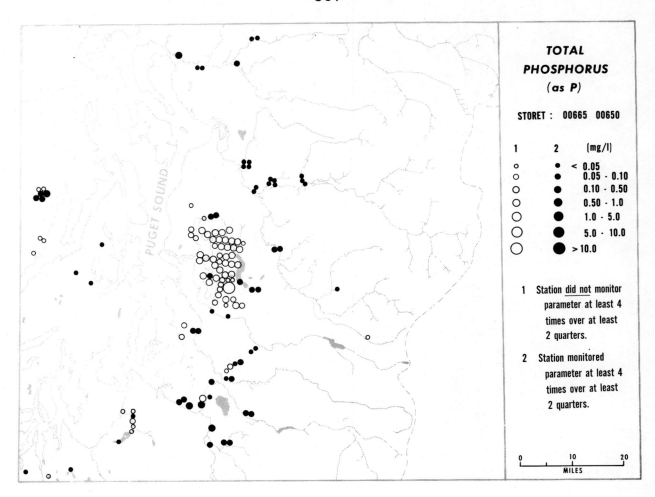

Figure 4.158

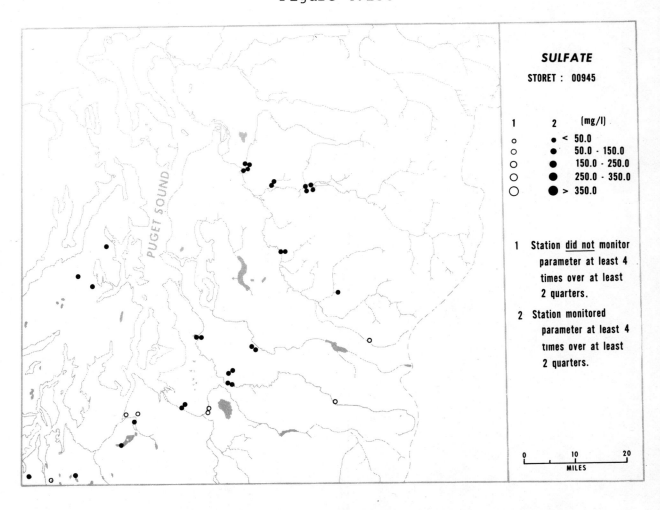

Figure 4.159

SAN DIEGO

The STORET retrieval polygon for San Diego corresponds to the San Diego planning unit used by the California State Water Resources Control Board (Basin 9). The basin description which follows is derived from that state agency's planning summary for Basin 9.

The San Diego Basin occupies approximately 4,000 square miles in the southwest corner of California. It includes 90 miles of Pacific coastline extending from Laguna Beach to the Mexican border. It also includes coastal lagoons which are subject to tidal action, San Diego and Mission Bays and 11 streams draining into the Pacific Ocean.

Physical relief ranges from sea level to more than 6,000 feet in the mountains of the coastal ranges. Precipitation varies from 10 inches per year along the coast to 30 inches per year in the mountains. The climate is true Mediterranean subtropical with the average rainfall of 15 inches per year falling predominantly during the four winter months. Because of climatic patterns and man-made modifications of the drainage system, most streams in the basin are ephemeral. Although most of the water supplied for municipal use is imported from outside the basin, very intensive use is made of all available surface and groundwater.

The San Diego polygon includes a wide range of land uses, ranging from protected state wild lands to naval air stations and ports. Large areas of land to the west and northwest are state-protected wilderness areas and parks. There are also a number of Indian Reservations in the rural areas of the polygon. Also, major portions of governmentally owned land are taken up by Camp Pendleton Marine Base, Miramar Naval Air Station, and naval installations in and around San Diego Bay. At the present time, much of the land in rural areas is unused, vacant land.

San Diego is, of course, the major urban center of the polygon, containing the major residential and industrial concentrations of the region; though Escondido also has a large industrial cluster. In San Diego, the major industrial activities are located around San Diego Bay, with another sizeable cluster situated in the northwest suburban area of the city. A major mining operation is located in the north position of the city.

Agriculture, in the rural sections of the polygon, consists of orchards, truck cropping, nursery stock, poultry and livestock, grain and pasture lands. Irrigation is often necessary because of climatic conditions.

San Diego Bay receives discharged wastewater from a number of surrounding industrial sites, municipal wastewater outfalls and runoff from the naval stations. Other important sites of industrial discharge are Ocean Side (from mining operations and industry) and Escondido. Municipal effluent is discharged in numerous locations from the small communities located mainly in the western half of the polygon.

The 1971 INVENT obtained for San Diego from STORET contained only three stations which monitored any of the biological and chemical parameters we had selected for appraisal. Supplementary water quality data were obtained from the California State Water Resources Control Board and added twenty-three additional stations to our maps.

Stations were well distributed throughout the polygon but were lacking near the mouths of most of the eleven stream systems in Basin 9. The majority of the sampling points were located on dams or on lakes or reservoirs. Four stations were located within the outer margins of the inner city, usually at filtration plants below municipal reservoirs. The number and distribution of surveillance stations needed to monitor the many industrial discharges and wastewater treatment plants was far from adequate.

For the limited number of stations for which data were provided, a surprisingly large range of parameters was monitored in 1971. All parameters used in this study with the exception of total and fecal coliform bacteria and MBAS were monitored. However, the overall insufficiency of stations precluded mapping of most parameters. To compound the problem, readings were taken monthly or quarterly at many sampling points and less frequently at others.

Keeping in mind the limited number of stations and parameters, as well as the less-than-ideal station locations, several generalizations can be made about water quality. Twenty-one stations were used in each map. Fluoride and pH maps show no marked concentrations of pollution. Public Water Supply reference levels were exceeded by 3 stations for chloride, 7 for sulfates and 2 for nitrates. Escondido Creek below Escondido and the San Diego River were above reference levels for all three parameters. Chlorides and sulfates were above recommended levels at the San Diego River. Sulfates were also above 250 mg/l at two stations on Murray Lake and one at the Miramar filtration plant.

Table 4.13

San Diego

Parameter	Total		Inner City		Remainder		Details by Water Use Designation						
								Inner City			Remainder		
	N	P	N	P	N	P	WD	R	E	PR	R	E	PR
PH	21	52	4	0	17	65	FA	0	0	-	0	0	-
							PS	0	0	-	0	0	-
							PC_1	0	0	-	0	0	-
							PC_2	0	0	-	1	6	100
TDS	22	55	4	0	18	67	AI_1	0	0	-	0	0	-
							AI_2	1	25	0	2	11	0
							PS	4	100	0	9	50	56
CL	21	48	4	0	17	59	PS	1	25	0	2	12	0
F	21	52	4	0	17	82	AI_1	0	0	-	0	0	-
							AI_2	0	0	-	0	0	-
							AI_3	0	0	-	0	0	-
							AL	0	0	-	0	0	-
NO_3	21	52	4	0	17	65	AL	0	0	-	0	0	-
							PS	1	25	0	1	6	0
SO_4	21	52	4	0	17	65	PS	4	100	0	3	18	0

Code:

N = Number of stations
P = Percentage of stations below cutoff value
E = Percentage of stations exceeding reference level
R = Number of stations exceeding reference level
PR = Percentage of stations exceeding reference level below cutoff

Water Use Designation (WD):

AI = Agricultural, Irrigation
AL = Agricultural, Livestock
FA = Freshwater Aquatic Life
MA = Marine Water Aquatic Life
PS = Public Water Supply Intake
UR = Undesignated Recreational
PC = Primary Contact Recreational
ST = Secondary Treatment Standard
NS = Nutrient Standard

Note: Subscripts refer to different standards, where more than one standard is specified for a given water use designation.

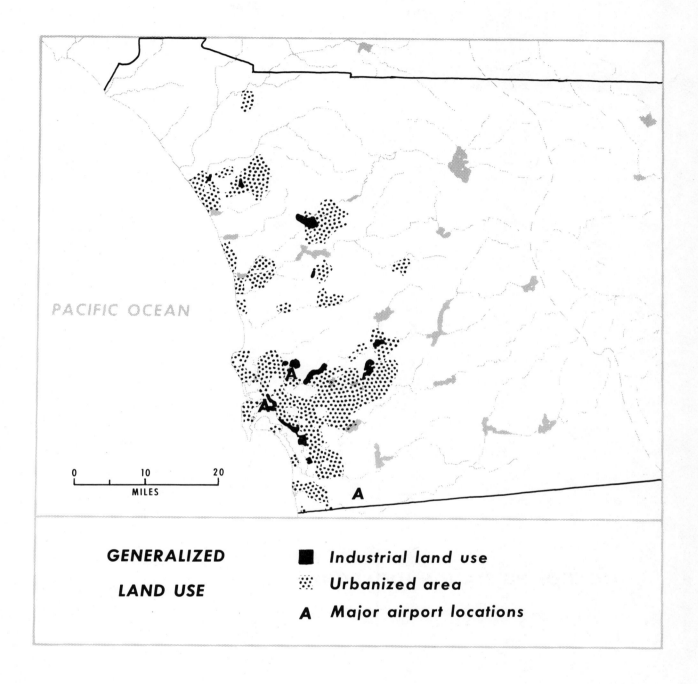

PACIFIC OCEAN

0   10   20
MILES

GENERALIZED

LAND USE

■   Industrial land use

⋮⋮   Urbanized area

A   Major airport locations

Figure 4.160

MONITORING STATION LOCATIONS

Figure 4.161

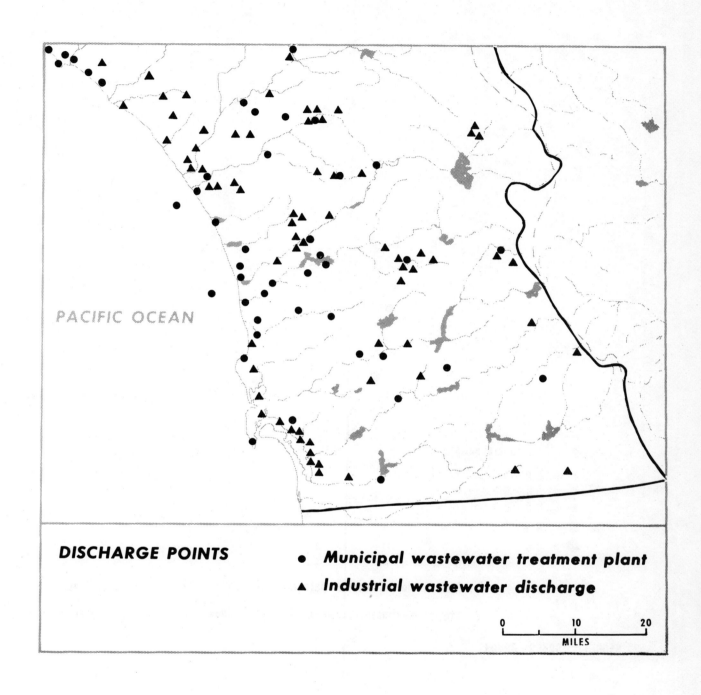

PACIFIC OCEAN

DISCHARGE POINTS

● **Municipal wastewater treatment plant**

▲ **Industrial wastewater discharge**

0   10   20
MILES

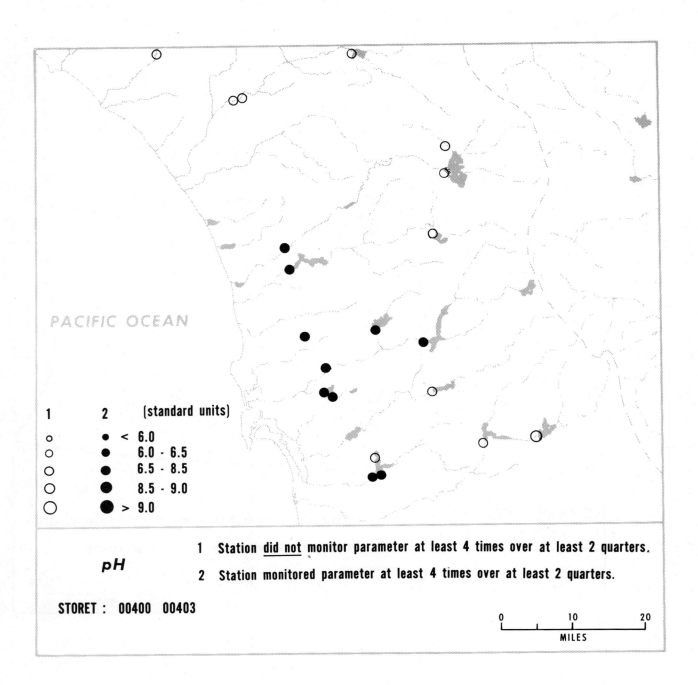

Figure 4.163

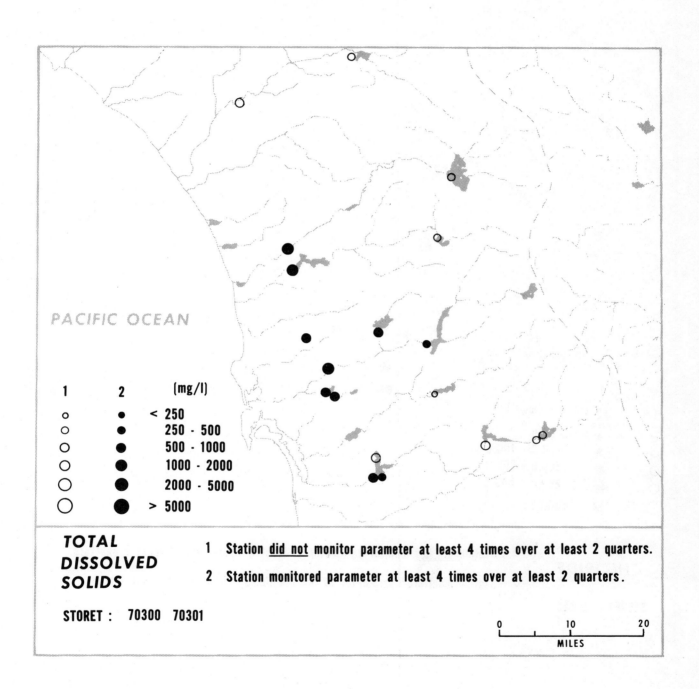

PACIFIC OCEAN

1	2	(mg/l)
○	●	< 250
○	●	250 - 500
○	●	500 - 1000
○	●	1000 - 2000
○	●	2000 - 5000
○	●	> 5000

TOTAL DISSOLVED SOLIDS

1   Station <u>did not</u> monitor parameter at least 4 times over at least 2 quarters.

2   Station monitored parameter at least 4 times over at least 2 quarters.

STORET :   70300 70301

0   10   20
MILES

Figure 4.164

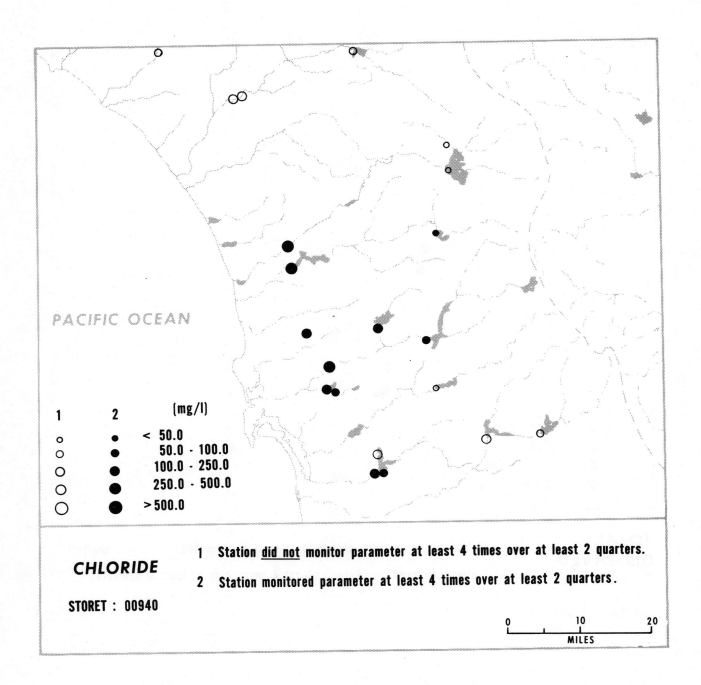

PACIFIC OCEAN

1	2	(mg/l)
○	●	< 50.0
○	●	50.0 - 100.0
○	●	100.0 - 250.0
○	●	250.0 - 500.0
○	●	> 500.0

CHLORIDE

STORET : 00940

1 Station <u>did not</u> monitor parameter at least 4 times over at least 2 quarters.

2 Station monitored parameter at least 4 times over at least 2 quarters.

0   10   20
MILES

Figure 4.165

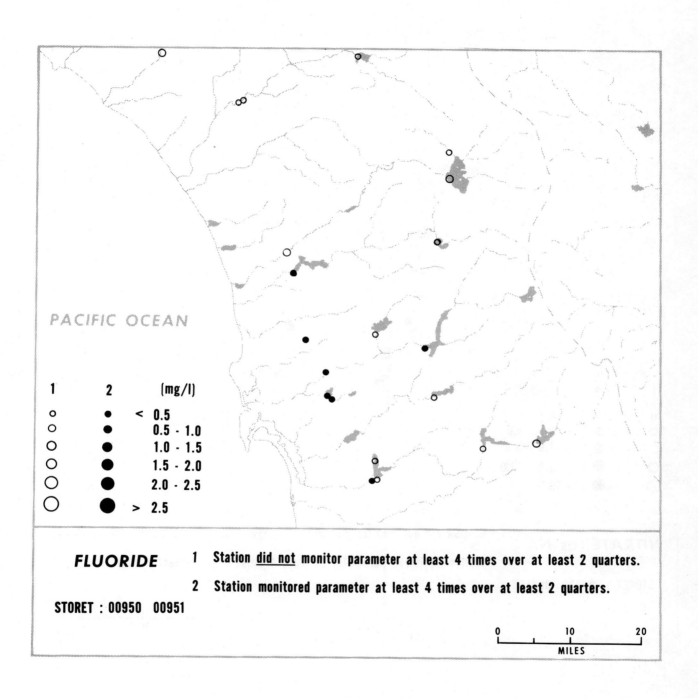

PACIFIC OCEAN

1	2	(mg/l)
○	●	< 0.5
○	●	0.5 - 1.0
○	●	1.0 - 1.5
○	●	1.5 - 2.0
○	●	2.0 - 2.5
○	●	> 2.5

FLUORIDE

1 Station **did not** monitor parameter at least 4 times over at least 2 quarters.

2 Station monitored parameter at least 4 times over at least 2 quarters.

STORET : 00950 00951

0   10   20
MILES

Figure 4.166

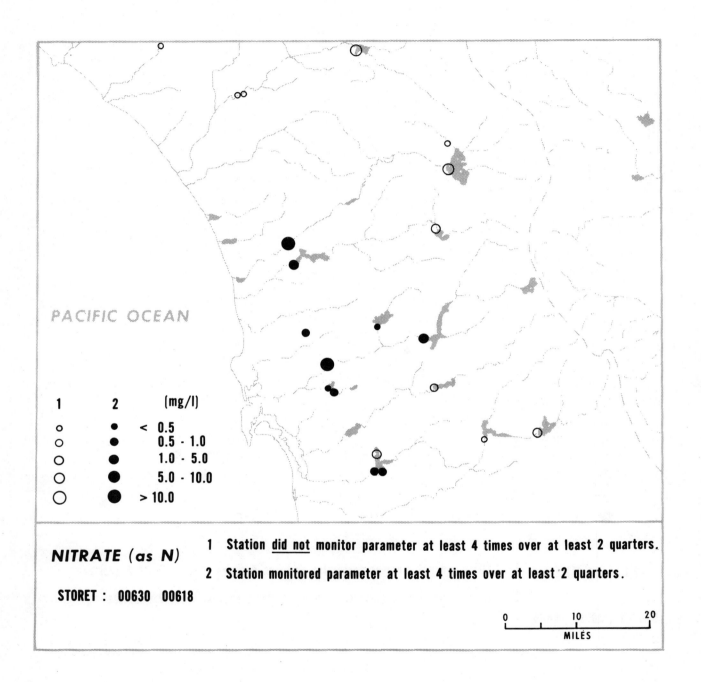

PACIFIC OCEAN

1	2	(mg/l)
○	●	< 0.5
○	●	0.5 - 1.0
○	●	1.0 - 5.0
○	●	5.0 - 10.0
○	●	> 10.0

NITRATE (as N)

STORET : 00630 00618

1 Station <u>did not</u> monitor parameter at least 4 times over at least 2 quarters.

2 Station monitored parameter at least 4 times over at least 2 quarters.

0   10   20
MILES

Figure 4.167

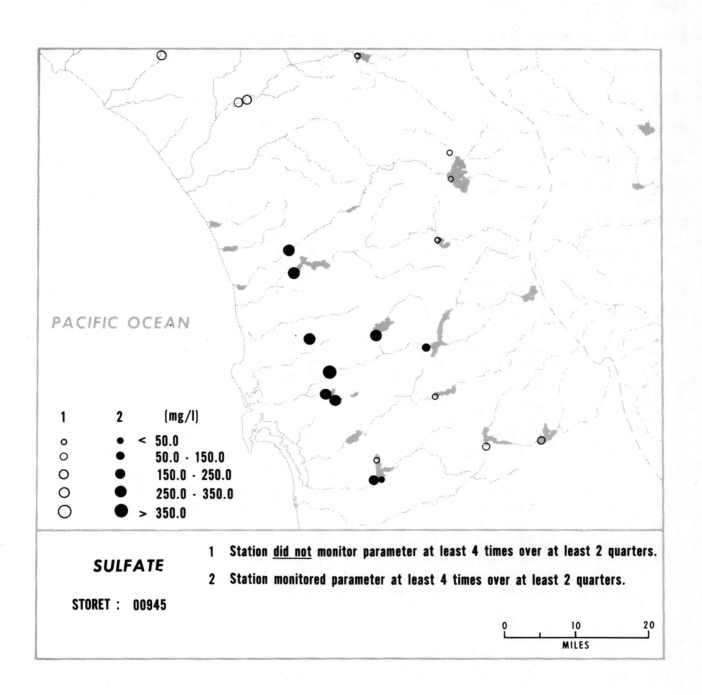

PACIFIC OCEAN

1	2	(mg/l)
○	●	< 50.0
○	●	50.0 - 150.0
○	●	150.0 - 250.0
○	●	250.0 - 350.0
○	●	> 350.0

SULFATE

STORET : 00945

1 Station _did not_ monitor parameter at least 4 times over at least 2 quarters.

2 Station monitored parameter at least 4 times over at least 2 quarters.

0   10   20
MILES

Figure 4.168

OVERVIEW: Similarities and Differences
in Metropolitan Water Quality

That major differences exist in the magnitude of water pollution from one metropolitan region to another should by now be evident. These differences are highlighted in Table 4.14, which summarizes the percentages of monitoring stations within each of the twelve polygons that fail to meet specified water quality standards. Few regions approach Seattle's cleanliness, and even Seattle's waters were far from perfect in 1971. In many of the nation's older industrial centers, most of the surface waters were seriously contaminated by pollutants of many kinds.

Allowing for these gross regional differences, there were a variety of _intraregional_ patterns of variation that the regional maps shared in common in 1971. Among these were the following:

1. Dissolved oxygen levels tend to reach their minimums immediately downstream from urban industrialized concentrations. The parameter maps for Denver, Birmingham and Cincinnati each attest to this. That the maps for the remaining cities do not show this pattern is due to a lack of central city data, or to location of the city at the head of an estuary or on a lake or ocean.

2. Salinity rates in areas where water is diverted for irrigation increase in a downstream direction. The Denver TDS map illustrates this salinity increase.

3. Contaminants resulting from human sewage discharges, specifically total and fecal coliform bacteria, were markedly higher in the vicinity of the urbanized areas, especially where adequate treatment and storage facilities are lacking, than they were in the rural parts of the polygons.

4. There was a correlation between the heavier trace metals and areas of heavy industrial concentrations, although the data for these contaminants were limited in nature.

5. Location of urban centers at the point where a river discharges into a large body of water helped to minimize the downstream effects of water pollution. Five of the twelve urban regions are located on estuaries: Providence, Washington, Baltimore, Jacksonville and Seattle. At each of these cities the flushing and mixing effects of the estuary favor rapid

Table 4.14

<u>Percentages of Monitoring Stations Failing to Meet Specified Standards</u>

	D.O. FA	D.O. PC	BOD ST	TOT. COL. PS	FECAL COL. PS	FECAL UR_1	FECAL UR_2	FECAL PC_1	FECAL PC_2	PH FA	PH PS	PH PC_1	PH PC_2	TDS PS	TURB FA_1	TURB FA_2	MBAS PS	NH_3 FA	NH_3 PS	NO_3 PS	P NS	SO_4 PS	CD FA_1	CD FA_2	CD PS	CU PS	FE PS	PB FA	PB PS	ZN PS
PROVIDENCE	18	32	--	26	15	4	15	19	26	6	0	0	19	--	0	0	--	100	43	0	93	--	--	--	--	PS	PS	--	--	PS
WASHINGTON	2	3	1	61	56	42	56	71	82	1	1	1	7	15	21	94	--	100	38	0	46	--	--	--	--	--	--	--	--	--
BALTIMORE	0	1	--	10	11	7	11	25	35	1	0	0	11	--	0	76	--	11	0	0	40	--	--	--	--	--	--	--	--	--
ROCHESTER	4	6	0	42	--	--	--	--	--	0	0	0	5	25	12	68	--	88	8	0	65	14	--	--	--	--	2	--	--	--
CINCINNATI	0	5	0	64	57	29	57	79	100	4	4	4	6	4	3	19	--	100	25	0	78	0	0	17	15	0	15	7	13	0
ST. LOUIS	13	20	--	59	39	34	39	76	79	4	2	2	10	31	57	78	58	96	23	4	69	15	0	18	18	0	--	22	23	0
BIRMINGHAM	40	69	--	--	--	--	--	--	--	7	0	0	21	--	--	--	--	--	--	--	--	--	--	--	--	0	--	76	76	0
JACKSONVILLE	3	10	5	0	--	--	--	--	--	25	0	0	35	0	0	10	--	--	--	0	61	--	--	--	--	--	--	--	--	--
DENVER	3	7	1	60	28	23	28	49	61	0	0	0	2	47	13	84	8	69	23	0	80	31	0	65	51	0	13	0	26	0
OKLA. CITY	NOT MAPPED			--	--	--	--	--	--	0	0	0	0	64	--	--	--	--	--	0	46	32	--	--	--	--	--	--	--	--
SEATTLE	3	4	2	2	5	1	5	18	25	3	2	2	16	0	4	41	--	63	1	1	30	0	--	--	--	--	--	--	--	--
SAN DIEGO	NOT MAPPED			--	--	--	--	--	--	0	0	0	6	60	--	--	--	--	--	10	--	33	--	--	--	--	--	--	--	--

dispersion of pollutants. On the other hand,
the back-flushing effect of many estuaries
occasionally transports contaminants far upstream only to have them return and be added
to by new urban effluent discharges. Such a
combination often has a disasterous impact
on the quality of marine waters adjacent to
the urbanized area. The 1971 STORET data used
in this study were limited in scope and failed
to show the effects of backflushing directly.
Indirect evidence is available, however: dispersion and diffusion of contaminants were
evident in the Seattle, Providence and Washington
parameter maps, but not in those for Baltimore
and Jacksonville.

Many of these conclusions, prepared as they were using STORET
data for 1971, remained true in 1974 according to EPA's National Water
Quality Inventory of that year. The EPA study focussed on the nation's
largest river basins including the Mississippi, Ohio and Alabama-Coosa
Rivers. Water quality evaluations were based on multiple-year data
records. Evidence was provided for St. Louis, Cincinnati, Birmingham,
Washington and Jacksonville.

Among the findings confirmed were these: Dissolved oxygen values
were above reference levels in the St. Louis area, indicating no serious oxygen depletion problem there. However, turbidity and dissolved
solids, particularly sulfates, increased below the confluence of the
Missouri and Mississippi Rivers. In addition, higher levels of BOD,
ammonia, phosphorus and nitrate remained around St. Louis, and were
associated with urban sewage pollution. Similarly, the substantial
increases in total and fecal coliform bacteria that persisted were
attributed to discharges from the urban centers. It should be noted
that the high levels of phenols and hydrocarbons derived from urban
industrial sources in St. Louis have resulted in the elimination of
the fishing industry over much of the Mississippi downstream from
St. Louis.

The EPA report also confirmed our findings for Cincinnati even
more closely than for St. Louis. In both 1971 and 1974 there were
excessively high coliform levels at Cincinnati. In both years, ammonia, phosphorus and turbidity levels increased below Cincinnati.

There were briefer comments on pollution problems in the Tusca-loosa-Birmingham area in the 1974 study. Discharges of large volumes of wastes into intermittent streams and reservoirs were considered responsible for the substantial pollution that existed. The 1971 STORET data, particularly the dissolved oxygen map, clearly illustrate the pattern.

Other pollution problems discussed in the EPA inventory were those in the Washington, D.C. and Jacksonville areas where domestic sewage and uncaptured urban storm runoff posed serious threats to local water quality. The parameter maps in this chapter substantiate the pollution problem in the Washington case but fail to show the same in the Jacksonville case where central city data were lacking.

※   *Chapter 5*

Metropolitan Air Quality Differentials

The procedures followed in assembling information on variations
in water quality in a sample of U.S. metropolitan areas were repeated
as data on air quality, noise, and solid wastes were accumulated.
In each instance, a detailed study of the Chicago region was followed
by the collection of a smaller set of comparable indicators for as
many of the twelve sample regions as was possible.

In the case of air quality, the detailed Chicago investigation
was limited to the Illinois portion of Air Quality Control Region 67
-- an area serviced by 94 monitoring sites, 30 in the City of Chicago,
32 elsewhere in Cook County, 8 in Du Page County, 1 each in Kane and
Kendall Counties, 6 in Lake, 2 in McHenry and 14 in Will County. Of
these, 20 are owned and operated either by the Federal or the Illinois
EPA, 32 by various cities, and 42 by counties and their Boards of
Health. Most of the locally-owned stations are not included in the
Federal EPA's SAROAD system, the National Aerometric Data Bank. This
situation apparently is repeated in other metropolitan areas, and it
means that a comprehensive set of air quality information can only be
assembled if SAROAD is supplemented by the information obtainable
from several other local governmental agencies.

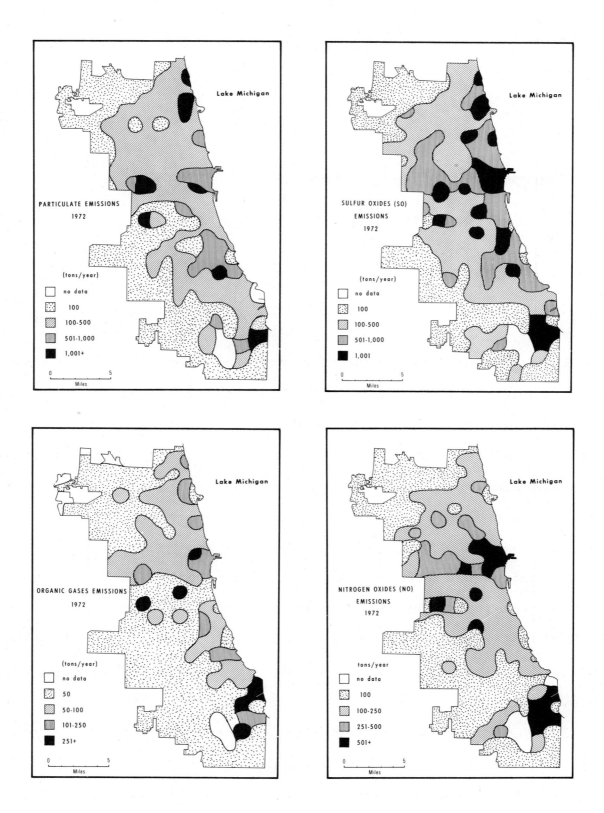

Figure 5.1. Emissions Data for the City of Chicago in 1972.

Such supplementation was in fact undertaken in the Chicago case, but the twelve-region comparisons were limited in some cases to data forthcoming only from SAROAD because not all state offices requested to send supplementary air quality data in fact did so. In the City of Chicago, the effort to supplement SAROAD paid off, for not only were spatially-disaggregated data on emissions available (Figure 5.1), but many of the monitoring points also yielded useful information concerning the presence of airborne trace metals such as lead and cadmium (Figure 5.2). These data aside, however, the Chicago case study was limited to the same set of air quality parameters as the SAROAD-based twelve-region comparisons: particulate matter, sulfur dioxide, nitrogen dioxide, carbon monoxide, hydrocarbons, and photochemical oxidents, including ozone. Each of these will be discussed in turn in what follows.

In the Chicago case, also, a special effort was made to examine whether the individual monitoring station data met the U.S. EPA's criteria for data adequacy when annual arithmetic or geometric means are being computed for comparison with the nation's air quality standards, viz:

1. For continuous data, there must be available:
    (a) 75% of all hourly values to create
        a daily average
    (b) 75% of all daily averages to create
        a monthly average
    (c) 75% of all monthly averages to create
        an annual average

2. For discontinuous data, there must be:
    (a) a minimum of five samples per calendar
        year quarter with at least two months
        possessing two samples per month
    (b) all four quarters must be present and
        meet the annual criteria

We concluded that, in the 1973 sample year that was studied, these requirements were met by the data on particulates and sulfur dioxide, but that the information on the other pollutants was seldom satisfactory, by EPA's standards. Further examination indicated that a similar problem exists elsewhere, so Chicago is not unique in this respect.

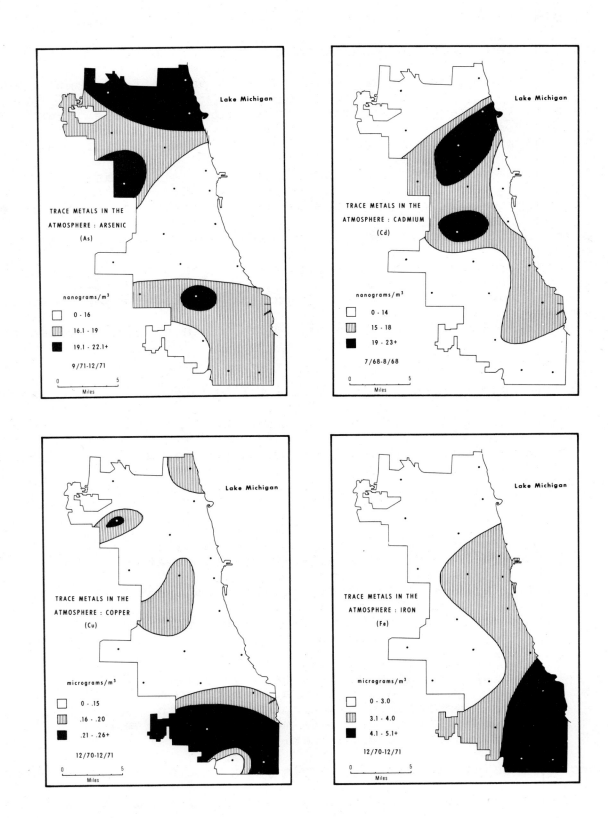

Figure 5.2a. Trace Metals Concentrations in the Atmosphere --
Arsenic, Cadmium, Copper and Iron.

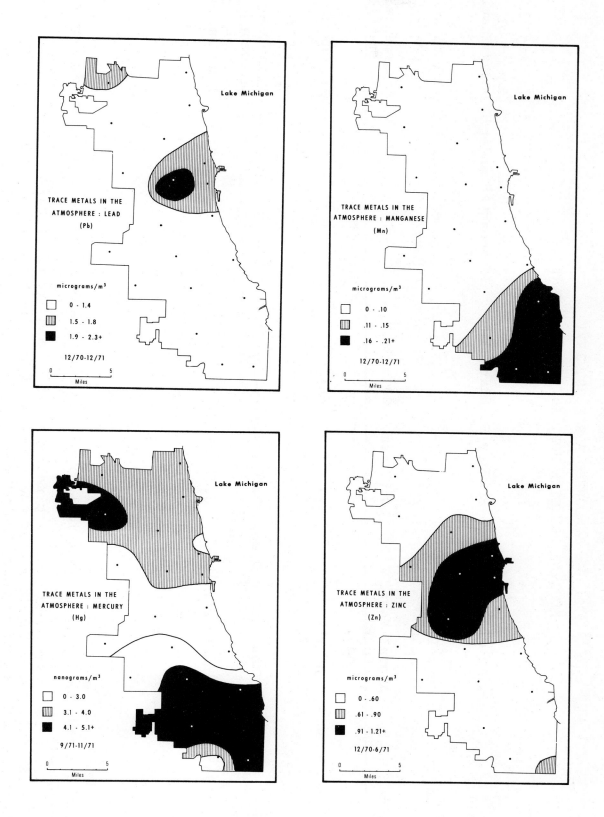

Figure 5.2b.   Trace Metals Concentrations in the Atmosphere --
Lead, Manganese, Mercury, and Zinc.

TABLE 5.1

SUMMARY OF NATIONAL AIR STANDARDS

ADOPTED APRIL 30, 1971

FEDERAL REGISTER VOL. 36, NO. 84, PART II[a]

Pollutant	Time of Average	Primary Standard[a]	Secondary Standard[b]	Method of Determination
Particulate matter	Annual Mean[c]	75 ug/m^3	60 ug/m^3	High Volume Sampler
	24 hour	260 ug/m^3 d	150 ug/m^3 d	Tape Sampler
Sulfur dioxide (SO$_2$)	Annual Mean	0.03 ppm (80 ug/m^3)		Pararosanaline
	24 hour	0.14 ppm (365 ug/m^3)d	0.5 ppm (1300 ug/m^3)	Coulometric
	3 hour	--------		
Carbon monoxide (CO)	8 hour	9 ppm (10 mg)d		Gas Chromatograph
	1 hour	35 ppm (40 mg)d		Non-Dispersive Infrared
Hydrocarbons (nonmethane)	3 hour (6 to 9 am)	0.24 ppm (160 ug/m^3)d		Flame Ionization Detector
Nitrogen dioxide (NO$_2$)	Annual Mean	0.05 ppm (100 ug/m^3)		Chemiluminescence
Ozone (O$_3$)	1 hour	0.08 ppm (160 ug/m^3)d		UV Absorption

aIllinois air quality standards are identical to the national standards, except for the proposed sulfur dioxide standard.

bConcentration in weight per cubic meter (corrected to 25 C. and 750 mm of Hg).

cUtilizes a geometric mean which indicates the midpoint of the distribution of values.

dConcentration not to be exceeded more than once per year.

Nonetheless, for comparative purposes, we did make use of the limited data at our disposal, and ultimately we were able to compare Chicago with maps of the other twelve cases--a process complicated by the much-delayed delivery from Raleigh, N.C. of the needed SAROAD output, slowed both by the conversion of SAROAD from one computer system to another, and by the misplacement or loss after receipt of our first two data requests! Once these data were received, the method that we followed was the one developed in the Chicago case--to map pollution levels at each monitoring station location by means of a graded series of dots, the grades being related to national air quality standards (Table 5.1). Where groups of stations exceeded the levels specified in the standards, contour lines also were interpolated to isolate the areas indicated to have substandard environments. The results are described in the sections that follow. The maps are only as useful as the monitoring networks are comprehensive. Of 388 monitoring stations in the twelve cities, the distribution is as follows:

City	No. of Monitoring Stations	Percent in Central City
Baltimore	35	32
Birmingham	6	100
Cincinnati	41	41
Denver	30	40
Jacksonville	15	80
Oklahoma City	22	73
Providence	32	22
Rochester	20	45
San Diego	9	22
Seattle	25	36
St. Louis	42	35
Washington, D.C.	69	10

We now present the maps, beginning with those for particulates.

PARTICULATES

It should not be assumed that all air pollutants are in the gaseous form. Small solid particles and liquid droplets, collectively called particulates, are also present in the air in great numbers, and may at certain times constitute a pollution problem. Particulates entering the atmosphere differ in size and chemical properties. The effects of particulates on health and welfare are directly related to their size and chemical composition.

Particulate pollutants enter the human body by way of the respiratory system, and, therefore, their most immediate effects are upon this system. The size of the particle determines the depth of penetration into the respiratory system. Particles over 5 microns (1 micron equals 1/25,000 inch) are generally stopped and deposited mainly in the nose and throat. Those that do penetrate deeper into the respiratory system into the air ducts (bronchi) are soon removed by ciliary action. Particles ranging in size from 0.5 - 5.0 microns in diameter can be deposited in the bronchi, with few reaching the air sacks (alveoli). Most particles deposited in the bronchioles are removed by the cilia within two hours. Particles less than 0.5 micron in diameter reach and may settle in the alveoli. The removal of particles from the alveoli is much less rapid and complete than from the larger passages. Some of the particles retained in the alveoli are absorbed into the blood.

High particulate concentrations have been associated with increased mortality and bronchitis. Long term effects due to the chemical nature of the particulate may be increased incidence of cancer and heart attack.

Plant surfaces and growth rate may be adversely affected by particulates. Particulate air pollution also causes a wide range of damage to materials, and includes corrosion of metals, and electrical equipment, and soiling of textiles and buildings.

Particulates were the most completely monitored pollutant in the Chicago SMSA (Figure 5.3). Ninety-two of the monitoring sites had high-volume air samplers; five of them did not take enough samples to be statistically representative of the 1973 ambient air quality. The particulate picture returned by the monitors is not a clean one. Over the whole area 44 percent of the sites exceeded the federal primary standard of 75 micrograms per cubic meter; 76 percent were above the 60 micrograms per cubic meter secondary standard, leaving only 24 percent of the readings in compliance with the standards. However, since the major source of particulates is industrial heating plants and domestic power plants the map of particulates is not a uniform one. Within Chicago 24 stations (83 percent) exceeded the primary and all exceeded the secondary level. Many of the readings were far above the standards; the worst site in 1973 for Region 67 was Washington High School in Chicago with an annual geometric mean of 163 micrograms per cubic meter. The rest of Cook County did not have such a great particulate burden. Only 8 sites (26 percent were above the primary standard, 19 (61 percent) monitoring sites had readings above the secondary standard and 12 (36 percent were below both. The other counties in the Chicago SMSA were relatively free of particulate problems, except around smaller cities in the SMSA such as Joliet to the southwest. But the pattern is not stable. Apparent gains in particulate pollution control between 1970 and 1972 appear to have been reversed somewhat in 1974 (Figure 5.4).

The twelve-city comparisons fare not much better (Figure 5.5). Allowing for widely-varying numbers of monitoring stations, most central cities and many suburban areas are seen to have serious particulate pollution problems.

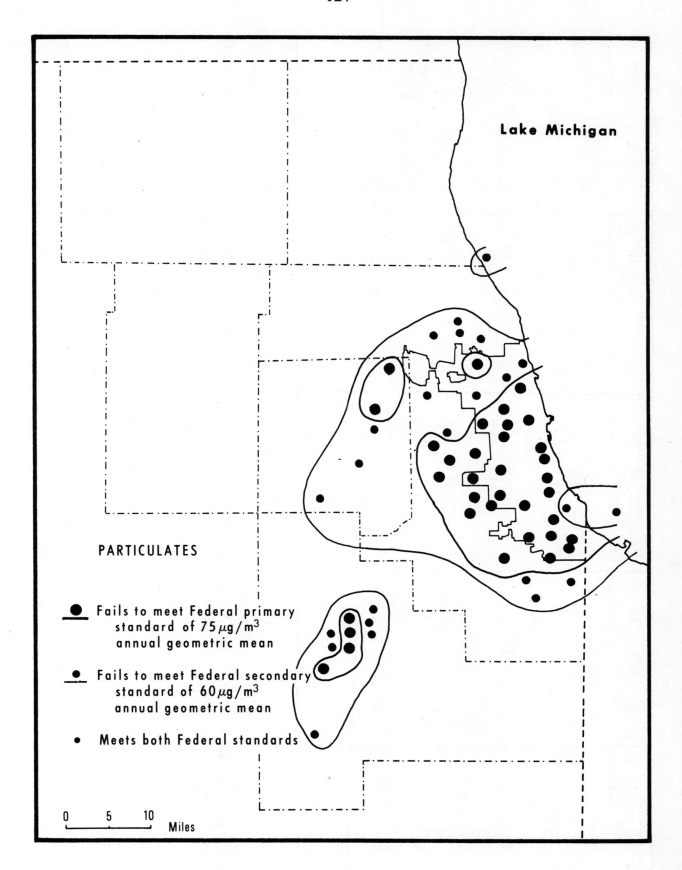

Lake Michigan

PARTICULATES

● Fails to meet Federal primary
standard of $75\,\mu g/m^3$
annual geometric mean

● Fails to meet Federal secondary
standard of $60\,\mu g/m^3$
annual geometric mean

• Meets both Federal standards

0   5   10
Miles

Figure 5.3

418

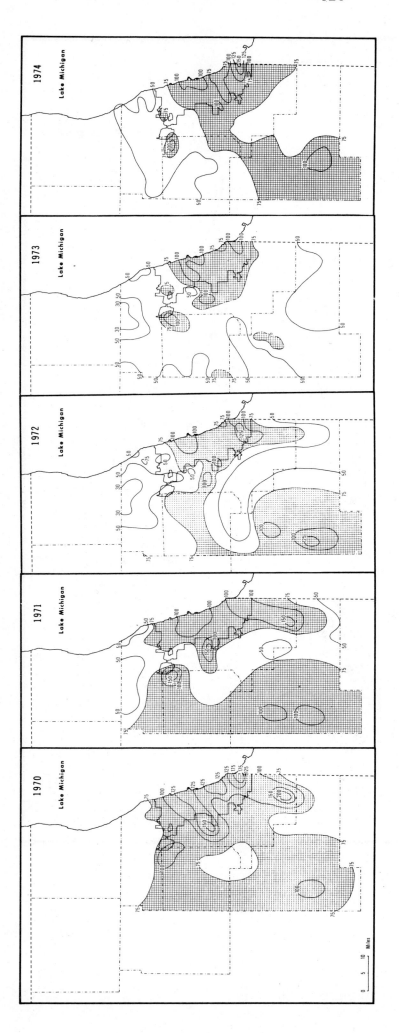

Figure 5.4. Variations in Levels of Total Suspended Particulates between 1970 and 1974. The shaded areas are those in which national standards are not met.

PARTICULATES

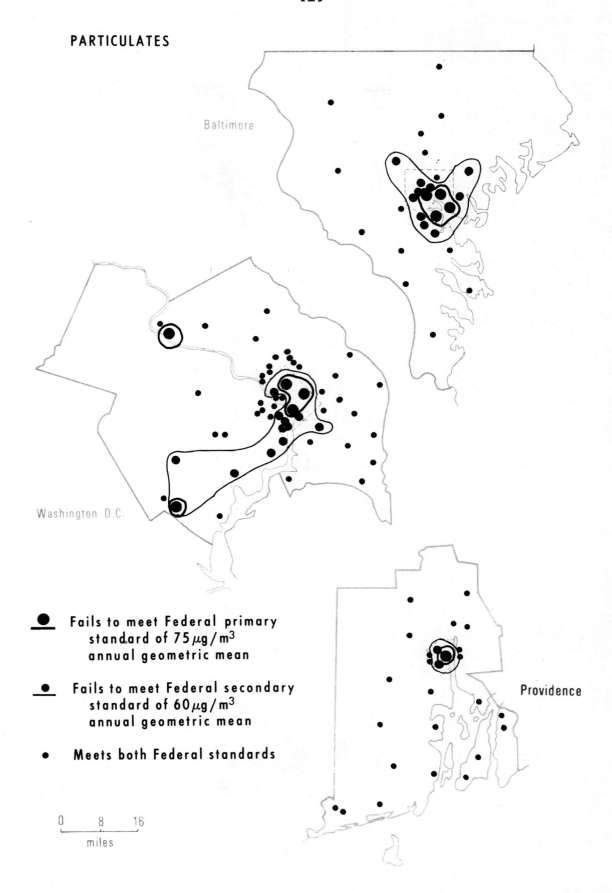

Baltimore

Washington D.C.

Providence

● Fails to meet Federal primary
standard of $75\,\mu g/m^3$
annual geometric mean

• Fails to meet Federal secondary
standard of $60\,\mu g/m^3$
annual geometric mean

· Meets both Federal standards

0   8   16
miles

Figure 5.5a. Particulates: Baltimore, Washington, and Providence.

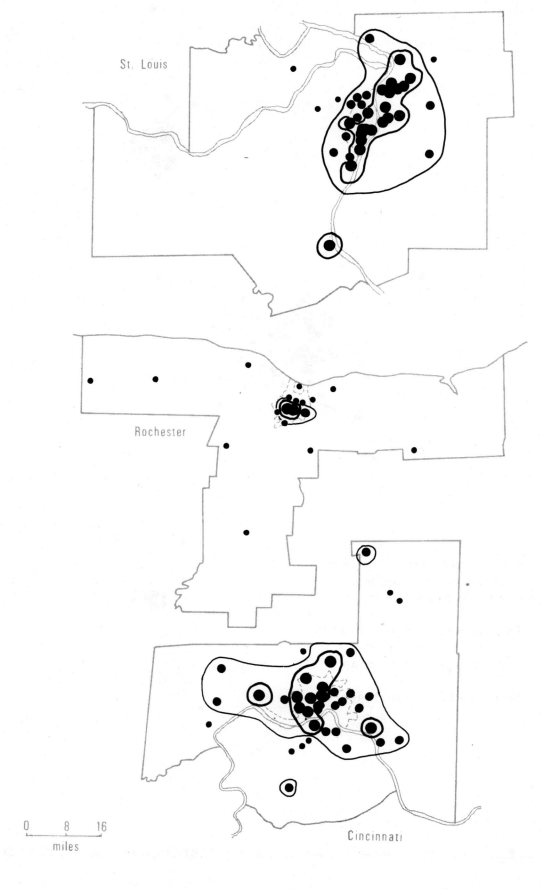

Figure 5.5b. Particulates: St. Louis, Rochester, and Cincinnati.

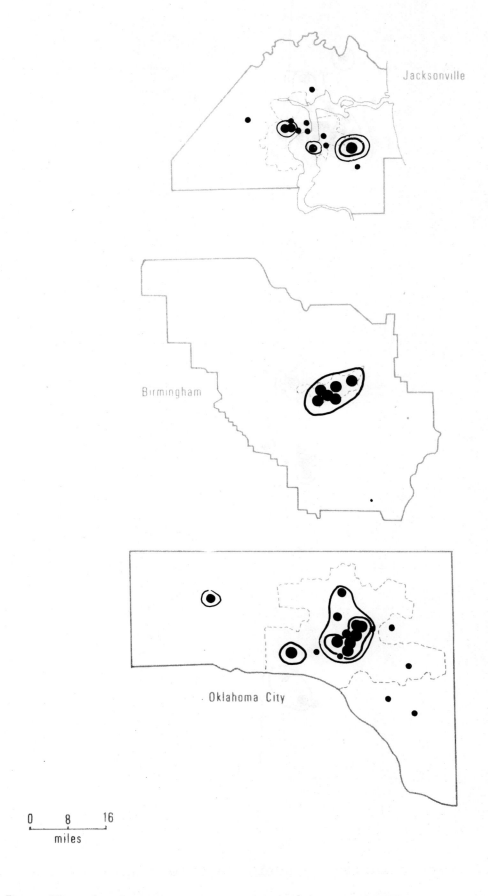

__Figure 5.5c.__ Particulates: Jacksonville, Birmingham, and Oklahoma
City.

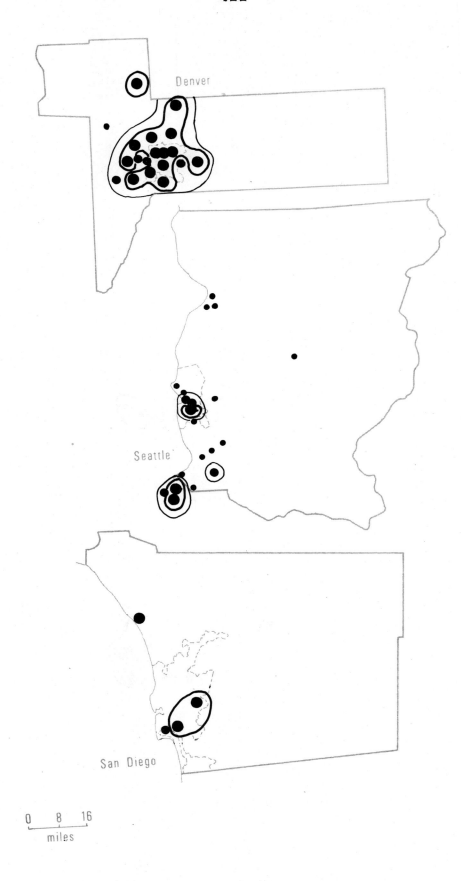

Figure 5.5d. Particulates: Denver, Seattle, and San Diego.

SULFUR DIOXIDE

The effects of the oxides of sulfur on health are related to irritation of the respiratory system. Such injury may be temporary or permanent.

The potentiation by particulate matter of toxic responses to sulfur dioxide (synergism) has been observed under conditions which would promote the conversion of sulfur dioxide to sulfuric acid. The degree of potentiation is related to the concentration of particulate matter. A threefold to fourfold potentiation of the irritant response to sulfur dioxide is observed in the presence of particulate matter capable of oxidizing sulfur dioxide to sulfuric acid.

Sulfur dioxide can cause acute or chronic leaf injury to plants. Acute injury, produced by high concentrations for relatively short periods, usually results in injured tissue drying to an ivory color; it sometimes results in a darkening of the tissue to a reddish-brown. Chronic injury, which results from lower concentrations over a number of days or weeks, leads to pigmentation of leaf tissue, or leads to a gradual yellowing, or chlorosis, in which the chlorophyll-making mechanism is impeded. Both acute and chronic injury may be accompanied by the suppression of growth and yield.

Corrosion rates are higher in urban and industrial atmospheres with relatively high levels of both particulate and sulfur oxides than they are in rural and other areas of low pollution. Sulfur oxide pollution contributes to the damage of electrical equipment of all kinds. Building materials and textile fibers are also harmed by atmospheric sulfur oxides.

Such problems appeared limited to very specific locations in the Chicago region in 1973 (Figure 5.6). However, Cook County was the only part of Region 67 that was monitored, with the exception of one site in Will County. There was a total of 43 sampling stations: 26 in Chicago, 16 in the rest of Cook County and the one in Joliet. The

only reading above the federal primary standard of .03ppm occurred
in McCook. In Chicago, at the University of Illinois Medical Center,
the average was .036ppm but not enough readings were made for this to
be statistically meaningful. Six other stations in Chicago failed
the secondary standard of .02ppm; as can be seen on the map the majority of these fall within the Loop. Most of the figures used to
produce the sulfur dioxide maps were annual arithmetic means. In case
this type of average did not provide a realistic picture of sulfur
dioxide in the SMSA we also looked at the 24-hour readings for this
pollutant. For the City of Chicago we counted the days that the
federal daily standards (primary 365 and secondary 260 micrograms per
cubic meter) were exceeded; few sites fell above the standards, supporting the picture of the annual averages. Over the years, too, the
story is one of progressive improvement (Figure 5.7). Figure 5.8
presents the data for the other twelve regions, where the same story
of general acceptability of sulfur dioxide levels is repeated.

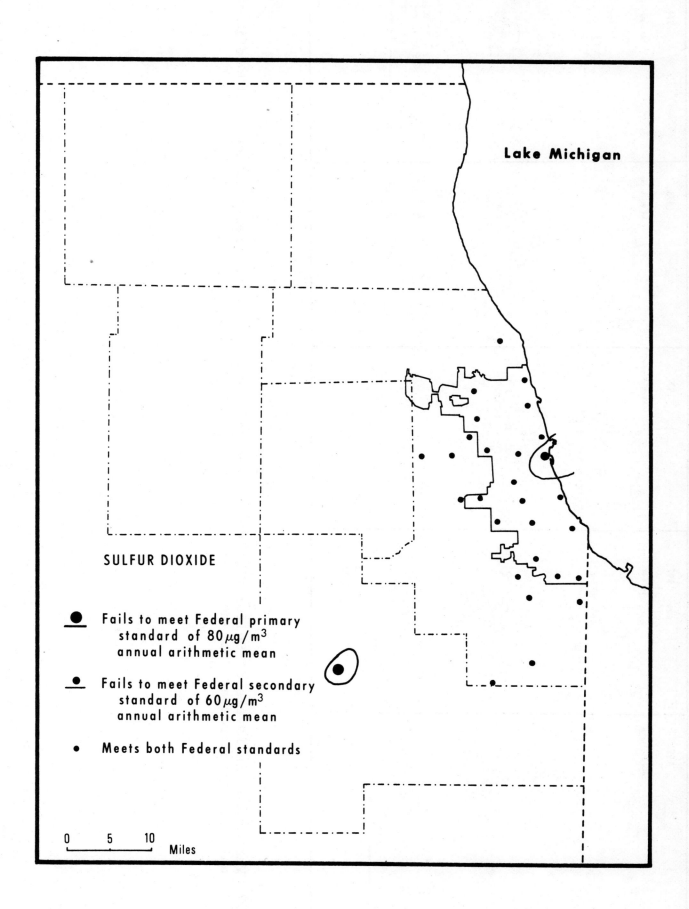

Lake Michigan

SULFUR DIOXIDE

● Fails to meet Federal primary
standard of $80 \mu g/m^3$
annual arithmetic mean

• Fails to meet Federal secondary
standard of $60 \mu g/m^3$
annual arithmetic mean

• Meets both Federal standards

0   5   10
Miles

Figure 5.6

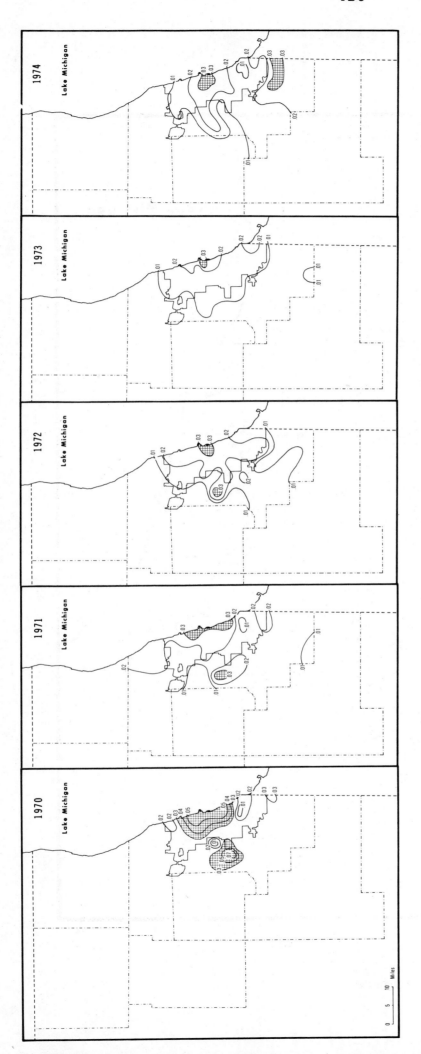

Figure 5.7. Variations in Levels of Sulfur Dioxide between 1970 and 1974. The shaded areas are those in which national standards are not met.

SULFUR DIOXIDE

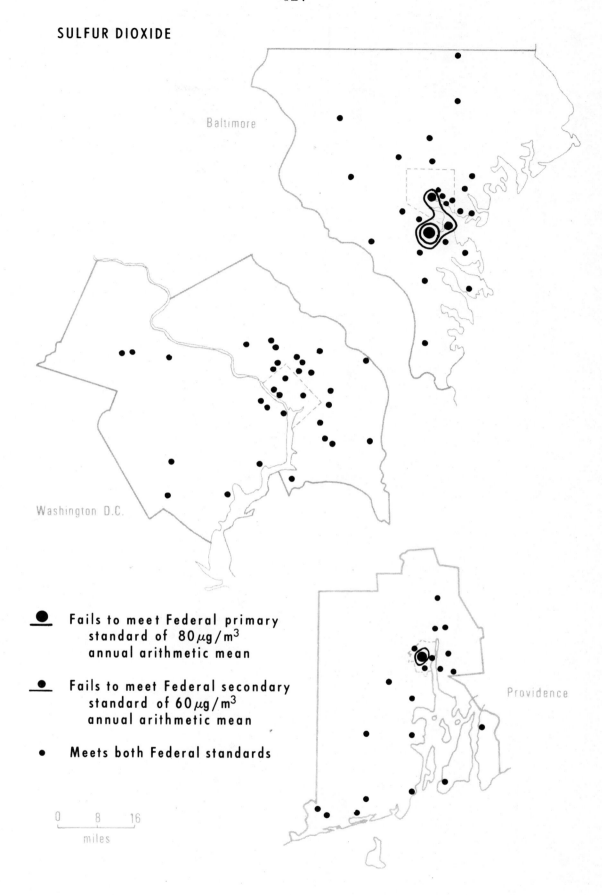

● Fails to meet Federal primary
standard of 80 μg/m^3
annual arithmetic mean

● Fails to meet Federal secondary
standard of 60 μg/m^3
annual arithmetic mean

• Meets both Federal standards

0   8   16
miles

Figure 5.8a.   Sulfur Dioxide: Baltimore, Washington, and Providence.

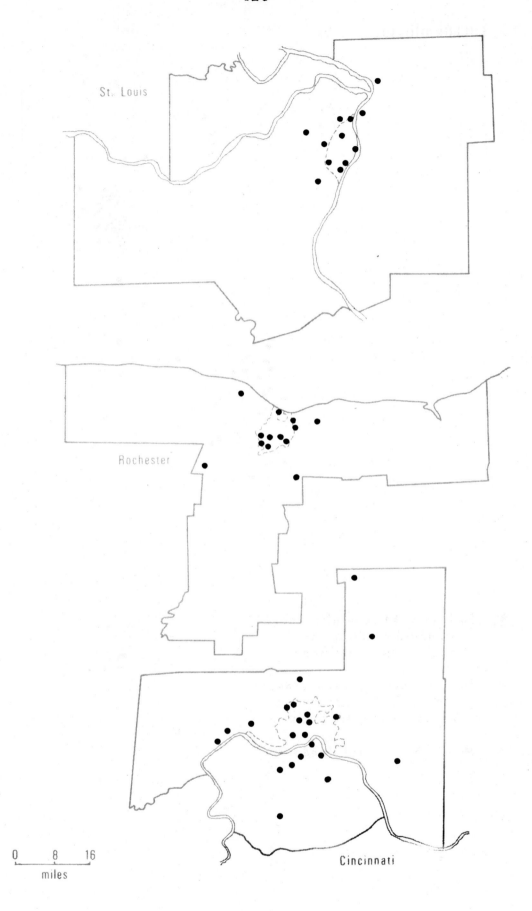

Figure 5.8b. Sulfur Dioxide: St. Louis, Rochester, and Cincinnati.

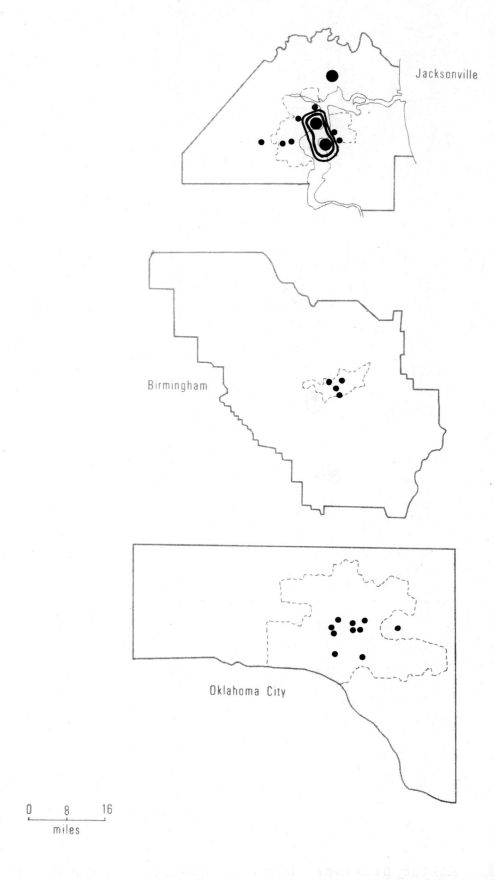

Figure 5.8c. Sulfur Dioxide: Jacksonville, Birmingham, and Oklahoma City.

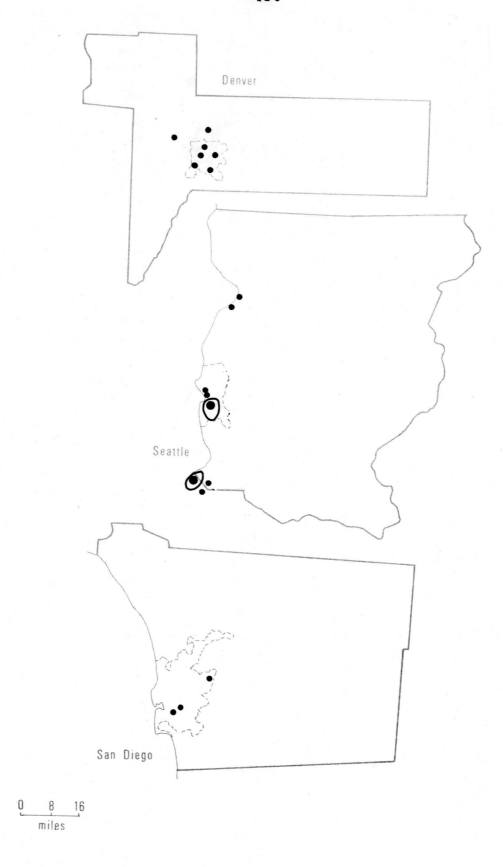

Figure 5.8d. Sulfur Dioxide: Denver, Seattle, and San Diego.

NITROGEN DIOXIDE

Nitrogen gas (N_2) is an abundant and inert gas which makes up almost 80 percent of the Earth's atmosphere. In this form, it is harmless to man and indeed very essential to plant metabolism. However, due to its abundance in the air, it is a frequent reactant in many combustion processes. When combustion temperatures are extremely high, as in the burning of coal, oil, gas, and in automobile engines, atmospheric nitrogen (N_2) may combine with oxygen (O_2) to form various oxides. Of these, nitric oxide (NO) and nitrogen dioxide (NO_2) are the most important contributors to air pollution. Other forms, such as N_2O, N_2O_4, and N_2O_5, may be present but NO_2 is the only form present in the atmosphere in any significant amount.

Nitric oxide (NO) is a colorless and odorless gas. It is the primary form of NO_x resulting from the combustion process. However, it immediately reacts with more oxygen to produce the irritant NO_2. NO_2 is a reddish-orange-brown gas with an unpleasant odor. It contributes to haze and a reduction of visibility. NO_x is also known to cause deterioration and fading of certain fabrics at concentrations between .6 and 2 ppm. Depending on concentration and extent of exposure plants may suffer leaf crop, lesions, and reduced crop yield. NO itself is not considered harmful to humans at concentrations found in the atmosphere, but NO_2 has been shown to cause inflammation in the lungs and bronchi in ranges from .062 to .109 ppm for a 24-hour mean concentration.

The term NO_x is therefore used to represent NO and NO_2. The ambient air quality standard for NO_2 is 100 micrograms per cubic meter ($\mu g/m^3$) or 0.05 parts per million (ppm). Until recently, reliable methods for measuring ambient NO_x levels were not available and, therefore, less information is available compared to oxides of sulfur and other pollutants. Even now, different sampling techniques may yield different results; therefore, the technique to be used must be chosen carefully in accordance with the purpose of the sampling.

NO$_x$ may also react with water to form corrosive acids, although this is not considered a serious pollution problem. NO$_x$ and various other pollutants (e.g., hydrocarbons) may react in the presence of sunlight to produce photochemical oxidants. These are extremely unstable compounds which damage plants and irritate both the eyes and respiratory system of people. Ozone (O$_3$) and a group of chemicals called peroxyacylnitrates (PAN) are the major kinds of photochemical oxidants.

Methods to control NO$_x$ emissions include the lowering of combustion temperatures and decreasing available oxygen needed for combustion. In automobiles, catalytic converters will help to cut down NO$_x$ emissions from exhaust fumes.

All of the NO$_x$ sampling sites in the Chicago region were located in the City of Chicago in 1973 (Figure 5.9) -- seventeen monitors in all taking 24-hour samples. In 1973 only seven sites took over 20 samples, which is the necessary number for statistical relevance. The ambient air quality standard is .05 ppm for the annual arithmetic mean concentration. None of the seven sites was above this; one station, with 16 readings, did have an average of .057 ppm. Figure 5.10 shows comparable data for the other twelve regions.

433

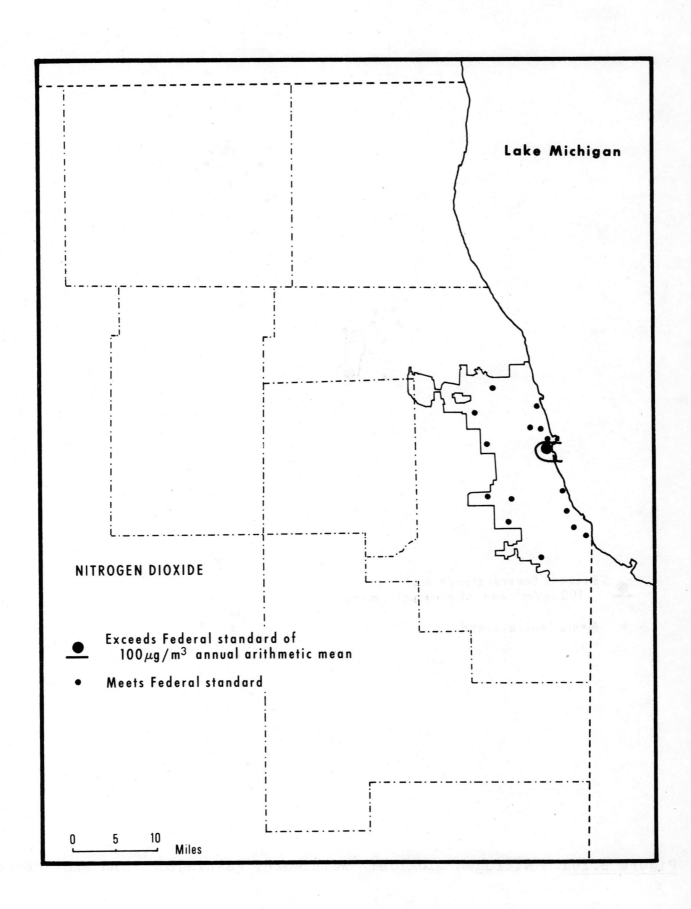

Lake Michigan

NITROGEN DIOXIDE

● Exceeds Federal standard of
  100 μg/m^3 annual arithmetic mean

● Meets Federal standard

0 5 10
Miles

Figure 5.9

NITROGEN DIOXIDE

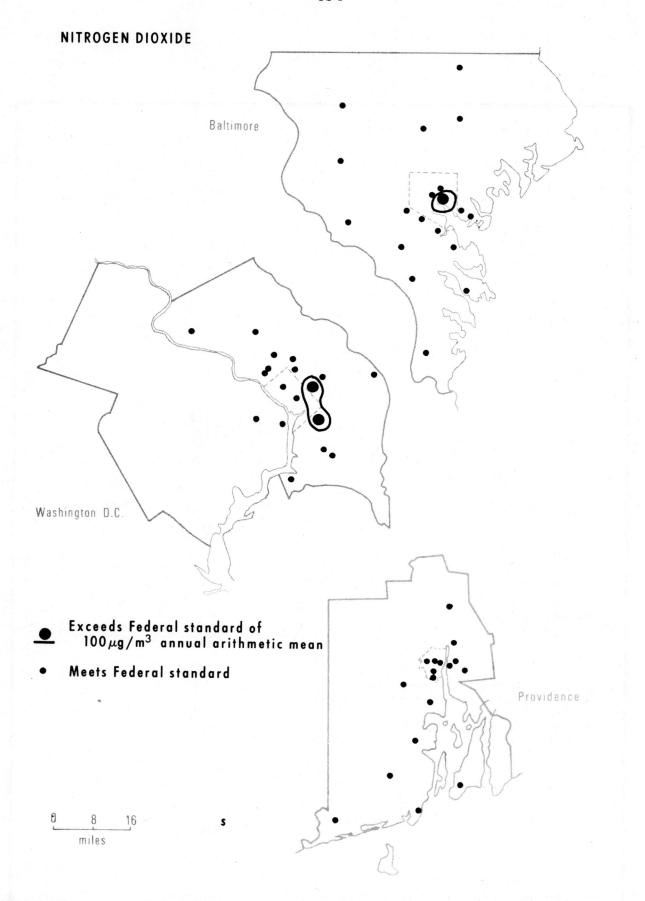

Figure 5.10a. Nitrogen Dioxide: Baltimore, Washington, and Providence.

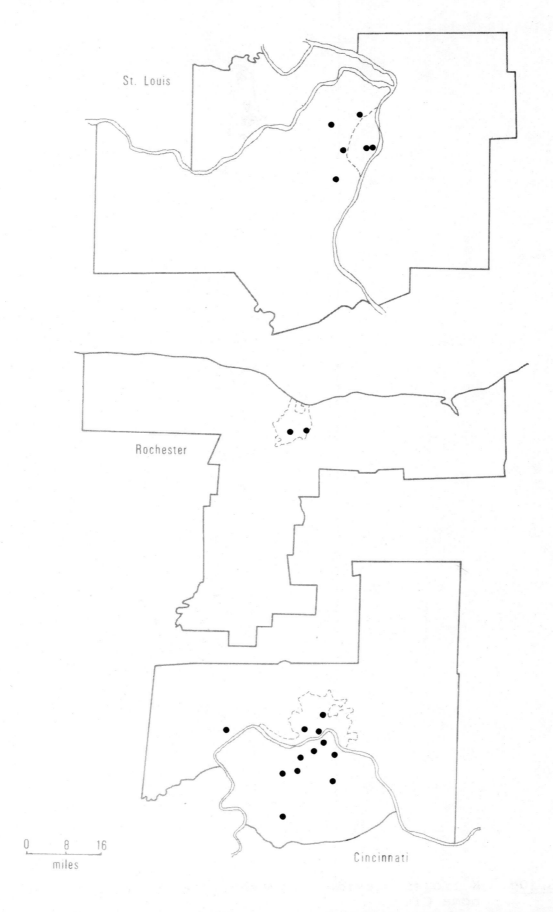

Figure 5.10b. Nitrogen Dioxide: St. Louis, Rochester, and Cincinnati.

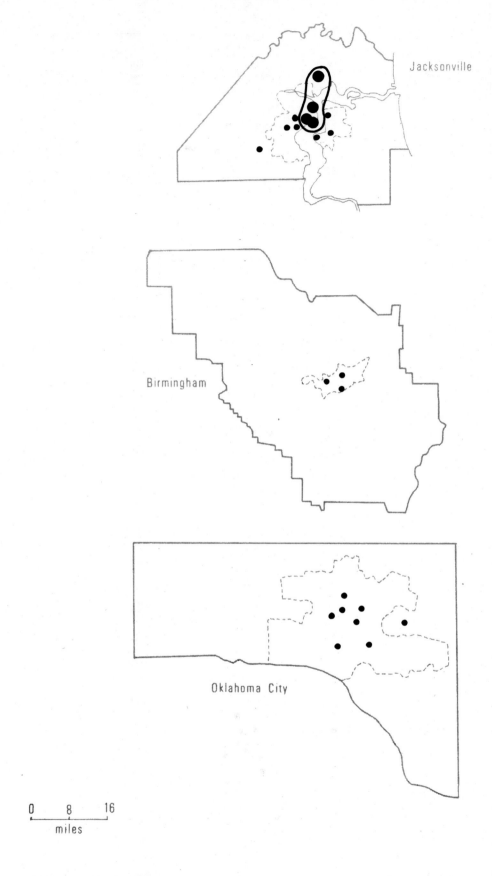

Figure 5.10c. Nitrogen Dioxide: Jacksonville, Birmingham, and Oklahoma City.

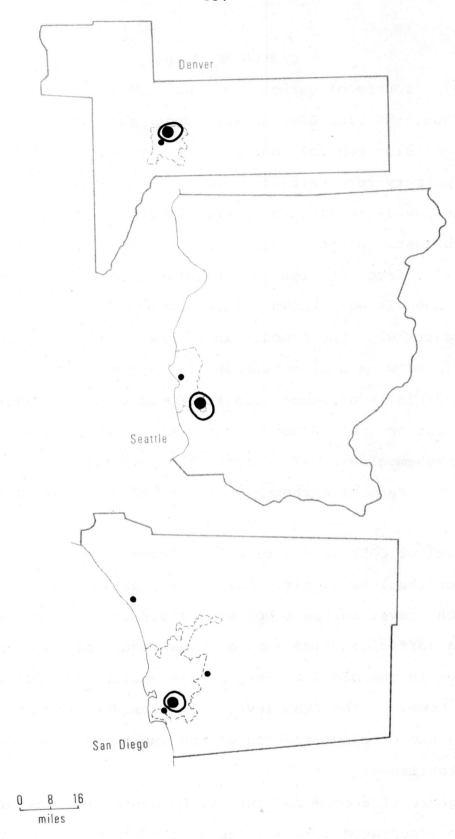

Figure 5.10c. Nitrogen Dioxide: Denver, Seattle, and San Diego.

CARBON MONOXIDE

The major source of carbon monoxide (CO) by far is the motor vehicle. Thus, the U.S. EPA has kept under its jurisdiction the regulation of emission control equipment on new motor vehicles, while the states primary responsibility for reducing excessive ambient carbon monoxide levels is limited to the development of transportation plans for congested urban areas.

The toxic effect of high concentrations of CO (greater than 100 ppm) on the body is well known. Carbon monoxide is absorbed by the lungs and reacts with the hemoglobin of the blood. The absorption of CO is associated with a reduction in the oxygen-carrying capacity of blood. The affinity of hemoglobin for CO is over 200 times that for oxygen, indicating that carboxyhemoglobin (COHb) is more stable compound than oxyhemoglobin. The higher the percentage of hemoglobin bound up in the form of carboxyhemoglobin, the more serious is the effect.

The level of COHb in the blood is directly related to the CO concentration of the inhaled air. For a given ambient air CO concentration, the COHb level in the blood will reach an equilibrium concentration after a sufficient time period. This equilibrium COHb level will be maintained in the blood as long as the ambient air CO level remains unchanged. However, the COHb level will slowly change in the same direction as the CO concentration of the ambient air as a new equilibrium is established.

An exposure of 8 or more hours to CO concentrations of 10 to 15 ppm has been associated with adverse health effects as manifested by impaired time interval discrimination, and levels greater than 30 ppm (episode level) can cause cardiac and preliminary functional changes in individuals with heart disease.

Studies on the existing ambient levels of CO do not indicate any adverse effects on vegetation, materials, or other aspects of human welfare.

Carbon monoxide was not monitored well in the Chicago SMSA. In 1973 no samples outside the city were significant. There are eight sites within Chicago; none of them had an annual geometric mean exceeding the federal standard of 9 ppm (Figure 5.11). Unfortunately, that picture is unrealistic. Independent studies have found very high levels of carbon monoxide in Chicago residents. Further, the Illinois EPA examined eight hour periods of carbon monoxide in Chicago and found 200 violations of the standard in 1973. Because of these exceptions, the state EPA is planning to redo the monitoring system for carbon monoxide so as to receive more accurate measures of this pollutant in the air. Figure 5.12 presents the twelve-city comparisons.

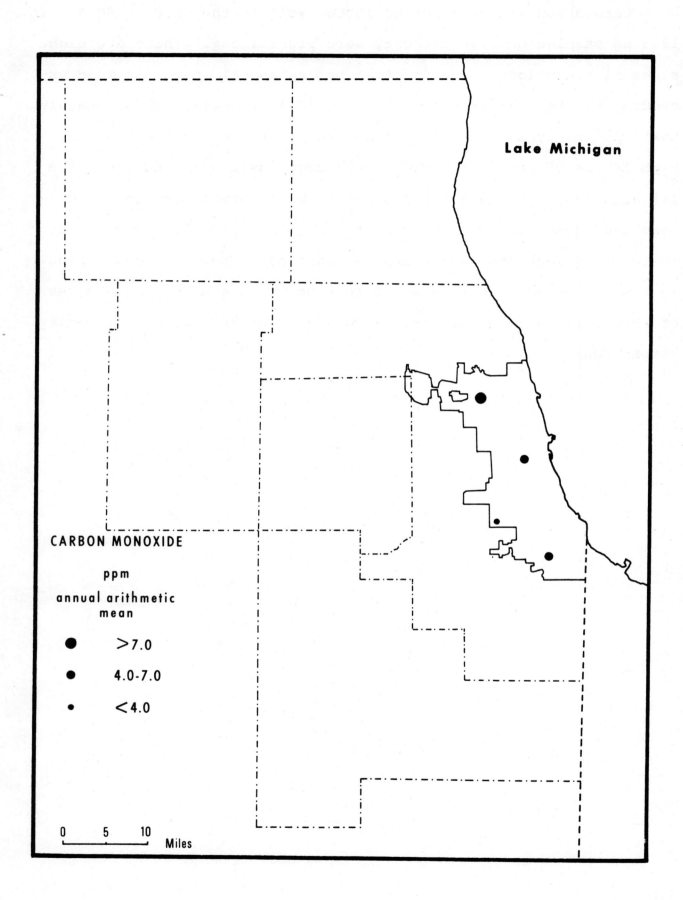

CARBON MONOXIDE

ppm

annual arithmetic
mean

● >7.0

● 4.0-7.0

• <4.0

Lake Michigan

0   5   10
Miles

Figure 5.11

CARBON MONOXIDE

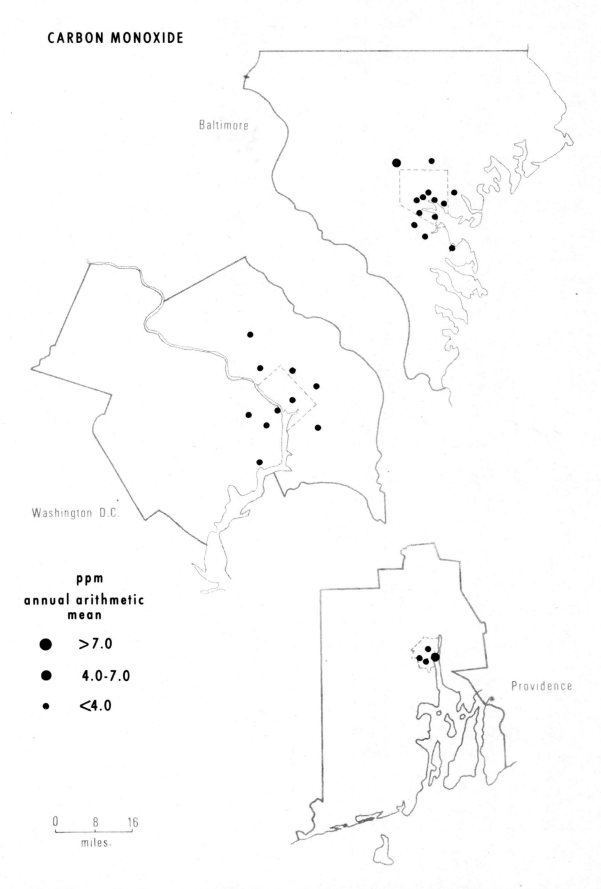

Baltimore

Washington D.C.

Providence

ppm
annual arithmetic
mean

●   >7.0

●   4.0-7.0

•   <4.0

0   8   16
miles.

Figure 5.12a.   Carbon monoxide: Baltimore, Washington, and Providence.

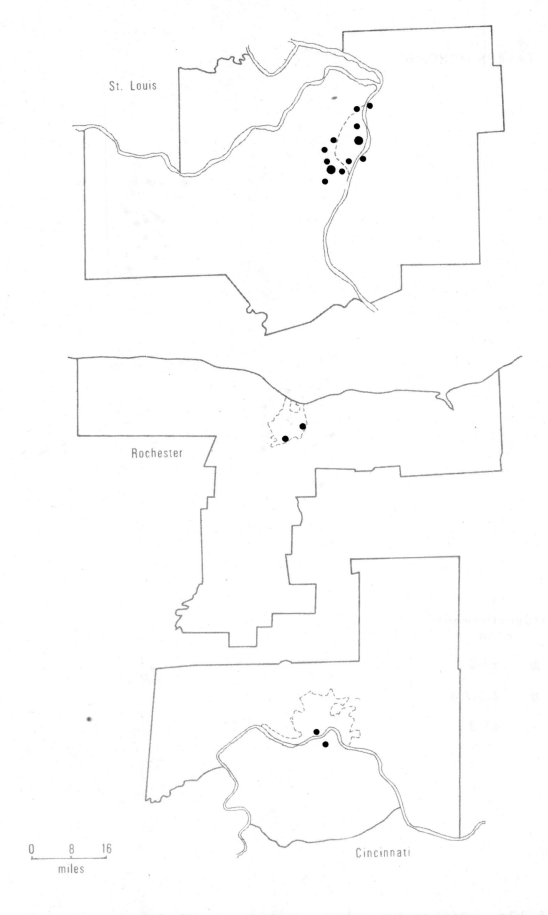

Figure 5.12b. Carbon Monoxide: St. Louis, Rochester, and Cincinnati.

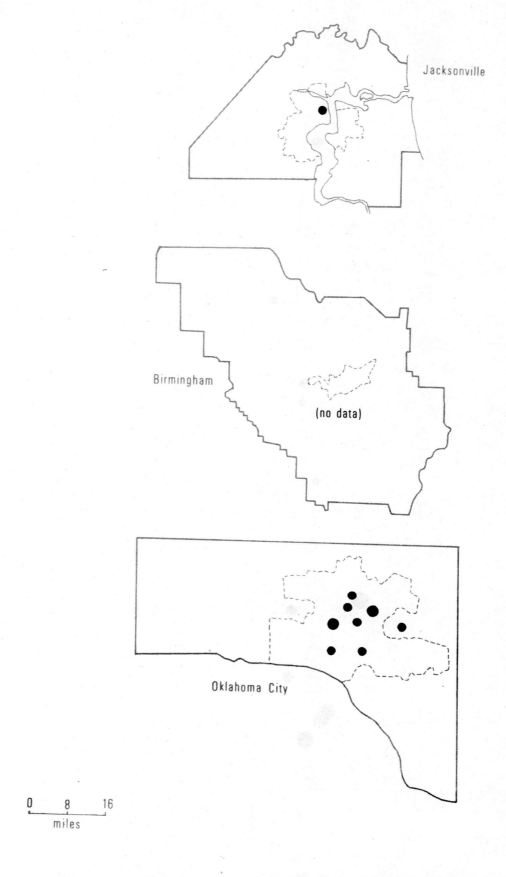

<u>Figure 5.12c.</u>   Carbon Monoxide: Jacksonville, Birmingham, Oklahoma
                City.

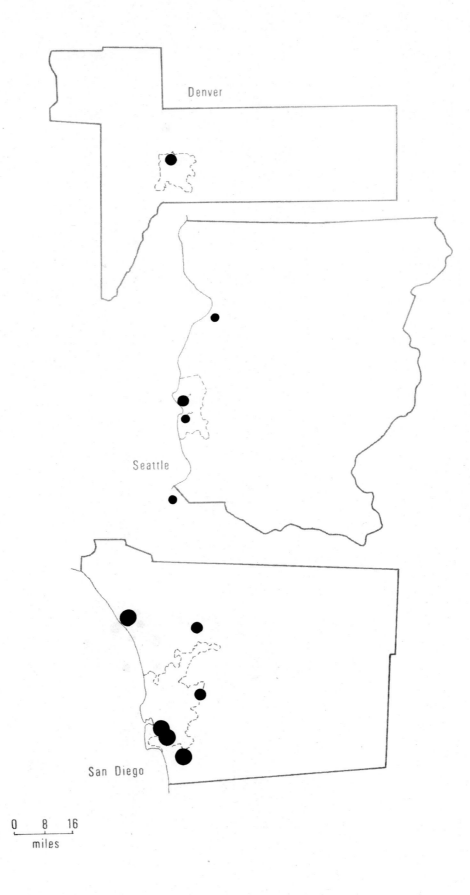

Figure 5.12d. Carbon Monoxide: Denver, Seattle, and San Diego.

HYDROCARBONS

Studies conducted thus far of the effects of ambient air concentrations of gaseous hydrocarbons have not demonstrated direct adverse effects from this class of pollution on human health. But, it has been demonstrated that ambient levels of photochemical oxidant, which do have adverse effects on health, are a direct function of gaseous hydrocarbon concentrations; thus, an air quality standard exists for hydrocarbons in order to take into account their contribution to the formation of hazardous photochemical oxidant.

Reasonable hydrocarbons data were unavailable in the Chicago case. Figure 5.13 presents such data as were available for the other twelve cases.

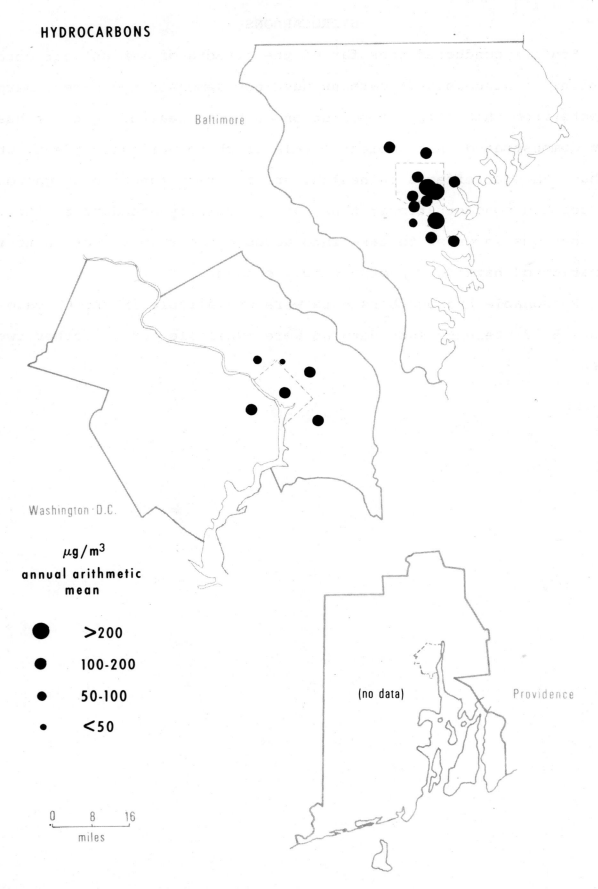

Figure 5.13a. Hydrocarbons: Baltimore, Washington, and Providence.

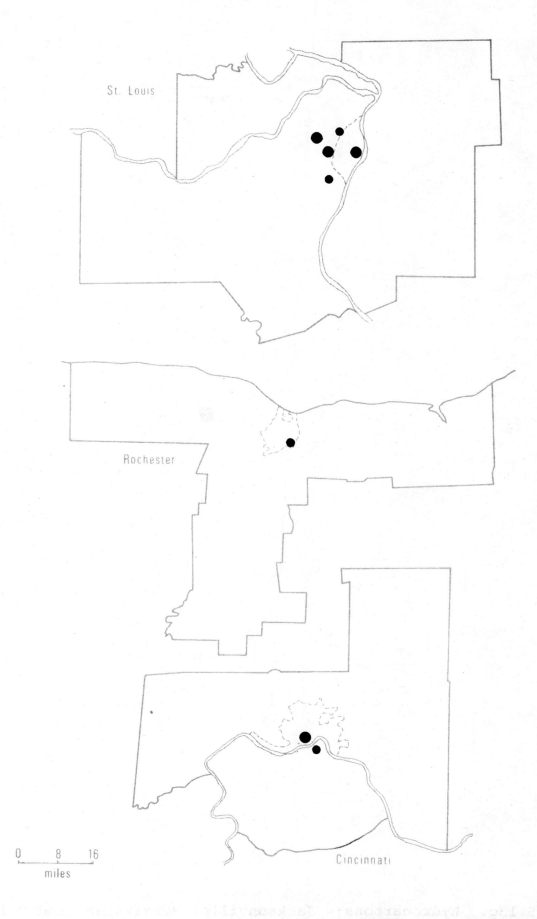

Figure 5.13b. Hydrocarbons: St. Louis, Rochester, and Cincinnati.

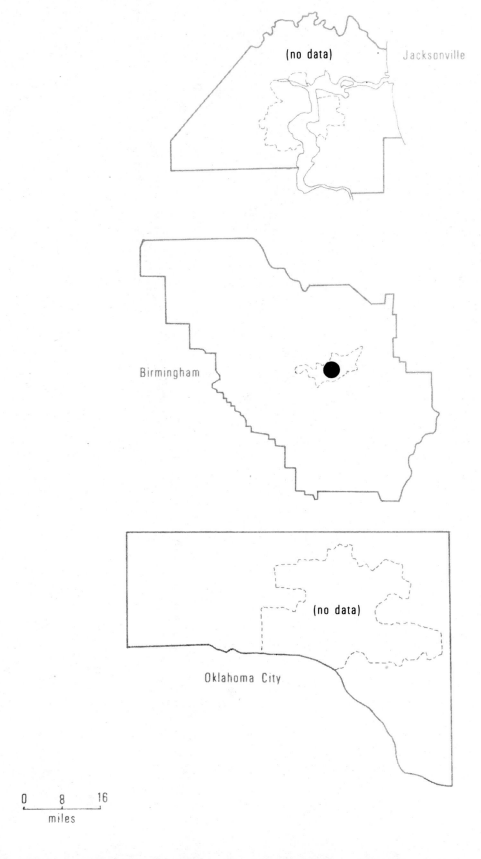

Figure 5.13c. Hydrocarbons: Jacksonville, Birmingham, and Oklahoma City.

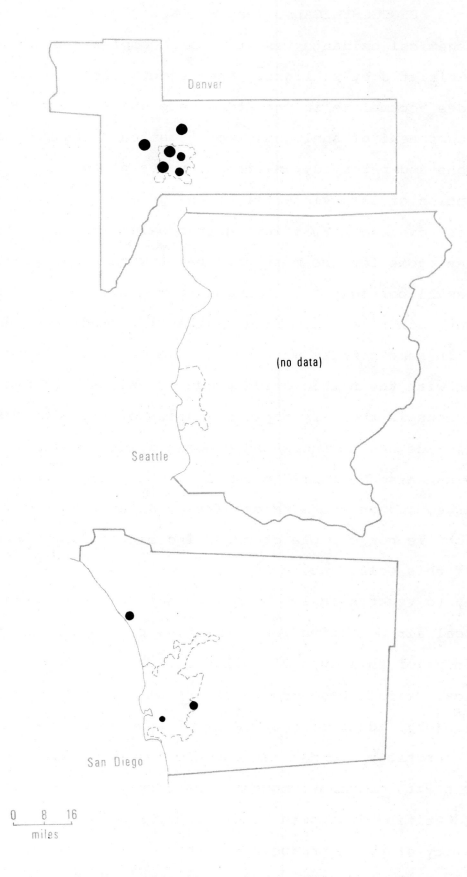

Figure 5.13d. Hydrocarbons: Denver, Seattle, and San Diego.

PHOTOCHEMICAL OXIDANTS, INCLUDING OZONE

Photochemical oxidants result from a complex series of atmospheric reactions initiated by sunlight. When reactive hydrocarbons and nitrogen oxides accumulate in the atmosphere and are exposed to the ultraviolet component of sunlight, the formation of new compounds, including ozone and peroxyacyl nitrates, takes place.

Absorption of ultraviolet light energy by nitrogen dioxide results in its disassociation into nitric oxide and an oxygen atom. These oxygen atoms for the most part react with air oxygen to form ozone. A small portion of the oxygen atoms and ozone react also with certain hydrocarbons to form free radical intermediates and various products. In some complex manner, the free radical intermediates and ozone react with the nitric oxide produced initially. One result of these reactions is the very rapid oxidation of the nitric oxide to nitrogen dioxide and an increased concentration of ozone.

Ozone can also be formed naturally in the atmosphere by electrical discharge, and in the stratosphere by solar radiation, both processes which are not capable of producing significant urban concentrations of this pollutant.

Injury to vegetation is one of the earliest manifestations of photochemical air pollution, and sensitive plants are useful biological indicators of this type of pollution. The visible symptoms of photochemical oxidant produced injury to plants may be classified as: (1) acute injury, identified by cell collapse with subsequent development of necrotic patterns; (2) chronic injury, identified by necrotic patterns with or other pigmented patterns; and, (3) physiological effects, identified by growth alterations, reduced yields, and changes in the quality of plant products. The acute symptoms are generally characteristic of a specific pollutant; though highly characteristic, chronic injury patterns are not. Ozone injury to leaves is identified as a stippling or flecking. Adverse effects on sensitive vegetation were observed from exposure to photochemical oxidant concentrations of about 100 µg/m³ (0.05 ppm) for 4 hours.

Adverse effects on materials (rubber products and fabrics) from exposure to photochemical oxidants have not been precisely quantified, but have been observed at the levels presently occurring in many urban atmospheres.

Under the conditions prevailing in the areas where studies were conducted, adverse health effects, as shown by impairment of performance of student athletes, occurred over a range of hourly average oxidant concentrations from 60 to 590 µg/m³ (0.03 to 0.3 ppm). An increased frequency of asthma attacks in a small proportion of subjects with this disease was shown on days when oxidant concentrations exceeded peak values of 250 µg/m³ (0.13 ppm), a level that would be associated with an hourly average concentration ranging from 100 to 120 µg/m³ (0.05 to 0.06 ppm). Adverse health effects, as manifested by eye irritation, were reported by subjects in several studies when photochemical oxidant concentrations reached instantaneous levels of about 200 µg/m³ (0.10 ppm), a level that would be associated with an hourly average concentration ranging from 60 to 100 µg/m³ (0.03 to 0.05 ppm).

Figures 5.14-5.16 show available data for Chicago and the other twelve cases.

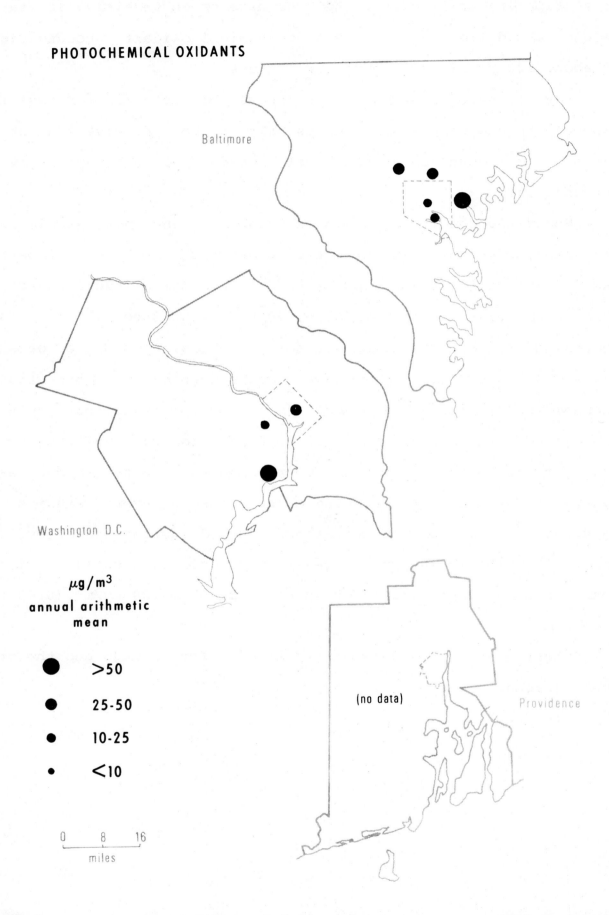

Figure 5.14a. Photochemical Oxidants: Baltimore, Washington, and Providence.

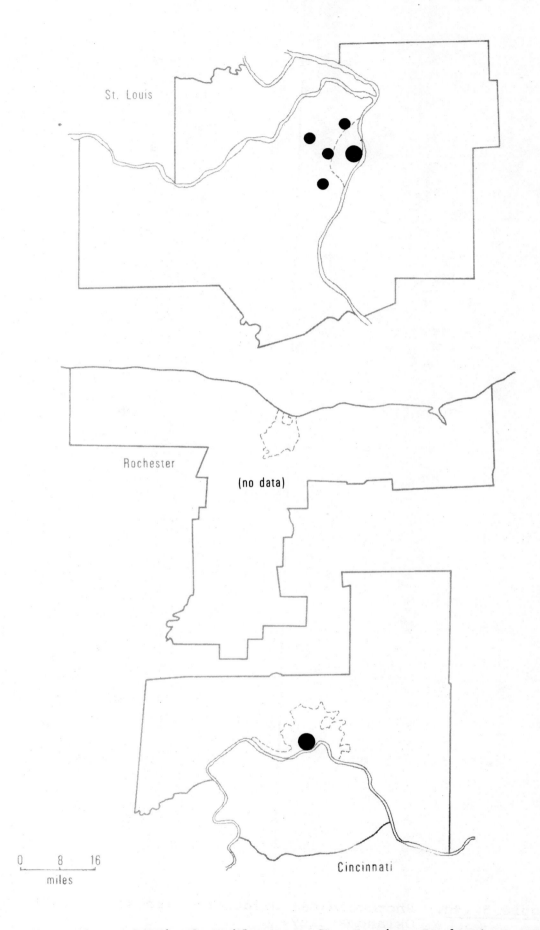

Figure 5.14b. Photochemical Oxidants: St. Louis, Rochester, and Cincinnati.

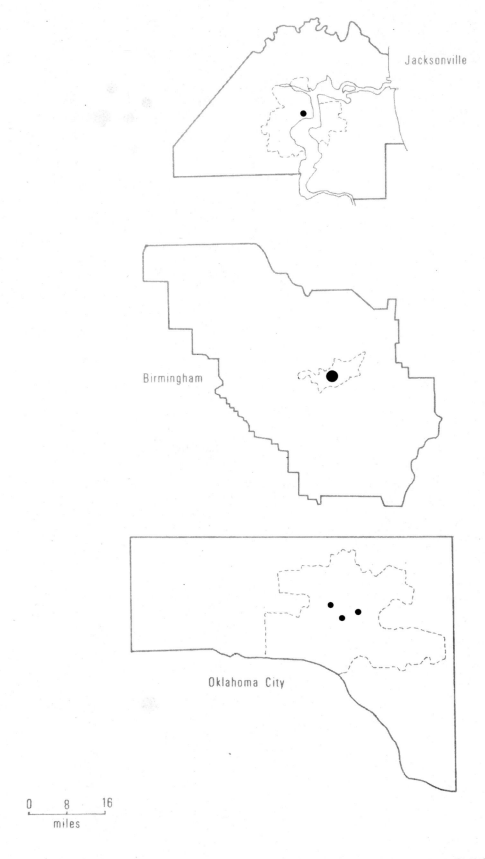

Figure 5.14c. Photochemical Oxidants: Jacksonville, Birmingham, and Oklahoma City.

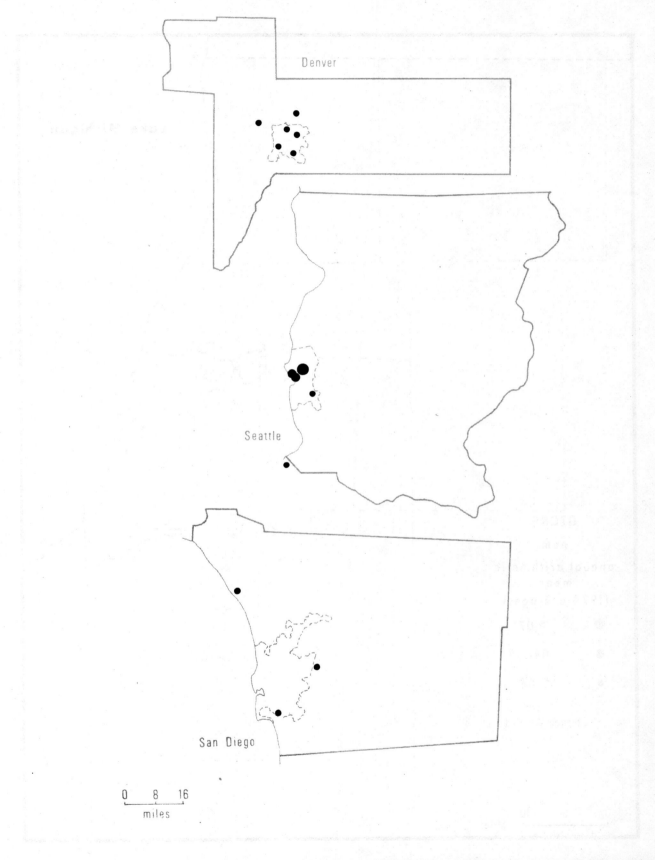

Figure 5.14d. Photochemical Oxidants: Denver, Seattle, and San Diego.

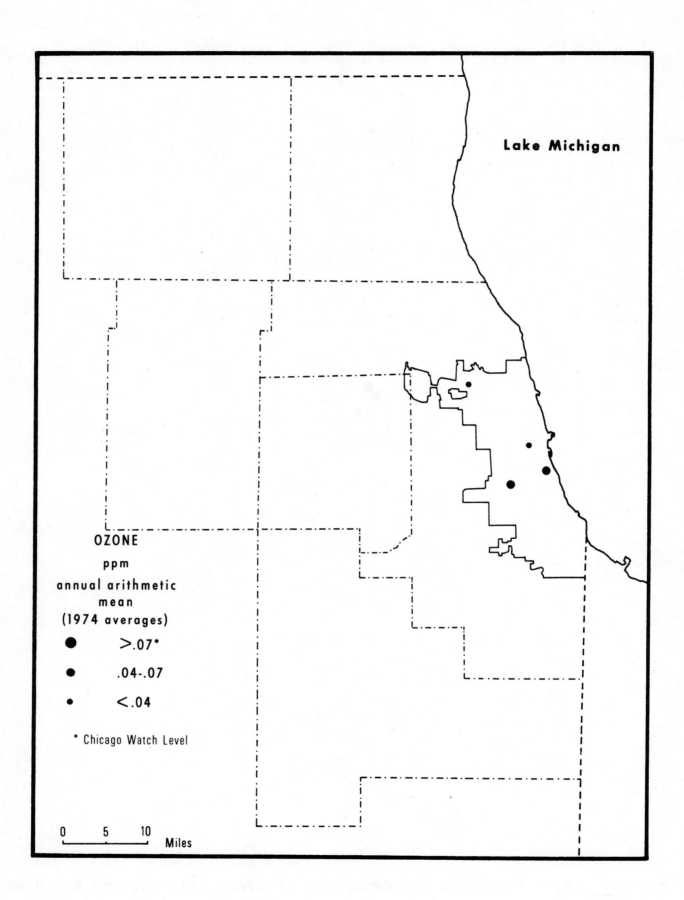

Lake Michigan

OZONE

ppm

annual arithmetic
mean
(1974 averages)

●   >.07*

●   .04-.07

•   <.04

* Chicago Watch Level

0   5   10   Miles

Figure 5.15

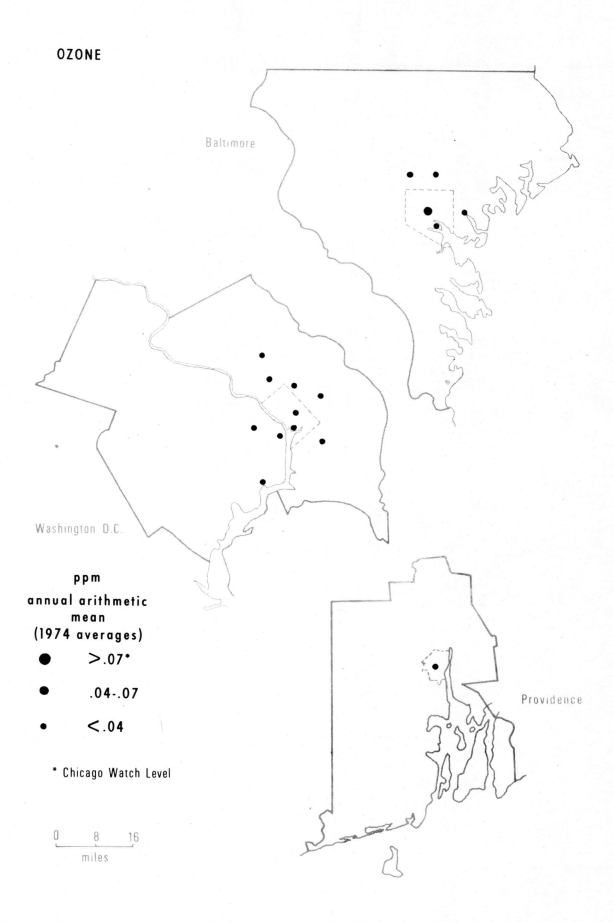

OZONE

Baltimore

Washington D.C.

Providence

ppm
annual arithmetic
mean
(1974 averages)

●   > .07*

●   .04-.07

•   < .04

* Chicago Watch Level

```
0    8    16
```
miles

Figure 5.16a.   Ozone: Baltimore, Washington, and Providence.

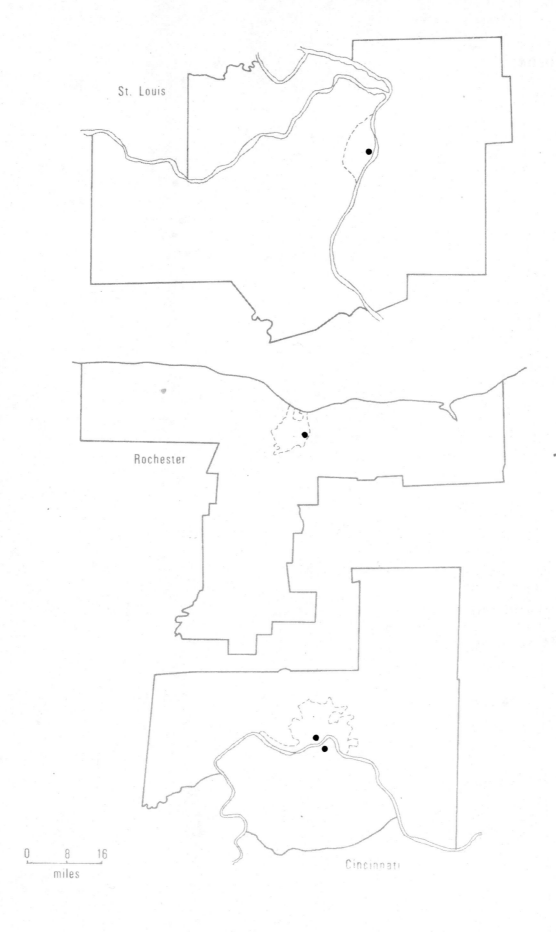

Figure 5.16b. Ozone: St. Louis, Rochester, and Cincinnati.

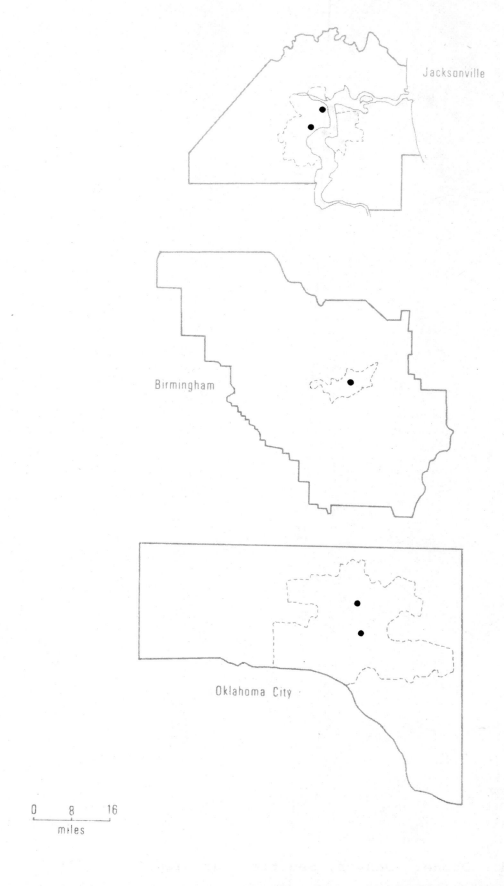

Figure 5.16c. Ozone: Jacksonville, Birmingham, and Oklahoma City.

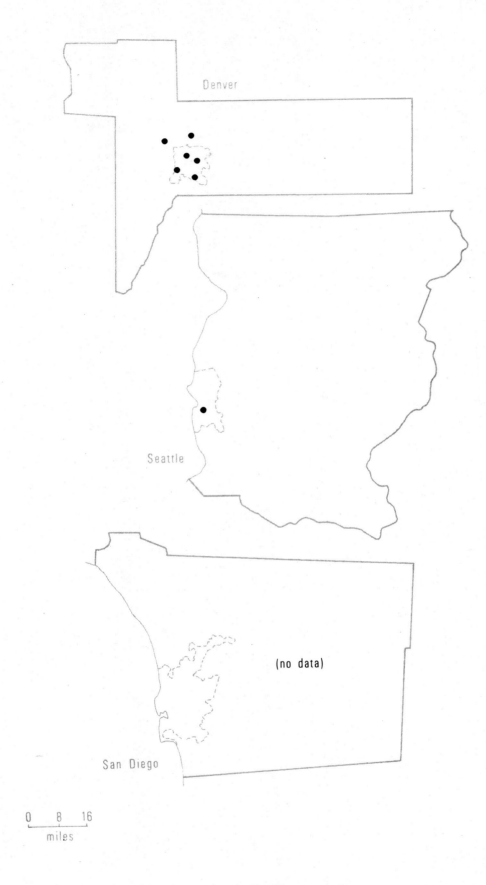

Figure 5.16d. Ozone: Denver, Seattle, San Diego.

✳ *Chapter 6*

The Urban Noise Environment

To understand the nature and incidence of noise pollution within

the nation's metropolitan regions, one first has to understand the

nature of sound, for as one consultant's report to the Congress put it:

> The key point about noise is that it is defined as
> 'unwanted sound,' and that the first thing one has
> to do in looking at a noise problem is to try to
> understand who doesn't want the noise and why he
> doesn't want it, and under what conditions he doesn't
> want it.

Sound is a wavelike vibration capable of being transmitted through

the atmosphere or other vibrating medium, and it is best described in

terms of the three parameters--magnitude, frequency, and temporal

structure. Magnitude, or intensity, is a measurement of the amount

of energy in the sound and is measured by calculating the amount of

pressure sound waves are capable of exerting on a surface. Each sound

wave is a cycle, and frequency is a measure of the number of cycles

per second created by the sound. The other important component is

duration, or the persistence of a sound in time.

The function of the human ear is to transform sound energy into

nerve impulses. The ear is sensitive to an extremely wide range of

sounds, and so a logarithmic scale, the decibel scale, has been devised
to provide a manageable representation that reflects the sensitivity
of the human ear. On the decibel scale, an individual perceives a
10 dB increase in the sound level as a doubling in loudness. The ear
responds to frequencies ranging from about 20 to 20,000 cycles per
second, though the range of human speech is generally concentrated in
the 500 to 2,000 cycles per second frequency range. High frequencies
are more easily perceived than low frequencies. When two sounds of
equal intensity but of different frequencies are heard at the same
time, the higher frequency is perceived as being the louder of the two.
This means that high pitched sounds "carry" further in the environment, as shown in Figures 6.1-6.5, which chart the distance decay
functions of a few common noises in the urban environment.

The modern urban place is characterized by a mosaic of communities interconnected by transportation and communications networks,
and each community has a distinct noise environment, dependent mainly
upon land use and proximity to major noise sources. The basic feature
of any noise environment is the background or ambient noise level--
the relatively constant noise level in which no single source is identifiable. The ambient sound level is, of course, subject to day-night
and seasonal fluctuations as well. Thus, a more refined definition
of the ambient sound level includes two components, one continuous,
of constant level and not attributable to an easily identifiable source,
and a second which is known (usually local traffic). The second definition is preferable because it recognizes that major land uses make
consistent contributions to the background noise levels with which
people must live, in the way that they affect the acoustical environment. The highly reflective surfaces of the central business district
contribute to the deafening din in most cities, while the grassy spaces
of a park reduce the reverberations of sounds and therefore lower the
ambient sound levels.

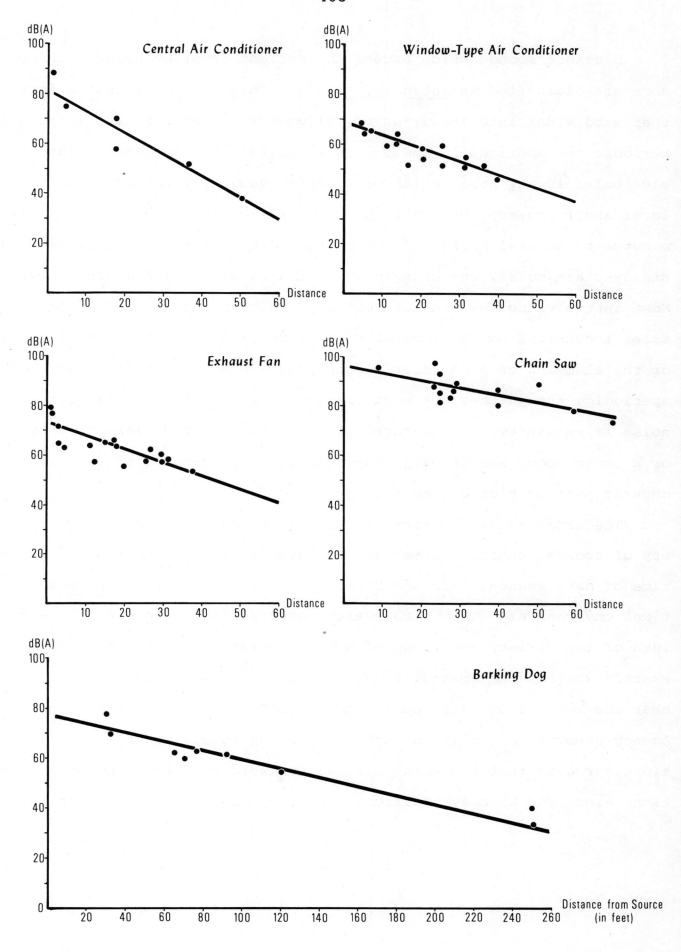

Figures 6.1-6.5. Distance-decay Functions of Common Noises in the
Urban Environment.

Distinct sounds which exceed the ambient level by about 7 dB or more are classified as intrusive sounds. This kind of sound is further subdivided into steady-state, fluctuating, intermittent (both periodic and aperiodic), and impulsive noise. A steady-state intrusive noise is any noise which persists at roughly the same decibel level and frequency for any length of time--be it anywhere from a few minutes to several hours. Fluctuating noise persists in time, as does steady-state noise, but changes in both decibel level and frequency. Most intrusive noises are intermittent, which means they are relatively brief incursions on the ambient noise level, such as the bark of a dog or the slamming of a car door. Such noises can be either periodic or aperiodic, though they are most frequently aperiodic. An impulsive noise is an extremely loud burst of noise such as the blast of a gun or a sonic boom, and is dangerous because it is capable of directly causing permanent damage to the ear.

The urban noise environment thus is characterized by a wide variety of sounds, exhibiting patterns related to location characteristics, time of day, season, land use factors, and the quality of the acoustical environment. The noise events depicted in Figure 6.6 give some idea of the variety and range of sounds in the urban setting. But exactly what is the spatial pattern of urban noises, and which groups bear the burdens of noise pollution? The Environmental Protection Agency reports the following data in its own sample-survey investigations, arguing that the most critical variable related to noise pollution, alongside highway traffic and airport noise, is urban densities:

Description	Typical Range L_{dn} in dB	Average L_{dn} in DB	Estimated Percentage of Urban Population	Average Census Tract Population Density, Number of People Per Square Mile
Quiet Suburban Residential	48-52	50	12	630
Normal Suburban Residential	53-57	55	21	2,000
Urban Residential	58-62	60	28	6,300
Noisy Urban Residential	63-67	65	19	20,000
Very Noisy Urban Residential	63-72	70	7	63,000

Noise from motor vehicles is of two kinds: the almost steady-state noise emanating from a highway adding to the ambient noise level of adjacent areas, and the intrusive noise of an especially loud vehicle which can be heard above the ambient level. The noise levels generated by moving automobiles start at around 65 dB for the particularly quiet models and extend up 85 and even 90 dB for the noisiest and those that are being abusively operated. Most trucks and buses create noise levels in the range of 80 to 95 dB, though sound levels as high as 115 dB have been recorded fifty feet away from trucks moving at highway speeds. Noise pollution from aircraft and airport operations also is a serious problem, and it threatens in the future, with the development of supersonic flight technology, to engulf not only urban areas with sonic booms, but rural areas as well.

Is EPA's emphasis on urban densities valid? What is the evidence in the Chicago case study and in the twelve comparative cases? How exactly do noise levels vary within metropolitan regions, and how do these levels relate to noise control standards, and therefore to legislatively-defined pollution? This is the problem addressed in this chapter, but it is one which presents great difficulties because comprehensive noise surveys are simply unavailable in most metropolitan areas. Thus, while we were able to obtain useful data for the Chicago case, only in Denver, Jacksonville and Washington, D.C. were we able to obtain satisfactory comparative evidence.

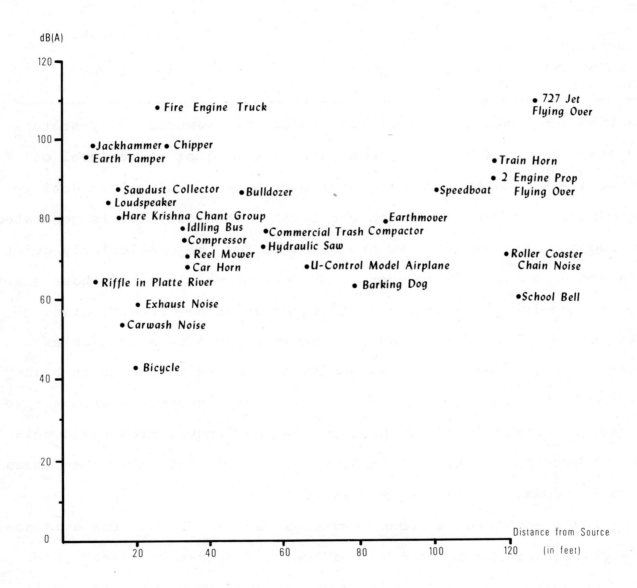

Figure 6.6. Noise Events Recorded by the Denver Community Noise Survey.

Figure 6.7 shows daytime background noise levels for various locations in the City of Chicago. These data were collected by a graduate student in economics at the University of Chicago who was researching his Ph.D. dissertation; the city has only spotty information for selected locations in and around the central business district. Generally, ambient noise readings below 60 dB provide a satisfactory residential noise environment for indoor activity, provided that there is a 15 dB reduction between the outdoor and indoor environments.

Chicago was one of the first cities in the United States to produce a strong comprehensive noise ordinance, which took effect on July 1, 1971. The ordinance is an outgrowth of the city's zoning ordinance and divides the city into districts: heavy manufacturing, general manufacturing, restricted manufacturing, business and commercial, and residential. These districts and the associated standards are presented in Figure 6.8. Noise limits are set for the outer boundaries of the districts for heavy, general, and restricted manufacturing. Where manufacturing districts meet residential districts noise limitations range from 55 to 61 dB(A). Where manufacturing zoning boundaries meet business and commercial zoning boundaries, the noise limit ranges from 62 to 66 dB(A). For business commercial and residential districts noise limits are set at the lot line. Noise coming from buildings in business and commercial districts cannot exceed 62 dB(A), while noise emanating from buildings in residential cannot exceed 55 dB(A).

The Chicago noise ordinance is an impressive piece of zoning legislation and is being held up as a model for similar legislation in other cities. There are, however, some problems associated with these laws. In many parts of Chicago, as measurements have shown, the background noise level never decreases to the levels at boundaries between land uses laid out in the ordinance. For example, at the

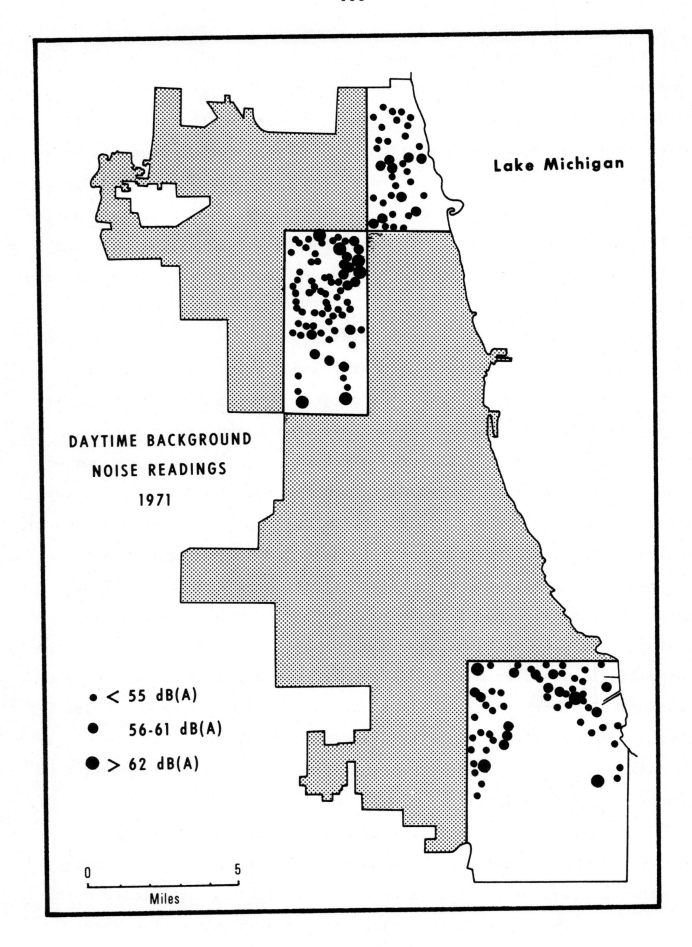

Figure 6.7. Monitored Daytime Background Noise Levels in Chicago.

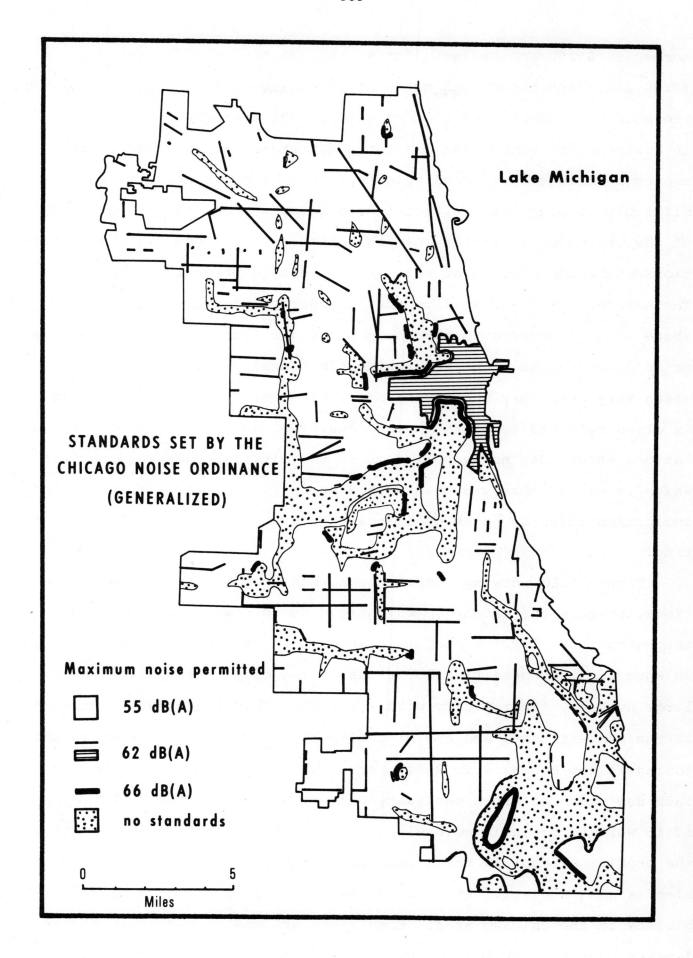

Lake Michigan

STANDARDS SET BY THE
CHICAGO NOISE ORDINANCE
(GENERALIZED)

Maximum noise permitted

☐ 55 dB(A)

▤ 62 dB(A)

▬ 66 dB(A)

⋰ no standards

0 _____ 5
        Miles

Figure 6.8.   Standards Set by the Chicago Noise Ordinance.

corner of State and Madison, during the quietest time of the day
(3:00 a.m.) the background noise level decreased to 63 dB(A). However,
the noise ordinance sets the limit at 62 dB(A) at the property line
in business and commercial districts for stationary sources in and
around buildings. The masking effect of background noise makes it
difficult to pick out the troublesome noise source, making enforcement
of the ordinance difficult in such situations. Figure 6.9 shows locations where the background noise levels exceed prescribed standards.
The extreme local variability that is characteristic of all the maps
where noise measurements have been plotted reflects the fact that the
prime determinants of noise--residential density and land use factors--
often vary over very short distances. This attribute of urban noise
is often referred to as the noise density of an area. The map of violations shows that noise pollution in the city is widespread, a fact
which is easily observed even with a sparsity of data. There is good
indication that the noise ordinance is not enforceable at the present
time.

Figure 6.10, showing intermittent noise readings at various locations, reveals the extent to which loud noise sources are dispersed
throughout the city. Zoning laws attempt to concentrate these sources
in specific, non-sensitive locations in the city. Because of their
large numbers, the rapidity with which the urban landscape is changing
at the present time, and the wide dispersion of the noise makers, such
zoning is not a realistic short term solution, however. Zoning and
land use planning are a necessary part of urban government, but even
if it were to begin immediately, it would still take years to correct
the problem evident in the noise environment. The extent of the problem is adequately illustrated by Figure 6.11, which shows noise complaints in the Chicago area. Complaints are most numerous in higher-
density central city locations, although not in the ghetto. However,
the causes of complaints do not show any particular spatial pattern.

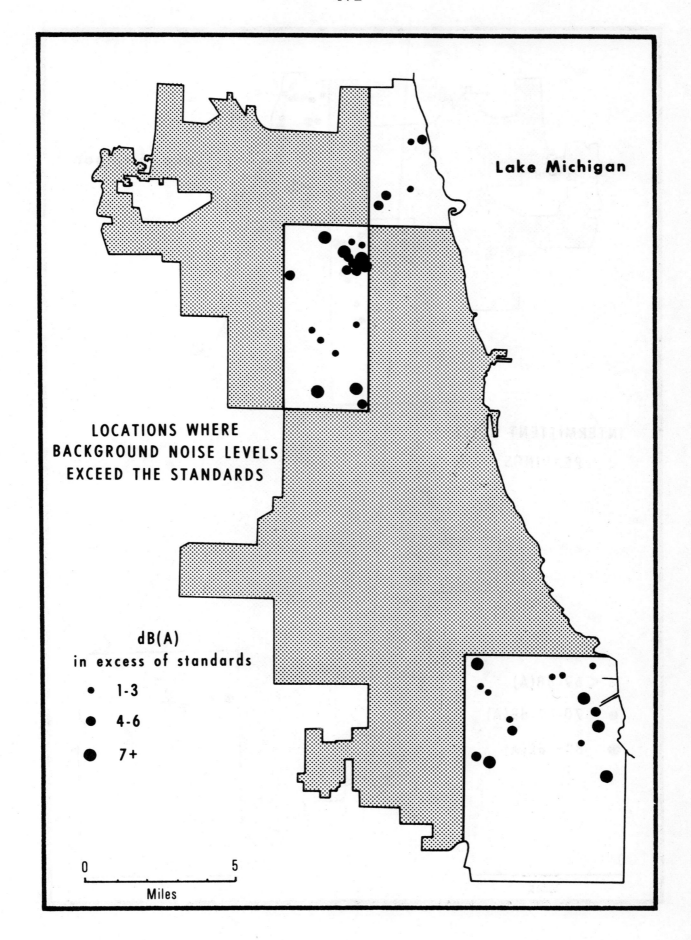

LOCATIONS WHERE
BACKGROUND NOISE LEVELS
EXCEED THE STANDARDS

Lake Michigan

dB(A)
in excess of standards

• 1-3

● 4-6

● 7+

0   5

Miles

Figure 6.9.   Locations in Chicago Where Background Noise Levels Exceed
the Standards Set in the Chicago Noise Ordinance.

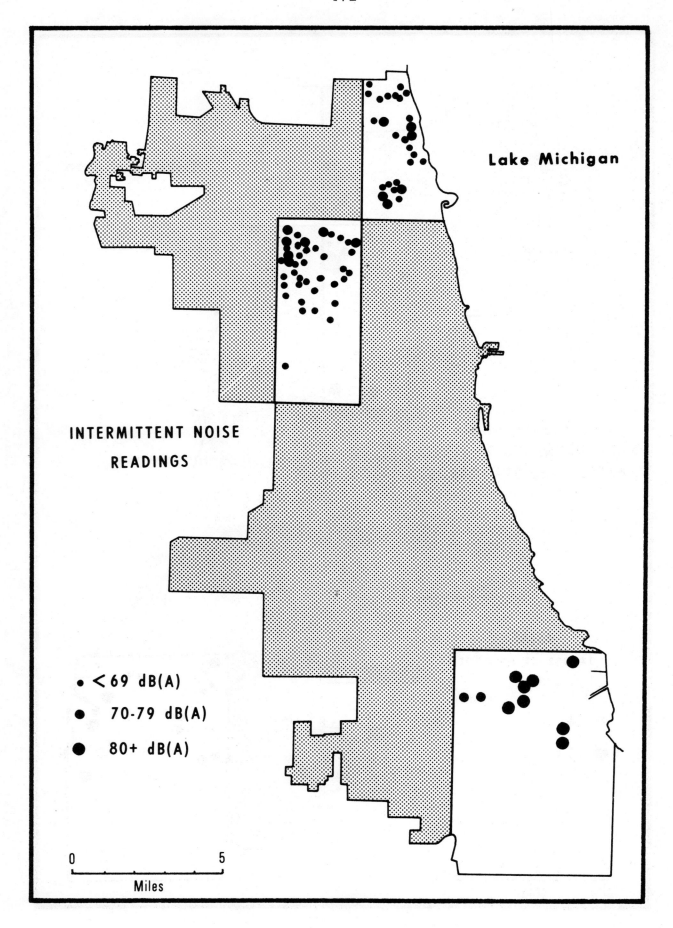

Figure 6.10. Intermittent Noise Readings in the City of Chicago.

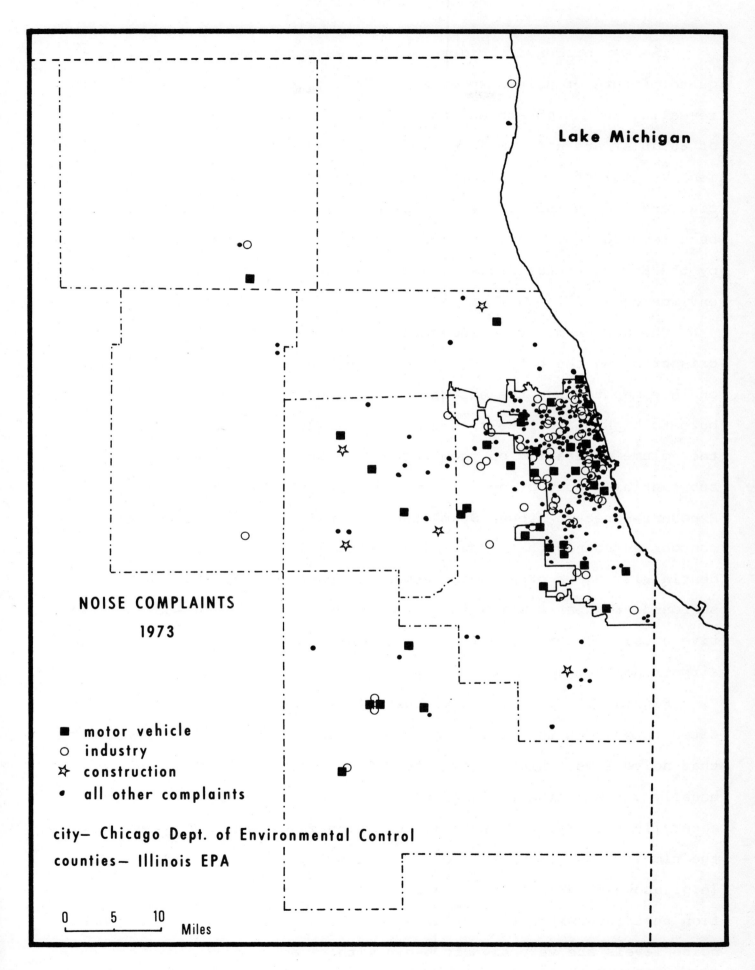

Lake Michigan

NOISE COMPLAINTS

1973

■ motor vehicle
○ industry
☆ construction
• all other complaints

city— Chicago Dept. of Environmental Control

counties— Illinois EPA

0   5   10
                Miles

Figure 6.11.   Noise Complaints in the Chicago Metropolitan Region in
               1973.

The map of Denver, Figure 6.12, presents perhaps the most adequate picture of noise exposure in the sampled metropolitan regions, revealing that high ambient noise levels (that is levels in excess of 60 dB(A)) are not a major problem in Denver in residential environments. Ambient noise levels above 60 dB(A) are found only in commercial and industrial areas; and in these areas, no ambient levels have been recorded above 70 dB(A)--the standard currently being proposed by the Environmental Protection Agency as providing a safe occupational environment.

The Denver map also shows the major surface transportation routes crisscrossing the city. It is not possible from the data presented on this map to know the extent to which these traffic arteries contribute to high noise levels in adjacent residential communities, though the volume of traffic on them suggests that they probably create a substantial amount of noise. In addition, the map shows the Noise Exposure Forecast around Stapleton International Airport. The NEF 40 contour surrounds that area which is "clearly unacceptable" for residential living or other noise sensitive uses, and the NEF 30 contour surrounds that area which is "normally unacceptable" for noise-sensitive uses. Obviously, quite a large part of the city is affected by airport noise.

Figure 6.13 provides a picture of mean noise levels at various sites throughout the city of Jacksonville. The mean noise level is that noise level which is exceeded 50 percent of the time, and is usually a few decibels higher than the ambient noise level, which is generally taken as that noise level which is exceeded 90 percent of the time. Thus, wherever the mean noise level is particularly high (e.g. above 65 dB(A)) in a residential environment, it is an indication that intermittent noise is a serious problem or that background noise levels are very high to begin with. Jacksonville has, at least at the sites recorded on the map, an excellent noise environment.

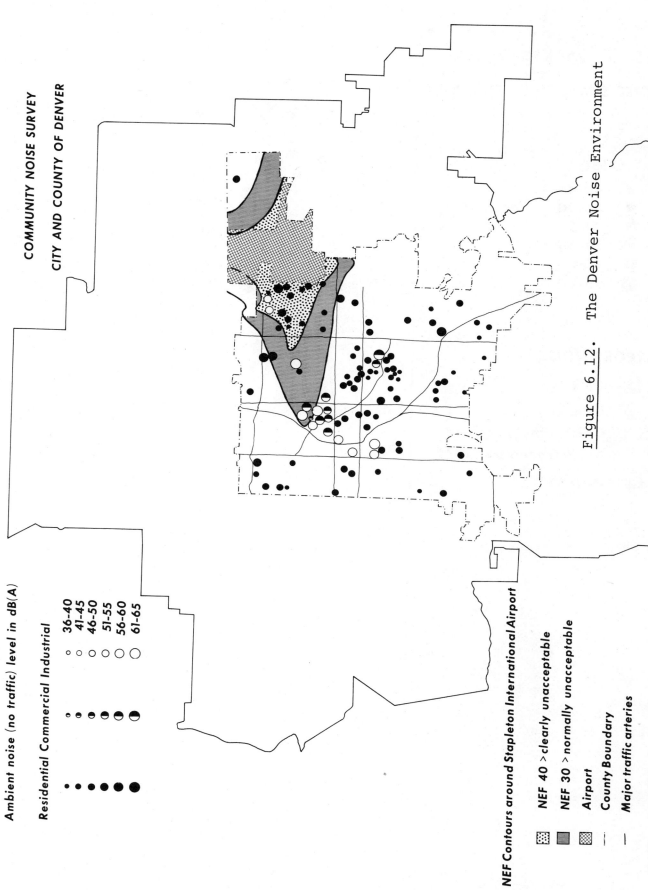

COMMUNITY NOISE SURVEY

CITY AND COUNTY OF DENVER

Ambient noise (no traffic) level in dB(A)

Residential Commercial Industrial

36-40
41-45
46-50
51-55
56-60
61-65

NEF Contours around Stapleton International Airport

NEF 40 >clearly unacceptable

NEF 30 > normally unacceptable

Airport

County Boundary

Major traffic arteries

Traffic volume 24 hours 26,000 and over

Figure 6.12.   The Denver Noise Environment

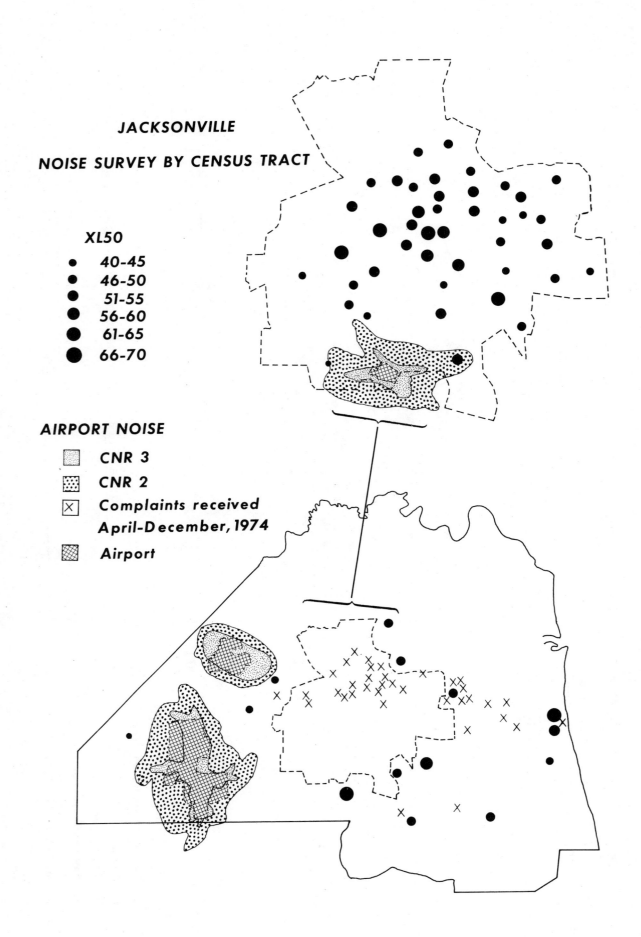

Figure 6.13. Average Noise Levels in Jacksonville, Florida.

Note: XL 50 is the noise level that is exceeded 50 per cent of the time.

The noise contours around the airport do not encompass large areas, though the potential for a problem exists. The complaints correlate with residential density fairly closely.

Figure 6.14 shows the average minimum and maximum for recorded noise levels over ten minute intervals at various sites throughout Washington, D.C.. Washington, like Chicago, is part of a major metropolis, while Jacksonville and Denver are middle-sized cities. The overall average of the minimum noise levels in Washington, which can be taken as a close approximation of the background noise level, is well above those of both Jacksonville and Denver: in Washington 61.7 dB(A), in Denver 48dB(A), and in Jacksonville 55.4 dB(A) (the average L_{50}). In Chicago the overall average is 55.6 dB(A).

It is difficult to draw any conclusions on the basis of these comparisons. The Jacksonville average is high because it is based on L_{50} measurements instead of ambient measurements. An average of ambient levels in this city would be a few decibels less, at least. Because the Chicago measurements are not representative of the entire range environments throughout the city, that average also may be misleading, and is probably on the low side. These averages do suggest, however, that the large urban regions are noisier than smaller cities such as Denver and Jacksonville.

Noise, Health, and Annoyance

An evaluation of the deleterious effects of noise in the urban environment must begin with the effects of noise on the human physiology. This is because adverse physiological consequences have the potential of disrupting all phases of life; and it is often extremely difficult, if not impossible, to restore complete physical health to someone who has suffered damage from noise pollution.

The most obvious effect of excessive amounts of noise on the human physiology, and the one that has received the most attention from researchers, is the reduction of an individual's capacity to

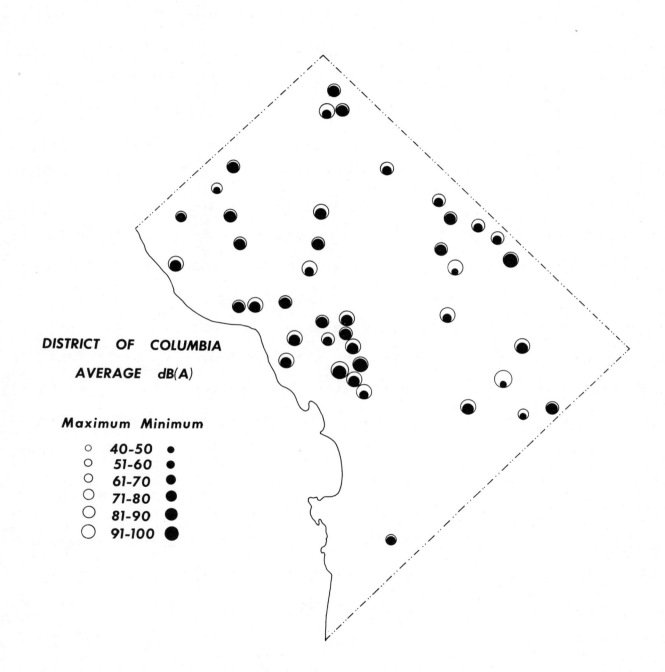

DISTRICT OF COLUMBIA

AVERAGE dB(A)

Maximum Minimum

○ 40-50   ●
○ 51-60   ●
○ 61-70   ●
○ 71-80   ●
○ 81-90   ●
○ 91-100 ●

Figure 6.14. Average Minimum and Maximum Recorded Noise Levels over
Ten-Minute Intervals in Washington, D.C.

hear sounds in the environment. Exposure to loud noises can lead to both temporary and permanent threshold shift. The threshold level is the level of a tone that can just be detected. While it is rare that a person will suffer any permanent damage from a single exposure to a high noise level, daily exposure to high levels of noise for long periods of time results in temporary threshold shift (TTS) that may last for several days after the exposure ceases and result in a threshold shift as great as 50 decibels. The possibility exists for developing permanent damage resulting from the accumulated effects of such a pattern of exposure. Permanent damage usually reaches a maximum after around twenty years of routine exposure, though the length of time varies in relationship to the intensity of noise to which there is daily exposure.

In recent years the theory that has become most attractive to governmental agencies and other organizations concerned with evaluating noise-induced hearing loss is the so-called "equal-energy" hypothesis. This hypothesis argues that the hazard to the hearing is determined by the total energy (a product of sound level and duration) entering the ear on a daily basis. While there does not yet exist hard experimental or empirical evidence to verify the equal-energy hypothesis, what is currently known about temporary and permanent threshold shift suggests this concept is the appropriate one for predicting the hazardousness of a particular noise environment, at least for relatively steady-state noise levels.

There is still uncertainty as to whether the energy principle accurately predicts the hazardousness of fluctuating noise levels and intermittent noise exposures, however. If the energy principle is inadequate in these situations, it is a serious flaw, for impulsive noise has been and continues to be a prominent cause of noise-induced hearing loss. One researcher who has studied the problem has concluded that fully developed, permanent threshold shift occurs more rapidly in impulsive noise exposure than steady-state noise exposure, that because the earliest and greatest change in threshold shift occurs at 6,000 Hz, there is a slightly different pattern of development of hearing loss in impulse noise than in steady-state noise exposure, and that permanent threshold shift stabilizes in time, as has been found with steady-state noise exposure.

In its most definitive publication on noise pollution so far, Information on Levels of Environmental Noise Requisite to Protect Public Health and Welfare with an Adequate Margin of Safety, the Environmental Protection Agency has published standards based on the equal-energy hypothesis. These standards are summarized below:

EFFECT	LEVEL	AREA
Hearing Loss	$L_{eq(24)}$ <70 dB	All areas
Outdoor activity interference and annoyance	L_{dn}<55 dB	Outdoors in residential areas and farms and other outdoor areas where people spend widely varying amounts of time and other places in which quiet is a basis for use.
	$L_{eq(24)}$<55 dB	Outdoor areas where people spend limited amounts of time, such as shcool yards, playgrounds, etc.
Indoor activity interference and annoyance	L_{dn}<45 dB	Indoor residential areas
	$L_{eq(24)}$<45 dB	Other indoor areas with human activities such as school, etc.

Note: $L_{eq(24)}$ represents the sound energy averaged over a 24-hour period while L_{dn} represents the L_{eq} with a 10 dB nighttime weighting. The hearing loss level identified represents annual averages of the daily level over a period of forty years.

To protect against hearing loss, the EPA has concluded that an L_{eq} less them or equal to 70 dB is sufficient. The equivalent A- weighted sound level is simply, the constant sound level that, in a given situation and time period, conveys the same energy as the actual time-varying A-weighted sound. The other major concern of these standards is that the population be protected against unwanted and unnecessary activity interference from environmental noise. An assumption behind this focus is that protection from other negative consequences of noise exposure, such as extra-auditory physiological responses detrimental to health, follow from adequate protection from both hearing impairment and activity interference.

The decision of the EPA to recommend the use of the long-term equiva-A-weighted sound level as a predictor of hazardous environmental noise is based on statistical analysis of data on individual cases of hearing loss. The EPA decided that, for purposes of hearing conservation alone, a level which is protective of that segment of the population at or below the 96th percentile will protect virtually the entire population. The validity of these standards must be held in question, however, because of weaknesses inherent in the data on individual cases of hearing loss. The collection of case histories of hearing loss has differed from research team to research team, and it has not always been undertaken with appropriate methodological caution. Furthermore, it is well known that there are large individual differences in susceptibility to permanent threshold shift. One researcher points out the problem with a statistically based standard this way: in any actual situation, the group of workers with elevated hearing levels will include both the susceptible and the unlucky. This fact causes all sorts of trouble when one tries to validate a susceptibility test based on a TTS with a cross-section study of a group of men who have been working in noise for many years and who have a wide range of hearing losses. In short, noise-induced hearing loss is related to total exposure over a lifetime and not just occupational exposure; though statistical studies have been forced to rely on the latter, since most of the data come from occupational studies. The inavailability of complete case histories for a wide cross section of society makes it virtually impossible to come up with realistic standards at the present time.

Another problem in measuring noise-induced hearing loss is that noise sometimes interacts with other factors in the environment to produce hearing loss. Some research suggests that a combination of effects of chemical agents (some of which are to be found among the pollutants in the air) and noise can bring about the loss of hearing. There is also a greater susceptibility to noise-induced hearing loss in persons undergoing treatment with antibiotics. Other researchers have found that vibration and noise together influence the dynamics of hearing loss. The failure of the equal-energy hypothesis to adequately account for the different effects of the several complicating factors may mean that in numerous individual situations a standard based on this hypothesis is not effective. It is agreed, however, that total exposure is the single most important factor in hearing loss, and that, at the present time, no better measurement for this quantity exists that the L_{eq}.

The EPA has put together a number of typical noise exposure patterns, each assuming a type of life style found in American cities. It is evident from these patterns that the factory worker suffers the most from noise exposure; and it may be that EPA's figures under-estimate average exposure of factory workers in the major urban areas, if is suggested by the preceding maps, ambient levels in residential environments in the large urban areas are often above 60 decibels. Ambient noise readings in Chicago and Washington in residential areas are often so high that there is not the chance for recuperation from possible temporary threshold shift from occupational exposure. If, for example, an individual is exposed for an 8 hour work period to an equivalent noise level of 75 dB(A), exposure for the remaining 16 hours of the day must not exceed an equivalent noise level of 60 dB(A) to achieve the prescribed standard of Leq of 70 dB(A). Since most factory workers work in noise levels far above 75 dB(A), they require serene noise environments for recuperative purposes; and it is quite obvious that, at least in Washington, D.C. and Chicago, many workers do not get what they need. It is probably even true that in some instances the residential noise environments even exacerbate occupationally developed hearing problems. Clearly, further research is needed to check the hypothesis that a large proportion of factory workers in the major conurbations in the United States are living and working in noise environments which are creating serious hearing problems for them.

Apart from damage to the sense of hearing, noise has other deleterious physiological effects, though the extent to which health is threatened by them is not adequately understood at the present time. What is of interest here are the typical, extra-auditory, physiological changes produced by noise--alterations in the circulation of the blood in peripheral areas of the body, disruption of the activity of the endocrine system, the fast responses of the voluntary musculature and response of the smooth muscles, and possible effects on the reproductive system.

There is wide disagreement concerning the extent to which the physiology of man is capable of adapting to repeated exposures to intense noise. There is wide acceptance of the idea that noise acts as a stimulator for activation of a group of physiological functions designated as arousal reactions.   In a physiological sense, the state of arousal is defined as an increase in the excitation level of certain systems of the body. One researcher in this field has concluded that in terms of abnormal vegetative reaction, noise stimuli in the range of 90 dB(A) to 100 dB(A) create a hazard to human health; and that possible disturbances might be found or manifested in various manners, even in psychic behavior, as there is no function in the human body exclusively affected by noise. Furthermore, the possibility of harmful effects on the body of loud noises exists even when there is no emotional or psychological reaction to the noise, or experience of annoyance. On the other hand, when there is the feeling of annoyance, it is aggravated at peak levels of 90 dB(A). One researcher concludes that as human health is endangered by single noise events as well, it seems justifiable to demand an assessment of noise not only by the calculated equivalent continuous noise level Leq, but also by limits for single noise events which must not be exceeded even if the Leq is below the criteria fixed in standards or laws. But as with noise levels associated with hearing loss, attempts to set standards to protect against the adverse health effects of impulsive or intermittent noise must be guided by the recognition of the fact that there is a large standard deviation in both psychological and physiological reactions to these kinds of noises.

Aircraft noise, in particular, may create health hazards of the kind which have just been referred to above. Laboratory experiments do not confirm the hypothesis of adaptive coping with aircraft noise; indeed, with increasing day-to-day aircraft noise exposure, the physiological response to the onset of noise in the laboratory increases. This response consists of a constriction of the blood vessels at the finger and at the temple, an increase in the electrical muscle activity, a decrease of the heart rate and an increase in the tracking error rate. This complex defensive reaction goes towards a blocking of information reception processes. The reaction correlates positively both with intensity and frequency of aircraft movements (r=.21). The greatest response is noted among persons of low mobility, and among those people with very high blood pressure. Quite clearly then, while aircraft noise and other disturbing environmental noises cannot at this time be directly linked to diseases other than hearing loss, they are capable of aggravating already existing health problems.

The modern city has evolved into an extremely complex stimulus environment in which it is becoming increasingly difficult for man to regulate his psychological and physiological responses. The frequency of situations charged with harmful noise levels encountered by individuals is directly related to the scale of the urban system. The larger the system, the more often noise is an additional stress in the environment. It is not simply that noise is another stimulus competing with other stimuli for the attention of man. As D.E. Broadbent puts it, noise is a stimulus which produces a change in the state of man and that this changed state is reflected in failures of selective perception. Even when an unwanted sound is not loud enough to directly stimulate the vegetative system, annoyance is always present and has a negative feedback on the psychophysiological state. This in turn may exacerbate a state of ill health, or it may affect the ability of an individual to perform a task, even though the main consequence has only been some psychological disturbance.

The relationship between environmental noise and the performance of tasks is another complex issue. For jobs in which verbal commands or exchanges of information are important, and for those jobs which require perception of auditory signals for their successful completion, unwanted noise can obviously interfere with performance. In regard to the performance of tasks not dependent upon the use of the sense of hearing, research results have been ambiguous and contradictory. In a detailed review of the research on this subject, Kryter concluded that, in general, because of adaptation, regular, expected noise has no adverse effects on mandatory mental or motor work performance or output. Some jobs most notably vigilance tasks and work requiring information gathering and analytical processes, appear to be far more sensitive to interference by noise than others; and of all the various forms of noise, non-rhythmic, intermittent and impulsive noises are the most disruptive. Singer and Glass found in their experiments that the only occasions when noise produces task decrements are those in which the individual is working on a highly complex task or is engaged in a vigilance-type task; even then, only unpredictable or uncontrollable noise will disrupt performance. In an article on some of the theoretical implications of perceived control over the environment and the opposite state of helplessness, these same authors point out the fundamental importance of the perception of control in the relationship of an individual to the environment. Inescapable and unpredictable noise they say, confronts the individual with a situation in which he is at the mercy of his environment. He is powerless to affect the occurrence of the stressor and he certainly cannot anticipate its onset. His psychological state under these circumstances as one of helplessness. In other words, it is not the stressful event itself that causes interference but the individual's lack of control over the event. This lack of control induces a state of helplessness in which there is an absence of incentives for initiating actions aimed at avoiding or escaping from the aversive stimulus. If on the other hand, the individual has learned that he can control the stimulus, escape and avoidance behaviors will be facilitated in subsequent exposures to the same and similar stressors.

One implication of the above is that an individual's response to aversive environmental noise may be part of a more encompassing pattern of learned responses to the environment. Noise in the urban environment and the perception of control over it are far more complex phenomena than their simplified counterparts in the experiments of Singer and Glass; though the experiments clearly indicate that a lack of control of a prominent stimulus in the environment is a serious source of psychological stress.

A further conjecture is that, to the extent that actual success in manipulating the environment depends upon socioeconomic factors such as income and education, social class is an important factor in learning how to cope with environmental noise. If the most desirable situation is one in which stimulus environment can be controlled, and this seems patently obvious, there is every reason to expect that the less affluent are forced to live in those environments in which noise is likely to be a problem, densely populated, innercity areas. Researchers have had difficulty in trying to verify this hypothesis, and it cannot be satisfactorily demonstrated by the data presented in this chapter, only suggested.

Community response to noise is a multifaceted problem, related to such variables as health attitudes, attitudes about the noise source, magnitude of the noise, what might be vaguely termed as environmental values (implying what an individual has a right to expect from his surroundings),and a variety of situational factors. One of the most thorough studies of community response to noise is Community Reactions to Sonic Booms in the Oklahoma City Area, conducted by the National Opinion Research Center in relation to the six month sonic boom test conducted by the Federal Aviation Administration. The study was conducted in 1964 with the purpose of discovering the long range acceptability of sonic booms, which because of the progress in the development of the SST, had the potential of becoming everyday features of the noise environment.

The Federal Aviation Agency's sonic boom test consisted of subjecting a large portion of Oklahoma City to a regular pattern of eight booms a day for a period of six months. The six months were divided into three time periods, for each of which the boom intensity was altered. In the first period the boom intensity was 1 psf (pound per square foot); in the second period it was 1.5 psf; and in the third period the boom intensity was 2.0 psf. In each of the three periods, extensive interviewing was conducted to monitor community reaction and correlate it with boom intensity. Many of the questions were designed to bring out information on the relationship between attitudes and feelings of annoyance with the booms.

Before the study began, it was found that there was a widespread sense of satisfaction with the living conditions in the area; so that once the booms began, they quickly became a prominent source of irritation and ranked very nearly at the top of the list of important local problems. Another initial factor affecting the overall response of the community was the importance of the aviation industry to the economic welfare of Oklahoma City and the widespread employment of local residents by this industry--about one third of all respondents in the interviews had direct or indirect connections with aviation industry. The Federal Aviation Administration preceded the tests with a publicity campaign and asked local leaders and the media to support the tests. The idea was promulgated that, if at all possible, sonic booms ought to be accepted by residents for the good of the whole community.

Throughout the study interferences with living activities were widely reported, and the number of reports of interference increased as the study progressed and the booms were intensified. House rattles and vibrations were the most commonly reported disturbances and were cited by virtually everyone. Having been startled or frightened was the next most common disturbance, reported by over a third of the respondents, followed by interference with sleep or rest. Disruptions with radio or television reception and conversation were reported by about 10 percent of all persons. While the types and patterns of interference reported were similar for all three interviewing periods, the intensity of annoyance over these disturbances increased over time for all disturbances; and sleep and rest interference produced the most vigorous negative reactions. These are indications that over the test period some residents developed negative attitudes regarding sonic booms, while many of those who were already against the booms became more vehement in this opinion. This is supported further by the finding that while almost 80 percent felt that they could accept the booms in the first interview period, only about 60 percent felt this way on the third interview when the intensity of the booms had increased.

Annoyance, however, is not directly correlated with the kind or extent of activity interference. Disturbance is a fairly objective and direct effect of sonic booms in many living situations; but how people feel about such disturbances and the intensity of the reaction is a largely subjective matter. It was found, before the FAA's tests began, that in general the complaint potential (the willingness to complain about a local problem if annoyed) was very low; and that actual complaint behavior during the tests was lower than the complaint potential--only 10 percent actually made complaints about the booms. Most people seemed to feel that complaints were of little or no effect in moving officials, including those who actually did make complaints. The socioeconomic characteristics are interesting to note: complainers were more often middle-aged females, with older children and smaller families. They had more education, a little higher income, and were about equally sensitive to noise.

Chapter 7

Solid Wastes: Generation, Collection and Disposal

There are three solid wastes "problems," those of generation, collection and disposal. One way of looking at potential pollution by solid wastes is by imagining what would accumulate if collection systems were not operating in our cities today; this is the "generation" problem that occasionally reappears when garbage workers strike. The second relates to methods of collection, whether public or private, regulated or otherwise, with attendant traffic, health and safety problems. The third is that of disposal, whether dumping, in sanitary landfills, or at incinerators, with the obvious questions of health and safety, attendant questions of recycling, reuse and recovery which might reduce the overall volume of wastes.

The study of solid wastes is beset by problems. Official attention has focused on disposal sites with new incinerator and landfill techniques, and only on the problem of collection to the extent that private and municipal haulers are licensed and governed by a municipal code. Generation, corporately or individually, is totally unregulated. One result is that record-keeping in most municipalities is incomplete at best. As the Northeastern Illinois Planning Commission (NIPC) concluded in 1973, "solid waste management suffers from a lack of the most basic information". The problem, NIPC points out, is fundamentally one of the numerous agencies handling solid waste. In the City of Chicago and most surrounding communities, for example, the municipality collects only from residences of four flats or less. All other industrial, commercial, and large multi-family buildings, are serviced by private haulers who are highly competitive and, consequently, secretive. Although they must be licensed by the city, there are no requirements that they report the areas they service, or the amounts they collect. Furthermore, even many of the city agencies which handle collection and disposal of various types of solid waste do not keep uniform records using standard definitions, or maintain meaningful measures of the amounts collected and dumped. In other words, there is no overall data system that would enable an effective solid waste management plan to be developed. From collection to incineration to landfill much of the information necessary to planning is simply non-existent.

Since so little comprehensive information exists on solid waste generation, collection, and in many cases, disposal, the problem we had was to seek out whatever data might be available, whatever the source. We were primarily interested in data which dealt with the sources of solid waste, the amounts collected, generated, or disposed, and some spatial unit to indicate where the waste originated (e.g. collection routes, solid waste management areas, or political boundaries such as the wards according to which the City of Chicago's collection system is organized). Also we were especially interested in subsidiary sources of solid waste (demolitions, street dirt, tree and stump removal, bulk collections, and abandoned cars) not normally reported, so that an accurate picture of solid wastes could be developed.

Information on disposal practices, and attempts by each city on resource recovery also was sought. Finally, any regulations on collection and/or disposal were sought after, as there are no national standards for collection and only a few standards for disposal (mainly health and sanitary regulations for landfills).

The data were obtained by contacting various city and county officials and agencies who dealt with solid waste. These included Sanitation Departments, Environmental Control Agencies, and Public Works Departments. Information was requested not only for city data, but also for the county. In the case of Chicago and St. Louis, information was obtained for the entire SMSA. Any planning documents or previous studies done by city or county agencies dealing with solid waste management were particularly sought after.

Because responses were so limited, the data painstakingly scoured for this present report are patently incomplete, and of variable quality and reliability. However, since the largely valueless National Survey of Community Solid Waste Practices conducted by the EPA in 1968 obtained no data for the Chicago area and little data for the other twelve metropolitan regions, the data presented here are of special importance.

Solid Wastes in the Chicago Region

As a result of our efforts, we were able to obtain for the City of Chicago, and in some instances for the whole Chicago metropolitan area, data on all major types of solid waste, including many subsidiary sources not normally recorded or reported. The principal source of information was NIPC's 1973 report on solid wastes, which provided data on collection and disposal outside the City of Chicago, including an excellent inventory of landfill and incinerator sites, although only sparse collection data for the 356 municipalities in the metropolitan area. Additional data on the metropolitan area were provided by the Center for Environmental Studies, Argonne National Laboratory, to fill in some of the gaps of the NIPC data.

The major source of generation data was the Department of Environmental Control, for the City of Chicago. The Department provided the computer output from the Solid Waste Report for the City of Chicago published in 1966, with a 1972 unpublished update.

Both reports made estimates of solid waste-residential, commercial, and industrial- on a square mile basis for the City of Chicago. The Sanitation Bureau provided figures on public collection in both cases. Private collection in 1966 was estimated from a survey of private scavengers with 80 percent of them responding. In 1972 the private collection figures were estimated on the basis of a survey of owners of buildings over four stories, with a 65 percent response rate. In other words, the 1966 survey asked the people collecting, and the 1972 survey asked the people generating to estimate the amounts of solid waste they were handling. The 1972 data also included the number of buildings and dwelling units in each square mile.

It is important to note that in 1966 about 45 percent of the solid waste from larger buildings was burned on site in incinerators or boilers, a practice subsequently banned, thus increasing the amount of solid waste to be collected by private companies. And finally it is important to emphasize that both data sets were generated for the purpose of air pollution control. The solid waste data were collected in the interests of controlling air pollution at incinerator sites, not for solid waste management or control.

Final sources of solid waste data were the City of Chicago's Department of Building's Demolition Division, which provided the data on residential demolition; the Bureau of Forestry, Parkways and Beautification, which gave us data on tree and stump removal; and the Department of Streets and Sanitation, which provided the data on special bulk collection, street dirt, and abandoned automobiles. Yet even with this, some data are missing, such as tree trimmings, street dirt from thoroughfares and special events, trash and tree removal by the Park District, leaf and landscape waste, private tree removal, sewage sludge, construction debris and non-residential demolition, even though our data on subsidiary sources greatly extends the usual figures on solid waste generation.

Our data for Chicago thus cover various years, although the major data are for the years 1972 and 1973. The emphasis is on collection and generation, which has been neglected in prior discussions of solid waste management.

Per capita generation rates were calculated for the entire metropolitan region, and are mapped in Figure 7.1. The lowest per capita generation occurs in the City of Chicago, and in northwestern Cook and Du Page counties. Those areas that are blank on this map and the following two maps are unincorporated. Figure 7.2 illustrates the per capita residential generation for the metropolitan region. As before, Chicago has one of the lowest generation rates. This map also shows the extent of suburban development, extending in a concentric ring around the city, and as far west as Kane County. Finally, Figure 7.3 shows the per capita industrial generation for 1970. Clearly those areas of heavy industry in the metropolitan area are highlighted around the immediate periphery of Chicago particularly to the northwest of the city, and the satellite cities of Joliet, Aurora, Geneva, and St. Charles.

Table 7.1 gives a summation of per capita generation per county in tons/person/year. In Table 7.2 this same information is given in pounds/person/day. As one can see, McHenry County has the highest generation rate followed by Will and Kane Counties.

TABLE 7.1

PER CAPITA GENERATION SUMMATION 1970

(tons/person/year)

County	Total Tons[2] (x 1000)	Total Population[3] (x 1000)	Total Tons/ Population	Domestic Tons (x 1000)	Domestic Tons/ Population	Industrial Tons (x 1000)	Industrial Tons/ Population
Cook*	3,944.29	1,964.08	2.01	1,893.19	.96	2,042.09	1.04
Chicago	2,752.67	3,366.90	.82	2,045.51	.61	208.23	.06
Chicago[1] Total Cook	4,495.25		1.34				
Du Page	525.84	382.09	1.38	421.98	1.10	99.31	.26
Kane	432.49	212.56	2.03	221.10	1.04	211.29	.99
Lake	422.00	298.91	1.41	294.62	.99	127.43	.43
McHenry	230.62	61.97	3.72	81.64	1.32	149.98	2.42
Will	385.99	161.65	2.39	204.09	1.26	171.97	1.06

*Excluding Chicago

[1] Includes tonnages from subsidiary sources

[2] Source: Larry Dyer, Argonne National Laboratory
             Center for Environmental Studies

[3] NIPC Report

TABLE 7.2

PER CAPITA GENERATION 1970

(lbs/person/day)

County	Total	Domestic	Industrial
Cook*	11.01	5.26	5.70
Chicago	4.49 [1] 7.34	3.34	.33
Du Page	7.56	6.03	1.42
Kane	11.12	5.70	5.42
Lake	7.73	5.42	2.36
McHenry	20.38	7.23	13.26
Will	13.10	6.90	5.81

*Excluding Chicago

[1] Including Subsidiary Service

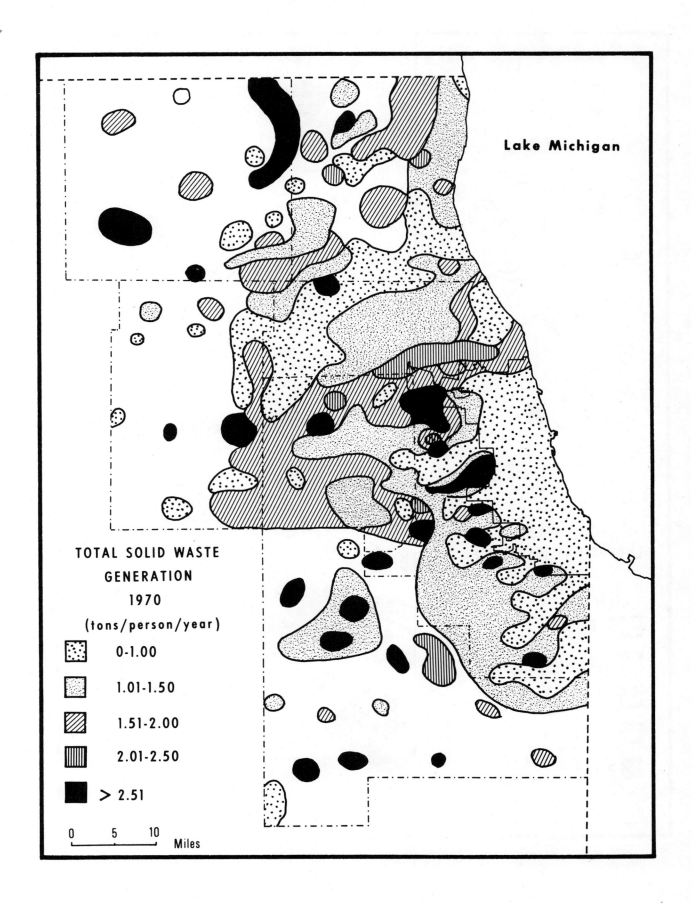

TOTAL SOLID WASTE
GENERATION
1970
(tons/person/year)

	0-1.00
	1.01-1.50
	1.51-2.00
	2.01-2.50
	> 2.51

Lake Michigan

0   5   10   Miles

Figure 7.1

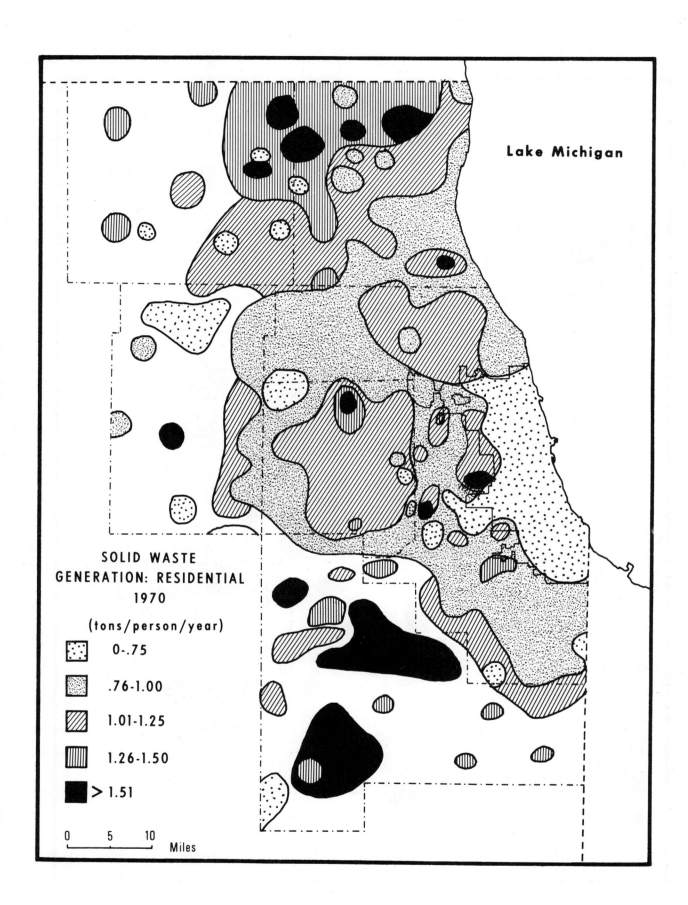

Lake Michigan

SOLID WASTE
GENERATION: RESIDENTIAL
1970

(tons/person/year)

▦	0-.75
▦	.76-1.00
▨	1.01-1.25
▥	1.26-1.50
■	> 1.51

0   5   10
Miles

Figure 7.2

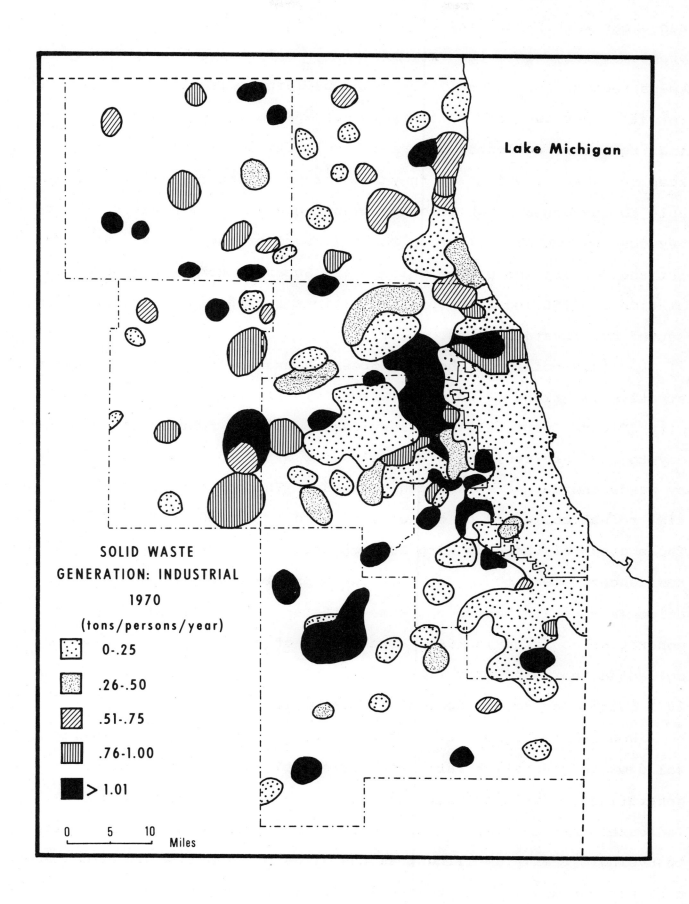

SOLID WASTE
GENERATION: INDUSTRIAL
1970
(tons/persons/year)

☐ 0-.25

☐ .26-.50

☐ .51-.75

☐ .76-1.00

■ > 1.01

0 5 10
Miles

Lake Michigan

Figure 7.3

More detailed data were obtained on solid wastes generated by
sub-areas within the City of Chicago, although even these data are
problematical, since the City of Chicago only weighs the amounts and
keeps records consistently for those buildings with 4 stories or less.
For all other dwelling units in larger apartment complexes, residential refuse is collected by private collection companies which do not
keep records, or which, if they do, are unwilling to make them available to the general public or to planning agencies. However, a survey done by the Air Pollution Control Board of the city was able to
get the cooperation of the Chicago and Suburban Refuse Disposal Association in 1966 and thus obtained estimates of solid waste and areas
served by private haulers.

At this point, we should digress to examine the political admin-
strative districts of Chicago, wards. There are 50 wards within the
city (Figure 7.4). All city services, political representation, and
day-to-day services including collection of solid wastes, are handled
by wards and data are recorded by wards. The percentage of residential refuse collected by the city by ward is mapped in Figure 7.5.
Those areas of the city with low densities, particularly single family
residences, stand out. The 1972 map of residential solid waste generation (Figure 7.6) shows the same pattern of high and low areas of
generation as found in 1966. The amount of residential solid waste
collected increased from 1,381,676 tons in 1966 to 2,045,506 tons in
1972 despite an actual decline in population.

However total collection figures by area are not as revealing of
solid waste generation rates as Figures 7.7 and 7.8 show, plotting
generation by dwelling unit and per person respectively. Figure 7.7
indicates that apartment dwelling units **may** produce more solid waste
than single family dwellings, as the areas of high-rise buildings show
a higher per dwelling unit generation. Figure 7.8 further refines this
conclusion, since dwelling units can harbor different numbers of people.

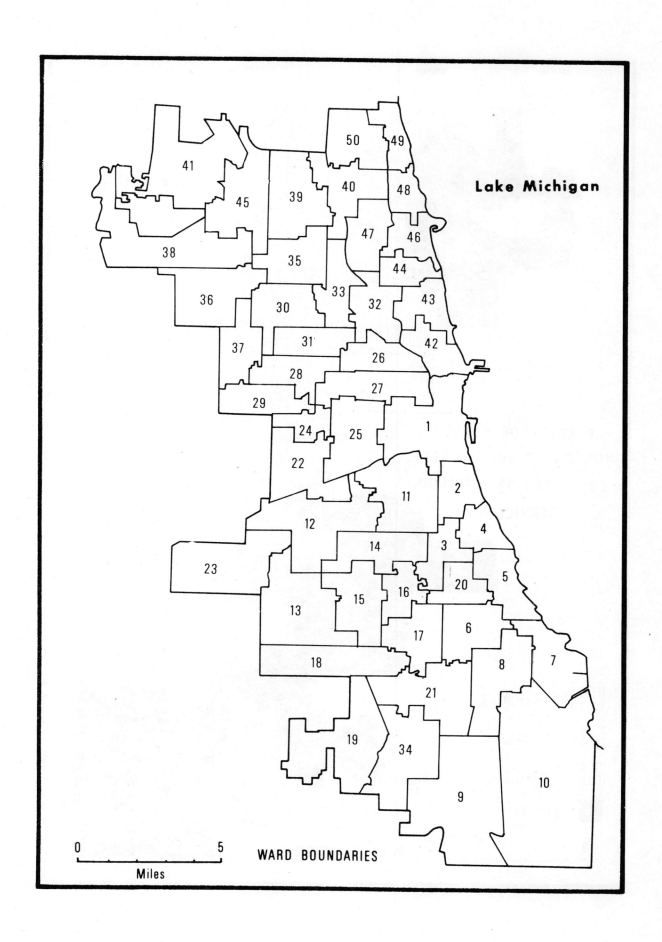

Lake Michigan

WARD BOUNDARIES

0   5
Miles

Figure 7.4

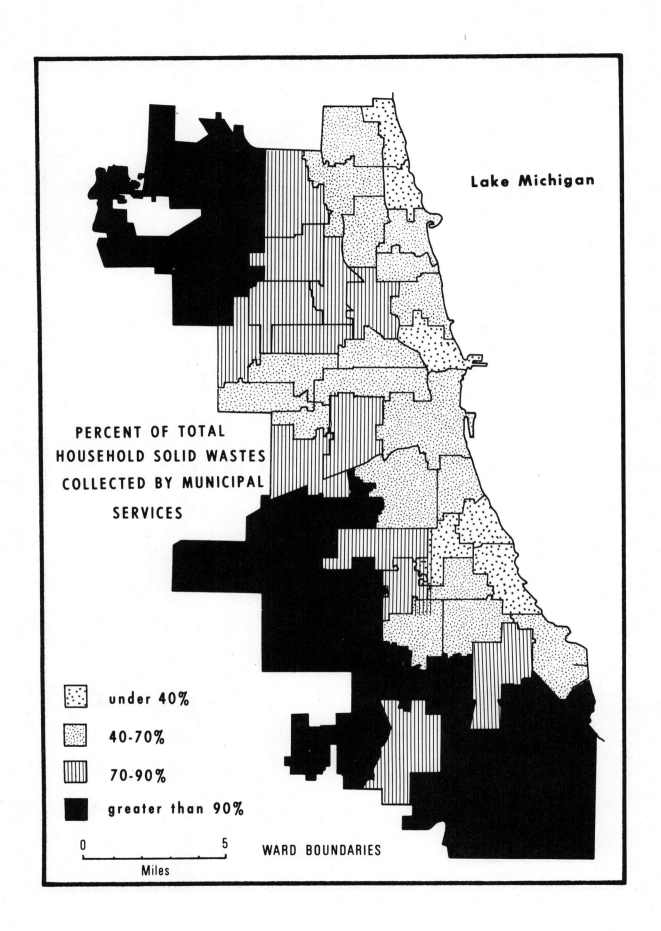

PERCENT OF TOTAL
HOUSEHOLD SOLID WASTES
COLLECTED BY MUNICIPAL
SERVICES

Lake Michigan

under 40%

40-70%

70-90%

greater than 90%

0   5

Miles

WARD BOUNDARIES

Figure 7.5

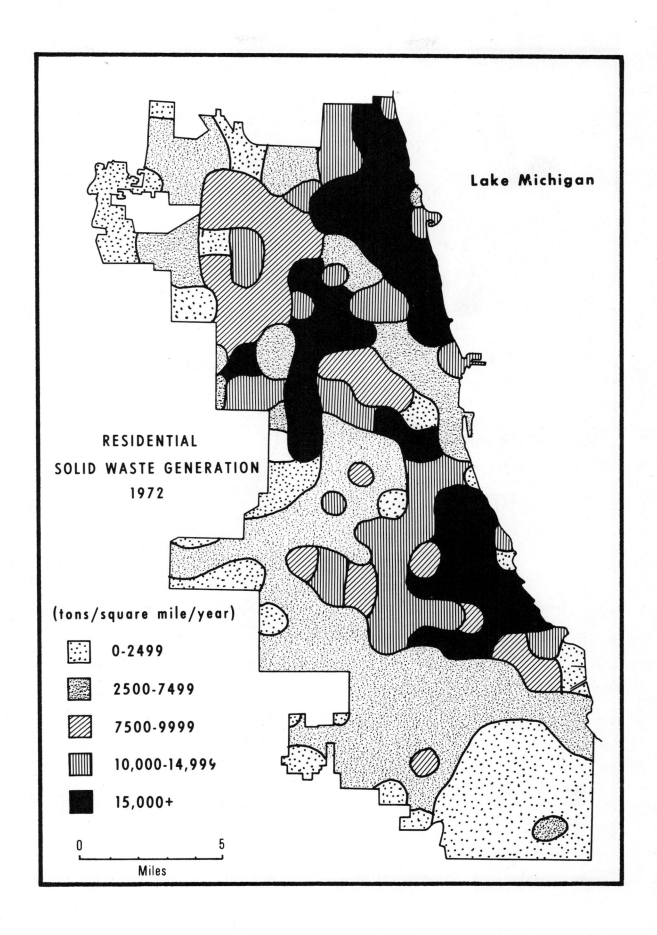

Lake Michigan

RESIDENTIAL
SOLID WASTE GENERATION
1972

(tons/square mile/year)

0-2499

2500-7499

7500-9999

10,000-14,999

15,000+

0   5

Miles

Figure 7.6

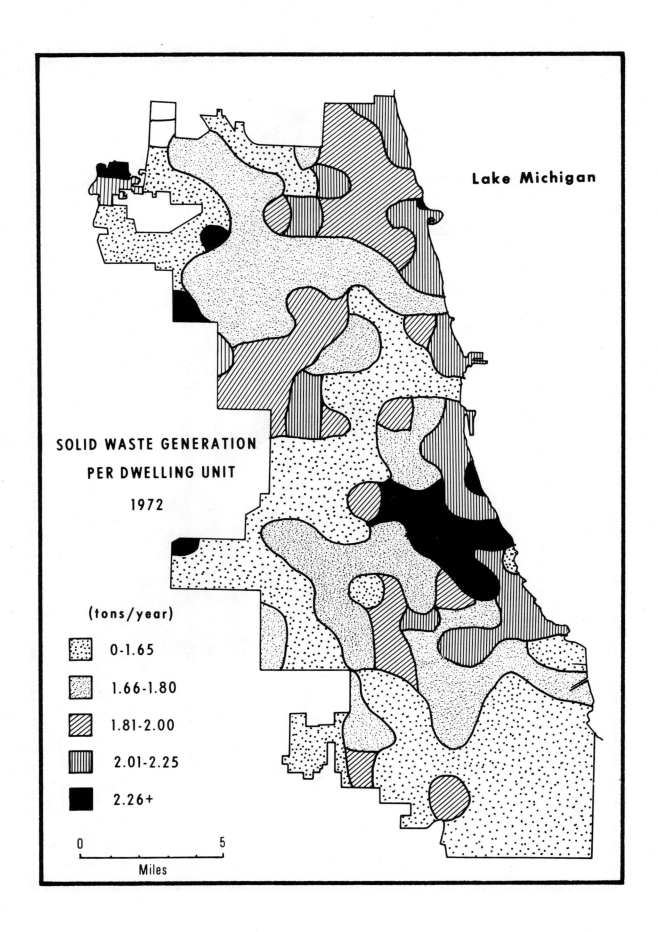

Lake Michigan

SOLID WASTE GENERATION
PER DWELLING UNIT
1972

(tons/year)

0-1.65

1.66-1.80

1.81-2.00

2.01-2.25

2.26+

0   5

Miles

Figure 7.7

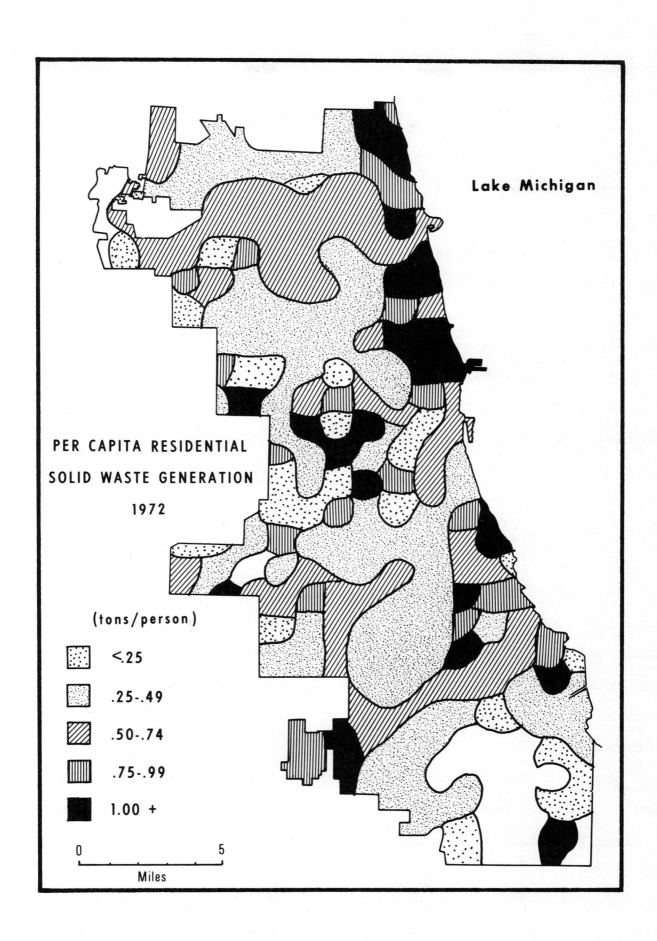

PER CAPITA RESIDENTIAL
SOLID WASTE GENERATION
1972

Lake Michigan

(tons/person)

<.25

.25-.49

.50-.74

.75-.99

1.00 +

0   5

Miles

Figure 7.8

Residences are not the only producers of waste. Of the total amount of solid waste generated within the city, approximately 11 percent originates in commercial sources. In 1966, 319,171 tons of commercial solid waste were collected. In 1972, 366,388 tons were generated. What is important is not that the amounts have increased over the six year period, but rather the decentralizing of the waste from the inner city to the outlying areas of the city (Figure 7.9). The Loop still predominates, but smaller centers of waste generation are found to the north and scattered throughout the south side of the city. This corresponds to the commercial structure of the city, which in recent years has witnessed an increase in the number of regional and community shopping centers located on the periphery. The city also collects 133 thousand tons of waste per year from combined residential and commercial sources. The combination units are usually located along busy thoroughfares, where commercial establishments are located on the ground floor and living quarters above, in those areas of the city with the highest densities.

Industrial sources of solid waste account for the lowest amount of total waste generated for the city, only 5 percent. The total amount of industrial solid waste has decreased approximately 50 thousand tons from 1966 to 1972. The pattern which is evident from this comparison is the movement of industry from the inner city to the suburbs. Industrial collections in 1966 showed a fair amount of industry clustered in the central part of the city, extending west from the Loop. This corridor follows one of Chicago's main expressways and is the terminus for rail transportation within the city. Also evident were industrial clusters located along major waterways, and scattered industrial areas on the city's South Side, particularly in the vicinity of Lake Calumet. However, the 1972 generation map (Figure 7.10) shows the decentralization of industrial activities from the older central industrial areas to the periphery of the city, and to the surrounding suburbs.

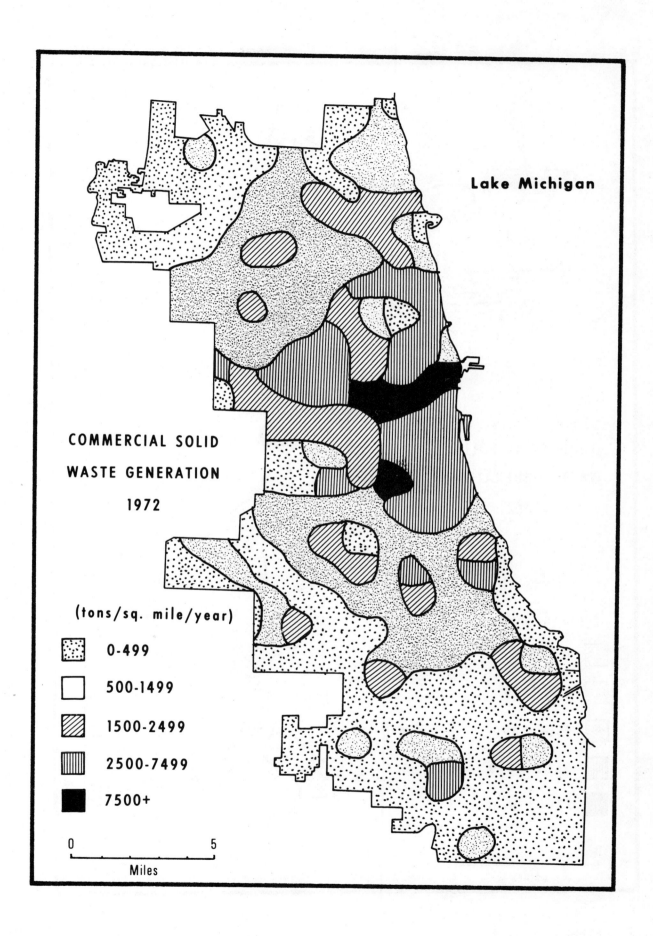

Lake Michigan

COMMERCIAL SOLID

WASTE GENERATION

1972

(tons/sq. mile/year)

0-499

500-1499

1500-2499

2500-7499

7500+

0   5

Miles

Figure 7.9

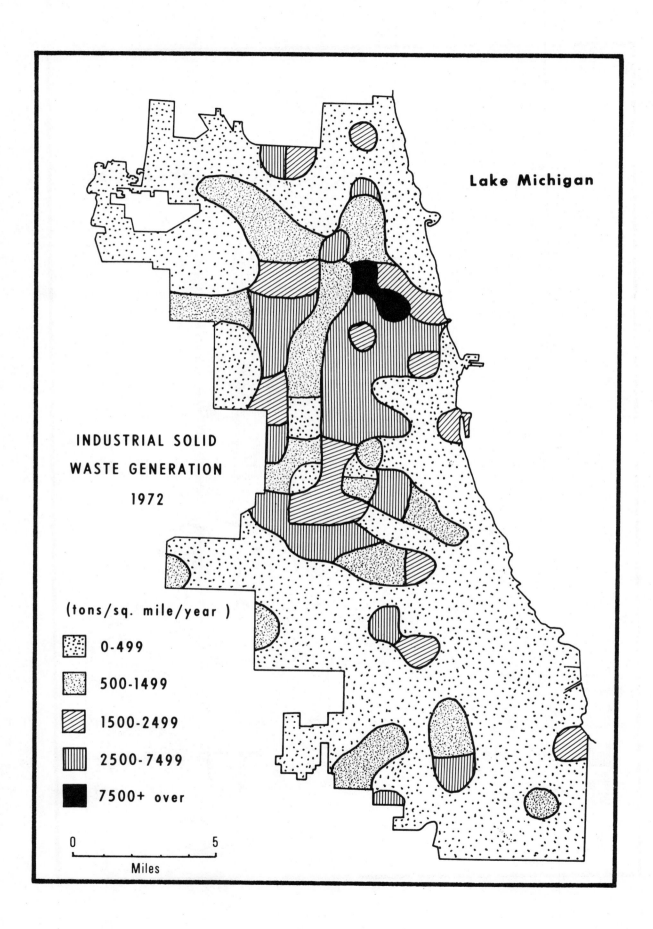

Lake Michigan

INDUSTRIAL SOLID
WASTE GENERATION
1972

(tons/sq. mile/year)

0-499

500-1499

1500-2499

2500-7499

7500+ over

0   5

Miles

Figure 7.10

Data for five "subsidiary" sources of solid waste also were obtained for the City of Chicago: bulk trash; mechanically swept street dirt; tree and stump removal; residential demolition; and abandoned autos. These data are for the year 1973, except for bulk collections which reflect a new city program fully operational only in 1974.

The maps (Figures 7.11 to 7.16) show the amounts in tons per square mile per ward, except for abandoned cars where the records are by police district. For comparability, all weights and measures were converted to tons. Bulk trash collections could simply be converted from pounds to tons, as the loads are directly weighed. However, for street dirt, The Bureau of Sanitation uses a factor of 800 pounds per cubic yard of dirt. The Bureau of Forestry estimates each tree removed averages 1 ton and each stump, 300 pounds of wood material. Factors of 200 tons per dwelling unit and 1.78 tons per auto were used to convert these often unwieldy figures of abandoned units.

Although all five subsidiary sources are considered part of the solid waste equation, it is important to note that some of these resources are recycled and reused rather than disposed. Virtually all of the abandoned automobiles are sold to scrap metal dealers, by the city, and most of the brick from demolitions is crushed and sold as road or landfill material with 5 percent going as reusable old brick. Eighty-five percent of the wood from tree removal is chipped and sold for low grade paper. So far, bulk trash is not salvaged, and street dirt has yet to be discovered as a reusable resource.

Estimates of the total solid wastes generated by the City of Chicago were obtained by summing the foregoing data--the 1972 information for residential, commercial and industrial sources, and the 1973 information on subsidiary sources. Separate totals were obtained and mapped by square mile (Figure 7.17) and by ward (Figure 7.18). The summary revealed that residential solid waste is the leading component of municipal solid waste for the City of Chicago comprising

510

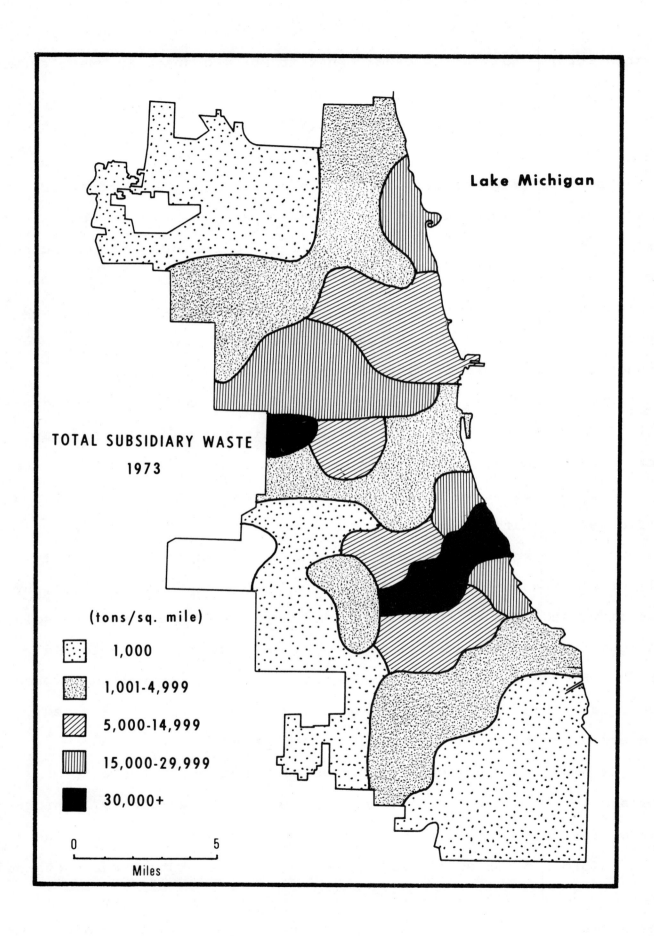

Lake Michigan

TOTAL SUBSIDIARY WASTE
1973

(tons/sq. mile)

1,000

1,001-4,999

5,000-14,999

15,000-29,999

30,000+

0   5
    Miles

Figure 7.11

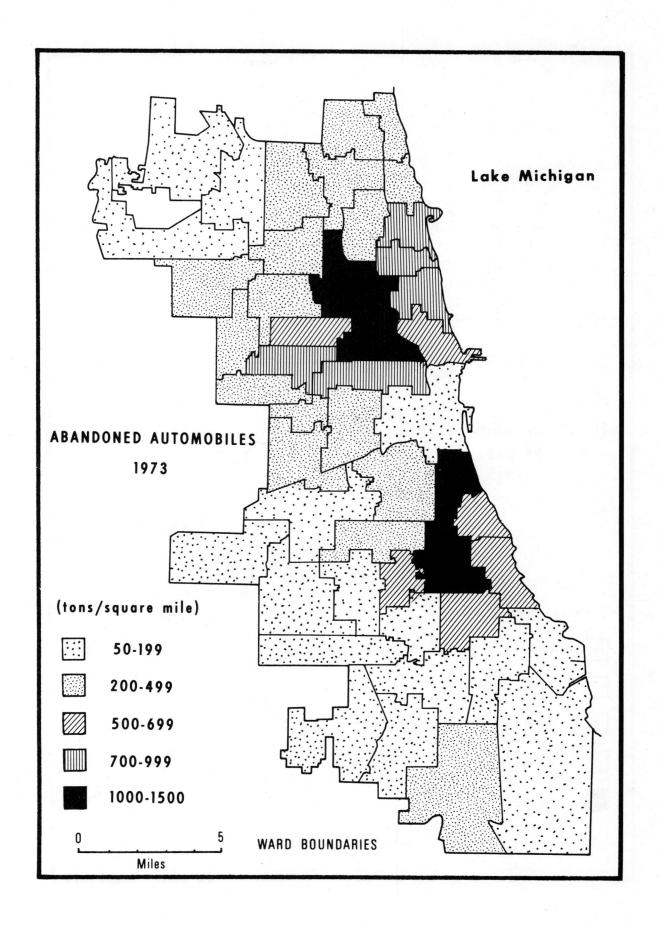

Lake Michigan

ABANDONED AUTOMOBILES

1973

(tons/square mile)

50-199

200-499

500-699

700-999

1000-1500

0   5

Miles

WARD BOUNDARIES

Figure 7.12

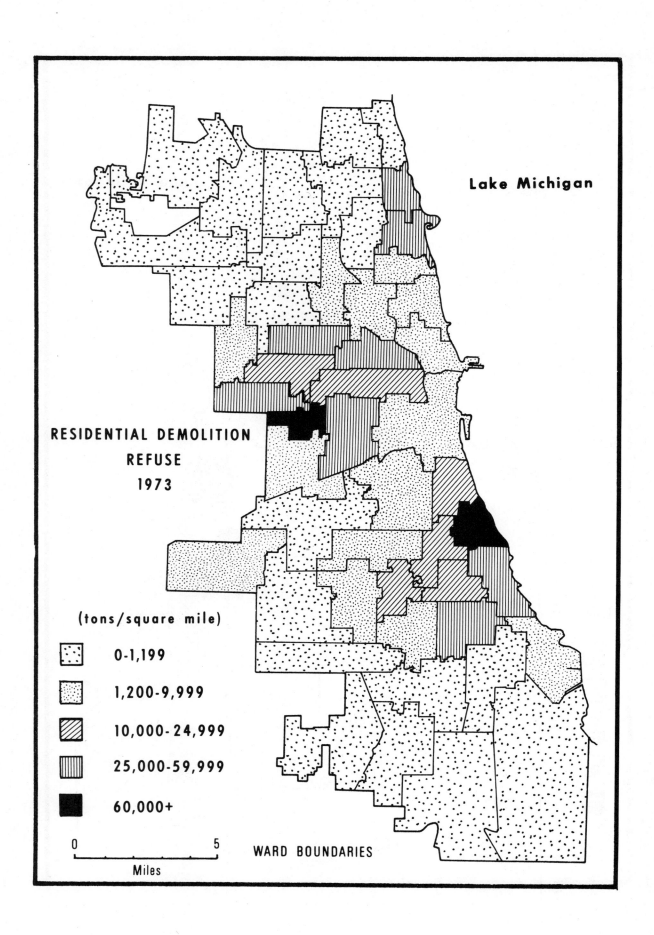

Lake Michigan

RESIDENTIAL DEMOLITION
REFUSE
1973

(tons/square mile)

0-1,199

1,200-9,999

10,000-24,999

25,000-59,999

60,000+

0   5   WARD BOUNDARIES

Miles

Figure 7.13

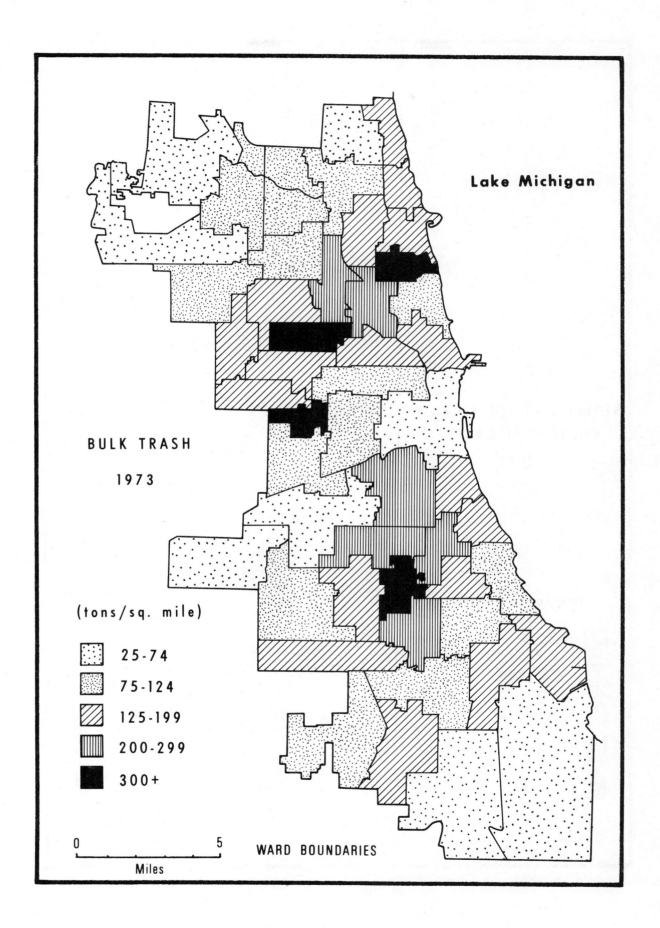

Lake Michigan

BULK TRASH

1973

(tons/sq. mile)

25-74

75-124

125-199

200-299

300+

0   5

Miles

WARD BOUNDARIES

Figure 7.14

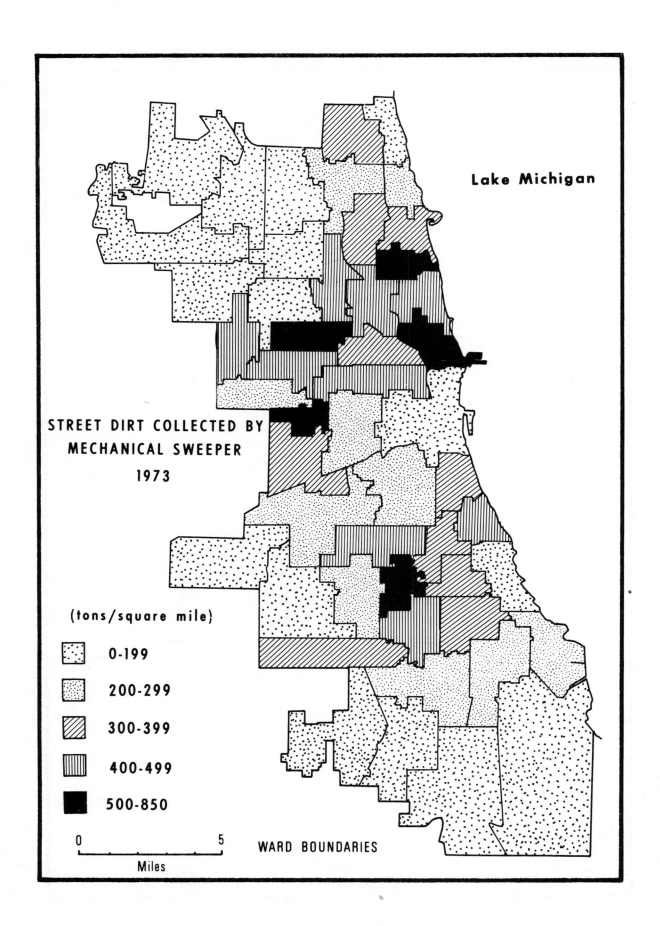

STREET DIRT COLLECTED BY
MECHANICAL SWEEPER
1973

Lake Michigan

(tons/square mile)

0-199

200-299

300-399

400-499

500-850

0   5

Miles

WARD BOUNDARIES

Figure 7.15

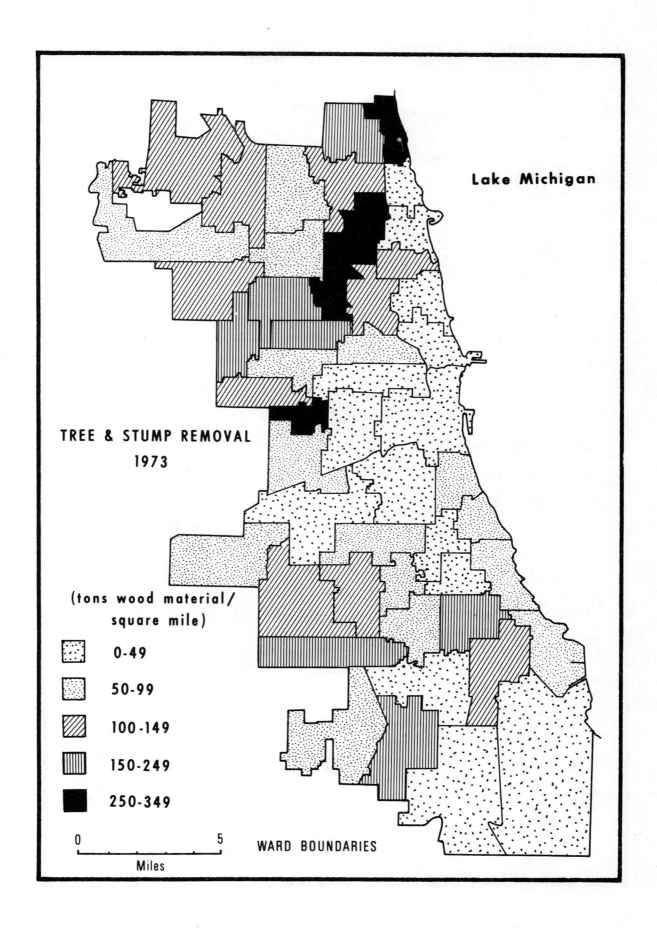

Lake Michigan

TREE & STUMP REMOVAL
1973

(tons wood material/
square mile)

0-49

50-99

100-149

150-249

250-349

0   5

Miles

WARD BOUNDARIES

Figure 7.16

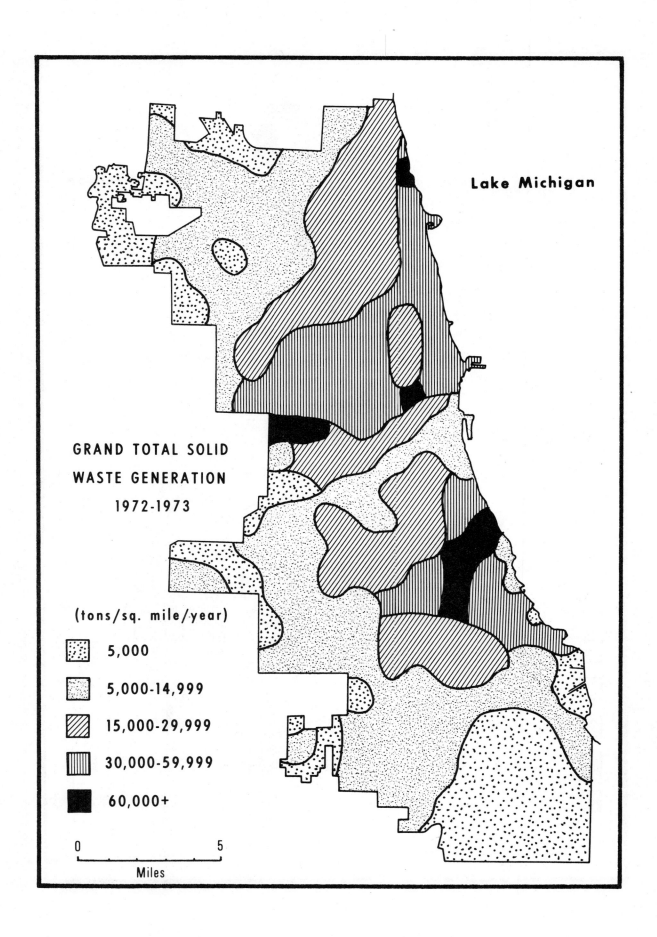

Lake Michigan

GRAND TOTAL SOLID
WASTE GENERATION
1972-1973

(tons/sq. mile/year)

5,000

5,000-14,999

15,000-29,999

30,000-59,999

60,000+

0   5

Miles

Figure 7.17

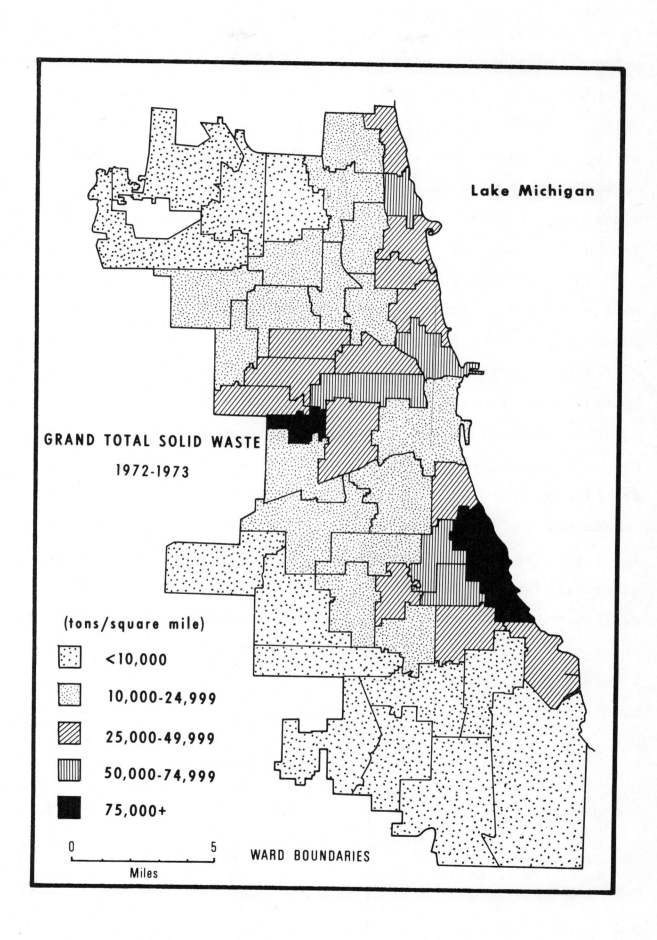

Lake Michigan

GRAND TOTAL SOLID WASTE

1972-1973

(tons/square mile)

<10,000

10,000-24,999

25,000-49,999

50,000-74,999

75,000+

0   5

Miles

WARD BOUNDARIES

Figure 7.18

45 percent of the total. This is followed by subsidiary sources, 39 percent; commercial sources 11 percent; and lastly industrial sources 5 percent. In many respects this is contrary to popular thinking which contends that more solid waste is generated by industrial sources, as is the finding that apartment dwelling units were found to produce more residential solid waste than single family dwelling units. The areas of high rise buildings show a higher per capita dwelling unit generation rate than the single family unit.

The "subsidiary" sources not commonly reported also are seen to be a significant factor in municipal solid waste. The leading component of the subsidiary sources, demolitions, shows the highest concentrations in the city core. Other subsidiary sources are concentrated in the poorer neighborhoods of the city.

Previous estimates for the amount of solid waste generated have been 4.1 pounds/person/day as a national average. In Chicago in 1966, the finding was 4.5 pounds/person/day. The evidence assembled here indicates that a generation figure of 7.31 pounds/person/day was the level in 1972. Table 7.3 compares these Chicago data to EPA's estimates derived from the 1968 survey of solid wastes. The EPA figures reflect only that material known or estimated to have been collected, where our figures are estimates of 1972 collections and actual 1973 figures for the subsidiary sources. In both cases, those wastes transported or disposed by the individual generator were not included.

Table 7.3

AVERAGE SOLID WASTE COLLECTED (LBS/PERSON/DAY)

Solid Waste	Urban[1]	National[1]	Chicago
Household	1.26	1.14	3.33
Commercial	0.46	0.38	0.60
Combined (municipal)	2.63	2.63	4.15
Industrial	0.65	0.59	0.34
Demolition, construction, street, alley and misc. (subsidiary)	0.72	0.58	2.84
TOTALS	5.72	5.32	7.31

[1]Source: U.S. EPA, Preliminary Analysis of the 1968 Solid Waste Survey.

It is apparent from both the EPA source and our data that these values are conservatively low. We therefore conclude that solid waste is a larger and more critical problem in Chicago than had previously been thought. While it is true that our total of 4,497,713 tons per year may overestimate the amount being hauled to landfills, as much of the tree, car, and demolition waste is recycled, it certainly underestimates the total amount of refuse generated which must be handled in some way, whether dumped, burned, or recycled -- dumped at sanitary landfills in suburbia (Figures 7.19 and 7.20), or burned at incinerators, compacted and then dumped in the City of Chicago and in Evanston, Melrose Park, Skokie and Stickney.

A Seven-City Comparison

Initially, 12 cities were selected for a cross city comparison, but due to a lack of data this was narrowed down to seven cities. Information on solid waste practices and management was unobtainable for the following cities: Oklahoma City, Seattle, and Washington, D.C. Providence provided monthly collection figures for 1974 but had no disposal, route information, or historical information. Birmingham provided information on how much they collected in 1974, but nothing substantial in terms of areas of collection, disposal sites, etc. Even in the cities providing information, data for all of the four types of refuse examined in the Chicago case study was generally unavailable. St. Louis provided the most comprehensive data concerning commercial, residential, and industrial sources of waste generation, but the majority of cities were concerned mostly with disposal, and with collection of solid waste from residences. Data acquisition for the St. Louis SMSA was helped by a report issued by the East-West Gateway Coordinating Council, which undertook a comprehensive survey and analysis of solid waste generation in that area. Information on collection and disposal of solid waste for San Diego was provided by

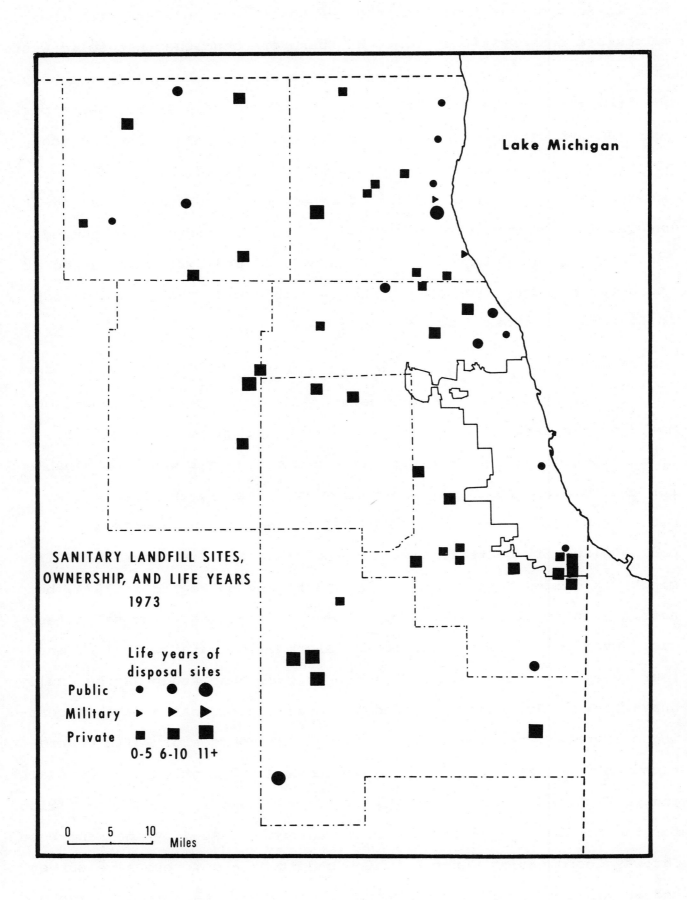

Lake Michigan

SANITARY LANDFILL SITES,
OWNERSHIP, AND LIFE YEARS
1973

Life years of
disposal sites

Public   ● ● ●

Military   ▶ ▶ ▶

Private   ■ ■ ■
              0-5 6-10 11+

0   5   10
|____|____|
         Miles

Figure 7.19

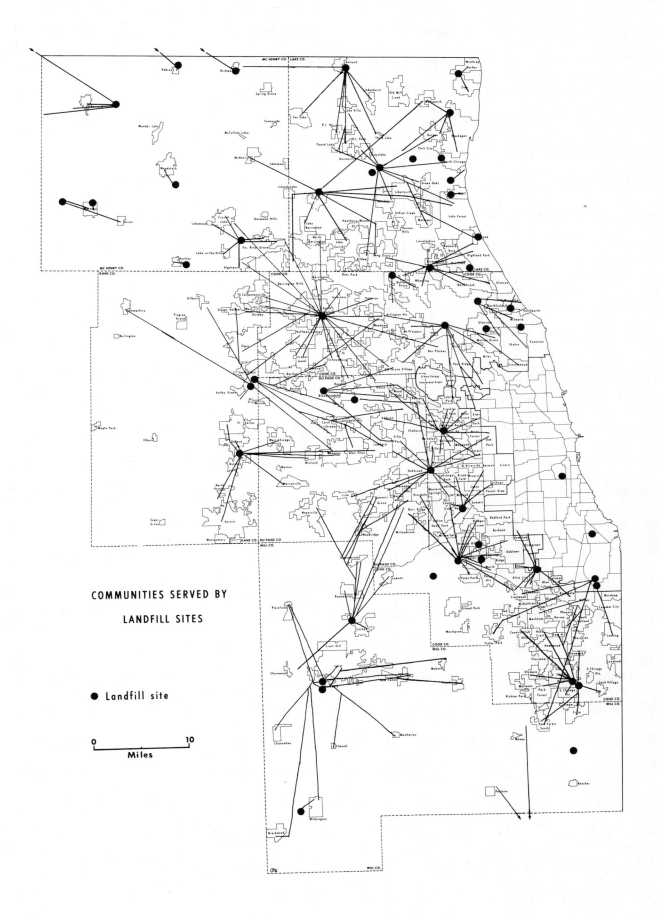

COMMUNITIES SERVED BY

LANDFILL SITES

● Landfill site

0   10

Miles

Figure 7.20

the Solid Waste Division of the City of San Diego, while data for the Rochester region was acquired from three sources: The U.S. Environmental Protection Agency, Region II, Rochester Field Office; the Department of Public Works for Monroe County; and the City of Rochester, Department of Public Works, and the Bureau of Environmental Services. In the Denver region, information was provided by the Division of Public Works, Sanitary Services Section, City of Denver, and by the Denver Regional Council of Governments and the Urban Drainage and Flood Control District's final report on Project Reuse (Renewing the Environment Through Urban Systems Engineering). The data was very limited in both areal distribution and quality. Collection figures were available for the previous two year period for the City of Denver but not for the rest of the metropolitan area. The Project Reuse report estimated collection figures which they calculated by establishing a per capita generation rate (in cubic yards/person/year). There is no indication as to how that particular rate was arrived at or what it actually means. Disposal information was also limited and highly variable in quality. The location of the landfills is reliable, but the amounts of refuse they dispose is only at best an estimation. Data for Cincinnati and Jacksonville were provided by their respective departments of Public Works, Division of Sanitation. The Cincinnati data was provided for a two year period and generally was of high quality, though not comprehensive. Jacksonville data was much less complete. Finally, sources of solid waste data for Baltimore were obtained for the Bureau of Sanitation, Baltimore County for the county, and from the City of Baltimore's Sanitation Division for the city. The county data were concerned with the disposal of solid waste and the sanitary landfills located in the county. The city data, on the other hand, were concerned with all aspects of the solid waste problem; collection, generation, and disposal.

In only two cases, then -- St. Louis and Rochester -- was there any information on collection and/or generation of solid waste for the entire metropolitan area. As is the case with Chicago, collection of solid waste varies by source. Residential solid waste collection in St. Louis is by municipal service, contracted service, or by private haulers (Figure 7.21). Contract service refers to a private operator who contracts with the city. Private service is by a private hauler who contracts with the individual owner of a building, or the residents of a building. Municipal services only collect residential solid waste. All the other sources of solid waste; commercial, industrial, some subsidiary, and agricultural, are collected by private haulers.

Tables 7.4 and 7.5 show the total amount of solid waste generation for 1973 per county in the St. Louis area. The commercial waste category includes commercial and institutional waste as defined in the Sverdrup and Parcel Associates report. Subsidiary sources are the same as the special sources indicated in the Sverdrup report except that in our category, water and sewage treatment sludge, and hazardous materials are not included. The reason for the high per capita generation rate revealed by Table 7.5 is that many primary manufacturing and heavy industrial operations are located in the St. Louis metropolitan region.

When solid waste generation by source is analyzed (Table 7.6), the heavily industrialized nature of the area becomes clear. In four of the seven counties in the metropolitan region, generation of industrial solid waste exceeds 3 pounds/person/day. Figures 7.22, 7.23 and 7.24 show the residential, commercial and industrial waste generation in the metropolitan region. The St. Louis City-East St. Louis corridors are the most striking features.

Table 7.4

SOLID WASTE GENERATION* 1973

(tons/year)

County	Res.	Comm.[1]	Ind.[2]	Agr.	Sub.[3]	Total
Franklin	18,800	7,300	22,000	600	3,600	52,000
Jefferson	38,800	9,850	17,700	180	6,600	73,100
Madison	94,400	52,650	298,800	7,140	32,300	486,300
Monroe	5,600	1,900	1,000	60	740	9,300
St. Charles	34,600	10,600	59,500	290	7,300	112,300
St. Clair	107,700	80,000	381,900	30,920	119,800	717,300
St. Louis City	249,800	288,000	559,100	–	558,200	1,655,100
St. Louis	364,700	244,400	318,700	45	332,500	1,260,400
TOTAL	914,400	696,100	1,658,700	39,420	1,060,900	4,365,800

*Figures are only estimates.

[1]Includes commercial and institutional waste as categorized by the Sverdrup and Parcel Associates, Inc. report.

[2]Includes industrial sludge; only includes 30% of all industrial waste due to recycling and/or disposal on the manufacturing site.

[3]Includes sewage sludge.

Source: East-West Gateway Coordinating Council, 1974, p.II-5.

Table 7.5

TOTAL SOLID WASTE GENERATION* 1973

County	Pop[1]	Solid Waste (tons/year)	Per Capita (lbs/person/day)
Franklin	55,100	52,000	5.17
Jefferson	105,200	73,100	3.81
Madison	250,900	486,300	10.62
Monroe	18,800	9,300	2.71
St. Charles	92,900	112,300	6.62
St. Clair	285,200	717,300	13.78
St. Louis City	622,200	1,655,100	14.58
St. Louis	951,200	1,260,400	7.26
TOTAL	2,381,500	4,365,800	10.04

[1]Population estimates for 1970.

*Source: East-West Gateway Coordinating Council, 1974, Table I-A (appendix).

COLLECTION OF RESIDENTIAL SOLID WASTE

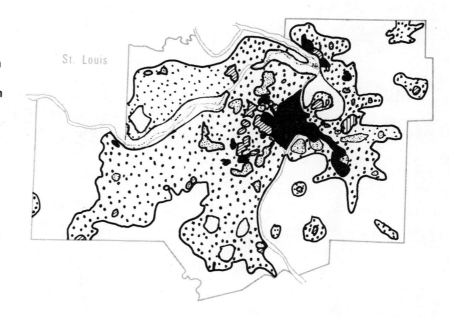

■ Municipal Collection

▨ Contracted Collection

▥ Both Municipal and
  Contracted

▨ Private Collection

▨ Collection Available

RESIDENTIAL SOLID WASTE GENERATION 1973

Tons

▨ 1 - 380

■ 381 - 7,200

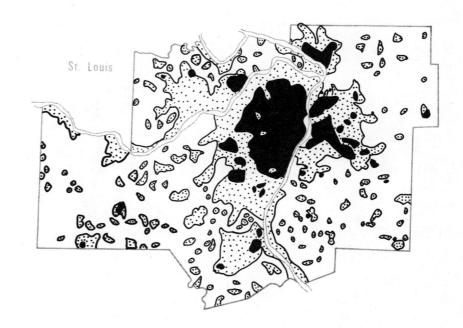

Figures 7.21- 7.22

COMMERCIAL AND INSTITUTIONAL SOLID WASTE GENERATION 1973

Tons

⊡ 1 - 500

■ 501 - 13,199

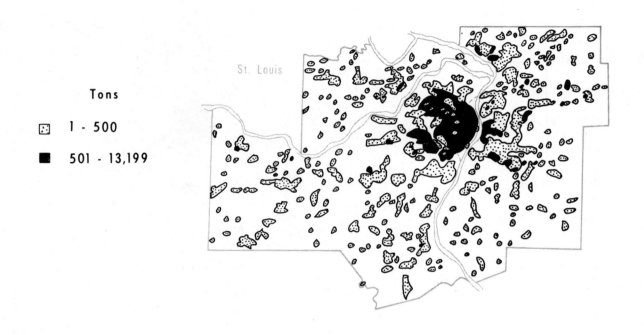

INDUSTRIAL SOLID WASTE GENERATION 1973

Tons

⊡ 1 - 1000

■ 1001 - 162,374

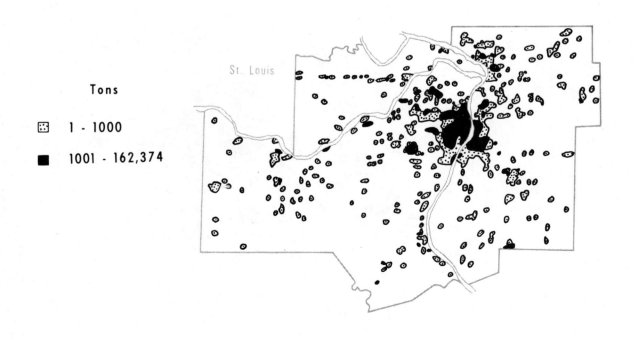

Figures 7.23-7.24

Table 7.6

SOLID WASTE GENERATION BY SOURCE 1973
(lbs/person/day)

County	Res.	Comm.	Ind.	Agr.	Sub.
Franklin	1.87	.73	2.19	.06	.36
Jefferson	2.02	.51	.92	.01	.34
Madison	2.06	1.15	6.52	.16	.71
Monroe	1.63	.55	.29	.02	.22
St. Charles	2.04	.62	3.51	.02	.43
St. Clair	2.07	1.54	7.34	.59	2.30
St. Louis	2.14	1.85	3.06	.00	3.10

Generation totals for the Rochester region were given in only the grossest manner. Estimates were provided for the city, and the surrounding municipalities in the county by quadrants, not by each individual municipality. It is obvious that this information, is not as comprehensive as that for St. Louis and is of little help in developing a picture of solid waste (all sources, not just residential) generation in the area.

For other cases, data were only available for legal cities. In Cincinnati, the responsibilities of the Division of Waste Collection include the following: collection of all residential refuse; collection of all combustible waste (as needed) from schools, hospitals, and public institutions; collection of all garbage from restaurants and food processors; and the collection of all dead animals. The total amount of waste that was collected by the city and disposed by the city in the last six years is reported in Table 7.7. This is further divided into its component parts, collection information only, for the two year period (Table 7.8). The waste paper category reflects an effort made by the city from 1972 thru 1974 to collect newspapers and magazines separately from the rest of the waste in order to recycle it. The papers were sold as salvaged paper and were not part of the tonnage that needed disposal. However, this collection service

Table 7.7

YEARLY TOTALS

Year	Tons Collected	Tons Disposed
1969	186,242.0	360,388.0
1970	182,958.6	360,843.1
1971	193,528.0	379,080.0
1972	195,263.0	379,066.0
1973	204,952.0	384,576.0
1974	198,185.7	404,097.7

Source: 1974 Annual Report, City of Cincinnati

Table 7.8

TONNAGE COLLECTED

Category	Tons	
	1974*	1973**
Household (load packer)	157,136	174,349
Household (container truck)	32,833	25,715
Special (appliances & Furniture)	4,894	1,320
Waste Paper (newspaper)	1,210	1,877
Dead Animal	223	224
Miscellaneous (model cities program)	1,890	1,467
TOTAL	198,186	204,952

*Not included in these are ash collections made for buildings (schools and other institutions) where coal is the source of heat.

**In addition 7078 yd^3 of non-combustible waste and ashes was collected from apartment buildings, schools and institutions where coal is still the main source of heat.

---

was discontinued in November of 1974 due to a dramatic decline in markets for the salvaged paper. The city is divided into ten collection districts (Figure 7.25). Collection figures for 1974 are found per district in Table 7.9.

The City of Baltimore is divided into five collection districts (northwest, east, northeast, west, and central), and then further subdivided into 26 boroughs. Maps of these districts were requested but were not made available to us. The city collected 400,565 tons of mixed refuse in the fiscal year 1972-73. Broken down to a per capita figure per year, this means that in 1971-72 every person in Baltimore generated 886 pounds of solid waste, and in 1972 this rose to 894 pounds.

Table 7.9

1974 COLLECTIONS (tons)

District	Tons	District	Tons
1	2,098	6	17,551
2*	32,832	7	18,158
3	17,768	8	18,036
4	21,173	9	16,616
5	21,432	10	21,115
		TOTAL	186,779

*District 2 is container collection city wide.
Source: Division of Waste Collection, City of Cincinnati, R.D. Behrman.

Table 7.10 shows the amounts of solid waste collected by source for the years 1971-72 and 1972-73. Included in this table are the subsidiary sources of solid waste. For the sake of consistency, all figures were given in tons. Therefore, the ashes, bulky trash, street dirt, leaves, and mechanical sweepers figures, originally given in cubic yards were converted using factors in Refuse Collection Practices, American Public Works Association, Chicago, Illinois, 1966, pp. 34 and 36.

The City of San Diego collects solid waste from residences only. No commercial or industrial waste is collected by the city. The municipal refuse consists of the usual components, garbage, paper, glass, rags, bottles and cans, but the city also picks up those components listed under subsidiary sources of solid waste; wood, ashes, sawdust, tree and shrub trimmings. The only restrictions on collection deals with those subsidiary components. Sawdust must be wetted down to prevent blowing and to lessen its potential as a fire hazard, and all tree trimmings must be in bundles not exceeding four feet in length

Table 7.10

BALTIMORE SOURCES OF SOLID WASTE

| | Total Collection (tons) | |
Source	FY 1971-72	FY 1972-73
Ashes	23	12
Market Refuse	8,385	7,593
Bulky Trash	348	354
City Collection	322	325
Model Cities	26	29
Street Dirt	427	389
Leaves	24	24
Mechanical Sweepers	35	29
Mixed Refuse	410,565	404,609
TOTAL	420,155	413,364

Source: Fiscal Year Report 1971-72, pg. 31-36 and Fiscal Year Report 1972-73, pg. 35-40.

---

or be too bulky or heavy for one person to carry. Also, the diameter for tree trunks cannot exceed eight inches and all branches must weigh less than 80 pounds in order for the city to pick them up.

Table 7.11 gives the total amount of solid waste collected by district for the years 1971-1974. Again, it must be emphasized that these figures do not represent the total amount of solid waste in the City of San Diego, but only that solid waste collected by the city from residential areas. The table also records the per capita generation rate of solid waste for the City of San Diego. Residential solid waste collection per capita/day is taken from the actual collection figures, and is differentiated from the total amount of solid waste generated per person/day which are merely estimates.

The City of Denver's sanitation services collects from all households up to 7 units in size, and collects garbage, trash, and yard debris. Bulk collections are made on the basis of citizen's requests and recorded in terms of how many loads and not tonnages thereby making this information useless in terms of this present report. Other services of the department include branch and tree limb collection

Table 7.11

TOTAL SOLID WASTE COLLECTION* (tons/year)

Year	Rose Canyon	Chollas	20th & B	Mission Beach	Total
1974[1]	46,038.75	41,103.93	32,260.13	1,294.23	120,697.04
1973	100,205.60	93,544.32	72,495.83	3,275.42	269,521.17
1972	95,126.89	86,333.72	72,032.14	2,866.29	256,359.04
1971	87,914.24	87,987.39	76,886.09	2,231.77[2]	255,019.49

[1]Only includes January-June 1974 data.

[2]Route opened March, 1971; consequently figures represent collections from March-December, 1971.

*Includes residential waste only.
Source: City of San Diego, Solid Waste Division

PER CAPITA GENERATION (San Diego)

	Population	Residential Solid Waste (tons)	(lbs/person/day)	Total Solid Waste	Total Generation
1974	771,000	120,697[1]	1.72	-[2]	-[2]
1973	-[2]	269,521		831,600	
1972	735,000	256,359	1.91	764,863	5.70
1971	696,566	255,019	2.06	606,745	4.77

[1]Only includes a 6 month period - figure was doubled and then the per capita generation computed.

[2]Figure unavailable

(measured in loads), hand sweeping downtown (measured in cubic yards), dead animals (also measured in loads), and rubbish collection in 10 low-income public housing projects.

The ten collection districts and the amounts of material collected for a two year period are found in Figure 7.26 and Table 7.12 respectively. As can be seen the areas of the heaviest amounts of material are in the suburban areas on the fringes of the city, areas H, J, and D.

The City of Rochester collects solid waste from all residences each week, and the Central Business District each day. There are no restrictions on multiple dwelling units, hence all the residential solid waste collected in the city is by city services. Bulk waste, commercial waste and institutional waste is also collected by the city.

Table 7.12

HOUSEHOLD COLLECTION BY REFUSE DISTRICT

District	1973 (tons)	1972 (tons)
A	17,497	16,780
B	18,128	17,722
C	13,548	13,962
D	20,094	18,359
E	16,354	16,018
F	15,127	14,227
G	16,270	16,055
H	20,299	19,370
J	20,249	19,362
K	17,263	16,762
TOTAL	174,829	168,667

Source: Department of Public Works, Sanitary Services Division, Annual Report, 1973. City of Denver, Colorado, pp. 31.

Table 7.13 shows the tonnage of solid waste collected for the fiscal year 1973-74. The city is divided into two collection districts, east and west. The east collection district has slightly more than half of Rochester's population of 300,000. Table 7.14 gives the tonnage figures for the amount of refuse hauled. As mentioned before, figures started being kept in 1973. This table gives an estimate of the amounts of waste being collected and the seasonal variation of the collection.

Table 7.13

SOLID WASTE COLLECTION BY SOURCE
Fiscal Year 1973-1974 tons

	Refuse	Bulk	Commercial E-Z Pack	Street Cleaning	Private Haulers
East	78,329	19,470	14,377		
West	54,159	8,515	6,902		
TOTAL	132,488	27,985	21,279	7,211	10,400

GRAND TOTAL 199,363

Source: Dept. of Public Works, Bureau of Environmental Services, Division of Refuse Disposal, City of Rochester.

Table 7.14

REFUSE DISPOSAL HAULED

	1973	1974
Jan.	13,958	12,219
Feb.	12,925	12,299
March	19,781	16,546
April	18,371	17,583
May	23,471	23,073
June	18,700	17,957
July	16,181	15,368
Aug.	20,343	19,955
Sept.	15,076	15,084
Oct.	15,515	15,221
Nov.	19,258	19,661
Dec.	13,322	12,719
TOTAL	206,901	197,685

Source: City of Rochester, Dept of Public Works

The City of St. Louis collects solid waste from residences only. Commercial and industrial solid waste is left up to the private haulers. The total amount of solid waste generated by source for the city is found in Table 7.15.

The only area of Jacksonville which is serviced by the Sanitation Division is within the old core city limits. The rest of solid waste collection for the city is handled by private companies which are paid by the city according to the following rate schedule: $37.50 per unit per year for residential sites, and $45.00 per unit per year for commercial sites. For purposes of classification, a unit which has six or more dwelling units is considered commercial.

Industrial solid waste is either disposed on site or collected by the industry itself. There is no involvement by the city in the collection or disposal of industrial solid waste.

City of Cincinnati's Collection Districts

☑ Not in city

City of Denver's Collection Districts

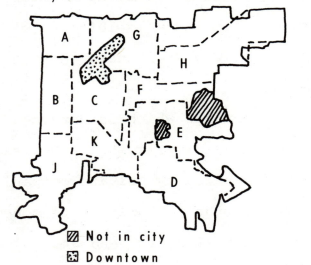

☑ Not in city

▣ Downtown

—— Collection District boundaries

Figures 7.25 and 7.26

Table 7.15

TOTAL SOLID WASTE GENERATION BY SOURCE - ST. LOUIS
1973

	Solid Waste (tons/year)	Per Capita[1] (lb/person/day)
Residential	249,800	2.20
Commercial	288,000	2.54
Industrial	559,100	4.92
Agricultural	-	-
Subsidiary	558,200	4.92

[1]Population from Table 7.5.

Overall, collection of solid waste in Jacksonville is not tightly monitored. According to their 1990 Solid Waste Plan, "The present system of municipal collection within the core area and the issuance of franchises to private operators have resulted in non-uniform service levels and excessive management problems by city officials (pp. 11-2)."

Disposal of Solid Waste in the Seven Cities

Traditionally, disposal of solid waste has been the most important aspect of solid waste management. It has been easier to keep records by weighing the material brought to the landfills than it has been to record collections let alone generation. Also, sanitary engineers have been concerned with the technical problems of landfill construction and maintenance, and not with the social problems of solid waste generation.

Rather than attacking the problem at the source, generation and collection, solid waste managers have chosen to deal with the final stage of the problem, disposal. Solid waste has not been thought of as a pollution problem until very recently, when many of the major urban centers have and are running out of space to dump their waste. This concern of where to put the waste generated by urban areas has made some people aware of the enormity of the problem, and that attention should be focussed on the generation side of the equation, not the disposal side as is currently being done. Ironically, in more than one city in this volume, accurate record keeping of disposal amounts only began in the early 1970's. Obviously, in those cities, information on collection and generation is virtually non-existant.

The evidence for the comparative cities is thus as follows:

1. Cincinnati. In late 1973, two of Cincinnati's incinerators and one of its landfills were closed. The incinerators were victims of the Federal Clean Air Act, as the high costs involved in bringing these two plants (originally built in 1930) into compliance with the act were economically prohibitive. The sanitary landfill (a public disposal site for solid fill only) was closed and most of the area was developed into a recreation facility. The city currently utilizes two incinerators (one of which was scheduled to close in late 1975) and three sanitary landfills which are private but which contract with the city. A summary of waste disposal by source and site is found in Table 7.16.

2. Baltimore. The City of Baltimore disposes of its solid waste by incineration. There are two incinerator plants which only incinerate flammable waste materials. There are three landfills which are run by the Bureau of Sanitation. These are Reliable serving the southeast and located in Baltimore Highlands; Hernwood serving the west and located southeast of Randallstown; and Texas serving the north and located in Cockeysville. Both Reliable and Hernwood handle residential and commercial refuse, while the Texas sanitary landfill handles residential and institutional waste only. A demolition landfill began operating in fiscal year 1972-73 for the explicit use of contractors in disposing of demolition refuse. There is also a private landfill serving the east portion of

the city, called the Norris Farm Sanitary Landfill. Table 7.17 points out the disposal of mixed refuse for the city versus private collection, amounts of materials incinerated, and finally the residuals which are landfilled. Table 7.18 shows the quantity of disposed materials by source and composition. Some of the figures were given in cubic yards and were converted to tonnages for the sake of consistency. Finally, Table 7.19 lists the tonnage of solid waste landfilled to the various landfills, again by source.

3. San Diego. The City of San Diego utilizes three landfills (Fig. 7.30). Chollas and Miramar are opened to the public for their use, while Arizona is limited to the city's municipal service. It is expected that the life years of the landfills (Arizona has 5, Chollas 10-13, and Miramar 6-10) will be less than those figures quoted due to the public use of two of the city's landfills. The four county landfills operated by the county, are too distant for use by the city, and hence are of no help in alleviating the disposal problem. As of this writing, there have been two efforts aimed at reducing the amount of material entering the landfills. One is a refuse baling operation. This involves compressing the waste material into closely packed cubes bound with wire. Landfill space is thus conserved due to this compaction. This is the alternative used by the city rather than incineration. The other proposal includes cooperation with a private enterprise. This venture is the collection of newspapers from the curb for recycling. As of this writing, there is no information available on the success or failure of these operations since their enactment in the fiscal year 1974.

4. <u>Denver</u>.   There are 20 general purpose landfills in the Denver metropolitan area and 8 special purpose landfills. Special purpose landfills mainly accept demolitions, rubble, organic liquids, and wood material.   Figure 7.27 shows the location, type of ownership, and the service areas of the landfills in the metropolitan area.   The service areas were determined by taking the point equi-distant from adjacent landfills.   This line was then adjusted to compensate for exclusive use or other special site entry conditions, and then this was further adjusted to reflect access (i.e. it was adjusted for topography, highway access, etc.).   Table 7.20 shows the estimated fill rate of each of the landfills in the metropolitan region.   Landfill 18 is omitted as it falls out of the SMSA boundary.   The City of Denver primarily disposes of its waste in landfills 2, 3, and 4 (Table 7.21) and a very small portion of the waste in landfills 6, 9, and 10.   Lowry Bombing range disposal site (6) is available for use by private individuals for the disposal of their own refuse and for the disposal of chemical and other wastes not allowed in the contracted landfills.

5. <u>Rochester</u>.   Rochester's waste is taken to the east and west transfer stations which were formally incinerators.   The waste is then transported 55 miles (one way) to the landfill site for Rochester which is located in Seneca Falls, New York. Prior to 1973, the city used a landfill site located in Rush Township for its disposal.   But, in July 1973 the site was termed unsanitary and was forced to close down.   This problem of disposal of Rochester's solid waste will be discussed in more detail in a later section.

Table 7.16

SUMMARY BY DISPOSAL SITE (CINCINNATI)

1973[1]

	Incinerator	Este Ave LF	Private LF	Total
Residential	78,971	56,949	66,931	200,851
Commercial	141,787	21,634	18,304	181,725
TOTAL	220,578	77,583	85,235	384,576

1974[2]

	Incinerator	SLF	Other	Total
Residential	46,425.5	150,418.2	1,342.3*	198,186
Commercial	114,963.6	88,175.5	2,772.9**	205,912
TOTAL	161,389.1	238,593.7	4,115.2	404,098

*Includes 1,210 tons of newspapers and 132.2 tons collected from Saylor Park following the tornado disaster.
**Includes solid waste destroyed on city-owned property (Este landfill before it was closed to the public in November).

[1]Source: 1973 Cincinnati Waste Collection Annual Report, Dept. of Public Works, Division of Waste Collection, City of Cincinnati, mimeographed, 16 pp.

[2]Source: 1974 Cincinnati Waste Collection Annual Report, Dept. of Public Works, Division of Waste Collection, City of Cincinnati, mimeographed, 18 pp.

Table 7.17

MIXED REFUSE DISPOSAL (BALTIMORE)
FY 1971-72[1], 1972-73[3]
(tons)*

	City	Private	Total Incinerators	Landfill	Total
Incinerator #3	104,048[1]	14,719[1]	118,767[1]		
	101,555[2]	17,574[2]	119,129[2]		
Incinerator #4	196,950[1]	12,559[1]	209,509[1]		
	199,527[2]	12,499[2]	212,026[2]		
TOTAL			328,276[1]	99,567[1]	427,843[1]
			331,155[2]	103,527[2]	434,682[2]

Source: FY 1971-72[1] Report, p. 31.
FY 1972-73[2] Report, p. 35.

*Tonnages are based on actual weights.

Table 7.18

QUANTITY OF DISPOSED MATERIALS (BALTIMORE)
FY 1971-72 and 1972-73

Location	Materials	Quantity (tons) FY 1971-72	Quantity (tons) FY 1972-73	Total (tons) FY 1971-72	Total (tons) FY 1972-73
#3 Incinerator	Mixed Refuse	118,767	119,129		
	Market Refuse	6,084	5,680		
	Street Dirt	716[1]	892[1]		
				125,567	125,701
#4 Incinerator	Mixed Refuse	209,509	212,026		
	Market Refuse	2,301	1,913		
	Street Dirt	–	–		
				211,810	213,939
Landfills	Mixed Refuse	99,567	103,528		
	Street Dirt	136,760[1]	124,519[1]		
	Ashes	7,456[1]	3,892[1]		
	Bulky Trash	6,964[2]	7,075[2]		
	Leaves	7,674[1]	7,604[1]		
	Mechanical Sweepers	11,239[1]	9,239[1]		
				269,660	255,857
	GRAND TOTAL			607,037	595,497

[1]Conversion factor of 800 lbs/yd used.

[2]Conversion factor of 200 lbs/yd used.

Source for conversion factors: Refuse Collection Practices, American Public Works Association, Chicago, Illinois 1966, pp. 34 and 36.

Source: FY 1971-72 report, p. 36.
FY 1972-73 report, p. 35.

Table 7.19

SOLID WASTE LANDFILLED (BALTIMORE)
FY 1973-1974[1]

Landfill	Residential SW (tons)	% of Total	Non-Residential SW* (tons)	% of Total	Total (tons)
Reliable	45,246	21	170,199	79	215,445
Texas	113,612	81	26,540	19	140,152
Hernwood	57,910	67	28,523	33	86,433
Norris Lane	92,326	100	–	–	92,326
Total	309,094		225,262		534,356

*Mainly consists of commercial and institutional waste.

[1]Source: Bureau of Sanitation Annual Report, Fiscal Year 1973-1974.

Table 7.20

FILL RATE   (DENVER)
(cubic yard/year)

Landfill Site	Cubic Yard/Year	Landfill Site	Cubic Yard/Year
1	250,000	11	900,000
2	212,000	12	50,000
3	1,400,000	13	42,000
4	180,000	14	108,000
5	200,000	15	360,000
6	1,000,000	16	n/a
7	11,000	17	n/a
8	900,000	19	n/a
9	259,000	20	n/a
10	2,000,000		

*These figures are merely estimates made by a private engineering firm reflecting observations of the landfills, and data acquired from the operating personnel (1971).

Table 7.21

CITY OF DENVER WASTE DISPOSAL

Landfill	1973 Cubic Yards	1972 Cubic Yards
Herbertson 4	393,714	396,591
Weeks 2	204,068	200,924
Arapco 3	153,026	142,632
Total	750,810	740,147

Source: Department of Public Works, Sanitary Services Division, Annual Report, 1973. City of Denver, Denver, Colorado, p.37.

Table 7.22

INCINERATION OF REFUSE (ST. LOUIS)
1972-73 (tons)

Source	North Incinerator	South Incinerator	Total
Refuse	93,088	107,334	200,422
Commercial[1]	1,101	866	1,967
Subsidiary[2]	5,780	614	6,394
Total	99,969	108,814	208,783

[1] Reflects waste from hospitals.

[2] Includes waste wood and bulky items only.

Source: Annual Report of the Dept. of Streets, 1972-1973 City of St. Louis, mimeographed, p.49.

Table 7.23

TONNAGE REPORT FROM DISPOSAL SITE (JACKSONVILLE)
(March-December, 1974[1])

Disposal Site	Private Haulers	City Haulers	Residents	Total
Imeson	79,010	60,350	111	140,214[2]
Pickettville	73,891	10,100	72	84,837[3]
Salisbury	70,125	1,968	19	72,112
Sandler	11,254	20	43	11,317
Stetson	23,936	1,319	70	25,325
Total	258,216	73,757	315	333,805

[1] Weighing of the material and accurate record keeping was not being done until March, 1974.

[2] Includes "summer clean-up '74" which added an additional 743 tons during the months of July and August.

[3] Includes "summer clean-up '74" which included 774 tons during the months of June, July and August.

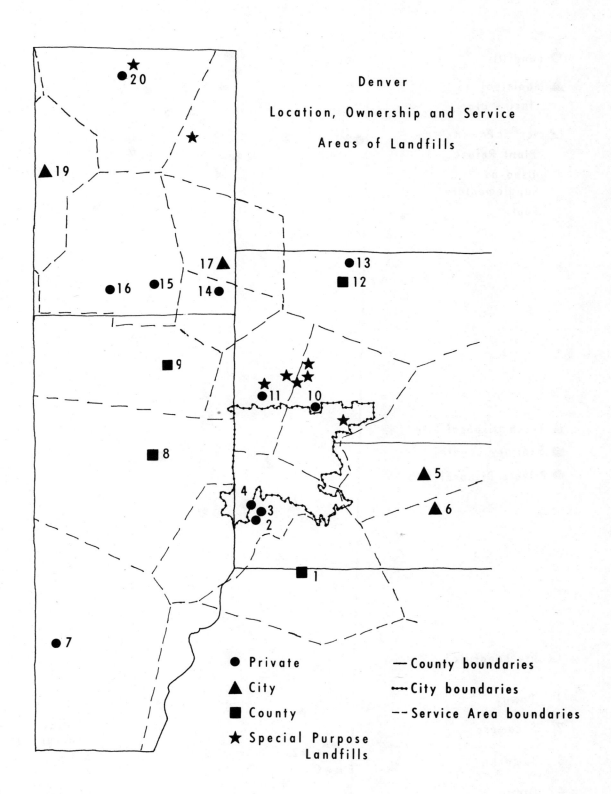

Denver

Location, Ownership and Service

Areas of Landfills

● Private   — County boundaries

▲ City   ┅ City boundaries

■ County   -- Service Area boundaries

★ Special Purpose
   Landfills

Figure 7.27

544

SOLID WASTE DISPOSAL SITES

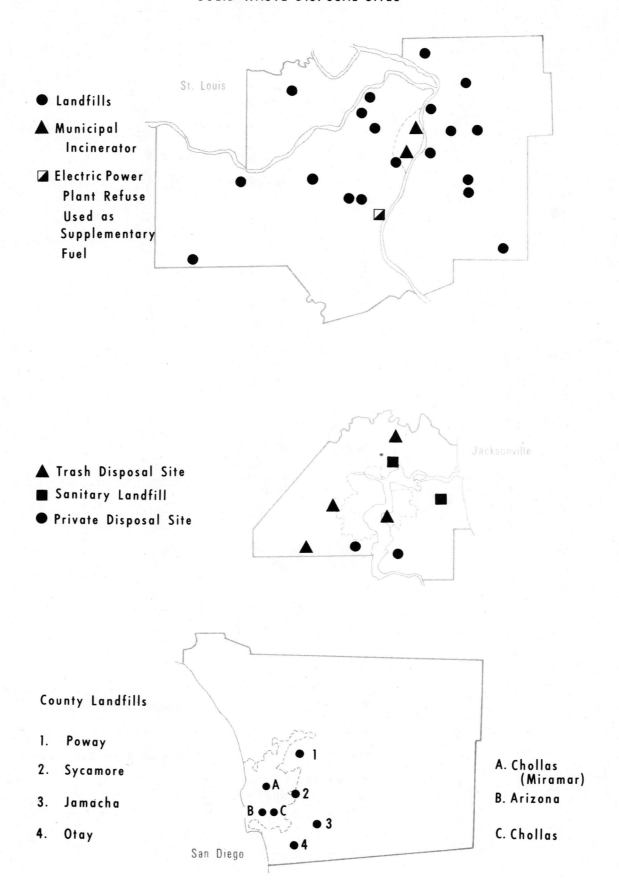

Figures 7.28 - 7.30

6. St. Louis. Disposal of solid waste in the St. Louis SMSA is mostly in sanitary landfills and in rural dumps. There is no incineration of refuse except for the City of St. Louis. Also, the rural parts of the metropolitan area are still permitted to burn their waste. Figure 7.28 shows the location of the disposal sites in the area.

The refuse collected by the City of St. Louis is incinerated in 2 incinerators. These divide the city in half; the north incinerator servicing the northern half, and the south incinerator servicing the southern half of the city. The total tonnage figures by source for each incinerator are found in Table 7.22.

Two unique aspects of solid waste disposal need to be mentioned for St. Louis. First, is that the city operates a bulky item shredder and a log processing plant which are separate from their incinerators. The second aspect is that the city in conjunction with Union Electric Company burns some of their municipal solid waste as supplementary fuel for the production of electric power.

7. Jacksonville. Accurate record keeping of the amounts of solid waste collected and generated by the City of Jacksonville are not kept. Instead, beginning in March 1974, weighing and record keeping was being undertaken at the disposal site. Table 7.23 is the tonnage report by disposal site. Those sites listed are used by the city and the private haulers who contract with the city. Figure 7.29 shows the disposal sites in the entire SMSA differentiated by type.

Disposal of Solid Waste in Metropolitan
Areas--Rochester Case Example

The problem of solid waste disposal by cities is becoming more
serious. Land within city boundaries is becoming scarce and the value
too high to be used as a landfill site. Incineration, although decreasing the overall amount of material, still needs to be disposed.
In many parts of the country, cities have utilized landfills and land
for dumps in the suburban areas surrounding the cities. Conflict
between city needs and suburban wants is becoming clearer, and the
political power and influence to obtain those needs and wants is being
used. The battle line, then seems to be drawn. Cities need places
where they can dump their waste, and the suburbs are the logical
choice. The suburbs feel that the city has no right to dump its refuse in their area, and hence zone or legislate against such action.
Such is the nature of the conflict in the Rochester area in regards
to solid waste disposal.

The City of Rochester dumped its refuse at the Emerson Street
dump for years until 1969, when it was closed because of the unsanitary conditions. In 1971 the city began using the Rush landfill which
was operated by the State Environmental Facilities Corporation. However, this dump was closed in 1973 again because of unsanitary conditions. Two incinerators were installed in the city, but were soon
shut down because of their violation of air quality standards. Meanwhile, garbage is piling up in the city.

Countless studies and proposals were put forth to the county
legislators and the city legislators. Yet, for various reasons, no
comprehensive solid waste management program was forthcoming. There
are three reasons, the first of which is financial. Rochester City
was unable to raise tax revenues due to a legislative action (the
Hurd decision). The other two reasons are best said in an article
appearing in the Times Union, Rochester, New York on February 22, 1974:

"First, no resident wants a landfill near him.
Second, following that certainty, no politician
wants to be the one vote for a landfill near his
constituents. And many other, not directly
affected THIS time, back off because their towns
may be next."

Rochester is currently working on a resource recovery plant for
its solid waste. However, this is a long range solution as the plant
will not be fully operational until 1978. Meanwhile the discussion
over where to put Rochester's waste continues. Currently, the city
is dumping its waste 55 miles away in Seneca Falls, New York. But,
the contract with Seneca Falls, ran out in June, 1975, and once again
the city was faced with the problem of where to put its waste.

Although this is one extreme example of solid waste mismanage-
ment, it is by no means unique. All major American cities will soon
be facing this dilemma as the suburbs have their own solid waste
problem and in many cases are unable or unwilling to add to their
own waste burdens by handling the city's refuse.

Recovery of Municipal Solid Waste

Recovery of municipal solid waste by recycling began in 1971 in
the City of Baltimore. The reclamation center was run by the city
and the profits from the recycling were returned to the general operating fund. The center collects glass, paper, and tin. Table 7.24
shows the amount of materials collected. In 1973-74 a white metals
(those items such as refrigerators, washers, heaters, etc.) recycling
operation was set up. A private firm contracting with the city, provides usage of a trailer and hauls the bulk items away for recycling
in exchange for dumping privileges at one of the county landfills sites.

One of the primary objectives of Project Reuse was to look at
the feasibility of implementing resource recovery operations for the
entire Denver metropolitan area. This is in keeping with the intended
results of the program; short and long range implementation programs
for drainage, flood control, and solid waste management in the urban
areas of the region.

Three citizen group recycling efforts were operational in the area in 1971 when the report was written. However, they are no longer operational. The possible reasons for their demise is that the markets for the materials did not appear; a significant portion of the material brought in for recycling ultimately ended up in landfills anyway; and finally, the overall amounts of materials brought in was in many cases, too great for the facilities to handle and consequently, they became a neighborhood nuisance and a potential health hazard.

Table 7.24

RECYCLING OF MUNICIPAL SOLID WASTE
(tons)

Material	March-June 1971	F.Y. 1971-72	F.Y. 1972-73
Cans	20	65	69
Paper	142	471	391
Glass	127	360	349

Source: F.Y. 1971-72 Report p. 28, and F.Y. 1972-73 Report p. 31.

The only industrial recycling operation is the "Cash for Cans" policy of the Coors Brewery. They offer a 10¢ per pound incentive for all aluminum scrap returned to the company redemption center.

As previously mentioned, St. Louis has developed a unique way of recovery of municipal solid waste; use as a supplementary fuel for the production of electric power.

In response to community sponsors, the Sanitation Department in Jacksonville has made available receptacles for glass and aluminum cans throughout the city for the purposes of recycling. The materials are crushed and taken to a private company for final recycling. The city is paid on a pound basis for the materials brought to the companies. However, this recycling is on a limited basis only.

Conclusions

What is to be concluded from the foregoing? Several points should be made at this time:

1. One of the most striking conclusions is the lack of data. On the municipal level very little accurate record-keeping is done for collection or disposal. It was not until 1974, for example, that Jacksonville even began weighing the solid waste that was being landfilled. Record keeping on the national level is non-existent.

2. Reliability of the data is highly questionable. Data is sparse for collection, except for residential collections (Table 7.25). Other sources of waste are not measured or monitored. There is no reliable information on generation rates, except for St. Louis. The reliability of the data can be questioned due to lack of information on the subject, and/or due to the particular data gathering methods utilized in this analysis.

3. Problems of measurement seem to be crucial. In Baltimore for example, the annual report of the Sanitation Division, in adding the amounts of solid waste collected, added numbers where tonnages were the units, and some where cubic yards were the units as though they were one. Also, converting from one unit to the other has resulted in some problems (e.g. converting street dirt measured in cubic yards to tons).

4. Generation rates for residential solid waste for the seven cities are consistently higher than both the urban average and the national average computed

by the EPA (Table 7.26). The EPA figures, as well as the seven city comparison, were computed for known collected amounts and are thus conservatively low. The EPA figures clearly reflect the inaccuracy of the EPA estimates of known collections or the out-of-dateness of the survey (completed in 1968).

5. Where data are available, subsidiary solid waste seems to be a large component of the total amount of solid waste within a given city.

6. Totals of solid waste per city generally reflect only residential sources and do not necessarily give an accurate picture of the total amount of solid waste collected within a city by all collectors. Also, the per capita generation figure for total solid waste also does not give an accurate picture of the real situation, as data for all the components of municipal solid waste (commercial, industrial, subsidiary, etc.) are not available.

7. The need for further information on solid waste generation in order to plan for control is apparent. There is no comprehensive solid waste planning at the national or state level and many municipalities are facing a crucial problem in terms of waste disposal (the Rochester case for example). Attempts have been made at the regional level for solid waste management. Sixteen solid waste management areas were defined by the Denver Regional Council of Governments. These areas (Figure 7.31) were then evaluated in terms of the generation of solid waste within them in order to facilitate a solid waste management plan for the entire

metropolitan area. The waste loads were based on the following: the per capita waste generation rate which is 6.5 cubic yards per capita per year, multiplied by the population gives the annual generation rate; an assumption that the amount of waste generated equals the amount of waste landfilled; and finally an assumption that the density of wastes which enter the landfills equals 559 pounds per cubic yard. There is no information on how these figures were arrived at or what the assumptions are based on which leads one to seriously doubt their validity.

8. Resource recovery appears to be a viable option (technically) to decreasing solid waste in cities, yet only three cities in this report have plans to pursue this. These are Denver and Rochester with resource recovery plants, and St. Louis which utilizes part of its waste as fuel for the generation of electricity.

Table 7.25

COLLECTION SUMMARY

Waste (tons)

City	1970 Pop.	Res.	Comm.	Ind.	Sub.	Total
St. Louis	622,236	249,800	288,000	559,100	558,200	1,655,100
Cincinnati	452,550	186,779				204,952
Baltimore	905,759	404,609			8,755	413,364
San Diego	696,566	269,521				831,600
Denver	514,678					174,829
Rochester	296,233	132,488	21,279		35,196	199,363[1]
Jacksonville	528,865					[2]
Chicago	3,362,825	2,045,506	366,388	208,228	1,742,576	4,495,250

[1] Includes private collections which are not differentiated by source.
[2] Jacksonville does not keep collection amounts.

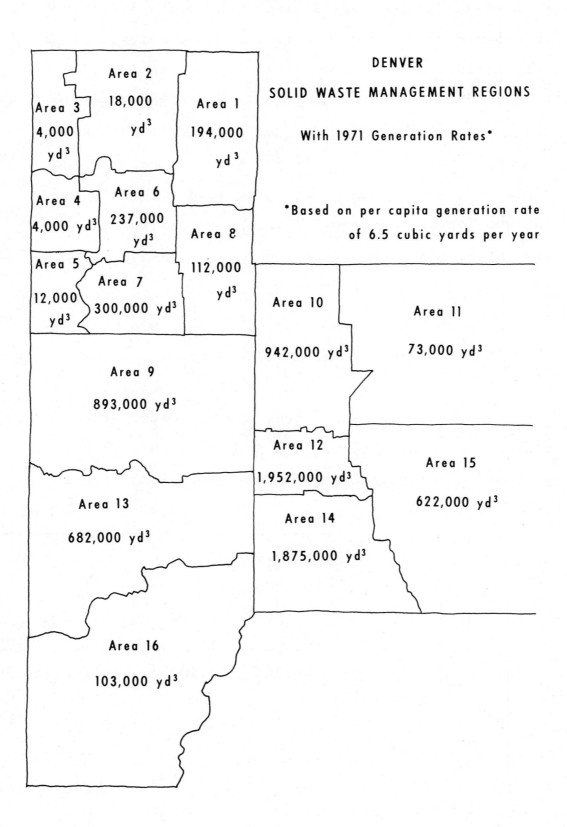

Figure 7.31

Table 7.26

Generation Rates*
(lbs/person/day)

	Res.	Comm.	Ind.	Sub.	Total
St. Louis[1]	2.20	2.54	4.92	4.92	14.57
Cincinnati	2.26				2.48[2]
Baltimore	2.45			.05	2.50
San Diego	2.17				6.54
Denver	1.86				1.86
Rochester	2.45	.39		.65	3.69
Jacksonville[3]	-				3.46
Chicago	3.33	.60	.34	2.84	7.31
Urban	1.26	.46	.65	.72	5.72
National	1.14	.38	.59	.58	5.32

*Calculated from collection amounts by source (where available) for each city in 1973, and 1970 Census Population figures.

[1]Generation summary not collection.

[2]Tonnage includes residential and some commercial.

[3]No data available for collection amounts. Rate is derived from disposal tonnage total for 1974 when records began to be kept.

✳ *Chapter 8*

Pollution Burdens in the Nation's Central Cities

So far, the report has all been prologue. In Chapter 1, we discussed the rationale for the study, albeit briefly, and in Chapter 2, we explored the social geographies of Chicago and the twelve metropolitan areas selected for comparative investigation. Chapters 3 and 4 presented the data on water quality, and Chapters 5-7, respectively, on air quality, noise, and solid wastes. What, then, are the relationships between the social geographies of the nation's central cities and environmental pollution? Which social groups bear the greatest pollution burdens? It is to that question that we now turn. As before, we examine the Chicago case first, and then turn to the twelve comparison regions because, as before, the essential methodology was worked out in the Chicago case and then applied in a streamlined form to the twelve comparisons.

Several limitations already will be apparent, however. As was pointed out in Chapter 3, the people residing within the nation's major central cities are provided by their respective utilities with drinking water that meets Public Health Service standards. It is the suburbanite or exurbanite whose private

drinking water supply presents the greatest problems, yet there

are not consistent state or national programs for monitoring or

assessing drinking water quality in such circumstances, let alone

a data system that permits meaningful comparisons. We therefore

do not discuss drinking water quality here.

Moreover, the entire question of the burdens arising from pol-

luted surface waters presents special problems. Whereas everyone

residing in an area perforce must breathe the air, a polluted

watercourse running nearby can be avoided. It becomes a burden to

users only in terms of the prospective uses they want to make of

it. Thus, water quality standards are set in terms of permitted

uses. But information is not readily available on uses and users

either in contiguous neighborhoods or areas more removed from

the watercourses we studied. Therefore it was not possible to

derive appropriate measures of exposure so that the risks and bur-

dens of poor quality surface waters could be calculated properly.

In consequence, while we presented detailed information on a vari-

ety of water quality parameters in Chapters 3 and 4, outlined in

a preliminary fashion the relationships between water quality and

land use, and did explore relative water quality among the metro-

politan areas, it was not possible to analyze the water pollution

burdens of different social groups residing in the nation's central

cities.

This chapter thus is restricted to three types of pollution:

air, noise, and solid wastes. As instructed by our program offi-

cer in EPA, the comparisons we make are for the central city popu-

lations, not the entire metropolitan areas. This difference

should be kept in mind:

	Central City Population	SMSA Population	Central City/ SMSA Percent
Chicago	3,366,900	6,978,950	48.0
Baltimore	906,000	2,070,670	43.0
Birmingham	301,000	739,270	40.0
Cincinnati	453,000	1,884,850	24.0
Denver	515,000	1,234,280	41.0
Jacksonville	529,000	529,000	100.0
Oklahoma City	366,000	640,890	57.0
Providence	179,000	910,780	19.0
Rochester	296,000	882,670	33.0
St. Louis	622,000	2,363,020	26.0
San Diego	697,000	1,357,850	51.0
Seattle	531,000	1,421,870	37.0
Washington, D.C.	757,000	2,861,120	26.0

In Chicago, monitored air quality information on particulates and sulfur dioxide was adequate enough to be combined with emissions data on nitrogen oxides and organic gases, and with specially-developed data on hazardous trace metals contained in atmospheric aerosols over the city, to enable assessments of air quality burdens to be made. Data on two other risks also were available and included in the study, pesticide poisonings and rat bites. Detailed information on the generation of solid wastes by six different sources enabled pollution risks to be studied in that case. However, the Chicago noise data were not rich enough to be studied in the manner that had been hoped.

In the twelve-city comparisons, the air quality monitoring networks were complete enough to permit systematic comparisons of exposure to particulates in all twelve cases. However, data limitations restricted comparisons of sulfur oxide exposure to only four cases and nitrogen dioxide to three. In the remaining cities, and with respect to the other air quality parameters, there were either too few monitoring stations to permit meaningful pollution contours to be interpolated, or the available monitoring information indicated that in the years studied there were no areas within the central cities that were at risk. Risk was defined as that circumstance in which federal long-term primary or secondary air quality standards were violated. Noise exposure comparisons were possible in three metropolitan areas where small area noise surveys had been completed. Two of these cases also provided data on airport noise exposure. However, no comparative small area data on solid wastes were available for any of the twelve comparative central cities.

The Chicago Case

The methodology for measuring pollution burdens was worked out in the Chicago case, and the results are presented in Tables 8.1-8.3. Turn, for example, to the first rows and columns of Table 8.1, which appear as follows in the table on page 560.

	Particulates		SO$_2$
	Primary Standards	Secondary Standards Only	Secondary Standards Only
Mean Family Income			
>20 (in $1000)	1.19[a] (100.0)[b]	0.00 (0.0)	0.00 (0.0)
17.5-20.0	1.93 (65.0)	0.97 (32.5)	0.07 (2.5)
10.0-17.5	38.09 (63.3)	18.71 (31.0)	0.15 (0.3)
7.5-10.0	29.26 (97.5)	0.74 (2.5)	0.37 (1.2)
<7.5	5.20 (93.3)	0.37 (6.7)	0.00 (0.0)

What this block of numbers shows is that 1.19 per cent of the city of Chicago's population lived in areas in which the mean family income exceeded $20,000 in 1970, and which also exceeded federal long-term primary standards for particulates, and that --the number in parentheses-- this was 100.0 per cent of the city's population that resided in such high-income areas. Similarly, 5.2 per cent of the city's population lived in areas in which mean annual incomes were very low (less than $7,500), and in which the primary particulate standards were violated. This was 93.3 per cent of the population living in such low income areas; the other 6.7 per cent (0.37 per cent of the city's population) lived in areas in which the secondary particulate standards were violated, but the primary standards were not. Of the 20.79 per cent of the city's population living in areas violating only the secondary particulate standard (0.00 + 0.97 + 18.71 + 0.74 + 0.37), the majority (0.97 + 18.71 = 19.68 per cent) resided in areas with mean incomes in the 10-20 thousand dollar range --over 30.0 per cent of the population residing in such areas.

How were these numbers derived? Maps of the city were gridded into a network of square miles and a point was placed at the center of each square mile cell. By overlaying this grid on a contoured population density map, the density at each point could be interpolated. This, in turn, provided an estimate of the population residing in each square mile, since the densities also had been calculated on a per square mile basis. Transferring the grid to the mean annual incomes map, the average income level of the population residing in each square mile was obtained. A similar process provided readings of pollution levels, and whether or not primary and/or secondary standards had been violated. The resulting data were cross tabulated, and the percentages computed. The process was repeated for each of the social indicators noted in the rows of Tables 8.1-8.3, and each of the pollutants and hazards reported in the columns. The same procedures were applied to each of the other twelve cities studied.

The Air Pollution Burdens

The air pollution burdens revealed for the city of Chicago by Table 8.1 are as follows:

1. The entire city violates secondary particulate standards, and 79.21 per cent of the population resides in areas violating the primary long term standards.

2. The 20.79 per cent of the city's population living in the areas least affected by particulate pollution are middle income--one third of that group--for both the

Table 8.1

PERCENTAGES OF DIFFERENT POPULATION SUB-GROUPS
RESIDING IN AREAS EXCEEDING FEDERAL AIR QUALITY STANDARDS,
OR IN HIGH-RISK ENVIRONMENTS WHEN STANDARDS HAVE NOT BEEN ISSUED.

	Particulates		SO$_2$
	Primary Standards	Secondary Standards Only	Secondary Standards Only
Mean Family Income			
>20 (in $1000)	1.19[a] (100.0)[b]	0.00 (00)	0.00 (00)
17.5 - 20	1.93 (65.0)	0.97 (32.5)	0.07 (2.5)
10 - 17.5	38.09 (63.3)	18.71 (31.0)	0.15 (0.3)
7.5 - 10	29.26 (97.5)	0.74 (2.5)	0.37 (1.2)
<7.5	5.20 (93.3)	0.37 (6.7)	0.00 (00)
Poverty Indicators			
0	20.49 (51.1)	15.89 (39.7)	0.00 (00)
1	14.63 (75.8)	4.68 (24.2)	0.00 (00)
2	13.51 (95.3)	0.67 (4.7)	0.22 (1.6)
3	16.34 (100.0)	0.00 (00)	0.37 (2.3)
4	7.20 (100.0)	0.00 (00)	0.00 (00)
5	2.82 (100.0)	0.00 (00)	0.00 (00)
% Black			
<10	38.61 (61.4)	20.05 (31.9)	0.37 (0.6)
10 - 50	8.24 (95.7)	0.37 (4.3)	0.15 (1.7)
>50	28.07 (98.7)	0.37 (1.3)	0.00 (00)
% Secondary Occup.			
0 - 20	26.51 (51.9)	18.71 (36.7)	0.37 (0.7)
>20	47.37 (96.8)	1.34 (2.7)	0.15 (0.3)
% Single Unit Housing			
0 - 20	47.08 (85.6)	7.94 (14.4)	0.59 (1.1)
20 - 40	13.29 (74.3)	4.46 (24.9)	0.00 (00)
40 - 60	11.29 (72.1)	2.45 (15.6)	0.00 (00)
>60	6.24 (54.6)	3.79 (33.1)	0.00 (00)
% Public Trans.			
<10	0.89 (75.0)	0.30 (25.5)	0.00 (00)
10 - 19.9	1.26 (34.0)	0.89 (24.0)	0.15 (4.0)
20 - 39.9	44.03 (72.5)	15.52 (25.5)	0.52 (0.9)
>40	30.15 (88.6)	3.86 (11.4)	0.46 (1.3)
Pop. Change 1970/1960			
<.75	10.17 (96.5)	0.37 (3.5)	0.37 (3.5)
.75 - 1.0	44.62 (79.6)	10.32 (18.4)	0.00 (00)
1.0 - 1.3	19.68 (67.3)	7.72 (26.4)	0.07 (0.3)
1.3 - 2.0	2.67 (92.3)	0.22 (7.7)	0.00 (00)
2.0 - 3.0	0.52 (100.0)	0.00 (00)	0.15 (28.6)
>3.0	0.00 (00)	0.07 (11.1)	0.00 (00)

[a] Percentage of the city's population

[b] Percentage of the population in the row class living in substandard areas.

Table 8.1 (cont.)

	Nitrogen Oxides Emissions	Organic Gases
	(>250 tons/ sq.mi./year)	(>100 tons/ sq.mi./year)
Mean Family Income		
>20 (in $1000)	0.00 (00)	0.00 (00)
17.5 - 20	0.07 (2.5)	1.56 (52.5)
10 - 17.5	4.83 (8.0)	3.42 (5.7)
7.5 - 10	7.80 (26.0)	4.31 (14.4)
<7.5	0.37 (6.7)	1.11 (30.7)
Poverty Indicators		
0	1.93 (4.8)	1.93 (4.8)
1	1.86 (9.6)	0.22 (1.2)
2	2.97 (21.0)	2.08 (14.7)
3	2.60 (15.0)	4.68 (28.6)
4	1.04 (14.4)	0.67 (9.3)
5	1.86 (65.8)	1.11 (29.5)
% Black		
<10	7.35 (11.2)	5.87 (9.3)
10 - 50	1.71 (19.8)	1.19 (13.8)
>50	4.53 (15.9)	3.79 (13.3)
% Secondary Occup.		
0 - 20	1.56 (3.1)	2.38 (4.7)
>20	11.36 (23.4)	8.54 (17.5)
% Single Unit Housing		
0 - 20	9.88 (17.9)	9.36 (17.0)
20 - 40	1.56 (8.7)	0.59 (3.5)
40 - 60	1.04 (6.6)	0.67 (4.3)
>60	0.44 (3.9)	0.67 (5.8)
% Public Trans.		
<10	0.00 (00)	0.00 (00)
10 - 19.9	0.00 (00)	0.37 (10.0)
20 - 39.9	8.32 (13.7)	2.75 (4.5)
>40	4.60 (13.5)	4.38 (12.9)
Pop. Change 1970/1960		
<.75	2.67 (25.4)	2.82 (26.8)
.75 - 1.0	7.50 (13.4)	5.05 (9.0)
1.0 - 1.3	2.23 (7.6)	2.00 (6.9)
1.3 - 2.0	0.52 (17.9)	0.74 (25.6)
2.0 - 3.0	0.15 (28.6)	0.00 (00)
>3.0	0.00 (00)	0.00 (00)

rich and the poor are concentrated in the most polluted areas. These middle income residents are predominantly white, employed in white collar occupations, living in stable areas, with a relatively high degree of dependence upon public transportation.

3. The 79.21 per cent of the city's population that resides in areas violating primary long-term particulate standards consist of all of the rich, most of the poor, and two-thirds of the middle-class; two-thirds of those living in predominantly white areas, but almost all of the black; 85 per cent of the population residing in apartment neighborhoods, but only 54 per cent of those residing in areas of predominantly single-family housing, etc.

4. Only one half of one per cent of the city's population resided in areas that violated secondary sulfur oxide standards in the year studied. These were lower income white residents of apartment neighborhoods, in the main.

5. Both nitrogen oxides and organic gases emissions were greatest in lower middle income apartment neighborhoods, both black and white, areas in which blue collar manufacturing employees made relatively heavy use of public transportation --areas, too, which declined in population between 1960 and 1970.

Exposure to Hazardous
     Substances

A very different story is told by the data on exposure to higher levels of trace metals in atmospheric aerosols in the city of Chicago (Table 8.2). These data come from the Chicago Air Sampling Network stations over various years and time periods, and their spatial configuration reflects the pattern of their sources. Elements like mercury, manganese and iron, which are by-products of the steel industry, are concentrated in the southeast, near the Indiana mills. Lead pollution is highest in the Loop, the focus for automobile exhausts in Chicago. For overall pattern the southeast has the greatest concentration of several trace metals. The residential near-south side has few of these pollutants in comparison. Likewise, the northwest has high mercury and arsenic but low levels of all other metallic aerosols. Thus, the middle income white population residing in single family neighborhoods has the greatest level of exposure to atmospheric mercury and arsenic, whereas the apartment-dwelling high income group is most exposed to atmospheric zinc. Atmospheric lead most burdens the low-income black, while cadmium levels are greatest in the atmospheric aerosols in lower income blue collar white apartment neighborhoods.

The final two hazards included in Table 8.2 are of another kind: pesticide poisoning and rat bite risks. The standards for pesticides are set in terms of water quality, but in a city where poisons are likely to be eaten and breathed, such a definition is incomplete. Almost all the pesticide problem in Chicago can be traced to areas with rodent problems, where the anti-rat devices fall into the hands of children. The map of pesticide poisoning risk was developed from the Chicago Department of Health data on poisoning and the number of children under fifteen in each census tract. The rat bite data came from Chicago's Model Cities program, and also were converted to data on risk per 1,000 children under age 15. See Figures 8.1 and 8.2.

Table 8.2 reveals that the highest risk of rat bites is in low income black apartment neighborhoods. These neighborhoods, plus lower income white apartment neighborhoods have the highest rates of pesticides poisonings.

Solid Wastes

In the case of solid waste, a different exposure pattern emerges. Exposure to solid waste by income reveals that over half of the population earning greater than $20,000 is at risk in five out of the six categories. On the other hand, only one in five middle-income residents appears to be at risk. Finally, the low income category reveals that more than 70 percent live in areas that generate high levels of residential waste, most residential demolitions, and most subsidiary wastes. They therefore have the highest per capita solid waste generation rates.

Table 8.2

PERCENTAGES OF DIFFERENT POPULATION SUB-GROUPS
RESIDING IN AREAS WITH HIGH EXPOSURE
TO HAZARDOUS SUBSTANCES.

	Mercury (>4 ngr/m^3)		Arsenic (>19 ngr/m^3)		Zinc Compounds (>.9 ngr/m^3)	
Mean Family Income						
>20 (in $1000)	0.00[a](00 ;[b]		0.00 (00)		1.89 (100.0)	
17.5 – 20	0.00 (00)		0.97 (32.5)		0.74 (2.5)	
10 – 17.5	19.16 (31.8)		21.31 (35.4)		4.97 (8.3)	
7.5 – 10	2.60 (8.7)		4.60 (15.3)		9.80 (32.7)	
<7.5	0.00 (00)		0.00 (00)		1.26 (22.7)	
Poverty Indicators						
0	13.22 (33.0)		15.59 (38.9)		0.74 (1.9)	
1	6.83 (35.4)		5.35 (27.7)		3.64 (18.8)	
2	1.78 (12.6)		3.34 (23.6)		5.05 (35.6)	
3	0.37 (2.3)		1.26 (7.7)		5.57 (34.1)	
4	0.00 (00)		0.74 (10.3)		0.37 (5.2)	
5	0.00 (00)		0.00 (00)		2.82 (100.0)	
% Black						
<10	12.55 (20.0)		21.01 (33.4)		9.88 (15.7)	
10 – 50	3.49 (40.5)		0.59 (6.9)		2.97 (34.5)	
>50	5.35 (18.8)		5.27 (18.5)		4.16 (14.6)	
% Secondary Occup.						
0 – 20	14.40 (28.2)		20.79 (40.8)		2.23 (4.4)	
>20	7.50 (15.3)		6.24 (12.7)		13.96 (28.5)	
% Single Unit Housing						
0 – 20	4.23 (7.7)		13.51 (24.6)		12.85 (23.3)	
20 – 40	3.79 (21.2)		8.17 (45.6)		4.68 (26.1)	
40 – 60	8.54 (54.5)		5.12 (32.7)		0.22 (1.4)	
>60	5.35 (46.8)		2.15 (18.8)		0.00 (00)	
% Public Trans.						
<10	0.96 (61.9)		0.00 (00)		0.00 (00)	
10 – 19.9	1.86 (50.0)		0.97 (26.0)		0.00 (00)	
20 – 39.9	16.19 (26.7)		16.86 (27.8)		9.88 (16.3)	
>40	2.52 (7.4)		8.17 (24.0)		7.05 (20.7)	
Pop. Change 1970/1960						
<.75	0.37 (3.5)		0.59 (5.6)		4.53 (43.0)	
.75 – 1.0	9.36 (16.7)		14.85 (26.5)		9.80 (17.5)	
1.0 – 1.3	9.58 (32.7)		11.29 (38.6)		2.08 (7.1)	
1.3 – 2.0	1.41 (48.7)		0.59 (20.5)		0.59 (20.5)	
2.0 – 3.0	0.37 (71.4)		0.00 (00)		0.00 (00)	
>3.0	0.67 (100.0)		0.00 (00)		0.00 (00)	

[a]Percentage of the city's population.

[b]Percentage of the population in the row class living in substandard areas.

Table 8.2 (contd.)

	Manganese ($>.15$ ngr/m^3)		Lead Compounds (>1.8 ngr/m^3)		Cadmium (>18 ngr/m^3)	
Mean Family Income						
>20 (in $1000)	0.00	(00)	0.00	(00)	0.00	(00)
17.5 - 20	0.00	(00)	0.00	(00)	0.89	(30.0)
10 - 17.5	6.24	(10.4)	0.00	(00)	8.17	(13.6)
7.5 - 10	0.96	(3.2)	2.23	(7.4)	10.17	(33.9)
<7.5	0.00	(00)	0.74	(13.3)	0.00	(00)
Poverty Indicators						
0	4.16	(10.4)	0.00	(00)	3.27	(8.1)
1	2.75	(14.2)	0.00	(00)	6.46	(33.5)
2	0.22	(1.6)	0.67	(4.7)	5.49	(38.7)
3	0.00	(00)	0.00	(00)	5.20	(31.8)
4	0.00	(00)	0.37	(5.2)	0.37	(5.2)
5	0.00	(00)	1.93	(68.4)	0.00	(00)
% Black						
<10	3.34	(5.3)	0.00	(00)	18.04	(28.7)
10 - 50	2.08	(24.1)	0.96	(11.2)	0.37	(4.3)
>50	1.71	(6.0)	1.93	(6.8)	2.38	(8.4)
% Secondary Occup.						
0 - 20	4.31	(8.4)	0.00	(00)	3.12	(6.1)
>20	2.97	(6.1)	7.05	(14.4)	16.19	(33.1)
% Single Unit Housing						
0 - 20	1.78	(3.2)	3.04	(5.5)	15.96	(29.0)
20 - 40	1.26	(7.1)	0.00	(00)	3.04	(17.0)
40 - 60	3.64	(23.2)	0.00	(00)	0.22	(1.4)
>60	0.52	(4.5)	0.00	(00)	0.00	(00)
% Public Trans.						
<10	0.00	(00)	0.00	(00)	0.00	(00)
10 - 19.9	0.22	(6.0)	0.00	(00)	0.00	(00)
20 - 39.9	6.16	(10.1)	0.00	(00)	12.70	(20.9)
>40	0.59	(1.7)	3.04	(9.0)	6.53	(19.2)
Pop. Change 1970/1960						
<.75	0.00	(00)	1.48	(14.1)	0.59	(5.6)
.75 - 1.0	3.49	(6.2)	0.67	(1.2)	15.07	(26.9)
1.0 - 1.3	3.12	(10.7)	0.00	(00)	3.79	(12.9)
1.3 - 2.0	0.52	(17.9)	0.59	(20.5)	0.00	(00)
2.0 - 3.0	0.00	(00)	0.00	(00)	0.00	(00)
>3.0	0.00	(00)	0.00	(00)	0.00	(00)

Table 8.2 (contd.)

	Copper Compounds ($>.2$ ngr/m^3)		Iron Compounds (>4.0 ngr/m^3)	
Mean Family Income				
>20 (in $1000)	0.00	(00)	0.00	(00.)
17.5 - 20	0.00	(00)	0.00	(00)
10 - 17.5	6.68	(11.1)	7.65	(12.7)
7.5 - 10	0.74	(2.5)	0.96	(3.2)
<7.5	0.00	(00)	0.00	(00)
Poverty Indicators				
0	3.49	(8.7)	4.23	(10.6)
1	2.23	(11.5)	3.56	(18.5)
2	0.00	(00)	0.89	(6.3)
3	0.00	(00)	0.00	(00)
4	0.00	(00)	0.00	(00)
5	0.00	(00)	0.00	(00)
% Black				
<10	4.60	(7.3)	3.86	(6.1)
10 - 50	1.86	(21.6)	2.45	(28.4)
>50	0.89	(3.1)	2.38	(8.4)
% Secondary Occup.				
0 - 20	3.12	(6.1)	5.27	(10.3)
>20	2.82	(5.8)	3.64	(7.4)
% Single Unit Housing				
0 - 20	0.44	(0.8)	2.38	(4.3)
20 - 40	0.44	(2.4)	1.34	(7.5)
40 - 60	2.75	(17.5)	4.08	(26.1)
>60	3.71	(32.5)	0.89	(7.8)
% Public Trans.				
<10	0.59	(38.1)	0.00	(00)
10 - 19.9	0.44	(12.0)	0.22	(6.0)
20 - 39.9	6.83	(11.2)	7.20	(11.9)
>40	0.00	(00)	1.34	(3.9)
Pop. Change 1970/1960				
<.75	0.00	(00)	0.59	(5.6)
.75 - 1.0	1.86	(3.3)	3.86	(6.9)
1.0 - 1.3	4.01	(13.7)	3.56	(12.2)
1.3 - 2.0	1.04	(35.9)	0.52	(17.9)
2.0 - 3.0	0.37	(71.4)	0.00	(00)
>3.0	0.00	(00)	0.00	(00)

Table 8.2 (contd)

	Pesticide Poisoning (at least 2.0% at risk)		Rat Bite Risk (children under age 15- risk per 1000)	
Mean Family Income				
>20 (in $1000)	1.19	(100.0)	0.00	(00)
17.5 - 20	0.96	(32.5)	0.00	(00)
10 - 17.5	22.72	(37.7)	0.00	(00)
7.5 - 10	14.63	(48.8)	5.49	(18.3)
<7.5	1.26	(22.7)	1.19	(21.3)
Poverty Indicators				
0	12.92	(32.2)	0.00	(00)
1	4.16	(21.5)	0.37	(1.9)
2	8.61	(60.7)	0.59	(4.2)
3	6.68	(40.9)	2.82	(17.3)
4	4.31	(59.8)	1.26	(17.7)
5	0.74	(31.6)	2.82	(100.0)
% Black				
<10	21.98	(34.9)	0.00	(00)
10 - 50	3.42	(39.7)	2.08	(24.1)
>50	17.08	(60.1)	5.79	(20.4)
% Secondary Occup.				
0 - 20	19.53	(38.3)	0.07	(0.1)
>20	19.97	(40.8)	7.80	(15.9)
% Single Unit Housing				
0 - 20	26.43	(48.0)	7.87	(14.3)
20 - 40	9.43	(52.7)	0.00	(00)
40 - 60	4.01	(25.6)	0.00	(00)
>60	0.74	(6.5)	0.00	(00)
% Public Trans.				
<10	0.00	(00)	0.00	(00)
10 - 19.9	0.07	(2.0)	0.00	(00)
20 - 39.9	26.06	(42.9)	4.83	(7.9)
>40	14.55	(42.8)	2.97	(8.7)
Pop. Change 1970/1960				
<.75	7.13	(67.6)	2.90	(27.5)
.75 - 1.0	24.80	(44.2)	3.19	(5.7)
1.0 - 1.3	8.39	(28.7)	1.19	(4.1)
1.3 - 2.0	0.59	(20.5)	0.59	(20.5)
2.0 - 3.0	0.00	(00)	0.00	(00)
>3.0	0.00	(00)	0.00	(00)

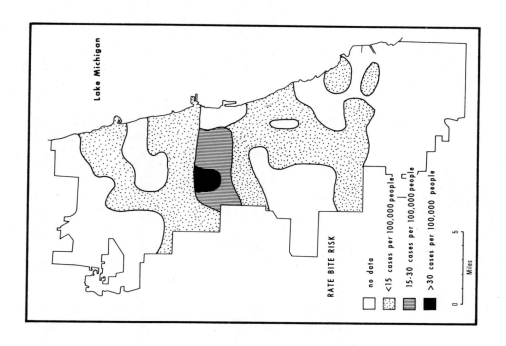

Figure 8.2

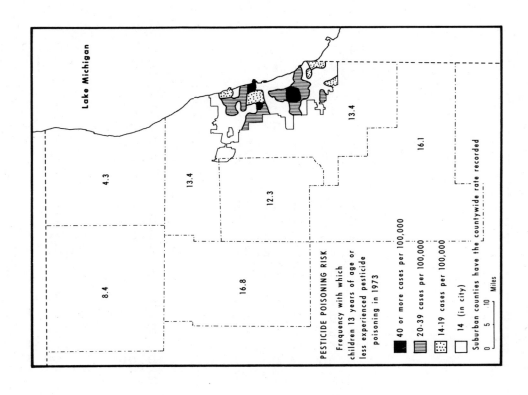

Figure 8.1

Those areas of the city with populations having three or more poverty indicators are most exposed to solid waste pollution especially to the residential demolitions and unspecified subsidiary categories. Racially, blacks are more at risk, but generally this is under 50 per cent of the total black population except in demolitions and subsidiary cases. Blue collar workers bear the burdens of industrial, demolition, and per capita solid waste pollution, although as with blacks, only about half of all the blue collar workers are at risk. Contrary to most of the solid waste literature, we found that apartment dwellers are significantly more exposed to solid waste pollution than those people residing in single family units. Also, the greater the percentage of people using public transportation, the greater the exposure to solid waste pollution.

What this analysis indicates is that there are two subsets of the population at risk. The first of these are those persons residing in high density apartment areas with high income levels that are predominantly white, who use public transportation, and whose communities have seen an increase in growth of population since 1960. The other subgroup are the low income poverty people, again residing in high density apartment areas. This group is predominantly black with occupations in the blue collar category and who rely on public transportation. The neighborhoods of these people have seen a decline in population over the last 15 years. Population decline leads to abandonment of buildings and general decay of the area. Those people who remain in these areas experience a high exposure level to various sources of solid waste, among them being residential demolitions.

Table 8.3

PERCENTAGES OF DIFFERENT POPULATION SUB-GROUPS RESIDING IN AREAS WITH HIGH EXPOSURE TO SOLID WASTE.

	Residential (>2 tons/year/ dwelling unit)	Commercial (> 2,500 tons/ mi^2)	Industrial (> 5,000 tons/ mi^2)
Mean Family Income			
>20 (in $1000)	0.59[a](50.0)[b]	0.59 (50.0)	0.59 (50.0)
17.5 - 20	2.52 (85.0)	1.11 (37.5)	0.00 (0)
10 - 17.5	13.59 (22.6)	2.82 (4.7)	10.17 (16.9)
7.5 - 10	7.65 (25.5)	8.39 (28.0)	11.29 (37.6)
<7.5	3.94 (70.7)	2.75 (49.3)	1.26 (22.7)
Poverty Indicators			
0	8.39 (21.3)	0.74 (1.9)	4.01 (10.0)
1	2.90 (15.0)	1.34 (6.9)	7.28 (37.7)
2	3.56 (25.1)	3.34 (23.6)	3.94 (27.7)
3	6.98 (42.7)	5.12 (31.4)	5.64 (34.5)
4	4.16 (57.7)	2.75 (38.1)	1.63 (23.7)
5	0.82 (29.9)	2.23 (78.9)	0.97 (34.2)
% Black			
<10	12.32 (19.6)	7.05 (11.2)	15.22 (24.2)
10 - 50	1.86 (21.6)	2.08 (24.1)	2.38 (27.6)
>50	12.32 (43.3)	6.38 (22.5)	5.94 (20.9)
% Secondary Occup.			
0 - 20	15.07 (29.5)	4.16 (8.2)	6.31 (12.4)
>20	11.58 (23.7)	11.29 (23.1)	17.23 (35.2)
% Single Unit Housing			
0 - 20	21.46 (39.0)	14.33 (26.0)	17.75 (32.3)
20 - 40	1.19 (6.6)	1.19 (6.6)	3.49 (19.5)
40 - 60	3.19 (20.4)	0.00 (0)	1.49 (9.5)
>60	0.96 (8.4)	0.00 (0)	0.74 (6.5)
% Public Trans.			
<10	0.00 (0)	0.00 (0)	0.00 (0)
10 - 19.9	1.41 (38.0)	0.00 (0)	0.00 (0)
20 - 39.9	7.50 (12.3)	4.46 (7.3)	14.78 (24.3)
>40	18.41 (54.1)	11.06 (32.5)	8.69 (25.5)
Pop. Change 1970/1960			
<.75	4.46 (42.3)	6.68 (62.7)	3.94 (37.3)
.75 - 1.0	13.36 (24.1)	6.46 (11.5)	14.92 (26.6)
1.0 - 1.3	7.80 (26.5)	0.96 (3.3)	4.53 (15.5)
1.3 - 2.0	2.15 (74.4)	1.35 (46.2)	0.00 (0)
2.0 - 3.0	0.15 (28.6)	0.15 (28.6)	0.15 (28.6)
>3.0	0.59 (88.9)	0.00 (0)	0.00 (0)

[a]Percentage of the city's population.

[b]Percentage of the population in the row class living in substandard areas.

Table 8.3 (contd.)

	Residential Demolitions (>10,000 tons/ mi^2)	Total Unspecified Subsidiary (>5,000 tons/ mi^2)	Per Capita (>1.5 tons/ year/mi^2)
Mean Family Income			
>20 (in $1000)	0.00 (0)	1.19 (100.0)	0.59 (50.0)
17.5 - 20	1.04 (35.0)	2.52 (85.0)	2.52 (85.0)
10 - 17.5	6.61 (11.0)	9.65 (16.0)	5.72 (9.5)
7.5 - 10	17.97 (59.9)	22.28 (74.3)	8.84 (29.5)
<7.5	4.31 (77.3)	4.83 (86.7)	4.83 (86.7)
Poverty Indicators			
0	2.23 (5.4)	3.34 (8.3)	2.82 (7.0)
1	2.90 (15.0)	3.86 (20.0)	2.75 (24.2)
2	5.72 (40.3)	9.43 (66.5)	2.38 (16.8)
3	12.84 (78.6)	14.78 (90.5)	6.16 (37.7)
4	4.31 (59.8)	5.94 (82.5)	3.86 (53.6)
5	2.45 (86.8)	2.82 (100.0)	1.34 (47.4)
% Black			
<10	8.54 (13.6)	14.11 (22.4)	8.91 (14.2)
10 - 50	2.38 (27.6)	3.71 (43.1)	3.56 (41.4)
>50	18.12 (63.7)	21.53 (75.7)	9.80 (34.5)
% Secondary Occup.			
0 - 20	5.20 (10.2)	32.00 (62.7)	6.61 (13.0)
>20	23.83 (48.7)	8.69 (17.8)	15.52 (31.7)
% Single Unit Housing			
0 - 20	27.92 (50.7)	36.83 (66.9)	19.01 (34.5)
20 - 40	1.19 (6.6)	2.38 (13.3)	1.34 (7.5)
40 - 60	0.67 (4.3)	0.74 (4.7)	1.19 (7.6)
>60	0.00 (0)	0.00 (0)	0.37 (3.2)
% Public Trans.			
<10	0.00 (0)	0.00 (0)	0.07 (4.8)
10 - 19.9	0.00 (0)	0.00 (0)	0.07 (2.0)
20 - 39.9	9.88 (16.3)	12.77 (21.0)	4.97 (8.2)
>40	19.82 (58.3)	4.75 (14.0)	15.07 (44.3)
Pop. Change 1970/1960			
<.75	4.53 (43.0)	7.57 (71.8)	5.05 (47.9)
.75 - 1.0	19.53 (34.7)	25.10 (44.8)	11.29 (20.1)
1.0 - 1.3	4.46 (15.2)	6.31 (21.6)	3.94 (13.5)
1.3 - 2.0	1.34 (46.7)	1.34 (46.2)	1.48 (51.3)
2.0 - 3.0	0.00 (0)	0.00 (0)	0.15 (28.6)
>3.0	0.00 (0)	0.00 (0)	0.00 (0)

The Twelve City Comparisons

As noted earlier, complete twelve-city comparisons were possible only in the case of particulates (Table 8.4). Inadequate monitoring systems and/or lack of evidence of pollution problems made the assessment of pollution burdens either impossible or unnecessary in the other cases (see, for example, the maps of air quality in Chapter 5). Thus, sulfur dioxide exposure is assessed in only four cases (Table 8.5), nitrogen dioxide in only three (Table 8.6), ambient noise levels in three (Table 8.7), and airport noise in two (Table 8.8).

Air Quality

Where systematic comparisons across the cities are possible, however, as in Table 8.4, the results are quite striking. In all areas, the very poor are most likely to be concentrated in the areas with the most serious particulate problems. A high proportion of the upper middle class always avoid such areas. The most affluent may avoid such areas totally, as in Rochester, St. Louis, or Seattle, or may be concentrated in a heavily polluted central location as in Birmingham. A high proportion of the poor are black or members of other ethnic minorities, living in older neighborhoods, and relying more than most upon public transportation. In some cases, the most polluted areas may also have heavy concentrations of the elderly (e.g. Oklahoma City); in others it is the young (e.g. Baltimore); and in yet others both of these (e.g. Birmingham).

Similar conclusions can be derived from Tables 8.5 and 8.6, although the problems are less. The black and the poor are concentrated in the much smaller parts of the central cities that are afflicted by problems of sulfur dioxide or nitrogen dioxide pollution.

Noise

Noise comparisons must be tempered by the fact that for Denver, we had data for only 10% of the population, while Jacksonville and Washington fared a little better (between 20-80 percent of the total population). This caveat realized, as was the case with air, high levels of noise pollution primarily affect low income groups (Denver and Jacksonville). In the Denver case, 59 percent of the black and Spanish populations were exposed as opposed to 100 percent of the black populations of Jacksonville and Washington. It is interesting to note that for Jacksonville and Washington all of the white central city population is at risk. Washington also had a high percentage of high income people exposed. Inner city residents using public transportation (Washington) had higher exposure levels. Denver and Jacksonville showed just the opposite, with private transportation users being more at risk. Older neighborhoods had higher exposure levels, and an examination of age differentials indicated that all age groups had the same exposure. Areas of high density in Washington and middle density in Denver and Jacksonville carried the highest burdens. Middle income white (Jacksonville) and low income black and Spanish (Denver) had the highest exposure levels to airport noise. Those neighborhoods built after 1950 were most exposed.

Comparisons from Table 8.7 show that the poor and the black are concentrated in those older central-city neighborhoods where ambient noise levels are the greatest. In contrast, Table 8.8 shows that middle income whites residing in mid-density areas are most exposed to airport noise which is hardly surprising given the outlying nature of airport locations. The reader will be able to confirm these conclusions by turning to pages 584-6.

TABLE 8.4

PARTICULATE EXPOSURE LEVELS:
SOCIAL GROUPS IN THE TWELVE CITIES

	BALTIMORE		BIRMINGHAM	
	Primary	Secondary	Primary	Secondary
Income ($)				
>17,500	0[a] (0)[b]	1.2 (34.9)	3.8 (100.0)	0 (0)
10,000-17,500	6.0 (14.3)	20.4 (49.1)	19.6 (83.6)	3.8 (16.4)
7,500-10,000	29.2 (66.9)	14.5 (33.2)	25.1 (100.0)	0 (0)
<7,500	11.3 (100.0)	0 (0)	47.2 (100.0)	0 (0)
Ethnicity				
>30% Black	21.9 (55.01)	16.6 (41.6)	66.9 (95.9)	2.8 (4.1)
10-30% Black	8.8 (43.4)	8.2 (40.4)	19.3 (97.1)	0.6 (2.9)
>30% Spanish	0 (0)	0 (0)	0 (0)	0 (0)
10-30% Spanish	0 (0)	0 (0)	0 (0)	0 (0)
Others	15.6 (39.3)	11.3 (28.4)	10.3 (98.1)	0.2 (1.9)
>10% Oriental or American Indian	0 (0)	0 (0)	0 (0)	0 (0)
Spanish & Black	0 (0)	0 (0)	0 (0)	0 (0)
% Use Public Transportation				
>20	40.5 (65.6)	19.9 (32.2)	24.6 (100.0)	0 (0)
10-20	3.6 (14.1)	9.9 (39.0)	29.2 (97.9)	0.6 (2.1)
1-10	2.4 (18.2)	6.3 (48.8)	34.7 (100.0)	0 (0)
<1	0 (0)	0 (0)	7.1 (68.9)	3.2 (31.1)
Housing Age				
20-40% built 1939/earlier	0 (0)	0 (0)	8.0 (100.0)	0 (0)
>40% built 1939/earlier	38.6 (57.9)	23.2 (34.8)	0 (0)	0 (0)
>20% built 1960-1970	3.3 (77.9)	0.9 (22.1)	1.7 (100.0)	0 (0)
Mixed	4.4 (15.7)	11.3 (39.8)	86.0 (95.7)	3.8 (4.3)
Stage in Life Cycle				
>10% over 64	16.6 (35.1)	17.1 (36.3)	4.0 (100.0)	0 (0)
>20% under 18	6.0 (95.6)	0.3 (0.4)	14.3 (98.6)	0.2 (1.4)
Others	22.5 (49.8)	18.7 (41.4)	77.9 (95.7)	3.5 (4.3)
Combination	1.3 (100.0)	0 (0)	0 (0)	0 (0)
Density				
>8,000	38.4 (47.5)	26.5 (32.8)	4.2 (100.0)	0 (0)
4,000-8,000	6.6 (41.7)	8.0 (50.0)	52.2 (100.0)	0 (0)
1,000-4,000	1.1 (36.4)	1.7 (54.6)	39.1 (93.8)	2.6 (6.2)
200-1,000	0.3 (100.0)	0 (0)	0.6 (33.3)	1.2 (66.7)
<200	0.0 (0)	0 (0)	0 (100.0)	0 (0)

[a]Percentage of the city's population

[b]Percentage of the population in the row class living in substandard areas.

TABLE 8.4 (cont.)

	CINCINNATI		DENVER	
	Primary	Secondary	Primary	Secondary
Income ($)				
>17,500	0 (0)	1.4 (100.0)	16.1 (88.2)	2.1 (11.8)
10,000-17,500	34.0 (64.8)	18.4 (35.2)	31.8 (96.3)	1.2 (3.7)
7,500-10,000	19.3 (86.1)	3.1 (13.9)	37.2 (100.0)	0 (0)
<7,500	15.3 (64.3)	8.5 (35.7)	11.4 (100.0)	0 (0)
Ethnicity				
>30% Black	22.1 (100.0)	0 (0)	0 (0)	0 (0)
10-30% Black	11.1 (54.6)	9.2 (45.4)	2.2 (100.0)	0 (0)
>30% Spanish	0 (0)	0 (0)	0 (0)	0 (0)
10-30% Spanish	0 (0)	0 (0)	38.3 (100.0)	0 (0)
Others	35.4 (61.4)	22.2 (38.6)	49.9 (93.7)	3.4 (6.3)
>10% Oriental or American Indian	0 (0)	0 (0)	0 (0)	0 (0)
Spanish & Black	0 (0)	0 (0)	6.2 (100.0)	0 (0)
% Use Public Transportation				
>20	15.5 (60.0)	10.3 (40.0)	2.4 (100.0)	0 (0)
10-20	32.3 (76.0)	10.2 (24.0)	26.8 (98.1)	0.5 (1.9)
1-10	21.7 (67.1)	10.6 (32.9)	62.1 (97.1)	1.8 (2.9)
<1	0 (0)	0 (0)	5.3 (83.9)	1.0 (16.1)
Housing Age				
20-40% built 1939/earlier	26.7 (64.2)	14.8 (35.8)	21.5 (100.0)	0 (0)
>40% built 1939/earlier	0 (0)	0 (0)	1.3 (100.0)	0 (0)
>20% built 1960-1970	0 (0)	0 (0)	5.0 (80.4)	1.2 (19.6)
Mixed	41.9 (71.7)	16.6 (28.3)	68.5 (96.6)	2.4 (3.4)
Stage in Life Cycle				
>10% over 64	1.7 (33.3)	3.4 (66.7)	7.3 (100.0)	0 (0)
>20% under 18	4.3 (100.0)	0 (0)	34.3 (94.1)	2.1 (5.9)
Others	62.6 (56.6)	28.0 (43.4)	55.0 (97.8)	1.2 (2.2)
Combination	0 (0)	0 (0)	0 (0)	0 (0)
Density				
>8,000	27.2 (66.7)	13.6 (33.3)	43.8 (100.0)	0 (0)
4,000-8,000	34.0 (80.0)	8.5 (20.0)	42.6 (97.2)	1.2 (2.8)
1,000-4,000	7.1 (43.5)	9.2 (56.5)	9.1 (81.8)	2.0 (18.2)
200-1,000	0.3 (66.7)	0.2 (33.3)	1.1 (90.0)	0.1 (10.0)
<200	0 (0)	0 (0)	0.0 (100.0)	0 (0)

TABLE 8.4 (cont.)

	JACKSONVILLE				OKLAHOMA CITY			
	Primary		Secondary		Primary		Secondary	
Income($)								
>17,500	0	(0)	0	(0)	0	(0)	3.5	(23.3)
10,000-17,500	0	(0)	1.0	(3.0)	13.3	(25.9)	13.2	(25.8)
7,500-10,000	0	(0)	4.1	(10.0)	25.2	(58.4)	6.7	(15.5)
<7,500	0	(0)	6.4	(27.8)	0	(0)	0	(0)
Ethnicity								
>30% Black	0	(0)	4.8	(19.6)	7.0	(77.0)	1.3	(14.0)
10-30% Black	0	(0)	2.0	(16.5)	3.0	(29.6)	3.3	(37.4)
>30% Spanish	0	(0)	0	(0)	0	(0)	2.0	(100.0)
10-30% Spanish	0	(0)	0	(0)	0	(0)	0	(0)
Others	0	(0)	4.8	(7.5)	27.5	(35.7)	17.0	(21.9)
>10% Oriental or American Indian	0	(0)	0	(0)	0	(0)	0	(0)
Spanish & Black	0	(0)	0	(0)	0.9	(58.6)	0	(0)
% Use Public Transportation								
>20	0	(0)	1.4	(9.0)	0	(0)	0	50.0)
10-20	0	(0)	5.6	(46.6)	8.5	(94.0)	0.3	(3.7)
1-10	0	(0)	4.6	(8.4)	13.3	(53.3)	7.7	(31.1)
<1	0	(0)	0	(0)	16.7	(25.2)	15.4	(23.1)
Housing Age								
20-40% built 1939/earlier	0	(0)	0	(0)	2.8	(75.9)	0.6	(16.7)
>40% built 1939 earlier	0	(0)	0	(0)	0.6	(83.3)	0.1	(8.3)
>20% built 1960-1970	0	(0)	0	(0)	8.6	(48.9)	1.5	(8.6)
Mixed	0	(0)	11.6	(12.6)	26.5	(33.8)	21.3	(27.2)
Stage in Life Cycle								
>10% over 64	0	(0)	0	(0)	1.2	(99.1)	0	(0)
>20% under 18	0	(0)	6.0	(22.1)	22.0	(49.2)	6.9	(15.5)
Others	0	(0)	5.6	(7.8)	15.2	(28.0)	16.6	(30.4)
Combination	0	(0)	0	(0)	0	(0)	0	(0)
Density								
>8,000	0	(0)	0.8	(16.7)	19.6	(60.0)	7.8	(24.0)
4,000-8,000	0	(0)	5.3	(20.6)	13.4	(42.0)	11.4	(34.0)
1,000-4,000	0	(0)	2.5	(3.9)	4.4	(25.0)	3.8	(21.9)
200-1,000	0	(0)	0.2	(15.2)	0.4	(2.9)	0.5	(3.8)
<200	0	(0)	0	(0)	0.3	(9.4)	0.1	(4.2)

TABLE 8.4 (cont.)

	PROVIDENCE				ROCHESTER			
	Primary		Secondary		Primary		Secondary	
Income ($)								
>17,500	0	(0)	6.4	(100.0)	0	(0)	0	(0)
10,000-17,500	40.4	(45.9)	29.0	(32.9)	22.1	(33.1)	21.0	(31.5)
7,500-10,000	3.2	(59.7)	0	(0)	20.3	(90.0)	2.2	(10.0)
<7,500	0	(0)	0	(0)	9.0	(100.0)	0	(0)
Ethnicity								
>30% Black	0	(0)	0	(0)	20.3	(100.0)	0	(0)
10-30% Black	0	(0)	0	(0)	9.0	(66.7)	4.5	(33.3)
>30% Spanish	0	(0)	0	(0)	0	(0)	0	(0)
10-30% Spanish	0	(0)	0	(0)	0	(0)	0	(0)
Others	43.7	(43.7)	35.5	(35.5)	22.1	(33.3)	18.8	(28.2)
>10% Oriental or American Indian	0	(0)	0	(0)	0	(0)	0	(0)
Spanish & Black	0	(0)	0	(0)	0	(0)	0	(0)
% Use Public Transportation								
>20	0	(0)	0	(0)	16.7	(88.1)	2.2	(9.0)
10-20	0	(0)	0	(0)	22.5	(53.3)	12.8	(30.2)
1-10	43.7	(43.7)	34.9	(35.2)	12.2	(31.2)	8.2	(21.2)
<1	0	(0)	0.5	(100.0)	0	(0)	0	(0)
Housing Age								
20-40% built 1939/earlier	0	(0)	0	(0)	37.0	(66.3)	13.7	(24.6)
>40% built 1939/earlier	0	(0)	0	(0)	4.5	(100.0)	0	(0)
>20% built 1960-1970	0	(0)	0	(0)	0	(0)	0	(0)
Mixed	43.7	(43.7)	35.5	(35.5)	9.9	(24.9)	9.6	(23.9)
Stage in Life Cycle								
>10% over 64	0	(0)	0	(0)	4.5	(82.8)	0.9	(17.2)
>20% under 18	7.3	(93.4)	0	(0)	9.0	(90.6)	0	(0)
Others	36.3	(39.5)	35.4	(38.5)	37.9	(44.7)	22.3	(26.3)
Combination	0	(0)	0	(0)	0	(0)	0	(0)
Density								
>8,000	0	(0)	0	(0)	36.0	(88.9)	4.5	(11.1)
4,000-8,000	10.3	(66.7)	0	(0)	13.5	(42.9)	11.2	(35.7)
1,000-4,000	32.2	(39.5)	34.4	(42.1)	1.9	(6.7)	7.5	(26.7)
200-1,000	1.0	(40.0)	1.0	(40.0)	0	(0)	0	(0)
<200	0	(0)	0	(0)	0	(0)	0	(0)

TABLE 8.4 (cont.)

	ST. LOUIS Primary	ST. LOUIS Secondary	SAN DIEGO Primary	SAN DIEGO Secondary
Income($)				
>17,500	0 (0)	0 (0)	2.1 (27.7)	5.4 (72.3)
10,000-17,500	37.4 (79.8)	9.5 (20.2)	28.8 (50.2)	28.6 (49.8)
7,500-10,000	34.6 (72.9)	12.8 (27.1)	27.6 (83.5)	5.4 (16.5)
<7,500	5.3 (100.0)	0 (0)	1.0 (52.9)	0.9 (47.1)
Ethnicity				
>30% Black	26.4 (64.0)	14.8 (36.0)	0 (0)	0 (0)
10-30% Black	14.9 (87.1)	2.2 (12.9)	4.2 (100.0)	0 (0)
>30% Spanish	0 (0)	0 (0)	0 (0)	0 (0)
10-30% Spanish	0 (0)	0 (0)	10.1 (85.0)	1.8 (15.0)
Others	36.0 (87.2)	5.3 (12.8)	30.2 (44.5)	37.7 (55.5)
>10% Oriental or American Indian	0 (0)	0 (0)	3.3 (100.0)	0 (0)
Spanish & Black	0 (0)	0 (0)	11.1 (87.7)	1.6 (12.3)
% Use Public Transportation				
>20	53.9 (80.1)	13.4 (19.9)	0 (0)	0 (100.0)
10-20	4.5 (45.9)	5.3 (54.1)	4.4 (93.3)	0.3 (6.7)
1-10	18.9 (83.7)	3.7 (16.3)	33.7 (62.6)	20.1 (37.4)
<1	0 (0)	0 (0)	21.7 (52.3)	19.8 (47.7)
Housing Age				
20-40% built 1939/earlier	0.9 (70.6)	0.4 (29.4)	2.3 (99.6)	0.0 (0.4)
>40% built 1939/earlier	67.3 (75.2)	22.2 (24.8)	0 (0)	0 (0)
>20% built 1960-1970	8.9 (100.0)	0 (0)	2.3 (21.9)	8.2 (78.1)
Mixed	0 (0)	0 (0)	54.7 (62.3)	33.0 (37.7)
Stage in Life Cycle				
>10% over 64	49.2 (76.1)	15.4 (23.9)	5.7 (77.6)	1.6 (22.4)
>20% under 18	0 (0)	0 (0)	17.3 (51.3)	16.4 (48.7)
Others	9.8 (100.0)	0 (0)	35.9 (62.3)	21.8 (37.7)
Combination	18.1 (71.8)	7.1 (28.2)	0 (0)	1.2 (100.0)
Density				
>8,000	68.7 (76.5)	21.1 (23.5)	44.8 (64.2)	25.0 (35.8)
4,000-8,000	7.9 (100.0)	0 (0)	12.0 (62.2)	7.3 (37.8)
1,000-4,000	0.7 (40.0)	1.1 (60.0)	2.4 (40.7)	3.5 (59.3)
200-1,000	0.3 (60.0)	0.2 (40.0)	0.4 (8.1)	4.1 (91.9)
<200	0 (0)	0 (0)	0.1 (18.0)	0.6 (82.0)

TABLE 8.4 (cont.)

	SEATTLE		WASHINGTON, DC	
	Primary	Secondary	Primary	Secondary
Income($)				
>17,500	0 (0)	0 (0)	7.9 (40.0)	9.2 (46.7)
10,000-17,500	12.7 (16.0)	21.6 (27.1)	25.4 (54.6)	19.4 (41.6)
7,500-10,000	2.5 (20.9)	7.5 (62.8)	17.0 (53.3)	13.2 (41.2)
<7,500	0 (0)	1.5 (100.0)	1.8 (100.0)	0 (0)
Ethnicity				
>30% Black	3.7 (35.7)	6.6 (64.3)	44.2 (60.7)	26.9 (36.9)
10-30% Black	3.7 (32.4)	5.8 (51.9)	6.1 (64.6)	2.5 (26.2)
>30% Spanish	0 (0)	0 (0)	0 (0)	0 (0)
10-30% Spanish	0 (0)	0 (0)	0 (0)	0 (0)
Others	7.9 (10.0)	18.8 (24.0)	1.8 (10.0)	12.4 (70.1)
>10% Oriental or American Indian	0 (0)	0 (0)	0 (0)	0 (0)
Spanish & Black	0 (0)	0 (0)	0 (0)	0 (0)
% Use Public Transportation				
>20	0.7 (8.3)	7.3 (83.3)	47.7 (53.5)	36.3 (40.6)
10-20	1.0 (5.4)	0 (0)	3.5 (40.6)	4.2 (49.2)
1-10	13.4 (18.6)	24.0 (33.3)	0.9 (41.4)	1.2 (58.6)
<1	0 (0)	0 (0)	0 (0)	0 (0)
Housing Age				
20-40% built 1939/earlier	13.7 (22.0)	25.4 (40.8)	14.9 (65.4)	7.9 (34.6) (
>40% built 1939/earlier	0 (0)	0 (0)	31.9 (78.3)	7.1 (17.4)
>20% built 1960-1970	0 (0)	2.2 (15.1)	0.9 (35.3)	1.6 (64.7)
Mixed	1.5 (6.3)	3.6 (15.8)	4.4 (12.9)	25.1 (74.2)
Stage in Life Cycle				
>10% over 64	11.6 (21.6)	9.5 (17.7)	12.3 (87.0)	1.8 (13.0)
>20% under 18	0 (0)	2.2 (42.8)	7.0 (85.0)	1.2 (15.0)
Others	3.7 (14.9)	6.2 (25.0)	20.2 (42.5)	25.5 (53.8)
Combination	0 (0)	13.5 (82.2)	12.6 (41.9)	13.2 (43.6)
Density				
>8,000	5.9 (14.8)	13.2 (33.3)	45.6 (55.3)	31.6 (38.3)
4,000-8,000	8.1 (17.2)	14.7 (31.3)	6.1 (41.2)	7.9 (52.9)
1,000-4,000	1.2 (9.3)	2.8 (20.9)	0.4 (14.3)	2.2 (85.7)
200-1,000	0.1 (25.0)	0 (0)	0 (0)	0.1 (100.0)
<200	0 (0)	0 (0)	0 (0)	0 (0)

TABLE 8.5

EXPOSURE TO SULFUR DIOXIDE POLLUTION IN FOUR COMPARISON CASES

	BALTIMORE		JACKSONVILLE	
	Primary	Secondary	Primary	Secondary
Income($)				
>17,500	0[a] (0)[b]	0 (0)	0 (0)	0.2 (16.7)
10,000-17,500	0 (0)	1.6 (3.8)	2.3 (6.5)	1.5 (4.3)
7,500-10,000	0 (0)	4.8 (11.0)	3.2 (8.1)	5.6 (14.2)
<7,500	0 (0)	5.3 (47.0)	2.0 (8.4)	13.0 (54.2)
Ethnicity				
>30% Black	0 (0)	7.4 (18.5)	2.5 (10.3)	11.2 (45.1)
10-30% Black	0 (0)	0.3 (1.7)	1.4 (11.2)	3.6 (30.0)
>30% Spanish	0 (0)	0 (0)	0 (0)	0 (0)
10-30% Spanish	0 (0)	0 (0)	0 (0)	0 (0)
Others	0 (0)	4.0 (10.0)	3.6 (5.7)	5.7 (9.0)
>10% Oriental or American Indian	0 (0)	0 (0)	0 (0)	0 (0)
Spanish & Black	0 (0)	0 (0)	0 (0)	0 (0)
% Use Public Transportation				
>20	0 (0)	10.7 (17.3)	1.8 (11.6)	8.9 (57.7)
10-20	0 (0)	0 (0)	0.4 (3.4)	4.6 (38.7)
1-10	0 (0)	1.0 (8.0)	4.8 (8.8)	5.8 (10.5)
<1	0 (0)	0 (0)	0.5 (2.9)	1.0 (5.9)
Housing Age				
20-40% built 1939/earlier	0 (0)	0 (0)	0 (0)	2.0 (44.4)
>40% built 1939/earlier	0 (0)	10.7 (16.2)	0 (0)	0 (0)
>20% built 1960-1970	0 (0)	0 (0)	0 (0)	0 (0)
Mixed	0 (0)	1.0 (3.4)	7.5 (8.2)	18.4 (20.0)
Stage in Life Cycle				
>10% over 64	0 (0)	1.3 (2.9)	0 (0)	0.5 (33.2)
>20% under 18	0 (0)	3.0 (40.3)	2.7 (10.0)	5.6 (20.6)
Others	0 (0)	7.3 (16.2)	4.8 (6.7)	14.2 (20.0)
Combination	0 (0)	0 (0)	0 (0)	0 (0)
Density				
>8,000	0 (0)	9.3 (11.5)	0.8 (16.7)	4.1 (83.3)
4,000-8,000	0 (0)	1.3 (8.3)	1.6 (6.4)	9.3 (36.5)
1,000-4,000	0 (0)	0.8 (27.3)	5.1 (7.4)	6.8 (9.9)
200-1,000	0 (0)	0.3 (100.0)	0 (0)	0.2 (14.7)
<200	0 (0)	0 (0)	0 (0)	0 (0)

[a]Percentage of the city's population

[b]Percentage of the population in the row class living in substandard areas.

TABLE 8.5 (cont.)

	PROVIDENCE				SEATTLE			
	Primary		Secondary		Primary		Secondary	
Income ($)								
>17,500	0	(0)	0	(0)	0	(0)	0.7	(10.9)
10,000-17,500	0	(0)	34.0	(38.6)	0	(0)	15.5	(19.4)
7,500-10,000	0	(0)	0	(0)	0	(0)	2.8	(23.5)
<7,500	0	(0)	0	(0)	0	(0)	0	(0)
Ethnicity								
>30% Black	0	(0)	0	(0)	0	(0)	0	(0)
10-30% Black	0	(0)	0	(0)	0	(0)	2.9	(23.0)
>30% Spanish	0	(0)	0	(0)	0	(0)	0	(0)
10-30% Spanish	0	(0)	0	(0)	0	(0)	0	(0)
Others	0	(0)	34.0	(34.0)	0	(0)	16.1	(20.5)
>10% Oriental or American Indian	0	(0)	0	(0)	0	(0)	0	(0)
Spanish & Black	0	(0)	0	(0)	0	(0)	0	(0)
% Use Public Transportation								
>20	0	(0)	0	(0)	0	(0)	0.7	(8.3)
10-20	0	(0)	0	(0)	0	(0)	1.8	(9.2)
1-10	0	(0)	34.0	(34.2)	0	(0)	16.5	(23.0)
<1	0	(0)	0	(0)	0	(0)	0	(0)
Housing Age								
20-40% built 1939/earlier	0	(0)	0	(0)	0	(0)	18.3	(29.3)
>40% built 1939/earlier	0	(0)	0	(0)	0	(0)	0	(0)
>20% built 1960-1970	0	(0)	0	(0)	0	(0)	0	(0)
Mixed	0	(0)	34.0	(34.0)	0	(0)	0.7	(3.2)
Stage in Life Cycle								
>10% over 64	0	(0)	0	(0)	0	(0)	10.7	(19.7)
>20% under 18	0	(0)	7.8	(100.0)	0	(0)	2.2	(42.9)
Others	0	(0)	28.8	(31.2)	0	(0)	6.2	(25.4)
Combination	0	(0)	0	(0)	0	(0)	0	(0)
Density								
>8,000	0	(0)	0	(0)	0	(0)	4.4	(10.7)
4,000-8,000	0	(0)	10.3	(66.7)	0	(0)	12.4	(27.4)
1,000-4,000	0	(0)	23.6	(29.0)	0	(0)	2.1	(15.9)
200-1,000	0	(0)	0	(0)	0	(0)	0.1	(25.0)
<200	0	(0)	0	(0)	0	(0)	0	(0)

TABLE 8.6

EXPOSURE TO NITROGEN DIOXIDE
IN THREE COMPARISON CASES

	BALTIMORE	JACKSONVILLE
Income($)		
>17,500	0[a] (0)[b]	0 (0)
10,000-17,500	1.3 (3.0)	2.0 (5.8)
7,500-10,000	13.9 (33.9)	7.9 (19.3)
<7,500	7.3 (64.7)	17.4 (75.6)
Ethnicity		
>30% Black	6.0 (15.0)	15.1 (61.5)
10-30% Black	5.3 (26.0)	3.9 (33.4)
>30% Spanish	0 (0)	1.2 (100.0)
10-30% Spanish	0 (0)	0 (0)
Others	11.2 (28.3)	7.1 (11.3)
>10% Oriental or American Indian	0 (0)	0 (0)
Spanish & Black	0 (0)	0 (0)
% Use Public Transportation		
>20	20.5 (33.3)	13.1 (84.6)
10-20	1.3 (5.2)	5.0 (41.2)
1-10	0.7 (5.1)	7.6 (13.8)
<1		1.7 (9.6)
Housing Age		
20-40% built 1939/earlier	0 (0)	3.1 (69.6)
>40% built 1939/earlier	19.9 (29.5)	0 (0)
>20% built 1960-1970	2.6 (62.3)	0 (0)
Mixed	0 (0)	24.2 (26.3)
Stage in Life Cycle		
>10% over 64	6.6 (14.4)	1.5 (100.0)
>20% under 18	1.3 (17.5)	7.6 (27.8)
Others	13.2 (29.3)	18.2 (25.6)
Combination	1.3 (100.0)	0 (0)
Density		
>8,000	18.6 (23.0)	4.9 (100.0)
4,000-8,000	4.0 (25.0)	11.4 (44.4)
1,000-4,000	0 (0)	11.0 (16.1)
200-1,000	0 (0)	0 (0)
<200	0 (0)	0 (0)

[a]Percentage of the city's population

[b]Percentage of the population in the row class living in substandard areas.

TABLE 8.6 (cont.)

	WASHINGTON, DC
Income($)	
>17,500	0 (0)
10,000-17,500	14.0 (30.1)
7,500-10,000	9.6 (30.2)
<7,500	0 (0)
Ethnicity	
>30% Black	22.8 (31.3)
10-30% Black	0.9 (9.2)
>30% Spanish	0 (0)
10-30% Spanish	0 (0)
Others	0 (0)
>10% Oriental or American Indian	0 (0)
Spanish & Black	0 (0)
% Use Public Tranportation	
>20	21.9 (24.6)
10-20	1.8 (20.3)
1-10	0 (0)
<1	0 (0)
Housing Age	
20-40% built 1939/earlier	2.6 (15.0)
>40% built 1939/earlier	4.4 (9.5)
>20% built 1960-1970	0 (0)
Mixed	16.7 (49.1)
Stage in Life Cycle	
>10% over 64	3.5 (24.8)
>20% under 18	0 (0)
Others	20.2 (42.5)
Combination	0 (0)
Density	
>8,000	19.3 (23.4)
4,000-8,000	4.4 (29.4)
1,000-4,000	0 (0)
200-1,000	0 (0)
<200	0 (0)

TABLE 8.7

EXPOSURE OF VARIOUS POPULATION SUB-GROUPS
TO AMBIENT NOISE LEVELS IN EXCESS OF 50 dBA:
THREE CASES

	DENVER			JACKSONVILLE		
Income($)						
>17,500	1.2[a]	(6.6)[b]	2.4[c]	0.6	(100.0)	50.0
10,000-17,500	3.6	(11.0)	7.1	17.1	(68.8)	61.1
7,500-10,000	2.9	(7.9)	5.8	22.8	(87.2)	84.9
<7,500	3.6	(31.8)	7.1	24.5	(100.0)	90.2
Ethnicity						
>30% Black	0	(0)	0	17.7	(100.0)	71.3
10-30% Black	0.5	(22.7)	1.0	9.7	(95.0)	77.8
>30% Spanish	0	(0)	0	0	(0)	00
10-30% Spanish	4.9	(12.7)	9.5	0	(0)	0
Others	2.4	(4.6)	4.8	26.8	(74.6)	58.0
>10% Oriental or	0	(0)	0	0	(0)	0
American Indian		(				
Spanish & Black	3.6	(59.0)	7.1	0	(0)	0
% Use Public						
Transportation						
>20	2.4	(100.0)	4.8	13.8	(98.8)	92.3
10-20	3.6	(13.4)	7.1	8.6	(100.0)	73.2
1-10	5.4	(8.4)	10.5	30.5	(82.5)	66.8
<1	0	(0)	0	3.8	(56.9)	36.8
Housing Age						
20-40% built 1939/earlier	3.6	(18.3)	7.1	3.9	(100.0)	88.6
>40% built 1939/earlier	0	(0)	0	0.2	(100.0)	100.0
>20% built 1960-1970	0	(0)	0	1.7	(100.0)	48.5
Mixed	7.8	(10.7)	15.3	48.5	(83.6)	53.5
Stage in Life Cycle						
>10% over 64	1.2	(16.7)	2.4	1.1	(100.0)	61.5
>20% under 18	5.4	(14.8)	10.5	10.7	(91.0)	48.5
Others	4.9	(8.6)	9.5	35.5	(83.5)	96.2
Combination	0	(0)	0	0	(0)	0
Density						
>8,000	2.4	(9.1)	5.6	5.7	(100.0)	100.0
4,000-8,000	8.5	(41.2)	19.4	20.2	(90.9)	74.5
1,000-4,000	0.5	(14.3)	4.6	36.8	(83.2)	69.5
200-1,000	0	(0)	0	0.7	(94.2)	46.3
<200	0	(0)	0	0	(0)	0

[a] Percentage of the city's population

[b] Percentage of the population in the row class living in substandard areas.

[c] Percentage of subgroup population for which data was available.

Table 8.7 (cont.)

	WASHINGTON, DC[1]			WASHINGTON, DC[2]		
Income($)						
>17,500	25.7	(100.0)	42.9	25.7	(100.0)	50.6
10,000-17,500	61.0	(100.0)	55.4	56.8	(100.0)	53.7
7,500-10,000	13.3	(100.0)	17.6	13.3	(76.2)	16.7
<7,500	0	(0)	0	0	(0)	0
Ethnicity						
>30% Black	53.5	(100.0)	32.2	55.6	(93.1)	32.3
10-30% Black	23.7	(100.0)	82.5	17.4	(100.0)	77.7
>30% Spanish	0	(0)	0	0	(0)	0
10-30% Spanish	0	(0)	0	0	(0)	0
Others	22.8	(100.0)	54.7	22.8	(100.0)	54.7
>10% Oriental or American Indian	0	(0)	0	0	(0)	0
Spanish & Black	0	(0)	0	0	(0)	0
% Use Public Transportation						
>20	91.0	(100.0)	44.0	84.6	(95.3)	40.9
10-20	9.0	(100.0)	50.0	11.2	(100.0)	55.1
1-10	0	(0)	0	0	(0)	0
<1	0	(0)	0	0	(0)	0
Housing Age						
20-40% built 1939/earlier	20.7	(100.0)	50.0	22.6	(100.0)	52.4
>40% built 1939/earlier	42.3	(100.0)	39.6	43.9	(100.0)	40.8
>20% built 1939/earlier	2.9	(100.0)	50.0	2.9	(100.0)	50.0
Mixed	34.0	(100.0)	41.4	26.5	(86.6)	33.8
Stage in Life Cycle						
>10% over 64	12.4	(100.0)	37.3	12.4	(100.0)	37.3
>20% under 18	7.1	(100.0)	36.3	9.2	(100.0)	42.4
Others	40.2	(100.0)	35.9	34.0	(89.1)	34.7
Combination	40.2	(100.0)	56.4	40.2	(100.0)	56.4
Density						
>8,000	32.8	(100.0)	39.6	31.0	(94.7)	37.5
4,000-8,000	7.8	(100.0)	52.9	7.8	(100.0)	52.9
1,000-4,000	1.1	(100.0)	42.9	1.1	(100.0)	42.9
200-1,000	0	(0)	0	0	(0)	0
<200	0	(0)	0	0	(0)	0

[1]Maximum readings   [2]Minimum readings
See Figure 6.14, p. 478.

TABLE 8.8

EXPOSURE TO AIRPORT NOISE

	DENVER NEF>30		JACKSONVILLE CNR>1		
Income($)					
>17,500	0 [a]	(0) [b]	0	(0)	100.0 [c]
10,000-17,500	3.7	(11.8)	1.4	(3.9)	96.1
7,500-10,000	8.7	(22.4)	3.8	(9.3)	90.7
<7,500	3.6	(31.8)	0	(0)	100.0
Ethnicity					
>30% Black	0	(0)	0	(0)	100.0
10-30% Black	2.2	(100.0)	0	(0)	100.0
>30% Spanish	0	(0)	0	(0)	0
10-30% Spanish	1.3	(3.5)	0	(0)	0
Others	7.8	(14.7)	5.2	(8.1)	91.9
>10% Oriental or American Indian	0	(0)	0	(0)	0
Spanish & Black	4.2	(67.2)	0	(0)	0
% Use Public Transportation					
>20	2.4	(100.0)	0	(0)	100.0
10-20	6.1	(22.3)	0	(0)	100.0
1-10	7.0	(11.0)	4.0	(7.2)	92.8
<1	0	(0)	1.2	(7.0)	93.0
Housing Age					
20-40% built 1939/earlier	3.6	(18.3)	0	(0)	100.0
>40% built 1939/earlier	0	(0)	0	(0)	100.0
>20% built 1960-1970	0.4	(6.6)	0	(0)	100.0
Mixed	11.5	(15.8)	5.2	(5.6)	94.3
Stage in Life Cycle					
>10% over 64	0	(0)	0	(0)	100.0
>20% under 18	12.0	(32.8)	0	(0)	100.0
Others	3.6	(6.4)	5.2	(7.3)	92.7
Combination	0	(0)	0	(0)	0
Density					
>8,000	4.8	(11.1)	0	(0)	0
4,000-8,000	8.4	(18.4)	0	(0)	0
1,000-4,000	2.0	(20.0)	5.1	(100.0)	7.4
200-1,000	0.8	(70.0)	0.1	(100.0)	8.8
<200	0.0	(100.0)	0	(0)	0

[a] Percentage of the city's population

[b] Percentage of the population in the row class living in substandard areas

[c] Percentage of subgroup population for which data was available.

Epilogue

We began on page 1 by referring to the Washington Center for Metropolitan Studies' report "Incidence of Pollution where People Live in Washington." As this last chapter of this study was being typed in final form for the publisher, an article entitled "Discriminatory Air Pollution" appeared in the journal Environment (18, 2: 26-31). This article, based on the Washington Center's Studies, concluded that "chances of being exposed to poor-quality air in urban areas are greatest for persons in poverty, in occupations below the management or professional level, in low-rent districts, and in the black population," and that, frequently, air pollution in the neighborhoods occupied by such people "is at a level linked to chronic disease."

With this conclusion we agree in general, but with several caveats appropriate from the base of a comparative nationwide study as opposed to examination of a single case. Where overall levels of air pollution are low, the minority poor tend to be clustered in the most polluted zones. Where levels of air pollution are high, the middle class are most likely to preempt the least polluted central city locations, for the most affluent either live far away in exurbia, or find that the other advantages of close-to-the-center apartment neighborhoods offset the disadvantages that higher levels of pollution impose upon such locations. However, the details of the relationship vary from city to city, because cities of different ages, locations and sizes have different social geographies, and because the nature and pattern of air pollution varies from place to place. Thus, the specifics of hazardous chemicals in Chicago show widely varying patterns of incidence among neighborhoods and social groups.

The above relationships hold not only for the most commonly monitored air pollutants, but for high levels of ambient noise and solid wastes, too: the minority poor, living in the oldest highest-density inner-city neighborhoods, are afflicted with the greatest pollution burdens --joined in some cities by the more-elderly apartment-living affluent. But these same inner city neighborhoods also are beset by a complex of other ills related to poverty and poor housing, including greater risk of rat bites, and of poisonings by the rodenticides and pesticides used to keep unwanted pests in check.

In one sense, the problems of the inner-city poor are overdetermined; a cure for one or two of the symptoms still leaves enough others to contain and absorb the likely benefits of having one or two symptoms cured.

The more affluent suburbanite does not escape to a pollution-free environment altogether, however. For some, expanding airports bring increasing problems of aircraft noise. For many others, unregulated private drinking water supplies fall far below the Public Health Service standards that are maintained by central city utilities, either because the ground water supplies tapped have natural mineral contents that are excessively high, or because the ground water reservoir has been polluted by unsatisfactory septic tank fields, improper solid wastes disposal, etc. In addition, all too frequently, the highest levels of pollution of surface waters are found in those suburbs downstream from major urban-industrial complexes, especially as the first flush following a major storm flows through. Yet this, also is overly-general; as our maps show, there is wide variation within each metropolitan region as to the nature and incidence of surface water pollution. The specifics must be determined in each particular case; the available raw materials those whose use is exemplified in this comparative metropolitan data source.

Selected References

GENERAL

Berry, Brian J. L., and Frank E. Horton. Geographic Perspectives on Urban Systems. Englewood Cliffs: Prentice-Hall, 1970.

_____ and Frank E. Horton. Urban Environmental Management. Englewood Cliffs: Prentice-Hall, 1974.

_____ et al. Land Use, Urban Form and Environmental Quality. Chicago: University of Chicago, Department of Geography, Research Paper #155, 1974.

Hagevik, George. Planning for Environmental Quality. Exchange Bibliography #97, Council of Planning Librarians. Monticello, Illinois, 1969.

Strahler, A. N. and A. H. Strahler. Environmental Geoscience: Interaction Between Natural Systems and Man. Santa Barbara: Hamilton Publishing Company, 1973.

PESTICIDES

Haus, S.A. "Strategic Environmental Assessment System: Pesticide Residuals," Draft technical memorandum for EPA Office of Research and Development, Environmental Studies Division. Mitre Corp, 1973.

Health Effects of Organophosphate Insecticides. IIEQ document # EHRC-6.

Pesticides Study 1972. Illinois Department of Public Health.

Petty, H. B. "The Impact of the Federal Environmental Pesticides Control Act." (mimeo.)

WATER POLLUTION

American Water Works Association. Water Quality and Treatment: A Handbook of Public Water Supplies. McGraw Hill: New York, 1971.

Association of Central Oklahoma Governments. "Regional Land Use Plan for Central Oklahoma," Oklahoma City. (Sept, 1972).

Benefits of Water Quality Enhancement. Department of Civil Engineering, Syracuse University, Syracuse University, Syracuse, New York, 1970.

Birmingham Regional Planning Commission. "Regional Development Plan," Birmingham. (June, 1972).

Brown, Eugene, M. W. Skongstad, and M. G. Fishman. Methods for Collection and Analysis of Water Samples for Dissolved Minerals and Gases. U. S. Geological Survey Techniques of Water Resource Investigations, Book 5, Chapter Al, 160 pp. 1970.

California State Water Resources Control Board. "Interim Water-Quality Control Plan for the San Diego Basin." San Diego Region. (June, 1971).

Ciaccio, Leonard. Water and Water Pollution Handbook. Volume 1. New York: Marcel Dekker, Inc., 1971.

Daley, Raymond D., Gary W. Issac, and Robert I. Matsuda. A Survey of Stream Conditioning in Issaquah Creek. Water Quality Series No. 3, Seattle, Washington, 24 pp., 1966.

Department of Health of the District of Columbia, Water Quality Control Division and the Environmental Protection Agency. "Water Quality Standards Summary," Doc. No. WQS 11-001.

Department of Public Health and Welfare of Missouri. "Water Quality of Big, Bourbeuse and Meramec River Basins," Jefferson City, Missouri, 1964.

Department of Water and Sewers. Annual Report 1972, and Chicago Water System. City of Chicago, Illinois, 1973.

Edmondson, W. Thomas. "Water Quality Management and Lake Eutrophication: The Lake Washington Case," in Water Resources Management and Public Policy. Seattle: University of Washington Press, pp. 139-178, 1968.

Engineering Consultants, Inc. Comprehensive Water Quality Management Plan-South Platte River Basin, Colorado. Water Quality Control Division, Colorado Dept of Health; Denver, Colorado, 1974.

Hern, John D. Study and Interpretation of the Chemical Characteristics of Natural Water. U.S.G.S. Water Supply Paper 1473, U.S. Government Printing Office, 363 pp., 1970.

Issac, Gary W. and Curtis P. Leiser. "Seattle's Efforts in Restoration of Bays and Estuaries," 32nd North American Wildlife and Natural Resources Conference, San Francisco, California, Transactions. (March 13-15, 1967) pp. 127-137.

Jacksonville Area Planning Board and Frederic R. Harris, Inc. "Interim Water Quality Management Report for Duval County, Florida," Jacksonville, Fla. (January, 1973).

Kiely-Irza and Associates. Extension and Modifications to Sanitary Sewers and Storm Drains for the Town of North Providence. Providence, Rhode Island (Sept. 1968).

Metropolitan Engineers. West Point Environmental Planning Study-Interim Report. 64 pp. (April, 1973).

Metropolitan Sanitary District. Geology and Water Supply. Technical Report Metropolitan Sanitary District, Chicago, Illinois. (December, 1972).

Metropolitan Washington Council of Governments. "Water and Sewer Plan and Program." Washington, D.C. (Sept, 1970).

_____"Water and Sewerage Plan and Program, 1971-72," Washington, D.C. 1971.

_____"The Changing Region," Washington, D.C., (no date).

Municipality of Metropolitan Seattle. Metro 71-1971 Report on Operations. Seattle, Washington, 1971.

Northeastern Illinois Planning Commission. Regional Water Supply Report. Technical Report #8, Chicago, Ill., 1974.

Office of Program Planning and Fiscal Management. State of Washington Pocket Data Book, 1972. Olympia, Washington. (January, 1973).

Ohio, Kentucky, Indiana Regional Planning Authority. "Regional Water System Plan," Cincinnati, Ohio. (March, 1971).

_____"Regional Sewerage Plan," Cincinnati, Ohio. (Nov., 1971).

Rhode Island Development Council. "Basic Economic Statistics," Providence, Rhode Island, 1972.

_____State Planning Section, "Analysis of Rhode Island Land Use," Providence Rhode Island, 1961.

_____State Planning Section. "Non-urban land: Present Use and Economic Classification." Providence, Rhode Island, 1972.

Rhode Island Statewide Planning Program and Rhode Island Department of Health. "Interim Water Quality Management Plan for the Woonasquatucket River Basin," Providence, Rhode Island, 1974.

_____"Water Quality Management Plan for the Moshassuck River Basin," Providence, Rhode Island. (January, 1975).

Regional Planning Council, Baltimore, Maryland. "General Development Plan, Baltimore Region," Baltimore. 1972.

Richardson, Donald, J. W. Bingham, and R. J. Madison. Water Resources of King County, Washington, U.S.G.S. Water Supply Paper 1852, Washington, D.C., 74 pp., 1972.

Santos, J. F., and J. Stoner. Physical, Chemical, and Biological Aspects of the Duwamish River Estuary, King County, Washington, 1963-1967. U.S.G.S. Water Supply Paper 1873-C, Washington, D.C., 74 pp., 1972.

Sasman, R.T., C.K. McDonald, W.R.Randall. Water Level Decline and Pumpage in Deep Wells in Northeastern Illinois 1962-1966. Illinois State Water Survey Circular 94, Urbana, Illinois. 1967.

Sheaffer, John R. and Arthur J. Ziegel. The Water Resource in Northeastern Illinois, Planning Its Use. Technical Report No. 4, Chicago, Illinois. 1966.

State of Maryland. "Potomac-Metropolitan Area Basin Water Quality Management Plan," Baltimore, Maryland. (January, 1974).

State of Oklahoma Department of Pollution Control, "Water Quality Management Plan, Canadian River Basin." Oklahoma City, Oklahoma. 1973.

Suter, Max et al. "Ground Water Resources of the Chicago Region, Illinois," Cooperative Ground-Water Report 1, State Water Survey, Illinois Geological Survey, Urbana, Illinois, 1959.

Sylvester, Robert O. and Carl A. Rambow. "Methodology in Establishing Water Quality Standards," in Water Resource Management and Public Policy, ed. by Thomas H. Campbell and Robert O. Sylvester, University of Washington Press: Seattle, pp. 110-122. (1968).

U.S. Environmental Protection Agency. Manual of Individual Supply Systems. Water Supply Division, Washington, D.C. 1973.

_____ National Water Quality Inventory: 1974 Report to the Congress Vol. 1, Washington, D.C.: EPA Office of Water Planning and Standards. 1974.

U.S. Federal Water Pollution Control Administration. Report of the Committee on Water Quality Criteria. Washington, D.C. 234 pp. 1968.

U.S. Geological Survey, Water Resources Division. Water Resources Data for Alabama, 1972.

_____ Water Resources Data for Oklahoma City. 1971.

_____ Water Resources Data for Maryland and Delaware. U.S. Geological Survey, Part 2. Water Quality Records 1970-71.

_____ Water Resources Data for Massachusetts, New Hampshire, Rhode Island and Vermont. 1971.

_____ Mineral and Water Resources of Missouri. Vol. XLIII, 2nd Series, Doc. No. 77-2780, Washington, D.C. 1967.

U. S. Public Health Service. Drinking Water Standards. Public Health Service Publication 956, Washington, D.C. 7 pp., 1962.

Walker, William H. "Illinois Ground Water Pollution," Journal of the American Water Works Association 61 (1) January, 1969.

Washington State Geological Survey. Water Resources Data for Washington, 1971, 1972. Tacoma: Washington State Geological Survey, Water Resources Divisions, 1973.

Washington Water Pollution Control Commission. <u>A Regulation</u>
<u>Relating to Water Quality Standards for Interstate and</u>
<u>Coastal Standards for Interstate and Coastal Waters of the</u>
<u>State of Washington and a Plan for Implementation and Enforce-</u>
<u>ment of Such Standards</u>, February, Olympia, Washington, 22 pp.
1967.

Water Pollution Control Board, New York State Department of Health.
"The Lower Genesee River Drainage Basin Official Classifi-
cations." Rochester, New York, 1959.

Wegert, N. <u>Urban-Metropolitan Institutions for Water Plannning,</u>
<u>Development and Management: An Analysis of Usages of the</u>
<u>Term 'Institutions'</u>. Colorado State University, Fort Collins, 1972.

Welch, Eugene. <u>Factors Initiating Phytoplankton Blooms and Resulting</u>
<u>Effects on Dissolved Oxygen in the Duwamish River Estuary</u>,
<u>Seattle, Washington</u>. U.S.G.S. Water Supply Paper 1873-A,
Washington, D.C.,62 pp. 1969.

AIR POLLUTION

Anderson, R., and T. Crocker. "Air Pollution and Residential
Property Values." <u>Urban Studies</u>. Vol. 8, pp. 171-180 (1971).

_____ and T. Crocker. "Air Pollution and Property Values: A
Reply." <u>Review of Economics and Statistics</u>. Vol. 54,
pp. 470-473 (1972).

Andrews, Richard B. (ed.) <u>Urban Land Use: The Central City</u>.
New York: Free Press, 1972.

Bednarz, Robert S. <u>The Effect of Air Pollution on Property Value</u>
<u>in Chicago</u>. University of Chicago Department of Geography
Research Paper No. 166. Chicago, Illinois, 1975.

Department of Health, Division of Air Pollution Control. <u>Air Qua-</u>
<u>lity Data Summary, National and State Ambient Air Quality</u>
<u>Standards, Sampling Location, Annual Summary 1972</u>. State
of Rhode Island and Providence Plantations (mimeographed),
41 pp., 1972.

Division of Air Monitoring, Bureau of Air Quality Control. <u>Mary-</u>
<u>land State Yearly Air Quality Data Report, 1972</u>. State of
Maryland, Department of Health and Mental Hygiene, Environmental Health Administration, Baltimore, Maryland, 120 pp.
1973.

_____ <u>Maryland State Yearly Air Quality Data Report, 1973</u>. State
of Maryland, Department of Health and Mental Hygiene,
Environmental Health Administration, Baltimore, Maryland,
134 pp., 1974.

Division of Behavioral Sciences, National Research Council.
<u>Environmental Quality and Social Behavior: Strategies for</u>
<u>Research</u>. Washington, D.C.: National Academy of Sciences,
1973.

Downing, Paul B. (ed.) Air Pollution and the Social Sciences: Formulating and Implementing Control Programs. New York: Praeger, 1971.

Drake, John W. et al. "Environmental Mutagenic Hazards." Science, Vol. 187 (2), pp. 503-514, 1975.

Engineering-Science Inc. Development of a Trial Air Quality Maintenance Plan Using the Baltimore Air Quality Control Region, U.S. E.P.A., Office of Air and Waste Management, Office of Air Quality Planning and Standards, Research Triangle Park North Carolina, EPA-450/3-74-050, 1974.

Freeman, A. Myrick, III. "Air Pollution and Property Values: A Methodological Comment." Review of Economics and Statistics, Vol. 53 (1971), pp. 415-416.

_____"On Estimating Air Pollution Control Benefits From Land Value Studies." Journal of Environmental Economics and Management, Vol. 1, 1974, pp. 74-83.

Haefels, Edwin T. "Environmental Quality as a Problem of Social Choice." Allen V. Kneese and Blair T. Bower (eds.). Environmental Quality Analysis. Baltimore: Johns Hopkins Press, pp. 281-332, 1972.

Hagevik, George. Decision-Making in Air Pollution Control. New York: Praeger, 1970.

Illinois E.P.A., Technical Services Section, Division of Air Pollution Control. Illinois Air Sampling Network Report 1973, Illinois E.P.A.: Springfield, 159 pp., 1974.

Kraus, Harold A., and Richard G. Kastner. Air Quality Data 1972: Data Summaries of Air Quality Measurements Made in Cincinnati and the Southwestern Ohio Air Pollution Control District During the Year 1972, Division of Air Pollution Control, Department of Sewers, Cincinnati, Ohio, 27 pp., 1972.

Lave, Lester B. "Air Pollution Damage: Some Difficulties in Estimating the Value of Abatement." in Allen V. Kneese and Blair T. Bower (eds.), Environmental Quality Analysis. Baltimore: Johns Hopkins Press, 213-242. 1972.

National Clearinghouse for Mental Health Information. Pollution: Its Impact on Mental Health. Rockville, Maryland: National Institute of Mental Health, 1972.

Puget Sound Air Pollution Control Agency. Annual Report 1971. Puget Sound Air Pollution Control Agency, Seattle, 36 pp. 1972.

Ridker, R. and J. Henning. "The Determinants of Residential Property Values with Special Reference to Air Pollution." Review of Economics and Statistics, Vol. 2, 85-103. 1975.

Record, Frank A., David A. Bryant, Gordon L. Deane, Benjamin Kincannon, and Michael Miles. Development of an Example 10-year Air Quality Maintenance Plan for Denver AQMSA. Final Report, U.S. E.P.A., Office of Air and Waste Management, Office of Air Quality Planning and Standards, Research Triangle Park, North Carolina, EPA-450/3-74-053, 1974.

San Diego County, Air Pollution Control District. Air Pollution Quarterly, Vol. 2, Annual Report, Calendar Year 1973 (mimeographed). 1974.

Special Studies Division, Air Quality Service, Environmental Health Services. Oklahoma 1973 Annual Ambient Air Quality Report, Oklahoma State Department of Health, Oklahoma City, Oklahoma, 68 pp. 1974.

⎯⎯⎯⎯ Oklahoma 1972 Annual Ambient Air Quality Report, Oklahoma State Department of Health, Oklahoma City, Oklahoma, 71 pp. 1973.

Strong, Ann L. "The Impact of Preemption on Environmental Regulation." Land-Use Controls Annual. Chicago: American Society of Planning Officials, pp. 15-35, 1972.

Technical Services Division, Puget Sound Air Pollution Control Agency. 1973 Air Quality Data Summary. Puget Sound Air Pollution Control Agency, Seattle, 37 pp., 1974.

TRW, Inc. Development of a Sample Air Quality Maintenance Plan for San Diego. U.S. E.P.A., Office of Air and Waste Management, Office of Air Quality Planning Standards, Research Triangle Park, N. Car., EPA-450/3-74-051. 1974.

Wright, Colin. "Some Political Aspects of Pollution Control." Journal of Environmental Economics and Management. Vol. 1, 173-187, 1974.

NOISE

Alexandre, Ariel. "The Social Impact of Aircraft Noise," Traffic Quarterly, pp. 371-383 (July, 1974).

Anthrop, Donald F. Noise Pollution. Toronto: D.C.Heath and Company, 1973.

⎯⎯⎯⎯ "The Noise Crisis," In Noise Pollution and the Law, James L. Hildebrand (ed.). Buffalo: William S. Hein and Company, Inc., 1970.

Anticaglia, Joseph R. "Introduction: Noise in Our Overpolluted Environment," in Physiological Effects of Noise, Bruce L. Welch and Annemarie S. Welch (eds.). New York: Plenum Press, 1970.

Beranek, Leo L. "Noise," Scientific American, pp. 66-73. (December, 1966).

Bolt, Beranek, and Newman, Inc. Chicago Urban Noise Study. Report No. 1411-143, Downers Grove, Ill. (November, 1970).

⎯⎯⎯⎯ Highway Noise: A Design Guide for Highway Engineers. Highway Research Board, 1971.

⎯⎯⎯⎯ Noise Exposure Forecast Contours For Aircraft Noise Tradeoff Studies at Three Major Airports. FAA-No.-70-7. (July, 1970).

Borsky, Paul N. Community Reactions to Sonic Booms in the Oklahoma City Area. National Opinion Research Center, Aerospace Medical Research Laboratories, AMRL-TR-65-37, Vol. II, (October, 1965).

_____ "The Use of Social Surveys for Measuring Community Response to Noise Environments," in Transportation Noises, J.D. Chalupnik (ed.) Seattle: University of Washington Press, 1970.

Bragdon, Clifford R. Noise Pollution. Philadelphia: University of Pennsylvania Press, 1970.

Broadbent, D.E. "Factors Increasing and Decreasing the Effects of Noise," in Proceedings of the International Congress on Noise as a Public Health Problem. Environmental Protection Agency, 550/9-73-008, 1973.

Burt, M.E. "Aspects of Highway Design and Traffic Management," Journal of Sound and Vibration, Vol. 15 (1), 1971.

Caccavari, C. and H. Schechter. "Background Noise Study in Chicago." Department of Environmental Control, City of Chicago, 1973.

Ceypek, Tadeusz, Jerzy J. Kuzniarz, and Adam Lipowczan. "Hearing Loss Due to Impulse Noise," in Proceedings of the International Congress on Noise as a Public Health Problem. Environmental Protection Agency, 550/9-73-008, 1973.

Chalupnik, James G. (ed.) Transportation Noises: A Symposium on Acceptability Criteria. Seattle: University of Washington Press, 1970.

"Chicago Noise Ordinance," Department of Environmental Control, City of Chicago.

Coles, R.R.A., C.G.Rice, and A.M. Martin. "Noise-Induced Hearing Loss from Impulse Noise: Present Status," in Proceedings of the International Congress on Noise as a Public Health Problem. Environmental Protection Agency, 550/9-73-008, 1973.

Colony, David C. "Expressway Traffic Noise and Residential Properties," United States Department of Transportation, Bureau of Public Roads, 1967.

Department of City Planning Reference Atlas, City of Chicago, 1961.

Dickerson, D.O. et al. Transportation Noise Pollution: Control and Abatement. Springfield, Virginia: National Technical Information Service, N 71-15557, 1970.

Dunsbee, J. and F. Billingsley. "Ambient Noise Levels in Residential Areas," in Acoustic Noise and Its Control. London: The Institution of Electrical Engineers, 1966.

Environmental Protection Agency. "Community Noise," EPA Report NTID 300.3. (December 31, 1971).

_____ "Information on Levels of Environmental Noise Requisite to Protect the Public Health and Welfare with an Adequate Margin of Safety," EPA Report 550/9-73-004. (March, 1974).

_____"Public Health and Welfare Criteria for Noise," EPA Report 550/9-73-002. (July 27, 1973).

_____"The Economic Impact of Noise," EPA Report NTID 300.14. (December 31, 1971).

_____"The Social Impact of Noise," EPA Report NTID 300.11. (December 31, 1971).

_____"Public Hearings on Noise Abatement and Control," Vol. IV, U.S. Government Printing Office, Stock No.5500-0036. (September 27-29, 1970).

Foster, C.D. and P.J.Mackie. "Noise: Economic Aspects of Choice," Urban Studies, Vol. 7. (June, 1970).

Gaskill, Daniel. "The Urban Noise Environment," Unpublished M.A. Thesis, Social Sciences Division, The University of Chicago, 1975.

Gatley, William. "Control of Urban Noise by Regulation," Missouri Municipal Review, pp. 16-19. (May, 1972).

Glass, David C. and J. E. Singer. "Behavioral Aftereffects of Unpredictable and Uncontrollable Aversive Events," American Scientist, Vol. 60. (July-August, 1972).

_____Urban Stress. New York: Academic Press, 1972.

Gulian, Edith. "Psychological Consequences of Exposure to Noise, Facts and Explanations," In Proceedings of the International Congress of Noise as a Public Health Problem. Environmental Protection Agency, 550/9-73-008, 1973.

Haider, M. "Influences of Chemical Agents on Hearing Loss," in Proceedings of the International Congress on Noise as a Public Health Problem. Environmental Protection Agency, 550/9-73-008, 1973.

Illinois Airport Directory, Department of Transportation, State of Illinois, 1974.

Jansen, Gerd. "Non-Auditory Effects of Noise, Physiological and Psychological Reactions in Man," in Proceedings of the International Congress on Noise as a Health Problem. Environmental Protection Agency, 550/9-73-008, 1973.

Kramon, James M. "Noise Control: Traditional Remedies and a Proposal for Federal Action," in Noise Pollution and the Law, James L. Hildebrand (ed.). Buffalo: William S. Hein and Company, Inc., 1970.

Kryter, Karl D. The Effects of Noise on Man. New York: Academic Press, 1970.

Leake, Chauncy D. "Summary of the Symposium," in Physiological Effects of Noise. Bruce L. Welch and Annemarie S. Welsh, (eds.). New York: Plenum Press, 1970.

Leonard, Skipton and Paul N. Borsky. "A Causal Model for Relating Noise Exposure, Psychosocial Variables and Aircraft Noise Annoyance," in Proceedings of the International Congress on Noise as a Public Health Problem. Environmental Protection Agency, 550/9-73-008, 1973.

McKennell, Aubrey C. "Complaints and Community Action." in Transportation Noises: A Symposium on Acceptability Criteria, James G. Chalupnik (ed.), pp. 228-244. Seattle: University of Washington Press, 1970.

Miller, James D. "The Effects of Noise on People," Environmental Protection Agency, NTID 300.7. (December 31, 1971).

Northeastern Illinois Planning Commission. "Metropolitan Aircraft Noise Abatement Policy Study: O'Hare International Airport, Chicago, Illinois." HUD/DOT IANAP-71-1, 1971.

Patterson, H.P. and Connor, W.K. "Community Response to Aircraft Noise in Large and Small Cities in the USA," in Proceedings of the International Congress on Noise as a Public Health Problem. Environmental Protection Agency, 550/9-73-008, 1973.

Pinter, Istvan. "Hearing Loss of Forest Workers and of Tractor Operators," in Proceedings of the International Congress on Noise as a Public Health Problem. Environmental Protection Agency, 550/9-73-008, 1973.

Rohrman, B. et al. "Interdisciplinary Study on the Effects of Aircraft Noise on Man," in Proceedings of the International Congress on Noise as a Public Health Problem. Environmental Protection Agency, 550/9-73-008, 1973.

Spater, George A. "Noise and the Law", in Noise Pollution and the Law. James L. Hildebrand (ed.) Buffalo: William S. Hein and Company, Inc., 1970.

Schultz, Theodore J. and Nancy M. McMahon. "Noise Assessment Guidelines," prpared by Bolt, Beranek, and Newman, Inc., for the U. S. Department of Housing and Urban Development, 1970.

U. S. Environmental Protection Agency. Community Noise. Report No. NT1D 300.3, Washington, D.C., U.S. Government Printing Office. (December, 1971).

Vaughan, Roger J. "The Impact of Noise on Property Values." University of Chicago, 1973.

Ward, W. Dixon. Susceptibility to TTS and PTS," in Proceedings of the International Congress on Noise as a Public Health Problem. Environmental Protection Agency, 550/9-73-008, 1973.

Welch, Bruce L. "Environmental Noise, 'Adaptation' and Pathological Change," in Physiological Effects of Noise," Bruce L. Welch and Annemarie Welch (eds.) New York: Plenum Press, 1970.

SOLID WASTE

Black, Ralph J., Anton J. Muhick, Albert J. Klee, H. Lanier Hickman, Jr., and Richard D. Baughan. The National Solid Wastes Survey: An Interim Report. U. S. Department of Health, Education, and Welfare, Public Health Service, Environmental Control Administration. 53 pp. 1968.

Bower, B.T., G.P. Larson, A. Michaels, and W.M. Phillips. "Waste Management," Ekistics, Vol. 26 , pp. 438-450. (November, 1968).

Bureau of Sanitation Annual Report, Fiscal Year 1973-1974. Baltimore County, Maryland.(Mimeographed).

Burke, William P. "Chicago's Abandoned Car Disposal Control Program," Proceedings of the Third Mineral Waste Utilization Symposium. Sponsored by the U.S. Bureau of Mines and the IIT Research Institute. Chicago, Illinois. (March, 1972).

Caris, Susan. "Reclamation, Reuse, and Recycling: Alternatives to Planned Obsolescence," Unpublished M.A. Thesis, Department of Geography, University of Chicago. 1974.

City of Chicago, Department of Streets and Sanitation. "1974 Recommended Appropriation of the Department of Streets and Sanitation to the Honorable Chairman and Members of the Committee on Finance, Chicago City Council, Chicago, Illinois. (Mimeographed). 1974.

City and County of Denver, Department of Public Works. Annual Operating Report. 123 pp., 1973.

Denver Regional Council of Governments. Solid Waste Management in the Denver Region- Final Report. HUD Project no. COLO-USE-1, 259 pp., 1972.

_____ Landfill Site Description, Analysis, and Recommendations. Supplemental Publication Project Reuse-Final Report, 67 pp. 1972.

_____ Recycling Activity Description. Project Reuse Final Report, Supplemental Publication, 57 pp., 1972.

_____ Collection System Description. Project Reuse Final Report, Supplemental Publication, 61 pp., 1972.

Department of Environmental Control. Inventory of Refuse-Solid Waste Estimate, City of Chicago. 1966.

_____ Emission Inventory-Fuel and Solid Waste Report, City of Chicago. 1972.

Dyer, Larry. Center for Environmental Studies, Argonne National Laboratory.(raw figures for suburban waste generation-unpublished data).

Hardin, Ernest L. Jr., and H. Lawrence Dyer. An Analysis of Solid Waste Management Systems for Northeastern Illinois. State of Illinois, Illinois Institute for Environmental Quality Document No. 75-7. May, 1975.

McFarland, Margaret. "The Burden of Blight: Subsidiary Sources of Solid Waste in Chicago," Unpublished M.A. Thesis, Social Sciences Division, University of Chicago, 1974.

Murphy, William J. "Solid Waste Management in Chicago," Municipal Solid Waste Management: Central City Waste Management. Washington, D.C.L National League of Cities and United States Conference of Mayors, 1974.

1972-1973 Annual Report of the Department of Streets, City of St. Louis, Missouri. 49 pp.

Northeastern Illinois Planning Commission. Solid Waste Report: Technical Report No. 7, Chicago, Illinois: Northeastern Illinois Planning Commission. (April, 1973).

Sanitation Division. 1972-1973 Fiscal Year Report of the Sanitation Division. Department of Public works, Bureau of Utility Operations. City of Baltimore, Maryland. (October, 1973).

_____. 1971-1972 Fiscal Year Report of the Sanitation Division. Department of Public Works, Bureau of Utility Operations. City of Baltimore, Maryland. (November, 1972).

Seeley, Richard J. and Peter A. Loquercio. Solid Waste Report for the City of Chicago: Phase 1 Solid Waste Estimate-1966, Engineering Services Division, Department of Air Pollution Control, City of Chicago. 1966.

Sheaffer, John R., George S. Tolley, et al. Decision Making and Solid Waste Disposal, University of Chicago, Center for Urban Studies. (March, 1969-April, 1971).

Sniffin, Willard. Analysis of Present Status and Recommendations for Future Use of Our Sanitary Landfills, City of San Diego, California Public Works Department (mimeographed). (September 14, 1967).

Sverdrup & Parcel and Associates, Inc. Solid Waste Management Plan for the Metropolitan St. Louis Area. Draft Summary Report, Prepared for East-West Gateway Coordinating Council, St. Louis, Missouri. (April, 1974).

Truitt, Marcus M., Jon C. Liebman, and Cornelius W. Kruse. Mathematical Modeling of Solid Waste Collection Policies. (Vol. 1 and 2). U. S. Department of HEW, Public Health Service, Environmental Health Service, Bureau of Solid Waste Management. PHS pub. #2030. 1970.

Index